return 5/6.

Praise for the first edition of *Ireland 1798–1998*

'Jackson's measured and ironic approach is a breath of fresh air. This book confirms his position in the leading rank of Irish historians.'

History

'Jackson's book cannot be bettered as the most up-to-date, comprehensive and readable account of the last 200 years.'

History Review

'Jackson presents a survey of modern Irish political history that is up-to-date and even-handed in its perspective . . . An important contribution that belongs in all college libraries. '

Choice

'A brief review cannot do justice to the richness and complexity of *Ireland 1798–1998*. Jackson's gracefully written interpretations of events, forces and personalities are based upon an extensive reading of secondary sources and thoughtful, perceptive and impartial judgements.'

Irish Studies Review

'A flowing narrative and sharp historical analysis . . . Jackson is to be congratulated for producing a finely researched, well-written survey, which scholars, advanced undergraduates and the general reader will find immensely informative and thought-provoking.'

Albion

'The book is a formidable achievement. Logically organised, lucidly presented and stylishly written, this is a first-class study that will enthrall all those interested in the history of Ireland in the modern period.'

Thomas Bartlett, University College Dublin

'Alvin Jackson offers an authoritative, reflective and refreshing analysis.'

Irish News

D1427337

i

For J.C.

SECOND EDITION

IRELAND
1798–1998
WAR, PEACE AND BEYOND

ALVIN JACKSON

WILEY-BLACKWELL

A John Wiley & Sons, Ltd., Publication

This second edition first published 2010
© Alvin Jackson 2010

Edition history: Blackwell Publishing (1e, 1999)

Blackwell Publishing was acquired by John Wiley & Sons in February 2007. Blackwell's publishing program has been merged with Wiley's global Scientific, Technical, and Medical business to form Wiley-Blackwell.

Registered Office
John Wiley & Sons Ltd, The Atrium, Southern Gate, Chichester, West Sussex, PO19 8SQ, United Kingdom

Editorial Offices
350 Main Street, Malden, MA 02148-5020, USA
9600 Garsington Road, Oxford, OX4 2DQ, UK
The Atrium, Southern Gate, Chichester, West Sussex, PO19 8SQ, UK

For details of our global editorial offices, for customer services, and for information about how to apply for permission to reuse the copyright material in this book please see our website at www.wiley.com/wiley-blackwell.

The right of Alvin Jackson to be identified as the author of this work has been asserted in accordance with the UK Copyright, Designs and Patents Act 1988.

All rights reserved. No part of this publication may be reproduced, stored in a retrieval system, or transmitted, in any form or by any means, electronic, mechanical, photocopying, recording or otherwise, except as permitted by the UK Copyright, Designs and Patents Act 1988, without the prior permission of the publisher.

Wiley also publishes its books in a variety of electronic formats. Some content that appears in print may not be available in electronic books.

Designations used by companies to distinguish their products are often claimed as trademarks. All brand names and product names used in this book are trade names, service marks, trademarks or registered trademarks of their respective owners. The publisher is not associated with any product or vendor mentioned in this book. This publication is designed to provide accurate and authoritative information in regard to the subject matter covered. It is sold on the understanding that the publisher is not engaged in rendering professional services. If professional advice or other expert assistance is required, the services of a competent professional should be sought.

Library of Congress Cataloging-in-Publication Data

Jackson, Alvin.
    Ireland, 1798–1998 : war, peace and beyond / Alvin Jackson. – 2nd ed.
        p. cm.
    Includes bibliographical references and index.
    ISBN 978-1-4051-8961-3 (pbk. : alk. paper)   1. Ireland–History–19th century.
2. Ireland–History–20th century.   I. Title.
    DA950.J34 2010
    941.508–dc22

                                                                        2009054211

A catalogue record for this book is available from the British Library.

Set in 10.5/13pt Minion by Graphicraft Limited, Hong Kong
Printed and bound in Malaysia by Vivar Printing Sdn Bhd

1   2010

CONTENTS

List of Plates   vii

List of Maps   viii

Acknowledgements   ix

List of Abbreviations   xi

1	INTRODUCTION	1
	1.1 Ends of the Century	1
	1.2 Modes and Frameworks of Interpretation	2

2	THE BIRTH OF MODERN IRISH POLITICS, 1790–8	6
	2.1 The Origins of the Crisis	6
	2.2 Constitutional Radicalism to Revolution, 1791–8	10

3	DISUNITING KINGDOMS, EMANCIPATING CATHOLICS, 1799–1850	23
	3.1 The Union, 1799–1801	23
	3.2 The Catholic Question, 1799–1829	27
	3.3 Justice for Ireland, 1830–41	37
	3.4 Utilitarians and Romantics, 1841–8	46
	3.5 The Orange Party, 1798–1853	58

4	THE ASCENDANCY OF THE LAND QUESTION, 1845–91	68
	4.1 Guilty Men and the Great Famine	68
	4.2 Pivot or Accelerator?	80
	4.3 Brigadiers and Fenians	85
	4.4 Home Rule: A First Definition	108
	4.5 Idealists and Technicians: The Parnellite Party, 1880–6	116
	4.6 A Union of Hearts and a Broken Marriage: Parnellism, 1886–91	131

5   GREENING THE RED, WHITE AND BLUE: THE END OF THE
UNION, 1891–1921   141
    5.1   The Irish Parliamentary Party, 1891–1914   141
    5.2   Paths to the Post Office: Alternatives to the Irish
        Parliamentary Party, 1891–1914   168
    5.3   The Parliamentarians and their Enemies, 1914–18   193
    5.4   Making and Unmaking Unionism, 1853–1921   212
    5.5   Other Men's Wounds: The Troubles, 1919–21   241
    5.6   Trucileers, Staters and Irregulars   254

6   'THREE QUARTERS OF A NATION ONCE AGAIN': INDEPENDENT IRELAND   272
    6.1   Saorstát Éireann, 1922–32   272
    6.2   Manifest Destiny: De Valera's Ireland, 1932–48   285
    6.3   Towards a Redefinition of the National Ideal, 1948–58   304
    6.4   The Age of Lemass, 1957–73   314

7   NORTHERN IRELAND, 1920–72: SPECIALS, PEELERS AND PROVOS   331

8   THE TWO IRELANDS, 1973–98   373
    8.1   The Republic, 1973–98   373
    8.2   Northern Ireland, 1973–98   390

9   IRELAND IN THE NEW MILLENNIUM   410
    9.1   The Republic, 1998–2008   410
    9.2   Northern Ireland, 1998–2008   415
    9.3   The End of Irish History?   423

Notes   426

Chronology   450

Maps   478

Select Bibliography   490

Index   512

Plates

1   Leaders of the 1798 rising   16
2   Daniel O'Connell acquitted, Dublin 1844   49
3   A funeral at Skibbereen of a famine victim, January 1847   72
4   Cahera 1847   74
5   Charles Stewart Parnell re-elected as leader of the Irish
    Parliamentary Party, House of Commons, December 1890   136
6   John Redmond   142
7   Irish Volunteers, Kesh, County Sligo, 1914   166
8   Arthur Griffith, c.1922   182
9   Patrick Pearse, c.1916   201
10 The General Post Office, Dublin, after the Rising   202
11 Colonel Edward Saunderson, September 1906   217
12 The Ulster Unionist Convention Building, June 1892   222
13 Sir Edward Carson, c.1910   228
14 Michael Collins and Richard Mulcahy, c.1922   264
15 Eamon de Valera   285
16 Seán Lemass and Terence O'Neill, Stormont, Belfast, January 1965   321
17 Charles Haughey, c.1970   324
18 Liam Cosgrave, Brian Faulkner, and ministers from the
    Belfast Executive and the Dublin coalition government,
    Hillsborough, February 1974   386
19 The aftermath of the Omagh bombing, August 1998   394
20 John Hume and David Trimble with Bono from U2, Belfast, May 1998   402
21 Bertie Ahern, Taoiseach of Ireland (1997–2008)   413
22 Ian Paisley, First Minister of Northern Ireland, and Martin
    McGuinness, Deputy First Minister, as the 'Chuckle Brothers'   420
23 United in support for the PSNI: Robinson, Orde, McGuinness
    at Stormont, 10 March 2009   422

Maps

1   Ireland: provinces, counties and county towns   478
2   The 1798 rising   479
3   The Orange Order, May 1798   479
4   O'Connell and Young Ireland: the repeal meetings, 1843; 1848 rising   480
5   The 1916 rising   480
6   The Anglo-Irish war: reprisals by British forces, September 1919–July 1921   481
7   Parliamentary constituencies, 1604–1800   481
8   Parliamentary constituencies, 1801–85   482
9   Parliamentary constituencies, 1885   482
10   Dáil constituencies, 1923   483
11   Dáil constituencies, 1935   483
12   Population density, 1841–91, by baronies   484
13   Population change, 1841–1926, by counties   485
14   Emigration, 1851–1911, by counties   486
15   Religious denominations, 1871, by counties   487
16   Distribution of Catholics and Protestants in Ulster, 1911, by district electoral divisions   488
17   Religious affiliations, 1971   488
18   Irish speakers, 1851–1961   489

ACKNOWLEDGEMENTS

I have taxed the patience, kindness and friendship of many in researching and writing this book. Sir Geoffrey Elton asked me to take on the project, and offered generous support in the early months: I remember him with respect and affection. Numerous friends and colleagues have read part, or all, of the typescript, but of course bear no responsibility for any shortcomings there may be in the final version. Tom Bartlett, Seán Connolly, the late Peter Jupp and Patrick Maume offered sharp insights and stimulus across the entire volume; Gordon Gillespie offered help with the later sections of the chronology and of the narrative. Roy Foster read the typescript and gave wise advice and vital affirmation. I have benefited, too, from the support of many other friends: Paul Bew, Richard English, David Hayton and David Livingstone at Queen's, Maurice Bric at University College Dublin, Oliver Rafferty at Oxford, and Kevin O'Neill, Peg Preston, and Rob Savage at Boston College. Blackwell Publishers' readers were – following the convention – anonymous; but their careful reports supplied both encouragement as well as important suggestions for improvement.

I am grateful to numerous individuals and institutions for help with research or copyright materials. Lesley Bruce and Alexandra Cann Representation kindly gave me permission to quote from the work of Stewart Parker. Michael Longley graciously and wittily recorded his willingness to see some of his verse used within these covers: the covers themselves carry an illustration made available through the great generosity of Brian P. Burns and drawn from his superb collection of Irish art. I am indebted, as ever, to the staff of the National Library of Ireland, the Public Record Office of Northern Ireland, the Library of Trinity College Dublin, and the Library of Queen's University Belfast. I must in particular acknowledge the help of Yvonne Murphy and her colleagues in the Northern Ireland Political Collection of the Linenhall Library. To those owners of copyright whom I have been unable to contact or whom I have omitted through oversight, I offer my apologies.

I owe other debts of gratitude. The powers-that-be at Queen's University and the University of Edinburgh arranged for sabbatical leave, without which the book might never have seen the light of day. The British Academy has funded my original and ongoing researches into modern Irish history, most recently through a Senior Research Fellowship (2008–9). The Burns Library and Irish Studies Program at Boston College appointed me to their Burns Visiting Professorship in 1996–7: this brought vital liberation from teaching and administration, as well as access to some splendid library resources. I have mentioned three Bostonian friends: let me also acknowledge the friendship and support of the late Adele Dalsimer, Kristin Morrison and Bob O'Neill, all of Boston College. My greatest debt is recorded in the dedication.

A.J.

LIST OF ABBREVIATIONS

ACA	Army Comrades' Association
AIA	Anglo-Irish Agreement
AOH	Ancient Order of Hibernians
APL	Anti-Partition League
CBS	Christian Brothers' School
CSJ	Campaign for Social Justice
DHAC	Derry Housing Action Committee
DMP	Dublin Metropolitan Police
DUP	Democratic Unionist Party
GAA	Gaelic Athletic Association
GOC	General Officer Commanding
ICTU	Irish Congress of Trade Unions
IDA	Industrial Development Authority
IFS	Irish Free State
ILPU	Irish Loyal and Patriotic Union
INLA	Irish National Liberation Army
INTS	Irish National Theatre Society
IRA	Irish Republican Army
IRAO	Irish Republican Army Organization
IRB	Irish Republican Brotherhood
ITGWU	Irish Transport and General Workers' Union
IUA	Irish Unionist Alliance
IWFL	Irish Womens' Franchise League
NICRA	Northern Ireland Civil Rights Association
NIHE	National Institute for Higher Education
NILP	Northern Ireland Labour Party
NIO	Northern Ireland Office
PD	People's Democracy: Progressive Democrats

PIRA	Provisional Irish Republican Army
PSNI	Police Service of Northern Ireland
PUP	Progressive Unionist Party
RIC	Royal Irish Constabulary
RUC	Royal Ulster Constabulary
SAS	Special Air Service
SDLP	Social Democratic and Labour Party
TD	Teachta Dála
UCD	University College Dublin
UDA	Ulster Defence Association
UDP	Ulster Democratic Party
UDR	Ulster Defence Regiment
UFF	Ulster Freedom Fighters
UIL	United Irish League
UPNI	Unionist Party of Northern Ireland
USC	Ulster Special Constabulary
UUC	Ulster Unionist Council
UVF	Ulster Volunteer Force
UWUC	Ulster Women's Unionist Council
YIB	Young Ireland Branch of the UIL

INTRODUCTION

We are trying to make ourselves heard
Like the lover who mouths obscenities
In his passion, like the condemned man
Who makes a last-minute confession
Like the child who cries out in the dark.

Michael Longley[1]

1.1 Ends of the Century

Irish history, it has been observed, is often written as a morality tale, with a pre-formulated structure and established patterns of triumph and travail.[2] Written in the aftermath of the paramilitary ceasefires of 1994 and 1997 and revised in the wake of the St Andrews Agreement of 2006, this story of Ireland might easily assume some of the characteristics of its predecessors in the field: a narrative of heroism and villainy with a happy resolution. The quality of the fairy-tale ending may not be fully perceived for some years yet, and the interaction of the book's themes may not coincide with the typology of other stories of Ireland. Yet the period under consideration here does appear to represent a discreet phase within Irish political history: while the book lacks the robust predestinarianism of earlier stories, it may at least boast a shadowy symmetry.

The book begins and ends with the turn of a century. The book begins with the creation of militant republicanism and militant loyalism in the 1790s – in the essential context both of European revolution and of a great international conflict: 'the events of 1793–4, in their total effect, marked a turning-point in the history of the protestant ascendancy', J.C. Beckett has noted; Thomas Bartlett has called the 1790s 'the crucible of modern Ireland when separatism, republicanism, unionism and Orangeism captured the Irish political agenda for generations to come'.[3] The book closes with, if not the demise, then at least the modification of militant repub-licanism and militant loyalism in the 1990s and after. Again, the dual context for this development has been European revolution and the apparent resolution of a great international rivalry. America and France fired Irish republican zeal in the early 1790s: the French wars indirectly brought about the militarization of this repub-lican enthusiasm after 1793. The fall of the Soviet empire in the late 1980s and the termination of the ideological and material conflicts between communism and capitalism have affected Ireland no less than the seismic political shifts of the 1790s. Militant republicanism can no longer appeal, even indirectly, to the resources of the eastern bloc; the British government no longer finds a wholly compliant partner in the United States.

Moreover, in both the 1790s and the 1990s social and economic developments broke through their constitutional constraints. The end of the eighteenth century was characterized by the consolidation of the Catholic propertied interest, and by its increasingly vocal opposition to a constitution which recognized property, but not Catholicism. The Irish Protestant constitution (even – especially – when revamped in 1782–3) proved unable to accommodate this newly arisen interest, and was abolished by the British government through the Act of Union (1800). The end of the twentieth century in Northern Ireland has been characterized by the proportionate growth of the Catholic population, and their increasing political and cultural confidence: the Protestant-dominated constitutional arrangements of the period 1920–72 proved unable to accommodate Catholic aspirations, and, after the Second World War, increasing Catholic political and economic strength. The constitutional development of Northern Ireland between 1972 and 1994 has involved a spasmodic retreat from effectively Protestant institutions, as Unionism has splintered and the political and cultural confidence of northern Protestants has waned. There is, however, some scattered evidence to suggest that this process has been temporarily halted. It would seem that 25 years of violence (1969–94) have brought not only some belated Catholic political victories, but at last a more crit-ical self-awareness and reorientation on the part of Ulster Protestants.

This of course broaches the characteristic *fin-de-siècle* theme of decadence. The late eighteenth century witnessed the first symptoms of the decay of Protestant ascen-dancy in Ireland, albeit a decay well screened by a luxuriant social and political culture. Whether the late twentieth century has witnessed the decay of Protestant predom-inance in Northern Ireland (screened again by an exotic political culture) will remain an open question for some decades. Whether the late twentieth century has witnessed the final decay of what has been euphemistically labelled the 'physical force' traditions of loyalism and republicanism is similarly uncertain. If there is, arguably, a symmetry in this story of Ireland, then its lines necessarily remain blurred.

1.2   Modes and Frameworks of Interpretation

Until recently the most common framework applied to modern Irish history has been that associated with the varieties of Irish nationalism. Work written in this

broad tradition has become much less common given the steady professionalization of Irish history writing since the 1930s, but some of its features live on. The
Irish history profession evolved alongside the development, in the late nineteenth
and early twentieth centuries, of the Irish revolution, and there was an inevitable
overlap or exchange. In 1886, at the time of the first Home Rule Bill, historians
from several traditions debated the achievement of Grattan's parliament, the
assembly abolished in 1800 through the Act of Union: nationalist commentators
saw an economic and cultural flowering in Ireland as a result of legislative independence, while unionist commentators stressed the merits of Union. Heroes of
the campaign to repeal the Union, such as Thomas Davis, were lauded in celebratory biographies (Charles Gavan Duffy, *Thomas Davis* (1890)). General histories of
Ireland (such as that by Mary Hayden) deployed a straightforward morality,
emphasizing the benefits of self-rule and the brutality of British imperial government. This work has supplied several starting points even for some contemporary
Irish historiography: an emphasis on the nobility of nationalist endeavour, on the
suffering of the Irish people under British rule, and on the inevitable success of the
national struggle. Such work, in its most direct expression, fell victim to the popularization of a more 'scientific' historical methodology with the creation, in 1938,
of the influential journal *Irish Historical Studies*; intellectual proponents of an
uncritical militant nationalism were also embarrassed by the more bloody aspects
of the IRA campaigns after 1969. The paramilitary ceasefires in 1994 and 1997 have,
however, permitted the renewal of a nationalist historical perspective on modern
Irish history.

An alternative and, since the mid-1960s, a highly influential interpretative
approach has been labelled as 'liberal'. Such work has its origins as a reaction against
the most elaborate and unconvincing nationalist rhetoric, and – certainly in the
view of critics such as Bradshaw – has substituted a rationalist aridity for nationalist floridity.[4] The characteristics of this work tend to be an intolerance of intolerance – a disdainful attitude towards popular political institutions and culture
– combined with a much more sensitive approach to the diversity of modern Ireland
than that adopted by the traditionalists. Neo-nationalists tend to see Ireland as an
ethnic nation subjugated by a neighbouring imperial power (Britain); 'liberals' place
greater emphasis on the 'varieties of Irishness' and are more wary about the crude
application of national labels.[5] 'Liberals' tend not to accept that Ireland was bound
by a simple colonial relationship with Britain.

The counter-revisionist critics of this dominant tendency within Irish historical
scholarship fall into a variety of camps (not all of which are discrete). Counter-
revisionism may at once be a reassertion of patriotic certainties: in this sense, counter-
revisionism may be seen as an Irish expression of the historiography of the radical
right prevalent in the 1980s. By extension, counter-revisionism may be seen as part
of the broader 'greening' of Irish society, as evidenced by the election of Mary McAleese
as President of Ireland, and – in terms of popular culture – by the phenomenal
success of Neil Jordan's film *Michael Collins* and Michael Flatley's *Riverdance*
(Flatley appeared on posters clad in the national colours, and the pounding rhythms
of his dancers suggested a militant Celticism to some – friendly – critics). But the

counter-revisionist tendency is as sophisticated as the revisionism which it seeks to subvert; and it is also arguable that counter-revisionism represents a post-modernist assault on the enlightenment verities of mainstream Irish history. In this interpretation revisionism is a liberal construction, and therefore as flawed and as dangerous as other constructionist readings. Indeed, just as some crusading post-modernists have seen the Holocaust as a bloody and perverted expression of the Enlightenment, so some 'green' post-modernists have seen 'enlightened' revisionists apologizing for what is occasionally described as the Irish holocaust – the Great Famine of 1845–51.[6]

Marxian interpretations of modern Irish history stem from the Irish commentaries of Marx himself, or – more frequently – the work of the socialist James Connolly, especially *Labour in Irish History* (1910) or *The Reconquest of Ireland* (1915). This work, predictably enough, is to be differentiated from mainstream nationalist commentary by its emphasis on class, and hostility towards organized Catholicism. It lays emphasis on the revolutionary potential of the Irish working class, seeing capitalism as an imperialist importation, and the middle classes as hopelessly corrupted: 'the middle class . . . have now also bowed the knee to Baal, and have a thousand economic strings binding them to English capitalism as against every sentimental or historic attachment drawing them towards Irish patriotism'.[7] The ineluctable problem which this work continually encounters is that of the Unionist working class in Belfast, a theoretical irritant (like the Tory working man in Victorian England) as well as an apparently practical obstacle to the socialist millennium. Connolly saw the Catholics and Presbyterians of eighteenth-century Ireland as united through their legal disabilities; he saw Presbyterians won to the cause of the Anglican 'master class' in the nineteenth century, and bound into an Orange working class whose servility was rooted in marginal superiority over Catholic unskilled labour. The influence of this model of sectarian and political relations in the north of Ireland since the late eighteenth century has been immense. Connolly's arguments have stimulated a continuous reappraisal, and even though his view of the servile Orange worker and rebel Catholic counterpart has been found to be oversimplistic, his rhetoric and assumptions continue to inform even highly respected contemporary portrayals of the north of Ireland in the nineteenth century.

This volume is not exclusively a part of any of these traditions. It is not neo-nationalist, because while the value of a free-ranging historical sympathy and empathy is warmly embraced here, a historical determinism forms no part of the critical approach. For much the same reasons the volume, though occasionally influenced by some Marxist scholarship on Ulster labour, is neither a socialist text nor a call to arms such as Michael Farrell's *Northern Ireland: The Orange State* (1976).[8] Similarly, while it shares the inclusivist vision of Irish identity explored in Foster's *Modern Ireland* (1988), the book is not a liberal document. It has been the fate of Ireland's liberal historians – Lecky, Beckett, Lyons – to see their rationalist faith in the power of scholarship smashed by popular political emotion: Beckett's optimistic projections of the political outlook in his *The Making of Modern Ireland* (1966) were soon shown to be ill-founded, while the mild, generous, confident nationalism of

F.S.L. Lyons's *Ireland since the Famine* (1971) was replaced by the bleaker tone of his last work, *Culture and Anarchy in Ireland* (1979). Written with this evidence of wrecked aspirations, and after 25 years of a low-grade but vicious civil war in Northern Ireland, this volume could not consciously be imbued with any Whiggish agenda, however subtle or artless.

Nevertheless, if post-modernist writing is a by-product of an age of crisis, then we in Ireland, and especially in Northern Ireland, are all post-modernists now. This book was written against a backdrop of political and social fluidity, with the ostensibly marmoreal political attitudes and institutions of Northern Ireland in flux: the book was begun in a post-Unionist Ulster, pursued in a post-nationalist Ireland, completed in a post-industrial United States and revised in a post-unionist Scotland. In common with much recent historiography, the volume addresses some of the contemporary predicaments of Northern Ireland and the island as a whole; there is no grand narrative, however, no 'Official Story', but rather an interest in what Richard Kearney has called an 'open plurality of stories'.[9] The work embodies no blind faith in the canonical 'facts' of Irish history. As Peter Novick has argued, the historian – and emphatically the Irish historian – can hope at best for plausibility.[10]

Readers, then, will not find here a universal narrative history, still less a history designed to serve as a basic introduction, or primer, for the subject. An analysis of Irish political parties, leaders, institutions and movements is sustained; and social, economic and cultural material relevant to the main political thrust is introduced and interwoven. Individual chapters highlight major political issues, and these are generally explored through the mapping of subsidiary themes or hypotheses: the material relevant to a given issue is often arranged thematically or within the context of a wider argument. This makes for a design which is intended to stimulate thought (or, indeed, to invite argument) about sometimes familiar historical issues or personalities: it is a design which (it is intended) will highlight some fresh conjunctions and configurations in the interpretation of modern Irish history. In addition, the design is meant to corral, not just the familiar hobby horses of students, but also some rarer creatures. An attempt has been made to give a place to some sections of Irish society not normally (or, at any rate, not adequately) represented within works such as this. Thus – once again – the volume is not conditioned exclusively by the contours of contemporary Irish life: the 'losers' of social and economic and political struggle are characterized as well as the 'winners'. There are Salieris here as well as Mozarts.

2

THE BIRTH OF MODERN IRISH POLITICS, 1790–8

We had the true faith, you see. Reason. The logical men. History was a dungeon. The people were locked into their separate compounds, full of stench and night-mare. But the dungeons couldn't stand against the force of rationalism. Let the people once unite, and we could burst open the doors, and they would flood out into the clean sunlight . . . all we've done, you see, is to reinforce the locks, cram the cells fuller than ever of mangled bodies crawling round in their own shite and lunacy, and the cycle just goes on, playing out the same demented comedy of terrors from generation to generation, trapped in the same malignant legend . . .
Henry Joy McCracken, in Stewart Parker's *Northern Star* (1983)[1]

2.1   The Origins of the Crisis

Ireland in the 1790s was a separate but dependent kingdom, united to Great Britain only through sharing a monarch, George III: the theoretical constitutional position of Ireland was similar to that of Hungary after the *Ausgleich* of 1867. Ireland boasted a separate bicameral legislature, which sat in Edward Lovett Pearce's splendid Italianate parliament house in College Green, Dublin: after 1782–3 this assembly enjoyed, at least in name, full legislative independence. There was a distinct Irish executive, headed by a lord lieutenant, and based in a sprawling administrative complex at Dublin Castle. There was a theoretically separate Irish judiciary, housed in Dublin's Four Courts, on the northern bank of the river Liffey.

But behind these elaborate institutions, and behind the florid rhetoric of the Irish parliament's patriot interest, lay the reality of British influence. The Irish parliament had, indeed, won what it was pleased to call 'legislative independence' in 1782–3; but while the strategies which secured victory had an immense significance, the limits of this triumph were soon apparent – and particularly after 1789 when, with the French revolution, an increasingly ambitious definition of parliamentary autonomy and authority gained currency.[2] In 1782 one of the keystones of the Irish constitution, Poynings' Law (1494), had been modified in order to award the Irish parliament sole rights over the introduction of legislation (the modifying legislation was known as Yelverton's Act): in addition an antique legislative irritant, the Declaratory Act (1720), which asserted the superior status of Westminster, was repealed and, in 1783, replaced by the Renunciation Act, a measure disavowing any British legislative ambition over Ireland. These tinkerings were hailed by Irish patriots as independence, but the chasm between this rhetoric and constitutional reality was wide, and ultimately dangerous.

The Irish political system in the 1790s was affected by British influence at almost every level. Though Yelverton's Act had emasculated the Irish privy council, its British counterpart still possessed a right of veto over Irish legislation, and this meant that the British government could spike any offensive measures (in reality it rarely did so). The constitutional settlement of 1782–3 did not directly alter the condition of the Irish executive, which remained firmly under the control of the British government. The chief executive, the lord lieutenant, was a British appointee, and was throughout the period 1782–1800 an Englishman; in the same period the Chief Secretaries – in effect the government managers in the Commons – were, bar one, Englishmen, and the unique Irish appointment, Robert Stewart, Lord Castlereagh, was deemed by his lord lieutenant in 1797 to be 'so very unlike an Irishman I think he has a clear claim to an exception in his favour'.[3] A triumvirate of powerful office-holders – John Foster, Speaker of the Commons, John Fitzgibbon, the Lord Chancellor, and John Beresford, Chief Commissioner of the Revenue – generally (though not uniformly) exercised their formidable political influence in the government interest.

The 'insistent treatment of Ireland as a British dependency' (as Nancy Curtin has described it) was made possible both by the British-controlled executive and by the peculiarly unrepresentative nature of the Irish parliament: strict British control over patronage combined with a narrowly based and therefore susceptible parliament to tarnish further the lustre of 'legislative independence'.[4] The Irish House of Commons at the end of the eighteenth century represented chiefly the Church of Ireland landed interest. Catholics were disfranchised between 1728 and 1793, and were excluded from parliament until the 'emancipation' of 1829; Presbyterians, while possessing the franchise, were in practice scarcely represented. Of 150 constituencies represented in the Irish House of Commons, 107 were 'close' – that is, under the control of an individual or a small group of patrons. By contemporary European standards even limited parliamentary representation was a democratic luxury, and by contemporary British standards a small and irregular electorate was unexceptional. In addition, A.P.W. Malcomson has warned against the uncritical assumption that close boroughs implied inefficient or unchallenged control.[5] What was unusual about Ireland was not that landed property should be overrepresented (however unevenly), or that there should be a religious dimension to political rights, but rather that the two principles should be combined in order to exclude two powerful and wealthy confessional communities from representative politics. This constitutional quirk was made all the more glaring given the inflated libertarian rhetoric which had preceded the achievement of legislative independence in 1782. Legislative independence therefore raised dangerous expectations in two separate, but related, spheres: the campaign encouraged the assumption that, while the British connection would remain, British influence would be constrained; and, further, it underlined Catholic and Presbyterian exclusion. The Renunciation Act (1783) has been described as 'a mere decorative flourish for which the indirect price was out of all proportion to the benefit obtained': the same aphorism might be applied to the whole settlement (1782–3).[6] Legislative independence was a Pyrrhic victory for the ascendancy parliament, bought at the price of long-term constitutional uncertainty.

Thomas Malthus, in a famous discussion of Irish demography, suggested that the political uncertainty of the 1790s was a product, not of this long-term constitutional instability, but rather of exceptional population growth.[7] In 1790 the Irish population stood at around 4 million, having doubled since the famine of 1740–1; by 1800 the population would be 5 million, an astonishing rate of growth by late eighteenth-century European standards. Explanations for this growth are never likely to be conclusive, but the widespread adoption of the potato through the eighteenth century, combined with the general economic buoyancy of the later part of the century, are clearly relevant factors. Early marriage, and (possibly) a falling mortality rate, were the immediate spurs to this population boom, but a political dimension has also been observed: the political exclusion of Catholics, an issue increasingly to the fore after legislative independence, and limited Catholic prospects for betterment, may have removed any social or economic restraint on marital fertility. It may well be that the political turmoil of the 1790s was simultaneously a cause and a result of this growth.

Economic growth, while related to the issue of population, clearly operated as an independent destabilizing influence. After the fluctuating, but generally depressed, conditions of the period 1691–1730, the Irish economy grew swiftly: agricultural output rose, trade with Britain and with North America prospered, new industries (such as cotton) and well-established industries (such as linen manufacture, brewing and distilling) all generally flourished (despite occasional, temporary downturns, such as at the end of the 1770s). It is difficult to be precise about the political implications of this growth. It may, however, be surmised that the political crisis of 1779–82, which resulted in the achievement of 'free trade' and legislative independence for Ireland, was related to contemporary economic conditions – a period of depression after sustained growth, and the creation of an early 'crisis of expectations' (such as has been identified for the 1870s). The complex inter-relationship between economic growth and political protest may be further illustrated through the example of eighteenth-century Armagh. David Miller has argued that the rise of the linen industry in late eighteenth-century County Armagh encouraged some limited Catholic economic mobility and tended to destabilize well-established family structures within every confessional tradition: the profitability of handloom weaving permitted young men to establish their independence much earlier than was usual within small farmer society, and freed them from the restraints of the rigid, patriarchal family.[8] This social liberation combined with Catholic advance and with the rapid rise in population to stimulate the sectarian violence endemic in Armagh from the mid-1780s through to the mid-1790s.

But economic growth was linked to other evolving forms of social and political interaction. Tom Bartlett has argued persuasively that in Ireland after *c.*1770 a new moral economy was developing in the Irish countryside, underpinned by the grow-ing 'sociability' of community activity.[9] The mounting prosperity of the country-side was reflected in the rising number of fairs and markets, and in the gradual commercialization of rural economic life. Relative prosperity therefore not only equipped many Irish people with new political and material aspirations, but also gave rise to increasing opportunities for communal mobilization and protest. Aside from the emergence of new political fora, older forms of public activity – sporting events, wakes, funerals, patterns – also now began to take on an additional significance: the politicization of funerals, for example, seems to have gathered pace in this era.

These processes of socialization were augmented and diverted by the increasing importance of military activity within everyday life: it has been calculated that between 1760 and 1820, perhaps as many as one in six Irishmen spent part of their lives in the ranks of one or other of the armed forces, and indeed it is possible that, given the stupendous demands of the Napoleonic wars, this proportion may have been higher.[10] For many this involved a liberation from the shackles of the local community, and brought – perhaps for the first time – tighter definitions of nationality and of religious identity. Indeed, it has been observed that this era also witnessed a spiralling sectarianism, or rather sectarianization, in part the by-product of these more communal forms of political expression and of the mount-ing conflicts between Catholics and the Protestant state: the army, for example, may have been the first arena where many Irish Catholics experienced the reality of their religious subordination.

A related range of destabilizing influences may be located in the realm of ideo-logy. Irish interest in the American and French revolutions was immense, and the ideological fall-out from these events was no less dramatic. The rationalist, liber-tarian and republican ideals of, especially, the French revolutionaries found an audience in Ireland already sensitive (for the reasons already noted) to the issue of individual political rights and national sentiment. However, the direct influence of the great writers of the French enlightenment is difficult to gauge: Montesquieu, Voltaire, Diderot, Rousseau can have had only a very few, privileged readers in Ireland. Popular appreciation of the ideals and events of the French revolution came, not from its intellectual architects, but rather from the press and from pamphlets. 'Illiteracy', as Nancy Curtin has observed, 'was no barrier to familiarising oneself with the polemics of a Paine or of a Tone': public readings from the newspapers and from radical literature were quite common.[11] Nor was it necessary to follow difficult abstract argument: handbills hammered home a clear-cut political message, while ballads celebrated the French revolutionary achievement in a universally accessible fashion. Popular prophetic literature foretold the liberation of Ireland by the French. In Ireland, just as in France itself, popular political resentments were cultivated and directed by this literature. The tyranny of Irish government was underlined by the experience of the French; moreover, the Irish oppressed had now an ally in the shape of a liberated French nation.

2.2   Constitutional Radicalism to Revolution, 1791–8

The two dominant Irish political issues of the early 1790s were certainly not spawned by the French revolution, but they were nurtured through revolutionary sympathy. Parliamentary reform had been a longstanding question, dating back to the late 1740s and to the campaigns of the radical Dublin apothecary, Charles Lucas: although initially more concerned with Dublin corporation politics than with parliament, Lucas had condemned the misgovernment of the Castle and its parliamentary allies, and – after his political comeback in 1761 – had supported a septennial bill in order to limit the duration of parliament. Lucas's views, as David Dickson has noted, 'were later to influence Catholic apologists arguing for relaxation of the penal laws, and political radicals seeking parliamentary reform'.[12] The constitutional settlement of 1782–3 raised the issue of parliamentary reform in a more direct manner than had been done in the previous generation, with the Volunteers of Ulster attacking the power of the great borough owners, and a National Convention of the Volunteers, held in Dublin in November 1783, declaring in favour of a reform bill. This was presented to the House of Commons, and summarily rejected. A revival of the reform question in 1784–5 was spear-headed by a new coalition, largely urban, and embracing both Catholics (hitherto largely silent on the question) and dissenters. This fed off other resentments – the Dublin guilds wanted tariff protection, Catholics wanted the removal of disabilities – but soon fell victim to internal division (especially on the question of Catholic relief) and to a ferocious and abusive press campaign orchestrated by the Castle. The rejection of William Pitt's proposals for reform of the British parliament, presented in 1785, confirmed the comprehensive failure of the Irish reformers.

In the later 1780s the most conspicuous proponents of limited reform were the Whigs, who were bruised by their misjudgements during the Regency Crisis (they offered over-hasty support for the Prince of Wales during George III's temporary incapacity in 1788–9), and who established a formal party in the Irish parliament in 1789: this supported place and pensions bills, a responsibility bill, and the disfranchisement of revenue officers. Even though Whig clubs were founded in Dublin, Belfast and other large towns to bolster the new grouping (the Northern Whig Club denounced corrupt boroughs), the new political challenge came to nothing: the elections of 1790 brought no sweeping Whig successes, and in fact served only to consolidate the parliamentary strength of the Castle. While the Whigs appear to have found some inspiration from France in the summer of 1789 (their manifesto was published a month after the fall of the Bastille), the revolution both directly and indirectly would prove to be disastrous for them. As the revolutionaries grew more radical and violent, so the Whigs grew ever more divided in their attitudes. Moreover, with the outbreak of war between Britain and France in 1793, the Castle sought to bolster support for the war effort through annexing and enacting some of the Whigs' policies (a Civil List Act, a Place Act, a Barren Land Act and a Hearth Tax Act). However, this conciliation was complemented – as so often in the history of Castle administration – with coercion, and three security measures were passed in the same parliamentary session of 1793: a Convention Act, a Gunpowder Act and a Militia Act. And neither the Castle nor – despite some equivocation – the Irish House of Commons was seriously interested in the prospect of parliamentary reform: a Whig reform bill, creating three member county constituencies and a uniform, if elaborate, borough franchise, was easily rejected in March 1794, with the opponents of reform arguing that such moderation had spawned eventual anarchy in France. Denuded in certain areas of policy, and blocked in others, the Whigs lost credibility, and constitutional reform initiatives fell into other, ultimately less genteel, hands.

The only substantial reform of the franchise to be won in these years came in January 1793, with the admission of Catholic 40-shilling freeholders to the county vote through Hobart's relief bill (and even the importance of this can easily be over-stated, given that the Irish parliament was a borough-dominated assembly). The political leadership of the Catholic community before 1789 pursued a distinctively gradualist and (on the whole) loyalist agenda, couching limited demands for ministerial 'indulgence' in highly deferential language. The Catholic Committee, created in 1760, was the chief representative body for the Catholic community, and emerged as a mild and aristocratic institution: this went into abeyance in 1784, after the failure of the parliamentary reform initiative, but was revived in 1790–1 with the accession of new, bourgeois and radical, leaders. Eamon O'Flaherty has warned against treating the Catholic community in the late eighteenth century in crudely homogeneous terms, and indeed even the political attitudes of the Catholic clergy varied significantly: the French revolution created divisions between the episcopate and the younger clergy which foreshadowed similar tensions during the Irish land wars and revolutionary era.[13] Indeed, the lessons provided by France for Irish Catholics were ambiguous: the revolution simultaneously promoted the religious tolerance and equality which had for long been sought by Catholic representatives in Ireland, while involving an assault on the institutions and property of the Church. Revolutionary ideals therefore fired a demand for Catholic relief in Ireland, while disturbing many Catholic gentry and much of the episcopate.

By December 1791 the old aristocratic masters of the Catholic Committee had withdrawn, leaving the field to the middle-class radicals (notably John Keogh and Thomas Braughall). The deferential and loyal petitioning of Lord Kenmare, the aristocratic Catholic leader, was now replaced by the French-inspired language of right. In addition, Keogh and the new Committee complemented this radical assertiveness with strategic innovation. The Irish government and parliament were clearly unsympathetic to Catholic claims and were soon written out of the

Committee's strategy (two relief petitions, submitted by the Committee to the Irish House of Commons in January and February 1792, were rejected amidst much anti-papist philosophizing). A highly tentative reform measure – sponsored by Sir Hercules Langrishe and dubbed therefore 'Langrishe's Act' (even though it had originated with the Castle) – did nothing to defuse Catholic protest: indeed, on the contrary, for as Tom Bartlett has argued, the significance of the measure 'lay in the debate it provoked (but did not resolve) on the nature of the Anglo-Irish connection, in the jealousies and suspicions it aroused concerning the British government's Catholic game, and in the fact that it was clearly incomplete'.[14] Moreover, the bill passed into law accompanied by the elaboration and enunciation of the new idea of 'Protestant ascendancy'. Even before these humiliations the Catholic Committee had been prepared to sidestep the Irish parliament through exploiting close links with its supporters at Westminster (pre-eminently Edmund Burke) and establishing communication with the British government: Burke's son, Richard, was appointed English agent of the Committee in September 1791. The appointment of Theobald Wolfe Tone to the secretaryship of the Committee in July 1792 signalled a more defiant and radical approach; and this was confirmed by the national Catholic Convention, held in Dublin in December, which voted to petition the king for total legal equality. 'The real achievement of the Convention', O'Flaherty has argued, 'was that it succeeded in inducing Pitt to bring irresistible pressure on the Irish executive to grant the principal Catholic demand'.[15] Hobart's relief bill, admitting Catholic 40-shilling freeholders to the franchise, was the fruit of this simultaneously more assertive and subtle approach to the advocacy of Catholic rights: it was the highpoint of Catholic constitutional endeavour in the 1790s, indeed before the 'emancipation' (the term gained currency in 1792–3) of 1829. Thereafter Catholic constitutional pressure encountered an ascendancy interest increasingly concerned and defensive about the European war, and therefore more in tune than hitherto with the British government. The Catholic Committee was forced to dissolve under the terms of the Convention Act (1793): Henry Grattan's Catholic Emancipation Bill (1795) was defeated in the Irish House of Commons, and Grattan's viceregal patron, Earl Fitzwilliam, removed from office after a tenure of scarcely two months. Yet, though this half-cocked emancipation did not in fact herald a greater liberation, its significance should not be missed: Hobart called the enfranchisement 'a most important revolution in the political state of this country', and Tom Bartlett has convincingly stressed the long-term importance of the arguments and strategies which were pursued in the search for reform.[16] Ominously, the comparatively genteel power struggle that was under way in Dublin was underscored by a more naked sectarian conflict in south Ulster.

The crucial points of contact between the radical tradition of parliamentary reform and the campaign for Catholic relief came with the United Irish Society, founded in Belfast and Dublin in 1791, and with Wolfe Tone, 'mid-wife' of the Society and an influential Catholic sympathizer. The Society was at first a constitutional radical grouping, hostile to English interference in the government of Ireland, but urging the comprehensive reform of government rather than its overthrow. The

'Declaration and Resolutions of the Society of United Irishmen of Belfast', published
in October 1791 and drafted by Tone, called for 'a complete and radical reform of
the representation of the people in parliament', and the unity of all 'Irishmen' in
order to pursue this end. The Society reflected Tone's dual enthusiasm for parliamentary reform and Catholic emancipation (a combination most famously articulated in his *Argument on behalf of the Catholics of Ireland* (1791)); and indeed the
Dublin United Irishmen, originally largely Protestant, soon attracted an influx of
Catholics, including leading members of the Catholic Committee. The Dublin United
Irishmen produced a reform plan early in 1794 which fleshed out the general ideals
expressed in the original declaration: equal constituencies, universal male suffrage,
annual parliaments, payment of members of parliament. The Belfast United
Irishmen had produced a similarly moderate reform proposal early in 1793 – 'the
last act of Ulster constitutional reformism', in Dickson's description.[17] But by this
time, and certainly by the time the Dublin scheme appeared, the prospects for a
radical reform of parliament, never bright, had been utterly extinguished. The war
had undercut the popular francophile radicalism of 1791–2, scaring many early enthu-
siasts. The government, sensitive to any prospect of sedition, had little difficulty in
suppressing the Society in May 1794.

Many, especially northern, United Irishmen had fostered republican and revolutionary sympathies behind the cloak of constitutional radicalism (although Tone,
in the opinion of Marianne Elliott, 'was not an active separatist until 1795').[18]
Government suppression in 1793–4 combined with the apparent futility of a constitutional strategy to realize the latent militancy of the United Irish movement. Before
1794 the United Irishmen of Ulster were informally supervised by a committee of
public welfare sitting in Belfast. But with a heightened militancy of purpose came
the need for a more cohesive and secret organizational structure. A new constitution was therefore drafted late in 1794, and accepted in May 1795, in the wake of
Fitzwilliam's recall, and the disappointment of constitutional reform aspirations:
the new constitution created a rigid committee structure, binding small towns
and rural 'half-baronies' ultimately to the Ulster provincial committee. By the end
of 1796 the Society had decided to create a parallel military structure, with elected
sergeants, captains and more senior officers. At the same time – 1795–6 – the United
Irishmen of the north (in contradistinction to their more cautious brethren in Dublin),
using former members of the Catholic Committee as go-betweens, began to court
the leaders of a popular Catholic secret society, the Defenders: Henry Joy McCracken
and other United Irish leaders boasted in the summer of 1796 'that there had been
a junction between the leaders of the United Irishmen and the Defenders . . . there
was a complete union between the Defenders and the United Irishmen'. This (in
Elliott's description) 'merger' underlined the numerical strength of the northern
revolutionary conspiracy, creating a movement which, in the spring of 1797,
boasted a membership of 118,000 and an armoury of 7,000 guns.

The union of the United Irishmen and the Defenders was once seen as the graft-
ing of a politicized and coherent leadership onto a less sophisticated and less
well-organized mass movement. This, however, is to misjudge the probably

wholehearted nature of the union, as well as to underestimate the quality of Defenderism. The Defenders had their origins in Armagh in the mid-1780s, formed in the dual context of sectarian rivalry within the linen industry and competition for land within one of the most densely populated counties in Ireland. Increasing Catholic self-confidence, which found a particular expression in the bearing of arms, seems to have unsettled traditional sectarian relationships and to have fuelled Defenderism along with its Protestant rivals and antagonists (gangs such as the Nappagh Fleet or the Peep o'Day Boys). By 1790 the Defenders had become a secret society, organized – like the Peep o'Day Boys – along masonic lines, and spreading from south Ulster into north Leinster. Defenderism eventually percolated into the poorest strata of Catholic Dublin. Recent scholarship has tended to stress the extent to which Defenderism not only outgrew its local and narrow origins, but may always in fact have had a degree of broader political awareness: certainly it seems probable that (in Curtin's words) 'the further the Defenders were separated from Armagh, the more they lost their sectarian character'.[19] The French revolution probably helped to change, if not some of the core economic motivation of the movement, then at least its language: Defender oaths and catechisms were larded with republicanism and French sympathies. There is some evidence to suggest contact between French emissaries and Defenders as early as 1792. It has been argued that the campaign for Catholic relief (1791–3) helped to further the politicization of the Defender movement to the extent that 'the Defenders came to see themselves as the armed wing of the Catholic Committee': Defender arms raids at this time appear to have been in preparation for a final assault on ascendancy power.[20] The movement gained confidence by the concession of Hobart's Relief Act in 1793; and it garnered further support from the government's decision to conscript Catholics, by ballot, into a new militia force in the summer of 1793. However, in September 1795 the Defenders, operating outside their normal boundaries, suffered a defeat at the Battle of the Diamond, near Loughgall in north Armagh; but the aggressive response of their Protestant victors (who organized themselves as the Orange Order) drove many Catholics out of the county and thereby helped to spread a newly embittered form of Defenderism, particularly into north Connacht. By 1795 Defenderism remained a movement that was partly motivated by economic grievances – the desire for cheap land, better-paid labour, the righting of ancient land confiscations – and partly by sectarian resentment. But it was also a mass movement highly sympathetic to the French revolution, hopeful of French aid, and influenced in organization and rhetoric by revolutionary precedents. Here, then, was the basis for cooperation with the United Irishmen.

The Castle responded to this developing seditious combination with an unusual ferocity. As has been noted, even the highpoint of the Castle's reform endeavour – the measures of 1793 – was characterized as much by repression as by concession. The prospect of French intervention was as frightening for the government as it was encouraging for the United Irishmen and the Defenders; and though ministers were anxious to secure broad-based Irish support for the war through a number of minor reforms, they were equally anxious to crush any latent hostility to this war effort. In fact the government went some way to realizing its own worst fears: the disappearance of constitutional avenues to reform undoubtedly stimulated, if it did not create, the mass revolutionary conspiracy that was in place by 1796. In that year the renewed prospect of a French invasion brought a further legislative reaction in the forms of the Indemnity Act (a measure designed to protect magistrates who, in pursuing Defenders, had acted illegally) and an Insurrection Act (a measure easing the application of a curfew in disturbed areas, and facilitating weapons searches and the arrest of suspects). In October 1796 the crown forces were augmented through the creation of the yeomanry, a body led by officially approved gentry and designed to police its own local patch: this would prove to be an important government resource during the 1798 rising, even though – as Allan Blackstock has shown – it soon became tinctured with Orangeism and progressively unruly.[21]

The much-vaunted French expedition set sail in December 1796, only to be dispersed by Atlantic gales rather than the Royal Navy: but the Castle was still shocked, for it had been ill-served by its intelligence networks. Although Lazare Hoche's French fleet had been aiming to land at Bantry Bay, in the south-west, the most likely area for a sympathetic uprising lay not in Munster but in Ulster, where the United Irish Society had established the most broadly based organization: and it was therefore in Ulster that, in 1797, the Castle concentrated its military resources. In charge of the military operations in Ulster after the end of 1796 was General Gerard Lake, a forceful commander who was not over-sensitive to political and legal subtlety. Suspected radicals were imprisoned (between September 1796 and September 1797, perhaps 500–600 political prisoners were held); weapons searches began at the end of 1796 and were scaled up in March 1797 (by 1 July 1797, 6,200 firearms in working order, and 4,400 in unserviceable condition, had been seized by Lake's troops). The houses of suspects were burnt, and troops were quartered in areas where sedition and the secretion of weapons were thought to be rife. These techniques, perfected in Ulster, were applied to the south of Ireland in the winter of 1797–8. Martial law was declared in March 1798, but it had in fact existed in all but name for months before.

The bloody disarming of first the north and then the rest of the island had a number of consequences for the conspirators. The movement was simultaneously divided and fired: the militancy of the authorities combined with the evident impossibility of constitutional change (a last reform bill was thrown out by the House of Commons in May 1797) to cow some of the rebels while underpinning the militancy of others. Arrests of prominent United Irishmen from late 1796 deprived the conspiracy of perhaps the most talented section of its leadership, while others – fearing official retribution – fled during the summer of 1797. Riddled with informants, the conspiracy fell an easy prey to the government: much of the Leinster directory of the Society was arrested in March 1798 as a result of the treachery of one of its members. The intensification of the government operations in April and May 1798 further damaged the enthusiasm of the militants, disrupting United Irish organization and removing weapons and personnel: the sheer brutality of much of this action served to (indeed was designed to) intimidate. The arrest and fatal

Plate 1 Leaders of the 1798 rising.
Source: Linenhall Library/Flying Fox.

wounding on 19 May of the military leader of the Society, Lord Edward Fitzgerald, brought further confusion and effectively forced the remaining disoriented leaders to choose between surrender or rebellion. It was of course a Hobson's choice. Despite the disastrous incursions made by the government into the leadership and armoury of the Society, surrender scarcely offered a more propitious alternative; and the national directory opted to rebel. In the event the Ulster leadership, cowed by General Lake and anxious for French assistance, chose to misinterpret this call, and delayed the northern uprising for a week.

The 1798 rising is to be located in the political, economic and ideological 'disequilibrium' of the 1790s, and much of this chapter has been devoted to exploring this variety of contexts. But the rising was a mass movement – at least 27,000 insurgents fought in Ulster alone – and a variety of confessional and political traditions were bound together in a not always comfortable alliance: the problem of interpreting motivation remains complex, therefore. There was clearly a generally high level of political awareness in both the United Irish and Defender traditions, and a generally high level of French sympathy and revolutionary idealism. But what made the rising so potent was that it combined an intellectually coherent, and indeed accessible, ideology of liberation with ancient historical resentments and religious prejudices. Numerous northern Presbyterians evidently fought under the United Irish banner, while remaining profoundly suspicious of their Catholic co-conspirators: as Ian McBride has remarked, 'to some extent Presbyterian radicalism represented the continuation of the war against Popery by other means'.[22] Many Defenders were evidently fired by the prospect of righting ancient wrongs, or correcting local economic injustice, even though they expressed their convictions at least superficially in a more universalist garb. The Defenders fought under distinctively Catholic emblems at the battle of Randalstown (7 June); Henry Munro, the rebel commander at Ballynahinch (13 June), and a Protestant, was accused by the Defenders of sectarian prejudice in his battle plan; Larry Dempsey, a Catholic officer of the largely Presbyterian Ballynure insurgents, sought to rouse his men with the comment that 'by J—s, boys, we'll pay the rascals this day for the battle of the Boyne'.[23] Thus if the political sophistication of the insurgents has been sometimes underestimated (and a good case has been made for supposing this to be so for County Wexford), then equally it would be imprudent to overlook religious conviction and local, communal grievance as a sustaining influence behind revolutionary conviction.[24] The root problem in approaching the '98 is that, even more than other pivotal events in modern Irish history, the evidence for the rising tends to be overlaid with later political expectations. As J.C. Beckett remarked in 1966, 'the insurrection of 1798 is seen not as it was in deed but as Tone had hoped for it to be' – and it might also be suggested that the '98 is seen in some quarters, not as it was, but as Lord Clare perceived it to be.[25]

The location and course of the rising present fewer problems of interpretation. There were three main areas of action: in Leinster, especially Wexford, in eastern Ulster, and Mayo, in Connacht. In Leinster it was planned that there would be several county revolts, which would unite in marching on Dublin. But although

Carlow, Kildare, Meath and Wexford rose in revolt, elsewhere the grand scheme broke down and the rising took the form of minor skirmishes or small-scale raids: even in Meath and Kildare, where the insurgents were more ambitious, the crown forces had little difficulty in gaining the upper hand.

The experience of Wexford was of a different nature, and Louis Cullen and Kevin Whelan have done much to explain why this should have been so.[26] Wexford offered the insurgents a rather more fertile loam than in much of the rest of southern Ireland. A peculiarly weak Protestant gentry, politically divided, was associated with a fractured and capricious magistracy: an earlier moral economy had broken down in the 1790s, as the conservative gentry grew more defensive and Orange, and as law enforcement grew at best more unpredictable and at worst more partial than hitherto. The Protestant sub-gentry was weakened by the collapse of middlemen leases. By way of contrast Catholic Wexford was prospering on the back of the late eighteenth-century agricultural boom. The survival of Catholic gentry families in the county produced a young body of politically articulate radicals who possessed unusually good links with France and who provided leadership to the insurgents. In addition the Catholic faith was in unusually good shape in the county, in terms of the high number of priests educated on the continent, church building, recruitment to the priesthood, and the impact of Catholic teaching orders: priests were more important than elsewhere in Ireland in providing rebel leadership. Good political and economic contact with Dublin completes Whelan's picture of a politically sophisticated and highly unstable community on the eve of the rising.

Given this peculiar combination of circumstances the rising in Wexford temporarily prospered. The insurgents, led by Father John Murphy, destroyed a unit of the North Cork militia on 27 May, and thereafter captured Wexford town and Enniscorthy. In Wexford town a remarkable political experiment was pursued with the creation of a 'republic', governed by a local directory, and possessing other revolutionary trappings: a committee of public safety, district committees, and even a republican navy. The rebels experienced their first serious reverse on 5 June, at New Ross, where their attack on the crown forces was repulsed; however, the decisive battle of the Wexford republic was fought at Vinegar Hill on 21 June, where the insurgents were defeated and scattered.

However, Wexford provided more than a working model of Irish republican administration: the highly sectarian nature of conflict in the county – Protestants were killed at Scullabogue and on Wexford Bridge – endowed the Wexford rising with a rather more sombre reputation and a rather more complicated political legacy. While the reality of these executions was in itself grim, exaggerated accounts circulated in Ulster and helped to jar the cautious sectarian harmony of the northern conspirators. Narratives of Wexford probably contributed to the initially dilatory nature of the northern rising. But there were other factors inducing timidity. General Lake's brutal disarming of the north undoubtedly discouraged those many United Irishmen who had been swept into the movement, and who lacked a passionate republicanism. The disruption created by Lake in the north helped to confirm the ascendancy of Dublin over the conspiracy as a whole, and this loss of initiative may also have encouraged the caution of the northerners. The arrest and flight of the bolder northern leaders also both disoriented the movement and created space for more cautious successors – the 'foreign-aid men', such as Robert Simms, the United Irish general in Antrim, who wanted to delay action until French aid was assured. And even though there was a strain of dependence on France, there was equally widespread disillusionment in the north of Ireland with the course of French revolutionary politics: not every United Irishman saw French aid as an uncomplicated asset, given their treatment of the conquered Dutch republic and other territories.

The northerners rose when the rebels elsewhere were beginning to lose momentum. There was little coordination with Leinster, but scarcely more within Ulster itself: the insurgents in Antrim and Down rose at different times, and could therefore be dealt with separately by General Nugent, commanding the crown forces. Minor rebel successes in Randalstown and Ballymena, County Antrim, on 7 June were offset by a crushing and decisive loyalist victory at Antrim town. In County Down the insurgents were victorious in a skirmish at Saintfield on 9 June; but the gentlemanly rebel commander, Henry Munro, led his forces to utter destruction at the battle of Ballynahinch, fought on 13 June. His victor, Nugent, skilfully defused the remnants of the northern revolt through applying an amnesty to all but the rebel leaders. Munro and his Antrim counterpart, Henry Joy McCracken, were executed, as were 32 other leaders of the Ulster rising: other leaders went into exile. The official policy of clemency was not uniformly respected, but on the whole the suppression of the rising in the north was a much more restrained affair than elsewhere on the island.

Some of the evident explanations for the failure of the rising in Ulster were unique to the north. The alliance between the United Irish movement and Defenderism, originally a source of numerical strength, in fact proved unwieldy, and at times counterproductive: despite the secular ideals of the United Irish leaders, there is evidence of a damaging undercurrent of sectarian resentment in the rebel armies of the north. Some of the reasons for the northern failure were applicable to the rising as a whole. The Castle profited from excellent intelligence and a proliferation of informants within the United Irish ranks: Thomas Reynolds betrayed his own Leinster directory to the authorities in March 1798; in early June three of Henry Joy McCracken's United Irish colonels had, on receiving their general's plan of campaign, immediately passed it on to Nugent. Leonard McNally, a Dublin barrister and United Irishman, and Nicholas Mageean, a County Down farmer and United Irish colonel, were two of the most damaging informants, and Mageean in particular did much to undermine the northern preparations for revolt. Treachery was linked with timidity: many United Irishmen clearly had little faith in their ultimate prospects of success, and either counselled caution in May 1798 (like Robert Simms in Antrim) or deserted in the course of the conflict or defected to the loyalist cause. Timidity was linked to the government assault of 1797–8: the movement was, as has been observed, disrupted as well as denuded of both competent leaders and weapons. The government simultaneously goaded the conspirators into open rebellion as well as diminishing their prospects of success.

In addition the rebels made some serious miscalculations. They had an inflated view of their following within the crown forces, especially the militia, and to some extent hoped that their own lack of experience would be offset by this republican fifth column. Above all, they looked forward to timely and effective French intervention. But French military priorities were shifting in 1798 – away from the English Channel towards the eastern Mediterranean and Egypt. The French came – but to Killala, County Mayo, far removed from the main centres of the revolt in the east, and at the end of August, when both the main areas of rebel activity, eastern Ulster and Wexford, had been reconquered by the crown. Moreover, they came in small numbers and, in the opinion of Jean-Paul Bertaud, with insufficient weaponry: 1,019 French soldiers set sail, armed with 2,520 rifles – enough for their own purposes, perhaps, but scarcely enough to equip their Irish allies.[27] A minor victory was won at Castlebar by the French commander, Humbert, a battle made memorable by the panic-stricken retreat of the Irish militia; but the invaders surrendered at Ballinamuck, County Longford, on 8 September, and lost their bridgehead at Killala on 23 September. The French were 'treated as guests rather than as prisoners of war'; on the other hand, around 2,000 Irish insurgents were killed in the aftermath of Ballinamuck. A larger invasion fleet set sail before knowledge of the final collapse of the Humbert expeditionary force reached Paris, and was dispersed off the coast of Donegal in October. The French flagship, the *Hoche*, was captured on 12 October by Sir John Borlase Warren and the Royal Navy, but an additional prize lay among the sullen ranks of the prisoners landed at Buncrana: Wolfe Tone.

The capture and suicide of Tone came as a quiet coda to a rebellion that was already all but crushed. The '98 was a devastating experience – a short but bloody civil war, which involved the explosive release of pent-up economic and sectarian pressures. Estimates of the fatalities vary: it is generally held that 30,000 died as a consequence of the rising, though some contemporary calculations put the number as high as 100,000. Perhaps as many as 50,000 rebels took to the field in the summer of 1798; they faced around 76,000 soldiers of the crown. Even these lurid statistics only dimly convey the much wider impact of the rising, its prelude and suppression: the widespread destruction of property by both the rebels and loyalists, the application of an arbitrary military justice by the crown forces, and the unnerving series of trials which often involved free-ranging confessions or indictment, and which continued to 1801. The slaughter of the Irish insurgents at Ballinamuck remained long in the western folk-memory; the charnel house at Scullabogue became a minatory image for northern Presbyterians.

The rising illustrates with bleak clarity some of the central issues in modern Irish political history. The rebel movement embodied an uneasy compromise between secular ideals and a sectarian reality. The secular republicanism of the Belfast Presbyterians involved a thoroughgoing hostility towards institutional Catholicism: local Defenderism was driven in part by sectarian resentment. A highly complex rebel alliance was therefore held in place by what ultimately proved to be the rather flimsy ties of secularism and hostility to the British connection. Of course the Castle cynically played up the religious trauma of the '98 – but it merely had to gild the putrid lily of Irish sectarian passion. Contemporary Irish republicanism has to some extent inherited this difficult combination of secular nationalism and Catholic fidelity.

John Whyte has argued, with some justice, that one of the historic causes of instability in the north of Ireland has been the distrust of Protestant for Protestant.[28] The rising illustrates neatly some of the inconsistencies within northern Protestant politics – the gap between the intellectual sympathies of northern Protestants in 1798 and their instinctive political positions. The hesitancy of many northern leaders of the '98, the prevalence of informants, suggests perhaps the dilemma of those who had been forced into more advanced political positions than they would otherwise have found congenial. These men, driven by official repression and by their intellectual enthusiasm, gave birth to violent Irish republicanism, and then in some cases shied away from their offspring. The history of the '98 in the north suggests a curious combination of heady Presbyterian republican rhetoric and a residual deference to authority. At the very least it seems to be the case that the northern Presbyterians' enthusiasm for civic virtue blinded them to the realities of winning a civil war: yeomen were rescued by the rebels from the burning market-house at Randalstown on 7 June; Henry Munro's unwillingness to launch a 'dishonourable' night raid on the crown forces at Ballynahinch on 12–13 June ensured that he and his officers went to the scaffold with the purity of their cause intact. If some of the apparent contradictions of contemporary republicanism are foreshadowed in the '98, then something of the often strained and paradoxical relationship between contemporary Protestantism and the crown is foreshadowed in the rising.

If the rising saw the birth of militant republicanism, then it made possible a constitutional union between Ireland and Great Britain: the rising induced the growth of unionist sentiment among part of the governing elite of the two islands. William Pitt resurrected his old schemes for union in the summer of 1798, and found general approval in London, and divided opinions in Dublin: he had, however, a formidable intellectual resource in the unionist Chief Secretary, Lord Castlereagh, and the Lord Chancellor, Lord Clare, 'the greatest unionist of them all', in J.C. Beckett's description.[29] But the rising not only stimulated unionist sentiment, it also helped to make a union realizable. Because of the '98 British ministerial authority in Ireland was strengthened: a greatly augmented military establishment was an all too tangible reminder of the reality of British power in Ireland (without this force Lord Cornwallis, the lord lieutenant, believed that 'all thoughts of uniting the two kingdoms must be given up').[30] And because of the '98 and the protracted instability of the country the Irish parliament came to accept, albeit reluctantly, what they had for long been told by Lord Clare – that their patriotism was a recipe for self-destruction. The rising had demonstrated both that the ascendancy was vulnerable and that it could not save itself from the revolutionary deluge: unionism was therefore a means of protecting the ascendancy from the consequences of its own limitations.

The United Irish Society staggered on after the rising, and indeed an effort was made in the otherwise unpropitious circumstances of 1799 to revive its fortunes. One of the key instigators was Robert Emmet (1778–1803), who sought to sustain the patterns of militant republicanism that had been laid down – apparently so fruitlessly – in the 1790s. The result was a half-cocked uprising in the Dublin Liberties in July 1803, which was easily suppressed by the yeomanry, and which in the short term was notable only in so far as it claimed the life of the Lord Chief Justice, Arthur Wolfe, Viscount Kilwarden; Emmet, Thomas Russell and other leading conspirators were captured and, with only the respite of formulaic state trials, duly hanged. Emmet was subsequently enshrined in the pantheon of nation-builders, but in truth his actions subverted his professed ideals. The failure of the rising of 1803 helped to fuel the sectarianism of Irish politics, undermining the proponents of Catholic relief and weakening the possibility of a broadly based constitutional union. On the other hand, the rising was widely interpreted by Protestants as a prelude to a general massacre, and its easy defeat contributed to the bolstering of ascendancy morale. The rising therefore helped to make the union function in the ascendancy interest; and it contributed to the gradual identification of Catholicism with the national struggle. Neither outcome would have been welcomed by the 25-year-old idealist, who went to the gallows with his elitist republicanism unshaken, and with an emotionally charged message for posterity. Posterity, however, would take the form of a tenaciously Catholic democracy that had little time for Emmet's exclusivist convictions.

Disuniting Kingdoms, Emancipating Catholics, 1799–1850

I am the tall kingdom over your shoulder
That you would neither cajole nor ignore.
Conquest is a lie. I grow older
Conceding your half-independent shore
Within whose borders now my legacy
Culminates inexorably.

Séamus Heaney, 'Act of Union'[1]

3.1   The Union, 1799–1801

The two issues that dominated Irish high politics in the first half of the nineteenth century were interconnected and had already assumed a recognizable shape in the 1780s and 1790s: the nature of the constitutional relationship between Britain and Ireland, and the civil rights of Catholics. A form of parliamentary union had been adumbrated in the 1650s, during the Commonwealth, and had been a matter of speculation for a number of political thinkers since that time: these colonial patriots saw that the best guarantee of their rights lay in effective legislative independence, but some (such as William Molyneux) were willing to consider a union as a substitute for a flawed or defective local parliament. If there was a strain of ascendancy thought that considered union as a tolerable, but second-rate, means of guaranteeing Irish liberties, then this strain grew weaker as the eighteenth century progressed. Still, it is possible to detect lines of influence connecting not only the late eighteenth-century parliamentary patriots with earlier ideologues such as Molyneux, but also late eighteenth-century Unionist ultras, such as Lord Clare, with earlier patriotic writers: Clare increasingly came to the view that union represented not a second-rate but rather the only effective defence for the Irish Protestant nation. Neither Clare's thoughts of union, nor those of Molyneux, extended to the issue of

Catholic representation: for both a parliamentary union was worth considering only as a means of guaranteeing the political rights of the Irish Protestant nation.[2]

William Pitt's view of a parliamentary union was predicated on rather different assumptions from these; but while there were important theoretical distinctions, in practice his vision differed little from that of the Irish loyalist defenders of the ascendancy. For Pitt a union was a means of consolidating British control over Ireland, a dependent kingdom, at a time when there was a general drift towards the centralization of legislative authority at Westminster. For Pitt, too, a union was a safe means of addressing the issue of Catholic emancipation, for within a united parliament Catholics could enjoy full political rights without threatening the essentially Protestant nature of the constitution. The feasibility of union had been investigated in the late 1770s by Lord North, but in the context of a heightened Irish patriotism the idea had not taken root. In May 1785, when in opposition, North defended a legislative union before the House of Lords, but Pitt, the Prime Minister, though probably already sympathetic, kept silent. A union was no more a practical proposition in 1785, in the wake of legislative independence, than it had been in 1779, in the midst of the agitation for free trade. In 1798, however, in the aftermath of the rising, the political prognosis for unionism was altogether more favourable: the country was still disturbed (as late as 1799 there was talk of a French invasion), British military reinforcements were in place and were needed, and the hitherto boundless confidence of the ascendancy interest was now badly bruised. Pitt, therefore, seized the opportunity to launch an idea which had evidently been gestating throughout his ministerial career: as early as May 1798, he wrote to Cornwallis urging 'the necessity of bringing forward the great work of union which can never be so well accomplished as now'.[3]

However, even allowing for the effects of the rising, Pitt and the Irish executive could not take for granted the acquiescence of the Irish parliament (although it seems that at first they were inclined to overestimate their own strength). The unionist case was therefore opened with some subtlety, as for example in the pamphlet *Arguments for and against the Union*, written by the undersecretary at the Castle, Edward Cooke, and published in December 1798: this work was, as R.B. McDowell has observed, 'the first shot in the great battle', and precipitated the rapid organization of anti-unionist opinion, especially in Dublin.[4] Dublin had prospered with legislative independence, and there was therefore a wide variety of commercial and professional interests in the city intimately tied to the anti-unionist cause: William Saurin, later an ultra-loyalist attorney general, led the Irish bar against the union in 1799. But the opponents of union were by no means confined to the city or to the legal profession. The Orange Order, rooted in (but by now spreading beyond) south and central Ulster, was committed to the Irish Protestant constitution, and thus to the Irish parliament, which had so trenchantly defended Protestant interests. Throughout Ireland the country gentlemen, who were well represented within the existing constitutional arrangements, were largely opposed to union. But this correlation between representation and support hinted paradoxically at the strength of the unionist case – for because the representative base of the Irish parliament was narrow, so its support, though vocal, was ultimately limited. The anti-unionists might have broadened their appeal by embracing emancipation but, in contradistinction to their opponents, they made little effort to court Catholic opinion; they were further weakened by a circumstance beyond their control – the strength of the unionist position at Westminster. These factors, combined with widespread popular apathy, again partly a reflection on the limitations of the parliament – gave the government its opportunity.

By January 1799, when the lord lieutenant, opening the parliamentary session, referred obliquely to the desirability of a union, the House of Commons was utterly divided: an opposition motion removing this reference to union in the viceregal address was carried on 24 January by 109 votes to 104. For the moment, therefore, the government had failed, and ardent Unionists like Castlereagh and Cooke were forced to reconsider their strategy: Cooke blamed the defeat on a combination of British ignorance and (a related point) Cornwallis's 'total incapacity', while Castlereagh – with perhaps greater practical insight – ascribed the vote to the threatened self-interest of the country gentlemen.[5] Castlereagh's diagnosis underlay government policy for the rest of the year. Patronage that would normally have been spread over a decade was concentrated within one year and devoted to one purpose – the construction of a unionist majority in the Commons. Pitt's Home Secretary, the Duke of Portland, gave Cornwallis and Castlereagh virtually a free hand in the distribution of honours, with the result that 16 peerages were created, 15 promotions in the peerage promised, and a host of more minor pensions and places dangled in front of the loyal or undecided. Anti-unionists, even the relations of anti-unionists, were dismissed from office: among the more conspicuous casualties was Sir John Parnell, Chancellor of the Exchequer. In addition to these direct appeals to self-interest, the government (like the opposition) sought to bludgeon the political intelligence of the Commons through propaganda (in the form of pamphlet literature) as well as through the orchestration of public opinion (in the form of public petitions). On the whole the government outpaced the opposition in both contests, but the ferocity of its campaign, and the lavish resources deployed, indicate that the issue was finely balanced.

By January 1800, after over one year of political and psychological warfare, the Castle had created a parliamentary majority for the union. The opposition had from the beginning nothing to offer beyond an atavistic patriotism and the stale constitutional arguments of 1782, and by now their logical and emotional resources were spent: the government, defeated by five votes in January 1799, was now sustained by majorities that held consistently in the low to mid-40s. On 6 February 1800, the House of Commons formally agreed to consider the proposals for union, and on 17 February the committee of the House approved the idea. By 28 March both Houses of the now moribund Irish parliament had agreed to the union. On 6 June the Commons approved the committee report of the Union Bill, which was subsequently laid before the British parliament: here opposition continued, but here, too, the government prevailed. On 1 August 1800, the royal assent was given to the new Act of Union, which duly took force on 1 January 1801.

The eight articles of the Act of Union defined the relationship between Britain and Ireland in a manner which, with slight modifications, lasted until 1920. But the authors of the Act did not only look forward to the nineteenth century, they also addressed, or sought to address, some of the central political controversies of the 1780s and 1790s. The terms of the measure require some attention, therefore. The first four articles determined the political aspects of the British–Irish relationship, striking the level of Irish representation in the new united parliament. The Irish peerage was to be represented by 28 members within the House of Lords of the new United Kingdom. The 300 members of the former Irish House of Commons were to be replaced both in type and in number: 100 representatives were assigned to Ireland in the united parliament, 64 from the counties, 35 from the boroughs, and one from the University of Dublin. The Act of Union embodied, therefore, a reform of Irish representation, replacing a borough-dominated body of represen-tatives (234 out of 300 Irish MPs in the Dublin parliament represented boroughs) with a county-dominated representation: the democratic aspect of Irish represen-tation was therefore enhanced at the expense of the oligarchic. The fifth article of the Act created a united Church of England and Ireland, and the eighth article for-malized the legal and judicial aspects of the new Union, confirming the existing legislation of the Irish parliament and the appellate jurisdiction of the House of Lords of the new United Kingdom.

The sixth and seventh articles of the Union dealt with commerce and finance, and were to prove, next to the principle of union itself, the most controversial aspects of the measure. The sixth article created a customs union to complement the political union of articles one to four (although in both cases perfect unity was neither sought nor attained). Article six was, as Ó Gráda has pointed out, shaped to meet the desires of the Irish manufacturing interest.[6] British duties on a variety of exports to Ireland and on some imports from Ireland were removed, while Irish duties on a range of foreign manufactured goods were to remain, but to be scaled down, and finally removed by 1826. Article seven of the Union provided for an Irish contribution to the revenue of the United Kingdom at a rate of two-seventeenths of the total, a figure which took account of the ratio of Irish to British foreign trade and the relative value of the main dutiable goods consumed in Ireland and Britain – a figure calcul-ated, that is to say, with some reference to the standards of living in the two countries.

The Union and its mode of passage were a focus of controversy throughout the nineteenth century, with many of Ireland's later political, social and economic ills being traced back, with a crisp monocausal logic, to this great fall. Grattan's parlia-ment was, in mid- and late nineteenth-century nationalist rhetoric, a prelapsarian idyll, a political and economic golden age: for Unionists the same parliament was as corrupt and parochial as the Home Rulers who sought to restore an assembly to College Green. On the whole, modern scholarly opinion places a much slighter burden of explanation on the Act of Union than did the polemicists of the Home Rule era. The short-term political fall-out from the Union was in certain respects profound: an independent parliamentary tradition dating back to the Middle Ages was interrupted, while the broader political culture of the island was temporarily subdued. But in other respects it is easy to exaggerate the loss of the parliament. Irish parliamentary life did not, of course, die, but instead was transplanted to Westminster where the leading figures of the Irish parliament – Castlereagh, Grattan, Foster – found new seats and a renewed prominence. And, just as it is easy to exaggerate the extent of legislative independence, so it is easy to exaggerate the impact of its loss: the Irish parliament, even after 1782, was heavily influenced by the British government, acting through Dublin Castle. Dublin Castle, and a semi-autonomous Irish executive, remained in spite of the Union.

It is also possible to exaggerate the economic consequences of the Union. Despite 'free trade' and 'legislative independence', Ireland's economy had in fact grown more thoroughly intertwined with that of Britain in the later eighteenth century: the Union did not, therefore, create British economic ascendancy in Ireland, nor was it even the single most important influence over the early nineteenth-century Irish economy. The Napoleonic wars were a much more substantial factor, stimulating Irish agriculture, the provisions trade and some Irish manufactures over the years spanning the Union debate: equally, the wars brought higher levels of taxation and a quadrupling of the Irish national debt from £27 million to £107 million in the period 1801–16. This high level of debt was linked to the growth of Ireland's contribution to the revenue of the United Kingdom, as the cost of the war escalated: the debt burden was therefore linked to the financial relationship settled in article seven of the Union. But of course it is by no means clear that, without the Union, the level of debt would have been contained during the war: Irish state finances were in chaos before the Union, and there is no reason to believe that they would have improved without the Union. The war brought some benefits and some losses: it created a climate of financial instability for both the government and its citizens. Its precise impact on the Irish economy and on the welfare of the Irish people is therefore hard to decipher (Ó Gráda has acknowledged that 'the period was one in which lots of things were happening at once . . . making the analysis of any one single factor's role almost impossible').[7] Nonetheless, whether as an agent of growth or of economic chaos, the war was a much more immediate influence than the legislative union. And the end of the war would prove to be a much more traumatic economic experience than the end of the Irish parliament.

3.2   The Catholic Question, 1799–1829

> *Oh Wellington, sure you know it is true,*
> *In blood we were drenched at famous Waterloo,*
> *We fought for our king to uphold his crown,*
> *Our only reward was – Papists lie down!*
> Irish ballad, *c*.1820[8]

The Union was designed to address a number of pressing political issues and to bolster an unstable Irish constitution. One source of instability lay with the Catholic community and with its uniform exclusion from representative politics; and it was Pitt's intention that, just as the Union dealt with several subsidiary political questions (such as parliamentary reform), so it should incorporate or accompany some settlement of Catholic claims. Informal negotiations were conducted through 1799 between Cornwallis and the Irish hierarchy, and the outline of an agreement was sketched whereby emancipation would be traded for the concession to the crown of a negative veto over episcopal appointments. The government had apparently concocted a constitutional wonder-drug: an informal alliance between the crown and the hierarchy on the emancipation issue would enhance the loyalty of Catholic Ireland, while through the Union the ascendancy would be saved from its own limitations – but not at the cost of the Protestant constitution. Though on this occasion the Catholic Church in Ireland was amenable, Pitt's strategies were thwarted elsewhere: Lord Clare, an ardent Unionist and equally ardent opponent of Catholic aspirations, argued against any link between union and emancipation (and in fact on narrowly political grounds, given the tenacity of Protestant patriotism in the Irish parliament, he may have had a case). The Union therefore passed into law in the absence of any Catholic settlement, and though in 1801 Pitt sought to complete his constitutional architecture with the introduction of an emancipation bill, he met further opposition, this time from George III (though probably acting on the constitutional advice of Clare) and Lord Loughborough, the Lord Chancellor. If, as Oscar Wilde claimed, men destroy the things they love, then Clare's unforgiving logic preserved the integrity of his Protestant constitution for the slaughter. 'Few things in our history', Earl Stanhope, the biographer of Pitt, apostrophized in 1862, 'are perhaps more to be lamented than the inflexible determination of the King, in February 1801, against the Roman Catholic claims'.[9]

Clare's death in 1802 removed one of the most vituperative and intelligent ascendancy ultras, but it did not materially advance the cause of emancipation. In fact there remained formidable obstacles. The emancipationist case needed a powerful Protestant advocate in the United Kingdom parliament, and until 1805, when Grattan was returned for Malton, this was lacking. The ascendancy interest did not, of course, die with Clare, and there remained powerful advocates of the Protestant constitution in the United Kingdom parliament, both in the House of Commons and, especially, the Lords: a Catholic petition, presented by Grattan to the Commons in 1805, was rejected, and further petitions were presented (and dismissed) in 1808 and 1810. William Plunket's Catholic relief bill was defeated in the House of Lords in 1821. However, the parliamentary opposition to emancipation was beginning to flag by 1812, when Grattan garnered 215 votes in the Commons in support of a motion to consider the laws in force against Catholics. Indeed, in 1813 Grattan came close to obtaining a measure of emancipation, winning a number of divisions before being finally thwarted by the wrecking amendments of Castlereagh, George Canning and the Speaker of the Commons, Charles Abbot.

Grattan's relative parliamentary strength depended on his tireless eloquence, but also on several other less certain factors. To some extent the tractability of the British government and parliament depended upon the European war (although there was certainly no simple correlation): in the absence of other forms of political pressure, the short-term prospects for emancipation were brighter before 1815 than after – because Catholic quiescence was of greater political value during the war than after. Daniel O'Connell, a rising star of the Catholic Committee (1804–11), seems to have accepted these calculations, because in 1812–13, when the European war was in the balance, he was arguing a much more extreme case than in 1819, when the broader political context was less favourable. Peace worked in two ways to disarm O'Connell: it stiffened official attitudes, but it also deflated popular anger – because with peace came severe economic disruption and the temporary redefinition of popular Catholic priorities: 'by no kind of means, by no manner of exertion, and he *did* look about for means, and he *did* use a thousand exertions, could he arouse the Catholics to action, or even to a defensive position', wrote John O'Connell of his father in these years after Waterloo.[10]

One further brake upon Catholic achievement lay within the movement for emancipation. The reformers faced not only intermittent government suppression, they were also hampered by their own divisions, and especially over the question of the veto: some Catholic activists were prepared to accept a royal veto over episcopal appointments as the price of mollifying Protestant suspicions, while others – O'Connell included (though not consistently) – took a more austere line, arguing for the integrity of the Irish Catholic Church. Grattan's speech in favour of the Catholic petition of 1808 helped to inflame this vetoist controversy, for he assumed that the hierarchy would accept the intervention of the crown (as they reportedly had done in 1799), while in fact they took exactly the opposite line: a national synod, held in September 1808, declared against the veto. Some comment has been made upon 'the degree of horror and the intensity of the passions' which the subject aroused; and indeed Tom Bartlett has gone so far as to suggest that 'in the veto controversy the Catholic nation of the early 19th century found its voice'.[11]

In the longer term, however, this episode exposed divisions that would restrain the reform movement until the 1820s: the main representative body of Irish Catholicism in the years 1812–14, the Catholic Board, fractured on the issue in May 1813, with a minority vetoist faction seceding, leaving the Board to the control of an O'Connellite rump. Neither O'Connell nor the Irish bishops (who maintained their opposition to crown interference) were moved by two papal rescripts, published in February 1814 and May 1815, each of which recommended the acceptance of a form of royal veto. In fact by this stage papal approval or disapproval mattered little, for it increasingly seemed as if the Catholic movement possessed little more than its divisions: the pro-Catholic press was silenced by the government in 1813–14, while the Board itself was suppressed in June 1814 – actions which certainly reflected the determination of the youthful Chief Secretary, Robert Peel, but which were also made easier by the schism among the reformers. O'Connell sought to keep the embers of an agitation alive through his Irish Catholic Association (1815–17) and a reorganized Catholic Board (1817–18), but the ending of the war and the uncompromising attitude of Peel merely compounded the difficulties created by the veto controversy. As late as 1821, over the Plunket relief bill, the divisions between English Catholic opinion (on the whole vetoist), liberal Protestant opinion (vetoist), Irish Catholic vetoists, and O'Connellite and clerical anti-vetoists were paraded for the amusement of the ascendancy interest. Little wonder, then, that it has been said of O'Connell in these years that he had 'a significant political past, but seemingly no political future'.[12]

O'Connell assured his political future and restored unity to the emancipation movement through the medium of the Catholic Association and a Catholic 'rent', or general contribution, each created in May 1823. At first there was little to suggest that these were especially important or original initiatives: there had been other similar schemes both within Irish Catholic and British radical politics, and indeed O'Connell had headed an earlier, short-lived Irish Catholic Association between 1815 and 1817. Nor was the new Association at first strikingly successful: a high subscription fee (one guinea a year) kept the membership figures down, and meetings often fell short of a quorum. However, the Association attracted a publicity out of all proportion to its membership, for its protests were treated in lavish detail in the three or four national papers under O'Connellite influence (the issues that fired the body in 1823 were the demonstrations of the Orange Order and the burial-ground question – a zealous Church of Ireland sexton in Dublin had defied convention and created a furore in September 1823 by prohibiting a Catholic burial in a churchyard under Anglican control). This publicity paved the way for the successful launch in February 1824 of an associate membership of the Association, costing a penny a month: its numbers accordingly spiralled and a substantial fighting fund was garnered. Both O'Connell and Catholic Ireland were, by the end of 1824, teetering on the outer edge of a whirlwind transformation: 'before March 1824', MacDonagh has remarked, 'O'Connell had been merely much the best known of a group of well-known agitators. Now he towered over the remainder'.[13] Equally, the Catholic question had been hitherto merely one of a number of important issues irritating the ascendancy interest and British government: after 1824 it towered over all rival distractions.

Some preliminary assessment of O'Connell may be offered at this point, the fulcrum of his career as an agitator (though in fact he defies easy description, whether in personal or political – to say nothing of spiritual – terms). He was born in 1775 into a wealthy Catholic family at Derrynane, County Kerry, and was an early Catholic recruit to the bar (he was called in 1798). He became the leader of Catholic Ireland, yet was – probably until 1809 – at best an unconventional Catholic, at worst a deist (he seems to have over-compensated for this in later life through a meticulous – mildly neurotic, it has been suggested – religious observance).[14] He was simultaneously a loving husband and father but also financially reckless, and was therefore often forced to throw himself into his work, to the neglect of his family. He was capable both of an enveloping personal and political affection (Charles Gavan Duffy, an opponent, said that 'his instincts were generous and cordial'), yet he was renowned for the abuse which he offered to his enemies and, indeed, to friends who crossed him.[15] This has been explained as being a means of deflating proud ascendancy or British political antagonists, and as a means of puncturing any popular deference that such figures might attract; but, while this may have been true in practice, O'Connell's rebarbative manner also threatened potential allies and diverted him into several wearing and personalized antagonisms. His personal-cum-political feud with the talented vetoist barrister Richard Lalor Shiel damaged the Catholic cause in the early 1820s, though a reconciliation was effected in 1823 (Shiel was a co-founder of the Catholic Association). And, though O'Connell was generally a highly cautious lawyer, he could be recklessly, indeed thoughtlessly, eloquent: Shiel commented (in 1825, after the reconciliation) that 'he is so confident in his powers that he gives himself little trouble in the selection of his materials, and generally trusts to his emotions for his harangues'.[16]

He had a powerful sense of his own political and legal talents – sometimes so marked as to speak of a defensiveness: he was certainly (in monetary terms) one of the most successful barristers of the age. His vitriolic temper may have been partly an expression of professional frustration for, while he laboured as a junior counsel, those of sometimes lesser merit but from a different confessional tradition or a different nationality won honours and preferment. Like Edward Carson at the end of the nineteenth century, O'Connell was ruthless in pursuit of his verdict, whether in the courts or in political life. But if the law underpinned his adversarial approach and his hardhitting eloquence, it also meant that he was an essentially constitutional agitator. O'Connell's political convictions will be examined later, but he has been tellingly described as 'a respectable, a rationalistic, and a moral force radical'.[17]

His ability was complemented by what Roy Foster has termed a 'protean energy': the institutions and stratagems which O'Connell created were rarely original, but the application of a ferocious energy to old ideas won unprecedented results (as in 1823–5 with the Catholic Association).[18] He was simultaneously a conviction politician and an opportunist: he was profoundly committed both to the Catholic cause and later to repeal of the Act of Union, but he could be strategically pragmatic. He could be scathing of trimming among his fellow Catholic activists (over the veto question, for example, or the disfranchisement of the 40-shilling freeholders) – but he was quite capable of condemning a strategy that he would later embrace: pragmatism was permissible, but only on his own terms.

Like later constitutional Irish radicals (Parnell, Carson), O'Connell combined a parliamentary and extra-parliamentary strategy in the years preceding emancipation. There was some evidence that the British government and parliament were growing more sympathetic to the Catholic cause: the Unlawful Oaths Act (1823) was designed to counter Orangeism, and the Suppression Act (1825), while it outlawed both the Orange Order and the Catholic Association, was at least demonstrating an evenhanded oppression (the Catholic Association reformed immediately as the New Catholic Association). In March 1825 O'Connell thought that, with Francis Burdett's relief bill, the Catholic millennium had arrived: Burdett's measure combined emancipation with 'wings' – disfranchisement of the 40-shilling freeholders and state payment of the Catholic clergy – but in effect offered less to ultra-Protestant sensitivities than the old veto. While O'Connell could derive some satisfaction from the form of the bill and from its success in the House of Commons, disappointment came from a familiar source: the bill was ultimately defeated (in May 1825) in the Lords. Thus, though O'Connell and the Catholic Association had clearly impressed a growing body of British parliamentary opinion, it was equally clear that Westminster would not grant emancipation unprompted. The success of the Catholic Association between 1823 and 1825 had fired some – insufficient – parliamentary enthusiasm, but O'Connell and his lieutenants had to turn to Irish electoral politics to provide the necessary further stimulus.

The general election of 1826 offered the New Catholic Association an opportunity to test its electoral strength. This was a less obvious initiative strategy than might at first seem apparent, and indeed to some extent was forced onto the Association through local pressures. For, although O'Connell had created a popular emancipationist movement through the Association and the Catholic rent, this support did not automatically translate into votes: the Irish electorate remained small and – because of the system of open voting – susceptible to landlord pressure. Indeed O'Connell had thought so little of the 40-shilling freehold voters ('votes in the landlords' pockets') that he had been happy to acquiesce in their disfranchisement through the Burdett bill.[19] However, there were a few straws in the wind: Catholic freeholders, though often pliant, had sometimes been willing to defy the instructions of their landlord (as with the widespread electoral 'revolts' of 1818). And in a number of constituencies there was widespread resentment, fired by Association activists, at the anti-emancipationist politics, however paternalistic, of the local gentry clans. Among these constituencies was County Waterford.

The Waterford contest of 1826 was viewed by contemporaries as a great electoral test for the Catholic Association, and its significance has not been overlooked by historians. The outcome, declared on 1 July 1826, was the victory of a 23-year-old liberal Protestant landlord, Villiers Stuart, over Lord George Thomas Beresford, brother to the Church of Ireland Archbishop of Armagh and a son of the Marquis of Waterford, one of the most powerful proprietors in Ireland: it was a victory of an emancipationist, a member of the Catholic Association, over ascendancy Toryism. Indeed, it has been suggested that 'it would not be enough to say merely that the Beresfords were pillars of the ascendancy. To a real extent they were the ascendancy'.[20] But the outcome, though highly significant, only partly explains the significance attached to this contest. Stuart's contest certainly inspired later campaigns and may have fired parallel Catholic struggles in Counties Louth, Monaghan, Cavan and Westmeath, but (as Fergus O'Ferrall has remarked) 'the great defeat of the Protestant Ascendancy in Co. Waterford had been well planned long before the general election was called' – and the means to victory was as important as the result.[21] For this was no freak result, nor was it the product of a twentieth-century-style political swing: the Waterford result was echoed in other county constituencies and was produced by a profound electoral realignment. The normally passive 40-shilling freeholders, whom the Beresford and Tory interest regarded almost as a form of political property, had defied the instructions of their landlords and had plumped for Villiers Stuart and emancipation. This rejection of political and social deference was all the more shocking because it was repeated in other constituencies where, like Waterford, a dominant ascendancy clan had represented the county for several generations. There was, however, a darker side to the contest, which, though fought between two landed gentlemen adhering to the established Church, was profoundly sectarian: at one level Waterford was a fight between the institutionalized and public sectarianism of the ascendancy and the abusive, rhetorical sectarianism of the agitators. As one of the most widely publicized contests of the nineteenth century, and one of the most divisive, the legacy of Waterford is ambiguous: it announced simultaneously the death-rattle of Protestant supremacism (at least in the south and west of Ireland) and the birth-pangs of its Catholic successor.

The Waterford contest and the general election of 1826 as a whole left some short-term problems for O'Connell and the Association. A great electoral agitation had been created, but given the normal seven-year life of parliament, it was not altogether clear how this might be sustained in a peaceful fashion if the opposition to emancipation continued. Moreover, there were numerous reports (some spurious) of landlords revenging themselves on their freeholders for the humiliations of the 1826 election: money was needed for tenant protection, and accordingly a New Catholic rent was launched on 7 July 1826. But of course the benefits of the victory – even the realizable, short-term benefits – were of incalculably greater significance than the problems, for O'Connell had secured the first of a series of significant victories over the ascendancy, and in doing so had copper-fastened a social alliance both within the Irish Catholic laity and between the laity and the clergy. Moreover, just as O'Connell's electoral authority in Ireland was being reinforced, so his opponents at Westminster were suffering reverses: the strongly Protestant Duke of York, heir to the throne, died in January 1827, while Lord Liverpool, the Prime Minister and a scarcely less tenacious opponent of Catholic claims, fell victim to a stroke in February. Liverpool's incapacity ('he may be reckoned as dead', noted Henry Goulburn, the Chief Secretary) helped to reinforce the importance of the Catholic question within British high politics while finally destroying the possibility of an exclusively ultra-Protestant administration; in addition the period of flux at Westminster which ended in April with the succession of Canning to the premiership seemed to O'Connell to augur well for his cause and brought a more conciliatory tone.[22]

But the Catholic hopes invested in the new administration were undermined, first, by the death of Canning in August, and later with the disintegration of the Goderich ministry at the end of 1827: O'Connell was forced out of the parliamentary game and back onto the playing fields of Irish politics. By the time the apparently unsympathetic Wellington had succeeded Goderich (on 22 January 1828), with 'Orange' Peel as Home Secretary, an agitation had already been launched in Dublin: a chain of Catholic meetings was held throughout Ireland on Sunday, 13 January. Wellington's elevation appeared merely to confirm the need for this renewed campaign in Ireland, since he was (wrongly) regarded as the most bitter and immobile opponent of emancipation: the prospect of his appointment a year before, in January 1827, had created 'a great affright' for O'Connell, who believed (or who professed to believe) that 'all the horrors of actual massacre threaten us'.[23] In reality the parliamentary outlook remained relatively bright. The Marquis of Anglesey, originally – like Wellington – thought to be an antagonist, was appointed as lord lieutenant at the end of 1827 and remained in office under the Duke as a strong, if quirky, pro-Catholic. Wellington himself had already privately conceded the inevitability of emancipation and appears to have been probing the alternative paths to concession in the first months of his premiership: in April 1828 his government acceded to the repeal of the Test and Corporations Acts, an action which, while it removed disabilities on non-conformists, looked forward to Catholic emancipation. Moreover, in the following month the Suppression Act (1825), which had proscribed the first Catholic Association and forced a reorganization upon the movement, was allowed by the government to expire. There is little doubt that the agitation in Ireland since 1824 had impressed Wellington, and that he would not otherwise have been so willing to move on the Catholic question; equally, there is little doubt that, after years of parliamentary disappointment, O'Connell could not yet trust that he was pushing against an open door.

The focal point of the 1828 campaign, indeed of the whole campaign for Catholic emancipation, came with the by-election for County Clare, held in June: Fergus O'Ferrall has claimed that 'it is no exaggeration to state that the Clare election began a new epoch in Irish politics, and in Anglo-Irish relations'.[24] Yet, while the earlier Waterford clash between the ascendancy and Catholic interests had been long pre-pared, the origins of this even more decisive election were curiously haphazard. In January 1828 the Catholic Association had, as part of its reactivated campaign, under-taken to oppose every supporter of the Wellington administration. In June William Vesey Fitzgerald, a Clare landlord and MP for his county, was appointed to the Presidency of the Board of Trade in Wellington's cabinet and was required, there-fore, to seek re-election. The Association was bound to contest the election, but Fitzgerald was a formidable opponent: he was a gifted speaker, an experienced junior minister, an indulgent local patron and – above all – in favour of emancipation. No liberal Protestant, accordingly, would stand against him. O'Connell and his lieutenants grasped that the Clare election offered a golden opportunity to apply pressure to the administration, and pursuing an idea formulated in the 1790s by the Catholic activist John Keogh, it was agreed that a Catholic – O'Connell himself – should contest the seat. The inspiration was supplied by an earlier generation of activist and the organization was created by local activists, but the necessary charisma, energy and rousing, acerbic rhetoric – a calculated mix of historical allu-sion, exaggeration and chauvinism – were the contribution of O'Connell. The result was declared on 5 July, after five days' polling, and brought a further and – with the benefit of hindsight – decisive victory for the Catholic cause: O'Connell polled 2,057 votes to Fitzgerald's 982. Even contemporaries recognized the seismic significance of the contest. The formidable forces of Catholic Ireland had been paraded for the benefit of the government, and O'Connell was quick to point out that 'three hundred soldiers threw up their caps for me since I left Ennis'.[25] In fact the government needed little persuasion that it was threatened at best with (as Peel called it) 'a revolution in the electoral system in Ireland', or, at worst (in the opinion of Wellington), with violent unrest: 'we have a rebellion impending over us in Ireland ... and we have in England a parliament which we cannot dissolve [because of the 40-shilling freeholder revolt in Ireland], the majority of which is of opinion, with many wise and able men, that the remedy is to be found in Roman Catholic emancipation'.[26]

The Clare election stimulated further Catholic organization, especially in the form of new Liberal clubs and a more confident and assertive tone from the Association; equally, it provoked an increasingly coherent, if defensive, Irish Protestant response in the form of the Brunswick clubs. Catholics were beginning, in their frustration, to adopt 'military formation' (the parallel with the 'semi-constitutional' agitation of the Ulster Unionists in 1912–14 is once again suggestive). Faced with the prospect of another rising (and some Orange factionaries publicly hoped for a decisive showdown), and faced with a parliamentary impasse, the government planned for emancipation. An announcement was made in the King's speech in February 1829 and a bill introduced into the Commons on 6 March. There was no veto, and no 'wings', but there were some minor, if irritating, qualifications: most offices were now open to Catholics (except a small number, such as the Lord Chancellorship, at the intersection between crown, government and the Church of England); Catholic bishops were prohibited from using territorial titles. In addition the Catholic Association was suppressed. But the chief casualty of the victory was the 40-shilling freeholder, the footsoldier of the emancipation campaign and now disfranchised. O'Connell had affirmed that he would never accept emancipation with disfranchisement, but this 'Houdini of Irish Political Promises' was too skilled a political dealer to fret over the irritating small print of his victory.[27]

The emancipation of 1829 opened the way to Catholic participation in parliament and to public office, but of course these boons affected only a small educated and propertied elite. Emancipation represented, however, a great political victory for a people who had lived in the shadow of the military and political humiliations of the seventeenth and early eighteenth centuries: emancipation was a Catholic victory, planned by a Catholic leadership and won on the playing field of the Protestant constitution. The measure was passed not out of the magnanimity of the Wellington government but because the government feared – and was seen to fear – the consequences of resistance (the lessons of this for later Irish agitators, Unionist and nationalist, would not be missed): emancipation, which might in different circumstances have reinforced Irish Catholic commitment to the Union and to British government, in practice helped to loosen the bonds of political and social deference. Moreover, the measure was passed with minimal assistance from liberal Protestants, who had kept the issue before the House of Commons since the Act of Union, but who were now utterly overpowered by the strength of popular Catholic agitation. O'Connell paid lip service to the contribution of these allies, but in reality they had no more than a symbolic value: their support might once have helped to quell British Protestant fears, but in 1829 it was British Protestant fears that permitted emancipation to pass. Emancipation, which might have fore-shadowed a national secular alliance, focused not even a pale ecumenical sympathy but rather a glaring sectarianism.

It is sometimes argued that emancipation was more important as a psychological victory for Irish Catholics than as an immediate practical boon. Equally, it is claimed that the means by which the victory was won were to prove almost as significant as the victory itself. Certainly, for most Irish Catholics participation in a successful struggle mattered more than the direct political and professional gains promised by the Emancipation Act: O'Connell's mass movement empowered the hitherto powerless and gave Irish Catholics a sense of control over their own future. The Emancipation Act opened the way to Catholic domination of Irish representative politics, but the emancipation movement determined the nature of this domination. For, by creating the most successful popular mobilization of Catholic opinion in Irish history, O'Connell provided a working model for later nationalist activists: indeed, by reinforcing a sense of the Catholic past, of historical grievance, by reinforcing popular antipathy towards the 'Saxon', O'Connell exposed a bedrock of nationalist sentiment upon which he, and the inheritors of his constitutional tradition, would attempt to build.

However, if the emancipationists looked forward to the Home Rule movement, then equally they looked back to a long tradition of Catholic activism. Emancipation is significant not just as the foundation of constitutional nationalist politics but as the culmination of 70 years of organized Catholic agitation: it is significant, therefore, as a historical intersection. Emancipation was made possible not just by the astonishing energy and political talent of O'Connell, but also through the broader condition of the Irish Catholic community. Emancipation was not of course the economic liberation of Irish Catholics; it was the measure by which the prosperity of Catholics began to be converted into social and political recognition. Some Irish Catholics had prospered since the mid-eighteenth century, profiting from the expansion in Irish agriculture and commerce, but they had at first only cautiously tested the political effectiveness of this economic strength. With the agitation of 1791–3, the tenor of Catholic politics changed; a more middle-class, more vibrant and more assertive movement emerged, and it was this (rather than the renewed caution of the Catholic activists after the '98, or the florid gentility of liberal Protestant emancipationists) which provided a model for O'Connell. O'Connell, like John Keogh and the men of the Catholic Convention, built upon Catholic prosperity; O'Connell, like Keogh, was able to bypass Irish Protestant opinion in order to exploit a British parliamentary opportunity for Catholic gain (Keogh in 1793, against the background of a continental war, O'Connell in 1829, against the background of an unstable ministry). O'Connell, much more than Keogh, created his own political opportunities, and the size and scope of his agitation bear little relation to the more modest endeavours of the Catholic agitators in 1791–3. But, if emancipation was made possible by the Clare election victory, then the Clare victory was made possible by the enfranchisement of the 40-shilling freeholders achieved by the Catholics of 1793.

3.3 Justice for Ireland, 1830–41

The hesitation in O'Connellite strategy in the late 1820s had been caused by the uncertainties within British high politics, and by the uncertainty therefore of the Catholic position at Westminster: O'Connell had oscillated between frenetic diplomacy in London and frenetic agitation in Ireland, depending upon his perception of the parliamentary scene. But the accession of the Whigs to power in November 1830, and their domination of British politics until 1841 (except for the interlude of the first Peel administration in 1834–5), helped to anchor O'Connell at Westminster: in addition, after February 1835 he was bound to the Whig government and to Westminster through the informal agreement known as the Lichfield House compact. The ascendancy of the Whigs, ostensibly sympathetic to popular Irish demands, did not altogether eliminate this manic form of political endeavour – O'Connell throughout the 1830s either threatened to reactivate local agitation or actually did so – but on the whole this was a period when the British parliament was trusted to provide what O'Connell called 'justice for Ireland'. 'Justice for Ireland', like other O'Connellite objectives, was left ill-defined, but it included tithe reform and both municipal and parliamentary reform. If this 'justice' were not forthcoming, if the Whig reformers appeared tardy, then O'Connell made sure that he had the weapon of agitation ready to hand.

This – as later militant nationalists saw it – 'collaborationist' policy was made possible not simply because of the Whigs' hold on office, but because O'Connell devoted his lavish energy to electioneering and to the construction of a 'tail' of support in the Commons. There were initial problems: first, in February 1830 the Catholic hierarchy had urged priests to desist from further political activity, and – given the importance of local clergy in the electoral contests of the emancipation campaign – this was likely to prove highly damaging. Second, O'Connell had acquiesced in the disfranchisement of one of his best electoral weapons, the 40-shilling freeholder, and though he held hopes of their readmission to the franchise, these in fact were not realized during his lifetime: the existing £10 household franchise in combination with the preponderance of boroughs favoured the Tory interest. And third, like Parnell in the 1880s, he was inclined to ride roughshod over local sensitivities, most notably in the general election of 1830 when, in trying to find a seat, he 'had disturbed arrangements, strained supporters' loyalties, alienated [Thomas] Wyse, and offended potential colleagues in at least half a dozen constituencies'.[28] But the contest of 1830 was only a beginning, and in the next general election, held in 1832, O'Connell campaigned more successfully, harnessing his organizations and press effectively and imposing a repeal 'pledge' on sympathetic parliamentary candidates. In fact the election was the highpoint of his electoral success: 39 'repealers' were duly returned, including three of O'Connell's sons, two sons-in-law, one brother-in-law and one cousin. O'Connell's personal authority and the repeal pledge looked forward to Parnell and the Home Rule era, but his 'party' was in fact both a premonition of modern political organization and an echo of an older clientilism. If

O'Connell's party, like the Liberator himself, was an amalgam of ultra-modernity and the antique, then the strategies that it pursued were also a mixture of eighteenth-century 'connection' politics and the machine-style precision of the Parnellites and Redmondites. The sometimes wayward O'Connellites required a more tactful handling than Parnell was wont to supply, but equally the manner in which they were deployed by their commander in (for example) 1835 looked forward to Parnell in 1885 or Redmond in 1910: in each case a weak British government was sustained by Irish votes, but at a cost. That cost, however, did not yet amount to repeal.

Repeal was, appearances notwithstanding, a governing principle of O'Connell's political career. In common with other lawyers, he had been an anti-Unionist in 1800, but unlike others (W.H. Saurin, for example) he had retained this hostility: in a speech to Dublin corporation in September 1810, he had affirmed with characteristic gusto that, were the Prime Minister 'to offer me the Repeal of the Union upon terms of re-enacting the entire penal code, I declare it from my heart and in the presence of God that I would most cheerfully embrace his offer'.[29] Fortunately for O'Connell's conscience, no offer came upon these (or any other) terms, and in the 1830s he used repeal largely in order to intimidate otherwise truculent Whig ministries. In the late autumn of 1830 O'Connell fired a repeal agitation, but only apparently as an experiment and as a means of increasing his political capital: he and his supporters fought the election of 1831 as 'reformers' rather than repealers. The constricted nature of the Irish parliamentary reform bill of 1831 (only five additional seats were awarded to Ireland, and the 40-shilling freeholders remained disfranchised) and the generally cool demeanour of the Whig government helped to bring O'Connell back to repeal in 1832, as has been observed. But he still saw repeal as a means to an end, namely Whig pliability, even if some of his supporters took a different line (in November 1833 Fergus O'Connor, representing the radical wing of the movement, argued that the vacillating O'Connell had created a Frankenstein's monster through the repeal agitation).[30] At the time of the Lichfield House compact, February 1835, O'Connell made quite clear to the Commons the contractual nature of his commitment to repeal: 'if I am asked if I give up the repeal of the Legislative Union, my answer is that I suspend it. But for what? To give time for carrying into operation the three measures I have described [tithe reform and parliamentary and municipal reform]'.[31]

By the late 1830s, when the limits of the Whigs' willingness or capacity to offer 'justice' to Ireland were clear, O'Connell raised the spectre of repeal once again. At first he acted with caution: the Precursor Society (founded in August 1838) was designed not as a forerunner of a repeal agitation (despite its title) but rather as 'a society to prevent the necessity of seeking repeal'.[32] This strategy survived as late as April 1840 when, after a series of half-baked organizational initiatives, O'Connell created the National Association for Full and Prompt Justice or Repeal, a title which concisely summarized the purpose and priorities of the new body. By July 1840, when 'full and prompt justice' had not been forthcoming, and when it seemed probable that the Conservatives would regain power from the Whigs, O'Connell finally abandoned the dilatory strategies of the last ten years. Even in plumping for repeal, however, he preserved an ambiguity, for his new organizational vehicle (the Loyal National Repeal Association) was not merely 'national' in scope but also 'loyal' as well.

This raises the question of the content of O'Connell's repeal convictions, and indeed of his relationship with Irish nationalism. That he has been claimed as a founder of the constitutional nationalist tradition is clear, and the reasons for this attribution are equally clear: he created a goal, devised political strategies and mapped political relationships for future nationalist leaders. Yet, characteristically, he never defined repeal, preferring to force legislative initiative onto the British government: he wanted a subordinate, Catholic-dominated parliament for (at least) Irish domestic concerns, but beyond these broad outlines he gave little clue as to his expectations. As always O'Connell was more full-blooded in denunciation than in advocacy, and it is easier to say what he did not endorse: he was not a physical force nationalist, nor was he a cultural nationalist. Irish was his mother tongue, but he was not an enthusiast for the language. He loved the increasingly common Irish national symbolism of the early nineteenth century: round towers, wolf-hounds, harps. He wore a green suit on some British speaking tours, and he wore 'the largest shamrock that could be had' when marooned in London on St Patrick's Day.[33] But though he embraced the national colours and the symbolism of Gaelic revival, he was no cultural ideologue and outlined no strategy for Irish cultural survival. Instead he inherited the eighteenth-century Catholic concern for loyalty: although his loyalty to the British crown has been compared to that of the Confederates and Jacobites, it might as well be seen as an inheritance from the genteel Catholic activists of the late eighteenth century, eager to pledge allegiance to George III in the hope of political concession. O'Connell was undoubtedly eager to demonstrate that the Orange interest had no monopoly over loyalty, and indeed took delight in the occasional displays of Orange unruliness and disloyalty. He was a devoted subject of Queen Victoria (she could only be an improvement on William IV, and her affection for her Whig ministers had an obvious political benefit): he and his sons were presented to the Queen in February 1838, and he was the author of a loyal address of gratitude in May 1839.

O'Connell practised the art of the possible, working within the bounds, though sometimes at the edge of, practical politics. Repeal was a sincere conviction, though equally it was a conviction that tended to surface when all else had failed. Despite O'Connell's flamboyant rhetoric of 1810, and despite his praise for Grattan's parliament, he did not seriously raise the issue of repeal until emancipation had been won – until, that is, the possibility of a restored Protestant parliament was out of the question: even then an agitation was raised only to be dropped. He toyed with repeal in the 1830s not out of cynicism, but because he believed both that Westminster might function as a useful assembly for Irish Catholics and that it needed to be spurred into action: repeal was simultaneously a desirable principle and a necessary goad. This constitutional ambivalence is well rooted in Irish politics (an inverted form is recognizable in modern Ulster Unionism), and it was famously expressed in 1836: 'the people of Ireland are ready to become a portion of the Empire . . . they are ready to become a kind of West Briton if made so in benefits and justice;

but if not we are Irishmen again'.[34] O'Connell, like the Ulster Unionists of 1912–14, urged local autonomy and regimented agitation when Westminster ceased to function in his interests (the Ulster Unionists of course went much further towards paramilitarism than the repealers, and they had an even slighter control over the pace of political change than O'Connell): O'Connell's nationalism was therefore as contractual as the loyalism of the Ulster Unionists. But for most of the 1830s it appeared to O'Connell that Westminster would indeed deliver reform, though – frustratingly – the Whig government wavered between lukewarm acquiescence and lukewarm hostility. There was never sustained, coercive opposition (which might have been successfully defied), but equally there was no flow of beneficence.

O'Connell's cautious attitude to repeal was determined not only by a conviction that it might be unnecessary, but also by the suspicion that it might be unattainable. The opposition forces were formidable. Although emancipation had attracted considerable sympathy in the Commons long before the Act of 1829, it was clear that repeal was an entirely different proposition. O'Connell's repeal motion, introduced on 22 April 1834, was defeated in the Commons by 523 votes to 38: there was thus a virtually complete unity of British opinion on the question. Equally, while liberal Irish Protestants had only a limited value to the campaign for emancipation, then at least they highlighted a division within Irish Protestant opinion and probably undermined the possibility of an effective Orange counter-assault. But, although O'Connell had successfully appealed to Orange anti-union sentiment in 1810, and sought to do so again in the 1830s, it had become a forlorn hope, and indeed partly because of his own success on other issues. The rise of Catholic influence, combined with O'Connell's own wide-ranging attacks on the Orange interest, ensured that the possibility of substantial Protestant support on the repeal question was remote.

Repeal in the 1830s, then, was an aspiration, a tool, an alternative, but it was not, like emancipation, a goal pursued with ruthless conviction. 'Justice for Ireland' was O'Connell's immediate ambition, and this, in so far as it was defined, meant tithe reform, municipal reform and parliamentary reform: that is to say, 'justice for Ireland' meant the gradual demolition of Protestant ascendancy. As has been noted, O'Connell was profoundly disappointed with Lord Grey's niggardly Irish reform bill, but equally this was only a part of his agenda for 'justice'. The Church of Ireland, as a keystone of the ascendancy which O'Connell so loathed, was an obvious target for his demands, but in fact here he merely had to harness an agitation that was already in full spate. From 1830 an agrarian protest movement had spread from the south-east throughout the Irish midlands: the grievance that was agitating in particular the middling and larger farmers was the tithe, a tax levied on certain types of agricultural income and applied to the maintenance of the state Church, the Church of Ireland. The immediate origins of the agitation seem to have lain with a tithe proctor in the parish of Graiguenemanagh, on the border of counties Carlow and Kilkenny, who seized the cattle of the local Catholic priest as compensation for non-payment of the tithe. But although religious feeling partly underlay the agitation – Catholics and dissenters were obliged to pay the tithe no less than members of the Church of Ireland – there was also a strong political and economic aspect. First, the tithe applied largely to tillage, and thus the great pastoral farmers and land-lords who had cleared their estates for livestock were unaffected. Second, the tithe, always an unwelcome additional tax, was an especially great burden when grain prices were low and profit margins constrained. This in fact was the case in 1830, at the beginning of the 'tithe war'.

With parts of rural Ireland in turmoil, the Whig government tested a variety of strategies. The agitation was immediately confronted with a harsh policing policy, which brought the crown forces and protestors into bloody confrontation on several occasions: in June 1831, at Newtownbarry, County Wexford, twelve demonstrators were killed by the yeomanry; later in the year eleven police and soldiers were killed in an ambush at Carrickshock, County Kilkenny, by tithe protestors. In 1833 a severe coercion bill was introduced in the House of Commons and – despite the opposi-tion and disruptive tactics of O'Connell (again a premonition of Parnell) – placed on the statute book. But there were other approaches. The government was deter-mined, before applying a political solution, to suppress disorder and to relieve the condition of the Church of Ireland clergy, some of whom had been reduced to destitution as a result of the agitation. In June 1832, through the tithes arrears bill, £60,000 was applied to the relief of tithe owners, predominantly the clergy, and through the same measure the government was empowered to collect the tithe arrears for 1831: this was (with the benefit of hindsight) a significant interference, for although it took the burden of collection from the tithe owners, it also annexed one of their rights. A further measure in 1832, the Tithe Composition Act, converted the tithe into a money payment and thrust responsibility for payment onto the landlord: this, too, would prove a significant initiative, since it highlighted the increasingly popular expedient of deflecting the attack on the Church onto the landlord class and it looked forward to the final legislative resolution of the issue. Both bills were opposed by O'Connell.

But the two measures which pointed to, indeed provided, a more lasting settle-ment both to the agitation and to O'Connellite opposition were the Irish Church Temporalities Act (1833) and in particular the Tithe Rent Charge Act (1838). Each of these tackled in some form the tithe question, but the approach in each case was quite different. The first of the measures, the Church Temporalities Act, pruned the luxuriant hierarchy of the Church of Ireland, suppressing ten out of the 22 sees, reducing the income of the remaining 12, and applying a graduated tax on benefices worth £200 a year or more. Catholic or dissenting tithe-payers would thus no longer be affronted by the task of supporting bishops from an alien church in princely style (O'Connell was fond of pointing to the Bishop of Derry, worth, so he claimed, between £25,000 and £30,000 a year). Furthermore, it was originally intended to create, under parliamentary control, a surplus fund out of the £60,000 or £70,000 released by these reforms (though this plan to 'appropriate' the income of the Church was later withdrawn). O'Connell was delighted with the original bill, recognizing (along with the High Church critics of the measure) that it represented a serious parliamentary incursion into the management of the Church: he laid great stress on the appropriation clauses, and was correspondingly horrified when they were ditched. But if the Catholics sought appropriation, and in the long run sought the demise of the ascendancy interest, then Presbyterians were much more divided: many welcomed reform of the Church of Ireland and the curbing of its pretensions, but an influential minority, led by Henry Cooke, came increasingly to view the legislative assault on the Church as part of a concerted attack on Irish Protestantism as a whole. The Church Temporalities Act, though in the end a bitter disappointment to the Catholic supporters of the Whig government, both anticipated the final settlement of the Church question and helped to shunt some Irish Presbyterians towards a closer sympathy with their Anglican brethren. The measure thus looked forward both to disestablishment and to Unionism.

The Church Temporalities Act, though it clearly had a bearing on the tithe question, was not in itself an answer to the issue. A series of tithe bills, introduced in 1834, 1835 and 1836, sought a more direct approach, but all failed – the measures of 1835 and 1836 foundering on the question of appropriation. The instrument by which the issue was finally laid to rest was the Tithe Rent Charge Act of 1838, which scaled down tithe payments and incorporated them into a rental charge: landlords, mollified by a bonus, still bore the responsibility of paying, although they were also able to pass any charges on to their tenants (except those holding annual leases). The substantial arrears that had mounted over the period 1834–7 were written off. The success of the Act owed something to these provisions, although it is generally seen as a disappointingly limited response to eight years of agitation. Indeed the measure fell short of O'Connell's demands, and it did not incorporate the vital principle of appropriation. It was acceptable as a compromise, but only because O'Connell, while seeing the utility of the tithe issue, was never really fired by it: he used the tithe agitation for his own ends, but he was not (consciously at any rate) a social revolutionary, and as a landlord he did not want to see the tithe abolished because of a peasant agitation over which he had little direct control. This ambivalence, combined with the improved market conditions against which the bill was launched, helped to reinforce its effectiveness.

In the absence of repeal, O'Connell laid great stress on the reform of Ireland's antique municipal corporations: indeed, statutory reform of the Irish corporations, the tithe and of parliament had been his terms for suspending the repeal agitation and for supporting the Whig government in early 1835. Corporation reform, like the tithe issue, was part of O'Connell's broader campaign against Protestant ascendancy. The tithe agitation had been to some extent forced upon him, but it had represented nonetheless a welcome means of curbing the pretensions of the ascendancy Church. Municipal reform was a still more congenial occupation for the town corporations, like the Church of Ireland, were ascendancy strongholds, disproportionately Orange and Tory: in 1835 all but four of the 60 surviving corporations were exclusively Protestant. In addition, admission to the corporations in most cases was at best quirky, and their size was generally highly constricted. Although the political influence of the corporations had declined after the Great Reform Act, some (pre-eminently Dublin) retained a real electoral clout. They were also vested with formidable powers of local patronage, an issue which cannot have escaped the attention of O'Connell, who was a bitter critic of Orange jobbery and the most devoted patron of his own, hitherto neglected, following. The corporations were simultaneously influential and – even by the standards of the 1830s – highly irregular institutions, and they were therefore of obvious concern to O'Connell.

However, if the tithe question were resolved in a manner that fell far short of Irish demands, then this was even more clearly the case with municipal reform. O'Connell had been – characteristically – bullish about the initial prospects of comprehensive reform: in February 1833 he had been invited to join a parliamentary select committee to enquire into municipal government throughout the United Kingdom, and he had brought over from Ireland as witnesses several highly critical commentators on the Irish corporations. The committee report highlighted abuses in the corporations of Belfast and Dublin and recommended a full commission of enquiry: this was set up in July 1833 and appears to have been packed with reformers, indeed with O'Connellite sympathizers. Its report echoed and amplified the findings of the select committee, offering a thoroughgoing condemnation of the state of Irish municipal government. But successive bills which sought to enact the findings of the commission met with strenuous opposition in the House of Lords; and the government, highly vulnerable after the Tory gains in the election of 1837, was not in a position to force through a radical measure. The Municipal Corporations Act of 1840, like the Tithe Rent Charge Act of 1838, was therefore unremarkable – except in the sense that it was astonishing that any type of reform should be enacted after the long and wearing parliamentary battles over the issue. The measure, in the words of Angus Macintyre, 'was in reality a scheme of municipal disfranchisement' rather than an intricate democratic revision: 58 corporations were dissolved and elective councils created in Belfast, Dublin and ten other boroughs.[35] Many of the detailed O'Connellite demands went by the board: the municipal franchise was restricted to the ten-pound rather than the more democratic eight-pound householder qualification; and the lord lieutenant, rather than the councillors, was awarded the right to appoint the sheriffs (who held great influence over the selection of juries and the conduct of parliamentary elections). The Act indeed created some 'islands of representative democracy' and permitted O'Connell to win a victory of some significance in 1841, when he was elected lord mayor of Dublin.[36] But it was a diminished version of the corresponding English measure of reform (passed in 1835); and it represented a poor return on the lavish hopes invested by O'Connell in 1833.

Of all the Whig reforms, the Poor Law Bill of 1837–8 was the one which O'Connell treated with the greatest asperity; and, unlike the tithe and municipal reform, it was never part of the price of his support. Poor law reform had a chequered history in the 1830s: in 1833 the Whig government of Earl Grey had appointed a commission to investigate the issue, chaired by the Church of Ireland Archbishop of Dublin, Richard Whately, but its findings, published in 1836, did not chime with ministers' expectations. The Whately commission argued against the English poor law system, which was organized around the workhouse, advocating instead that poverty might be alleviated through employment, and that employment might in turn be created through public works. But the government, as in so much else, evidently wanted to apply English solutions to Irish problems, and in 1836 a second enquiry was launched. This provided the judgement that the government had clearly wanted all along. The new report, the work of an English poor law commissioner, George Nicholls, urged that the new English arrangements should be imported into Ireland; and this recommendation was speedily incorporated into legislation in early 1837. The Poor Relief (Ireland) Bill, introduced in February 1837, called for the organization of parishes into unions, each union being served by a workhouse: boards of guardians, using money raised from the rates, would administer both the new poor law unions and the new workhouses. The boards, in turn, were to be composed partly of elected representatives of the rate payers, and partly of the local magistrates.

O'Connell's response to the bill at first glance seems confused: in February he was welcoming, though by December – when the measure was reintroduced – this greeting had turned sour (he muttered darkly about 'social revolution' and complained about 'the new and heavy charge on property').[37] In reality neither the bill nor O'Connell's fundamental attitude had changed: it was the political context that had shifted. O'Connell had originally been prepared to support the Poor Law Bill as the price of effective municipal and tithe reform. However, both these measures now seemed to be slipping from his grasp, and in any event it was clear that the Tories were prepared to support the Whig Poor Law initiative: there was thus no tactical reason for O'Connell to mask his feelings, and he moved the rejection of the bill in February 1838. He believed that the new poor law would beggar the country, and in particular his own landed class: he believed, too, that the workhouses would serve both to weaken private charity and (in the absence of outdoor relief) to imprison the defenceless poor. In fact, in so far as it was political principle rather than humanitarian sympathy which underlay O'Connell's attitude, then his opposition was utterly misjudged. For the new boards of guardians, as largely elective bodies with increasing powers, helped to enhance the democratic influence over local government; and – in the absence of other fora – they proved to be an essential training ground for future nationalist politicians. On the other hand, and more importantly, neither the Poor Relief (Ireland) Act nor O'Connell's proposed remedies for Irish poverty had taken into account the possibility of a widespread crop failure: the new poor law system was certainly not designed for a cataclysm, and the threat of a disaster like the Great Famine would never have occurred to the Gradgrindian ideologues who were the architects of the system.

It should not, however, be supposed either that O'Connell's concerns were limited to his tripartite agenda of February 1835 or that his relative loyalty to the Whigs depended on a small number of half-hearted legislative initiatives (let alone unwanted measures such as the poor law reform). O'Connell had helped to curb, however modestly, the pretensions of the ascendancy Church and the influence of the ascendancy within the municipal corporations, but he also recognized the importance of undermining the 'Orange' dominance over official patronage and in the administration of the law. In fact, arguably the chief benefit of his relationship with the Whigs came from a sympathetic executive in Dublin Castle, headed by the second Earl of Mulgrave as lord lieutenant (1835–9), and by Lord Morpeth as Chief Secretary (1835–41): completing this anti-Orange trinity, and perhaps the most talented of the three, was a young Scots engineer, Thomas Drummond, who in 1835 was appointed undersecretary and in effect head of the Irish civil service. Drummond earned a remarkable reputation within the constitutional nationalist tradition of the nineteenth century: 'His record is unique', proclaimed his nationalist biographer, R. Barry O'Brien (author, too, of a famous 'life' of Parnell and editor of the autobiography of Wolfe Tone); 'He was a success. Why? The answer lies on the surface. He knew Ireland. He loved the people, he had a policy, and he stood to his guns'.[38] Drummond, as a middle-class Scots Presbyterian and as a technocrat of a Benthamite tendency, had as little affection for the Orange and ascendancy interest as O'Connell, and set about curbing its influence at all levels of the Irish administration: this task was made somewhat easier after 1835, when a parliamentary select committee issued a scathing condemnation of the insidious influence of the Orange Order. Drummond and his political masters were particularly keen to reform the administration of justice and pursued a policy of centralization combined with a mild catholicization. Catholics were admitted to the judiciary for the first time: the appointment of magistrates was taken out of the hands of the local (and often ascendancy-dominated) magistracy and vested in the Castle (Charles O'Connell, Daniel's son-in-law, eventually won one of these positions). The local magistrates themselves came under scrutiny, with the increasing appointment of Catholics and the corresponding dismissal of Orange sympathizers (such as Colonel Verner, Deputy Lieutenant for Tyrone, removed from the magistracy after giving an Orange toast at a dinner to commemorate the Battle of the Diamond). Jury lists were compiled under new regulations. The police system was regularized and centralized, with the creation in 1836 of the Irish Constabulary: a considerable number of Catholics – including, pointedly, a brother of Michael Slattery, the Catholic Archbishop of Cashel – were appointed as officers of the new force. Four Catholics in succession held the office of attorney general for Ireland under the Whigs, appointments to which O'Connell attached particular importance: the reason for his anxiety is not hard to locate, for the attorney general, who offered legal advice to the executive and who represented the state in the courts, bridged the divide between government, the judicial system and the general public.

By 1840–1 it has been estimated that one-third of the key legal and executive positions in Ireland were held by 'anti-Tories', as opposed to the virtual Tory and ascendancy monopoly at the beginning of the 1830s: O'Connell himself had emerged as a significant patron for petitioning Catholics (and indeed, occasionally, Protestants).[39] By 1840, however, Drummond was dead and had been succeeded in office by Norman Macdonald, a Scot, too, but 'out of sympathy with national feeling': Lord Mulgrave, the nominal head of the executive team which O'Connell so favoured, had already in 1839 been translated from Ireland to the War and Colonial Office.[40] If the increasingly embattled Whig government had delivered modest (if symbolically significant) reform at a snail's pace, then the

Mulgrave–Morpeth–Drummond troika had demonstrated the reality of Catholic emancipation with a brisk efficiency. But by the summer of 1840 this troika was broken, and their masters at Westminster looked set to fall victim to the Tories. The first instalment of 'justice for Ireland' had – viewed in the round – not been inconsiderable, but O'Connell's difficulty lay in knowing when, indeed if, the next instalment would be forthcoming. Little wonder, then, that with a Tory succession imminent, he should have reverted to repeal and to an extra-parliamentary agitation.

3.4   Utilitarians and Romantics, 1841–8

The creation of the Loyal National Repeal Association in July 1840 was the effective starting point for the repeal campaign, although neither with emancipation nor with repeal was an agitation instantly created. The success of the emancipation campaign in 1829 rested partly on the effort invested by agitators from the late eighteenth century; and, equally, the achievement of a mass agitation for repeal by 1843 was a long-term effort, depending on the (albeit uncertain) evangelism of the late 1830s and early 1840s. But besides this generic explanation, there were other reasons for the dilatory start to the repeal campaign. The fall of the Whig government and the accession of Peel and the Tories in June 1841 precipitated an election which, while it scarcely caught the repealers unawares, did catch them underfunded: only 18 firm repealers were returned at this election, and there were strategically significant Tory victories in Dublin city and in County Carlow (where O'Connell's youngest son was standing). This has been described as a 'comparatively respectable showing' by O'Connell's most sanguine modern biographer, but in fact it may well have helped to demoralize the repealers, rendering them both an unattractive proposition for the Whig opposition and an insignificant threat for the Tories.[41]

In addition to this setback, at once a reflection and a cause of weakness, O'Connell was temporarily diverted into the municipal arena. The corporation elections of October 1841 brought the repealers some local compensation for their earlier reverses, and particularly in Dublin where – thanks to O'Connell's meticulous generalship – they gained 47 out of 60 available seats. This assured him both the lord mayoralty of Dublin ('a legally recognised lordship from the people, utterly unconnected with court favour or aristocratic usage', enthused John O'Connell) and an opportunity to realize the (admittedly limited) benefits promised by the Municipal Corporations Act.[42] In fact O'Connell's year as lord mayor was the municipal equivalent of his parliamentary strategy in the 1830s, and a part of his broader assault on the bastions of the ascendancy: the year served as a political bridge linking emancipation with repeal, for as lord mayor O'Connell was simultaneously demonstrating the reality of emancipation and the potential of a repeal administration in Dublin. He promised to act impartially, and seems to have done so, although his earnest religious convictions and his strong sense of the theatrical led to some provocative gestures (he threw off his mayoral finery on New Year's Day 1842 before entering church because, as he explained, while he was a Catholic, his robes were

Protestant).[43] Such lapses were probably inevitable in the context of decades of Orange domination within the corporation and the heightened sectarian atmosphere of the early and mid-nineteenth century, but they reflected attitudes which contributed in the end to the demolition of the repeal movement and which sustained divisions about its legacy.

Success and domination within the local arena seem to have empowered O'Connell after years of an enervating dependence upon the Whigs. By the end of his term of office, in the autumn of 1842, he was ready to activate the plans for a repeal agitation which had been laid down in the early 1830s and, with apparently greater seriousness, in the years 1838–40. As with emancipation, so with repeal, the Catholic clergy were central to the organization of the agitation, and as an opening gambit in August 1842 O'Connell commanded that lists of the parish priests and leading Catholic laity in Leinster be compiled. But the repeal movement echoed the emancipation movement in other respects: the hierarchy of the Repeal Association, the repeal rent, the local repeal wardens, the associate membership fee of a penny a month – all these details were inherited from the emancipation movement. The idea of formal public debate, so enthusiastically pursued in the 1820s between Catholic and Protestant advocates, was revived in February 1843, with the great contest in the Dublin corporation between the repealers, led by O'Connell, and the Unionists, led by Isaac Butt. Naturally public meetings were of central importance to the emancipation and repeal agitations, but between March and September 1843 an unprecedented campaign of 'monster' meetings – the adjective was supplied by *The Times* – was held, attracting audiences of half a million and more (the largest was held at Tara, County Meath, on 15 August, with an attendance estimated at between half a million and three-quarters of a million). These meetings fulfilled the same significance in the repeal campaign as the electoral contests of the 1820s did for emancipation: the shock of Waterford or Clare could not be recaptured because there was no longer any novelty in electoral upsets, but the scale and discipline of the public meetings of 1843 were just as sensational, and even more intimidating. The meetings were entertainments, just as the election campaigns of the 1820s had been: there were 42 bands at the Tara meeting, 10,000 horsemen, a harpist, and above all a cathartic oratory. O'Connell's election rhetoric of the 1820s was reworked and elaborated at these rallies, with a strong emphasis on belligerence and on the historical grievances of Irish Catholics: two militant speeches, at Kilkenny and (famously) at Mallow, County Cork, in June 1843 followed an apparent hardening of attitude on the part of the government and looked forward to a bloody confrontation. But, as in the 1820s, so in the 1840s, there was an ambivalence in O'Connell's attitudes, whether as a result of careful political calculation or (equally probable) his fatal gift of fluency: a comparison might be made with the ambiguities of Carson's position in 1912–14, where there was a counterpoint of public defiance and private conciliation, and an oscillation between pellucid logic and hazy emotionalism. But Asquith was no Peel, and the Ulster Unionists' resolve was not tested in 1914 as was the militancy of the repealers in 1843. For the climax of O'Connell's campaign, which was to have been a meeting at Clontarf, County

Dublin, on 8 October, never occurred. The posters announcing this gathering suggested that it would have a paramilitary dimension, and the government seized the opportunity to issue a ban: O'Connell – true to his essential constitutionalism – acquiesced. His apparently unexceptional speech at Skibbereen on 22 June ('I am not determined to die for Ireland, I would rather live for her') had in fact revealed his convictions more honestly than the celebrated 'Mallow Defiance' of 11 June ('they may trample on me, but it will be my dead body they will trample on, not the living man').[44]

O'Connell's decision to abandon the Clontarf meeting had been an act of principle, one which was decried by choleric theoreticians of war such as John Mitchel: even the more constrained, if susceptible, Thomas Davis was moved to write that 'Earth is not deep enough to hide the coward slave who shrinks aside; / Hell is not hot enough to scathe the ruffian wretch who breaks his faith'. The allusion to O'Connellite rhetoric and, indeed, to O'Connell himself, seems clear.[45] However, it is all too easy to accept the argument that Clontarf represented a decisive, indeed a disastrous, turning point in O'Connell's fortunes and in those of his movement. O'Connell himself, no less than his difficult Young Ireland protégés, helped to affirm this view: he had decreed that 1843 was to be repeal year, and he continually proclaimed, even in private correspondence, his belief that repeal would be granted before the year was out. The Young Irelanders (Denis Gwynn compared them patronizingly but not unhelpfully to restless and impatient undergraduates) tended to accept O'Connell's messianic conviction at face value, and tended, too, to be persuaded by their own passion.[46] Even though Davis and other Young Irelanders were uneasy about the 'monster' meetings, it is clear that, by the summer of 1843, O'Connell had convinced many, possibly even himself, that he had achieved a political momentum similar to that won by 1828–9. The apparent surrender at Clontarf, followed by O'Connell's four-month imprisonment (May–September 1844) on a charge of sedition, seemed a pathetically meek dénouement to months of political protest and confident political prophecy: 'We promised loud and boasted high', intoned Davis, ' "to break our country's chains, or die"; / And should we quail, that country's name will be the synonym of shame'.[47]

There are other perspectives on Clontarf. Clontarf may be seen as a decisive moment in the history of repeal, only if it is assumed that repeal was, in the 1840s, a realizable ambition. This, however, is to underestimate the strength of the opposition, and in particular to neglect the already tenacious Unionism of eastern Ulster. In fact, neither O'Connell nor the Young Irelanders attached any particular significance to the increasingly divergent political traditions of the north. Neither, however, can have been completely unaware that the north presented potential difficulties: during the emancipation campaign the levels of Catholic rent collected in Ulster had been unusually low, and in September 1828 an attempt by John Lawless, an O'Connellite lieutenant, to rouse support and to expose the weakness of Orange influence had led to a humiliating, and potentially disastrous, confrontation with Orangemen at Ballybay, County Monaghan. The episode demonstrates O'Connell's bullish conviction that dissent in the north could be managed no less than in the

MR. O'CONNELL, IN HIS TRIUMPHAL CAR.

Plate 2   Daniel O'Connell acquitted, Dublin 1844.
Source: Mary Evans Picture Library.

rest of the country, and – characteristically – there is nothing to suggest that his confidence was damaged by the encounter. In January 1841, despite the still hesitant nature of the repeal movement in the south and west of Ireland, O'Connell planned a triumphal progress north into Belfast to evangelize for the cause; but, as so often in his career, rhetoric and reality diverged, and he had to be content with what his opponents saw as a skulking entry. He was snubbed by northern liberal Protestants, barracked by Orangemen, derided by the able northern Unionist leader, Reverend Henry Cooke, but still able to preen himself on 'so triumphant a result'.[48] This attitude was, of course, a genial provocation and typical of O'Connell's great ability to mask adversity, and it reflected an unwillingness to judge northern Unionism as anything other than a conventional, and therefore negotiable, problem.

The Young Irelanders, though comparatively well informed, appear to have taken much the same attitude. Several Young Ireland leaders – Charles Gavan Duffy, John Mitchel – were Ulstermen and there were northern contributors to the *Nation*, including one of the celebrated women poets, 'Finola' (Elizabeth Willoughby Treacy), but none treated Ulster as an impediment to their cultural or political ambitions: it was unfortunate, but scarcely surprising, that Mitchel, the only Ulster Protestant in the high command of the Young Irelanders, should have been so marginal, both in terms of his convictions (he was a lapsed Unitarian) and his personality (he was 'possessed by hate' and had a 'volcanic' temper).[49] In fact the insouciance of the repealers should not come as any great surprise: from the perspective of both Young Ireland and O'Connell, the great institutions of the ascendancy had been shown to be vulnerable, and there was no immediate reason to suppose that the popular Orangeism of the north would prove to be any more tenacious than the propertied Orangeism of the south. And as yet the political culture of the north, though perhaps subliminally Unionist, was still not overtly or comprehensively so: there was as yet no organized Unionist movement, and political divisions within northern Protestantism, though easing, remained noticeable. Moreover, memories of the United Irish tradition in Belfast were still fresh – indeed, there were some hardy survivors from the period, such as Mary Anne McCracken – and the most influential northern secular leader of the period, William Sharman Crawford, while no friend to O'Connell, was equally neither an advocate of ascendancy nor a conventional Unionist.

Had O'Connell not encountered the convinced and militant Unionism of Peel at Clontarf, then – like later nationalist leaders – he would have had to deal with northern political dissent. The Clontarf incident, while certainly a personal political tragedy for O'Connell, cannot therefore realistically be viewed as 'the reason' why repeal failed (and all the more so, given the failure of the potato crop in 1845 and its impact on Irish political activity). Clontarf certainly broke the momentum of the repeal agitation, but then this would in any event have been disturbed with the onset of winter and the suspension of agitation. Clontarf helped to expose damaging divisions within the repeal movement between the O'Connellites and the Young Irelanders – but then these divisions were already present and ran deeper than mere matters of strategy. In fact the agitation, judged as a whole, was not without profit: while the Clontarf episode may have demonstrated the impossibility of repeal, the campaign of which it was a part helped to keep the problem of Irish government before the House of Commons and to energize British legislators. O'Connell's strategies had changed, as had the party in office, but the repeal issue served precisely the same function in the early 1840s as in the years of the Whig alliance. O'Connell had created repeal – his 'Frankenstein's monster', according to Fergus O'Connor – as a tool; and despite the elaboration of his ambitions, it remained a tool.[50]

The agitation highlighted both a problem and an opportunity for the Tory government: the mass meetings revealed the scale and social diversity of Irish disaffection, while the confusion among the repealers after Clontarf provided a chance to act. Peel, like his protégé Gladstone, believed in the efficacy of political timing, and after Clontarf he could offer judicious concession without being seen to surrender to the threat of violence (as ultra-Tories charged that he had done over emancipation). In fact the agitation had already goaded Peel into some (albeit quiet) conciliatory gestures: after June 1843 he urged on the reluctant lord lieutenant, Lord De Grey, that 'considerations of policy and also of justice demand a *liberal* and indulgent estimate of the claims on the favour of the Crown of such Roman Catholics as abstain from political agitation'.[51] Rewarding 'well-affected' and competent Catholics was only a part but nonetheless (given O'Connell's patronage concerns in the late 1830s) a significant part of a more ambitious strategy. Although Peel had declared that he would resist repeal and the dismemberment of the Empire by force, he recognized equally that 'mere force . . . will do nothing as a permanent remedy for the social evils of that country [Ireland]': despite the evidence of the Clontarf episode, he sought not to crush the repeal alliance but rather to undo it, by isolating and pacifying its component parts.[52] Satisfying the professional aspirations of 'well-affected' Catholic lawyers, doctors and policemen was therefore necessary, but a much more pressing, if related, problem was the close cooperation between the repealers and the Catholic clergy. 'Sever the clergy from the agitators, and agitation must cease' advised James Kernan, a Catholic resident magistrate, in a report submitted to the cabinet in May 1843: the suggestion did not go unheeded, for this 'severance' would prove to be a central ministerial objective over the next three years.[53]

After Clontarf, Peel, his Home Secretary Sir James Graham and the liberal Tory Chief Secretary Lord Eliot were united in promoting a policy of modest conciliation towards the Catholic clergy. Clontarf provided the opportunity, and the demolition of the repeal agitation provided a key motive, but in fact the origins of some of the initiatives long predated 1843. Peel's Charitable Donations and Bequests (Ireland) Bill (1844) addressed a longstanding Catholic grievance, which had been highlighted by O'Connell in 1830 and again in 1844: Peel's measure established a broadly based board, numbering 13 and including five Catholics, which was charged with the location and administration of charitable bequests for the Catholic clergy. Hitherto such bequests had been administered by a largely Protestant board, which had exercised unsatisfactorily wide discretionary powers and which accordingly had been distrusted by the Catholic laity. The new measure in fact did not satisfy either O'Connell, who favoured a board comprising the Catholic bishops, or his episcopal sympathizers (pre-eminently Archbishop MacHale of Tuam), but a significant body of clerics (including the Archbishops of Armagh and Dublin, and the Bishop of Down and Connor) were prepared to accept the bill as an improvement, however flawed, on the existing arrangements. Had the bill originated with a Whig ministry, doubtless O'Connell would have followed Archbishop Murray of Dublin in welcoming an 'instalment' of reform. As it was, the Tory government had successfully driven a wedge between the Repeal Association and a significant body of senior bishops. Little wonder that the new lord lieutenant, Lord Heytesbury, could gloat that 'we have erected a barrier – a line of Churchmen – behind which the well-thinking part of the Roman Catholic laity will conscientiously rally'.[54]

Peel's courtship of the Catholic Church continued in April 1845, with his Maynooth Bill. By this measure the annual grant to the seminary at Maynooth was trebled (to £26,360) and was rescued from an annual political controversy by being made a permanent charge: in addition a one-off payment of £30,000 was provided for building work. The political price paid for this act of conciliation was high (the resignation of Gladstone, the heightened anti-pathy of ultra-Protestants within both the Anglican and dissenting traditions, the renewed hurtful accusations of bad faith), but the bargain was not entirely one-sided: Peel hoped for a better-educated and more anglophile priesthood, and he gambled that his stand against English

Protestant fury would be repaid with Irish Catholic respect. In the short term (the only timespan within which it is possible to judge) Peel's gamble worked, and even his unrelenting political enemy, O'Connell, offered a muted and grudging approval (he had in fact little choice). But the intervention of the Famine destroyed the Irish political landscape within which both Peel and his O'Connellite critics operated, and his experiment in (what Donal Kerr has called) 'killing Repeal by kindness' was therefore cut short.[55] Neither the Charitable Bequests Act nor the Maynooth grant could in themselves satisfy the exuberant hopes that O'Connell had aroused in 1843: but these modest measures helped to demonstrate that Toryism was not wholly bound to the ascendancy interest, and that Tory reform was not crudely related to militant pressure. Peel had indicated that the Union might be made to work for Irish Catholics no matter what party was in power, just as his constructive Unionist successors 50 years later would seek to demonstrate that the Liberals had no monopoly over Irish reform. Each generation of Tory won an understandably sceptical response from the politicians; but each generated some (albeit ephemeral) popular goodwill.

Scepticism was, however, among the more favourable reactions won by Peel's third Irish initiative, the Academical Institutions (Ireland) Bill. As with the Charitable Bequests Act and the Maynooth grant, Peel's immediate political motivation in broaching the issue of university reform was the repeal movement, but – like these earlier measures – there was also a broader and more generous perspective. Ireland lacked an extensive system of higher education such as existed in Scotland, and Irish Catholics in particular possessed no university which was in keeping with their faith and culture. Peel's measure, introduced in May 1845, sought to balance generous educational provision with the non-denominational principle, and the creation of three new colleges was proposed from which the teaching of theology and religion would be excluded. As with charitable bequests, much hinged on the attitude of the Catholic bishops: at first they were disposed to bargain, presenting Heytesbury on 25 May with severe – though apparently negotiable – demands, but their attitude subsequently hardened. Led by the redoubtable MacHale of Tuam, with the assistance of the able Rector of the Irish College at Rome, Paul Cullen, a majority of the hierarchy came to condemn the 'infidel' colleges as a threat to the faith and morals of the Catholic laity: the two senior archbishops, Crolly of Armagh (who hoped for a college in his own city) and Murray of Dublin, were effectively isolated in their willingness to work with an amended version of Peel's proposal. A meeting of the hierarchy, held in Dublin in November 1845, although divided 18–6 in opposition to the bill, agreed to submit the measure to Rome for a decision: the majority's advice to Pius IX was pointed ('Time, Beattissime Pater, time Anglos et dona ferentes'), and the bill was duly condemned on 13 July 1846.[56]

There were similar, perhaps even more serious, divisions within the repeal movement over the issue: Davis in the *Nation* offered guarded approval, while the O'Connellite organ, the *Pilot*, followed the bishops' lead in condemning the colleges plan. These divisions came to a head on 26 May 1845 at a celebrated general meeting of the Repeal Association, when Davis and O'Connell sparred cruelly with one another and were reconciled only after tears from Davis and an affectionate embrace from O'Connell ('more like the clumsy pantomime of an ox than any display of manly sincerity' grumbled one of Davis's friends).[57] Davis's early death (in September 1845) prevented the issue developing, but the damage had been done and there were other issues to which the bitterness of the colleges debate could be, and was, transferred.

Peel's bill provided no lasting solution to the vexed question of Irish university education – a lasting compromise came only with the Irish Universities Act of 1908 – and the failure of the potato crop in 1845 reduced the importance of the bill, and indeed the issue, even for the government. But if the measure failed to satisfy Peel's genuine aspirations for the better administration of Ireland, then it nurtured some political advantages: a temporarily divided hierarchy, and a repeal movement torn by internal political, indeed sectarian, tension. Peel's acute tactical sense should not, however, obscure his commitment to what he called in his resignation speech 'a complete equality of municipal, civil and political rights' in Ireland; nor should his contribution to the demise of the repeal movement detract from, as Donal Kerr puts it, 'the credit of being the first Tory premier to make a serious effort to solve the Irish problem by conciliation'.[58]

Peel's legislative programme laid the foundations for the 'coercion and conciliation' strategies of the late nineteenth century; the programme helped to define the political vocabulary of nineteenth-century Ireland ('godless colleges', 'Castle bishop', 'Castle Catholic', 'Young Ireland' were all formulations popularized as a result of the debate on Peel's measures).[59] But, while it is important to appreciate Peel's achievement, and important to grasp that he was pursuing a consciously divisive strategy, it should be emphasized that he did no more than precipitate the tensions within the repeal movement: the chasm between Young and Old Ireland was not excavated by Peel alone. The Young Irelanders and the O'Connellites were united by their commitment to repeal, but divided in almost every other respect: they had separate newspapers (the *Nation*, founded on 15 October 1842, was the focal point for the Young Irelanders), separate strategies (the Young Irelanders were sniffy about mass agitation, preferring to politicize through education) and – repeal aside – separate goals (the Young Irelanders were primarily cultural nationalists, though they helped to revitalize the Irish republican tradition). These comparisons merit some expansion. The *Nation* helped to define the Young Ireland grouping, for the leaders – Davis, Gavan Duffy, Mitchel – were intimately involved in the task of publication, while the large circulation achieved (10,000 copies were sold of each edition, with perhaps 250,000 readers) provided them with a wide political influence. The paper, though initially loyal to O'Connell (after Clontarf it proclaimed that 'the man who dares to adopt any policy not sanctioned by O'Connell will deserve the deepest execration') became increasingly sceptical, and there were divisions over several issues (including, as has been observed, the university question).[60]

The *Nation* was used to publicize other distinctive Young Ireland initiatives: 'educate that you might be free' was one of the most celebrated of Davis's injunctions, and he helped to provide both reading facilities (the repeal reading rooms) and a nationally minded literature (the Library of Ireland, dubbed by George Boyce 'the Irish forerunner of the Left Book Club').[61] The Young Irelanders, despite some disingenuous and self-indulgent allusions to their plebeian credentials, were in some respects strongly elitist. Davis in particular seems to have been uneasy about the vulgar and dangerous nature of O'Connell's 'monster meetings', while cherishing a hope (like Parnell) that Protestants would retain a position of leadership in a free Ireland: like Parnell, Davis hoped to win over the Irish gentry to the cause of nationality. A revitalized Protestant leadership was not of course part of O'Connell's political agenda, but then neither was the wide-ranging cultural nationalism of the Young Irelanders. Davis was a Carlylean romantic, imbibing German nationalism through the writings of the sage of Chelsea: he was in addition bitterly anti-utilitarian, savaging what he called 'the horde of Benthamy'.[62] O'Connell shared some of Davis's prejudices (the two men plundered Irish history with a missionary zeal), but he professed himself a loyal Benthamite, and he had no interest in many of Davis's cultural passions – pre-eminently the Irish language. He was a grudging sponsor of some of Davis's initiatives (for example, the repeal reading rooms), but he was basically a practical agitator rather than a nationalist theoretician. Even setting aside the question of religion, there was a gap in understanding between the two men, which O'Connell's exuberant goodwill and Davis's propriety scarcely bridged.

Given these deep practical and ideological divisions, permanent schism within the repeal movement could have occurred over any one of a number of issues: the breakdown in fact came with the question of violence. The paradoxical relationship between Young Ireland and O'Connell is nowhere better illustrated than here: the Young Irelanders prided themselves, as Sinn Féin would do, on their austerity and discipline, yet in fact it was O'Connell, in their eyes grubbing and shambolic, who was more vigorously legalistic and a more effective, because a more subtle, authoritarian. O'Connell was convinced of the need for legality and order within the repeal movement, but equally he struck a balance between firm discipline and often highly militant rhetoric: the two features in fact were complementary, for invigorating, possibly incitative, speeches were only possible within the context of a carefully policed movement. On the whole Young Ireland echoed this position, though the ambiguities were undoubtedly more marked: both Davis and O'Connell referred vituperatively to the failings of the 'Saxon', and both promoted an expurgated reading of Irish military history. Davis wrote martial verse, but generally qualified his calls to arms with the suggestion that 'wisdom' or 'thought, courage, patience' would prevail.[63] Writing in the *Nation* after Clontarf, he decried the prospect of violence – yet at the same time he sublimated his anger in bitter, militant poetry. On balance, however, Davis was a moderating influence among the Young Irelanders: only after his death did the militancy of his colleagues become noticeably crude, culminating in November 1845 with a notorious article in the *Nation*, wherein John Mitchel ruminated on the techniques of guerrilla warfare. Mitchel sought to justify himself by explaining that he saw violence only as a last resort and as a response to official coercion – but this did not mollify O'Connell. Motivated partly by principle, but also doubtless by the desire to impose his authority on a united movement, O'Connell demanded that the Repeal Association affirm its unqualified repudiation of violence. This stimulated a bitter debate within the Association in July 1846, after which William Smith O'Brien and the Young Irelanders withdrew. Despite some diplomatizing in December 1846, the secessionists formed their own rival organization, the Irish Confederation, in January 1847. But by this time the discussion of violence and its applications was becoming increasingly bizarre, for while the repealers talked metaphysics, Ireland starved.

O'Connell's strategies had depended upon combining a ferocious but constitutional agitation with sharp high-political skills. By 1846–7 neither of these was attainable: O'Connell himself was declining, both physically and intellectually, and his last parliamentary performances were rambling and tragic. Even had he had the ability, it would have been impossible to sustain an agitation in the context of the Famine. Even earlier he had stepped back from repeal (just as he had done in the 1830s), proposing alternatives in January 1844 to the 'present ardent desire for repeal', and toying with federalism in October 1844.[64] In the last months of his life he retreated to his estate and to matters of local patronage. One of his last political acts, in January 1847, was to call for greater Catholic admission to the Dublin magistracy. It was bathos, perhaps, but nonetheless appropriate – for even at the end he was chivvying the ascendancy interest and seeking the consummation of his great victory of 1829.

If the Repeal Association and O'Connellite gradualism were killed by the Famine, then the militancy of the Young Irelanders was both fired and destroyed. The desperate condition of the Irish cottiers and small farmers encouraged some in the Irish Confederation to hope that agrarian crisis would promote an enhanced national spirit (among the most influential of these theorists was James Fintan Lalor). Certainly Mitchel believed that the impoverished farmers might prove to be a political weapon, and in December 1847 he called on the peasantry to arm themselves in defiance of the government. He was still well in advance of the opinions of his fellow Confederates, however, and in an echo of the Repeal Association schism of July 1846 he and his allies withdrew from the Irish Confederation in February 1848, launching a newspaper, the *United Irishman*, to promote their militant convictions. The French revolution of 1848, like its predecessor in 1789, bolstered a generally more belligerent attitude, and Mitchel felt able to return to the Confederation in March 1848. But, ironically, this, the most aggressive of the repealers, was robbed of his martial ambitions by the government, who ordered his and other arrests in May 1848. The command of the Irish rebellion was left to the more genteel William Smith O'Brien, whose forces were crushed with a contemptuous ease by the Irish Constabulary at Ballingarry, County Tipperary, in July 1848. If there was a hint of bathos in O'Connell's last political acts, then this was all the more evident with the Confederation – for Davis's carefully honed martial verse and Mitchel's furious editorials had fired nothing more glorious than 'a cabbage-garden revolution', in the sneering description of a *Times* journalist.[65]

Viewed in a wider perspective, however, this bathos is less oppressive. The Young Irelanders provided a literature, role models and a vision of history to later generations of nationalist. They were influential, not primarily as failed revolutionaries but rather as propagandists: it is a pleasing paradox that, through cogent journalism and the exploitation of the past – through perfecting an O'Connellite methodology – they simultaneously influenced later nationalists and marred the reputation of their original patron, O'Connell. The 'Library of Ireland' provided a curriculum for young nationalists throughout the mid- and late nineteenth century, and helped to keep alive the memory of Davis and the other contributors to the series. John Mitchel's bitter prose resonated long after his death, with his *Jail Journal* (1854), many times reprinted, emerging as one of the classics of modern Irish nationalism. Mitchel provided a coruscating view of O'Connell, which became an orthodoxy for young Sinn Féiners: 'Poor old Dan! Wonderful, mighty, jovial and mean old man, with silver tongue and smile of witchery and heart of melting ruth – lying tongue, smile of treachery, heart of unfathomable fraud'.[66] It was a view that complemented the Young Ireland self-image of discipline and integrity of purpose – an image that was also of course bequeathed to the Sinn Féiners; it was a view that was confirmed, albeit in a much more subtle guise, by Charles Gavan Duffy. The Young Ireland veterans of the 1848 rising, exiled on the continent, provided a vital personal link with the Fenian rebels of 1867; but Gavan Duffy's longevity and prolific output as an author ensured that the influence of Young Ireland reached not just the succeeding generation of militant nationalist, but more distant generations as well. Gavan Duffy, the founder of the *Nation*, died in 1903 having, in the last 20 or so years of his life, written sympathetic accounts of the Young Ireland movement and its personalities in his autobiography (*My Life in Two Hemispheres* (1896)), in his *Thomas Davis* (1890) and his *Young Ireland* (1880). Gavan Duffy's work ensured that, even had it not been for Davis and Mitchel, the influence of the cultural and militant nationalists of the 1840s reached the generation that won Irish independence. James Connolly, bitterly critical of O'Connell, and indeed equivocal about some Young Irelanders, wrote sympathetically of Mitchel and Lalor. Arthur Griffith pledged allegiance to the memory of Davis rather than to that of O'Connell. And it was a telling detail that on the centenary of Davis's death, in 1945, the Irish government published a celebratory volume (*Thomas Davis and Young Ireland*), where it was left to Professor Michael Tierney, the President of University College Dublin, to publish – two years after the event – a centenary volume for O'Connell.[67]

And yet the achievement of O'Connell, however much disputed, remains inescapable. The problem of interpretation which O'Connell posed for contemporaries, and for historians, is akin to that presented by Parnell: but where Parnell veiled his convictions, if any, in taciturnity, O'Connell achieved the same effect through loquacity. Both were highly skilled and subtle tacticians, with bold demands, but with numerous fall-back positions. Both spoke dogmatically, but acted pragmatically: both were suspicious of doctrinaire rigidity. The political malleability of each explains the malleability of their respective reputations, and their lasting fascination. O'Connell's fame, though damaged by the historiographical ascendancy of Young Ireland at the end of the nineteenth century and of little value to the revolutionary generation, was gradually restored once the independent state was secured: the centenary of emancipation, in 1929, and Seán Ó Faoláin's *King of the Beggars: A*

Life of Daniel O'Connell (1938) brought a revival of popular appreciation, for O'Connell, no role model for revolutionaries, had an undoubted didactic value in the new conservative Catholic state. His individualism, his constitutionalism and his trenchant faith were also recognizable virtues after the Second World War, in a landscape scarred by death and by totalitarianism; Michael Tierney was keen to emphasize O'Connell's claim to be the 'creator' of Christian Democracy, 'which is today [1949] . . . the bulwark of Europe against the pagan doctrine of state supremacy'.[68]

If this was perhaps a bold assertion, then O'Connell certainly inspired the liberal Catholic movements of his day, and his contribution to a Catholic and constitutional nationalism in Ireland is equally beyond question. He was an influence on Montalembert and on French liberal Catholics for whom he was 'the man of all Christendom': Montalembert, Lamennais and Lacordaire created, in December 1830, the General Agency for Religious Freedom (the Agence Générale pour la Défense de la Liberté Religieuse), an association of militant Catholics modelled consciously on 'the miracles of the Catholic Association'.[69] O'Connell also attracted the interest of a wide range of German intellectuals and churchmen: the Katholischer Verein Deutschlands, founded in October 1848, like earlier French organizations, drew on the inspiration provided by O'Connell and the emancipation movement.[70] Peter Alter has suggested that the great mobilization of the Irish Catholic masses, which was O'Connell's central achievement, helped to inspire the revolutions of 1848–9 in central Europe.[71] There is, however, an irony here: it is a pleasing quirk that the Young Irelanders, who were strongly influenced by continental European romantic nationalism, and who were ultimately fired by the French revolution of 1848, should have had so slight an impact on Europe; while O'Connell, who – as Desmond Williams affirmed – was at best mildly interested in matters beyond Ireland and Westminster, had a lasting European significance.[72]

O'Connell politicized the Irish people using the most accessible tools: the Catholic faith and the Catholic clergy. He sought an independent parliament for all Irish people, using the same tools to effect this end. He was generous in his perspectives, but he was also a product of the penal era, and his ardent faith and his hostility to the ascendancy promoted a suspicion of, and defensiveness towards, all Protestants – even those nominally his allies. Catholic and Protestant emancipationists, and Catholic and Protestant repealers generally (not always) spoke the language of tolerance; but they were seeking the impossible – to marry a public generosity with the private conviction that they each held a monopoly of spiritual truth. Both O'Connell and Davis were products of an era of peculiarly bitter sectarian feeling, and neither completely rose above this – even if, within this context, they were each convinced both of their own benevolence and the lurking 'bigotry' of others. As Brian Girvin has pointed out, 'O'Connell's protestations that his politics were not sectarian can be taken seriously, yet he himself was always quick to denounce Protestant concerns as sectarian and not sincerely held': much the same sentiment might be applied to Davis.[73]

If the parentage of Christian Democracy is questionable, then the parentage of Parnellism is clear. O'Connell provided a political constituency for Parnell, and a political strategy. His 'tail' in the 1830s, his alliance with the Whigs, his relationship with the Church, his gradualism – the willingness to accept 'instalments' of justice – all foreshadowed Parnell. They shared a broadly similar relationship to violence, communicating with the militants while channelling popular aggression into constitutional paths. They each successfully applied the lever of militancy to truculent British governments. Above all, O'Connell defined a goal, repeal, which Parnell inherited and mildly elaborated. They were apparently (and in respects actually were) worlds apart, the garrulous, pious Catholic lawyer and the taciturn, impious Protestant squire, but they were political clones.

3.5   The Orange Party, 1798–1853

> *Likewise yeze Presbyterians that for the truth contend*
> *Come forward now and manfully your chartered rights defend*
> *From Fenians and from Paypishes that fiercely youse assail*
> *And hope throughout Green Erin's Isle to carry a repeal*
> 'The Boys of Sandy Row' *c.*1870[74]

Daniel O'Connell was a political colossus and his influence – though interrupted in Ireland – has been both lasting and widespread. The repeal movement created a particular tradition of constitutional political involvement – what Tom Garvin has called 'a strong general understanding of the mechanisms of representative democracy combined ultimately with a disregard for, or unawareness of, the ethical principles that lie behind those mechanics'.[75] The broader repeal movement also helped to revive, through the agency of Young Ireland, the militant republican tradition within Irish nationalism. The competition between these distinct (though related) visions of Irish politics was bitter and has tended to dominate narratives of nineteenth-century Irish political history: this, in turn, has meant that what O'Connell saw as the true political opposition, what he called 'the Orange party', has been relegated to a position of negligible significance. But, while the achievements and tribulations of nineteenth-century nationalism have naturally formed the staple of Irish political historiography, the electoral success and political consolidation of this 'Orange party' were formidable and represent one of the more striking themes of modern Irish history. Only through the work of Theo Hoppen has this theme begun to receive an appropriately careful scrutiny.[76]

'Orange party' was a deliberately vague and pejorative formulation, but in essence it was a reference to Irish Toryism. O'Connell looked forward fondly to the demise of Toryism (and indeed to the demise of Protestantism), and there were clear grounds for optimism. The series of political victories which O'Connell secured in the 1820s and 1830s were also, at least ostensibly, defeats for the ascendancy interest and for its party political manifestation, Toryism. O'Connell, through the Catholic Association, liberated Catholic voters from their traditional subservience to their landlord – and, while this affected both Whig and Tory magnates, it was the Tories who were O'Connell's preferred victims. Catholic emancipation had been strenuously resisted by leading Irish Tories, although, viewed in a wider perspective, it had also divided Irish Protestants (whose interests Toryism purported to represent). The passage of the Emancipation Act was both a humiliation and a material setback for the ascendancy interest, and it was capped by the passage of the two parliamentary reform measures, British and Irish, in 1832. Ecclesiastical and municipal reforms in the 1830s represented further, if more minor, affronts. The Orange Order, which enjoyed a close though often difficult relationship with Toryism, was forced into a humiliating dissolution in 1836.

But O'Connell's predictions of the death of 'the Orange party' were misjudged. Irish Toryism matured into a successful popular Conservatism which, as late as 1859, was the largest Irish party at Westminster. O'Connell himself proved to be not so much the assassin of Irish Toryism as its tutor; indeed (however paradoxical it might at first seem), it could well be argued that the two greatest influences over the birth of modern Irish Conservatism were O'Connell and his bête noire, Robert Peel. O'Connell's indirect but profound influence over Irish Tories operated at two levels: first, like Parnell at the end of the nineteenth century, he provided a model for his opponents to copy and adapt; second, and again like Parnell, his sweeping successes forced his opponents into defensive action. O'Connell therefore provided both a stimulus and a paradigm for his Tory opponents. Peel, a no less important if more distant influence, was reviled by many Irish Tories for his 'apostasy' over emancipation. However, he provided his nominal Irish allies with both a theoretical and practical political model, for he offered an accessible Conservative philosophy through the Tamworth manifesto, and demonstrated its successful application in the British Conservative recovery of the mid- and late 1830s.

If the achievements of O'Connell in many ways anticipated the Parnellite era, then equally the successful adaptation of Irish Toryism in the 1830s and 1840s was a precursor to popular Unionism. The outstanding features of this adaptation mirrored the achievement of O'Connell: the creation of a Conservative electoral organization and the creation of a Protestant political consciousness. O'Connell's electoral triumphs in the 1826 general election and after, and the challenge of parliamentary reform in 1832, each underlined the need for organization, and to some extent O'Connell supplied a blueprint for success. The early aspects of this organization are somewhat shadowy. The Brunswick clubs, formed in 1827–8 in the wake of the first dissolution of Orangeism, fulfilled different functions in different parts of the country, but they operated broadly as a popular anti-emancipationist organization and as an adjunct to Toryism. Certainly the Cork Brunswick Constitutional Club was effectively a Tory electoral organization and originally quite distinct from the Orange Order: like later Conservatives it appealed, at least nominally, to all 'constitutionalists', regardless of religious affiliation. The spread of the clubs in 1828 was, like the New Catholic Association, based upon a parish organization; and, again like the New Catholic Association, the clubs simultaneously recorded electoral triumphs (such as the victories of Gerard and Daniel Callaghan in Cork city in the by-elections of 1830) while providing a much-needed boost to Protestant political morale.[77]

But the Brunswick clubs, though functioning broadly in the Tory interest, were not fully coequal with Toryism. The first attempt at a popular 'Conservative' organization in Ireland – the Irish Protestant Conservative Society – came in 1831, in the prelude to the Reform Acts of 1832 and the general election of December 1832. The O'Connellite influence is clear: the denominational appeal in the title of the body echoed that of the Catholic Association, and the Society organized an appeal, a 'Protestant rent', which was an unmistakeable borrowing from the emancipationists.[78] The Society oversaw the creation of a network of local registration clubs, which were often – again, an O'Connellite feature – under the control of the (Protestant) clergy. If, as Tom Garvin has suggested, O'Connell bequeathed a passion for the form, if not the ethics, of representative democracy, then this was a legacy seized as much by Conservatives as by later nationalists: the Conservative registration drives were often defined by sharp practice, and nowhere more clearly than in Belfast, where the black arts practised by the party apparatchik John Bates ensured the ascendancy of his cause.[79] A characteristic scam involved the registration of £10 householders: Bates retained numerous Belfast architects in the Conservative interest, whose task was to place a low value on Liberal-owned houses and thereby to disfranchise their occupants.

The Irish Protestant Conservative Society marked the beginning of a successful elaboration of Conservative organization. The Society was superseded in 1836 by the Irish Metropolitan Conservative Society, created in the aftermath of the Tamworth manifesto and ostensibly a more moderate and thoughtful body. The Metropolitan Society possessed formidable intellectual and technical resources, bolstered as it was by the likes of Isaac Butt, and it helped to reinvigorate Irish Toryism throughout Ireland by supplying funds and (in the case of the Metropolitan Society) a consensual Peelite philosophy: anti-Catholicism was an additional electoral tool. Working in partnership with the Conservative Registration Society, the Metropolitan continued the tradition of electoral gamesmanship laid down by the Protestant Society. In 1837 the Tories were able to launch a broad electoral campaign, running candidates (as did the Irish Unionists at the end of the century) in no-hope constituencies to bolster local morale and to irritate their opponents. The fruits of this campaign were relatively modest (34 seats were won, as compared to 30 in December 1832), but even this showing placed the Conservatives ahead of their O'Connellite rivals (who won 31 seats, as compared to 39 in 1832). Moreover, the foundations for the more sweeping success of 1841 were laid, when it seemed – momentarily – that the Conservatives had emerged as the largest Irish party, winning 43 seats (this total was later pared to the still impressive figure of 40 as a result of successful election petitions).

This organizational revival was also effective within the realm of municipal politics. Here the challenge to the Tories was much the same as at the level of parliamentary politics – a combination of, on one hand, an effective O'Connellite opposition with, on the other, rule changes in an electoral game which had hitherto suited the Tory interest. O'Connell had viewed municipal reform as a priority, for it seemed likely to hasten the demise of the 'Orange' interest. But, while the Municipal Corporations

Act (1840) was unquestionably a serious setback to Irish Toryism, costing them the control of both Dublin and Cork, it was also a spur to local organization; and, while the Tories remained in a minority on both the Dublin and Cork corporations, they were equally a growing and influential minority. Efficient organization together with the comparatively high franchise qualification helped to spare Toryism from electoral annihilation in the south and west of the island, but the same combination of assets produced even more remarkable results in areas where the party had traditionally been strong. In Belfast the first election after the passage of the Municipal Corporations Act produced a clean sweep for the Tories: every place on the 40-strong corporation was captured by a Conservative, and John Bates, the astute and ruthless manager of the new Belfast Conservative Society, was returned to the strategically crucial position of town clerk. It was, as Cornelius O'Leary has remarked, the 'apogee' of his long political career.[80]

If Bates and the Belfast Tories peaked in 1842, then the national party reached its electoral summit in the period from the late 1850s through to the mid-1860s. The ultimate origins of this success were earlier, however, dating back to the shock of the new experienced by Tories in the era of emancipation and reform. After generations of apathy Conservative organization was created, modified and re-created with a scientific precision and an evangelical enthusiasm, the most frenetic tinkering coming in the early and mid-1830s. The last major overhaul before the invention of a new party structure in the 1880s came with the Central Conservative Society (1853) – what Theo Hoppen has judged as 'perhaps the single most significant development in the history of the party's electoral and political machinery'.[81] This appears to have been in part a response to the new electoral conditions created by the Irish Franchise Act (1850), and by the momentarily burgeoning Independent Irish Party, though there were also distant echoes of the National Repeal Association in its constitution and function. The new Society instructed (where necessary) local Tories in the gamut of political intelligence, promoting – like its predecessors – creative registration work, and gathering and collating all forms of relevant information. The Society simultaneously encouraged effective and coherent Irish Tory action at Westminster, while struggling to maintain friendly links with British Conservatism (some landed ultras had sought in the 1840s to break the connection with the British party). By the late 1860s it was flagging in confidence, 'stoic resolve' (in Hoppen's description) replacing 'erstwhile optimism' – but more than any other single organization the Central Society should be credited with the electoral success won by Irish Tories in the mid-nineteenth century.[82] Moreover, the achievements of the Society had a wider resonance: as a broadly representative Tory organization, with good local and cross-channel connections, the Central Conservative Society provided a model both for English party reformers in the late 1860s as well as Ulster Unionists in the era of Home Rule.

Skilful registration work by bodies such as the Central Conservative Society depended upon, but did not in itself create, a flourishing supply of Tory voters. The broader missionary activities of the Society may have won a few to the cause, but there was clearly no mass conversion. The importance of the Society, and of its precursors, rests primarily in the mobilization and invigoration of Tory support – in the exploitation of more fundamental realignments within Irish Protestant politics and society. These shifts occurred most obviously in the wake of the campaign for emancipation, and in the prelude to the Reform Acts of 1832 – just as the successful mobilization of Unionist opinion was originally a response both to Parnellite agitation and the parliamentary reform measures of 1884–5. In the late 1820s and after, Toryism began to develop from its origins as a remote establishment creed towards a more popular and consensual formulation. To an extent this popularization built upon the reaction to O'Connell, but some voters – particularly dissenters – needed a more positive inducement before being enfolded in the Tory embrace, and this, arguably, was supplied by Peel's new inclusivist vision of the party. Two obvious aspects of this new openness may be found with the accession of both Orangemen and (more tentatively) some Presbyterians to the Tory faith.

The relationship between Toryism and Orangeism in the early nineteenth century was thoroughly ambiguous. Certain convictions were held in common – there was, for example, an anti-Catholic sympathy binding many ultra-Tories and the Orange Order. But the plebeian origins of the Order, and its reputation for aggression (it was founded in September 1795 after a sectarian affray, the Battle of the Diamond) meant that it held an uncertain appeal for the 'respectable' classes. Its credibility was bolstered in 1797–8 because of its usefulness at a time of widespread conspiracy and eventual rebellion; and as a consequence it spread both geographically and socially. The membership of the Order was around 100,000 in the 1820s, drawn from all levels of the social hierarchy: it attracted many Conservative landowners in Ireland, and even came to enjoy royal patronage (in the shape of the Dukes of York and Cumberland, brothers to George IV), but it never completely shed its original, flawed reputation. The Order was a potential asset to Tory government but it was also (because of its rowdiness) a continual threat to political stability; and while it prospered under certain administrations (especially during the reign of William Saurin as attorney general (1807–22)), there was no uniform sympathy for its actions (it was dissolved for the first time along with the Catholic Association in 1825). Peel's attitude – cautious support for the principles of the Order, combined with suspicion of its secret oath-bound existence – is probably broadly indicative of the mind of parliamentary Toryism. However, both Orangeism and Toryism were, in the 1820s, diverse institutions encompassing (within admittedly clear parameters) a range of values and convictions; and, while there was a clear sympathy between some Tories and the Order, there was no coherent alliance such as existed during the Home Rule era.

These ambiguities were beginning to be resolved in the late 1820s. The pressures created by emancipation and reform helped to consolidate gentry support for the Order, and thereby to clear the way for a more complete (though still occasionally tense) relationship between Orangeism and Toryism. Orangemen, in turn, no less threatened by the legislative challenges to Protestant ascendancy than the gentry, found refuge within the developing institutions of Conservatism, and there was widespread Orange participation in Tory electioneering in the mid-1830s. After the formal dissolution of the Order in 1836 (as the result of a highly critical parliamentary report), Orangeism maintained a half-concealed but often thriving existence, sometimes (as in Belfast) under the cover of the Protestant Operative movement. The prominent Dublin Protestant Operatives' Association, founded in March–April 1841, was characterized by a strong evangelical and apocalyptic Protestantism, and in part filled the gap created by the dissolution of formal Orangeism: the Association's driving force, the Reverend Tresham Gregg, had Orange contacts and sympathies. Some residual social tensions plagued the relationship between the Dublin Operatives' Association and local Conservatism, for, while the Operatives were clearly anxious to play a role in local Conservative electoral politics, the Conservatives were less anxious to admit plebeian representatives into their counsel. The revival of the Grand Orange Lodge of Ireland in 1845–6 brought a restoration, indeed an elaboration, of the active links with Toryism which had been so conspicuous in the early and mid-1830s. It has even been suggested that the key Central Conservative Society of Ireland (1853) was an Orange initiative.[83]

However, there had been a longstanding bond between (at least) ultra-Toryism and the Orange Order, and the consolidation of the links between the new Conservative institutions and the Order, though highly significant, was not, perhaps, very surprising. More remarkable, perhaps, was the growing relationship between a small but significant section of Irish Presbyterians and the developing Conservative movement of the 1830s. This tentative Presbyterian affiliation was remarkable on a number of grounds: first, the Church had traditionally been associated with political dissent, and second, its members had on the whole remained aloof from Orangeism. Presbyterians were therefore beginning to align themselves with what had for long been a repugnant political tradition, but they were also doing this at a time when Orangemen were becoming noisy proponents of Conservatism. The radical nature of this emerging political union underlines the extent to which a new Protestant political consciousness was being formed at this time – a new mentality incorporated within new party institutions. Catholic organization and politicization had therefore a Protestant equivalent; and equally Irish Protestantism gave birth to a political-cum-spiritual leader who shared some of the characteristics of Daniel O'Connell – Reverend Henry Cooke.

Cooke was one of the key strategists of this political realignment. Although he had been a moderate emancipationist in the mid-1820s, he was an opponent of the bill of 1829, and he viewed with alarm the rapid consolidation of the Catholic position. In particular he was disturbed by the cooperation between the Whig leadership and O'Connell, and he sought to counteract this by projecting a vision of a grand Protestant alliance, bound within a Peelite Conservatism. He was not in sympathy with the 'prelatical' forms of the Church of Ireland, but he saw the O'Connellite assault on its privileges as part of a broader assault on Irish Protestantism – and within these terms he was prepared to offer his support. At a famous united Protestant gathering at Hillsborough, County Down, in October 1834 (the form of a mass meeting and the strategic location suggest an O'Connellite inspiration), Cooke called for greater cooperation between the two main Protestant denominations: 'a sacred marriage of Christian forbearance where they differ, of Christian love where they agree, and of Christian co-operation in all matters where their common safety is concerned'.[84] He acknowledged his Conservative convictions and was careful (with a view, presumably, to disarming Presbyterian criticism) to affirm the details of his creed: 'to protect no abuse that can be proved, to resist reckless innovation, not rational reform; to sacrifice no honest interest to hungry clamour; to yield no principle to time-serving expediency; to stand by religion in opposition to every form of infidelity'.[85] Nor were these Conservative convictions passive: Cooke was deeply involved in the formation of the Belfast Conservative Society and worked alongside John Bates, whom he warmly commended ('[he] never loses an opportunity of doing his duty').[86] In addition he corresponded directly with Peel on the subject of the regium donum (March 1835) and on various Scots and Irish Presbyterian issues in the early 1840s (though not always successfully). Cooke did not create Presbyterian Conservatism, nor did he overcome the inherent distrust of the majority of Irish Presbyterians for Toryism. But as the single most influential Presbyterian cleric of the first half of the nineteenth century his endorsement of Conservatism had a vital significance, for it helped to make respectable an alien creed: he capitalized on Presbyterian fears of the Catholic revival, and he popularized the political vision embodied in the Tamworth manifesto.

Nor did Cooke create Presbyterian Unionism, yet here again his prominence as a clergyman meant that his politics had a much broader resonance than would otherwise have been the case. In any event, he was unquestionably the most conspicuous Irish Unionist of the age. Presbyterian disillusion with radical politics had evolved in the aftermath of the '98, the result both of lurid accounts of the treatment of loyalists in Wexford and of the confusion and treachery which accompanied the rising in Ulster. Cooke fired the latent anti-repeal sympathies of a broad range of Protestant opinion, both Presbyterian and Church of Ireland, emerging as the single most prominent northern opponent of O'Connell. He was a leading spirit behind the resistance to O'Connell's Belfast visit of January 1841, and was perhaps the chief political beneficiary of O'Connell's failure on this occasion. He was certainly the star performer at a great Conservative victory celebration, where he defined his Unionist sympathies in an O'Connellite formulation: he alluded to the sufferings of Irish Protestants in the past, emphasized his own impeccable lineage as a descendant of one of the defenders of Derry, and appealed in patronizing and ambivalent terms for tolerance. The most famous passage of his speech celebrated the growth of Belfast under the Union: 'Look at Belfast, and be a repealer, if you can'.[87] Of course, even without Cooke repeal would have won few converts among northern Presbyterians, for distrust both of the principle and of its promoter was already widespread. But Cooke fired and rationalized these convictions. Moreover, he expressed Presbyterian Unionism in Conservative terms: he dominated the Conservative celebration and (according to one newspaper report) was supported by over 100 Presbyterian clergymen. As in the early 1830s, only a minority of his co-religionists as yet supported this flirtation with the old Tory enemy: but it was becoming increasingly clear, given the Whig alliance with O'Connell, that Cooke's radical vision of a general Protestant alliance with the new Conservatism had merit. When he died in 1868, this vision still had not found general acceptance and the Presbyterian association with Liberalism remained vital. But, viewed through a wider lens, Cooke anticipated the Unionist architects of Protestant union in the early 1880s; and he forged a bond between Presbyterianism and Toryism and (ultimately) Ulster Unionism which retains a political significance to this day. As Ian McBride has remarked, 'Cooke fused together in his own person a particular combination of conversionist theology, social conservatism and anti-Catholicism which would eventually come to dominate popular politics in the north of Ireland'.[88]

Cooke contributed vitally to the creation of a broader Protestant political identity – but (like O'Connell with Catholicism) he was capitalizing upon several fundamental shifts of attitude within his community. Some of these are already clear: Cooke harnessed Protestant bewilderment at the rapid evolution of Irish Catholicism from political passivity and legal subjection in the late eighteenth century to political assertiveness and (at least nominal) legal equality in the 1830s. In particular Cooke expressed the general Protestant confusion with the multifaceted politics of O'Connell. Cooke's attempts to 'marry' the two main Protestant denominations had a negative, anti-O'Connellite stimulus, therefore, but these efforts were also rooted in some other centripetal tendencies within Irish Protestant politics. First, the Whig and O'Connellite critique of the Church of Ireland, though part of a broader assault on Protestant ascendancy, in fact addressed and corrected abuses within the Church and thereby ultimately removed it from political controversy: the Church emerged as a comparatively more effective and attractive institution, viewed whether by its own adherents or by Presbyterians. Second, the very tentative sympathy between Irish Presbyterians and the Church of Ireland that was publicized by Cooke in the 1830s was assisted by the consolidation of Presbyterianism itself. The fissile condition of Presbyterianism in the eighteenth century had given rise to the secessionist schism (over lay patronage in the Church), and the anti-burgher schism within the secessionist church (over the acceptance of the burgess oath enjoining loyalty to 'the true religion presently professed within this realm'). In addition there was a latitudinarian non-subscribing Presbyterian tradition as well as a reformed or covenanting church. Crucially, some of these divisions were being reconciled in the first half of the nineteenth century: the burgher/anti-burgher schism within the secessionists was resolved in 1818, and the secessionists themselves (numbering 141 congregations) were able to reunite with mainstream Presbyterianism in 1840. This union was, in turn, made possible by the campaign, urged by Cooke in the late 1820s, for a more rigorous and orthodox theology, and in particular for an Athanasian as opposed to an Arian view of the Trinity. The removal, in 1829, of latitudinarian and Arian elements within the Church cleared the way for a more precise definition of Presbyterian belief as well as a definition more comprehensible to Anglicans. As Finlay Holmes has cautiously remarked, Irish Presbyterianism emerged in 1840 and after as a more conservative institution, both in terms of its theology and its churchmanship.[89] And, while the majority of Presbyterians remained wedded to their suspicions of Anglicanism and to a Whiggish liberalism, it is clear that the origins of the socially cohesive and conservative Protestant alliance of the 1880s were being formulated in the era of Cooke and O'Connell. The unification of Presbyterianism was thus an essential precursor to the unification of Protestant identity – and to the creation of those political institutions which rested upon a unitary Protestant identity.

Another important source of cohesion within early nineteenth-century Protestantism rests with evangelicalism: this shared interpretation of Christian spirituality (with its emphasis on the cross, on personal conversion, on the authority of scripture and on mission work) helped, arguably, to overcome traditional denominational boundaries within Irish Protestantism. It is important not to exaggerate this point, however. Evangelical Protestant religion arrived in Ireland in the mid-eighteenth century, an import from England and from the Hapsburg empire: the French revolution underpinned a popular evangelical passion, for it heightened political uncertainties and brought the apparent threat of godlessness. Evangelicalism had the capacity to create religious disorder, not simply between spiritually renewed and confident Protestants and their Catholic counterparts, but also within and between Protestant denominations. Evangelical zeal within the Church of Ireland in the early nineteenth century occasionally threatened to create division between the hierarchy and evangelical activists; the divisions within Presbyterianism in the 1820s were at one level a conflict about the supremacy of an evangelical wing over traditional 'broad church' intellectuals such as Henry Montgomery. The evangelical vanguard, the Methodists, originally a movement within the established Church, split in 1816 into, on the one hand, 'a church offering full ecclesiastical rites to its people', and, on the other hand, 'a religious society within the Church of Ireland'.[90] In addition to these internal divisions, there was a certain amount of competition between different forms of evangelical Protestant, and between evangelicals of one persuasion (such as the Methodists) and the non-evangelical clergy of another (the Church of Ireland).

How, then, given this evidence, did evangelicalism serve as a spiritual and political cement for Irish Protestantism? Despite its divisive potential, evangelicalism served in the long term to reduce the labyrinthine eschatological and liturgical divisions within Irish Protestantism to a simple, individualistic creed that stressed the primacy of personal salvation. Protestant denominations, hitherto divided by politics or by theology, could increasingly share the same spiritual language and experience (this was most obvious at the time of the 1859 revival). The efficacy of this evangelical bond was most clearly apparent at times of external threat, as in the 1820s and 1830s, in the context of a resurgent and assertive Catholicism. Evangelicalism bolstered Protestant confidence at a time of crisis, imbuing a sense of spiritual superiority – a confidence in the inevitability of salvation, as well as a sense of purpose and of mission.

But the broader importance of evangelicalism should not be missed. Its political benefits were, for example, quite clear: a shared spirituality helped to underpin evangelical overtures to the Anglican Tory establishment, while a robust evangelicalism shunted the Conservative party towards a more thoroughly Protestant, indeed anti-Catholic, posture (though there were variations in emphasis between the years of government and of opposition). The shared experience of conversion or, more broadly, of revival helped to create a cohesive Protestant spiritual and political identity in the mid- and late nineteenth century. The influence of prominent evangelical and Tory landlords in south Ulster (the Annesleys, Crichtons and Farnhams) served to bolster the connection between Conservatism and evangelical spirituality: and the potent brew of a paternalistic and inclusivist Protestant Toryism which they distilled was widely exported and dangerously addictive. Irish Unionism was ultimately influenced, both in its political theology and its language, by its evangelical creators (men such as Edward Saunderson); to some extent Irish Unionism depended for its electoral survival on an evangelical Protestant consensus. The great paradox of Irish evangelicalism is therefore that it simultaneously encouraged an individualistic pietism as well as a communitarian form of politics.

The history of Ireland in the first half of the nineteenth century is therefore not simply the 'story' of emancipation and repeal, of the formation of the varieties of Irish nationalism. As always shifts in the perspective highlight obtrusive, but often overlooked, features of the historical landscape. From the vantage point of the third quarter of the century one of the most remarkable of the many Irish political edifices was Conservatism, which housed a minority constituency, certainly, but with effectiveness and (often) with flamboyance. A political ruin by the second quarter of the twentieth century, submerged partly under the gothic complexities of Ulster Unionism, Irish Toryism had in fact been threatened with destruction 100 years before, in the era of emancipation and reform. But it survived splendidly, and ultimately provided foundations for several new political constructs (the early Home Rule movement, the varieties of Unionism). The importance of Toryism in the history of Irish political artifice should be beyond question.

The Ascendancy of the Land Question, 1845–91

4.1 Guilty Men and the Great Famine

It was equally impossible to do the plainest right and undo the plainest wrong without the express authority of the Circumlocution Office. If another Gun-powder plot had been discovered half an hour before the lighting of the match nobody would have been justified in saving the parliament until there had been half a score of boards, half a bushel of minutes, several sacks of official memoranda, and a family-vault full of ungrammatical correspondence on the part of the Circumlocution Office.

Charles Dickens, *Little Dorrit*[1]

An Gorta Mór, the Great Famine (1845–51), weighs heavily on the contemporary conscience.[2] Originating in an ecological disaster, the Famine brought starvation and disease which claimed one million lives and stimulated a mass emigration which, in the ten years after 1845, totalled one and a half millions. The death toll, taken as a proportion of the Irish population, gives the Great Famine the grim distinction of being perhaps the most costly natural disaster of modern times. Out of this apocalypse springs much political and intellectual controversy. The horrendous loss of life helps to invest discussion of the Famine with a passion which, even by the standards of Irish political and historical debate, is unusual. Conflicting interpretations of the Famine have fuelled the 'revisionist' debate within modern Irish historical scholarship, and have caused some soul-searching within the history profession: the 150th anniversary of the disaster renewed political rancour and stimulated calls for an official British apology (an expression of regret was in fact proffered by Tony Blair, newly elected as Prime Minister, in May 1997); the anniversary created an opportunity to remember just how completely the public memory of the Famine had been suppressed in Ireland. The Famine victims have become pawns in political and academic debates which, at root, have little to do with the Ireland of the mid-1840s. In truth, the Great Famine remains a source of pain and guilt and confusion and anger for the contemporary Irish, just as other natural or human-made disasters have created similar responses elsewhere in Europe. The Famine dead pose questions which Irish liberalism and conservative nationalism are as yet unable to answer. The Famine dead bequeath a guilt which both the British and the Irish have difficulty in facing.

At the root of this tragedy, and the ensuing political controversies, was a virulent fungus, *phythopthora infestans*, which was noted in the United States in 1843 and which began to attack the Irish potato crop in the late summer of 1845. Irish dependence on the potato had been growing since the early eighteenth century, and by the mid-1840s it constituted the staple foodstuff of the labouring poor: any prolonged interruption of the supply, therefore, threatened the welfare of the cottiers who formed the bulk of Ireland's population of 8.2 million (in 1845). But in 1845 this threat did not seem to be immediate, for the fungus had attacked late in the growing season and over one half of the potato crop was saved. There was still distress, but comparatively few casualties: the as yet limited nature of the crop failure combined with the prompt and effective measures of the Peel government to stave off high levels of excess mortality. The controversy over the extent of the problem was resolved in 1846, when there was a virtually complete failure of the potato crop, and the poor were reduced to eating the seed potatoes – where they were available – which were vital for the following season. The result of this desperation and collapse in morale was a sharp fall in the acreage of potatoes planted (there may well have been a reduction from around two million acres in 1845 to under 300,000 acres in 1847): and thus, while there was a limited recovery in the crop of 1847, the harvest was small, and the level of distress very great. Moreover, despite the (admittedly tenuous) grounds for hope in 1847, the harvest of 1848, like that of 1846, was a near-complete failure, and mortality levels soared. Thereafter there was a slight improvement in the yield, but this was completely overshadowed by the devastating impact of the failure of 1846–8: disease was rife, and the number of famine-related deaths remained high until 1850–1. The completeness of the failure in two years, 1846 and 1848, combined with the false hopes of 1845 and 1847 to break both the health and the will of the Irish poor.

Beyond this narrative, however, lies a series of interpretative problems or controversies. Even the level of mortality during the Famine years has been a matter of some dispute, since a great deal of politically nuanced argument rests upon rival calculations of the death toll. Modern econometric analysis favours the traditional estimate of one million deaths, as opposed to lower figures in some 'revisionist' accounts, or exaggerated totals in some polemical literature: some texts have placed the total number of Famine dead (both the victims of starvation as well as of hunger-related disease) as low as 500,000 to 800,000, while James Connolly (for example) claimed in 1910 that 'at the lowest computation 1,225,000 persons died of absolute hunger; all of these were sacrificed upon the altar of capitalist thought'.[3]

The mortality figures are generally related to the performance of the government relief measures, and this issue – essentially the issue of culpability – has attracted considerable notice in the recent historiography of the Famine.

As with the narrative of crop failure, so it is much easier to describe government attitudes and activity in the years of the Famine than to assess their effectiveness. On 1 November 1845 the Prime Minister, Robert Peel (who had considerable experience of Ireland, having served as Chief Secretary) proposed the creation of a special relief commission: this in turn was charged with the management of a supply of £100,000 worth of maize and meal, which the government had ordered from the United States. This grain arrived in Ireland only at the end of January 1846, and had therefore little impact upon the distress arising from the partial crop failure of 1845: the comparatively few famine-related deaths in 1845 had more to do with the limited capacity of the agrarian economy to surmount a temporary and partial dearth than with the efficacy of the government's measures. The purpose of these grain purchases was to permit the government some influence over the food market – the intention 'was not to replace private traders but rather to control them': the sales of this grain, which began in March 1846, were designed to counter rising prices and were closed to commercial speculators.[4]

The second element of the Peelite strategy involved the encouragement of local relief committees (staffed by junior officials, poor law guardians and the clergy), which were designed to augment the official commissariat. These committees were enjoined to seek subscriptions, and they received official support in proportion to the amount that they raised from private sources: the government subvention occasionally matched the private funding, but was often limited to two-thirds of the locally raised sum. In addition these committees were charged with the distribution of food, ostensibly within strict guidelines but in practice (fortunately) more liberally than the official dictates permitted. Food was sold at cost price, or where appropriate (and against the official ruling) it was given freely. A type of outdoor relief was thus in existence long before the Poor Law Extension Act (1847), which formally sanctioned the first aid outside the workhouse.

The third and more traditional remedy applied by Peel to ameliorate conditions in Ireland was the provision of work. The work schemes, initiated by three measures early in 1846, were intended to complement the food distribution system that was being inaugurated simultaneously. The government was (at least in theory) endeavouring to augment the food supply while providing a source of earnings for labourers, but in practice its acute concern for the freedom of the market created problems: wages, for example, on the public schemes had to be less than those prevailing in the locality so that (again in theory) workers would not be drained from other forms of employment. The limited nature of the cash economy in many parts of Ireland combined with delays in the movement of currency and with the limitations of the official commissariat meant that some labourers were forced to buy on credit and at high prices from private food dealers.

However, dysfunctions such as these (which would become prevalent) were still comparatively rare by mid-1846, when Peel's administration fell. On the whole Peel's initiatives coped well with the still embryonic disaster. Peel had of course discovered free trade principles (he used the Irish crisis as a political tool to repeal the Corn Laws), but he was a highly pragmatic economic liberal: as T.P. O'Neill remarked, 'he showed an initiative unusual in that era of laissez faire and undertook tasks at variance with current economic theory'.[5] He mitigated the dogmatism of his Treasury officials while simultaneously defeating what Dickens called 'the great study and object of all public departments' – inertia or, in Dickensian terms, 'how not to do it'.[6]

The normal functioning of the market had been an abiding concern, but Peel was clearly prepared to intervene in order to ensure that the market worked in the interests of the public good. His fall from power in June 1846 opened the way to a much more doctrinaire administration, and to a number of disastrous modifications in the administration of relief. The government of Lord John Russell was highly susceptible to the *laissez-faire* dogma of Treasury officials, especially the arrogant and priggish Assistant Secretary, Charles Trevelyan: indeed, it is hard to escape the impression that Russell and his Chancellor of the Exchequer, Charles Wood, were – at least in the matter of Irish relief – mere ciphers for their civil service underlings. This new dogmatism found expression in a number of forms. Peel's importation of Indian corn (which had been inaugurated against Treasury advice) was not continued, for – as Trevelyan opined – 'the supply of the home market may safely be left to the foresight of private merchants': in fact it was not until mid-1847 that the impact of imports on food prices began to be felt.[7] The food depots that had been established under the Peel regime were controlled in a manner which betrayed a greater sensitivity for the rights of traders and the equilibrium of the market than for the starving poor: meal which had been sold at cost in early 1846 was sold at, or above, the average market price. Peel's relief commission was wound up and its functions transferred to central government.

Centralization was in fact a hallmark of the new dispensation. The Board of Works was reorganized, and the schemes of public employment relaunched under a closer management and with an at times brutal rigour. While central government took a controlling influence in the reconstitution of the public works, its desire for tight control did not stretch to payment. Where the Peelite schemes had been financed either by central government or through loans, the revised public works were to be funded exclusively by 'persons possessed of property in the distressed districts': half of the cost was to be borne directly by local taxpayers, while the other half was borne indirectly (in the form of government loans).[8] Moreover, though it seems that Peel intended to stimulate works of a high 'reproductive' value (that is, socially and economically profitable works), it is clear that the Whig government was much more agitated by the dangers of individual profiteering than by the desire to maximize the benefits arising from the investment (this pathological caution and negativism were more general characteristics of the administration): local cesspayers were therefore expected to pay for work which brought them little benefit.

Aside from the burden of ideology, the Whigs were also hampered by the extent of the crisis that they confronted. Peel's public works had recruited at most some

[COUNTRY EDITION.]   THE FAMINE IN IRELAND.—FUNERAL AT SKIBBEREEN.—FROM A SKETCH BY MR. H. SMITH, CORK.—(SEE NEXT PAGE.)

Plate 3   A funeral at Skibbereen of a famine victim, January 1847.
Source: Mary Evans Picture Library.

100,000 labourers, where the Whig scheme was employing around 750,000 by the spring of 1847: the government had in fact surpassed the farmers as the biggest source of employment. The task of mobilizing perhaps 10 per cent of the Irish population was enormous, and T.P. O'Neill is surely right to distinguish the practical achievement of the local Board of Works from the strategic ineptitude of Whitehall; Christine Kinealy also distinguishes the energy of Irish administrators from the detached, even cynical, ideologues in London.[9] However, this scale compounded the weaknesses of central policy. Wage payments were often delayed, sometimes for five weeks or more. The labourers could not therefore acquire food, except by taking on extortionate loans, and in any case they were often so weak through fatigue and malnourishment that they could not work. Labour was paid at a piece rate, and the wage was assessed so that a worker might earn between 10d(4p) and 1s 6d(7.5p) a day, depending on his exertions: this, while an unexceptional stimulus in normal commercial conditions, was of course an appalling requirement in a time of distress for it penalized precisely those who were most in need of a wage. In addition, given the context of high food prices, these miserly wages offered little hope except to the desperate.

Nor were the works completed of widespread value. Although the government eventually relented and permitted more reproductive employment, this decision was delayed and was so swathed in bureaucratic technicality that it had little effect. Most of the £4.8 million outlay on public works went on roads and quays, which were often left incomplete when the works scheme was axed in May 1847. A proposal to reactivate the schemes in 1848 with a view to relieving distress and finishing the abandoned projects was quashed by an imperious Trevelyan. These bloody and costly monuments have been seen as a material embodiment of the flaws of Whig dogmatism – (in Roy Foster's eloquent phrase) 'the celebrated (and often mythical) piers where no boats could land, walls around nothing, roads to nowhere, are poignant metaphors for a policy that was neither consistent nor effective, but which expressed economic beliefs held by the governing classes in both countries'.[10]

The public works had been the chief prop of the government's relief policy through the grim winter of 1846–7, and they had failed. The scheme had been (if nothing else) a bureaucratic wonder, and might well have proved effective if there had been a cheap supply of food to complement the wage payments. But the works were in fact an administrative Tower of Babel: a magnificent edifice, founded and sustained on dubious principles, and the source, ultimately, of much human misery. The extent of the failure was recognized in February 1847 through the Destitute Poor (Ireland) Act and a U-turn in policy: the Act brought a shift away from efforts to provide the poor with work and money towards a much more direct approach – the provision of free food. Using the existing network of local relief committees, the government established a battery of soup kitchens, which were maintained by contributions from the rates, from private charity and from central funds. Not all were eligible for relief under the provisions of the new Act, but in practice the coverage was wide: in addition one of the problems encountered in the operation of the public works – sustaining the able-bodied in the context of high food prices – was addressed by making food available at cost price. The soup kitchen scheme has been judged a success, and again, in purely administrative terms, it is difficult to question this judgement: by the middle of August 1847 over 3 million people were being fed through the kitchens, a remarkable achievement by any standards, and especially by those of the early Victorian period.[11]

But, as with the public works, the administrative spectacle should not divert attention from a number of serious problems. First, once the kitchens were in operation they did good work, but there was a fatal delay between the abandonment of the old relief scheme and the inauguration of the new scheme: this was bridged, albeit imperfectly, by the work of private agencies such as the Quakers and the British Relief Association. Second, the soup kitchens provided the cheapest form of gruel which, in all probability, had only a slight nutritional value. It is difficult to gauge the precise impact of the kitchens on the mortality rate since they were in operation only during the summer of 1847, and it has been suggested that the fall in mortality at this time was merely 'a seasonal phenomenon'.[12] Third, the organization of the kitchens, though impressive, still meant that the hungry poor often had to trek long distances to be fed. And fourth, there is some suggestion that the queues for food, though probably inevitable, brought both further degradation and demoralization to the poor, as well as – more seriously – the increased risk of succumbing to infectious disease. The soup kitchens prevented starvation, but they may well have heightened the threat of typhus.

Even with these manifold problems, the soup kitchens were probably the most effective of the relief measures inaugurated by government. They were, however,

BOY AND GIRL AT CAHERA.

Plate 4   Cahera 1847.
Source: Hulton Getty.

designed merely as a temporary expedient, to buy time for a more permanent relief initiative. For this reason the scheme, though hampered by red tape, ran counter to a number of Whig shibboleths: the provision of food at cost price, for example, overthrew the Whig commitment to market forces and represented a turnaround from the earlier administration of the food depots. The more considered Whig response to the Great Famine came with the Poor Law Amendment (Ireland) Act of June 1847. This amounted to a modification of the existing poor law to cope with the demands of a near-permanent crisis, and it was launched against deceptively auspicious circumstances (falling food prices, an anticipated rise in the demand for labour). A separate Irish poor law commission was created, and the number of Irish poor law unions increased to ensure a more effective supervision of relief. The most controversial aspect of this initiative, however, came with the funding arrangements, for the full cost of relief in any union was to be borne by its ratepayers. In practice this outrageously parsimonious decision was inoperative, and the government had to support numerous unions from 1847 through to 1849: private charity, transmitted through the British Relief Association, also helped to support impoverished areas. In May 1849 a measure was passed to permit the Poor Law Commission to transfer levies from the more prosperous east of the country to the devastated areas of the south and west; and in 1850 the Treasury advanced a loan of £300,000 to bail out the indebted unions. But, while these measures were welcome, they encapsulated the grudging and wrong-headed approach of the Whig government to relief: the Treasury, ever concerned with cost and with market freedom, held firm to its disastrous principles until the evidence of appalling mortality forced those actions which should have been taken in the first place.

Perhaps the most important and potentially beneficial aspect of the Poor Law Amendment Act was the institution of widespread outdoor relief. The categories of people eligible for this aid were tightly defined, but could be relaxed under certain conditions; and, indeed, during the winter of 1847–8 the Poor Law Commission extended the operation of outdoor relief in 70 out of the 130 unions. However, an amendment to the measure – the infamous 'Gregory clause' – excluded from relief those who held more than one-quarter of an acre of land. Moreover, the structures and provisions of the Act, though apparently adequate, once again foundered on the rock of official parsimony. Because the local ratepayers were in the first instance responsible for the cost of relief, their representatives on the local poor law committees were often afraid to incur large-scale expenditure. The financial state of many unions remained parlous until at least 1849. The rations issued to those on outdoor relief, or those sheltering within the workhouses, were therefore often minimal, and in addition many were denied relief on the slightest pretext. The workhouses were not built to cope with a natural disaster, and though many were extended through the erection of temporary accommodation, this building was done speedily and poorly, and conditions remained dreadful. Overcrowding was rife, and the opportunities for the spread of disease were appallingly great. Many more were given outdoor relief than were contained within the workhouses, though this balance shifted slightly as more workhouse accommodation was provided. The numbers involved indicate the extent to which the population had been impoverished: in 1849 some 930,000 people were housed at one time or another in the workhouse (this was the peak figure), while around 1.21 million were given outdoor relief (outdoor relief had peaked in 1848 with 1.43 million beneficiaries). The overriding impression is of a stupendous administrative performance which might easily, with a more liberal expenditure, have been converted into a stupendous humanitarian achievement.

Complementing these gargantuan, if plodding, official efforts were individual philanthropists and private relief agencies. No clear picture of landlord effort during the Famine has emerged, although the evidence suggests that, as minor casualties in the holocaust, they were not always in a position to supply aid. Irish landlords were longstanding hate-figures for zealous Whigs and utilitarians, and the Poor Law Amendment Act, in forcing the burden of Irish poverty into the uncertain grasp of Irish property, was merely the legislative expression of deep-seated anger and impatience (one thinks of Drummond's famous remarks about the responsibilities of Irish property). Indeed, the parentage of Whig policy is not hard to trace, for it rests unquestionably with the utilitarian initiatives of the 1830s: the creation of the Irish poor law system along English utilitarian lines, the thrusting of responsibility onto Irish landlords over the tithe question, the disruption of the old patronage networks of the gentry – all clearly prefigured the expedients adopted, and the prejudices exposed, during the Famine. Denuded of rental income and threatened with the burden of relief, few landlords could be great philanthropists, and indeed many, following the logic of the Whig relief measures, or stimulated by economic desperation, initiated large-scale evictions from their estates. The burden of debt among the landed classes grew to the extent that the government saw the need for the Encumbered Estates Act (1849), which was designed to facilitate the sale of the many estates 'encumbered' with debt – designed, in the words of George Boyce, 'to encourage free trade in land'.[13] It was also hoped that the measure would attract capital from outside Ireland (again the Whigs placed great faith in the smooth operations of the market place); but in fact Irish property proved to be an unappetizing prospect for any other than Irish investors, and the influx of new funds never materialized. Between 1849 and 1857 there were 3,000 sales under the terms of the Act and of the £20 million paid out only £3 million came from outside Ireland: only one in every 24 of the new purchasers came from Britain. The overall effect of the Act was therefore to divert investment capital away from other Irish enterprise and into the land, where – for proprietors – speedy and secure returns were not to be had.

If Irish property as a whole was not sufficiently prosperous to bear the burden of relief which the government was anxious to impose, then individual landlords offered good-hearted but minor acts of philanthropy. This was true of other classes. The clergy of all denominations were active in relief work, though some priests of the Church of Ireland were guilty of the sin of 'souperism' – of proselytizing among the hungry poor.[14] All the churches, however, paid a heavy toll for their relief efforts, with mortality rates among the Catholic clergy doubling during 1847 (in the same year 40 Protestant ministers died from typhus or relapsing fever). But the religious denomination which was most conspicuously associated with famine relief was also one of the smallest – the Society of Friends, or Quakers. In November 1846 a group of Dublin Quakers formed a Central Relief Committee to coordinate efforts in Ireland and to communicate with interested Quakers in England. As Mary Daly has pointed out, the strength of the Quaker contribution rested in a combination of disinterested compassion (the Society was unconcerned with evangelism) and disproportionate wealth and business skill (the denomination, though small, included leading business families such as the Pims and Bewleys).[15] The scale of Quaker relief was, by private standards, enormous – around £200,000 – but of course it could only be a small fraction of government expenditure (around £10.5 million) and it was therefore only a partial solution to the widespread misery in the Ireland of the late 1840s. Moreover, Irish Quakers tended to be more constrained than their English counterparts. Like the government, they were initially reluctant to distribute free food and equally unwilling to undermine private commercial effort: though compassionate, they believed in the doctrines of political economy almost as fervently as the officials of the Treasury. In this sense their business acumen cut two ways. Still, the overall importance of the Quaker contribution was not seriously impaired by these ideological qualms, or by the necessarily modest scale of relief, because the timing of their effort offset these limitations: in particular their soup kitchens, which were operating in the spring and summer of 1847, helped to alleviate distress in a hiatus between official relief enterprises. Well-timed private charity could have a disproportionate impact, but as the hard-pressed and exhausted Quaker philanthropists readily acknowledged, it was government alone which in the long term could 'carry out the measures necessary in many districts to save the lives of the people'.[16] A massive and prolonged crisis such as the Great Famine ultimately sapped the energy of private relief agencies and numbed the compassion of private donors. Only government had (in theory) the financial and human capacity necessary to tackle famine relief: it was therefore a tragedy for the starving millions that the Great Famine should have coincided both with a financial trough in Britain and with the ideological ascendancy of utilitarianism.

Accounts of relief strategy dominate the literature on the Famine, and they are related to the issue of accountability. One million died in the Famine years, and both the Irish public and (to a lesser extent) Irish historians, in coming to terms with the disaster, have mulled over the ways in which it might have been avoided: a concomitant of this task has been the apportioning of blame. One distinguished commentator, Cormac Ó Gráda, has suggested that there has been a tendency in modern Irish historiography to 'normalize' the Great Famine and to evade the issue of culpability; and he has seen this apparent timidity as part of the academic reaction to the violence in Northern Ireland.[17] Some (though not all) recent historians of the Famine have returned in tone and judgement, if not in methodology, to older narratives, illustrating the pain and brutality of the period as well as emphasizing the great burden of responsibility borne by dogmatic government ministers and civil servants. On the whole recent work, mainly that of the 'new' economic historians, has convicted the government of heartlessness and miserliness and a near contempt for Irish lives: Trevelyan is restored as the flawed protagonist of a bloody gothic tragedy ('Trevelyan perhaps more than any other individual represented a system of response which increasingly was a mixture of minimal relief, punitive qualifying criteria, and social reform').[18] A now famous illustration of the cheapness of Irish misery was made in 1983 by Joel Mokyr, who pointedly compared British expenditure on the Famine (£10.5 million) with the outlay 'on an utterly futile adventure in the Crimea' (£69.3 million).[19]

Only time and further detailed scholarship will tell whether these judgements stand, or whether they merely represent a temporary swing of the historiographical

pendulum away from an apparent 'revisionist' orthodoxy. Some preliminary sum-
mation might, however, be ventured at this stage. Criticisms of British government
policy date back to the Famine, and a tradition of impassioned denunciation began
with the young radicals of the *United Irishman* newspaper: John Mitchel remarked
famously that 'the Almighty indeed sent the potato blight, but the English created
the Famine' by permitting food exports from Ireland while people starved. Mitchel's
disciple, Thomas Devin Reilly, elaborated upon this view by describing the government's relief efforts as being an ill-concealed attempt at mass murder: for Reilly the
poor law system was designed so that the Irish population 'which once numbered
nine millions may be checked in its growth and coolly, gradually murdered'.[20]
Unfavourable comparisons between the expenditure on famine relief and on warfare are much older than the work of Mokyr, dating back (again) to the Famine
era and contemporary criticism. This form of analysis was of immense importance,
partly because of the general influence of the Young Ireland historical perspective
throughout the late nineteenth and early twentieth centuries. But it was also the
case that such a critique chimed with popular anger, incomprehension and suspicion in the wake of an unprecedented natural disaster; and, furthermore, it was
readily comprehensible to people who had become attuned in the O'Connell years
to bitter denunciations of Saxon oppression. Accusations of genocide made sense
to many Irish people on the basis of their own painful experiences; but do they
make sense in the light of government attitudes and actions?

The government was undoubtedly characterized by a cussed faith in a self-
regulating market and by an exaggerated view of the economic strength of the
Irish landed class: no other interpretation can adequately explain the emphasis on
public works in 1846–7 at the expense of cheap food, or the burden imposed on
Irish property by the Poor Law Amendment Act (1847). Influential civil servants
such as Trevelyan had an at times brutally legalistic conception both of religion and
of the economy: Trevelyan's reluctance to tamper with what he saw as the fixed laws
of the market place was as firm as his faith in a vengeful God. Equally his confidence
in his own judgement was as secure as his condescension towards the 'Celtic peoples'
(an ironic prejudice, given the Cornish origins of his own family).[21] The Whig
government (in contrast to Peel) tended to react to events, and even then to react
very tentatively: even though the total sum spent on relief by the Whigs was large and
might have been yet larger, it could unquestionably have been employed in more timely
and productive ways. The painfully slow manner in which relief schemes were inaugurated in 1846–7 reflected the government's abiding fear of perverting market forces
and undermining the economy (sustaining the natural laws of the market seems at
times to have been much more of a priority than preventing deaths): this tardiness
cost lives, in particular because the great killers of the Famine – typhus, relapsing
fever – were able to take root at this time and to spread. In addition, Christine Kinealy
and others have argued that some in the government came eventually to see the
Famine as a crude mechanism for social reform ('these included population control and the consolidation of property through a variety of means'), and to tailor
relief strategies accordingly: 'this was a pervasive and powerful "hidden agenda"'.[22]

In all this there was arrogance and officiousness and (at the very least) the appearance of coldness; but there is no evidence of a genocidal impulse or a murderous conspiracy. Even the most unsympathetic officials worked exhaustively to set up the painfully elaborate official relief schemes, and they achieved bureaucratic – but not humanitarian – marvels. More money might well have been spent on relief, and this in fact was the plea of many contemporaries (Ó Gráda has suggested that a great protest meeting of Irish peers, MPs and landlords held at the Rotunda, Dublin, in January 1847 'was unique in Irish history'): it is clear that many compassionate observers deemed the various initiatives to be inadequate; it is clear, too, that condemnation of the British effort was not confined to later, and politically embittered, critics.[23] On the other hand, comparisons between the cost of the relief schemes and expenditure on the Crimean War, though superficially shocking, are less impressive on reflection. Such comparisons demonstrate merely that many nineteenth-century European governments spent more on military endeavour than directly on social welfare, and to expect otherwise is to apply humane but anachronistic values: as Ó Gráda has remarked, 'even today the welfare of the underclass and the famine-prone often plays second-fiddle to military adventures'.[24] Moreover, as has been noted, the Famine coincided with a profound economic downturn in Britain and a broader European food shortage, so that there were apparently some grounds for cautious expenditure. The historiographical emphasis has traditionally (and naturally) been on the immense level of mortality and on the missed opportunities ('if', Kinealy has argued, 'the measure of success is judged by the crudest yet most telling of all measures – that of mortality – the British government failed a large portion of the population'); but, as the eminent Irish physician William Stokes remarked, 'if many were lost, perhaps ignorantly, let us think on the number saved. We cannot be suddenly wise'.[25]

The Famine has bequeathed a variety of painful legacies. It creates awkwardness for both Unionists and nationalists: there is no clear reason to suppose that an Irish repeal administration would have performed any better than the British, and there is some reason for imagining that, bereft of resources, it would have performed a good deal worse. It is true that in the subsistence crisis of 1782–4, which struck after the winning of legislative independence, an embargo had been placed on food exports: but the initiative here was taken by the British-appointed lord lieutenant, and came in defiance of some Irish commercial protests. In addition the O'Connellite tradition was heavily tinctured with the utilitarian convictions that were at the cancerous root of British policy: the great O'Connell pursued his life-long antagonism towards Peel and Toryism to the point of supporting the Whig dogmatists whose relief policies proved so tentative (few of the repeal MPs, for example, opposed the Gregory clause). But equally, however, the Famine demonstrates the narrow constraints of Unionism: the Whig conviction was that Irish property should pay for the cost of relief, whether immediately (in the form of rate payments) or in the mid-term (through the repayment of loans advanced by the Treasury). There was some effort to direct funds from wealthy areas of Ireland to impoverished areas, but no attempt was made to raise funds through a levy in Britain. And, although the Treasury loans were written off in 1853, this was only as part of a deal whereby income tax was extended to Ireland (so that, in effect, the loans were repaid by a different medium).

But the Famine created a much wider pain. As after any great tragedy, the burden of self-imposed guilt carried by the survivors was heavy. The Famine revealed some of the most prosaically heartless aspects of Victorian government; but equally it exposed some of the grimmer aspects of Irish social relations in the nineteenth century. In the struggle for survival or for marginal advantage, there was much ruthlessness. Landlords and farmers evicted impoverished cottiers; private traders insisted on the free export of grain in the Famine years, and were angered by the official importation and distribution of food; gombeenmen exploited the inadequacy of the official relief system by lending money at exorbitant rates, or by supplying food at an immense profit. The wealthier parts of Ireland showed great reluctance when called upon, in 1849–50, to aid the more impoverished areas of the country. At a more local and intimate level, the burden of hunger and disease reduced many of the poor to actions which they would otherwise have thought shameful. Little wonder, then, that the decimated and broken Irish looked to find guilty men in the corridors of Whitehall.

4.2   Pivot or Accelerator?

No less politically charged than the question of culpability is the debate over the impact of the Great Famine: indeed, no issue illustrates more clearly the sensitivities that still enshroud the historiography of the Famine years. For the 'debate', as with so many other aspects of the 'revisionist' controversy, is not so much about absolute difference as about questions of emphasis and political nuance. Thus, few would claim that the Great Famine had any other than a profound impact upon Irish politics or Irish society; but perceptible differences open up in deciding precisely how profound this impact might have been. Though the metaphors vary slightly, the debate is now (and indeed has for long been) about whether the Famine was, on the one hand, a 'watershed' or 'a turning point', or, on the other hand, 'a catalyst' or 'an accelerator'. Traditional historiography has on the whole favoured the stronger metaphors, while much recent scholarship prefers to place an emphasis on continuity. Some irritation has been expressed, however, at a perceived 'trend to de-sensationalise the Famine' and at 'the tendency to remove the Famine from the centre stage of nineteenth century history', and (as with the issue of accountability) there is some evidence of a mild reversion to older perspectives.[26]

Whatever the emphasis, it is clear that the Famine touched almost every aspect of Irish life in the mid- and late nineteenth century. The death of one million people in a population of (at its peak) around 8.25 million, combined with the migration of 1.5 million in only ten years (1845–55), could not fail to have devastating and lasting consequences. Ireland was altered beyond recognition after the Famine, and this is surely of greater importance than counter-factual, and necessarily speculative, argument about the role of the Famine in generating or accelerating change. The chief casualties of the Famine were the cottiers, who lived at a subsistence level and who were therefore particularly susceptible to starvation and disease: cottiers were also those most given to migration, now, as Oliver MacDonagh has argued, a reflection of profound despair (though the socially 'superior' nature of the emigrants after 1849 has also been noted).[27] The near-disappearance of the cottiers or labourers was linked to the consolidation of holdings in the Famine years and after, for the death, migration or eviction of the poor created opportunities for substantial farmers and landlords: one-quarter of all farms disappeared between 1845 and 1851, while the average size of farms increased in the same period (thereafter a sort of stasis was reached). The disappearance of the poor, combined with the economic vulnerability of the gentry, meant that the Ireland of the post-Famine years was a country of middling farmers: 'Irish society', Mary Daly has observed, 'tended to be dominated by the values, mores and lifestyle of the farmer'.[28]

If the condition of the agriculturalist changed, then so did the nature of agriculture itself. During and after the Famine there was a considerable shift away from tillage, which had been a mainstay of Irish agriculture since the late eighteenth century, towards animal husbandry and pastoral products. The origins of this change have been debated and were at one time located in the aftermath of the French wars, but Ó Gráda's investigation of agricultural output on the eve of the Famine reveals a continuing emphasis on tillage: his comparative analysis of Irish agriculture in the 1850s suggests that the impact of the Famine had induced a rapid shift to pastoral farming.[29] It is now clear that the increasing scarcity of effective labour in the Famine era meant that successful tillage was out of the question. Moreover, the repeal of the Corn Laws in 1846 opened Irish tillage production to a much wider array of competition, and therefore to much greater commercial uncertainty than had been the case in the protected and cushioned past. In addition the persistence of blight continued to damage confidence in the potato, and indeed yields remained miserably low until the discovery by Alexis Millardet of the copper sulphate remedy in the 1880s. The consolidation of greater holdings and the rapid shift to pastoral agriculture gave rise to a new feature of the Irish rural landscape – the great cattle 'ranches' of the east and the midlands.

Other aspects of the social and political life of Ireland were affected by the Famine, though less clearly or less directly. The Famine brought an immediate reduction in the Irish population, and seems to have popularized a range of attitudes and actions which ensured further decline. Late marriage and celibacy were increasingly common options within the socially ambitious farming community, as was emigration for those not in line to inherit the family property. However, there is no simple relationship between these various trends and the Famine. The average age at marriage was already growing in the pre-Famine period, and the proportion of those remaining unmarried was also increasing. Moreover, as Daly has observed, early and frequent marriage in the post-Famine period was associated precisely with those localities which had been hardest hit by the Famine (such as Connacht and west Cork): marriage age and marriage rates would seem therefore not to be solely related to Famine experience but rather to be partly contingent on prosperity, or lack of it.[30] Indeed, the hard-hit areas of the west and south-west were also those which demonstrated the slightest shift from tillage to pastoral agriculture, and the most tenacious commitment to the potato, indicating again the complicated regional and economic variations in the Irish response to the Great Famine.

Emigration was also, of course, an established feature of Irish life before 1845, indeed from the early eighteenth century on. Throughout the eighteenth century there was a low-level though fluctuating migration from Ulster to North America; but this was interrupted by the French wars (1793–1815) and in any event had produced an Irish-born population in the United States of only 44,000 by 1795. The end of the conflict coincided with an economic downturn and with food shortages (in 1816–17) and this, combined with the wartime suppression of emigration, stimulated a renewed flight: indeed, it has been argued – by W.F. Adams – that the end of the war saw new characteristics in emigration (the development of sustained mass migration, the beginning of a cheap emigration trade, the first widespread signs of poor migrants).[31] Though there were some later troughs in transatlantic and cross-channel emigration (often depending on relative economic conditions), the overall trend was upwards, and in 1842 alone over 100,000 left Ireland for the United States and Canada. However, if emigration during the Famine years and after built upon older traditions and structures, equally there were grimly novel features of this exodus. Though emigration had been rising in the early 1840s, the figures did not approach those of the later 1840s and early 1850s. The scale of the Famine emigration was therefore unprecedented, as was the scale of its casualties: in 1847 220,000 emigrated, while in 1852 368,764 left Ireland. One sixth of those on the passage to Grosse Ile, Quebec, died, with 4,572 deaths in a particularly grim two-month period in 1847.[32] This mass exodus and the permanence of high emigration levels combined with the pattern of infrequent and late marriages to produce a long-term population decline. In the pre-Famine period the same factors, operating at a lower level of intensity, helped to depress the rate of population growth; but, with fewer victims of famine, and with progress towards the eradication of smallpox, the population itself continued to rise.

The massive emigration figures of the Famine and post-Famine eras reflected a more profound shift. A contemporary observer, Lord Monteagle, believed that the despair of 1846 had wholly changed the attitude of the peasant towards emigration: emigration, once the path to exile, was now a welcome and necessary escape route. Oliver MacDonagh has developed this viewpoint, arguing passionately that the Famine brought 'a real change in essence', whereby emigration became an immediate personal option rather than a remote contingency which happened to others.[33] Emigration, thus, which was generally related to wage differences and to perceptions of relative advantage, became less of an economic calculation and more a panic-stricken reflex.

The life of those left behind changed, although – once again – the relationship between this change and the Great Famine is real, though opaque. The long-term decline in population which began with the Famine and which promoted the dominance of the farmer had a wide variety of implications for Irish society. Real wages rose for the survivors, as did living standards. The housing stock improved: in 1841 the single-roomed homes of the cottiers constituted over one-third of Irish housing, while by 1861 this fraction had fallen to less than one-tenth. The dominance of the potato in the Irish diet was overcome (although ironically, as has been noted, the areas that clung most tenaciously to the potato – in Connacht – had also been those most savaged by the blight). Literacy levels rose in the course of the Famine, 'a reflection', in Daly's observation, 'not of a revolution in schooling, but of the heavy mortality among the poor and consequently among illiterates'.[34] Daly has argued that the long-term rise in literacy may be attributed as convincingly to the retreat of the labouring classes as to the impact of the national school system.

The Famine was at one time blamed for the demise of the Irish language. It is now widely accepted that Irish was under challenge well before the arrival of the potato blight, and that the anglicization of Ireland, though hastened by the Famine, depended upon other circumstances. The spread of the national schools after 1831 encouraged use of the English language – Thomas Davis was angered by the exclusive use of English textbooks in the schools – though it would be wrong to overemphasize this point. The political direction supplied to Catholic Ireland in the first half of the nineteenth century was also an influence: O'Connell's emphasis on Catholic opportunity and on upward mobility was at the expense of the Irish language (even though he was a native speaker). There were other more subtle factors at play: the increasing ease of communication with Britain, the continuing development of British government and British economic influence in Ireland. Around half the population were Irish speakers in 1845. The Famine dramatically accelerated this process of decline, removing well over one million Irish speakers either through death or emigration: by 1851 the Irish-speaking survivors of the apocalypse numbered 1.5 million (23 per cent of the population), of whom 319,000 were monoglot (5 per cent).[35]

The Famine had an impact on Irish religious practice, though again, as with so much of this debate, there are differences of emphasis in rival interpretations. A 'devotional revolution' has been discovered, hingeing on the Famine years and involving a shift from traditional lax and heterodox practice towards a more formal and rigorous Catholicism. In this analysis a marked contrast is sketched between the old mixture of pagan and Christian celebration and the new Roman liturgical practice associated with the episcopal rule of Cardinal Cullen; equally a development in Church discipline has been noted, with higher attendances at mass in the post-Famine period and with an enhancement of the social and political authority of the priesthood. These shifts have been explained very largely in terms of the social impact of the Famine: those most devoted to the traditional religion, the cottiers, were decimated by hunger and disease, while the value of the old practices for the survivors was now, given the horrific nature of the disaster, highly questionable. The rising standard of living in the post-Famine period combined with the reverberating shock of the tragedy meant a greater popular acceptance of a more elaborate Church establishment and a more elaborate liturgy.

The neatness of this interpretation has, however, been disputed. In particular Seán Connolly has highlighted the pre-Famine evidence for this 'devotional revolution', emphasizing the spread of church-building and the retreat of traditional practices in the more prosperous part of the country well before the arrival of the blight.[36] The popular authority of the priest from the 1820s through to the early 1840s was simultaneously demonstrated and bolstered through O'Connellite politics, and the movements for emancipation and repeal. The basis for the priests' later ascendancy was thus apparently laid long before 1845.

This thesis and counter-thesis are reconcilable. The Famine may not indeed have been the original or sole stimulus for the spiritual reorientation of the farmers and wealthier sections of Catholic society: long-term economic and political consolidation within Catholic Ireland may help to explain these changes. On the other hand, the spread of the 'devotional revolution' owed much to the impact of the Famine, for this brought the consolidation of precisely those classes which had for long been susceptible to change. Nor should the profound spiritual trauma inspired by the Famine be written off. It seems a plausible speculation that, just as the Famine – in MacDonagh's judgement – promoted a 'sea change' in popular attitudes towards emigration, so a 'sea change' in attitudes towards religion was also promoted.[37] Change may have been prevalent before 1845, but it assumed a wholly different quality and completeness during and after the Famine.

Just as with religion, so with politics: the Great Famine exercised an immense though not exclusive influence. The popular perception of ministerial ineptitude or malevolence in the administration of relief inflamed anti-English sentiments, both within Ireland and among the many panic-stricken Irish emigrants. Again, however, it cannot be claimed that the Famine was the ultimate origin of hostility in Ireland to the 'Saxon', since (even setting aside the longer tradition of British–Irish bitterness) O'Connell had inflamed Irish national sentiment partly through an appeal to populist notions of England's wrongdoing. Moreover, the Famine emigration did not create an Irish community in North America hostile to the British Empire, since this was already in existence, albeit at a modest size: migration in the eighteenth century had often been linked to a combination of economic downturn and political exclusion, and numerous emigrants had been prominent critics of British tyranny.

Nor did the Famine bring any immediate reinforcement to Irish nationalism: despairing anti-Englishness did not automatically imply a more full-blooded commitment to repeal or to independence. The repeal movement foundered during the Famine, damaged both by the illness and death of O'Connell in 1847 but also by the perceived irrelevance of its core demand at a time of starvation and death. It has been suggested that the Famine undermined the confidence of many repealers in the goal for which they had so strenuously fought.[38] O'Connell himself had reordered his political priorities in the last stage of his career, giving emphasis to Famine-related issues rather than to the constitutional question (he was a supporter both of the Whig administration and of its measures of 1846). The Famine also immobilized the rebels of 1848, simultaneously firing their republican passion and disarming its practical potential. Later generations of Irish nationalist – particularly those indebted to Mitchel – would look back on the Famine as the nadir of British misrule in Ireland, and gain inspiration from their perception of a heartless, indeed murderous, colonial administration; but, for these nationalists of the revolutionary era the Famine was merely the worst of many examples of British tyranny, more potent than other memories because more recent and more widely accessible.

Nevertheless, it would be wrong to underestimate the significance of the Famine, whether in terms of popular Irish politics or Irish political thought. The Famine did not create but it surely transformed the anti-English hostility that underpinned much of the Irish nationalist movement in the mid- and late nineteenth century. Before the Famine anti-English sentiment was deep-seated, but perhaps remote: memories of the suppression of the '98 would have been fresh, but then the rising affected only a comparatively small part of the country and loyalties were more bitterly divided than has often been allowed. The Famine brought much more sweeping casualties and a much more vivid, because painful and immediate, sense of the injustice of British government. In the context of disease and starvation this hostility could find no immediate expression; but, in the aftermath of the Famine, the combination of irreducible anger and relative prosperity among the farming population would provide the foundations for a successful nationalist movement.

The Famine also marked Irish political thought. O'Connell, a landlord, had eschewed any serious attempt to tackle the fundamental problems of the Irish tenurial system (indeed, it is not at all clear that he accepted that there was an issue to tackle). The Famine changed the emphases of the O'Connellite era, for the scale of the disaster and the growing suspicions of British malevolence highlighted the severe limitations of the Liberator's social radicalism and of his constitutionalism. The Famine, with the spectre of starvation and disease and bureaucratic inanity, stimulated the rebirth of the physical force tradition. But perhaps of greater importance than the half-baked rebellion of 1848 was the fact that the Famine helped to highlight the profound problems with the Irish land system and to popularize the radical agrarian agenda of Fintan Lalor. It was the Famine that forged the bond between land and the national question, indeed the bond between land and violent nationalism; it was therefore the Famine that determined the direction of Irish politics for the next 50 years.

4.3   Brigadiers and Fenians

> *God save Ireland, said they loudly;*
> *God save Ireland, said they all;*
> *Whether on the scaffold high,*
> *Or the battlefield we die,*
> *What matter, if for Erin dear we fall!*
>   T.D. Sullivan[39]

The Famine simultaneously destroyed the immediate possibility of mass agitation and underlined the need for effective Irish political representation: it defeated O'Connell's army of cottiers, while it lent weight to the political clout of the substantial farmers. The Famine defused the urgency of repeal, while simultaneously arming the land question. It brought the intensification of religious sensitivities, with widespread suspicions of souperism and of anti-Catholic conspiracy. In these ways the Great Famine defined the structures and concerns of Irish politics in the mid-nineteenth century.

One of the issues that was highlighted by the disastrous state of the Irish agrarian economy was tenant right. The failure of the potato crop brought economic pressure on Irish landlords who were confronted both with diminishing rentals and with the immediate burden of the poor law: many were swift to transfer this pressure to the tenantry, either through severe measures to collect the available rent or through eviction. The level of eviction, which in the more prosperous conditions of the mid- and late 1850s was under 10,000 persons in a year, stood at 104,000 in 1850, having risen from 90,000 in 1849. These evictions, in themselves a substantial cause of distress, highlighted a related issue – the absence, outside Ulster, of any compensation for improvement to a holding. This was both a barrier to agricultural development and a very great source of injustice, for there was no incentive to improve a property and those few tenants who ventured their capital in a holding had, in the event of eviction, no right of redress. Nor was this issue hidden from the gaze of Westminster: the Devon Commission, which reported in 1845, accepted the advice of its witnesses and recommended that a landlord should be legally bound to compensate an outgoing tenant for any improvements. But, though several bills were constructed around this principle, none ever made it to the statute book. Moreover, a private effort to legalize the Ulster custom by the radical MP for Rochdale, William Sharman Crawford, failed by a very large margin (112 votes to 25) in June 1847: Sharman Crawford's bill, had it been successful, would have given legal recognition to the payments customarily offered by incoming tenants to their predecessors in a holding. It was evident, therefore, that Irish farmers faced a mounting economic challenge from the landlords and that they could expect no balm from within the existing British and Irish party system. They therefore took refuge in an autonomous organization, the Tenant League.

The farmers' defensive reflex was identifiable as early as 1847, when a series of tenant organizations was founded (including one at Holycross, Tipperary, inaugurated by Fintan Lalor). But these never grew beyond their local origins, and it took a further two years before a national farmers' movement began to emerge: the first body to establish itself on a permanent footing was the Tenant Protection Society of Callan, County Kilkenny, launched by two Catholic curates in October 1849. The Callan initiative coincided with an upsurge in evictions and the continued devastation of the Famine. In addition to this generally bleak (if important) context, there were also particular problems for those prosperous market-led farmers who cultivated wheat and barley: Paul Bew and Joe Lee have remarked that the Callan Society and, indeed, the subsequent tenant organizations were formed after especially poor wheat harvests in 1849 and 1850.[40] In any event, Callan marked the beginning of an organizational campaign which extended throughout all of Ireland and which, in the opinion of J.H. Whyte, had emerged by the summer of 1850 as the dominant feature of Irish political life.[41] Directed by Charles Gavan Duffy, Frederick Lucas and S.M. Greer, plans were laid to coordinate these formidable but as yet centrifugal forces: a conference of the separate organizations met in August 1850 and declared in favour of the fair evaluation of rent, security of tenure and the free sale of the tenant interest. In order to realize these goals it was agreed to found a permanent governing organization, the Irish Tenant League.

The new Tenant League assumed a larger significance in the extensive writings of Gavan Duffy, one of its most enthusiastic patrons, than in the broader political history of mid-nineteenth century Ireland: it was he who baptized the organization as the 'League of North and South'.[42] In fact the chief significance of the League rests in the fact of its creation rather than in any long-term, or even mid-term, impact. It might be possible to argue that the League popularized the demand for the three 'fs' – fair rent, free sale, fixity of tenure – and thereby laid the foundations for the agitation of the 1880s; but in fact the connection was at best tenuous, for there was no history of sustained farmer pressure or continuous organization, and the League rested on a socially more elevated prop than its populist and inclusivist successors. Yet the architects of the League had apparently succeeded where the movements for emancipation and repeal had failed, creating a national political organization that united farmers of all denominations in a radical programme of reform. This unity was short-lived, for the northerners demonstrated a less intense commitment to agitation than their southern counterparts; but the 'League of North and South' provided an all too rare stimulus to good-hearted ecumenical politicians such as Duffy, and it also provided an (in fact deceptive) exemplar to the Land Leaguers of 1880. And, though the Irish Tenant League swiftly withered, it survived long enough to spur the creation of an independent Irish Parliamentary Party dedicated, in part, to the cause of tenant right.

There were, however, other and much more immediate influences behind the formation of a distinct Irish Parliamentary Party: chief amongst these was the pressure of outraged Catholic opinion. The rise of the farmer movement coincided with a sharp deterioration in sectarian relationships, both in Ireland and in Britain, and an increasingly pronounced division between the Catholic sense of pastoral responsibility and Protestant sensitivities concerning civil authority. It is hard to identify any golden age of sectarian harmony in nineteenth-century Ireland, and certainly the passage of Catholic emancipation in 1829 did not inaugurate anything other than a temporary calm. In fact, with the development of evangelical Protestantism and of Catholic wealth and assertiveness, there was a steady worsening of relations: a number of episodes in the mid- and late 1840s contributed to this decline and highlighted the need for a new and distinctive Irish Catholic response in the House of Commons. The Famine fuelled the widely held suspicion that the British government had engineered an act of genocide against Catholic Ireland; moreover, allegations that the Protestant clergy had demanded the conversion of the hungry as a condition of supplying relief – that they had bartered Indian meal for souls – reflected both an isolated reality as well as mounting sectarian hostility. At the level of high politics, Peel's scheme of Queen's Colleges had provoked an anger among the Catholic bishops, which festered long after 1845 and which was renewed at the Synod of Thurles in 1850. But the episode that sparked the most concentrated sectarian anger coincided with the Synod, but had otherwise no connection. In August 1850 Pope Pius IX announced the constitution of a new Catholic hierarchy in England, and shortly afterwards the new Archbishop of Westminster, Nicholas Wiseman, proclaimed that 'we govern, and shall continue to govern, the counties of Middlesex, Hertford and Essex': the Liberal government of Lord John Russell immediately sought to channel and exploit Protestant outrage at these apparent pretensions, and in February 1851 a measure was launched which prohibited the use by Catholic bishops of British place names.[43] Russell's Ecclesiastical Titles Bill, and his increasingly trenchant Protestantism, created immediate problems for his Irish Liberal supporters, many of whom were Catholic or who represented Catholic constituencies. These were resolved in March 1851, when a large body of Irish Liberals began to act in opposition to their own government and to assume the appropriately defiant title of the 'Irish Brigade'.

In August 1851 the Brigadiers acquired their own extra-parliamentary organization, the Catholic Defence Association; and in the same month the leaders of the Tenant League (who were losing out in the battle for rural Catholic support) and of the Brigade were brought into an informal alliance. Sharman Crawford was the intermediary, and the basis for agreement was a tenant right bill which was acceptable to the more timid of the Brigadiers without sacrificing all of the Leaguers' demands. This marked the beginnings of a tentative and imperfect, but still vital, coalition between the religious and land movements: it was, in its way, an early prototype for the broad union of forces – religious, economic and constitutional – which drove the Home Rule movement in the 1880s. Certainly the role of the Catholic clergy in promoting this union was very great ('never perhaps did their influence reach greater heights than in 1852'), and prefigured the clerical endorsement of Home Rule 30 years later.[44] This coalition prepared to fight the general election of July 1852, pledged to Sharman Crawford's proposed reform and to the policy of independent opposition; and the local political magnates and fixers (whose importance Theo Hoppen has stressed) showed themselves to be impressed with the mixture of religious fidelity, limited tenurial reform and mildly patriotic opposition which the independents promoted.[45] In fact, before the polling took place another and in some ways more important battle had occurred to decide the nature of Irish Liberal representation: and here the Independents had won out, forcing their more Protestant Whig counterparts into retreat. The election of 1852, fought in the context of heightened sectarian bitterness (in particular rioting at Stockport), marked what John Whyte has called 'the zenith of the independent Irish party': around 48 MPs were returned in the Independent interest, and two conferences, held on 8–9 September and on 28 October to decide on land and religious policy, reinforced the new parliamentary grouping's commitment to the strategy of independent opposition.[46]

To compare the new Independent Irish Party with its later Parnellite and Redmondite successors is to court errors of scale or anachronism, but it does help to highlight a variety of features. Like the Home Rule movement, the Independent

Irish Party rested on a formidable union of clerical and farming support. However, despite the enthusiastic endorsement of many priests, the Independents soon encountered the opposition of Archbishop Paul Cullen, who saw revolutionary passions and Mazzinian godlessness beneath the middle-class piety of Independent leaders like Duffy, and who was therefore opposed to the widespread involvement of his clergy in party propaganda and electioneering: Cullen's tough-minded attitude provoked a succession of Independent appeals to Rome, the strain of which brought the petitioning Frederick Lucas to an early grave.

Like the later Home Rule Party, the Brigadiers and Independents exercised influence by holding the balance between the main parties inside the House of Commons: the Brigadiers had helped to topple the Russell government, and the Independents helped to create the Aberdeen coalition. Like the Parnellites, the Independents were apparently quite content to endorse the Tories in preference to the Whigs, should there appear to be any temporary advantage in so doing. Like the later Home Rule Party, the Independents lost ground in the context of relative agrarian tranquillity or prosperity: just as the Parnellites appear to have suffered from the effective government assaults on the Plan of Campaign in the later 1880s, and just as the Redmondites lost direction after the success of British land legislation, so the Independents were damaged by the rising rural prosperity of the later 1850s.

But there were also sharp distinctions between the two generations of independent Irish parliamentary protest. The Irish Party of the 1850s had no coherent constitutional platform, and was not nationalist in any meaningful sense. It built upon transient religious and economic passions, and was vulnerable to collapse when those passions dissipated. If it differed in purpose to its successors, then it also differed in structure: it was a much more inchoate body than later Irish parties, imposing a loose and ineffective form of discipline. The party was pledged to act in a policy of independent opposition, but this was never fully defined; members of the party were originally bound to accept majority decisions upon the threat of expulsion, but this principle – similar to that imposed by the Parnellites – was soon broken. Even more seriously, the party possessed no strong national organization such as that which supported both the earlier O'Connellite movement and the later Parnellites: neither the Tenant League nor the Catholic Defence Association were effective as local electoral machines, and in any case the latter was very short-lived. The party was therefore highly susceptible to setbacks within its leadership, and indeed a good case has been made out for supposing that the party eventually failed because of failures of personality.[47]

These contrasts broach the separate but related issue of the party's demise. From a highpoint in 1852, when 48 MPs were returned on the Independent platform, the party had sunk to a membership of only 11 in 1859, when it split on the issue of the Tory government's reform bill, and effectively collapsed. In the 1860s a sizeable number of Irish members continued to express their (somewhat hazy) commitment to 'independent opposition' – perhaps as many as 18 in 1865 – but these expressions seem at this stage to have been an aspiration rather than a political reality, and were in any event soon silenced. The former Young Irelander, John Blake

Dillon, staging a genteel political comeback in 1865 as MP for County Tipperary, sought to capitalize on the shifts in British Liberal politics that were occurring after the death of Lord Palmerston; and he succeeded in reuniting the old Independent factions around a policy of support for the new and apparently more 'advanced' Liberal leadership. In 1866 the Independent opposition was confronted once again with a measure of parliamentary reform, the issue which had all but broken the party in 1859; now, however, Dillon's endorsement of the Liberal government carried the day, and the Independents voted solidly for the government on the second reading of the new reform bill (27 April 1866). A form of unity within the Independent tradition had therefore been reconstructed, but at the cost of abandoning the central tenet upon which the tradition rested. As Vincent Comerford has observed, 'it is to 27 April 1866, and not to any date in the late 1850s that we must look for the demise of an independent opposition party in parliament'.[48]

The reform question was thus the proximate cause of death, but there had in fact been symptoms of mortality from at least 1852: in that year the party had lost two of its leaders, John Sadleir and William Keogh, who fell victim to personal ambition, and – in defiance of earlier pledges – accepted junior ministerial office in the Aberdeen coalition. The party had little better luck with its other leaders: Frederick Lucas died, aged only 43, in October 1855, while Charles Gavan Duffy, disillusioned with the attitude of Rome towards clerical support for the Independent cause, left Ireland for Australia in the following month. The most eminent remaining survivor in the leadership, George Henry Moore, was unseated on petition after the election for County Mayo in 1857, and failed to win County Kilkenny in the general election of 1859.

The issues of discipline and organizational support have been outlined, and were undoubted sources of weakness to the party. But perhaps its single greatest flaw was that it was founded on a paradox: it was a small Liberal splinter group which, harnessing Catholic and farming passions, affected independence from British Liberals and was prepared to support the Tories – the traditional party of Irish Protestants and landlords – in order to demonstrate the seriousness of its aspirations. It encountered the problem which Irish Unionist parliamentarians faced in 1885–6 – that of preserving the credible fiction of autonomy while in reality possessing very limited room for political manoeuvre. The Irish Unionists resolved their paradox by effectively and speedily abandoning all but the shadow of parliamentary independence; but the Irish Party of the 1850s sought to preserve their fiction, combining loose political discipline and a flaccid constitution with high principles, and bringing forth as a result confusion and division and acrimony. In the end the Independents shared the fate of the Unionists, trading their autonomy for subservience and a modest influence within one of the British political traditions.

The Independent Irish Party failed, therefore, sinking from a dominant position in Irish electoral politics in 1852 to a marginal significance by the end of the decade, and final destruction in 1866. Moreover, before their effective surrender to Gladstonianism, the Independents appear to have inflicted damage on the wider liberal family and to have created special, if transient, opportunities for Tory electoral scavenging: certainly in 1859 the Tories emerged – uniquely, in the history of post-reform parliamentary politics – as the largest single Irish party, garnering 54 seats as compared to the Liberals' 51. More specifically, a quirky, limited alliance between the Tories and those sections of the Independents under the influence of G.H. Moore seems to have operated in the later 1850s, with the Whigs as the intended victims: indeed Lord Naas, the astute Tory Chief Secretary, gave some financial assistance to likely Independent candidates.

But the Independents were more than an electoral curiosity. They were significant in their own terms as (however momentarily) an ascendant force in Irish politics: to a very great extent they flagged issues – the three 'fs' of tenant right, the disestablishment of the Church of Ireland – that were taken up by later generations of popular politician. And though the Independents soon foundered, their wreckage provided a marker buoy for future Irish political enterprises. There is certainly a danger, as Roy Foster has identified, of overplaying the benefits of hindsight in assessing the Independent Irish Party; but equally there is little doubt that the party supplied an important reference point, not just for historians but for later political activists.[49] The failure of the Independents and of constitutional pressure may well have assisted the resurrection of the physical force tradition in the later 1850s (certainly the creation of Fenianism only occurred when the disorientation of the Independent Irish Party was beyond question); and the Home Rulers of the 1870s and 1880s were well versed in the errors of their precursors. Political failures can indeed 'be as interesting as successes'.[50]

The Independent Irish Party was in some respects a piece of O'Connellite nostalgia: its fluid structure, its loose external connections, its emphasis on popular Catholic concerns – all recalled the heyday of O'Connell's 'tail'. The party was an old-time reaction to the increasingly inflexible nature of British parliamentary discipline, an Irish response to the formalization of British party politics. Fenianism was also, in part, a reaction to the inflexibility and exclusivity of parliamentary politics; through its strong connections with Young Ireland and the Irish Confederation, Fenianism, too, was partly rooted in the O'Connellite past. But here the connections end. For the Independents developed within an exclusively Irish and parliamentary context, and for most of their political lifetime they satisfied neither constituency. They responded only turgidly to Irish electoral pressures and to British political conventions: their deliberate inaccessibility within the Commons and their enforced remoteness from Ireland doomed them to failure. Fenianism, on the other hand, was highly dependent on a range of international conditions, and its apparently bitter inflexibility, its simplicity and (paradoxically, for a secret society) its openness confirmed its status as one of the most influential of all Irish nationalist organizations. Fenianism tapped several Irish and European political traditions and answered a variety of contemporary needs, both political and social: where the Independents offered only carefully crafted electioneering and the remote prospect of minor reform, the Fenians offered rhetoric (they were 'incurably verbal'), and recreation and status, and the prospect of immediate patriotic glory.[51] In fact neither the Fenians nor the Independents achieved much in isolation; but the marriage of the two traditions under Parnell – the militant and the constitutional – would prove irresistible.

Fenianism sprang from the wreckage of the 1848 rising and developed in the context of a fissile but active nationalist popular culture in the late 1850s. The exiled veterans of the Irish Confederation in France and in the United States were crucial to the survival of an 'advanced' nationalism, and two in particular – James Stephens and John O'Mahony – carried their enthusiasms and experience into Fenianism. These men, who had been enthusiastic proponents of Young Ireland, were brought into contact with the demi-monde of Blanquist insurrectionary societies in Paris; later, moving to the United States, they encountered other veterans of the '48 and also the as yet untapped financial and sentimental resources of the Irish American community. Stephens returned to Ireland in 1856 and journeyed through different parts of the country in a reconnaissance which he later glorified as his 'Three Thousand Mile Walk': this introduced him to like-minded nationalists, and in particular to the Phoenix literary societies, the most prominent of which was located in Cork and was under the direction of Jeremiah O'Donovan Rossa. By March 1858 Stephens was able to unite his network of Irish sympathizers with his knowledge of European secret organizations and his access to American funding: and the result, fashioned in Peter Langan's timber yard in Lombard Street, Dublin, was a body called initially merely 'the organization', but later dubbed 'the Fenians' or the 'Irish Republican Brotherhood' (IRB).

The timing of this nativity is significant. Speaking in 1881 the prominent Irish American Fenian, John Devoy, defined what he saw as necessary conditions for an insurrection: 'Ireland's opportunity will come when England is engaged in a desperate struggle with some great European power or European combination, or when the flame of insurrection has spread through her Indian Empire, and her strength and resources are strained'.[52] The creators of Fenianism, with their varied experience of exile in France, America and (for some) Australia, were as sensitive to the international scene as the United Irishmen whom they claimed as their forebears. The later 1850s may be seen, with the benefit of hindsight, as a less propitious time for Irish sedition and insurrection than the later 1790s; but there were still several encouraging features. Britain had fought a costly and unglamorous war against the Russians in the Crimea, which – though it delivered a victory of sorts – had cast doubts on aspects of British military efficiency. Moreover, though the French were British allies on this occasion, the campaign highlighted petty national tensions and brought no permanent understanding between the two powers. On the contrary, by the end of the 1850s a variety of episodes – the Orsini bomb plot against Napoleon III, for example, which was planned in London – had damaged the Anglo-French relationship. While the British army was diverted to India and the suppression of the 'Mutiny' or Rising (1857–9), the French were consolidating their navy through the construction of new iron-clad steamships and fighting an apparently efficient campaign against the Austrian Empire in north Italy (in May 1859). By 1858–9, a war between France and Britain was a real possibility; and the British acknowledged the seriousness of this threat through a programme of fortification and – even more remarkably – through the volunteering craze. For James Stephens it seemed as if the international conditions which had fired the 1798 rising were being recreated; and he and his co-conspirators prepared for the coming Anglo-French war through the creation of the Fenians.

The war with France did not come, but Fenian hopes of a British military humiliation, or at the very least, a military diversion, were kept alive into the mid-1860s by other means. Irish patriots had looked to France, as Britain's traditional continental European rival, for succour; but the rapid growth both of American power and of the Irish community in America suggested alternative possibilities. Indeed, America had for long offered blessings to the Irish patriotic cause. The British preoccupation in North America in the late 1770s had indirectly stimulated Irish national aspirations; and the newly formed United States had provided a haven both for political as well as economic refugees from Ireland throughout the early nineteenth century. The Anglo-American war of 1812–14 coincided with the dispersal and demoralization of the Irish rebels after the twin failures of the '98 and the Emmet rising, and had therefore little impact upon 'advanced' nationalism; but the possibility of a renewed conflict after 1861 – the possibility of British involvement in the American Civil War – developed against, for Fenian conspirators, a much more encouraging context in Ireland. The *Trent* episode (which arose when federal naval officers stopped a British vessel and arrested two confederate envoys) brought Britain close to war with the North at the end of 1861 and stimulated a wave of American sympathy in Ireland: this reached a climax at a mass demonstration in the Rotunda, Dublin, on 5 December 1861, which was suborned by the Fenians. Not only did the Civil War seem likely to draw in the British, it also provided many Irish Americans with military experience and with an eagerness to take on the true, Saxon, enemy. The Civil War therefore seemed to create unique opportunities for the Irish revolutionary cause; and the Irish Fenians, who were well grounded in American and Irish American politics, were keen to respond.

The Fenian leaders were sensitive to the international scene, and to some extent cast their plans in accordance with the state of international relations. But Fenianism flourished not simply because it channelled Irish American passion and money, and continental revolutionary fervour, but also – and indeed, primarily – because it responded efficiently to developments within Irish society. Estimates of the strength of Fenianism vary, and are marred by the hyperbole of Stephens and other leaders, but it seems likely that by 1864 – only six years after the creation of the movement – there were some 54,000 recruits. This figure, though modest enough in the context of O'Connellism, suggests nonetheless a more than superficial appeal. Fenianism was rooted in the social changes of the post-Famine years: the consolidation of the middle classes, especially the lower middle class, the development of towns, especially county towns, and the elaboration of a retail and service sector which hinged on the prosperity of the small farmer. Fenianism appealed to artisans and shop assistants, to travelling salesmen and to farmers' sons: it appealed to the 'class above the masses' which was educated and status-conscious, but debarred through poverty and through the constrictions of mid-Victorian Irish society from social advancement.[53] Fenianism was therefore a means of sublimating social and political frustration.

But, paradoxically, the growth of Fenianism also reflected a modest degree of social liberation. For Fenianism, more than any earlier popular Irish movement, was eventually controlled by the classes that it represented rather than by wealthy professionals or successful businessmen or déclassé ascendancy figures (some degree of upward social mobility within the movement should, however, be noted). Fenianism therefore marked an important transition in Irish politics, representing a shift away from the politics of deference (whether deference to a landlord, or to a priest, or even to a wealthy and autocratic populist figure such as O'Connell) towards a much more self-sufficient form of political expression: police observers noted that there was a Fenian 'type', embodied in a confident demeanour and gait, and a quiet defiance of everyday authority figures such as the priest or constable.[54] Fenians were not generally bound to a landlord or to a factory master; and they were frequently in employment which offered them not just freedom from unsympathetic domination, but also free time. The Fenian movement channelled popular lower middle-class political tensions, but it did so – at least in part – through providing both recreation and status. The (often nominal) secrecy of Fenianism generated a mystique, which combatted the humdrum in small town life, while its modest degree of social exclusivity offered members some affirmation of status: comparisons might be evoked both with freemasonry and with the artisan organizations of mid- and late Victorian Britain.

But if the Fenian movement addressed social insecurities, it also provided entertainment and recreation: indeed, given the relatively small numbers who turned out in 1867 to fight, it might well be argued that this recreational dimension was the most important aspect of contemporary Fenianism. The movement also satisfied the Victorian infatuation with military skill, and might be compared with the volunteering fad that swept through England in 1859; Fenianism, like the later Ulster Volunteer Force (UVF), offered its recruits the opportunity to play wargames – to drill, to train with weapons and, for some, to enjoy military rank. But, more broadly, just as the UVF was related to an intricate Unionist popular culture, so Fenianism fed off the widespread respect accorded to the Irish revolutionary tradition, and indeed generated its own popular revolutionary culture: it had its own paper, the *Irish People*, founded by Stephens in 1863, propagated its own literature (Charles Kickham, the author of *Knocknagow: or the Homes of Tipperary* (1873) was the most renowned Fenian literator), and provided more informal recreation in the shape of rambling, picnics and soirées. In common with continental nationalist organizations, and in common with late nineteenth-century popular Irish nationalism, there was a sporting dimension to Fenianism, with gym-training and boxing on offer besides armed insurrection. While picnics and gymnastics might seem to be unlikely forms of revolutionary expression, such activities helped to consolidate the romantic nationalism and the ties of kinship and friendship which made Fenianism such a potent political movement.

Fenianism also satisfied the widely felt need for spectacle and ceremonial: in some respects it was a curiously public and theatrical conspiracy. In common with other political and religious movements, the Fenians were keen to exploit the ever-expanding rail and road networks; for cheap and easy travel created opportunities both for efficient proselytism as well as mass mobilization. There was thus a popular appetite for mass ceremonial as well as the technology to create such displays. This was perhaps most evident with the campaign of the Amnesty Association in late 1869, when 54 mass meetings were held to demand the release of Fenian prisoners: one of these demonstrations, held at Cabra, attracted an estimated 200,000 protesters and recalled the heyday of O'Connellite agitation. But the most famous and influential example of Fenian street-theatre came earlier, with the funeral of the Young Irelander, Terence Bellew MacManus, who died in exile in San Francisco on 15 January 1861.

The idea to exhume MacManus and convey his body to Dublin came probably from the IRB's sister organization in the United States, the Fenian Brotherhood, whose motivation may well have had more to do with sectional rivalries in Irish America than any higher principle. There was no initial coordination with the Irish Fenians, but while the body was in transit a MacManus Funeral Committee was created to superintend the arrangements in Dublin: this was in effect a Fenian front organization. MacManus's remains arrived in Dublin on 4 November, and there began an elaborate ceremonial which lasted until the final committal, at Glasnevin, on 10 November: the journey to the cemetery was the climax of the week's public mourning, for at least 7,000 or 8,000 accompanied the hearse, forming a procession about a mile in length and flanked by an enormous crowd of respectful onlookers. The numbers in themselves were impressive, but the restraint of the crowd was equally startling; and the visual impact of the occasion was heightened by the presence of funeral marshalls, dressed in mourning and on horseback, and by the widespread use among the processionists of black and white armbands. Although the Catholic Archbishop of Dublin, Paul Cullen, was hostile to clerical involvement, a Fenian sympathizer, Father Patrick Lavelle, conducted the necessary religious ceremonials and provided a suitably trenchant oration.

The significance of the occasion, though undoubted, is nevertheless hard to define. The MacManus funeral was a formidable display of Fenian organizational skill, and it provided a model for later republican ceremonial: there are parallels between this and the funeral of O'Donovan Rossa in August 1915, when Patrick Pearse, echoing Lavelle in November 1861, delivered the graveside eulogy. The funeral also reveals a characteristic Fenian *modus operandi*, for the Brotherhood controlled the occasion, not directly but through its command of a subsidiary, or front organization, the MacManus Funeral Committee (such apparently innocuous patriotic bodies proliferated in the 1860s, often under the influence of Fenianism). Yet, whether the funeral reveals much about the state of contemporary Irish public opinion is open to question. Vincent Comerford has convincingly questioned any automatic connection between attendance on such occasions and endorsement of the political views of the organizers: certainly the MacManus funeral cannot be used uncritically as evidence for the extent of active popular approval of Fenianism.[55] Archbishop Cullen attracted a crowd estimated by the police (who were rarely sanguine about such matters) at around 100,000 in July 1862, when he opened a new building for the Catholic University at Drumcondra. Even the Prince and Princess of Wales, visiting Ireland in April 1868, attracted great crowds and apparently widespread popular enthusiasm (especially when the Prince visited the Punchestown races). Such occasions reveal little other than transitory popular moods and a lively sense of occasion: they do not demonstrate fundamental political convictions. Fenianism certainly won credibility and gained in confidence through events such as the MacManus funeral; but spectators were not necessarily revolutionaries and sympathetic curiosity was not in itself the basis for a new order.

It would also be misleading to emphasize the social and recreational aspects of the movement to the exclusion of political and ideological themes. Fenianism was formed as a revolutionary conspiracy, and its leaders actively sought to promote the destruction of British rule in Ireland and the establishment of an Irish republic: the formal title of the movement, the Irish Republican Brotherhood, was frequently rendered as 'the Irish Revolutionary Brotherhood'. T.W. Moody has observed that Fenianism was the only Irish revolutionary organization of the nineteenth century which was committed to insurrection from the very moment of its foundation: where the United Irishmen and the Young Irelanders had begun life as purely constitutional bodies and had only gradually, and reluctantly, turned to revolt, the Fenians always professed themselves to be revolutionaries, only occasionally and guiltily toying with constitutional action (as in 1869–70, and in 1873–6).[56] Insurrection, then, was a fundamental tenet of Fenianism, as was the attainment of Irish independence: but the objectives of the movement seem at the start to have been more negotiable than its strategy. For, though the formal goal of Fenian insurrection was a republic, and though a trenchant republicanism was a feature of some Fenian leaders, it is clear that others would have been prepared to accept a more modest constitutional settlement. Both John O'Leary and Charles Kickham were prepared to acknowledge the nominal supremacy of the British crown in a self-governing Ireland. Isaac Butt launched the Home Rule movement in 1870 having sounded out members of the Supreme Council of the IRB; and although relations between the Council and parliamentarianism subsequently became strained, a close if informal connection remained. Even Parnell, the icon of the parliamentary creed, was, it has been cautiously suggested, a recruit to Fenianism.[57]

The social attitudes of the Fenian leadership are even more elusive than their constitutional convictions. On the whole the priority of the movement was national independence, but in so far as certain rural social groupings seemed to be an impediment to this goal, then the Fenians evinced hostility: the landlords were occasional targets, as were the graziers ('those men of bullocks' or 'boors in broadcloth'), and the newly prosperous farming class.[58] Over-weening social ambition and greed were seen as diversions from a necessarily single-minded nationalism, and were therefore constantly denounced (this concern may have reflected the social insecurities of the Fenians themselves as much as high-minded nationalist principle). The cry of the movement was 'the land for the people', and this combined with the apparently 'advanced' views of leaders like Stephens (who in 1866 became a member of the First International) suggested a highly socialistic organization. Unsurprisingly, therefore, the wealthy and professional classes stayed well clear from early Fenianism; and, equally, the farmers (who had no desire to see their hard-won property lost to 'the people') often remained aloof.

But these generalizations demand some qualification. There were personal and territorial and chronological distinctions in the social critique offered by Fenians. Different Fenian commanders offered different social perspectives: John O'Mahony, though a minor gentleman, described himself as 'an ultra-democrat', and his later writings (in the opinion of Desmond Ryan) 'foreshadowed the social teachings of Pearse and Connolly on the eve of 1916'; Charles Kickham, on the other hand, looked back nostalgically to the patriotic aristocracy of 1782, and at the opening of the Land War, in 1879, he and John O'Leary showed themselves to be highly sensitive to the plight of moderate or reasonable landlords.[59] Kickham, as President of the Supreme Council in the early 1880s, was 'passionately opposed both to the Parnellites themselves and to Fenian dealings with them'.[60] Moreover, despite the spirited rhetoric of the *Irish People* between 1863 and 1865, and despite the lurid condemnation of 'the aristocratic locusts . . . who have eaten the verdure of our fields' in the Fenian Proclamation of February 1867, the movement proved itself in practice to be sensitive towards the rights of property: the rebels of 1867 were, in this respect, peculiarly respectful and undestructive.[61] This feature, combined with the widespread sympathy for Fenian prisoners and the three 'Manchester Martyrs', helped at last to win some farmer support for the movement (especially in the province of Munster). Indeed the austerity of Fenian nationalism could prove to be as much of a burden in the countryside as the allegation of socialism: in 1879–80, at the opening of the Land War, the smallholders of the west effectively abandoned the IRB in preference for the more immediate and worldly temptations held out by the Land League.

Fenianism was thus a revolutionary conspiracy and not a coherent social doctrine; and the most complete (if highly flawed) expression of the Fenian ideal came not in any socialistic treatise but with the intensive revolutionary plans of 1865–7 and the rising of 1867. The Fenian leadership had long promised such a rebellion, and James Stephens had initially and brazenly decreed that 1865 would be the year of action. Large sums of money were sent from America by John O'Mahony, who also directed sympathetic veterans of the Civil War across the Atlantic in order to command the putative Irish rebel army. On 5 August 1865 Stephens directed O'Mahony to issue 'the final call' for American support, an initiative which involved the sale of 'Irish Republic' bonds and which indirectly signalled to Irish American sympathizers that the liberation of their homeland was at hand.[62] Yet the rebellion of 1865 never came: Stephens was gambling on the state of international relations, and, as the likelihood of an Anglo-American war faded and as British security seemed insurmountable, he was forced into bluster and prevarication. In fact delay, rather than bringing any immediate tactical advantage, played into the hands of the authorities, for while Stephens's mixture of enthusiasm and procrastination sapped Fenian morale, the flow of intelligence into Dublin Castle (from informants such as Pierce Nagle) grew ever greater. The offices of the *Irish People* were raided by the police on 15 September, the paper – one of the chief vehicles of popular Fenianism – was suppressed and its files scrutinized for evidence of illegality: leading Fenians – T.C. Luby, O'Donovan Rossa, O'Leary – were arrested at the same time and bound over for trial. Stephens was apprehended a little later, but was sprung from gaol by John Devoy on 23 November: he remained in hiding in Ireland as his movement collapsed around him.

Uncertain of the effectiveness of normal judicial procedures, the government suspended the Habeas Corpus Act in February 1866, initiating a further and more intensive round of arrests. The cumulative impact of these assaults was disastrous, with the detention of hundreds of suspects, the disappearance of legal boltholes and the disruption of the Fenians' carefully crafted organizational structure. Stephens, however, continued to elude the authorities and managed to slip out of Ireland in March, bound, by a circuitous route, for the United States. In truth the government's actions can have caused him some mixed emotions, for, while his work was overturned, he was temporarily spared the recriminations of those whom he had raised to a fever pitch and abandoned. The respite was only temporary, however: as his promises of revolt were renewed throughout 1866, along with periodic private arguments for delay, the murderous frustration of his lieutenants grew. His teasing, schizoid leadership was finally rejected amidst a welter of personal abuse in New York in December 1866, when he was ousted from the command both of the American and Irish Fenian movements. In the end Stephens was a victim of his own charisma, for his prophetic style had deceived himself as much as the frustrated rebel heroes under his command.

Stephens's difficulty was akin to that of Carson in 1913–14: he was the leader of an armed conspiracy, the vitality of which depended on the lure of action. Promises of military glory were necessary to sustain popular morale; but, equally, such promises created the general expectation that they would be shortly redeemed. Both men grasped that, under existing circumstances, their movements would be annihilated in any conflict; and both sought to prevaricate in the Micawberish hope that 'something would turn up'. Carson's luck held out, for 'something' – in the shape of the Great War – *did* 'turn up', and both his leadership and the morale of his movement survived unimpaired, where Stephens was swept away by a tide of distrust and frustrated aggression. They were two vain and charismatic men with a shared instinct for political survival; but Carson had a lawyer's sense of the limits of persuasiveness and a firmer grasp on political realities.

When the Fenian rising came, in February and March 1867, it came without any direct intervention from Stephens. Indeed, partly because of the damage sustained by Irish Fenianism during the government offensive, and partly because of the wealth of Irish American military experience, the leadership of the impending revolt fell into the hands of several ex-officers of the Federal army, the most prominent of whom was Colonel T.J. Kelly. Kelly, like Stephens (whose place he nominally filled), saw little hope of success for the revolutionary enterprise, but he had a stronger sense that the personal honour of the Fenians and the broader credibility of the movement were at stake: he was an energetic, indeed a calculating and ruthless soldier, but no desperado. Arriving in London at the end of January 1867, he found that a group of Irish Fenian refugees had – Stephens's procrastination notwithstanding – plans for a revolt well in hand, and though his own immediate preference was for caution, these schemes were put into action in mid-February. Over 1,000 Fenians gathered on 11 February in preparation for a raid on the well-stocked and (so it was thought) lightly guarded arsenal at Chester: but in fact the authorities had been informed of the rebel plans and had strengthened the garrison to the point where the Fenians lost heart and dispersed. A more minor uprising took place near Cahirciveen, County Kerry, where on 12 February around 100 Fenians under the command of a Colonel John O'Connor seized a coastguard station and its weapons before discovering – through the capture of a police dispatch rider – that their plans were also known to the authorities. They, too, like their English counterparts, dispersed. They, too, like their English counterparts, appear to have been the victims of an informer, John Joseph Corydon, who was well connected with the Fenian community in Liverpool.

The failure of the February insurrection discredited its architects and created an opening for a new executive committee, comprising representatives from each of the four provinces of Ireland. This met in London on 10 February and appears to have immediately transformed itself into a self-styled Provisional Government of Ireland: two further members, one representing the British Fenians, and Colonel Kelly (who surrendered his authority to the new body), were co-opted. At about the same time the new Provisional Government declared in favour of a further uprising, which was provisionally scheduled for the end of February but subsequently postponed to early March. This furious impulse to fight, in the teeth of failure and regardless of the damage done by the government and by informers, reflects both the desperation of the Civil War veterans and a general disgust at Stephens's dithering and apparent cowardice in 1865–6.

The manifesto of the rebels was published on 19 February and declared war on the 'aristocratic locusts, whether English or Irish': the document, which was republican and internationalist in tone, reflected the political sensitivities not just of the Provisional Government but also of its English sympathizers, and especially Charles Bradlaugh. As Vincent Comerford has remarked, the cooperation between the Provisional Government and English republicans highlights a context for Fenian development beyond that which might normally be supplied: the Fenians certainly operated within a tradition of militant Irish republicanism, but in the later 1860s they were also part of, and sought to exploit, a broader republican connection in the United Kingdom.[63] However, neither these new English allies nor, indeed, the older American support networks delivered much by way of military aid. The Fenian rising of 1867 was launched with the support of English rhetoric and the questionable support supplied by Irish American officers; but no allied expeditionary force was sent to Ireland and there was no diversionary uprising in Britain or in British North America.

The uprising had two main focuses, Dublin and Cork, with lesser out-breaks in Tipperary and Limerick: there were skirmishes in Clare, Louth, Queen's County and Waterford. The broad strategy (there was no detailed plan of campaign) was to hold out until the appearance of Irish American reinforcements; and this meant that set-piece battles with the crown forces (such as had broken the '98 rising) were unwelcome, and that raids on well-guarded barracks (such as the fiasco at Chester) were equally unwelcome. A number of rallying points were selected (Tallagh Hill, Dublin, and Limerick Junction): the choice of Limerick Junction reflected a general recognition of the importance of railways, and indeed a characteristic rebel action was the uprooting of track. Beyond these highly preliminary and defensive plans, there seems to have been little except a faith in improvisation. Perhaps this reflected despair, or a conviction that the purposes of Fenianism were sufficiently served by the fact of the revolt – the 'propaganda of the deed' – rather than its out-come.[64] But it may also be the case that, in the light of the betrayals of February, the leaders were suspicious of devising premature and over-elaborate plans which might easily have fallen into the hands of their enemies. If the impulse towards vague-ness was the fear of treachery, then it was not entirely misplaced: for, as before, the authorities were well informed of the insurgents' schemes. Any gaps in their knowledge were helpfully plugged by a General Massey, who was arrested on 4 March and who graduated from being the most senior conspirator in Ireland to the role of chief witness for the crown in the prosecution of his former associates.

The Cork Fenians numbered perhaps 4,000 men, but though they carried out some minor operations – the capture of a coastguard station, the destruction of a police barracks – they never reached their designated muster-point and soon lost heart and dispersed. In Limerick the Fenians attacked a small police station at Kilmallock on 6 March (a premonition, it has been remarked, of the strategies of 1919–21); and there were similar minor confrontations between the rebels and the Irish Constabulary in Tipperary.[65] As in the aftermath of the '98 (though on a much smaller scale), these skirmishes were often conducted by small, broken bands and were devoid of any overall strategic purpose: as in the aftermath of the main battles of the '98, these skirmishes continued for several weeks after 5–6 March.

Though estimates vary, the most substantial manifestation of the 1867 rising came in Dublin. Here there were three intended points of mobilization on the night of 5–6 March – Tallaght Hill, Palmerston and Killakee at Rathfarnham: it appears that Killakee was to be the main centre of activity, for it was here that the military leader of the Dublin Fenians, General Halpin, had stationed himself. The other rallying points were probably chosen for diversionary purposes. If this was (as seems likely) the strategic purpose of the Dublin insurgents, then their plans went utterly awry: the lines of communication collapsed and Halpin waited at Killakee for a force that never arrived, while at Tallaght Hill a substantial gathering of Fenians waited for leadership that was never supplied. There were some, albeit very minor, successes:

the group of Fenians who gathered initially at Palmerston were led by two army veterans (Lennon, a deserter from the 9th Lancers, and Kirwan, a sergeant in the Irish Papal Brigade) and captured the police stations at Stepaside and Glencullen before dispersing. At Tallaght Hill a large body of Fenians assembled – the Irish Constabulary suggested (probably erring towards generosity) as many as 7,000– 8,000 – but, aside from the lack of organization and direction among this body, they were demoralized by the results of a minor affray at Tallaght police station, where the Constabulary routed a small body of Fenians and inflicted two casualties. The insurgents on the Hill either slunk away in despair or were dispersed and driven off by British troops. The overall result of the Dublin rising was, for the rebels, utterly disastrous. Recent scholarship has laid emphasis on the relatively large numbers that the Fenians were able to mobilize (despite the failures of February and the impact of arrests), but the complete failure of the Fenian leadership to exploit this support has also been stressed. As the latest scholar of the episode has remarked: 'the conduct of the rising amply confirmed the dangers of a headquarters staff of American officers totally divorced from the centres, the effective leaders of the individual circles'.[66] Given the plight of Halpin, a disoriented leader separated from his dispirited troops, this judgement seems hard to fault.

If the 1867 rising was a diminutive version of the '98, then Bompard's expedition was echoed in the arrival, in May 1867, of *Erin's Hope*, a solitary vessel carrying a handful of Irish American sympathizers, who were rounded up by the authorities with the same efficiency that had been applied to Tone and his allies. The scale of the two risings at first glance scarcely bears comparison: it is doubtful whether the rebels of 1867 mustered 10,000 men in total, where perhaps 50,000 turned out in 1798; estimates of the casualties of the '98 vary between 30,000 and 100,000, where the total fatalities of the 1867 rising amounted to 12. However, both rebellions had an apparently decisive impact on British policy, and both supplied the revolutionary cause with martyrs. Tone, sentenced to hang long after the rebels had been crushed, was the most celebrated victim of the '98 rising (even though he took his own life); and equally the most celebrated casualties of the 1867 rising fell after the battles had been lost, and met death on a British scaffold.

Just as the bloody aftermath of the '98 contributed greatly to the folk-memory of the rising as a whole, so the aftermath of the 1867 rising had in some ways a much more fundamental political impact than the military episodes of February and March: the immediate fall-out from the '67 certainly stimulated a much more intense and sympathetic popular interest than the botched manoeuvres of the rebels. On 11 September Colonel T.J. Kelly and a fellow Fenian officer, Timothy Deasy, were arrested in Manchester; a week later they were escorted in a Black Maria from their gaol in order to make a brief court appearance. These legal formalities gave would-be rescuers a chance, while the spectacular (and politically profitable) rescue of James Stephens in 1865 provided an exemplar: returning from court, the Black Maria was attacked by 30 armed Fenians, who liberated both Kelly and Deasy but in so doing also shot and killed one of the (unarmed) police guards, Sergeant Brett. Twelve suspects were later charged with involvement, and of these five men were sentenced to hang: two of the five were reprieved, but Allen, Larkin and O'Brien went to the gallows at Salford Gaol on 23 November.

The three men had saved their leaders (Allen said that he would die for Colonel Kelly), but – more remarkably – they had also saved their movement: they succeeded in rescuing the 1867 rising from the ridicule which had been applied to the '48, and which might easily have been transferred to the confused and futile skirmishes that constituted the Fenian uprising. For Allen, Larkin and O'Brien were executed despite what Catholic Ireland viewed as their innocence of calculated murder, and as a result of what was seen as British injustice. (For their part the British author-ities had little doubt about the guilt of the accused: the two presiding justices and Cranbrook, the not unkindly Home Secretary, were convinced that Allen had fired the fatal shot and that he and the other two Fenians had led the ambush.) There may also, paradoxically, have been an element of surprise and shock in the Irish reaction: the public was accustomed to a relatively lenient judicial response to insur-gency (there were no executions after the 1848 rising, or indeed as a result of the main unrest in 1867), and this complacency was confirmed by the general assump-tion that the suspects were innocent, by the youth of the accused (Allen was only 19), and by the two reprieves that preceded the hangings.

The political repercussions of this confusion of anger and shock and sympathy were profound. As with the 1916 rising, so in 1867 the execution of Irish rebels created a consensus of support for Fenianism which had hitherto been conspicu-ously lacking. As in 1916, so in 1867, Irish parliamentarianism and Irish militancy achieved a shaky sort of rapprochement; after each rising the Catholic hierarchy and Irish militancy were able to establish a cautious understanding. The full force of sentimental nationalism was mobilized in the interests of the militant leaders: pro-pertied Irish people could now, through the patriotic sacrifice of the Manchester Martyrs, appreciate those whom they had once suspected of propagating socialism and anarchy.

This political reorientation deserves some further attention. The title of 'martyr' that was bestowed upon Allen, Larkin and O'Brien hinted at a shift in the relation-ship between popular Catholicism and the Fenian movement. The Church had hitherto been divided on the issue of the Fenian threat: MacHale of Tuam had refused to condemn the movement and had offered some protection to the most out-spoken of the Fenian priests, Patrick Lavelle; Moriarty of Kerry, a Gallican like MacHale, was a vehement critic of Fenianism, who cooperated with the crown author-ities and (much to Archbishop Cullen's disgust) maintained good relations with the local Protestant clergy. On the other hand, Cullen (a cardinal after 1866) differed from Moriarty only in degree, seeing Fenianism less in terms of its nationalism than its (in his skewed perspective) rampant anti-clericalism; he therefore damned the movement as an Irish manifestation of the prevalent continental godlessness. Cullen, predictably, was a more imaginative critic than Moriarty (whose indictment of the IRB did not extend far beyond the conviction that 'eternity was not long enough and hell not hot enough for the Fenians'); indeed, Cullen sponsored an initiative designed to divert electoral attention away from the Fenian movement and to win popular endorsement for several essentially Catholic political concerns (although tenant right also featured alongside disestablishment of the Church of Ireland and state funding for Catholic education).[67] But the new National Association of Ireland, founded on 29 December 1864, returned only three MPs at the general election of 1865 and soon limped into the political sidelines.

Cullen has been seen (in certain respects, at any rate) as a more innovative political radical than his Fenian opponents, for, while the Fenians stood in a familiar tradition of insurrection, Cullen was attempting to formalize the subjection of Catholic Ireland to clerical political leadership: 'it [the creation of the National Association] will generally be regarded as only a fresh attempt to Ultramontanise the Irish people', opined the (Conservative) *Dublin Evening Mail*.[68] His failure kept alive both the fluid relationship between Catholicism and the IRB, and the broader possibility of a non-sectarian nationalism.

The implications of Cullen's failure became clear after the execution of Allen, Larkin and O'Brien. Free from the discipline of the National Association, or indeed any other secular body directed by the Cardinal, Catholic priests and the Catholic laity united in a widespread public display of mourning. At mass on the day following the executions, Sunday 24 November, priests prayed for the souls of the three Martyrs; in the following weeks requiem mass was widely celebrated in commemoration of the Martyrs' sacrifice and for the peace of their souls. Priests and laity collaborated in solemn mock funerals, one of the largest of which took place on 1 December in Cork: another massive procession, attracting some 30,000 participants, marched in Dublin on 8 December. Some of the burning sense of injustice which fuelled these demonstrations was dissipated by the Fenians' attempt to spring one of their number, Richard Burke, from Clerkenwell gaol: this enterprise depended on a bomb, which, when detonated on 13 December, killed over 20 people living in the neighbourhood but failed to effect Burke's escape. But although the Clerkenwell explosion caused a momentary hesitation, it fired English outrage and indirectly helped to intensify national hostilities; so that the pro-Fenian alliance of priests and people, though shaken, remained substantially intact.

This clerical endorsement of the Martyrs, though it was by no means a blanket approval of Fenian aims or strategy, encouraged many of those who had hitherto kept the Brotherhood at arm's length. The farmers were amongst those who were most susceptible to the influence of the Church, and were therefore amongst those who were most influenced by the very public shift in clerical attitudes. In addition, the rising of 1867 had brought none of the feared despoliation of property, and had instead delivered three heroes: the rising could therefore be interpreted not necessarily in the light of the anti-clericalism or apparent social radicalism of the *Irish People*, but rather in a more traditional and comprehensible way as a conventional demonstration of Irish gallantry and patriotism, and of British repression and duplicity. After the executions at Salford gaol farmers and others who had been sceptical could accept Fenianism as an honourable expression of Irish patriotic aspirations. Fenianism became identified with the cause of tenant right, and indeed served increasingly as a blank screen onto which all manner of social and national grievances might be projected. By 1871 the ribbon movement – the secret rural combinations of small farmers and labourers – had been won to the cause of the Brotherhood (although Paul Bew has suggested that the high price paid by the Fenians was 'an acceptance of the traditional methods and objectives of agrarian outrage').[69]

The popularization of the Fenians meant, inevitably, a blurring of the distinctions between the constitutional and physical force traditions. This process had a number of aspects: first, as it attracted greater numbers of sympathizers, so the Brotherhood lost some of its militant integrity. Second, if Fenianism was moving closer to constitutionalism, then the constitutionalists were also edging towards the Fenians. Third, Liberalism, freed from the Whiggish preoccupations of Palmerston, was simultaneously evolving as a more inclusivist political force, appealing in particular to the concerns of the Celtic peoples. Thus by 1869–70 a great (if often vulnerable) coalition of Irish constitutionalists and militants, allied with British Liberals, was evolving – an alliance which would later be reconstituted under Parnell and which would dominate Anglo-Irish relations until 1916.

Aside from the Martyrs themselves, the two most influential figures in the early stages of this evolution were Isaac Butt and Gladstone. Butt occupied a political position of great strategic importance, standing at the intersection of several Irish political traditions. He was a great lawyer and constitutionalist who had applied his talents to the defence of, first, the Young Ireland prisoners in 1848, and, later, the Fenian prisoners of 1866–8. Butt was closely involved, therefore, with the creation of Fenian apologetics; and he carried his arguments as defence counsel out of the courtroom to a broader public in 1868–9 through a campaign for the release of the Fenian prisoners. He helped to propagate this initially somewhat fissile campaign, and in June 1869 he emerged as President of a united Amnesty Association: the Association sponsored a series of popular meetings in the summer and autumn of 1869 which, though starting somewhat shakily, peaked on 10 October, when an estimated 200,000 people gathered at Cabra to hear Butt, G.H. Moore and other proponents of an amnesty. Thereafter the Association, fearful of creating the conditions for another Clontarf, suspended these 'monster' meetings. The movement had only a partial success, therefore, and not only because the Association was scarred by the memory of O'Connell: for although the government was prepared to release some Fenian prisoners immediately, it was not prepared to release all, nor was it willing to free the most prominent (save Charles Kickham).

However, as Butt's biographer has remarked, the success of the Amnesty Association rested less with this very qualified outcome than with more intangible and long-term benefits. Militants and constitutionalists were united for the first time in 'constitutional action for a common object'.[70] The meetings at which this Association developed worked not just in the interests of an amnesty but at a more fundamental level: just as with O'Connell's meetings for emancipation and repeal, violent and emotive rhetoric was used, which roused a patriotic fury and which (in the words of John O'Mahony) brought 'the resurrection of a nation from its death-like torpor'.[71] The Amnesty movement helped to create a nationalist coalition and to fire nationalist sentiment, but it also helped to enhance the political reputation of Butt. Butt was able to exploit his popular standing and his influence with the Fenians to direct this national coalition towards a new body and a new goal: the Home Government Association (founded on 19 May 1870 with the tacit sanction of some of the Fenian Supreme Council); and Home Rule.

While tame constitutionalists such as Butt were luring the Fenians away from their revolutionary purity, Gladstone and the British Liberals were luring Butt and his Fenian allies towards the cage of parliamentary politics. The more anaemic Irish Republican Brotherhood of 1869–70 now confronted not the full-blooded British chauvinism of Palmerstonian Whiggery but rather the much more sympathetic, populist and celticized Liberalism of Gladstone. The general election of 1868 was fought and won by Gladstone on the question of the disestablishment of the Church of Ireland; for he had found in the Church an issue that attracted support from British non-conformists of all hues as well as from Irish Catholics. This revision of British Liberalism, coming in the wake of the Fenians' military failure as well as of John Blake Dillon's conciliatory initiative of 1865–6, reaped immediate electoral dividends in Ireland: the total of 66 seats which the Irish Liberals won was the high-water mark of their success in the nineteenth century. Almost certainly Gladstonian 'justice for Ireland' was immediately rooted in these psephological calculations rather than in panic: as Vincent Comerford has eloquently argued, 'justice for Ireland' was offered by Gladstone 'initially and primarily in order to win seats in Ireland; he did so, not because Fenians had guns and gunpowder, but because other Irish catholics had votes'.[72] A contrary view is apparently supplied by Gladstone himself, who in the House of Commons on 31 May 1869 declared (amidst characteristic layers of qualification) that 'the Fenian conspiracy has been an important influence with respect to Irish policy'.[73] Gladstone's argument was that the Fenian outrages awakened British public opinion to the broader condition of Irish politics; but he was keen to emphasize that, in spite of this electoral awakening, the Fenians had not altered his own convictions 'in the slightest degree'. These apparently divergent glosses are in fact easily reconcilable: Gladstone was indeed moved by electoral considerations, as Comerford has argued; but the electorate, in turn, was moved by the Fenian threat. Indeed, the very fact that Gladstone was able to win the election of 1868 on an Irish issue (referring to the landed ascendancy in terms which would not have been misplaced in the Fenian Proclamation) highlights some of the electoral implications of the uprising in the previous year.

Gladstone's second instalment of 'justice for Ireland' undermined the renewed tenant right campaign of 1869–70, but brought less popular Catholic satisfaction than the Irish Church Act of 1869. The new farmer agitation was launched in 1869 by Sir John Gray, the constitutionalist proprietor of the *Freeman's Journal*, who was reviving the old Tenant League agenda of the early 1850s but under apparently more propitious circumstances: as in its earlier manifestation, the movement was founded on farmers' clubs which eventually united under a national Irish Tenant League. Butt, who privately saw the farmers' movement as a diversion from the amnesty and broader constitutional questions, offered a highly insipid support; but he was concerned to hedge his political bets and therefore attended the meeting (held on 28 September 1869) at which the new Tenant League was launched. He was also present on 2–3 February 1870 at a great Land Conference, which was held in order to thrash out a coherent reform proposal: but he appears to have been disingenuous, persuading the delegates into making lavish demands which he knew would not be satisfied – and which he calculated would stand in the way of any premature reconciliation between the farmers and the apparently benign Liberal administration. Gladstone's Landlord and Tenant (Ireland) Bill, which was published on 15 February, compromised the principles of free contract and *laissez-faire* (the Ulster custom was legalized, and some tenants were given greater security of tenure and an enhanced right to compensation for improvements); but the radical precedents created by the measure were concealed by its apparently tentative nature and by the modest defence offered by its author (Gladstone may well have been as concerned to settle his own nerves as to allay proprietorial suspicions). Butt's tactical judgement was therefore once again affirmed; and he was able to quietly direct the disappointed tenant activists towards a higher goal – Home Rule.

Butt had therefore succeeded in diverting many Fenians as well as many farmers towards the cause of Home Rule. Fenianism had flourished in the context of a divided and directionless Irish parliamentary representation; and, equally, it withered when a constitutional movement emerged which supplied a coherent leadership to Irish Catholics and captured their political imagination. The success of Butt's Home Rule agitation – 60 Home Rulers were returned at the general election of 1874, as opposed to only 10 Liberals – reflected the extent to which it had replaced Fenianism as the political vessel into which all Irish political and social aspirations were poured. The Fenians themselves were captivated (in part, at least): at a grand Fenian Convention held in March 1873 the Supreme Council decreed that the day of insurrection might be postponed, pending the approval of the Irish people; and that in the meantime the IRB might 'lend its support to every movement calculated to advance the cause of Irish independence consistently with the preservation of its own integrity'.[74] This reflected partly a hesitant acceptance of the Home Rule initiative as well as a deep-seated passivity within the Fenian movement – a passivity which owed much to Kickham, by 1874 the President of the Supreme Council, and which offended the much more gung-ho approach of American Fenianism (dominated after 1867 by John Devoy and the Clan na Gael movement). It was Clan na Gael that was instrumental in purging the Irish leadership of those who appeared to be falling for Home Rule: a decision of the Supreme Council, taken on 10 August 1876, bound all Fenians to abandon 'active cooperation' with the Home Rule movement, and as a result the Council lost four of its members, including two MPs (Joseph Biggar and John O'Connor Power).[75] Only when a suitably 'advanced' and apparently ruthless parliamentarian emerged on the scene, in the shape of Charles Stewart Parnell, did the possibilities of the constitutional approach dawn on the Clan na Gael: this turnaround was enshrined in Devoy's 'New Departure' telegram of October 1878, in which he offered conditional support to Parnell, and by his protracted courting of the 'Chief' in 1879. Even then, however, Kickham and the Supreme Council of the Irish Fenians remained aloof, attempting to preserve the old militant austerity while their movement, broken by the attractions of the Land League and of the Parliamentary Party, collapsed around them.

Fenianism was overshadowed but not suppressed: it survived, providing a cabbalistic underpinning to the dominant parliamentary movement until in 1916, as in 1858–9, constitutionalism was judged to have failed and the Fenian moment recurred. However, the highpoint of nineteenth-century Fenianism came unquestionably, and ironically, in the wake of the defeats of 1867. The 'martyrdom' of Allen, O'Brien and Larkin created a massive patriotic movement out of a limited insurrectionary conspiracy. Fenianism was now tolerated, if not blessed, by the Church; an equally reverent popular institution, W.E. Gladstone, supplied some indirect and unwilling encouragement. But the basis for this brief popular expansion had been laid much earlier: by the eloquent propagandizing of Fenian journalists and literators, and through the social Fenianism of the early and mid-1860s.

Fenianism looked to 1798, and to 1848, and indeed in some senses was a direct by-product of Young Ireland and the Irish Confederation. In certain limited respects it also anticipated the later Irish Republican Army (IRA), most clearly in its militant constitution, its organization and its self-reliance: there was a substantial Fenian presence in the higher ranks of the IRA (to be found most obviously with Michael Collins and his lieutenants). The Fenians also greatly enriched the popular culture of late nineteenth-century and twentieth-century republicanism, supplying icons, ballads and a popular literature: the numerous memorials to the Manchester Martyrs are evidence of the material culture supplied by the IRB; T.D. Sullivan's song, 'God save Ireland!', inspired by the courtroom utterances of the Martyrs, supplied an unofficial anthem both to later republicans as well as constitutionalists.

But in other respects the Fenians were a premonition of militant loyalism – and indeed the parallels between Fenianism and the Ulster Volunteer Force of 1912–14 are as compelling as those between Fenianism and later militant republicans. Both the UVF and IRB were very public militant conspiracies; both, however, were serious military institutions. But where the Fenians had been trained in the battlefields of the American Civil War, the UVF leaders had in many cases gained experience in South Africa, fighting the Boers. Both bodies depended on gun-running for their weaponry, the UVF profiting from the cast-offs from the Edwardian arms race, and the Fenians benefiting from the glut of cheap weapons on the market after the Civil War. Both movements were launched against strained international contexts and a heightened popular militancy: both movements to some extent supplied otherwise peaceful civilians with a spurious military glory. Each body had its adventurers: Devoy's rescue of six Fenian prisoners held in Western Australia using the ship *Catalpa* is reminiscent, in its derring-do, of Fred Crawford's Childeresque escapades with the gun-running vessel the *SS Fanny* (or indeed his plan to kidnap Gladstone and transport him by yacht to the Antipodes).

But the UVF, like Fenianism, attracted immense popular support because it was simultaneously a military threat and a means of recreation. Both bodies provided bored, patriotic clerks and shop assistants and salesmen with a purposeful hobby; both bodies helped to cement family ties, and social and commercial connections.

Membership of the UVF was as much a commercial asset to a small businessman in Protestant Belfast in 1914 as membership of the IRB was to a Catholic shop-keeper in (say) Cork in 1865. The success of each body depended, therefore, not simply on its political or military aspirations: each body thrived because it was rooted in the social and commercial insecurities of Irish society.

4.4 Home Rule: A First Definition

While British legislation
Afflicts our Irish nation,
And no amelioration
*   Of that misrule is near;*
Parnell the Pertinacious,
O'Donnell the Audacious,
Will prove how efficacious
*   Our strategy is here.*
Popular doggerel (*c.*1879)[76]

The Independent Irish Party and Fenianism each exercised an influence over the early evolution of the Home Rule movement. The Independent Irish Party supplied a strategy of unencumbered parliamentary opposition, and it also suggested a loose (in fact destructively loose) form of party organization and discipline: in addition there were some veterans of the Independent Party who survived to contribute to the foundation of the Home Rule movement, the most prominent of whom was G.H. Moore. Both parties expressed a mild-mannered and ultimately ineffectual interest in education and in tenant right.

The contribution of Fenianism to the Home Rule movement was (paradoxical though it may seem) much more profound than that of the Independents. Superficially the resemblance between the Independent Irish Party and the early Home Rule Party appears close (both were genteel, inchoate, sometimes directionless parliamentary bodies), but in truth the dependence of the Home Rulers on the achievement of Fenianism was much greater than their debt to any constitutional predecessor (with the arguable exception of O'Connell). For the Fenian movement achieved, through the three Manchester Martyrs and through the Amnesty move-ment, a degree of popular politicization which had not been reached since the days of repeal. Contemporary commentators and historians interpret this point in slightly different ways, but there is a shared sense of the dependence of Home Rule on the Fenian achievement. Theo Hoppen has emphasized the extent to which the Amnesty movement of the late 1860s overcame what he sees as the 'natural' local-ism of Irish politics: the Amnesty Association achieved a political 'breakthrough', creating a national movement and popularizing a national issue, especially in rural constituencies where narrow parochial concerns had for long been predominant.[77] These, for Hoppen, were the national foundations upon which the Home Rule movement built. The egotistical and tendentious F. Hugh O'Donnell introduced his *History of the Irish Parliamentary Party* (1910) with a more crude and flamboyant expression of the same argument: 'it would be quite useless for me to write this history; this history would lack its essential significance, if I were to omit or attenuate the significance of Fenianism in reviving all the forces of Irish protest against the Act of Union'.[78]

Even in its first tentative organizational form, Home Rule embodied very considerable political potential. The Home Government Association was formed in May 1870 by Isaac Butt, who was uniting Protestant Conservative dissidents with Catholic Liberals in a constitutional initiative which was blessed with the 'benevolent neutrality' of an insurrectionist body, the Irish Republican Brotherhood.[79] The demand itself, a call for the re-establishment of an autonomous Irish parliament in Dublin, had a very high level of brand recognition among Irish voters, for it was basically a resurrection of the O'Connellite call for repeal of the Union. In addition the Association benefited from the high level of national political awareness achieved by the Fenians and the Amnesty campaign; and (linked to this) it benefited from growing disillusionment with Gladstone's promises of 'justice for Ireland'. Popular Catholic expectations had been aroused by disestablishment and shattered by the prosaic reality of the Land Act (Irish Protestant disillusionment had come earlier, with the Irish Church Act, which had stimulated some limited Conservative support for the Home Government Association); Catholic liberals were also dissatisfied with Gladstone's Irish University Bill (1873), and thunderstruck by his vigorous and truculent assault on the Vatican council (his pamphlet, *The Vatican Decrees*, first published in November 1874, went through 110 editions and stands as by far the most popular of his writings).

Some aspects of this rich potential were realized; other aspects withered with a depressing swiftness. Voters were interested in the idea of Home Rule, but there was no great passion and – more important – no great willingness to subscribe; the contrast with the repeal movement in both these respects was therefore marked. In addition sectarian tensions in Ireland (and beyond), while rarely offering scope for encouragement, had taken a turn for the worse in the wake of the promulgation of papal infallibility. Butt's hopes of a propertied patriotic coalition seemed initially justified by the nervous union of Protestant and Catholic gentry which launched the Home Government Association. But in practice the suspicion entertained by the hierarchy that the Association was a Tory ruse discouraged widespread Catholic participation; and when – after the failure of Gladstone's university proposals and after his Vatican pronouncements – the bishops evinced a cautious interest in the Association, it was the turn of Protestant Tory nerves to fail. The Protestant Conservatives who had helped to create the Association feared, and particularly after the passage of the Ballot Act (1872), that they would be entrapped and overwhelmed within a popular Catholic movement. These proto-Home Rulers (men such as Edward King-Harman) would eventually find a more comfortable station within organized Unionism, and would indeed bring to Unionism a quirky sense of Irish patriotism which it has often hidden, but never entirely lost.

Some of these burdens on the Association were beyond Butt's ability to remove (though he might affect to ignore them); others (primarily the question of organizational inadequacy) were lightened when, in November 1873, the Home Government Association was superseded by a new Home Rule League and by its British sister organization, the Home Rule Confederation. Organizational defects remained, but the new League benefited from the popularity of the Home Rule concept with the farmers' clubs and – to a more qualified extent – with the Catholic Church; and, drawing upon these ancilliary but crucial resources, it managed to return 59 MPs to the House of Commons in the general election of February 1874. Many of these men were perhaps pragmatic patriots: one putative Home Rule candidate explained to a Liberal minister that his separatist manifesto was his 'only chance. I do not think anyone can make much of my Home Rule'.[80] Many were also anxious, once elected, to retain at least a nominal independence: J.G. Biggar's efforts to impose a more rigorous discipline on the party failed (fortunately for himself, in fact, since his own 'advanced' convictions and defiant obstructionism in the years 1874–7 would otherwise have been smothered). In many cases these Home Rulers owed their seats to farmers: but they were a very gentrified crew, and indeed contained many landed Liberals who had trimmed their sails to accommodate the prevailing farmer gale. There was, however, some premonition of the shape of things to come: even though the new Home Rule Party was largely landed, and even though the House of Commons as a whole was still a landed institution, two tenant farmers had been returned on the Home Rule ticket. Moreover, although Biggar's efforts to create an Irish caucus at Westminster had failed, the Home Rule Party 'demonstrated a remarkable degree of voting cohesion on Irish issues in the Parliament of 1874–80' (in contrast to the more chaotic condition of the Liberal stand on Ireland).[81]

Still, the contrasts between the Buttite party and the Parnellite party are striking. A sharp if acerbic commentator, F. Hugh O'Donnell, highlighted six areas where he felt that there were distinctions between the first Home Rulers and their (in his view) tainted 'Parnello-Gladstonian' successors.[82] Butt's party sought the restoration of an Irish parliament, as did the Parnellites, but the strong federalist tinge to Butt's (and O'Donnell's own) convictions meant that his party was concerned to promote an Irish contribution to imperial affairs in any future parliament governing 'the common Empire'. Buttite Home Rule was both federalist as well as gentrified in tone: the first Home Rulers looked to a bicameral Irish parliament, which would represent the Irish peers and command their intellectual and political resources. The first Home Rulers also repudiated any tendency towards machine politics (this in contradistinction to the formidable Parnellite caucus that emerged in the 1880s); allied with this was the original conviction that Home Rule MPs should be representatives of local opinion, and not delegates. Finally, O'Donnell stressed that the original Home Rulers repudiated any hint of sectarian ascendancy (this evidently in contrast to the influence of the Catholic Church within the Parnellite movement); and that they rejected agrarian revolution.

These characteristics stemmed in large part from the leadership supplied by Butt, which was moderate and reasoned, and – as befitted a lawyer and scholar – respectful towards British constitutional practice. This rationality and caution was deeply felt, but it was also designed to impress British parliamentarians: it was thus a subtle combination of conventionality and deference, and as such (and especially in the context of the somewhat remote and facetious Tory leadership) it was utterly ineffectual. Butt's polite demand for the consideration of Home Rule was swept aside in March 1874, when first tentatively presented ('He did not at present ask the house to concede Home Rule to Ireland. That question remained to be discussed, and perhaps to be discussed for many years').[83] His land bill, submitted in 1876, was easily defeated (45 of his own nominal supporters helped to vote it down); he was unable to satisfy his ever-suspicious clerical supporters by devising a suitable university bill; and the more raucous elements within his own support broke free from his genteel example in May, when they staged a 'scene' over the question of the Fenian prisoners. The resubmission of his demand for Home Rule in June 1876 created further uproar, with his 'supporters' offering rival and contradictory definitions of legislative independence, and the Chief Secretary, Michael Hicks Beach, and the young member for County Meath coming into conflict over the Manchester episode. This new MP, elected only in April 1875, was Charles Stewart Parnell, and his cool and simple defence of the 'Martyrs' in the face of the intimidating 'Black Michael' (as the Chief Secretary came to be known) won the sympathetic attention of Fenians.

These early trials of Butt's leadership highlighted a variety of problems. There was no firm party discipline and no clear characterization of policy: Butt defined his 'party' as a group of independent and sympathetic representatives rather than as a disciplined, machine-driven body. He had a strong respect both for property and for the Empire – a respect which tended to limit his room for manoeuvre in the Commons and his popular appeal in Ireland: he was too much of an imperialist and too much of a gentleman to regard Britain's difficulties as anything other than Ireland's difficulties, and – like Carson – his instinct was to rein in Irish opposition when Britain's diplomatic or imperial adventures looked set to bring war. In addition he did not regard parliament as a full-time occupation or commitment, and was guilty (in common with his moderate support) of frequent absenteeism: his catastrophic personal finances meant that, despite an admittedly somewhat modest 'tribute' fund, he had to maintain his career at the bar. These qualities and convictions were treated as problems by an increasingly influential and militant element within the Home Rule Party, and they were to provide the grounds for the attempted overthrow of Butt's leadership in the years between 1877 and his death in May 1879.

To argue that Butt inspired this opposition is not simply to suggest that his failings conjured it into existence: on the contrary, he created both problems as well as solutions. To a certain extent the opposition to Butt arose not from contrary strategies or convictions, but rather from a caricatured interpretation of Butt's own vision: problems arose because Parnell and his truculent allies were young men in a hurry, where Butt was an old man who appeared quite content to mark time. The anger of these young turks arose because the party was achieving little or nothing, and their response took two forms: parliamentary obstruction and the strengthening of ties with the 'advanced' nationalists outside the Commons.

Yet, while these strategies were a reaction against Butt's passivity, they owed something to his initiatives. Butt was interested in the possibility of parliamentary obstruction, although he was not prepared to carry obstruction to what he regarded as an indiscriminate or undignified level. At the conference that launched the Home Rule League, held in November 1873, he admitted that 'extreme cases might justify a policy of obstruction', though he confessed that he regarded the benefits as limited and possibly counter-productive.[84] Nevertheless, once elected, he embarked on a moderate and brief campaign of obstruction to the Conservative government's Expiring Laws Continuance Bill (1874), which brought no tangible gain but rather – for Butt – the acceptable alternative of a moral victory. The battle was renewed in the spring of 1875, with the Peace Preservation (Ireland) Bill, a measure which Butt promised to oppose with vigour: 'we believe that we can promise that the Irish party will in this matter, at least, exhaust all the forms of the house to attain their just and righteous object'.[85] But what David Thornley has called Butt's 'policy of argument' – the policy of debating and questioning in detail – was tempered with an unrelenting concern for the dignity both of the Home Rule Party and of the Commons, and in practice he could be relied upon to go to the verges of wilful obstruction, and there to stop.[86] This procedural brinkmanship caused frustration among some of his colleagues from the start: already in 1874 a different and more thorough-going version of Buttite tactics was being tested by J.G. Biggar, the MP for Cavan, a hard-dealing Belfast man with little respect for genteel conventions. By the parliamentary recess of 1876–7, it was clear that Butt's more moderate obstructionism was winning moral victories, and gentle compliments from the Conservative front bench, but little else; and there emerged within the Home Rule Party a small coterie, centred on Biggar and Parnell, who (though differing somewhat in their ultimate convictions) were prepared to develop a more ruthless approach to parliamentary procedure.

Biggar and Parnell were joined by Frank Hugh O'Donnell, returned at a by-election in January 1877, and by Edmund Dwyer Gray, the proprietor of the *Freeman's Journal*, returned for Tipperary in May 1877; there were three other obstructionists, including John O'Connor Power. Together these men abandoned the restraints of their nominal leaders and embarked upon a campaign of disruption aimed at government business. Every procedural opportunity was exploited: measures were talked down, and where natural eloquence failed, the reading of Blue Books provided a substitute. These tactics were summarized under four headings, called facetiously (by Parnell, evidently) 'Biggar's Four Gospels': '1. To work in Government time. 2. To aid anybody to spend Government time. 3. Whenever you see a Bill, block it. 4. Whenever you see a Raw [a sensitive issue?], rub it'.[87] Two episodes in this season of parliamentary warfare were of particular significance. First, in April 1877 Butt was stung by Parnell's obtuseness into making a public rebuke ('an unforgiveable sin for an Irish nationalist', F.S.L. Lyons has commented, 'to condemn fellow countrymen in a foreign country').[88] Second, the obstructionist campaign reached a well-publicized climax at the end of July 1877, with the protracted debate on the South Africa Bill, a measure designed to formalize the annexation of the Transvaal. This resulted in an all-night sitting of the House on 31 July–1 August and brought the mounting tensions between an appalled Butt and his wayward following to a head. Butt attempted to reassert his authority at a meeting of Home Rule MPs held on 6 August, but succeeded only in providing a forum for the bitter animosities that were brewing within the party. Hereafter the confrontation grew more direct, and more acrimonious.

The obstructionist tactics of the Biggar–Parnell coterie brought as little tangible gain as the genteel parliamentary gamesmanship of Isaac Butt: they did, however, arouse tremendous popular interest and enthusiasm (press reports of 'seven Irish agin the English' were calculated to fire patriotic emotions).[89] The well-publicized cussedness of Biggar and Parnell helped therefore to rally popular support for a party and for a parliamentary strategy which had otherwise failed to capture the imagination. Their actions helped to redefine Irish parliamentarianism in other ways. The obstructionists divided the Home Rule Party, humiliating Butt and discrediting his policies with a broad section of the Irish electorate: the confrontation of August 1877 was swiftly followed by Butt's deposition (at the hands of Parnell) from the Presidency of the Home Rule Confederation. But the actions that divided the obstructionists from their moderate leadership simultaneously helped to fashion links with an alternative source of support: the Fenian movement. In fact Butt's humiliation with the Home Rule Confederation probably owed much to the Fenians, who had heavily infiltrated this body.

The sudden fame of the obstructionists was attained at precisely the moment when the Clan na Gael were consolidating their influence within British and Irish Fenianism. Butt had of course launched the Home Rule League with the tacit support of some leading Irish Fenians, and his leadership had been originally sustained by memories of his defence of the Young Ireland and Fenian prisoners. However, although he pioneered the relationship between parliamentarianism and the Irish Republican Brotherhood, he reaped only scanty political profits: for, while the constitutional Fenianism of the late 1860s had helped to create the Home Rule movement, the senior leaders of the Brotherhood remained doggedly (if passively) insurrectionist. In addition, John Devoy and the Clan na Gael were decidedly unimpressed by Butt's delicate pirouetting, and put pressure on their Irish counterparts to reinforce a traditional, militant line: the influence of Clan na Gael lay behind the purge of 1876–7, when those sympathetic to the parliamentary experiment were expelled from the Brotherhood. Devoy's influence over Irish Fenianism was further affirmed with the creation in 1877 of a joint committee of the IRB and Clan na Gael, and by the high levels of funding that the Americans were supplying to their Irish brethren. But it would be wrong to infer from this either that Devoy and the Clan na Gael were all powerful, or that they were opposed in principle to parliamentarianism: the problem for Devoy lay partly with the Buttite formulation of Home Rule (his colleague William Carroll described the Home Rulers of 1879 as offering 'a heart-sickening picture, a miserable caricature of the movement of

Grattan without a scintilla of its fire and spirit'); another problem lay with the influences behind parliamentarianism.[90] Devoy and Clan na Gael were ultimately prepared to accept the parliamentary experiment, but only if it were redefined along more aggressive lines and only if they were able to exercise some degree of control over this redefinition.

The last months of Butt's leadership were characterized by two distinct but related developments. First, the animosity between the old leader and the obstructionists was becoming more overt and more highly charged. The increasingly complex and dangerous entanglements of British diplomacy at the end of the 1870s highlighted both Butt's imperial sympathies and the distance between him and his more radical following: the party was divided over the pro-Turkish policy of Disraeli's government, and over the wars in South Africa (1877–9) and Afghanistan (1878–80). Butt's humiliation of August 1877 was confirmed in 1878, when Parnell was re-elected as President of the Home Rule Confederation. In February 1879, at a conference of the by now somewhat demoralized Home Rule League, John Dillon attempted to carry a vote of no confidence in Butt's leadership: though this failed, the public condemnation of the leader's alleged near-treachery was a renewed blow. The stand-off lasted until May 1879, when Butt died; and indeed the divisions continued to ache until May 1880, when Parnell was able to over-throw the stop-gap leader (William Shaw) who had been nominated by the dying Butt and sustained by the moderates.

While Butt was increasingly beleaguered, Parnell was winning allies: Butt's isolation in 1878–9 was paralleled by the consolidation of Parnell's position, and in particular by the strengthening of his ties with Fenianism. In early 1878 Parnell met the Clan na Gael ambassador William Carroll on several occasions, including once, in March in London, when, ever slippery, he remarked that 'the Fenians want to catch us, but they are not going to': Parnell was aware that the endorsement of Clan na Gael came with a price.[91] On 24 October 1878 this price was fixed: Devoy telegraphed Parnell from the United States offering the support of the Clan na Gael, but under certain conditions including, significantly, the call for a 'vigorous agitation of the land question on the basis of a peasant proprietary'.[92] In effect the relationship between Fenianism and parliamentarianism was being recast, with a new emphasis on American financial and political support and on the centrality of the land question: the United States and Clan na Gael had played only a marginal role in Butt's calculations, and while land was important to constitutional Fenianism and to the early Home Rule League, the movement shied away from anything smacking of revolution or even agitation (the early connections between land, Fenianism and Home Rule remained, and – according to Paul Bew – provided a foundation for the agitators of 1879).[93] Devoy also wanted an abandonment of federalism – the, for Butt, crucial imperial dimension to Home Rule – and the substitution of a more general demand for self-government (a call which in fact thoroughly suited Parnell's preference for ambiguity). Devoy sought a generally more active and 'aggressive' parliamentary policy, an apparently subsidiary condition which was in fact a subtle commentary on Butt's passivity and gentility.

Parnell had substantial informal support from Fenians in Britain, Ireland and the United States, and he had no need to offer any precise response to Devoy's overture. In addition, this first 'New Departure' was rejected by the Supreme Council of the IRB in January 1879, although individual Fenians were free to pursue its tenets. The proposal was further and more fundamentally undermined by the rapidly shifting and deteriorating condition of the Irish economy, which created new political demands and opportunities. Parnell's silence, the truculence of the Supreme Council and, above all, the rural economic crisis compelled Devoy into further negotiations with the constitutionalists in the spring of 1879, which produced a reformulation of the 'New Departure' on 1 June: this offered a more specific defence of the insurrectionary position, while also defining a little more exactly the forms of land and constitutional settlement that would be satisfactory to those subscribing to the agreement. This second 'New Departure' also called for 'an absolutely independent party' created by those MPs 'elected through the public movement'.[94] But, although this informal contract apparently brought American militants and Irish parliamentarians into an agreement, it not did embody the core convictions of either partner. The Fenian commitment even to a more aggressive constitutional strategy appears to have been somewhat cool; while they saw a substantial land reform – they called for compulsory purchase – as being unattainable by normal constitutional means. For his part, Parnell had hitherto placed little emphasis on the Lalorite view, held by Devoy and Michael Davitt, that the land and national questions were insepar-able; and, unlike Devoy and Davitt, he believed that land reform was attainable by constitutional means, and might indeed prove to be the way by which landlords would be finally lured into the national movement. The great compact of 1 June therefore fudged as much as it settled; and almost certainly Parnell's agreement was highly tentative and highly qualified. Parnell had profited too much by silence and by ambiguity to be bound by the Fenians in potentially damaging ways. He was content to accept their support, while smiling icily at the terms.

One of the strengths of Parnell's political leadership rested with his cool, noncommittal appraisal of his options. Another strength, however, lay with the genial plundering of the ideas and initiatives supplied by others. For, above all, Parnell's political strength lay in opportunism. In the later 1870s his opportunity came. He was promoted to a national prominence on the strength of the tenacious obstructionist policies pioneered by Biggar; he had been taught by Butt the political potential contained within constitutional Fenianism. Now, in 1878–9, Devoy supplied a political alliance and a political agenda, resurrecting the ideas of Fintan Lalor and indeed of Butt; Michael Davitt, a recently released Fenian prisoner, supplied an organizational initiative in the shape of the Land League of Mayo, created in August 1879. More important than all this, however, was a deepening agricultural crisis, which broke the prosperity of the early and mid-1870s, and the moderate political attitudes and institutions which depended, partly, on a sense of well-being: the crisis of 1878–9 created a broadly based economic threat and widespread distress, in effect forging a rural coalition of different types of farmer and agricultural

labourer. These were the formidable tools available to the new leader of Irish nationalism at the time of his accession, in May 1880.

4.5   Idealists and Technicians: The Parnellite Party, 1880–6

> *O pallid serfs! whose groans and prayers have wearied Heav'n full long,*
> *Look up! there is a law above, beyond all legal wrong,*
> *Rise up! the answer to your prayer shall come, tornado-borne,*
> *And ye shall hold your homesteads dear, and ye shall reap the corn!*
>   Fanny Parnell, 'Hold the Harvest!' (1879)[95]

The style of Parnell's following was to a very great extent a determined reaction
against the Butt era: discipline replaced a gentlemanly freedom, vulgar demonstration
replaced eloquent remonstration, and popular militancy replaced elite diplomacy.
Isaac Butt's bourgeois homeliness was superseded by the authentic hauteur of the
Irish gentry; Butt's legalistic and scholarly precision gave way to Parnell's aristocratic and enigmatic vagueness. Butt's gradualism, indeed his resigned approach to
political debate, were replaced with ambitious demands and a compelling urgency.
Charles Stewart Parnell and his lieutenants looked elsewhere for political models
(Tim Healy, for example, drew spiritual inspiration from O'Connell and rhetorical
stimulus from John Mitchel); but their movement makes sense as much as the conscious negation of its predecessor as the lineal descendant of earlier popular protest
movements.

Parnell, despite his rather studied indifference to Irish history, acknowledged a
debt to the Independent Irish Party of the early 1850s, and this analogy provides
a valuable, if ambiguous, guide to his strategic thinking.[96] The Independents wielded
influence within the House of Commons as an – at least nominally – autonomous
grouping, content to endorse either of the main British parties and willing to exploit
any available parliamentary impasse. There were some survivors from the Independent era – the O'Gorman Mahon, Sir Charles Gavan Duffy – who were either
members of the Parnellite Party or who otherwise facilitated the Home Rule cause
(Gavan Duffy, for example, was an important agent easing communication between
the Parnellites and Tories in 1885). Like the Parnellites, the Independents were actively
endorsed by the Catholic clergy, and secured a brief electoral ascendancy through
a passionate identification with a Catholic cause (opposition to Lord John Russell's
Ecclesiastical Titles Act); like the Parnellites they combined a spiritual as well as
secular urgency, for they also drew heavily on the discontents of Irish farmers. But
Parnell was never unduly anxious about historical detail (except perhaps in the case
of his own family's ancestry and attainments), and his interest in the Independents
of the 1850s simultaneously reflected his assessment of his own achievement as well
as unconsciously flagging its limitations. For while the party benefited from the fragile
sectarian unity embodied in the Tenant League, it developed as a predominantly
Catholic institution: in addition, despite its much-vaunted 'independence', the party

was continually prey to the seductions of British parliamentary politics, as witnessed most notoriously by the case of Sadleir and Keogh. The constraints imposed by a primarily Catholic electoral base and by a Liberal parliamentary alliance would also later jeopardize the Parnellite project. Moreover, just as the Independent Irish Party was founded on tenant grievance and yet eventually lost the votes of substantial farmers, so too Parnellism – at least as defined by Parnell in 1890–1 – lost the support of those who had once been its electoral life-blood.

Parnell's career – and by extension the life of the movement which he spawned – has been defined in terms of three 'classic' phases: the years from 1875 to 1885, from 1885 to 1890, and the last brutal months of the Split, from December 1890 to October 1891.[97] In the first of these periods the Parnellite alliance was constructed – an improbable amalgam of graziers, small farmers and labourers, Dubliners and country people, Catholics and Fenians; in the second period this alliance was brought into association with an equally unwieldy electoral coalition, Gladstonian Liberalism; and through the third and last period Parnellism was either redefined or, according to recent arguments, properly articulated for the first time. Each of these phases displays Parnell's tactical skills and his alarming self-confidence in a varying light; viewed as a whole they reveal the essential but also fatal complexity of his movement.

Between 1879 and 1882 Parnell succeeded, partly through skill and partly through good fortune, in helping to raise a protest that was sufficiently potent to give him leverage over the British government, while also falling far short of the agrarian revolution that some of his more radical lieutenants had envisioned. Although Parnell had encouraged the cautious suit of the Fenians and of the Clan na Gael, and although he had emerged as one of the most prominent hardliners within the Home Rule Party, his commitment to a full-scale nationalist revolution remained decidedly cool: he identified himself with extremist agrarians, he condoned violent activity, but he remained an ardent parliamentarian with a curious concern for his own landed class, and indeed for the good order of society as a whole. His initial response to the mounting land agitation in the west of Ireland was therefore highly cautious: although he attended a key meeting at Westport, County Mayo, on 8 June 1879 (one of the gatherings which led to the creation of the Land League of Mayo in August of that year), and although he accepted the Presidency of the Irish National Land League, founded on 21 October in Dublin, he seemed to be torn between exploiting the political potential of the new land movement and shying away from the risks involved. Only after November 1879, by which time it was clear that the agrarian crisis was more than transient, did Parnell align himself irrevocably with the agrarian militants. When, in May 1880 (in the aftermath of the general election) he was elected as chairman of the Irish Parliamentary Party, he was able to add a constitutional dimension to the popular authority and the Fenian endorsement which he already possessed: one of the foundations for Parnell's later ascendancy lay with this rationalization of political leadership inside Catholic Ireland.

How did the Parnellite leadership view the rural problems that were driving the agitation of 1880–1? The essential achievement of Parnell here, as with later issues, was to preserve a semblance of unanimity within what was, in fact, a very diverse ideological environment. The Parnellite Party that developed in the House of Commons after 1880 contained a spectrum of opinion on the land question, encompassing advocates of nationalization like Davitt as well as conservatives (or pseudo-radicals) like Healy who favoured proprietorial solutions: it encompassed 'Whigs' like Captain W.H. O'Shea alongside those, like J.G. Biggar, of more 'advanced', often Fenian sympathies, who saw the land agitation as a prelude to a national peasant uprising. In fact Biggar and his like hated their 'Whig' colleagues with a passion which, if anything, exceeded their detestation of Orange Toryism: Barry O'Brien observed that 'in Ireland the Tory is regarded as an open enemy, the Whig as a treacherous friend. It is the Whigs, not the Tories, who have habitually sapped the integrity of Irish representation'.[98] The value of Parnell to his movement was that he generally occupied a mediating position between these extremes, and that, with his aristocratic credentials and personal charisma, he could create consensus out of the most unpromising materials: even Healy, his most outrageous critic in the months of the Split, accepted that one of Parnell's political talents lay in minimizing the differences that divided individual followers. Barry O'Brien, again, noted that 'Parnell's great gift was the faculty of reducing a quarrel to the smallest dimensions'.[99]

Parnell himself did not favour any *Jacquerie*, and while he was interested in the idea of a widespread peasant proprietorship, he (sometimes openly) derided the views of Davitt and other radical colleagues who looked forward to the nationalization of the land. He saw unjust legal and economic privilege as the barrier that divided landlords from active participation in the national movement, indeed perhaps national leadership: he certainly saw the hostility of the landed interest as a major obstacle to the success of the Home Rule movement. But he addressed this problem not by advocating the abolition of landlordism ('we do not want to exterminate the residential Irish landlords', he once declared) but by seeking a comprehensive redefinition of agrarian relations in a manner which removed farmer grievance without alienating the proprietor interest: the specific form that this desire took, at any rate in 1880, was voluntary land purchase on the basis of 35 years' rent payment.[100] Although recent scholarship has tended to emphasize the integrity of Parnell's political thought, it is difficult to question Paul Bew's judgement that this prescription was 'naive': Parnell evidently believed that the land war might be directed in a manner which would underpin the unity of the Irish nation and create the conditions for subsequent landlord participation.[101]

Edward Saunderson, the parliamentary leader of the Irish Unionists, once observed that Parnell controlled the 'throttle-valve of crime'; and while this was the rhetoric of partisanship, there is indeed a sense in which Parnell sought, where possible, to regulate the Land League agitation.[102] By the second half of 1880, with the more solid farmers of the south and east joining their impoverished western counterparts in the League, and with mounting bitterness and violence, there was little scope for moderation or for elaborate reflections on the future of Irish landlordism. Nevertheless, Parnell, while promoting the most radical objectives of the League, all the while underlined the need for non-violent action. Although the dividing line between 'non-violence' and violence in the activities of the League was generally pretty thin, Parnell does seem to have actively sought to redirect potentially criminal passions along a more tolerable pathway: his celebrated endorsement of 'moral suasion', or the boycott, at Ennis in September 1880 was at least in part an attempt to create a politically effective, legal strategy which might in addition provide parliamentary leverage.[103] The idea of the boycott, although not Parnell's own inspiration, came naturally to a man who knew how to cut intimates and to sustain frosty silences: the boycott was in fact Parnell's personality expressed as a policy. And although it scarcely operated in the disciplined terms which he envisioned, the boycott did at least provide the semblance of a constitutional alternative to a murderous chaos.

The London government's response to the Land League served initially to consolidate Parnell's ascendancy within the national movement. An attempt to prosecute Parnell and other leaders of the League between November 1880 and January 1881 hinted at official desperation: it was a lame, hopeless attempt to assert the authority of Dublin Castle, which promised only disaster regardless of whether the defendants were convicted or acquitted. Parnell *was* in fact acquitted, and the government rebuffed: but a conviction would have only served to further enshrine the League leaders in the popular estimation. Similarly, another legal initiative – the Protection of Person and Property (Ireland) Bill, which was enacted in March 1881 – provided Parnell and his lieutenants with a splendid parliamentary opportunity to defend Irish liberties: the climax of this measure's passage came on 3 February with the ejection of Parnell and 35 of his followers from the House of Commons. Such ministerial initiatives presented little difficulty for the Irish Party, for the arguments against coercion had been well rehearsed and the popularity within Ireland of a libertarian stance was of course assured.

But British policy in Ireland was traditionally a mixture of coercion and conciliation (even if this label has generally been applied only to Unionist policy before 1905); and it was always the conciliatory gestures that created the greatest tactical difficulties for popular Irish leaders. Gladstone's constructive approach to the land agitation came with the Land Law (Ireland) Act, passed in August 1881, and it was this measure, rather than the earlier coercive initiatives, which offered the true test of Parnell's political dexterity. The Land Act of 1881 added another component, the Land Commission, to the already labyrinthine bureaucratic machinery of the British government in Ireland: the measure made provision for the adjudication of rent levels within the courts of the Commission, and in addition it drastically curtailed the landlord's right of eviction. Tenants had the right of free sale under the terms of the new Act. This was an astonishing measure from Gladstone, a politician otherwise passionately concerned with the sanctity of contracts, with the size of government and with the status of the (English) gentry; and it was indeed recognized as a substantial concession by many in the Land League. However, the radicals within the League (such as the young John Dillon) were not prepared to perceive victory in the shape of a highly technical and ambiguous piece of legislation; nor were American militants content to see their agrarian revolution die in so miserable a fashion. Parnell therefore faced the possibility that the League would fragment over the issue, with moderates prepared to accept Gladstone's good faith, and a radical minority ('the Kilmainham party') seeking to develop the agitation. At a League convention, held in September 1881, he therefore backed a compromise formula which squared the circle of these divisions, combining elements of both positions and urging that the measure should be tested in the courts. This was in fact a brilliant piece of Parnellite ambiguity, for it simultaneously involved the effective acceptance of the measure while enabling Parnell to reassure his radicals that legal tests would expose its utter 'hollowness'. Unfortunately, Parnell's desire not to be seen to be outmanoeuvred by Gladstone and his desire to mollify his left wing each outpaced the essential caution of the test strategy (F.S.L. Lyons has called it 'fabian'); and his speeches in the autumn of 1881 were sufficiently extreme to convince the government that he was, after all, seeking to wreck the Act and thereby to destabilize the country.[104] The reality was, as Barry O'Brien observed, that Parnell's own political position rested on his ability to charm the militants, without actually offering any commitment: 'Parnell derived his political ascendancy in no small degree from the fact that he walked all the time on the verge of treason felony'.[105] But unsurprisingly, the skill of this performance did not impress the Chief Secretary for Ireland, W.E. Forster, or (at any rate in 1881) Gladstone: and on 13 October Parnell's high-wire act took him into Kilmainham Gaol.

Imprisonment does not seem to have been a conscious goal for Parnell. Nor was it a particularly grim experience, to the extent that he had a comfortable cell and was allowed various freedoms (including, curiously for a suspected traitor, the opportunity to practise his marksmanship with an airgun). However, despite its cushioned nature, imprisonment appears to have scarred Parnell: he was separated from his mistress, Mrs Katherine O'Shea, while she was pregnant with their child; in addition gaol brought constant supervision and indeed (paradoxically) greater accessibility for a man who was distinguished by his pride and by his need to escape periodically from all forms of society. But, as he readily understood, the petty humiliations of Kilmainham brought with them certain political opportunities. Parnell prophesied famously that, when imprisoned, 'Captain Moonlight' – agrarian terrorism – would take his place; and he and his gaoled lieutenants – Dillon, Sexton, Brennan and Kettle – went some way to fulfilling this prediction by issuing a call for a rent strike to be maintained 'until the government relinquishes the existing system of terrorism and restores the constitutional rights of the people'.[106] In fact Parnell's 'place' within the national movement, though ascendant, was hard to define; and he and his imprisoned colleagues were replaced not simply by crime but by a mixture of agrarian violence, constitutional procedures and women's political action. With the suppression of the League on 20 October, the agitation threatened to break: some farmers were willing to take advantage of the new Land Act, while there was simultaneously an increase in the numbers of those willing to commit crime in the interests of their vision of agrarian justice. The women activists of the Ladies' Land League, founded in January 1881 and led by Anna Parnell, sought to maintain the League journal, *United Ireland*, to reinforce the 'No Rent' manifesto and to look after the welfare of the manifesto's casualties – the evicted tenants: some

£70,000 was paid out by the Ladies' Land League between October 1881 and May 1882 by way of relief to these victims of the Land War. One of the statistical wonders of the women's operation (as well as one of its key weapons) was a detailed rent dossier, the so-called Book of Kells, which assembled estate information from all parts of Ireland and which attracted the bemused interest even of the men.[107] In general, however, the women had few friends among their male counterparts (Davitt was an exception): the grudging respect that was occasionally offered came only as a result of the remarkable moral courage and quick-wittedness of women activists such as Hanna Reynolds. Magnanimity came more easily with time. The significance of the women's League and its trenchant pursuit of its goals came eventually to be recognized even by aggressively unsympathetic commentators such as F.H. O'Donnell, for whom Anna Parnell was the 'Grande Mademoiselle' and the women Leaguers 'Captain Moonlight in petticoats'. The veteran Fenian John O'Leary offered a crisper and less patronizing verdict: 'they may not have been right, but they were suppressed because they were honester and more sincere than the men'.[108]

The arrest of Parnell and the other leaders of the League had been decided by the British cabinet; and it was the belief of ministers, in particular Forster, that this decapitation of the League would render it lifeless. But though the operations of the League were undoubtedly checked by the imprisonments, its connection with crime was more shadowy than ministers understood; and it became clear during the winter of 1881–2 that the detentions did not present any quick-fix solution to the problem of agrarian violence. Forster's essentially coercive strategy was by this stage discredited within the cabinet, many of whom felt that 'Buckshot' had not only strayed too far from the path of Liberal righteousness but (more unforgiveably) had done so without evident gain: certainly by early 1882 Forster appears to have lost the confidence of Gladstone. Forster's vulnerability was scented by the Parnellites, who sought successfully to by-pass the Chief Secretary in order to gain direct access to the more amenable Prime Minister: the self-regarding F.H. O'Donnell, operating evidently on his own initiative, put himself in touch with Gladstone's son, Herbert (the tactic was repeated by Healy in 1885, using Henry Labouchere as an intermediary); more famously, and more productively, Captain W.H. O'Shea opened up a channel of communication between the imprisoned Parnell and both Joseph Chamberlain (one of Forster's cabinet critics) and Gladstone. The end product of this diplomacy was the so-called Kilmainham 'treaty', a political understanding which bound Gladstone to deal with the leaseholders and with the rent arrears question while obliging Parnell to accept this elaboration of the Act of 1881 as 'a practical settlement of the land question' and a basis for future cooperation.[109] Gladstone was thus prepared to accept Parnell at his own valuation – that is as a substitute for 'Captain Moonlight'; and, accordingly, he and fellow inmates were released from Kilmainham on 2 May 1882, their freedom coinciding with the resignation of the weary and undermined Forster.

Parnell's release was greeted with enthusiasm by most nationalists except his radical lieutenants (who saw the 'treaty' as a climb-down) and his own family (who exhibited the studied passionlessness of their caste). But any militant protest or party division was out of the question, for on 6 May 1882 the new Chief Secretary, Lord Frederick Cavendish, and T.H. Burke, the Under-Secretary for Ireland, were murdered in Phoenix Park, Dublin, within sight of the Viceregal Lodge and to the bemusement of the lord lieutenant, Earl Spencer, who witnessed, uncomprehendingly, the fatal scuffle. Radical and moderate Leaguers were broadly united in their attitude (sympathy for the newly arrived Englishman, Cavendish, was sometimes greater than for Burke, an Irish Catholic gentleman who had been associated with earlier coercion); certainly Parnell, and the more militant Davitt and Dillon, together signed a popular manifesto which condemned the two murders in trenchant language. Radicals and moderates were also united in opposing the vigorous coercion bill that was introduced, perhaps inevitably, in the wake of the murders and in the context of English popular outrage. The Phoenix Park 'outrage' therefore temporarily prolonged the unity of the Leaguers; but, in reality, just as (in the words of Margaret O'Callaghan) the 'murders had a direct but not qualitative impact on Liberal policy', so they affected the shape but not the form of nationalist politics.[110] The Liberals brought coercion and an arrears settlement, as in fact they had planned; and Parnell, stimulated and aided by the Phoenix Park murders, continued on the more centrist path which he had charted with the Kilmainham 'treaty'.

In the heat of the Split, in October 1891, Parnell lamented that the 'terrible tragedy of the Phoenix Park' had robbed him of the opportunity to secure many legislative benefits for Ireland; but this was hyperbole.[111] In fact, although the murders temporarily cut off the possibility of any constructive relationship between Irish nationalists and the British government, such a bond – even when attainable – was always highly problematic for the Irish: as Parnell himself remarked in March 1884, 'I do not depend upon any English political party. I should advise you not to depend upon any such party'.[112] Rather, the murders, in temporarily discrediting a hardline position, permitted Parnell to reconstruct the national movement without the burden of his radicals, and along lines closer to his own political preferences. In May–June 1882 he was able, with little difficulty, to distance himself both from Dillon's renewed defence of boycotting and from Davitt's advocacy of land nationalization: indeed, Dillon, threatened with tuberculosis and dismayed by his leader's apparent change of direction, subsequently went into temporary retirement. Davitt published at this time his conversion from the standard League goal of peasant proprietorship to the more radical and, by the standards of the day, eccentric aim of land nationalization: his earnest efforts to detail his new-found principles were swotted with ruthless ease by Parnell ('if I were Davitt I would never define. The moment he becomes intelligible he is lost').[113] In addition, and with the reluctant consent of Dillon, Parnell moved against the radical and independent-minded Ladies' Land League, cutting off their funds and trading the discharge of their debts in return for their 'voluntary' disbandment; but the suppression of the Ladies' Land League was in keeping not simply with Parnell's concern for radical dissent but also with his interest in the funds of the movement (the Ladies' Land League, with its generous concern for the evicted tenants, was an extremely expensive machine). Moreover, the women's sometimes flippant attitude towards Parnell's leadership can scarcely have helped their cause: on one occasion Parnell and Dillon were greeted in the Ladies' Land League office by a sarcastic rendition of Gilbert and Sullivan's '20 love sick maidens we'.[114] With the 'left' wing of the land movement temporarily stunned, and with a tightened grasp on finance, Parnell (as F.H. O'Donnell observed) had achieved the freedom 'to make the next league'.[115] On 17 October 1882 the new Irish National League was launched, a body which differed from its banned predecessor both in having self-government as its primary function and in having Parnell as its effective creator and undisputed master. The 'uncrowned king' of 1880 had at last found a throne of sorts.

The hallmark of the new structure was organizational discipline and centralization. Although Davitt argued for substantial local representation in the government of the National League, the extent of his temporary eclipse may be measured by the fact that the League was effectively run by the Irish Parliamentary Party; it need hardly be repeated that the Parliamentary Party was by now effectively run by Parnell. In time this discipline was further tightened: heterodox local opinion on matters of strategy was efficiently smothered, as were several feeble efforts to reject central advice on the selection of parliamentary candidates. When the next general election loomed – at the end of 1885 – a rigorously policed organizational hierarchy was in place, responsible largely to Parnell himself: a small group of MPs, chaired by Parnell, vetted the lists of prospective parliamentary candidates, who were then presented to the appropriate county or borough conventions of the League. These had all the trappings of representative democracy, albeit with a clericalist colouring: each local League body had the right to forward four delegates to the county convention, where they were joined by any interested Catholic priest and one or two representatives of the Parliamentary Party. The candidate who emerged from this process was self-evidently the creature of the parliamentary leadership; and this subservient relationship was made explicit through the famous party pledge (introduced in 1884) by which the candidate undertook to 'sit, act and vote with the Irish parliamentary party' and, furthermore, to resign from his seat if called upon to do so by a majority of the party.[116]

All the parties in the United Kingdom were seeking to come to terms with the 'management' of democracy in the decades after the Parliamentary Reform Act of 1867; but – certainly in the opinion of its detractors – the Parnellite structure owed more to Tammany Hall than to any British exemplar. What was unusual about the Irish National League was not the concealment of central authority by the plumage of local representation (common enough within parallel British party organization), but rather the completeness of this central authority. For Parnell's party was a more formidable electoral machine than anything produced by contemporary British or northern Irish politics (and there were numerous organizational initiatives within British and Irish Toryism and British Liberalism); and, where the League's constitution did not function satisfactorily, then Parnell's charismatic leadership generally made good any shortcoming.

The party thus had a popular and enigmatic leader, and a local organization which masked central manipulation with a semblance of local authority. In addition to this battery of secular resources, the Parnellites now – by 1883–4 – added the author-ity of the Church. Viewed in a certain light this was a rather remarkable develop-ment. Parnell, a member of the Church of Ireland, had demonstrated some sympathy with Fenianism (according to one suggestion, recently revived, he actu-ally joined the Brotherhood immediately after his release from Kilmainham); aside from his Protestantism and his Fenian affinities (both distasteful to the hierarchy of the 1880s), Parnell had given support to the famous freethinker, Charles Bradlaugh, in his efforts to take his seat as MP for Northampton.[117] Moreover, for most of the hierarchy the Land League had been a highly suspect organization, partly because of the involvement of individual Fenians and partly because of its associ-ation with agrarian violence. But the new National League, though it still attracted some Fenian interest, was not the threat to social order that its predecessor had been. The Land League of 1879 had been founded among the impoverished small farmers of Connacht, and while it had developed from these origins, it never lost its association with what Tom Garvin has defined as the 'pre-modern, unsustained and sporadic' politics of the west: the National League of 1882, by contrast, was rooted in the relatively prosperous midland counties, where there was traditionally less violence and where the middling farmers and shopkeepers were loyal sons of the Church.[118] In addition Parnell, though a Protestant, had at least the merit of being a bad Protestant; and by 1883–4 he had also abandoned his Bradlaugh sympathies and was as deferential to the bishops as the most staunch clericalist.

The Church rewarded this obeisance, and the general rightward shift of Parnellism, with a cautious endorsement. The Parnell testimonial (a national fund designed to rescue Parnell from debt and to reward him for his patriotic achievement) was effec-tively launched by Dr Croke, the flamboyant, nationally minded Archbishop of Cashel, in March 1883. A much more significant affirmation came in October 1884, when the hierarchy entrusted the care of Irish Catholic educational interests to the Irish Party and its Protestant leader. By 1885 the clergy were effectively being built into the local League organization and were given an honoured position within the county conventions: in return they strived to maintain contact with the League headquarters in Dublin and worked to ensure the enactment of central policy at the local level. In addition shifts within the hierarchy favoured the Parnellite cause: the death of the highly circumspect Cardinal McCabe in February 1885 and the succession of William Walsh to the archbishopric of Dublin were particularly useful developments for the Irish Parliamentary Party.

Parnellism brought together the Church with elements of Fenianism (this, accord-ing to Barry O'Brien, had been a particular goal for Parnell); it united shopkeepers, farmers of all descriptions and the Dublin working and middle classes.[119] As always, it remained to be seen where the manufacturer of this formidable alliance planned to take his creation: as J.J. O'Kelly had remarked of Parnell in 1878, 'I am not sure he knows exactly where he is going'.[120] Indeed, to a certain extent the details of the Parnellite agenda evolved pragmatically, and in response to the opportunities supplied by British parliamentary politics. Moreover, it was also easier to define Parnellism in terms of what it was professedly *not*, rather than as a more proactive ideology: after 1882 Parnellism was clearly not a land agitation, nor was it a radical agrarian philosophy (in April 1884 Parnell repeated his condemnation of land nationalization and of the supra-national class alliance favoured by Davitt).[121] Nor, despite this gradualism, was the movement ever going to be a magnet for northern Protestants: an attempt to launch a Parnellite 'invasion of Ulster' in 1883 had certainly brought an electoral victory for T.M. Healy in Monaghan, but it had also inspired a loyalist backlash culminating at Rosslea, Fermanagh, in October when rival Orange and League crowds met in angry confrontation (this was a key event in the political education of notable early Unionists such as Edward Saunderson). Even some of the most celebrated expressions of the League's nationalism were notable for their ambiguity: Parnell's famous declaration at Cork on 21 January 1885 that 'no man has the right to fix the boundary to the march of a nation' was as evasive as it was idealistic.[122]

In fact there is a sense in which the growth and definition of the party and the League occurred in ways which were antithetical to Parnellism. Parnellism was partly an exercise in electoral technique: it was concerned with the effective regimentation of popular politics. For this reason, Parnell greeted the parliamentary reform and redistribution measures of 1884–5 with some coolness: these Acts expanded the Irish electorate from around 4.4 per cent of the population to some 16 per cent, incorporating small farmers and labourers and shifting seats from old underpopulated boroughs such as Dungannon (which boasted 279 voters in 1881) to burgeoning new cities such as Belfast (21,989 voters in 1881). But if Parnell was not overly concerned with the adequate representation of the industrial north-east, neither was he anxious to promote the democratic rights of the rural poor, whom (in the opinion of Lyons) he saw as susceptible to 'subversive influences'. In fact the existing electorate, created through the Irish Franchise Act of 1850, had served Parnellism well, for it was not only small but also socially well defined – that is to say, it was open to easy and efficient management. And yet, despite these qualms, the reform and redistribution measures of 1884–5 not only failed to radicalize the Irish electorate, but in fact helped to consolidate the Parnellite stranglehold over popular Catholic politics (85 Home Rulers were returned from Irish constituencies at the general election of 1885, while one English constituency – the Scotland division of Liverpool – returned an additional nationalist in the shape of T.P. O'Connor). Furthermore, this accession of strength occurred at a time when neither of the main British parties was thoroughly secure. The parliamentary reform of 1884–5 served therefore to strengthen decisively both the Parnellite ascendancy in Ireland as well as the party's leverage inside the House of Commons.

Moreover, the essence of Parnellism was its commitment to the idea of an Irish Parliamentary Party, untrammelled by compromising English alliances. And yet the search for Home Rule brought Parnell, perhaps inevitably, into harness alongside Gladstone and the Liberals. It was the Liberals who, through the Kilmainham 'treaty', had first tried to establish some form of working relationship with the Irish Party; and it was one of the progenitors of the 'treaty', the Liberal cabinet minister Joseph Chamberlain, who in November 1884 sought to excavate the idea of an understanding between the parties. Chamberlain's diplomacy, which again involved Captain O'Shea as an intermediary with Parnell, was based upon the offer of local government reform and administrative devolution in the shape of a Central Board for Ireland. By May 1885 a deal had emerged along the broad lines of the 'treaty' of 1882, whereby a legislative concession was traded for Parnellite cooperation: Parnell affirmed that he and his party would oppose but not obstruct a renewal of crimes legislation, provided that the government conceded a local government reform by way of return. Chamberlain's proposal was rejected by the Liberal cabinet in its dying weeks (the government fell on 9 June); and in any event Parnell had all along made clear that local government was not a substitute for Home Rule. But, though the Chamberlain initiative died, the lure of Irish votes and the desirability of an alliance with a skilled and dangerous parliamentary grouping remained.

Indeed, at first glance these temptations seemed to influence the incoming minority Tory government no less than the retiring Liberal ministers. And yet, it is hard to escape the impression that the Tory leadership, though concerned not to have the Parnellites as obstructive opponents, was not in fact overly keen to acquire them as allies. There were certainly tentative overtures: the Tory and Parnellite chief whips met at the time of the formation of the first Salisbury government, in June 1885, as did Parnell and Lord Randolph Churchill, a talented but unpredictable young-ster among the new ministers. The most famous of these meetings occurred on 1 August between Parnell and the Tory lord lieutenant for Ireland, Lord Carnarvon. But, though this diplomacy evidently left Parnell with the impression that the Conservatives might well deliver a reform (Carnarvon had apparently expressed his sympathy for Irish Home Rule and his hopes for the satisfaction of Irish 'national aspirations'), the fact was that, unlike the Chamberlain 'Central Board' exchanges, there was never any concrete proposal, nor indeed anything approaching a sustained and purposeful negotiation.[123] Moreover, if the Tories were courting the Parnellites, then – despite some impatient and offensive outbursts from Churchill – they were also making sure of their own Irish party, through the effective application of patronage. Irish Tories were in fact well represented within the new ministry; and it is often forgotten that an Irish Tory – the Lord Chancellor for Ireland, Lord Ashbourne – was to have been present at the Parnell–Carnarvon interview, but for some reason (almost certainly regard for his own political skin) stayed away. Thus it would be quite wrong to underestimate the political subtlety of Parnell's Tory opponents: there is every indication that, while there were some rare figures, like Carnarvon, who were broadly sympathetic to the Irish case, and some pragmatists, such as Churchill, then the most influential elements of the leadership, especially Lord Salisbury, were in principle too far removed from Irish nationalism to toler-ate any worthwhile understanding between the parties. Salisbury's celebrated speech at Newport on 7 October 1885 'could not be, indeed was not misunderstood' as an expression of Unionist conviction and gradualist reformism.[124] And aside from issues of principle, political practicalities militated against any serious relationship with Parnell: such a deal would have delivered the support of the Irish nationalists, but at the price of losing not just the Irish Unionists but also their backbench Tory sympathizers (it is important to remember the influence of militant Protestantism and Orangeism in British, no less than Ulster constituencies). A deal with Parnell would have won disciplined but no doubt demanding and troublesome Home Rule allies, while simultaneously dividing the British Tories and throwing the Irish Tories into rebellion. The general thrust of Tory policy was therefore to keep its options open, and to keep the Parnellites dangling. Indeed, by the time of the general election, in November–December 1885, British Tories had been able to win the endorsement of Parnell at no cost whatever to themselves.

The Tories were in fact of greater value to Parnell than he was to them. Parnell appears to have been initially overawed by Gladstone, but he also seems to have been lastingly embittered by his gaol sentence, and for this in part he blamed the Grand Old Man (Tim Healy, on the other hand, was a significantly more fervent convert to the Gladstonian mystique). Gladstone, with his high moral tone and didactic approach to political life, was (despite his high opinion of Parnell's political talent) far removed from Home Rule realpolitik; while, for his part, Parnell seems to have cultivated a private contempt for Gladstone, which was only fully aired through the infamous Manifesto of 29 November 1890. Temperamentally, Parnell was therefore closer to Churchillian cynicism than to the rarefied atmosphere of Gladstonian Liberalism; but he must also have recognized that only the Tories, with their control of the House of Lords, were in a position to deliver a major constitutional reform such as Home Rule. In addition Paul Bew has identified the fundamental significance, for Parnell, of an alliance with the Tories: 'it was his old dream of a "class conservative" government which inspired him'.[125] Practical politics, as well as personal – perhaps even ideological – affinities all help to explain Parnell's interest in the Tories. But it was a profitless suit: the general election brought a Liberal majority over the Tories of 85, with the Irish Parliamentary Party holding the balance between the two. By mid-December it was evident that the outgoing Tory government would not launch any Home Rule proposal either by themselves or in concert with the Liberals; and at the same time it was becoming increasingly clear that, given this coyness, Gladstone was prepared to act on his own for Ireland.

The tentative announcement of Gladstone's conversion to Home Rule on 17 December – the 'Hawarden Kite' – marks, perhaps, the summit of Parnell's achievement. The comprehensive shake-down that occurred in British and Irish politics between January and July 1886, bringing a hardening of the division between Unionist and Home Ruler, simultaneously defined the extent and the limitations of this Parnellite victory. Gladstone's espousal of Home Rule certainly brought an end to the studied ambiguity of Tory policy: after January the Tory leadership came out firmly on the side of loyalism and of coercion. The auction which Parnell had sought to encourage between the two British parties for the Home Rule trophy had therefore abruptly ended, with Gladstone emerging as the inevitable purchaser – but a purchaser who could not in fact pay the price of legislative success. For the flinty attitude of the Tories meant that, short of a major constitutional upheaval, Gladstone's conversion would always remain a symbolic rather than a substantive victory.

If the disposition of forces in the British parliament secured the fate of Home Rule, then neither Gladstone's diplomacy nor his actual measure did much to challenge the force of the inevitable. When Gladstone formed his administration in early February 1886 there remained some confusion about his intentions towards Ireland – this despite the 'Hawarden Kite'. If (as has been remarked) Parnell was a master of 'opaque inertia', then equally Gladstone was adept at opaque activity: having promised his colleagues that no decision on Home Rule would be taken without full cabinet discussion, he proceeded in private to draft an interconnected settlement which linked a land purchase measure with (more famously and controversially) a Home Rule bill.[126] Senior Liberal ministers were kept in the dark about this initiative until the end of February (for the land bill) and the beginning of March (for Home Rule): equally, but perhaps less surprisingly, there was little contact in this period with Parnell or his lieutenants. It would be futile to argue that this brusque treatment of colleagues and general lack of consultation scuppered the Home Rule proposal, for Gladstone would in any event have faced great opposition (the Whig elder, Lord Hartington, had in fact refused to join the ministry on the suspicion of its Home Rule sympathies). But Gladstone's prayerful sense that he had embarked upon a divinely blessed course, and his practical desire to bind Parnellism into a conservative settlement, both allowed him to underestimate the convictions and sensitivities of his own colleagues. He banked rightly on the party loyalty of some, like his Leader of the House of Commons Sir William Harcourt; but even Harcourt was amazed at the 'criminal lunacy' of Gladstone's proposals and frightened by his bland approach to the possible departure of influential ministers such as Chamberlain.[127] Indeed, when Gladstone's hand was at last called, at a cabinet meeting held on 13 March, Chamberlain and a fellow radical, G.O. Trevelyan, both resigned, thereby threatening both the future of the bill and of the administration itself.

If the politics of the Home Rule Bill were problematic, then the details of the measure caused equal difficulty, even for those who were sympathetic to the Irish claim for self-government. The bill was introduced into the House of Commons on 8 April, followed by the Land Purchase Bill on 16 April. Home Rule was at last given a definition – as a single-chamber assembly in Dublin, comprising two 'orders' of representative, one elite and one more popular, who together would legislate for Ireland but within strict parameters. All issues affecting the crown, defence and foreign affairs were reserved for Westminster, whose general supremacy over the Irish assembly was affirmed. Control of customs and excise, where the bulk of Irish revenue sprung, remained in London. Irish customs revenue would, it was proposed, be used to fund Ireland's 'imperial contribution' of just under £4.25 million and an Irish contribution of £360,000 to the United Kingdom national debt. Any remaining balance might be returned to Dublin, where, together with any direct taxes levied by the new assembly, it would constitute the revenue of the Home Rule administration. But, while the United Kingdom parliament continued in effect to tax Ireland, at the same time Gladstone proposed that Irish representation at Westminster be abolished. Vernon Bogdanor has defined three broad areas of difficulty with this measure, of which the issue of representation is one; Gladstone in fact had to promise to reconsider this question, and his second Home Rule measure contained an alternative formula.[128] The second area of difficulty relates to the problematic division of taxation powers between the London and Dublin authorities (Parnell was unhappy with the British retention of customs and excise duties, and – even setting aside his particular case – it is clear that the proposed settlement contained the potential for a longlasting friction between the two parliaments). The last and related area of difficulty rests with the claimed supremacy of Westminster, which would certainly have been an irritant for nationalists, while in no sense appeasing the fears of Unionists that Home Rule implied imperial disintegration.

The broad approach of the Parnellites to the challenge of the Home Rule debate combined an ongoing concern for party unity and discipline with a desire to dampen any potentially damaging and distracting unrest in Ireland. Even in February, before the new government had announced its proposed settlement, Parnell was fighting to sustain the discipline of his movement: Justin McCarthy observed that his chief was 'nervously afraid of anything being said or done which might give our enemies the slightest chance or handle against him'.[129] It is partly (though only partly) in this context that the Galway by-election of February 1886 should be judged: here Parnell sought to impose Captain W.H. O'Shea as the nationalist candidate. But O'Shea, whom Parnell was simultaneously advancing and cuckolding, was unacceptable to many senior nationalists; and a serious rift was avoided only because Parnell announced, startlingly, that he held 'a parliament for Ireland in the hollow of my hand' and that he and the nation therefore required loyalty from both the electors of Galway and the party.[130] Elsewhere in Ireland T.C. Harrington, the Parnellite MP for Dublin (Harbour), fought to reinforce the rule of the National League and to rein in the agrarian militants. Even John Dillon, normally aggressive, spoke at this time (16 February) in favour of moderation.

This caution remained the hallmark of the Parnellite movement, both within and beyond Westminster, until the summer of 1886, by which time the fate of the Home Rule Bill had been decided. Although party members recognized problems with Gladstone's proposal (voting by orders, the imperial contribution, customs, the ongoing British control of the Royal Irish Constabulary were all mentioned), their tactic was to provide a qualified welcome while postponing the consideration and amendment of detail to the appropriate moment in the parliamentary timetable: the committee stage. Parnell's own chief contribution to the discussion on the measure came on 7 June, in the final stages of the second reading debate. On this occasion he accepted the bill as a final settlement of Irish national demands, while explaining the modification of his earlier call for a restitution of Grattan's parliament; he offered some rather formulaic reassurances to the Ulster Unionist minority, couched in the language of 'one nation' patriotism. He sought to rattle Tory complacency by revealing some of the details of his conversation with Lord Carnarvon in the previous summer. But even if all this constituted (in the words of John Morley) 'one of the most masterly speeches that ever fell from him', it was to no avail.[131] For the issue had already effectively been decided a week earlier, on 31 May, when Joseph Chamberlain and some 50 disaffected Liberal MPs had agreed to rebel against their party leadership and vote against the bill. With these defections, and others, and stolid Tory resistance, the bill was rejected on the second reading division by a majority of 30 votes. Gladstone immediately dissolved parliament in order to take the issue to the country; and at the ensuing general election (of July 1886), while Ireland reaffirmed its commitment to Home Rule, Britain, especially England, pronounced in favour of the Union. This was to remain the broad pattern of United Kingdom politics until at least 1906, and arguably until 1918.

It is sometimes said that in 1886 Parnell 'undid' Parnellism, and the grounds for this suggestion are not hard to locate.[132] In 1886 Parnell bound his movement to Gladstonian Liberalism, repudiating his earlier conviction that the Irish Party should be free to scavenge for political gain. In 1886 Parnell accepted Home Rule as a 'final' settlement of Ireland's claims, thereby in fact agreeing a boundary to the march of his nation and repudiating his earlier grandiloquent claim at Cork. In 1886 Parnell moved to distance himself further from the agrarian militants who had been an essential element of the Parnellite alliance. Moreover, if the essence of Parnellism was a cool technical fascination with the mechanisms of power, and if Parnell had hitherto allowed this fascination to conquer any personal or family feeling (as in the suppression of the Ladies' Land League), then the Galway by-election witnessed a damaging confrontation between private sensitivity and political advantage. In sum, Parnell seemed to be redefining the ideals, the strategies, even the very substance of Parnellism.

But a true estimate of the changes wrought in 1886 depends on the original definition of Parnellism. Parnell's political make-up included a core of idealism which was swathed in pragmatism and egocentricity. Parnellism was in practice a combination of hazy patriotic principles and well-defined bargaining skills: its essence was as much negotiation as anything else. By implication Parnellism, changing subtly with the settlement of each bargain, was a fluid concept. Parnell's understanding with the Liberals in 1886 certainly carried echoes of the 'treaty' of 1882 and the abortive deal on Chamberlain's Central Board scheme in 1885; but – as was made patently clear in 1890–1, Parnell did not see the new alliance as an article of faith for his movement, but rather as a transient phase in its ongoing development. For as long as the Tories remained committed to, indeed dependent on, the Union, then the opportunities for political brokerage at Westminster remained painfully constrained. Viewed in this light, the 'union of hearts' formed in 1886 represented not the negation of Parnellism but rather its affirmation. For Parnellism was as much about deals as ideals.

Finally, although 1886 is frequently seen as a turning point in Parnellite development, perhaps the true redefinition of Parnell's politics came earlier, in 1882. After 1886 Parnell pursued a comparatively rightward course, distancing himself from the renewal of agrarian agitation and emerging in 1889, unscathed by the Pigott forgeries, as the darling of Gladstonian Britain. But the irony of the Pigott letters was that they purported to show Parnell's sympathy with the Phoenix Park assassins of 1882: the reality was that, while Parnell had certainly kept some very strange company (he had met the future Clan na Gael bomber, William Lomasney, in February

1881), he was clearly horrified by the murders of Burke and Cavendish. Margaret O'Callaghan and others have identified an increasing distance between Parnell and those militant nationalists in the IRB and elsewhere with whom he had once flirted (if Patrick Maume is correct, and Parnell – with spectacular mistiming – had joined the Fenians on 2 or 3 May 1882, then his concern may have been all the greater).[133] The formation of the vigorously disciplined gradualist National League in October 1882 may or may not have been a partial response to the threat perceived in the Phoenix Park murders; but it marked an acceleration in Parnell's drift towards a much less radical political position than that which he had occupied in 1880–1. Viewed in this light, Parnell's political stand between 1886 and 1890 was not so much a centrist novelty as merely the fulfilment of an agenda laid down in 1882.

4.6   A Union of Hearts and a Broken Marriage: Parnellism, 1886–91

Although it has been argued that the core of Parnellism was laid bare in the months of the Split (November 1890–October 1891), in fact the initial illumination both of Parnell and of his movement came earlier, beginning in 1886. Thereafter Parnell's increasingly cool attitude towards agrarian militancy was exposed, as was his ambivalent attitude towards cooperation with the Liberals. The early history of Parnellism was unmasked by the Special Commission appointed to investigate the Land League and, inferentially, the Pigott forgeries; the private history of Parnell and Mrs O'Shea, known for some years to parliamentarians, was finally revealed to a broader public in December 1889, when Captain O'Shea filed for divorce. One unremarked casualty of the polarization of British and Irish politics at this time was therefore the Parnellite enigma. It would be wrong to argue that Parnell ceased to exercise a charm and a fascination; but it is clear, however, that his room for manoeuvre was constricted, that his political options were limited and difficult, and that, lacking cover in the political limelight, he was becoming both increasingly high-handed and inaccessible even to favoured colleagues. It is hard to question Paul Bew's judgement that, had it not been for the divorce case revelations, Parnell would have survived as Irish leader; but equally, it does not seem unduly fanciful to suggest that Parnell's strategic confinement between 1886 and 1890, and his irritability and allusiveness, all inspired tensions among his followers which were aired only during the Split.[134]

Parnell had for long been divided from some of his lieutenants on the issue of land agitation: his ambiguous response to the Land Act of 1881 had disappointed some militants, as had the Kilmainham 'treaty' and the gradualism of the National League. Davitt was distressed to learn from Parnell that he saw land agitation as having little role to play in a future Home Rule Ireland; and he may have been more dismayed than amused by Parnell's sardonic observation that he, Davitt, would in all probability be arrested by the new Home Rule executive ('the first thing which I should do [as Irish Secretary] would be to lock you up').[135] But, these differences

aside, Parnell had been President of the Land League and had been careful to associate himself, at least in spirit, with some of his most hardline colleagues. With the
renewal of the land agitation between 1886 and 1890, Parnell's relationship with
the hardliners became more distant. He was probably consulted by the authors of
the Plan (though he later denied this); he certainly counselled O'Brien to 'set bounds'
to the operations of the Plan otherwise 'we shall be bankrupt and the Liberals
will shake us off'.[136] In general his attitude was one of mild sympathy and disdain:
in public pronouncements in 1887 he distanced himself both from the origins
and operation of the Plan, urging restraint on the Irish people. In both private and
in public the integrity of the Liberal alliance was professedly his chief concern (although
even here – as will be made clear – there was some ambiguity).

Some of the economic conditions that had combined to fuel the Land War of
1879–81 (especially a fall in crop and livestock prices) re-emerged in the late 1880s;
and there was a corresponding effort by some veterans of the Land League to regen-
erate an agitation. This initiative was led by John Dillon, William O'Brien and
T.C. Harrington; and in October 1886 Harrington published a 'Plan of Campaign'
in the Parnellite organ, *United Ireland*. The Plan has been described by F.S.L. Lyons
as 'a device for collective bargaining on individual estates' – a proposal by which
tenants on an estate would combine to establish an acceptable level of rent, which,
if it was refused by the landlord, would be pooled in an estate fund: this would
then be used to pay the maintenance and legal costs of those tenants who suffered
eviction as a result of their defiance.[137] It was accepted that the National League
would make good any shortfall in funding. The most recent historian of the Plan,
Laurence Geary, has argued that, although 'it was more extensive than has hitherto
been realised', still only some 203 estates (or 1 per cent of the total number) were
affected.[138] In most of these cases the targeted landlord was chosen with care, the
chief consideration being his (occasionally her) financial state: indebted – that is
to say malleable – landlords were favoured victims.

The new Tory and Unionist ministry responded to the challenge of the Plan in
a variety of ways. The original Tory administrative team (Sir Michael Hicks Beach
as Chief Secretary, Sir Redvers Buller as Under-Secretary) adopted a comparatively
emollient tone, highlighting a link between hardship and violence and looking benignly
at some of Parnell's legislative suggestions; but Hicks Beach was replaced in March
1887, and Buller survived him by only a few months. The new Chief Secretary, Arthur
James Balfour, combined preciosity and ruthlessness (he had a background both
as an evicting Secretary of State for Scotland as well as a china-collecting, philosophizing dandy). His Under-Secretary, Sir Joseph West Ridgeway, adapted himself
well to the tenor of the new regime, possessing what Balfour deemed to be 'an advantage of immeasurable proportions for developing a proper approach to Irish
administration' – namely a complete ignorance of the country.[139]

As with the Liberals and the Land League, so the Tories sought to enact special
crimes legislation: the Criminal Law Amendment Act, or 'Jubilee Coercion Act' of
1887, a permanent rather than renewable measure, was used with effect by crown
lawyers such as the young Edward Carson, and undoubtedly helped to undermine

the Plan. A hardnosed policing policy was put in place, exemplified by the 'Mitchelstown Massacre' of September 1887 when the Royal Irish Constabulary opened fire on a menacing crowd, killing three protestors and wounding two (Carson, again, was present on this occasion); the Chief Secretary, soon to be known as 'Bloody Balfour', was unabashed by this controversial episode and vigorously defended the crown forces. In addition British emissaries at the Vatican were active and helped to win the condemnation of the Plan by Pope Leo XIII in May 1888; exactly five years earlier the Liberal government had attempted to influence Leo XIII over the issue of the Parnell Testimonial. Confidential government diplomacy was also effective in another area: the Dublin Castle administration was active in shoring up one key estate targeted by the Plan (the Ponsonby lands in Cork), and Balfour promoted a syndicate of solvent proprietors whose task was to buy out the hapless Ponsonby.

Just as Liberal coercionists (such as Earl Spencer) had generally favoured a more constructive legislative approach to the administration of Ireland, so too the Tories sought to balance coercion with conciliation. Land legislation in 1887 and 1888 helped to 'kill by kindness' what coercion had failed to achieve in a more direct manner: the Land Act of 1887 extended the scope of Gladstone's measure of 1881, admitting leaseholders to the benefits of the earlier Act while the Land Purchase Act of 1888 contributed an additional £5 million to the funding of the pioneering Ashbourne Purchase Act of 1885. There was an effort (for the moment abortive) to supply Ireland with a comprehensive reform of local government. There was investment in public works.

The combination of these measures with the coherent leadership supplied by Balfour and the unusual boldness of the Castle lawyers (Peter 'the Packer' O'Brien, Carson) helped to suffocate an agitation which was, in addition, rather thinly rooted in Irish popular favour. Although recent research has sought to strike a balance between the exaggerated claims of the Plan's authors and the sometimes dismissive attitude of later commentators, and although it is true that the Plan worked to secure rent reductions, it was never a national agitation, and it seems to have peaked early and to have suffered a protracted demise.[140] It undoubtedly suffered from the frigidity of Parnell. There were however some victories, dearly won: the 'Mitchelstown Massacre' provided a focus for sympathy and support, especially in British Liberal circles; and in addition the whole of the nationalist movement was enthused by the revelations of the Special Commission hearings of February 1889.

Neither of these transient successes was without cost. The Mitchelstown episode bought sympathy for the Plan and for nationalism at the price of the lives of three demonstrators. The cost of the Special Commission victory was less bloody and less tangible, but also high. The Commission was formed by an Act of parliament, passed in July 1888, and it was charged with the task of investigating a series of charges made by *The Times* newspaper against leading Irish nationalists. In 1887 and 1888, *The Times* had published a number of letters which were allegedly the work of Parnell, and which seemed to prove the existence of a close and sympathetic relationship between the Irish leader and violent nationalism: in the most controversial of these missives, dated 15 May 1882, the author condoned the murder of T.H. Burke, one of the two Phoenix Park victims. These letters were only one aspect, but by far the most notorious, of the Special Commission hearings, which were held between October 1888 and November 1889. In a merciless cross-examination by the brilliant Ulster Catholic lawyer Sir Charles Russell, the author of the letters was revealed as Richard Pigott, a journalist and pornographer, who personified the sleazy demi-monde of late Victorian Dublin as well as the vicious intimacy of its political life. Russell's interrogation of Pigott stands (alongside Carson's examination of Oscar Wilde) as one of the classic set-piece confrontations of the late Victorian judicial system: and it was this, rather than the broader investigations of the Commission, which enthralled contemporaries.

Pigott, a talentless but pathological liar, linked the worlds of Fenianism, Dublin Castle and Irish Unionism, and sought to milk each of these three sources: he found a willing dupe in a recklessly ambitious young Unionist apparatchik, Edward Caulfield Houston. Houston offered generous expenses and a commission in return for any evidence that might compromise Parnell; and, having gone through the motions of an investigation, Pigott duly put pen to paper and supplied his credulous patron with the required materials. Pigott had genially exploited the gullibility of those who wanted to believe in Parnell's guilt: Houston and his colleagues in the Irish Loyal and Patriotic Union made little effort to verify the evidence that they had bought so dearly (the letters cost £500 and Pigott, who of course pocketed this sum, cheekily claimed an additional £105 'for himself').[141] But, except for those needing faith, Pigott was clearly a doubtful political messiah: the Parnellites got at the truth well in advance of the Special Commission hearings, and even the government belatedly and fearfully grasped at the disaster that threatened. On 20–2 February 1889 the forgeries were exposed with a brisk efficiency; and while their true author escaped to shoot himself in a Madrid hotel, their purported author basked on the high ground of Liberal morality.

But the exposure of Pigott and the humiliation of *The Times* placed Parnell on an extremely vulnerable pedestal. The adulation of the Liberals was certainly welcome, and Parnell seemed to respond warmly and for the most part in a conciliatory manner: on 8 March 1889 he attended a dinner organized by the Liberal Eighty Club, where he spoke sympathetically on the value of working within the constitution and, in a highly charged symbolic gesture, shook the hand of the former lord lieutenant of Ireland, Earl Spencer (Healy's Duke of Sodom and Gomorrah). A series of moderate speeches followed in the summer and autumn of 1889 and in December he journeyed to Hawarden to be blessed by Gladstone. But even here, when he was apparently at his most straightforward, there was ambiguity: Gladstone thought that the Hawarden visit had been delayed because Parnell was concerned to see whether the Tories would first commit themselves to an Irish Catholic university. There was other evidence of Parnell's old and – even in these most unpropitious circumstances – undying interest in courting Toryism. In July 1890 Parnell alarmed his *soi-disant* Liberal allies and his own followers by offering to deal with Balfour on the land question: in what Morley called a 'plunge into unexplained politics' Parnell proposed that by a remodelling of Balfour's new land bill, the Plan of Campaign might be brought to an end.[142] But although this might have consti-tuted 'unexplained politics' for Morley and Gladstone, more worldly commentators such as Dillon divined Parnell's intent and feared that it would 'spread a kind of uneasy feeling among the Radicals that our opposition to Balfour and the Tory party is after all not so real'.[143]

These spasmodic gestures towards Toryism were not the only unsettling aspect of the apparently healthy Liberal alliance. Parnell, though professing concern for Liberal sensitivities, was continuously worried that the 'union of hearts' might develop into an effective institutional union between the two parties, and that the fate of earlier Irish national endeavours (incorporation into Liberalism) might be repeated. He was therefore particularly keen to guard against the assimilation of the Irish within Liberal political society. Moreover, occasional speeches in the period hinted at his old extremism, the most controversial of these being an address to Irish town coun-cillors in May 1889 when he referred to the parliamentary policy as 'a trial' which 'we did not ourselves believe in the possibility of maintaining for all time'.[144] This was not a language comprehensible to Gladstonian Liberalism; nor were these the 'very conservative' Parnellite doctrines that were so soothing to the Liberal leader. Such statements helped to keep open a range of strategic options, but they did little to consolidate the middle ground that Gladstone believed he had charted between the two parties.

For the Parnellites this middle ground might well in time have become unin-habitable, parched through lack of legislative concession. It was also possible, though much less likely, that the Parnellite–Liberal consensus might have been threatened by some constructive working relationship with the Tories: the Unionist alliance was clearly not going to deliver Home Rule, but in 1898 it did deliver democratic county councils, and by 1903–4 some advanced Unionists were toying with the pos-sibility of administrative devolution for Ireland. But in truth the idea of a significant political space shared between Salisbury's Unionists and the Irish Party was merely a Parnellite fantasy, a recurring image from 1885 which occasionally and temporarily teased the Irish leader. Parnell's alliance with the Liberals did not crumble because the Irish were cut off from tangible political concession, nor was it replaced by an understanding with the Tories: the alliance ended because what Gladstone saw as the moral harmony between the parties suddenly gave way to dissonance. And the origin of this lay not in Parnell's occasional militant lapses, but rather in the divorce court.

Parnellism was a magnificent, though fragile, achievement; and Parnell was a dazzling, though vulnerable, political performer. The strain of operating at every one of the tiers of the multi-decked Anglo-Irish relationship was overwhelming, and there seems to have been little compensating support or intimacy from the Parnell clan (this in contrast to the affirmative relationship between Parnell's chief antag-onist, Healy, and his family networks). The crucial oasis at the centre of Parnell's searing political career was provided not by adoring parents or siblings, or by a conventional marriage, but rather by Katherine O'Shea, the wife of a colleague in

Plate 5   Charles Stewart Parnell re-elected as leader of the Irish Parliamentary Party,
House of Commons, December 1890.
Source: Mary Evans Picture Library.

the Irish Parliamentary Party: Mrs O'Shea was in addition an Englishwoman, who
had certain tenuous connections with the Liberal political establishment, but who
was pleasingly remote from the Irish networks where Parnell sought ascendancy.
The relationship began in 1880 and provided some of the psychological bedrock
for Parnell's successful political career in the following years; but it was of course
a flawed stratum. The first warnings of disaster came only in February 1886 with
the Galway Mutiny, and there were serious tremors in December 1889 when Mrs
O'Shea's estranged husband petitioned for divorce, citing Parnell as co-respondent.
But the quake came only in November 1890, when O'Shea pressed his (uncontested)
claims in court and called evidence that not only depicted Parnell as a moral repro-
bate, but – much worse – also defined him as a skulking fool.[145]

There had always been a Micawberish element to Parnell's strategy, and until very
late in the day he seems to have been complacent in the belief that 'something would
turn up': before November 1890 he expected that O'Shea might eventually be bought
off, and even after the courtroom revelations he seems to have banked on the Irish
instinct for unity in the face of political disaster. But here the luck that had accompanied his boldness through the 1880s ran out. Initially it seemed that Parnell would
indeed pull off the greatest tactical coup of his career, by sustaining the silence of

the Church and the endorsement of the party in the face of his adultery: the bishops were at first disapproving but reticent, while on 25 November the Irish members (who were kept in the dark about the Liberal attitude) were prepared to re-elect him as their leader. However, British non-conformist leaders such as Hugh Price Hughes, whose Home Rule convictions were – like those of Gladstone – interlinked with Christian principle, now saw Parnell as a blight on a moral cause; and, lacking some of the political finesse of their Irish brethren, they were fierce in their denunciation (an uncomprehending F.S.L. Lyons has called them 'hysterical').[146] Gladstone made it clear that Parnell's continued leadership of the Home Rule movement was incompatible with his own command of Liberalism; and this forced the Irish members to reconsider their earlier and instinctive closing of ranks. On 1 December 1890 73 out of the 86 members of the party reconvened in Committee Room 15 at Westminster; and on 6 December, after a prolonged and highly acrimonious debate, Justin McCarthy led 44 of those present away from Parnell's leadership and into secession.

This 'Split' was the central feature of Irish politics until Parnell's death in October 1891: indeed it remained a dominant theme until the reunification of the Irish Party in 1900. It would be easy to interpret the arguments which drove Parnell to his death and which resonated beyond his grave as being rooted in private personality clashes and public moral affront; indeed many sensitive contemporaries (such as William O'Brien) seem to have been diverted by Parnell's personal tragedy away from the ideological conflict that was being played out in 1890–1.[147] But, while a degree of narrow animosity undoubtedly fed the peculiarly bitter exchanges between Parnell and Tim Healy ('the most acute Catholic nationalist intelligence of his time'), there was more at stake in the conflict than this.[148] Healy (whose 'rhetoric disclosed a disquieting fanaticism') spoke for middle Ireland – for popular Catholic morality, and for the prosperous farmers and their economic dependents in the countryside and in the small towns: in other words, he represented the core of what had been Parnellism, and indeed it has been suggested with some truth that it was this 'Parnellism [which] destroyed Parnell'.[149] Parnell's campaign, which for years was seen as an incoherent postscript to his political career, is now judged as a revelation – albeit a crude revelation – of his fundamental convictions and strategies ('a laboratory of his political technique, in necessarily coarsened form').[150]

The Split should thus be seen less as a disjunction in Parnell's political evolution than as an unveiling. His strategy was as of old – to build a coalition of forces around a simple cry, that of 'independent opposition'; he emphasized that the anti-Parnellites, by submitting to Liberal 'dictation', were compromising the parliamentary independence which alone benefited Irish nationalism. He reactivated the sentiments contained within the speech of May 1889, which he had delivered to the town councillors of Ireland: he stressed that constitutionalism was only a highly fallible means to the end of legislative independence. He flattered the Irish Republican Brotherhood, without wholly abandoning this qualified parliamentary creed; he and his supporters looked for endorsement both to veteran Fenians as well as to intellectuals and fellow travellers of the younger generation. He elaborated his indictment of the Plan of Campaign, while continuing to express the concern for smallholders and evicted tenants that he had been offering from the time of the Land War: indeed, in the months of the Split, he sought legislation that would discriminate in favour of the small farmer interest and against the substantial farmers who bolstered his opponents. He reaffirmed his faith in a non-sectarian nationalism, though in a more liberated and therefore cruder manner than before: his attacks on the Church's intrusion into politics became ever more aggressive, buoyed by his own passionate convictions on this score as well as the evolving alliance between the clergy and his opponents. He carefully guarded his reputation for religious toler-ance (especially since Healy was accusing him of sectarianism); but a heightened concern for the role of his fellow Protestants within the new Ireland (one of the central if neglected themes of his career, according to Paul Bew) was also evident in these months of the Split.[151]

But Parnellism was not merely a political philosophy and a strategy, it was also a political style; and if the Split was merely an unveiling of the core of Parnellite thought, then this very process involved a fatal demystification. Parnellism was revealed, demystified and destroyed in one single process. This had begun before the Split with the Special Commission which, while vindicating Parnell on the crucial issue of the Pigott forgeries, had also published much that was distinctly unflattering about the operations of the Land League and its leaders. The O'Shea divorce hearing had supplied the details of Parnell's sometimes furtive and farcical courtship; and the ensuing political struggle had provided the anti-Parnellites with the chance to fur-ther embroider this humiliating evidence. Healy's recklessly sarcastic and abusive rhetoric gave begrudgers an opportunity to laugh publicly at a man whose haughty English manner had inspired much private resentment. Indeed, the emotional release provided by the Split brought not just taunts but also violence: Parnell, who had once been reverenced as a demi-god, was assaulted not just verbally but also phys-ically (most famously at Castlecomer in December 1890). His own style – passionate idealism expressed in tones of frosty restraint – was modified and debased: his dis-play of force and aggression during the Parnellite capture of the *United Ireland* offices in December 1890 involved an abandonment of the political cool for which he was renowned and respected. The very fact that he was forced back into Ireland and onto public platforms after a very long absence hinted at a desperation which had little role in the public image of a detached, omniscient political intelligence. James Bryce argued in 1903 that Parnell's self-confidence was an essential cement for his movement ('a chief ground of their obedience to him and their belief in his supe-rior wisdom'); Frank Callanan has observed that Parnell's 'composed audacity, and his mystique of invincibility, belied his vulnerability'.[152] But when this 'composed audacity' began to grow dishevelled and the self-assurance cracked, Parnell lost sup-port. He who had once brazenly defied the conventional laws of politics became simply a conventional, over-ambitious nationalist failure.

Parnell's position after December 1890 was indeed desperate, and he recognized his plight by his determination to fight – even though a superficially attractive com-promise was available. He rejected comparatively favourable terms for a settlement at Boulogne in January and February of 1891; but accepting any diminution of status at a weak point in his career would have been a humiliation and therefore a much more dangerous concession than might otherwise have seemed apparent. His intense personal involvement at three by-elections (Kilkenny in December 1890, North Sligo in April 1891 and Carlow in July 1891) was distinctive not merely because of his passion but because he had for long disdained participation in such contests: the three successive defeats that his candidates sustained overturned his reputation for electoral invincibility. He had been famous not as a fluent public speaker but as a careful and (when appropriate) a precise speaker. But this precision evaporated as the stress of the contest began to tell, and some of his later speeches degenerated into confusion: Dillon, noting Parnell's last speech at Creggs, Roscommon, on 27 September 1891, wrote tersely – 'Parnell at Creggs yesterday, incoherent scurrility – sad, sad'.[153]

What changed during the Split was not perhaps Parnell's rather eclectic political philosophy, but rather his political style: frenetic campaigning replaced an indifference to the Irish campaign trail, a Byronic gusto replaced an Augustan frigidity, an intellectual confusion born of stress and exhaustion replaced a taut precision of language. Parnell had perhaps little choice but to fight his corner – and to fight viciously; but, whether he had won or lost, his relationship with his movement would have been irremediably altered. He would have survived, cut off from English support and from the effective sanction of the Church, not as the disdainful autocrat of old but as the poltroon who had betrayed one of his own supporters and who had hidden from his vengeance on a fire-escape. He would have survived, haunted by the woundingly accurate assaults of Healy and by the private contempt of ordinary Irish people, like the old woman at Castlebar for whom he was merely an 'ould blackguard'.[154] But in reality the chances of survival were slim, given the forces which swiftly ranged against him; and if there had been any doubt as to the outcome, then the alteration in Parnell's public conduct that was evident from the moment he returned to Ireland in December 1890 would have signalled the depth of his political despair. For the Victorian Unionist Edward Dowden, Parnell was the fallen archangel Lucifer; for F.S.L. Lyons, Parnell was Macbeth, 'bear-like' fighting his course.[155] But Parnell was also Shakespeare's Richard III: a ruthless political warrior who at the end fought because there was no alternative; a vicious technician of power whose personal and political sins were for long contained, but in the end combined to ensure his downfall.

Parnell died on 6 October 1891. He had helped to direct an agitation which produced the most important single land reform of the nineteenth century: the Act of 1881. He had created a disciplined Parliamentary Party and popular movement dedicated to the restoration of Irish legislative independence; he forced Home Rule onto the political agenda of a reluctant British parliament. He united the Church and Fenianism in one national movement; he brought together farmers of all descriptions, the urban middle classes and the Dublin working class in the call for Home Rule. He alone of Irish popular leaders in modern times, as an Irish Protestant nationalist who was interested in the role of Protestants in Irish society, had the capacity to overcome the endemic sectarian and cultural divisions of the island. His appeal was great, his philosophy eclectic and vague, and his opportunism boundless. He applied (as did Edward Saunderson) eighteenth-century modes of thought and expression to the task of organizing a late nineteenth-century popular movement. In death, as in life, his appeal transcends the murky boundaries of constitutional and physical force nationalism. His legacy spoke both to the Irish upper middle classes who, before the accession to the eurozone, carried an icon of the Uncrowned King on their £100 notes and to the ideologues of Provisional Sinn Féin who found a home in Dublin's Parnell Square.

Greening the Red, White and Blue: The End of the Union, 1891–1921

5.1 The Irish Parliamentary Party, 1891–1914

Parnellism, like Sinn Féin, was a brilliant but artificial alliance; and the pressure of sustaining an elaborate semblance of unity caused the explosion of 1891, as indeed it would later cause the meltdown of 1921–3. For most of the 1890s, until the rather cosmetic reunion of 1900, three former lieutenants of the Uncrowned King, while differing in attitude towards the legacy of their dead master, tried independently to create at least the structural elements of his political success (a parliamentary presence, extra-parliamentary organization and an uncritically loyal press). For most of the 1890s there were at least three competing nationalist organizations – the National League, the National Federation and T.M. Healy's People's Rights Association – with attendant newspapers; for most of the decade these bodies were locked into a mutually damaging rivalry where minor political differences were pursued with a passable imitation of fury, and where deep-seated ideological divisions were blurred by ruthless tactical manoeuvring.

To some extent the political maturation of the 1890s was the natural consequence of Parnell's autocratic rule in the previous decade – a delayed reaction to an era when internal debate was carefully regulated and when able senior nationalists were kept in a curious state of partial dependence and subservience. But the divisions of the 1890s were not simply the indirect by-product of Parnell's political style; they were also a commentary on the variegated nature of his movement as well as on its ideological inconsistencies – and, indeed, on the highly complex nature of the Parnell Split. There was at least a coherence to the Healyite position where local political rights and the authority of the Church were simultaneously underlined, in contra-distinction to the classical emphases of Parnellism; but even this had roots in Parnell's half-hearted concern for the dignity of local elites and for that of the hierarchy. And Healy, who was the most ferocious of the anti-Parnellites and who in 1891 enjoyed a peculiarly sympathetic relationship with Gladstone, came to favour the characteristic Parnellite nostrum of an independent parliamentary stand.[1]

There were other, indeed more marked, curiosities within the main Parnellite and anti-Parnellite traditions. The Parnellites, who were led until the reunification

Plate 6   John Redmond.
Source: Hulton Getty.

of 1900 by John Redmond, tended towards centrism and participation in consensual initiatives such as Horace Plunkett's Recess Committee of 1895. To some extent this reflected Parnell's pragmatism and his tempered concern for the Irish gentry caste; but it was perhaps a more direct by-product of the minority status of the Parnellite cause. It has been said that the Parnellites, buffeted by none too scrupulous and powerful opponents, learned to respect conciliation and in particular to be tolerant of vulnerable minorities.[2] It is certainly the case that Redmond, having assumed the leadership of the united party, balanced a sympathetic (if ineffectual) interest in Irish minorities with a consensual style of leadership. It is an ironic reflection that this proud inheritor of the Parnellite tradition should have been in practice a highly submissive and reactive leader: in the (admittedly unsympathetic) judgement of William O'Brien, Redmond's tendency 'to sacrifice to the bad gods on the calculation that the good ones would not hurt him led into errors which turned awry some of the best opportunities in his life'.[3] Redmond himself, in a curiously frank admonition, recommended that it was better to be 'united in support of a short-sighted and foolish policy than divided in support of a far-sighted and wise one'.[4]

It is an equally ironic reflection that, of the main anti-Parnellites, none had the lasting significance of John Dillon; and few, whether Parnellite or anti-Parnellite, were as loyal to the Uncrowned King's conception of party organization, or indeed – in practical terms – the Liberal alliance. Parnell had upheld the primacy of the alliance while subscribing to the theory of independent opposition; and this, despite the ferocious divisions on strategy revealed in 1890–1, was essentially Dillon's stand in the years after Parnell's death. In addition Dillon betrayed his classical Parnellite roots in advocating a disciplined party machine, in association with a party pledge: this was Dillon's antidote to the freebooting years of the Split, as it had been Parnell's response to the indiscipline of the Butt era. Furthermore Dillon, like Parnell, was not above setting aside his own theories of party unity when the occasion required: Parnell had imposed Captain O'Shea on the Galway constituency in 1886 and Dillon blithely ignored party feeling in his 'Swinford Revolt' of August 1903. And Dillon, of all Parnell's former lieutenants, was the closest in terms of political style to his former Chief: an acute tactician who was also politically nimble, sometimes outrageously pragmatic or bold, capable of hauteur, and inclined to disappear from the limelight when occasion suited. 'His promulgation of Parnellite tenets' was, however (as Frank Callanan has noted), 'depressingly mechanistic'.[5]

The politics of the 1890s were thus partly about the appropriation of the Parnell legacy – even by those who ostensibly rejected any association with the fallen hero: they also reflected the highly personalized and highly confused ideological contours of the Split. But, while the politicians of this era looked back to the 1880s and to the traumatic year 1890–1 in establishing their political bearings, it would be wrong to define this decade exclusively in retro-political terms. These years of division are important, not merely for their roots but also for the dangerous spores that were produced and which had later consequences. This period produced an introspection within mainstream constitutional nationalism which represented a major disability, both when the party was confronted with militant Ulster Unionism in 1912–14 and when it was challenged by militant Sinn Féin after 1916. The period produced personal and factional animosities which were only soothed, and never healed, and which contributed both to the permanent fragility of the party and to popular suspicion about its effectiveness. The abiding concern for unity brought the snubbing of conciliatory opponents within Ireland and the repudiation of not unfriendly British ministerial initiatives; it helped to encourage the brutalization of the party's disciplinary machinery, as evidenced most notoriously by the 'Baton' Convention of February 1909.

On the other hand, the party was successful in maintaining a semblance of internal unity as well as in pursuing a broadly nationalist agenda. In fact, the problem was that, in certain respects, the party was too successful: the unrelenting critique of British rule and the abiding fear that nationalism might be undermined by conciliatory legislation were certainly natural reactions to the Split, but they also opened up a fatal inconsistency within party strategy. For the party – certainly in the years of Dillon's influence – was committed to its Liberal alliance and therefore to the British constitutional forum: but the abusive rhetoric which the Split had helped to spawn was systematically directed against British government, including even relatively friendly administrations. The party had thus created an elaborate mechanism for its own destruction. It helped to maintain contempt for British rule, and therefore contempt for its own association with British rule. In addition the ferocious rhetoric of the party implied a standard of consistency and achievement which allowed little tolerance for the necessary compromises of political life: it became a victim of its own contemptuousness and an easy prey to hypocrisy. The Irish Parliamentary Party had thus taken a steam-hammer to the superficially impressive shell of the British administration in Ireland; but it was Sinn Féin who picked up the kernel.

Not the least of the ironies associated with the fall of Parnell was the fact that he was the victim of an alliance in which he had invested much of his political capital. With the Liberals in opposition this alliance had delivered political frustration and personal destruction, but within ten months of Parnell's death the Liberals had been restored to office and the costly nationalist investment looked set to mature. Whether Parnell's presence in the Commons in 1892–3 would have made any difference to the Home Rule cause is debatable; but it is clear that the fratricidal nature of the Split, and the divided nationalist parliamentary representation, made the Home Rule cause less formidable than it would otherwise have been and its advocates correspondingly less confident. The challenge of defending a second Home Rule Bill, in 1893, did not inspire any reunification of the nationalists, even though in certain respects the outlook was more favourable than in 1886 (the cause had a majority in the House of Commons) and even though the bill was arguably more favourable to the Irish position (Gladstone was now proposing, in addition to the new Home Rule assembly in Dublin, the retention of 80 Irish MPs at Westminster). Nor could the continued disunity of the nationalists be justified through any relaxation of the Unionist cause: indeed the coherence and discipline of the Unionists was, if anything, more impressive in 1892–3 than in 1886. Nationalist division undoubtedly helped to demoralize Liberal believers like Gladstone and to affirm doubters like Lord Rosebery; it helped to ensure that Gladstone did not in fact use the defeat of the second Home Rule Bill as an opportunity to lead the country in a constitutional crusade for the empowerment of the Irish and the sequestration of the Lords. Nationalist division was one of several factors which helped to turn the Grand Old Man's final years into a miserable diminuendo rather than the Wagnerian climax that he had planned for so long.

The division between Parnellite and anti-Parnellite did not disappear, though it was clear already in the last months of Parnell's life that his supporters were in a decided minority: this was confirmed by the general election of 1892 (when the Parnellites won nine seats) and by the election of 1895 (when they captured 11 seats). Nor (as has been noted) was this the only line of fracture within nationalist politics: the divisions among the anti-Parnellites were, if anything, more profound than any external animosity, and in particular the rivalry between Healy and Dillon was pursued with a fury which would not have been out of place in the first vengeful months of the Split. Dillon's position was consolidated by the general election of 1895, after which the insidious semi-private competition between him and Healy was made public. By the end of 1895 Dillon had been able to further strengthen his hold on mainstream anti-Parnellism, winning the expulsion of Healy from the National League of Great Britain (7 November 1895), from the National Federation (13 November 1895) and from the committee of the party (14 November 1895): he crowned this succession of victories by capturing the chairmanship of the party in February 1896, replacing the veteran Justin McCarthy. But ejecting the vituperative and fluent Healy was an easier enterprise than winning his silence; and Healy fought on as an independent, siding with other marginalized figures such as William O'Brien and digging into the flesh of the Irish Parliamentary Party until his retirement in 1918. He became, and remained, 'the enemy within'.[6]

Behind the personalities and behind the superstructure of a shared nationalism lay ideological tensions. Healy represented the clericalist right wing of the party, and during his ferocious campaign against Parnell he had successfully mobilized the prosperous Catholic farming interest. Even though he exploited the disrupted relations between Parnell and Gladstone in order to oust his former Chief, and even though he seems to have respected Gladstone's conservative reformism, Healy opposed nationalist subservience to the Liberal alliance and was as content in the company of Tory ministers like Gerald Balfour and George Wyndham (with whom he was on quite intimate terms) as in that of senior Liberals. Like other conservative Catholics Healy may have been more comfortable with Tory Anglicanism than with Liberal non-conformity, even though – paradoxically – he had exploited the qualms of the non-conformist conscience in 1891. In the late summer of 1894 he remorselessly opposed Dillon and McCarthy's efforts to rescue the ailing finances of the party by appealing to the generosity of Liberal 'friends'; and in the 'Omagh scandal' of 1895 he exposed an attempt by the party leaders to hand over four expensive northern constituencies to the Liberals.[7]

Dillon was closer, both personally and ideologically, to another senior veteran of Parnell's campaigns, William O'Brien: the two men were longstanding friends and had cooperated closely on such tactically sensitive matters as the Plan of Campaign of 1886–91 and the Boulogne negotiations in January–February 1891. But both had a fundamentally different view of the party's relationship to popular opinion (O'Brien tended to favour the Land League model, Dillon was more impressed by the National League's subservient relationship), and both held different attitudes towards the Liberal alliance: both, to a certain extent, were victims of Parnell's ambiguous legacy. O'Brien had settled in County Mayo in 1895 and had been profoundly moved by the precariousness of life in the impoverished west: as Paul Bew has pointed out, Mayo was simultaneously the birthplace of the Land League and the county that had been most thoroughly disillusioned by its achievement.[8] In a rejection of Dillon's stentorian discipline, O'Brien went outside the party in order to address the social and political problems that impressed him: in January he launched an agrarian protest movement, the United Irish League (UIL), a body designed to represent the Connacht smallholders and to curb the growing ascendancy of the grazier interest. But the League was not simply a social initiative; from the moment of its inception O'Brien seems to have had in mind the continuing division between the Parnellites and their anti-Parnellite rivals. And he seems to have grasped the potential of a popular forum where both party traditions might coalesce without compromising their sectional convictions. Indeed, the UIL seems to have been designed partly as a mechanism for social protest, but also as a means of identifying one aspect of Parnell's complex legacy that everyone – the Chief's allies and his detractors – might accept.

Dillon's acceptance of the UIL was highly qualified, for he was offended by the creation of a body largely beyond his own jurisdiction as leader of the anti-Parnellite party; and in particular he was offended by the highly localized nature of the UIL constitution. His own view of the path to a reconciliation with the Parnellites was essentially high-political, and he resented the urgent pressure applied by external forces on the parliamentarians: in an expression of dudgeon he resigned from the anti-Parnellite leadership in February 1899. The voluntary retirement of the doctrinaire and sensitive Dillon undoubtedly eased the sectional rapprochement: the reunification of the party came exactly one year later, secured on the foundations of the League (which was formally integrated into the party in June 1900) and on a reconciliation between the Parnellite leader, Redmond, and the most acerbic of the anti-Parnellites, Healy. Dillon's role in this diplomacy was minimal. Like O'Brien he was content to see Redmond elected to the chair of the reunited party; but, like O'Brien, he was not so much concerned with Parnellite sensitivities as with securing a malleable leadership. Indeed, it seems that his original intention was to support another even more vulnerable Parnellite candidate with the hope eventually of ousting him.

These different interpretations of Parnell's legacy as it affected the internal workings of the party carried over inevitably into the arena of constructive unionism. Dillon's Liberal sympathies, his austere nationalism and his freely ranging suspicions rendered him immune to Tory blandishments: his rival, O'Brien, referred cattily to Dillon's 'unhappy faculty for misjudging any new state of facts by the light of the narrow suspiciousness which took the place of imaginative insight in his mental equipment'.[9] The novelty of the 'new state of facts' in the later 1890s may in fact be exaggerated. The Conservatives, who returned to power in 1895, did not so much embark on a new strategy as refurbish old ideas; indeed their 'policy' of 'killing Home Rule by kindness' seems to have been less a coherent philosophy than a series of pragmatic responses, based on earlier initiatives, to the shifting opportunities supplied by parliamentary politics.[10] Gerald Balfour, who held the Chief Secretaryship between 1895 and 1900, devised a Land Act in 1896 and a local government reform in 1898, each of which built upon ideas supplied by his brother, Arthur, who had been in Ireland between 1887 and 1891. The Local Government (Ireland) Act of 1898 established democratic county councils and urban and district councils, all based on a wide franchise (which included women): it owed much to the democratization of English local government in 1888 and to an earlier Irish bill, launched in 1892. The other key reform of Gerald Balfour's tenure was enacted in 1899, when he made provision for a separate Irish Department of Agriculture and Technical Instruction: again this was not so much Balfour's inspiration as that of his mentor, Horace Plunkett. Plunkett was a Liberal Unionist MP who was the ideologue behind the constructive policies of the later 1890s: he is best remembered for his efforts to improve Irish agriculture, in particular the advancement of technical education and of cooperation, and in 1895 he created a cross-party body, the Recess Committee, with these ends in view. The Recess Committee's report, published in 1896, provided the foundation for Gerald Balfour's Act of 1899; and in a recognition of this debt, Balfour appointed Plunkett to head the new Irish department.

These measures had difficult consequences for both Irish nationalists as well as Irish Unionists. By taking these various initiatives, Balfour threw both the Irish Unionist and nationalist leaderships onto the defensive and succeeded in galvanizing a variety of their internal divisions. The Parnellite leader Redmond accepted the conciliatory gestures of Plunkett and the Tory government at face value, cooperating with Unionists on the Recess Committee and (to his subsequent embarrassment) hailing the rather modest Land Act of 1896 as an end to the Irish land question. Redmond sat alongside both Liberal Unionists like Plunkett as well as Orange Conservatives such as Colonel Edward Saunderson on the All-Ireland Committee of 1897, a body designed to press for a more favourable financial relationship between Britain and Ireland. He regarded the Local Government Act as a monumental achievement, and he looked forward to the election of popular talented landlords to the new councils: 'all we say is', wrote a Redmondite editor in May 1897, 'that Ireland needs their services as men of intelligence and culture . . . we have no sympathy for those who preach the doctrine that all the Landlords deserve of Ireland is a single ticket to Holyhead'.[11]

But these expressions of goodwill did not last, nor were they shared by the mainstream anti-Parnellite tradition. On the contrary, Dillon viewed these Tories bearing legislative gifts not as philanthropists, but rather as subverters of nationalist morale and discipline. Where Redmond saw the lavish potential of gradualist reform, particularly in terms of the reconciliation of different Irish political and confessional traditions, Dillon saw only a conspiracy to undermine Home Rule. Like the Orange Tory Saunderson, Dillon refused to sit on Plunkett's Recess Committee; he was highly suspicious of the All-Ireland Committee and pressed so extreme a line that he spoilt any chance of consensus. He was a late and unenthusiastic supporter of the local government reform, apparently failing to grasp the extent to which this measure had, in the words of Redmond, inaugurated a 'social revolution'.[12]

However, Dillon, unlike Redmond, had at least the merit of consistency: he remained loyal to the Liberal alliance and to the primacy of Home Rule as a legislative goal. For Dillon Home Rule came first, and with it an Irish parliament to address the different social and economic problems faced by the country. These, along with a sure sense of personal advantage, were the guiding principles of his political career; and – certainly in the eyes of opponents – they implied a single-mindedness and an inflexibility that were damaging to an inclusivist nationalism. Where Dillon remained immoveable, then other leading nationalists took part in one of the most striking political realignments of the era. William O'Brien, disappointed by the results of his UIL agitation, which was losing momentum by 1901–2, turned from the familiar politics of agitation and embraced instead a Redmondite gradualism. But – paradoxically – O'Brien's centrist shift was occurring at precisely the same time that Redmond was fleeing the middle ground in search of a safer billet with nationalist fundamentalism. By 1903 Redmond had accepted Dillon's view of party strategy; and O'Brien, whose life had been devoted to rural agitation, found himself stranded, along with numerous ascendancy and Liberal exotics, in the barren middle ground of Irish politics.

Behind this realignment lay a variety of stimuli. The first was the arrival in Ireland in 1900 of a new Chief Secretary, George Wyndham. Wyndham was one of the few British Chief Secretaries, whether Conservative or Liberal, who rose above partisanship, even above a paternalist sympathy for Irish problems, to achieve something approaching an empathy with the mind-set of Irish nationalism. Like other Chief Secretaries, Wyndham was highly ambitious (the office tended to serve either as the birthplace or the charnel house of political reputations); but unlike other conventional careerists, Wyndham was a romantic English nationalist with a yearning for a purer medieval past and with an aesthetic High Church sensitivity. For the Irish he spoke the language of romantic nationalism, albeit with an excessively refined English accent; and even this jarring Englishness was offset by his kinship with the great Fitzgerald family, and in particular his (somewhat tenuous) descent from the patriot-hero of 1798, Lord Edward Fitzgerald. In addition, he had a gift for friendship which helped him to transcend the bunker of Dublin Castle society. Wyndham looked like a conventional Tory: he was a squire, married into the aristocracy, and with a background of military service; his earlier experience in Ireland had been as 'Bloody' Balfour's private secretary and henchman during the years of coercion. He had been Under-Secretary for War during the South African campaign which had so aroused Irish national anger. But by October 1902 Wyndham had demonstrated that these appearances were profoundly deceptive: for, in the first major appointment of his tenure, he chose a Liberal and Catholic Irishman, Sir Antony MacDonnell, for the strategically vital office of Under-Secretary for Ireland. Moreover, in his anxiety to secure MacDonnell's skills and experience, Wyndham promised that the new Under-Secretary would be more than a mere bureaucratic underling, and would instead be given an influence over the direction of administrative policy.

The forgotten context to the appointment of MacDonnell and to the broader centrist tendency within Irish politics in 1902–3 was – for the British government – the successful conclusion of the South African war on 31 May 1902. Yet the combination of an overall British victory and the memory of individual defeats gave little credence to political fundamentalism, providing scant satisfaction either to Irish loyalists or to Irish nationalists. Moreover, this ambiguous outcome was bought at an enormous cost to the Empire, both in terms of casualties and of capital. But these wartime sacrifices indirectly highlighted the attractions of centrism; and they did help to open up some temporary space in the middle ground of both British and Irish politics. MacDonnell's appointment would probably not have been possible in the context of an easy British victory and a triumphalist Tory imperialism: nor would other private initiatives towards a more consensual form of political culture have been viable. In fact the protracted and expensive conflict in South Africa was mirrored by the protracted, expensive and inconclusive land war that had been fought out in Ireland since the days of the Plan of Campaign. And, just as the end of the war heralded a brief centrist heyday in Britain, so in Ireland the flagging of O'Brien's land campaign heralded a momentary abandonment of conventional adversarial politics.

The first evidence of this new departure came with two public letters from minor landlords, the first of which was written by Talbot Crosbie and was published in June 1902; the second and more influential letter appeared in the press on 3 September 1902 under the name of Captain John Shawe-Taylor. Hitherto the main voice of landlordism had been supplied by the Irish Landowners' Convention, an institution that was dominated by conservatives and which had not been distinguished by its willingness to compromise the rights of proprietorship. Shawe-Taylor's letter, which called for a land conference between the different interested parties, did not therefore herald any liberal revolution among the ranks of the Convention; but it certainly flagged the presence of a body of conciliatory landlords whose small numbers were partly offset by the encouragement they were receiving from Dublin Castle. In addition to striking a chord with Wyndham, these proprietors appealed to the Parnellite centrist tradition, as represented by the veterans of the Recess Committee of 1895 and the All-Ireland Committee of 1897. Redmond, who had participated in both these earlier initiatives, was sympathetic to the idea of a conference. William O'Brien, perhaps the most pragmatic of the senior anti-Parnellites, had exhausted the possibilities of agitation through the UIL campaign and was also susceptible to a more pacific strategy. Even though what O'Brien called 'the pontiffs of the Landowners' Convention' remained sceptical, and even though Dillon's opinion was unknown (he was out of the country at this time), there was a sufficiently strong body of sympathetic landlords and tenants to make Shawe-Taylor's proposal viable.[13] Accordingly, representatives of the two interests came together on 20 December 1902 and speedily reached an agreement, which was published on 4 January 1903. In two weeks these delegates had outlined a resolution to a 300-year-old conflict: they were able to do this not because of some preternatural bargaining skills, but because they were a self-selected group of moderates who had taken a political gamble in attending the conference and who were urgently committed to its success. But they were also proposing to spend their way towards a solution using someone else's credit. For Wyndham was willing to smooth the path of this diplomacy, and incidentally to buy a sunny place in Irish history for himself, by the lavish application of British state funding.

The conference report provided the basis for the great Wyndham Land Act of August 1903. The report and the Act were neither new nor radical in the principles that they advocated: both were framed around the idea of voluntary land purchase, which had been a feature of legislation since the Irish Church Act of 1869 and Irish Land Act of 1870. Both the report and Act rejected the notion of compulsion that was becoming increasingly popular, especially among the followers of the northern radical Unionist T.W. Russell. But where Wyndham and the conference delegates departed from earlier precedents was in their ambition – for although they owed a great deal to pioneering voluntary purchase measures such as the Ashbourne Act of 1885, the scale of their new initiative was vastly greater. The lavish amount of available finance was a novelty, as was the legislative ingenuity involved in making sure that this money would be spent. The Ashbourne Act provided £5 million in total to fund a modest purchase scheme, where the Wyndham Act provided £12 million merely as an inducement to selling landlords: both the amount of the funding and idea of an inducement were quite new. Moreover, this landlord 'bonus' was offset by a legislative guarantee that the purchase annuities would be uniformly less than rental payments: the new Act fixed price zones within which landlords and tenants had to strike their deals, and which were adjusted so as to allow a modest discount to the tenants without breaking the hearts of the proprietors. Both the vendor and the buyer were therefore being tempted into negotiation by more or less brazen appeals to their economic self-interest.

The involvement of veteran agitators such as O'Brien and Russell in this initiative indicated that at least some radicals were prepared to abandon spending Irish money in social and political coercion in favour of spending British money as an economic blandishment to the landlord caste. For O'Brien the conference and the Land Act did not simply signify the end of Irish land-lordism: they marked as well the beginning of a new consensual approach to reform, and indeed the dawning of a new, admittedly slowly evolving, inclusivist national spirit. For O'Brien 'conference plus business' replaced confrontation plus stalemate: the Land Act of 1903, the outcome of this strategy, was as superior to Wyndham's earlier unaided legislative efforts on the land question 'as the plays of Shakespeare are to the chap books which they were taken from'.[14] Unfortunately from the point of view of consensual dialogue, this attempted reform of the institutions and procedures of Irish politics was greeted elsewhere with a profound scepticism: O'Brien's 'conference plus business' was seen by Michael Davitt as 'loyalism and water' and by some conservative Irish Unionists as part of a damaging nationalist conspiracy which included the British Tory government.[15] From the centrist perspective, the distressing irony of this brief political experiment was that it certainly brought the unity of nationalist and Unionist – but a strategic rather than a substantive unity, and a unity based on the repudiation of consensual politics.

The evangelical liberalism of O'Brien, Russell and – on the Unionist side – Lord Dunraven, Shawe-Taylor and others had echoes in some centrist overtures within British politics; but, whether in Britain or in Ireland, this centrism represented such an apparent break both with the recent convictions of its advocates and with mainstream party politics that it disoriented many, and achieved little. Until 1902–3 O'Brien and Russell had been ferociously critical of landlord influence and of the Unionist government's tepid reformism (for Russell the two were interconnected); now they were seemingly discrediting their earlier positions by fraternizing with the demons of landlordism and by cooperating in a serious reform initiative with the British government, which for so long had been judged to be irredeemable. Both O'Brien and Russell appear to have lost electoral ground as a result of these ideological spasms: both men were certainly at the peak of their popular authority before 1903, and both lost out to political fundamentalists thereafter. O'Brien's actions were jealously watched by Dillon, who on 25 August 1903, speaking at Swinford, Mayo, outlined his objections to the new land measure: this 'Swinford revolt' against what had been mainstream opinion in the Irish Parliamentary Party and the UIL was backed by the *Freeman's Journal*, and helped to capitalize on widespread distrust of landlord cooperation and of the settlement that had been incorporated within the new Land Act. Dillon's case resolved down to the conviction that the new Land Act incorporated a better deal than the landlords deserved, and that the centrists had bound the farmers to paying higher prices for their land than was necessary. Dillon's motives were complicated: he certainly felt strongly enough about this issue to defy the party discipline that he otherwise held so dear. Like other nationalist leaders, he may have been privately less concerned with the compromise struck in 1903 than with its authorship: in other words, his problem was that it was O'Brien's deal and not his own (there may be a comparison here with de Valera and the Treaty of 1921). However, Dillon had also a history as an irreconcilable: he had adopted much the same attitude to the Gladstone Land Act of 1881 as to the Wyndham Act of 1903, and with much the same results. For, just as in 1881 Dillon had kept Parnell on a more leftward course than might otherwise have been the case, so in 1903 Dillon compelled his new leader, Redmond, to shift away from the O'Brienite centre of the party towards a more radical and aggressive posture. Dillon's fighting stand in 1881 predated Parnell's informal alliance with the Liberals: it is therefore possible, and especially given Dillon's later Liberal sympathies, that he was annoyed by the Unionist origins of the land settlement. But the core issue for Dillon was evidently not a practical concern for the farmers, for his mixture of negativism and elusiveness in 1903 was calculated to unsettle Irish tenants, but not to provide constructive leadership. Nor was the core issue any undue sensitivity about the Liberal alliance – for even here Dillon was highly distrustful and often uncertain. What motivated Dillon in 1903 was rather (as always) his own position within the nationalist leadership; and also his abiding fear that British cash would divert Irish voters from the national question. Indeed, in 1903, as in 1881, Dillon feared that a comprehensive land reform would immobilize the Irish Parliamentary Party: 'if this Act [of 1903] is allowed to work', he prophesied to an American politician, 'there will be an end to the national movement before 12 months are over'.[16] And in 1903, as in 1881, Dillon was determined to avert this threat by cultivating popular doubts and ill-will, and thereby eradicating the conciliationist virus. Just as in 1881, he was unable to prevent Irish farmers exploiting a beneficial measure: but, as has been pointed out, he was fully capable of ensuring that the Act of 1903 would work in an atmosphere of sustained bitterness and suspicion.[17] Dillon, like the centrists, was heavily influenced by the South African war: his goal, after 1902, was legislative independence for Ireland along lines no less generous than had been applied to the former Boer republics in southern Africa. However, to this end he was prepared to sacrifice virtually all – the material welfare of the farmers, where it appeared to clash with his own definition of the national interest, the friendship of old allies like O'Brien, and (it need hardly be pointed out) the health of the Anglo-Irish relationship. Where there was the potential for an Anglo-Irish reconciliation, as in the Land Conference and the Wyndham Act, Dillon saw only a national crisis. The dire consequences of this tunnel vision for both Irish capitalism and Irish unity have been graphically and persuasively analysed by Philip Bull.[18]

Dillon's unacknowledged allies in this anti-centrist endeavour were conservative Irish Unionists, and also the British Treasury. After 1903 and the divisions within the Tory government over tariff reform, it was becoming clear that the days of Unionist ascendancy were numbered and that Wyndhamite conciliation had no long-term future. This only served to underpin both Dillon's acerbic critique of the centrist initiative as well as his expectations of a Liberal–Home Rule administration. When the Land Conference reconvened in 1904 as the Irish Reform Association its devolutionist manifesto was subjected to a scathing review from Dillon. And here he was joined by conservative Ulster Unionists, who – hypothesizing from a mixture of leaks and from the well-known close relationship between Wyndham and the Land Conference – detected the presence of devolutionist heresy inside Dublin Castle and, indeed, within the Unionist government. When the House of Commons reconvened in January 1905 Wyndham was subjected to a two-pronged attack: from Dillonite nationalists, who offered a general critique of the government of Ireland, and from Ulster Unionists, who accused Wyndham and his Under-Secretary Antony MacDonnell of complicity in a scheme of devolution. Befuddled by drink and disoriented by the speedy twist by which his legislative triumph of 1903 had turned sour, Wyndham resigned in March 1905. There is a fair possibility that, despite his denials, he had been aware that MacDonnell was involved in discussions about some form of limited devolution: he certainly knew of MacDonnell's sympathies in this direction, he had expressly granted MacDonnell considerable freedom of action, and indeed he had been briefed by MacDonnell concerning 'conversations' with Lord Dunraven and other devolutionists which had taken place in the summer of 1904 (Wyndham allegedly misplaced the vital letter containing this information).[19] But Wyndham's culpability is perhaps beside the point: neither the Dillonites nor the Ulster Unionists were primarily interested in whether or not the Chief Secretary was tenuously connected with a modest scheme of administrative revision. Instead, Dillon was concerned with the integrity of the Home Rule movement and with the possibility that the goal of legislative independence would be compromised by a more minor concession. And, for their part, the Ulster Unionists were concerned not in any immediate devolutionist threat, but rather in re-energizing their – by this stage – rather bedraggled forces, and in countering the challenge provided by the Independent Unionist movements led by T.W. Russell and, in Belfast, by Tom Sloan. The apparent paradox of Unionists expressing their concern about Home Rule by uniting with Home Rulers against a Unionist government is to be explained by this often forgotten alternative focus.

Administrative devolution did not die with the political immolation of George Wyndham in March 1905: nor did it die with the defeat of the Unionist government in December 1905. The incoming Liberal administration of Sir Henry Campbell-Bannerman resurrected the notion, as a compromise between nationalist aspirations and what was, from the perspective of Westminster, politically attainable. Like the Dunraven scheme upon which it was based, the Liberals' Irish Council Bill of 1907 was a modest affair, proposing the transfer of eight departments of the byzantine Irish administration to the control of a partly elected council. Redmond, whose instincts were generally moderate and consensual, was sympathetic to the proposal; so, more surprisingly, was Dillon. But Dillon's original antagonism to the Irish Reform Association's devolutionist agenda was founded on his suspicion of the Unionist predominance within the body and its associations with the Wyndham administration: he was happy to accept the same broad proposal from a Liberal government, and as part of a creeping approach to the attainment of full legislative independence. The bill was presented on 8 May 1907, after extensive consultation between the government and the leaders of the Irish Party. But herein lay the origins of the tactical problem that swiftly emerged – for the Liberal Chief Secretary, Augustine Birrell, believing that the Irish leadership had been squared, concentrated instead on defusing Unionist opposition and therefore played down any radical dimension to his measure. Redmond and Dillon were thrown onto the defensive, and broader Irish opinion was frankly derisive. At a National Convention held on 21 May Redmond decided to pre-empt any attack on the bill from the floor by leading the condemnation. William O'Brien, who was an informed but partial commentator on this 'Convention of Misunderstandings', believed that Joseph Devlin and his Hibernian followers were a crucial and antagonistic influence on 21 May; O'Brien also believed that Devlin would have been a 'less aggressive' critic of the bill had his patron and mentor Dillon been present and able to exercise a restraining influence.[20] But, as it was, the Convention was united in its condemnation and in its desire for 'a policy of fight': the bill was immediately withdrawn, and with it disappeared the last significant fragment of the consensual and gradualist approach of the Land Conference to the constitutional question.

Why had Redmond and – more strangely – Dillon so badly miscalculated the mood of the broader Irish Party? It should be said to begin with that it might have been possible for Redmond, had he been a different type of leader, to retrieve the situation at the ill-fated Convention by spelling out his own convictions. But Redmond, though nominally the guardian of the Parnellite tradition, was no Parnell, possessing little of the passion or the charisma of the Uncrowned King: he was temperamentally incapable of the sort of bravado which had allowed Parnell to face down political opposition (as, for example, during the Galway 'Mutiny' in 1886). Redmond not only lacked the moral courage of Parnell, he also lacked his former master's secure political anchorage: Redmond, after all, was leader of the party only because of the self-denial and on the sufferance of the predominant anti-Parnellite tradition. His abiding concern was thus the insecurity of his own position: and this was all the more understandable given the somewhat qualified allegiance of senior lieutenants such as Dillon and O'Brien.

But the Irish Council Bill debacle had other roots. There were new movements within the party and within the broader nationalist tradition, with which the veterans of the Land League era were only imperfectly acquainted. Of these the one with the most immediate significance was the Ancient Order of Hibernians. The Hibernians were a Catholic fraternity, rooted originally in Ulster, but (as with the Defender movement of the late eighteenth century) subsequently spreading southwards: the movement enjoyed a rapid growth after about 1902, and, through its tough-minded boss Devlin, it became a significant influence within the Irish Parliamentary Party. Devlin was a protégé of Dillon and (as has been noted) was susceptible to his influence. But even though Devlin was closely connected with the party hierarchy, and was indeed arguably the most influential of the younger nationalist MPs, there was still a chasm separating him and his movement from the nationalism of a Redmond or an O'Brien. Redmond, who was if anything over-sensitive to potential internal threats, recognized the significance of the Hibernians and was careful to bring Devlin into his counsel. But, whether in terms of ideology or temperament, he was far removed from the vibrant sectarian nationalism of the northern movement.

The modest development of the Sinn Féin movement in the mid- and later Edwardian era is also important as a context for the 'Convention of Mis-understandings'. A full discussion of this may be found in a later section, but it should be emphasized here that – given the increasingly coherent pressure from advanced separatism – the Irish Parliamentary Party leadership had little chance of arousing any passion behind a cry for administrative devolution. There was some slight support within the party for a form of abstentionism, but this was as yet a mere premonition of the drastic ideological realignments of 1916–18: still, even the six or so MPs who advocated this course of action represented a radical core which could not be completely ignored.

A final aspect of the Irish Council Bill episode which merits some attention relates to the style and rhetoric of the Parliamentary Party. To a very marked extent the party leadership was still operating to an agenda devised by Parnell, and in a manner reminiscent of him. None of the Irish leaders of the period had the personal authority of Parnell; yet all to a certain extent mimicked his passion and occasional extremism. But, where Parnell had an authority that enabled him to defy conventional notions of political consistency, none of his lieutenants fully inherited his gifts. Like Parnell, Dillon and Redmond oscillated between moderate and more 'advanced' positions; but neither could carry out these manoeuvres with the same skill as their Chief. The Irish Council Bill affair illustrates this point clearly: Dillon had mocked the devolutionist ideals of the Irish Reform Association, but two and a half years later was endorsing what he had so witheringly condemned. Dillon defined political leadership in Parnellite terms – that is to say, he expected that a disciplined party, trusting in the patriotic integrity of its leaders, would loyally follow their strategic perambulation. This miscalculation, combined with Redmond's apparent susceptibility to internal party pressure, helps to explain the damage that was sustained to the party leadership and to its relations with the Liberal government through the 'Convention of Misunderstandings'.

Catholic education and land had been central to Parnell's agenda, and they remained of concern to his successors; Catholic education and land had also been central to the agenda of the Dunravenite centrists, and indeed – in the case of land – an essential element of their political achievement. But, despite the centrist initiative, and despite the skill and interest of constructive Unionists like Wyndham, both these issues remained alive after the accession of the Liberals in 1906. Both Wyndham and his predecessor, Gerald Balfour, had tried to address the demand for Catholic university education, but had encountered – even by the standards of Edwardian Irish politics – a minefield: even the recklessly ambitious Wyndham was soon scared off the territory by the certainty of an explosive failure. The basic political difficulty lay in reconciling the Catholic demand for a state-aided denominational university with Protestant opposition among the Ulster Unionists and British Conservative backbenches. But beyond this familiar interplay between Catholic protest and Protestant outrage was a complex of political and economic and denominational interests. Restructuring Irish university education in order to meet Catholic aspirations meant addressing the existing colleges, with their attendant vested interests: of these the Anglican-dominated University of Dublin (Trinity College) and the Presbyterian-dominated Queen's College Belfast were perhaps the most formidable, but the two remaining Queen's Colleges (Galway and Cork) were not without influence. The alumni of all these institutions were represented in the House of Commons and in public life, and Trinity College had an additional resource in the two MPs which its graduates returned. Aside from these vested interests, constructive Unionist ministers faced the unrelenting suspicion not just of Orange Tories but also of anti-centrist nationalists such as Dillon. Even if a Balfour or a Wyndham had succeeded in squaring the circle of Irish educational interests, they were likely to encounter imaginative and destructive criticism from this quarter.

For all these reasons, the constructive Unionist record on the higher education question was barren, not of initiative but certainly of achievement. It was therefore left to Birrell to translate the aspirations of these centrist and constructive Unionist idealists into legislative reality. Birrell certainly could not flaunt Protestant sensitivities, but neither did he have Orange backbenchers to mollify. Nor was he likely to encounter the flamboyant criticism of the Dillonites: Dillon's commitment to the Liberal alliance clearly did not mean (as the Irish Council Bill episode proved) that Birrell's legislation would win automatic favour, but it did perhaps ensure a serious and considered reception. Birrell had an additional resource in an unexpected quarter: Edward Carson, though the senior MP for Trinity College, had for long been sympathetic to the demand for a Catholic university, and by this time he had emerged not merely as one of the most influential Irish Unionists but also – given the electoral massacre of Tories that had occurred in 1906 – as one of the most influential British Unionist frontbenchers. Birrell therefore had relatively more freedom than his predecessors, and in addition he benefited from their mapping of the political quagmire. His Irish Universities Act of 1908 effectively conceded if not the principle, then certainly the practicality of state-endowed Catholic higher education; but it also proposed to buy off some of the traditional opposition to this strategy by offering concessions to the different Protestant interests. Birrell planned to create a new federal National University of Ireland, with Maynooth and the colleges at Cork, Dublin and Galway as its key constituents. This National University was technically non-denominational, thus satisfying the qualms of the secular purists; but in practice it offered such wide opportunity for Catholic clerical influence that it also satisfied the hierarchy and the Irish Parliamentary Party. The pay-off for the Protestant interests came partly with the Anglican shrine of Trinity College, which – as its defenders sought – was left unmolested, while the predominantly Presbyterian Queen's College Belfast was advanced to full university status. The Act therefore followed the Wyndhamite practice of fudging irreconcilable difficulties of principle, while offering something to all of the contending Irish interest groups. But the difference of course was that the Act could be represented as one of the blessings of the Liberal alliance; and, in apparent contradistinction to the constructive Unionist endeavours, such measures could be seen as landmarks on the road to Home Rule, rather than the paving stones of a diversion back to the Union.

In all of this – the Wyndham Act, the Irish Council Bill affair, the Irish Universities Act – the extent to which the leadership of the Irish Parliamentary Party had distanced itself from O'Brienite conciliation was clear, but there were still some ambiguities: the leadership, especially Redmond, had been interested in devolution as a first tentative step to Home Rule, and they were broadly supportive of the Irish Universities Act – a measure which even the embittered O'Brien judged as 'neither very good nor very bad' and 'to be reckoned among the salvage' of the conciliationist strategy.[21] However, the direction of the party and the distribution of forces within it were exposed, partly through the 'Convention of Misunderstandings' in 1907, but unambiguously through the drift of the party's agrarian policy after 1906. The first symptoms of this radicalization of party policy had come with Dillon's 'Swinford revolt' in August 1903, and with O'Brien's resignation from the party in November 1903. O'Brien's retirement removed the single most significant conciliationist influence from the party command, giving free rein to the suspicions and defensiveness associated with Dillon. But the demise of the Conservative government brought even Dillon back, not to the conciliationists but certainly to some of their policy concerns; and by late 1907 O'Brien felt that sufficient common ground had been re-established between himself and the leadership for it to be possible to rejoin the party. He was quickly to be disillusioned.

The centre-piece of the conciliationist achievement had been the Land Act of 1903, but this was almost immediately attacked by radical agrarians in the party for the prices that it imposed, and for its sluggish operation in crisis areas such as the west of Ireland. Here there was a large population of the landless and of smallholders, the casualties of the Famine era and of the land wars. These families eked out a precarious existence beside the great farms of the cattle ranchers, the class of sub-stantial farmer or investor which had emerged since the Famine years and which had benefited greatly from land purchase legislation and from the general improvement in the agrarian economy. It was these remaining inequalities in the Irish country-side which focused attention on the inadequacies of the Wyndham Act and which created the opportunity for a revival of the Irish Party's radical agrarian tradition.

This revival was led by Laurence Ginnell, the leading agrarian militant within the party, and it began in October 1906 at Downs, County Westmeath: here Ginnell laid down what became known as the 'Downs policy', which amounted to a cam-paign of cattle-driving directed against the ranchers of the midlands and the west. This initiative, neglected by scholars until comparatively recently, was of the greatest significance for the future development of parliamentary nationalism.[22] Ginnell was exploiting the radical traditions of the party in an assault on the Wyndham Act, and he was able to win considerable endorsement from within the ranks of the UIL, the party organization: it appears, for example, that the UIL Standing Committee helped to arrange all of Ginnell's campaign meetings. But Ginnell's 'ranch war' brutally exposed not merely the smugness of 'bullockdom', but also the dangerous conflicting interests within parliamentarianism. At one level the ranch war involved a clear-cut rejection of the conciliationist approach to agrarian questions: in April 1908 O'Brien proposed that the party should return to the policy of 'conference plus business', but he failed to convince Redmond, and he lost the vote by a sub-stantial margin (42 to 15). The party had thus decisively confirmed the 'fighting policy' which had been first enunciated at the National Convention of 1907; and in February 1909, when O'Brien's conciliationist stand was again rejected (at the violent and rowdy 'Baton' Convention meeting), it was quite clear that the militants were the dominant influence on the party and on its leadership. O'Brien finally gave up his fight for the centrist cause within the party, and he returned to his political base in Cork and the politics of popular agitation. This time, however, he was agitating for the conciliationist cause, and his vehicle, the All for Ireland League, had a dramatic if short-lived electoral impact in Cork politics.

But the ranch war also exposed the chasm between the Irish Party's condition and its aspirations. The party aspired to be a vehicle for social radicalism, as it had appeared to be in the Parnellite era. But the difficulty was that, as British reforms affected an ever greater section of Irish society, so the radical critique of the party came ever closer to its own membership. In part this was a problem of rhetoric: the party fed off a tradition of aggressive posturing which was rooted in the platform style of Daniel O'Connell, and which had been of proved effectiveness in arousing audiences throughout Ireland. But ferocious criticism became not merely an expression of humane anger at social injustice, but also a means of crushing even comparatively mild-mannered critics (such as, in this period, Horace Plunkett and John Shawe-Taylor); and it implied a standard of righteousness on the part of the parliamentarians, and a standard of baseness among their opponents, which had often only the slightest anchorage in the truth. The rhetoric of the party became a tool for its own mutilation: the lurid accusations exchanged during the Split of 1890–1 inflicted a lasting damage on the party's credibility. But the ferocious assault on landlordism created problems for a party which contained some influential land-lord members: Parnell was periodically embarrassed on this score, and in 1903 John Redmond was damaged by the accusation that he was selling his estate at an inflated price. The ranch war illustrates this point further: the party endorsed a violent cam-paign against the grazier interest, while at the same time harbouring within its ranks many influential representatives of this interest. It has been pointed out that 'a remark-ably high proportion of the principal leaders of the ranch war either were or became graziers'.[23] This meant in practice that, as in the Parnell era, the party tried, Janus-faced, to look two ways: graziers sat on public platforms denouncing the very system from which they were profiting. This often created tensions among the audi-ences at such gatherings; but in the mid-term it also undermined the credibility of the party.

The fundamental problem was, of course, that the party was a social coalition. It was united by a shared national sentiment, but it also attempted to consolidate its shaky solidarity by aggressive attacks on its enemies, real or imagined, and through a ferocious reformist rhetoric. But with the retreat of Irish landlordism through-out the later nineteenth century, and particularly after the Wyndham Act, and with the parallel rise in the fortunes of some of the Irish Party's supporters, this strat-egy gave rise to, at best, hypocrisy and, at worst, self-mutilation. A familiar escape route for the leadership was to divert political attention away from potentially divi-sive campaigns such as the ranch war and onto the ancient Anglo-Irish antagonism (in 1907 the normally benign Redmond sought the cover of history): but even this created difficulties for a party committed to a relationship with the Liberals and dependent upon a British government for legislative favours. What was beyond doubt, however, was that neither the traditions nor the dynamics of the party permitted much scope for conciliationist politics on the O'Brien model.

If the ranch war underlined the extent to which the party had rejected O'Brienism, then the legislative response of the British government mirrored this anti-conciliationist posture. It should be emphasized, however, that Birrell's Land Act of 1909, though of great importance, was as much a response to a British crisis as to the problems of the landless and the impoverished in the west of Ireland: though it coincided with the ranch war, and though it originally addressed some of the demands of the radical agrarians, in its final form it offered little economic comfort to few outside of the British Treasury. For the Act of 1909 was designed to address a crisis of which the ranch war was, in part, only a symptom: a crisis of liquidity. One of the fundamental problems with Wyndham's Act was that it was in fact too successful, and that the large number of voluntary sales outpaced the capacity of the Treasury to provide funding. In addition the general financial context should not be forgotten: Irish land purchase was only part of a massive upsurge in British state expenditure which had begun with the South African war, and was reaching crisis proportions with the welfare reforms of the New Liberalism and the arms race of the later Edwardian period. The 'People's Budget' of 1909 was an attempt to recoup some of the costs of welfare legislation through an increase and redistribution in taxation; and (as is frequently forgotten) Birrell's Land Act of 1909 was an attempt to recoup funds through a more tight-fisted revision of the land purchase mechanism.

Here the financial interests of the British government coincided with the political interests of the Dillonites, who had always claimed that the deal struck in 1903 had been outrageously generous to the landlords. The political consensus upon which Birrell's Act was based was therefore very different from that which Wyndham had constructed: where Wyndham had used an agreement between moderate landlords and tenants to coerce the Treasury, Birrell used an unspoken alliance between the Treasury and hardline tenant opinion to coerce the landlord interest. The Wyndham Act had been based exclusively on the principle of voluntary purchase and upon a series of incentives for potential landed vendors: a bonus of 12 per cent on the purchase price was a particular inducement, as were the regulatory zones within which a price might be established and the promise of cash payment once the sale had been agreed. Birrell's proposal involved the modification, or threatened modification, of each of these particulars. The flat-rate bonus was abandoned in favour of one that was linked to the price of the land (the cheaper the sale price, the more of a cash bonus was on offer). In addition, the agreed price of an estate was now to be paid not in cash but rather in a guaranteed government stock. The voluntary principle was also adjusted: Birrell sought to introduce a sweeping element of compulsion into his measure, but this was later toned down and compulsory sale was limited to the relief of the congested districts of the country. There was originally provision for the landless families whom the ranch warriors had championed; but this was rejected in the House of Lords and abandoned with minimal regret by Birrell.

The Land Act of 1909 was hailed by the Irish Party as a victory, and, in a highly limited sense, this triumphalism was justified. For Birrell's measure, even when modified by the Lords, presented a tougher deal to Irish landlords than that which they had enjoyed since 1903. In addition Birrell had made provision, through the innovation of compulsory purchase, for some of the poorest and most congested areas of the country. But, as many contemporary critics observed, the true beneficiaries of the Birrell Act were not purchasing tenants, or the poor of the congested districts, but rather the officials of the Treasury: in fact the Act was occasionally

described as a 'Treasury relief measure'.[24] For the removal of some of the inducements for landlords to sell was also in effect the removal of opportunities for
tenants to buy. The Act certainly took the pressure off state finance by cooling
landlord enthusiasm; but in fact it went beyond this, for to a certain extent it was
also less attractive for tenants to buy, since the Act balanced a slight reduction in
the annuity term with an increase in the rate of repayment. A number of cosmetic
political flourishes helped, therefore, to disguise what was in reality a brake upon
the rollercoaster of Wyndhamite land purchase.

The Irish Party had rejected conciliatory politics and what was a generally effective, if expensive, land purchase agreement; instead the party shifted towards a more
confrontational strategy – the 'policy of fight' – and offered violent support for
a purchase scheme which clothed its meanness by some scraps of anti-landlord
rhetoric. It is difficult to understand Irish Party strategy except in terms of the constitutional question and the totem of the Liberal alliance. The party was committed
to Liberalism and therefore preferred to endorse this union, since it was the mechanism that would eventually produce Home Rule. The Tories might offer alternative,
superficially more attractive blandishments, but their motives were suspect and, even
setting aside the issue of their willingness, their capacity to advance Irish national
aspirations was limited by the bond with Ulster Unionism. Shifting to a more cynical
mode of interpretation, it might be argued that a penny-pinching Liberal purchase
measure was in some ways ideal, certainly for those in the party leadership who
shared the views of Dillon. For such a measure indicated the productivity of the
Liberal alliance without offering any permanent land settlement in advance of Home
Rule, and without offering enough (assuming that it were possible) to lure Irish
nationalists into the British embrace.

Such cynicism may not be inappropriate, for by the time that Birrell's measure
passed into law the first clashes between the Liberal government and the Tory-
dominated House of Lords had occurred, and the first tremors of the constitutional
crisis of 1910–11 had already been felt. If the Irish Party was prepared to claim
a victory in the somewhat unlikely shape of the Birrell Act, then for some of the
same reasons it was prepared to endorse a highly unpopular budget. In fact Lloyd
George's 'People's Budget' was almost as repugnant to the Irish electorate as it was
to the House of Lords: the Chancellor's threats of land taxes were as horrific to the
new peasant proprietors of Ireland as they were to the ancient landed families of
Britain; his proposed hike in the cost of liquor licences and in the duties on spir-
its and tobacco was possibly more threatening to the Irish distilling and brewing
interests than to the British Tory drink trade. But if Lloyd George's budget created
some resentment amongst Irish nationalist voters and created a window of opportunity for O'Brienite politics, then it also created opportunities at Westminster for
the Home Rule movement. Mindful of popular opinion in Ireland, the Irish leaders
were also anxious not to mitigate any conflict between the Liberal government and
the House of Lords; and, accordingly, they abstained during the division on the
third reading of the Budget. In November 1909 the Lords voted the Budget down;
and Asquith went to the country in search of a mandate. He needed Irish support

in British constituencies, but he also clearly wanted to avoid a potentially damaging contest on the Home Rule question. He therefore pledged himself to Home Rule at the beginning of the contest, but allowed the issue to drop in the weeks that followed. The result of the general election – a hung parliament in which the Irish Party was crucial to the survival of the government – ensured, however, that Home Rule would prove to be more than merely a campaign phantom.

In 1910–11 the Irish Party reached what may be regarded, with the benefit of hindsight, as its apogee. Liberal dependence on the party was confirmed in a second election, held in December 1910. The stalemate over the 'People's Budget' was forcefully resolved, and in the manner that best suited Irish political needs: a constitutional amendment, contained within the Parliament Bill of 1911, abolished the veto of the Lords over legislation originating in the Commons and replaced it with a mere suspensory power. The Lords had now no authority to delay, let alone reject, money bills. It was such a bill, of course, that had precipitated the constitutional crisis of 1910–11, but the issue of the Lords' powers was for long inextricably linked with Home Rule. Redmond had pressed a sometimes flagging Asquith to pursue the confrontation with the Lords to a successful resolution; and his urgency had underlined the intense Irish interest in this ostensibly British and parliamentary battle. But for those who remembered that the second Home Rule Bill had been defeated by the Lords, and who remembered that there had been rumours of a retaliatory Gladstonian strike against the Upper House, such promptings were unnecessary. The Parliament Act was therefore a victory for the Irish no less than for the Liberals: indeed, it was a triumphant vindication for those, like Dillon, who had steadfastly banked upon the productivity of the Liberal alliance. The parliamentary vulnerability of the Liberals made them more dependent upon the Irish, and at least superficially more serious about Irish national aspirations: Liberal vulnerability almost concealed (but not quite) the narrowness of the parliamentary options available to the Irish leaders. The parliamentary configuration in 1910–11 was therefore a triumph for Redmond and Dillon's strategy: but while it illustrated what might be achieved by a mixture of shrewd calculation and good fortune, it also underlined the limitations of what any Irish party might gain from a clientilist relationship with one of its British counterparts.

The Irish Party could, and did, reactivate the old but often hesitant Liberal commitment to Home Rule; but they had comparatively little control over the legislative shape that this commitment might assume. If a Home Rule Bill was the price that the Liberals had to pay for Irish support, then unsatisfactory detail was the compensating price paid by the Irish for their dearth of political options. The Irish were thus highly successful in exploiting the conditions of 1910–11 in order to induce the rebirth of Home Rule; but thereafter their power was slight. When Asquith launched the third Home Rule Bill in April 1912 the peak of Irish euphoria had already been reached, and indeed disappointment was beginning to set in. For the bill contained a highly ungenerous definition of financial autonomy, devised by Herbert Samuel and superseding a much more lavish proposal associated with the Primrose Committee of 1911. The Irish leaders supported the Primrose report, but had to make do with the (otherwise highly controversial) Samuel proposals. It was a foretaste of the succession of humiliations and disappointments which the Irish Party would experience as their strategic achievement began to sour.[25]

Part of the Irish Party's difficulty lay in the real weakness – even when, comparatively, it seemed strongest – of its parliamentary position. But there were other problems. The Irish Party's strongest advocates also tended, generally for other non-Irish reasons, to be the weakest members of the Liberal cabinet. The Irish Party's most sympathetic advocate was the Chief Secretary, Birrell, who during 1911, when a cabinet committee was deliberating on the Home Rule question, had kept in touch with the nationalist leadership and represented their views to ministerial colleagues. In early 1912, when the bill was in evolution, Birrell was the main point of contact between the government and the Irish Party, and again acted as a sympathetic mouthpiece for Irish opinion within the cabinet. But Birrell's authority over Irish policy grew weaker as the political ramifications of Home Rule became increasingly more apparent: Birrell and the Irish Party's loss was the gain of Lloyd George and, to a lesser extent, Winston Churchill. Certainly by the end of 1913 it was clear that Lloyd George had emerged as the single most proactive influence on the evolution of the Home Rule Bill. Churchill, too, was applying his unpredictable genius to the Home Rule question in a manner which made life more difficult for the prosaic intellects inhabiting the Irish Office.

The ebb and flow of personal influence within the cabinet affected matters of first-rate significance for the Irish. Chief amongst these was the question of Ulster. The majority of Ulster Protestants, numbering one million or so, allied with a scattering of sympathizers throughout the south and west of Ireland totalling no more than 250,000, constituted a movement in support of the maintenance of the legislative union between Ireland and Britain; but it was the Ulster Unionists who were, because of their concentrated strength, the most formidable opponents of Home Rule. The original bill had contained no substantial concessions to their point of view, for Asquith – supported in this case by Redmond – treated the bill as a bargaining position and not necessarily as a fixed programme of action. As the Ulster Unionists organized and became progressively more militant, it was clear that the bill would have to be amended; but the difficulty lay in reconciling Ulster Protestant anxieties with Irish national aspirations. By early 1913 Dillon and (later) Redmond had moved to the view that some form of 'Home Rule within Home Rule' – that is to say, some form of regional weighting within the new Ireland and its devolved parliament – would be necessary to appease their increasingly fraught northern compatriots; but Ulster Unionists were clear that they would not accept any settlement, however cushioned, that would place them under the control of a predominantly nationalist assembly in Dublin. As time passed and Asquith continued to equivocate, so Ulster Unionist militancy grew more pronounced and the chances of an equitable settlement grew more remote. Painful concessions, urged on the nationalists by the Prime Minister and by rising ministers such as Lloyd George, served only to humiliate Redmond and the Irish Party, without effectively answering the, by now, impassioned Ulster Unionist case.

Some senior Liberals had long toyed with the idea of excluding either the whole province or part of Ulster from the operation of the Home Rule Bill. Though a submission to the cabinet was made along these lines in February 1912 by Lloyd George and Churchill, their colleagues decided to wait: their idea seems to have been to test the strength of Ulster Unionist opposition before squandering any bargaining power by making (perhaps) unnecessary concessions. When the Home Rule Bill was launched the only mention of exclusion came from the Liberal backbenches, and from T.G. Agar-Robartes, a Cornish MP who in June 1912 suggested that the four predominantly Protestant counties of the north-east be excluded from the operation of the bill. This was the parliamentary debut of partition, but it was in this instance a brief performance: Redmond had little difficulty in damning the idea, pointing to the Unionists' declared strategy of using the Agar-Robartes amendment as a wrecking mechanism. But the debate on the amendment included a significant contribution from Lloyd George, who emphasized the practical objections to exclusion while ominously avoiding any comment on the under-lying principle.

This mixture of ministerial evasion and isolated backbench distress heralded a series of much more devastating interventions in the Home Rule debate. Churchill's partitionist sympathies were advertised in a speech delivered at Dundee in October 1913; and in the following month Lloyd George, who by now had upstaged Birrell as the dominant influence on Irish policy, began canvassing support among senior ministerial colleagues for an exclusion scheme. This amounted to a combination of county option and temporary exclusion, and was eventually presented to the Unionists in March 1914. Carson's verdict was that he did not want 'a sentence of death with a stay of execution for six years'.[26] But the Liberals did not have the political space to grant a reprieve; nor did they have the imagination to devise some alternative form of correction. Lloyd George's 'sentence of death' was therefore delivered again in May 1914, through an Amending Bill introduced in the House of Lords; and it provided the basis for the abortive talks held between the government, Unionists and nationalists at Buckingham Palace in late July, in the shadow of the Great War.

But though there was no miraculous settlement at Buckingham Palace, or in the weeks afterwards, there had in fact been considerable political movement on both sides of the Irish dispute. The evolution of the Unionist cause is reviewed elsewhere in this volume and need not be detailed here, but it may be emphasized that within two years Carson had led his movement away from an (in democratic terms scarcely defensible) all-Ireland Unionism and away from nine-county exclusion, abandoning in the process first southern Unionists and then the Unionists of the three outer counties of Ulster. He and his movement had settled on six-county exclusion by late 1913 as their minimum terms for a settlement, and to this they adhered throughout 1914. But the Irish Party had covered a similar, indeed in some respects a greater, political distance. Redmond had perhaps a greater faith in the righteousness of the nationalist movement than Carson had in Unionism: certainly, Redmond affected to believe that the checks and balances contained within the Home Rule Bill were both offensive and unnecessary. He wanted a unitary Irish state and seems to have been less enthusiastic about 'Home Rule within Home Rule' than his ostensibly more trenchant colleague, Dillon: when in February 1914 Asquith outlined his 'Suggestions', a proposal for 'Home Rule within Home Rule', Redmond 'shivered visibly'.[27] His aspirations are relatively clear, as is his dismissal of Unionist opposition: he relied on Joseph Devlin, his (or rather Dillon's) lieutenant, for information about the north, and Devlin persisted in interpreting Unionist militancy as a charade. But Redmond's tactical vision is more obscure. It seems probable that like Asquith, his fellow lawyer, Redmond was not prepared to offer politically difficult concessions where they might not be necessary; but, if this was the case, then like Asquith he paid dearly for the luxury of perspective.

In two years Redmond had modified his uncomplicated all-Ireland nationalism by accepting a six-year term of exclusion for those Ulster counties seeking a reprieve from 'Papish' rule. By June 1916, after the Easter Rising, he was prepared to shift further, accepting the temporary exclusion of the six counties where the Unionist population was concentrated. This retreat was in part the price that Redmond paid for ignoring northern resentments in 1912; indeed, it was arguably the price that he paid for abandoning O'Brienite conciliation in 1903. The Irish Party had made the most of the parliamentary opportunities in 1910, exploiting their ties with the Liberals and their relative voting strength, but they were dealing with Liberal ministers who for the most part lacked any passion for the Irish cause and who responded primarily to tactical considerations. Redmond's collapse indicates the difficulties that the Irish faced in dealing with a party which had moved on from its Gladstonian agenda and which spent its evangelical passions in promoting social welfare throughout the United Kingdom. The tragedy of the Irish Party was that, having thwarted the constructive Unionism of the Tories, they encountered in Asquithian Liberalism a party whose instincts were often both constructive and (sometimes) unionist. It was doubly frustrating for Redmond to observe that the rising star of the Liberals, Lloyd George, while simultaneously exploiting Celtic nationalism and religious dissent, was also thoroughly assimilated within British parliamentary politics and more obviously sympathetic to his co-religionists in Ireland than to his fellow Celts. Here then was the painful outcome of the meeting between Parnellism without Parnell and Gladstonianism without Gladstone.

Redmond's relationship with the Liberals was therefore difficult. He and his lieutenants were effectively excluded from the early ministerial discussions on the Home Rule proposal: indeed, for virtually a year (1911), the Irish leaders relied on sporadic intelligence supplied by Birrell, who 'acted as watch-dog for Irish interests'.[28] In 1912 Redmond and Dillon were rather better briefed, working closely again with Birrell. But their influence was minimal: even though they detested the financial settlement contained within the bill, they had clearly little power to effect major alterations. More alarmingly, this was the Liberal–nationalist relationship at its best. By 1913–14 the most sympathetic minister, Birrell, had become a forlorn, almost marginal influence within the formulation of Irish policy, and other rising stars of the party were moving in on the issue. This diversification of responsibility and interest meant that it was often difficult for the Irish leaders to interpret the direction of cabinet thought, let alone seek to apply any coherent pressure: for example, in late 1913 Redmond was receiving three contradictory accounts of cabinet policy from three different ministers. Advice from the Irish leadership was frequently ignored; on 4 February 1914, Redmond urged that no concessions to the Unionists should be offered in the early stages of the final circuit of the Home Rule Bill, but by 27 February he and his lieutenants were being pressed for serious concessions as a matter of urgency. Indeed, the week from 27 February through to 6 March 1914 illustrates with a brutal clarity the comparative insignificance of the Irish as an influence over what was ostensibly their own Home Rule measure; within these few days Redmond had first conceded county option and three-year exclusion, then five-year exclusion, and finally – on 6 March – a six-year term of exclusion. By any standards this was a humiliating retreat: it reflected the difficult clientilist relationship borne by the nationalists, as well as the extent to which they had lost political initiative to the Ulster Unionists. It illustrated the basically contemptuous attitude of even friendly ministers; and it advertised the strategic weakness of the party to its following. Nor, as has been mentioned, was this the limit of Redmond's degradation: he had accepted three different forms of exclusion, insisting that each was a final concession, but he at least held to the last 'final' concession through the difficult spring and summer of 1914. However, the First World War brought further pressures on Redmond from both the British and republican militants, and in June 1916, during the talks headed (inevitably) by Lloyd George, he accepted the abandonment of county option in favour of the temporary exclusion of a bloc of six northern counties. This in fact very nearly secured a settlement and was only scuppered by southern Unionist objections, but one of the more intriguing counterfactual problems in modern Irish history is broached by the notion of an at least partially successful finale to the constitutional nationalist struggle.

The hydra that threatened Redmond sprang in part from Ulster Unionist militancy: one of the heads of the beast was Liberal contempt, another was republican militancy, and it was this which would eventually despatch Redmondism. The separatist movement is discussed elsewhere in the volume, but its relationship with parliamentary nationalism is of interest and relevance here. The strength of Parnellism had lain partly in the fact that it represented an informal alliance between the Fenian and constitutional traditions within nationalism: the New Departure, or series of new departures, in 1878–9 was the clearest expression of this understanding, though Parnell's alleged recruitment to the IRB (if authentic) is an equally useful illustration of the ambiguities of his career and of his movement. On the other hand, the vulnerability of Redmondism sprang partly from the fact that, while it repudiated an effectively conciliationist policy, it also became progressively detached from Fenianism: it was thus neither a particularly convincing force for moderation nor an effective vehicle for militant nationalism. The leaders of the Irish Party had rejected the opportunity, presented by William O'Brien, for a continuing dialogue on the land question and related issues. Indeed, it was the misjudgement, or misfortune, of the parliamentary leadership to become embroiled in agrarian militancy (through the ranch war) at precisely the moment when popular support for such causes was waning. It was, however, scarcely coincidental that while the parliamentary movement was threatening to divide on the electorally unprofitable issue of the cattle-drives, other nationalists, seeking a purer form of political expression, sought to reactivate the Fenian tradition. The Edwardian Irish Parliamentary Party contained a group of Fenians and ex-Fenians, veterans of the Parnellite era; but this older generation was pushed to the sidelines during a comprehensive reorganization of the Brotherhood that was undertaken by Thomas J. Clarke after 1907. Where Fenianism and Parnellism had been interlinked, these neo-Fenians had little contact with or sympathy for parliamentary nationalism, and indeed would ultimately prove to be its nemesis.

One of Redmond's most conspicuous failings as the Irish leader was that he contrived to be identified with militant elements inside the parliamentary tradition, without gaining any of the benefits that might have arisen from any calculated militant initiative. This was simultaneously a definition of his concern for national unity, as well as his abiding concern for the unity of the party. Where Parnell had simultaneously identified himself with hardliners and applied a brake to their endeavours, Redmond seemed to be the victim of initiatives taken by others: he was the embarrassed chairman of the Baton Convention of 1909, when O'Brien and his supporters were driven from the party by the hurley sticks and hazel switches of Devlin's Hibernians and the cattle-drivers of Longford and Westmeath. He was the

Plate 7   Irish Volunteers, Kesh, County Sligo, 1914.
Source: Hulton Getty.

effective victim of Ulster Unionist militancy, which seems to have taken him by surprise and to have forced him into the humiliating political retreat of early 1914. And he was a by-stander in the initial stages of the parallel drift towards paramilitarism among nationalists. The Irish Volunteer movement, the nationalist response to the UVF, was founded in November 1913 by Eoin MacNeill together with Michael Joseph Rahilly ('The O'Rahilly') and Bulmer Hobson, and was soon infiltrated by the re-energized Fenian movement. Only after its initial success, and after the escalation of militant activity in the north (with the Larne gun-running), did Redmond move to establish his authority over the Volunteers; in June 1914 he forced the Provisional Committee of the movement to accept 25 new members, the nominees of the Parliamentary Party. But this was a late and a desperate move, for, while Irish Party sympathizers were well represented in the ranks of the Volunteers, the organizational structure was already under the influence of the IRB. The 25 Redmondites, middle-aged and uninterested, seem to have cut a poor figure when compared with the active younger zealots of the original committee. Even after their appointment, Redmond's control of the movement remained tenuous (as evidenced by the Howth gun-running in July 1914, when – clearly without his knowledge or support – 1,500 rifles and 45,000 rounds of ammunition were landed north of Dublin). The success of this enterprise was tragically marred by the subsequent confrontation between British soldiers and an unarmed crowd at Bachelor's Walk, where three of the civilians were killed. But these killings were also a graphic illustration of the increasing precariousness of Redmond's constitutional politics.

Redmond's coup created, therefore, a merely cosmetic unity. When he committed the Volunteers to the British war effort in September 1914, he precipitated – perhaps intentionally – a split in the movement; and while the overwhelming majority (numbering around 158,000) endorsed his position, a minority (some 12,000) were bitterly opposed to any form of military collusion with the British. In Dublin, the old heartland of Parnellism, there was a particularly significant concentration of dissidents, totalling perhaps 2,000 as opposed to some 4,700 Redmondite loyalists. But the military importance of the dissidents (who retained the title of Irish Volunteers) was enhanced by the fact that they stayed in Ireland, while large numbers of the Redmondites (or National Volunteers) obeyed the command of their leader and set off to their deaths on the Western Front.

Redmond wanted a blood sacrifice for Ireland in France and Flanders, and this he got in full: the Great War claimed the lives of his brother, Willie, and of colleagues like T.M. Kettle, along with those of perhaps 30,000 fellow Irish soldiers. Through his call to arms, through urging a distinctive contribution to the British and Allied war effort, Redmond had sought to underline the dignity of Irish nationality; Patrick Pearse and his fellow IRB activists within the Irish Volunteers sought to achieve much the same end through their stand at the General Post Office on Easter Monday, 1916. But this congruity only serves to highlight the final paradox of constitutional nationalism. For the constitutionalists had, in the end, been forced into a militant stand, first through their fear of the emerging Irish Volunteer movement and, second, through their participation in the British military drive. It is hard not to sympathize with the frustration of Captain Stephen Gwynn, an Irish MP and loyal Redmondite, who argued that 'the constitutional party ought either to have dissociated itself completely from the appeal to force or to have launched and controlled it from the outset'; in other words, that the party would have done better to remain true to its constitutional aspirations, or, failing that, to use militancy as a parliamentary lever, as Parnell had done and O'Connell before him.[29] In any event Redmond, acting from the most honourable motives, had effectively vindicated the need for a militant strategy and a blood sacrifice. From then on the difference between him and the separatists lay less with the issue of armed force than with the question of its purpose. For the essential failure of Redmond lay in the fact that he urged men to bear arms in the pursuit of a chimerical and thoroughly prosaic measure of devolution; while his militant opponents fought and died for a chimerical republic. It was inevitably the embittered and vituperative William O'Brien who summarized the dilemma of Redmondism, its paradoxes and ambiguities, with the most brutal clarity: 'constitutionalism in a country whose historical grievance is that she possesses no constitution is', he declared, 'an historical humbug'.[30]

5.2   Paths to the Post Office: Alternatives to the Irish Parliamentary Party, 1891–1914

The death of Parnell in 1891 not only exposed the different strains within the parliamentary tradition, it also helped to encourage cultural and political alternatives. This, at any rate, was the thesis favoured by the poet W.B. Yeats, who saw the temporary collapse of the Irish Party as a pivotal moment in his personal and artistic development, no less than in the history of the national movement (this idea was elaborated in his 'The Intellectual Revival in Ireland'). Historians, as ever, have been suspicious of the notion of a watershed (even in terms of Yeats's biography); and they have been more comfortable in identifying the long-term continuities spanning the last years of Parnell and beyond.[31] Even the most cautious, however, has observed the wider cultural and political resonance of Parnell's demise.

Yeats favoured the idea of 'hammering one's thoughts into unity'; and his Parnell thesis involved a necessary amount of pummelling and simplification.[32] In truth the roots of the new nationalism – of the Irish political and cultural efflorescence of the 1890s and beyond – lay not only in the (temporary) decay of parliamentarianism but also in many other, equally rich, seed-beds. The ideologues of this revival drew inspiration from a variety of precursors in the eighteenth and nineteenth centuries, and were responding to a variety of social and political questions which the parliamentarians had either answered inadequately or simply passed over. The British government, aided by the Irish Party, had enacted a variety of social reforms which, in turn, had facilitated a measure of popular educational and material progress. The British Liberal Party, in alliance with the Irish, had held out the always imminent prospect, but never attainable reality, of Home Rule. British politicians, following the agenda and concerns of Irish parliamentarians, had focused on addressing the needs of Irish farmers and of the wider countryside. Irish parliamentarians invoked the names of cultural nationalists like Thomas Davis or fiery rebels like John Mitchel, while not actively pursuing the manifestos of these men. In sum, British liberal reform allied with Irish Party strategy created a crisis of rising expectations. The Irish Party had helped to excite expectations of social mobility and of national fulfilment which it could not ultimately gratify. John Hutchinson has strenuously argued that the late nineteenth-century Irish cultural and political revival owed much of its force to the thwarted ambitions of educated lower middle-class Catholics, men and women who aspired to a place in the sun but found that it was already occupied by Protestants (or by Englishmen).[33]

At one level, then, the revival may be explained in terms of a Weberian 'blocked mobility' thesis. At another level, the cultural efflorescence owed its origins, at least in part, to a crisis of declining expectations among Irish Protestants. Vivian Mercier joked that 'the true purpose of the Irish Literary Revival was to provide alternative employment for the sons of clergymen after disestablishment had reduced the number of livings provided by the Church of Ireland', but the humour was pointed.[34] Protestants were still disproportionately represented in many areas of Irish official and professional life; they still held a disproportionate amount of the country's wealth. However, successive Land Acts ravaged the Protestant landed elite; and for these men and women, and for their co-religionists in the police or civil service or the professions, insecurities multiplied as the threat of a Catholic nationalist Home Rule administration loomed. Many, particularly in the north, took refuge in Unionism (as will be recounted later in the volume); but there was also a small but vibrant tradition which pursued a more constructive and proactive engagement with the national movement. Parnell had sought to define a role for Protestants in an autonomous Ireland; but Parnell had also helped to consolidate a powerful Catholic farmer interest upon which his political fortunes, and those of his party, largely depended. In a sense, then, Parnell had simultaneously outlined a future for Irish Protestants and refuted his own definition. If the future of Ireland, as envisaged by the parliamentarians, rested with the substantial farming interest, then this was not a vision which many urban intellectuals, both Catholic and Protestant, were prepared to share. The Anglo-Irish literary revival of the 1890s and beyond was in part the reaction of Protestant and other intellectuals to what was seen as the new, grasping rural middle class (what the dramatist J.M. Synge characterized as 'the groggy-patriot-publican-general shop-man who is married to the priest's half-sister and is second cousin once-removed of the dispensary doctor', or, with greater violence, as the 'ungodly ruck of fat-faced sweaty-headed swine'); these antipathies may have reflected the modified religious or social prejudices of the waning ascendancy, but they were also shared by some Catholic ideologues, and notably by D.P. Moran (editor of the *Leader* and philosopher of the nativist Irish Ireland movement).[35] The literary revival, and indeed Irish Irelandism, were of course not merely expressions of profound social resentment. The leaders of the literary revival were interested in the role of the artist within the national movement and they were concerned to promote a national literature in the English language. But they were also, in part, a group of Protestants who were seeking to explore their Irishness and to define a workable relationship with the national tradition. It was clear that, certainly until around 1910, these men and women saw little prospect of working within the mainstream parliamentary movement.

So far two key social focuses of the revival have been defined: the Catholic urban middle class, and southern Protestants of a middle-class or landed background. One important, though not pre-eminent, event in the history of the revival has been highlighted: the death of Parnell. But the revival was rooted in other crucial social and political movements; and there were other dates of equal significance to 1891. Underlying some of the political transformations of the late nineteenth century was a relative economic boom, which was sustained, though not without fits and starts, through to the First World War. It has been argued that this tended to exacerbate some of the social inequalities in British and Irish society; and it has also been suggested that the very rapid growth in trade union activity – known in Ireland as 'Larkinism', after the most prominent union leader, Jim Larkin – was rooted in these widening social disparities and in the increasing social resentment of to the poor.[36] The rise of Larkinism is not generally treated in the context of the broader cultural and political revival in Edwardian Ireland; but in so far as it represented the growth of an indigenous trade union movement and promoted the formation of an indigenous labour party, then it takes its place among the central themes explored in this chapter. The roots and final flowering of Larkinism also touched on many wider aspects of the revival. The economic upturn that helped to sustain union organization also helped to strengthen the material well-being of the farming interest and of the rural middle classes; and it helped to shape the resentments of an educated urban elite that enjoyed some mobility and prosperity, but only within the cage of the *ancien régime*. The final showdown between Larkin and the forces of Dublin capitalism in 1913 brought a number of key figures in the revival – Yeats, Patrick Pearse, the poet, educationalist and rebel, and George Russell, the dramatist and mystic – to the workers' cause.

Mysticism is a further connecting theme within the very diverse history of the cultural and political revival. There was a remarkable upsurge in mystical thought and practice in late nineteenth-century Ireland and Britain, which helped to energize the ideologues of the revival and shape their thoughts. Eastern spirituality was a fertile source of inspiration. It is not necessary to explore at length the origins of this broad phenomenon; and to do so might be to risk an overly prosaic reading of the determinedly mysterious. Still, it might be ventured that mystical religious practice reflected dissatisfaction with conventional religion as well as an enthusiasm for exclusive secret societies which had other, marginally less bizarre, forms of expression in Ireland (freemasonry, Orangeism, the Fenian tradition, the Ancient Order of Hibernians). Mysticism may have been partly about social and religious insecurity; its practice demanded a certain amount of leisure time and expense. For Protestants like Yeats or Synge or George Russell, mysticism and an interest in pre-Christian belief perhaps reflected a desire to step outside the sectarian arena of conventional Irish religion and to engage the national tradition on different, more neutral terms: 'I have longed to turn Catholic', the dramatist Lady Gregory announced to Yeats, 'that I might be nearer the people, but you have taught me that paganism brings me nearer still'.[37]

In some senses paganism was highly convenient for nationally minded Protestants. For mystical Catholics like Pearse, or the poet and revolutionary Joseph Plunkett, the rich spiritual resources of the universal Church offered a means of escape from the mundane realities of Irish religious life and practice: Plunkett found inspiration in the writings of St John of God, while Pearse wove his Christian and pagan Irish enthusiasms into a unique system of belief. Stephen MacKenna, the journalist and Irish Irelander best known for his translation of Plotinus, moved from Catholicism to a form of Buddhism to – at the end of his life – unitarianism. At the risk of irony, it might be tentatively argued that the Marxism of the great labour leader James Connolly also falls into the category of mystic conviction.

The death of Parnell was important in furthering the political and cultural revival. But there were other events and other individuals that also played a pivotal role in the shaping of affairs. Earlier cultural revivals – in the mid- and late eighteenth century, and in the 1830s and 1840s – provided precedents, heroes, an essential literature and the materials for later controversies. The intellectual and political activity of the 1830s and 1840s had a particular importance, as will become clear: Yeats and his circle were influenced by the scholarly activity of patriotic Unionists like the poet and archivist Samuel Ferguson, or George Petrie, the archaeologist, or – from a slightly later period – the popular historian Standish O'Grady. For Protestant nationalists these earlier scholars, though loyalist (Lady Gregory called O'Grady 'the Fenian Unionist'), illustrated the ways in which Protestants could express their Irishness and – without any humiliating or violent renunciation – align themselves with an advanced national tradition.[38] At a wider level, Ferguson and O'Grady illustrated the ways in which an authentically Irish national literature might be constructed in the English language, and at the same time without doing violence to their artistic integrity.

The cultural nationalists within Young Ireland, pre-eminently Thomas Davis, provided a reference point for all forms of revival activity in the late Victorian and Edwardian period. Davis highlighted the necessary connection between language and nationality, and advocated the revival of Irish; but he took his analysis little further. On the other hand, he promoted the celebration of Irishness through the English language (in, for example, 'The Library of Ireland', 1845); and, together with the broader Young Ireland movement, he appeared to subordinate his art to the demands of the national struggle. Thanks to his friend and admirer Charles Gavan Duffy, the teachings of Davis were made available to the nationalists of the 1880s and 1890s; and the questions that he raised about the role of artist and of the English language were focal points for debate among late Victorian and Edwardian intellectuals. His more vituperative and violent colleague John Mitchel provided a bitterly anglophobic analysis and rhetoric, which was a profound influence over later advanced nationalists such as Arthur Griffith, the founder of Sinn Féin, or Patrick Pearse. Pearse, in a series of pamphlets published in 1915–16, saw Davis and Mitchel as two of the five founding fathers of modern nationalism (the others were Tone, Lalor and – not so much because he was a thinker as because he was 'a flame that seared, a sword that stabbed' – Parnell).[39]

Some general features of the background to the revival have been highlighted by way of introduction. The different aspects of the revival, and their individual origins, may now be examined. These are explored separately, but the intellectual community in Ireland was (and is) comparatively small, and the close connections between different forms of cultural and political activity, and between ostensibly very different individual ideologues, should not be overlooked. Indeed, these connections represent one of the themes of the chapter. If the relationship between different types of revival activity is complex, then this complexity is even more evident in approaching the relationship between the mainstream parliamentary tradition and the apparent alternatives. This rich and ambiguous connection represents a further motif in what follows.

The debates about the form and purpose of Irish literature in the late Victorian and Edwardian period might be represented as a sort of patriotic spectrum, with at one end O'Grady and Ferguson, the Unionists, and at the other D.P. Moran, the ferocious advocate of a Catholic Gaelicism who wanted to convert English speakers to Irish and who argued that an authentic Irishness was rooted exclusively in the language; Moran, while wavering a little, was basically hostile to the 'mongrel' Anglo-Irish literary revival. The Parliamentary Party might, in this construction, be placed in the middle of the spectrum in that, while it contained a wide range of thought on this as on other questions, it broadly sustained the Davisite tradition of a literature in English serving the national interest. Between the Irish Party and Moran might be placed language advocates like Douglas Hyde, who saw a literature in English as a useful and inevitable transitory arrangement; here, too, might be found those (like Stephen MacKenna) who sought a genuinely cosmopolitan modern literature in Irish. Locating Yeats and his circle highlights the difficulties with any system of categorization, but, given his loyalty to O'Grady and Ferguson, and given his concern for a national literature in English, he might tentatively be placed between the patriotic Unionists and the parliamentarians.

This system is necessarily crude, but it provides a starting point. Ferguson, through his poetry and translations, and through his involvement with the pluralist *Dublin University Magazine*, demonstrated a combination of Protestantism, patriotism and literary accomplishment that exercised a powerful influence over Yeats. O'Grady, through his popularization of the ancient Irish epics (*The History of Ireland: The Heroic Period*, 1878), and through his attempts to formulate a programme of leadership for the old Protestant landed elite, was also of interest to Yeats. But, paradoxically, the rhetoric and analysis of these respectable patriotic Unionists were in places indistinguishable from some expressions of Fenian sentiment; and of course it had been perfectly possible for Isaac Butt, the pillar of the *Dublin University Magazine* and of the Orange establishment, to develop into the most notable defender of Fenian prisoners and the herald of Home Rule. The combination of literary ambition, 'soft' Fenianism and a concern for cultural fusion became a hallmark of Yeats's endeavours: Yeats, like Butt, conducted forays into advanced nationalism, but ultimately mellowed.

But Yeats and his movement were also very much products of the mid-1880s and the contemporary upswing in political and cultural debate. In a sense, therefore, it was not so much the absence of Parnell that was an intellectual stimulus as his presence: the growing possibility that Parnell would deliver a form of legislative auton- omy for Ireland encouraged numerous Irish intellectuals to think about the future cultural life of their country. A series of important initiatives dates from around this time: the growth of the Young Ireland societies ('whose ethos was distinctly armchair- Fenian'), the creation of the Contemporary Club and the founding of the *Dublin University Review* (a sort of revival of Butt's *Dublin University Magazine*).[40] Yeats was introduced to Fenianism and inducted into the IRB at this time: virtually simul- taneously, he was lauding the achievement of Ferguson. His agenda, and that of his wide circle, was – as Roy Foster has argued – 'not about creating an alternative to politics; it concerned what to do when politics delivered Home Rule'.[41]

The death of Parnell, and the consequent sullying and disorientation of the par- liamentary tradition, of course created opportunities for Yeats and other patriotic intellectuals. Still, while it would be quite wrong to dismiss the long-term signifi- cance of Parnell's demise, it is possible that the cultural activity of the early 1890s was stimulated almost as much by the renewed possibility of Home Rule (in 1893) as by the felling of the Uncrowned King. Initiatives such as Yeats's Irish Literary Society of London (December 1891) coincided with the death of Parnell; but the important National Literary Society, with which Yeats and the old Fenian John O'Leary were closely associated, was formed in June 1892, at the time of the fall of the Unionist government in London. And Yeats's influential lecture, 'Nationality and Literature', in which he argued for a national literature rooted in a cosmopolitan context, was first delivered at the height of the controversy over the second Home Rule Bill (May 1893). But there were other patriotic climacterics that had a strong cultural dimen- sion: the Greco-Turkish war of 1897 fired the spirit of some Irish nationalists, but the centenary of the 1798 rising and the outbreak of the South African war had a much more decisive importance. Yeats was President of the 1898 Centennial Association of Britain and France; and, while his ambitions for a national literature were long- standing, the centenary provided an immediate inspiration and context for the foundation of the Irish Literary Theatre in December 1898.

The Irish Literary Theatre, and its successor organization (the Irish National Theatre Society (INTS) of February 1903), reveal much about the ambiguities and the audac- ity of Yeats's cultural project. Yeats and (to some extent) his collaborators, Lady Gregory and Edward Martyn, sought to create a national drama which at the same time had a wider artistic appeal and intellectual credibility. They were interested in furthering the national cause, albeit primarily in the English language; they were also not immune to the blandishments of the Castle establishment. Yeats sought to emphasize that, while all meaningful art should be derived from the people, the artist could not set out to court popularity. This complex agenda meant that the Irish Literary Theatre enjoyed the patronage of hardline Unionists such as Lord

Ardilaun and advanced separatists such as Maud Gonne; it meant that the Theatre could mount essentially patriotic pieces such as Yeats's *Countess Cathleen* (staged in May 1899), which at the same time contrived to offend popular nationalist sensibilities. Yeats's political gymnastics involved a condemnation of the British campaign in South Africa (though only in March 1900); these also meant that in April 1902, in the last weeks of the war, he and Lady Gregory could stage *Cathleen ni Houlihan*, set during the 1798 rising and elaborating the theme of personal sacrifice to the cause of militant patriotism. The reaction of the Protestant Home Ruler Stephen Gwynn is much quoted – most famously by Yeats himself: 'I went home asking myself if such plays should be produced unless one was prepared for people to go out to shoot and be shot'.[42] Yet a year and a half later (in October 1903) the Chief Secretary for Ireland, George Wyndham, was in the audience for one of the productions of Yeats's Irish National Theatre Society (J.M. Synge's *In the Shadow of the Glen*). In June 1904 Yeats 'bumped into' Queen Alexandra at a society function.[43] And in August 1910 he cheerfully accepted a civil list pension from the British government. Perhaps all this says as much about the intimate nature of Irish society, and about the curiously flippant tone of much of the British establishment in Ireland, as about the literary movement: it certainly illustrates a genial British contempt for the posturing of advanced nationalism. But it also reflects upon the ambiguities of the Anglo-Irish literary revival and upon the skill with which these were defended by its chief ideologue, Yeats.

The Irish Literary Theatre and its successor, the INTS, could provide a safe literary Fenianism for an Irish audience and for the Castle establishment. But they also sought to balance a commitment to a national drama, rooted in the concerns of the people, with avant-garde aspirations. In 1901 James Joyce was arguing (in 'The Day of the Rabblement') that the Theatre had got this balance wrong, and indeed had sold out to a stultifying parochialism.[44] But this was a premature verdict: a different and more awkward relationship between modernism and nativism would soon emerge in the work of Synge, perhaps the most celebrated dramatist of the literary revival. Synge used in his work materials garnered from his home turf of Wicklow as well as the west of Ireland, and especially his beloved Aran Islands: folk-tales and reminiscences were recorded in his notebooks, as were the vocabulary, idioms and cadences of the westerners (whether English or Irish speakers). He used traditional materials but in a hyperrealistic and unsentimental form: he united parochialism and modernism. The result was work of European distinction which, for the moment, offended the patriotic sensitivities of some Irish theatregoers. His *In the Shadow of the Glen* depicted a young woman, Nora Burke, caught in a loveless marriage to an aging Wicklow farmer, who eventually finds freedom by eloping with a tramp: the play was first staged in October 1903 and was widely condemned (by Arthur Griffith, for example) as a cynical fraud, and as a calumny on Irish womanhood. Synge's *The Playboy of the Western World* offered to the Irish public Christy Mahon, a would-be parricide, protected and celebrated in a Mayo village. The boisterous vulgarity of the villagers, their respectful attitude towards a supposed murderer, and the robust language of the play (the mention of women's 'shifts' was a particular issue) all seemed to represent a calculated slander on the Irish people and a caricature of Irishness. The first staging of the play, on 26 January 1907, brought riots and a classic show-down between the modernists and nativists within the broad national revival.

In a sense this clash, bitter though it was, soon ceased to have a commanding urgency or relevance. For after 1910 the mainstream parliamentary tradition came into its own, propping a minority Liberal government in return for a commitment to a third Home Rule Bill. Constitutional reform in Britain in 1911 meant that Home Rule was no longer a pious aspiration, but rather an immediate prospect. The parliamentarians, always a centripetal force in Irish politics and culture, were now capable of inspiring a broader realignment within the national movement and among the leaders of the national revival: Griffith, Pearse and also Yeats were pulled into the orbit of Home Rule by the powerful gravity of a reinvigorated parliamentary cause. For Yeats and for his circle, this mellowing brought a separation from the Fenian linkages of the 1880s and 1890s. It was also associated with a reawakened and more overt identification with the fading world of the southern Protestant gen-try: Yeats was moved by 'the sense of a disappearing past, acquiring as it receded the enhanced and idealised allure of nostalgia'.[45] But this did not mean any marked revision of the cultural ideals of the literary revival, or any obvious retreat from its pluralist agenda: the Abbey Theatre (home of the INTS since December 1904), aided perhaps by the national realignment behind Home Rule, staged a passion play by Patrick Pearse in 1911 as well as gritty drama written in Ulster dialect by the north-ern Protestant St John Ervine (later a trenchant convert to Ulster Unionism). Nor, of course, did Yeats's obeisance to the parliamentary tradition exorcise the Fenian past: it could not annul the influence that powerful propagandist work like *Cathleen ni Houlihan* exercised over a generation of separatists. Tom Kettle quipped in 1906 that 'Mr Yeats had done more than anyone else to create an Irish theatre, and he had also done more than anybody else to prevent anybody going there': but while this judgement reflected popular hostility to the modernist challenge, it did not acknowledge the profound impact of unambiguously patriotic work.[46]

Yeats and his circle had sought to demonstrate the value of the artist to the national movement: they had also sought to defend the autonomy of the artist from sub-servience to the national interest. They had argued for an authentically Irish liter-ature in the English language. Their pluralist approaches, though not immediately popular, have come ultimately to dominate independent Ireland. But others, who engaged Yeats and Synge and Gregory in debate, approached the issue of a national literature from a different set of perspectives and with a more immediate popular impact. The Irish Irelanders of the Gaelic League and Sinn Féin were interested in the questions raised by the ideologues of the Anglo-Irish literary revival; but though they shared a patriotic vocabulary with the *littérateurs*, the answers that they provided were quite different. The intellectual roots of these Irish Irelanders were for the most part separate from those of the Anglo-Irish dramatists, and their political and cultural priorities were also distinctive. There were frequent points of communion between the two groups of intellectuals, but it is hard to escape the impression that the faiths were different.

If Yeats and his circle were concerned to create a literature for the new Ireland, then many of the Irish Irelanders believed that this creation should be in Irish and that it should be subservient to the national cause. Many Irish Irelanders, while not blind to the value of literature, defined the challenge of nationality in terms of the language: the Irish language was inseparable from Irish identity, and a national literature in English could be at best a transitory arrangement, and at worst a contradiction in terms. Irishness, in this definition, was bleeding away: the census statistics demonstrated that both the population of Ireland and the proportion of Irish speakers had dangerously declined since the Famine. In 1845 around 50 per cent of the population spoke Irish; in 1851 this had fallen to 23 per cent. The year 1891 brought not only the death of Parnell but also the revelation from the census that Irish speakers constituted only 14.5 per cent of the population.

As for Yeats and other anglophone intellectuals, Parnell's death created opportunities for the defenders of Irish. But, just as Yeats's creativity had been fired by a complex range of influences, so the advocates of the language depended not simply on political space but also on earlier scholarship and activism. The work of philologists in both the cultural revival of the mid- to late eighteenth century and that of the 1830s–1840s was important as an inspiration as well as a scholarly foundation: Johann Kasper Zeuss's *Grammatica Celtica* (1853) 'laid a sound basis for all future study of old and Middle Irish'.[47] British policy, held to blame for the disasters that the language experienced, was not without some meagre benefits: the Ordnance Survey (1824) was not only an exercise in mapping, it also brought together a body of Irish scholars committed to the garnering of information on place names and antiquities. As noted, in 1851 and after census-takers documented the retreat of Irish and thus helped to arm its defenders. Some earlier patriotic intellectuals, notably Thomas Davis, drew attention to the importance of the language; some earlier writers – James Hardiman, author of *Irish Minstrelsy* (1831), Ferguson, O'Grady – helped to popularize Irish-language material in translation.

Political campaigns in support of Irish and organizations devoted to its propagation also predated the main period of the cultural revival in the 1890s and after. The Society for the Preservation of the Irish Language was founded in 1876 by David Comyn and Father Nolan, and with Isaac Butt as a vice-president. It scored some early and significant political victories: in 1878 official permission was given for the limited use of Irish within the national (primary) school system. Also in 1878, an Intermediate Education (Ireland) Act was passed which, amongst its other provisions, gave a role to Irish within the new secondary schools. The Gaelic Union, formed in 1880, continued the work of the Society for the Preservation of the Irish Language: the Union sought to stem the retreat of Irish within the Gaeltacht and to evangelize for the language among English speakers. Its publication, the *Gaelic Journal*, attracted contributions from (among others) Michael Cusack, later founder of the Gaelic Athletic Association (GAA), and the young Douglas Hyde.

It is Hyde who is credited with inspiring the most successful of the language organizations, the Gaelic League. His argument on 'The Necessity for De-Anglicising Ireland', delivered as a lecture in 1892 (and published in 1894), called for a sweeping

Irish cultural revival for fear that 'we will become . . . a nation of imitators, the Japanese of Western Europe, lost to the power of native initiative, and alive only to second-hand assimilation'.[48] This address had a wide and profound influence: in the short term it helped to forge the ambition of a young Dublin clerk, Eoin MacNeill, to establish a popular organization for the propagation of the Irish language. From this emerged, in July 1893, the Gaelic League, with Hyde, MacNeill and the professor of Irish at Maynooth, Father Eugene O'Growney, at its head.

In his lecture Hyde had envisaged a cultural revival which would be above politics, and which would be of as great interest to Unionists as to nationalists. This, broadly, was the position from which the Gaelic League embarked: it aspired to be a non-sectarian and non-political organization, which would provide an inclusivist forum for those committed to the language. And, indeed, the League's early success owed something to the humanistic appeal made by Hyde and others to secular nationalists and to liberal Protestants: some loyalists or ex-loyalists were tempted within its confines, including – remarkably – the trenchant Orange pastor Reverend R.R. Kane, and also the second Lord Ashbourne, President of the Gaelic League of London and son of a Tory Lord Chancellor of Ireland. But the increasingly tense sectarian context within which the League was operating, especially after 1900, meant that it became increasingly difficult to uphold the pluralist ideal (D.P. Moran's narrowly Catholic vision of Irishness was one strong brake upon ecumenism); and the popular politicization that accompanied the third Home Rule Bill meant that the exclusively cultural agenda which Hyde had originally advocated became impossible to sustain. After 1914, as John Hutchinson has observed, cultural nationalism was swiftly transformed into the instrument of an elitist revolutionary movement.[49] At its ard-fheis of 1915, the constitution of the League was changed to acknowledge an active commitment to 'a free Gaelic-speaking Ireland', a modification which reflected an assumption shared by many – but not, significantly, Douglas Hyde.[50] Looking ahead a little, in September 1919 the British recognized, through proscription, the seriousness of the political threat posed by the League.

Like the Society for the Preservation of the Irish Language, the Gaelic League focused on the role of Irish within the educational system. An early success was the creation, after lobbying by the League, of a lectureship in Irish in University College Cork. League concerns were soon articulated in the higher reaches of the Castle regime: Douglas Hyde sat on the government commissions investigating secondary education (1901) and the universities (1906). What was arguably its greatest success came in 1910, when (despite forceful opposition from John Dillon) Irish was made a compulsory subject for matriculation in the new National University of Ireland. Building on this, the ard-fheis of 1913 voted to demand that Irish should be taught in every national school in Ireland, and that it should be made a requirement for entry into all the teacher training colleges on the island.

There was also pressure from the League to expand the use of Irish within public life. In 1896 its members called upon candidates in the East Kerry by-election to deliver speeches in Irish. In 1897 the League was successful in expanding the rights of Irish speakers giving testimony in the law courts. Its Dublin branches agitated for, and won, the instatement of Irish as a requirement for employment by Dublin corporation. In 1905 the League launched a campaign to force the Post Office to accept mail that was addressed only in Irish.

The means by which these cultural goals were pursued were sometimes ends in themselves. The need for a popular Irish-language newspaper was filled by *An Claidheamh Soluis*, the 'sword of light', which was launched in 1899 and which in 1903 acquired Patrick Pearse as editor (Pearse had joined the League in 1896 and had been a member of its Coiste Gnotha, or executive committee, since 1898). *An Claidheamh* articulated League policy, advertised its activities and provided an outlet for new writing in Irish (not least from Pearse himself): along with the *Leader*, edited by Moran, and the *United Irishman*, edited by Arthur Griffith, *An Claidheamh* represented a crucial vehicle for the wider Irish Ireland movement. But there were other more functional literary endeavours: the League issued large quantities of propaganda and basic educational materials (in 1900–1 over 100,000 copies of 18 different pamphlets were printed in order to spread the League's case on, for example, the role of Irish within the school system). Organizers were appointed to promote a commitment to the language in the Gaeltacht and other areas of the country. Classes and social events were organized to encourage Irish speaking: a particular effort was made to provide a grounding in the language for school teachers.

As has been noted, the League provided a forum for the young, educated lower middle classes. It originally provided a forum for a few Protestants who were dissatisfied with formal Unionism and who sought a more constructive engagement with the Gaelic tradition. More importantly, it offered an outlet for the social and political resentments of those Irish Catholics who were blocked by the institutions of the British regime, and who saw little attraction in the Home Rule movement. As with Fenianism in the 1860s, the League also offered recreational diversion: it satisfied not only national conviction but also a distinctively Victorian thirst for self-improvement and for the constructive use of leisure time. Membership of the League in the country areas consisted largely of farmers' sons. But the roots of the League were essentially urban: T.F. O'Rahilly, writing in 1932, lamented that 'the weakness of the League from the beginning was that it was essentially a townsmen's organisation, centralised in Dublin, and never took real root in the Irish speaking, or semi-Irish speaking, districts'.[51] The urban branches of the movement were filled with commercial clerks and shop assistants. Branch leaders, concentrated in the towns, were recruited from the lower ranks of the professional classes and from the intelligentsia.

It would seem, pursuing this analysis, that the success of the League was rooted in the failings of the Irish Parliamentary Party. But, as noted, there is a case to be made against any glib acceptance of a Parnell-centred, Yeatsian reading of the chronology of intellectual revival. The Gaelic League was indeed created in the confused aftermath of Parnell's death, when cultural activity seemed to offer a convincing alternative to the temporarily exhausted and discredited parliamentarians; it retreated somewhat after 1906, with the resurgence of the Irish Party and in the context of heightened class-based tensions in Dublin and elsewhere. But the League built upon a more ancient history of interest in the language; and it peaked in the early Edwardian period at a time when the Irish Party was already reunited and was clawing its way back to pre-eminence. The prosperity of the League and the Irish Party was not in fact determined by a fixed inverse relationship: both the League and the Irish Party (and indeed the wider national movement) benefited from the energizing effects of the South African war and from the broad upsurge in anti-imperial spirit that gripped the south and west of Ireland at this time. From a relatively modest position in the late 1890s, the League had reached a peak of 985 branches and some 75,000 members by 1906: the Irish Party was consolidating in the same period.

Moreover, there are dangers in positing too complete a separation between the Irish Party and the Gaelic League (or, indeed, other forms of the new nationalism). Patrick Maume has pointed out, through his study of D.P. Moran's weekly *Leader*, that 'the Irish Party had [not] entirely lost touch with the new Irish Ireland movements'.[52] Looking back to the 1870s, Butt had been a vice-president of the Society for the Preservation of the Irish Language. There were later gestures of solidarity: in 1901 an Irish Party MP attempted to address the House of Commons in Irish; in 1904 Douglas Hyde was offered a parliamentary seat by John Redmond. Stephen Gwynn, MP for Galway City (1906–18), was (like Pearse) for a time on the executive committee of the Gaelic League. The *jeunesse dorée* of parliamentarianism – the Young Ireland branch of the UIL – contained a number of bright young UCD graduates who attempted to keep the party in touch with the League and with other aspects of the new nationalism. But their quest was on the whole forlorn, and many of these Young Irelanders later migrated out of Redmondism into more receptive company (Maume has cited the example of P.J. Little, who matured into a Fianna Fáil cabinet minister).[53]

In general the Irish Party ran scared before the organized assaults of the League, and it was never able to assimilate its more ardent proponents. Other external challenges to the party, such as that supplied by William O'Brien and the UIL after 1898 – were containable, partly because they were expressed in the language of the Parnell era: the party elders could understand and respond to a popular land agitation since many of them had cut their teeth in the Land War or during the Plan of Campaign. The UIL, as recounted earlier, was eventually adapted as the machinery of the reconstructed Irish Parliamentary Party; but – while it continued to use the vocabulary of Parnellism – it did so in English, offering few concessions to the Gaelic League. The UIL constitution contained a commitment to Irish, but meetings were invariably conducted in English, even in communities where the national language retained a considerable hold. Moreover, influential party leaders like Dillon opposed key League demands (such as the enshrining of Irish as a matriculation requirement for the National University, and the compulsory teaching of Irish throughout the national school system). It was also ironic that the most influential parliamentarian who had any serious interest in Irish – Tim Healy – should also have been (except for brief rapprochements in 1900 and after January 1908) one of the party's most damaging critics: Healy, along with his brother Maurice, supported a more phonetically based spelling reform.

The party had a similarly complicated relationship with another important expression of the new nationalism, the Gaelic Athletic Association (founded in November 1884 in Thurles, County Tipperary, by Michael Cusack). Referring to the GAA and to the League, Stephen Gwynn wrote in 1919 that 'the bulk of both these bodies was always antagonistic to the parliamentary movement'.[54] This was a common perception, which had its origins in the very strong connections between the GAA and the Fenians, and in the hazy notion that organizations like the GAA represented an alternative, often a more extreme alternative, to parliamentarianism. While the Irish Party accommodated itself to British parliamentary traditions, the Association built upon continental European precursors – upon the example of young German and Czech patriots who, through their *Turnvereine*, sought to use athletics as a means of improving the physical and moral preparedness of the nation. Cusack was also actively impressed by the dangers of British cultural domination, of what he called in his opening manifesto, published in October 1884, 'the tyranny of imported and enforced customs and manners' and of 'foreign and hostile laws and the pernicious influence of a hitherto dominant race'.[55] Cusack argued that the Irish were being inveigled into playing foreign games, to which they were unsuited, and that the result was regular defeat, humiliation and demoralization. Once an enthusiastic rugby player and cricketer, Cusack now advocated the resurrection or propagation of the ancient sporting traditions of the country, and in particular hurling and athletics. A distinctively Irish version of football was codified (in 1885) and swiftly emerged as the most popular spectator sport in the country.

On the other hand, certain aspects of the relationship between the GAA and the party – or, at any rate, the Parnellite Party – were clearly symbiotic. The birth and early development of the Association coincided with the hey-day of Parnellism, and the connection was scarcely coincidental: the GAA clearly fed off the national self-confidence that Parnell had helped to cultivate and benefited from the politicization that Parnellism brought in its wake. The Uncrowned King himself seems (predictably) to have had little interest in Irish sports; but other MPs (Michael Davitt, Justin McCarthy, William O'Brien and Timothy Harrington) welcomed the arrival of the GAA with enthusiasm. There was, perhaps, some tension between the GAA and Parnellite strategies in the later 1880s; but Parnell's appeal to the extremes in 1890–1 restored the connection between the Association and the parliamentary movement. His last speeches, particularly in Dublin, were often accompanied by GAA demonstrations, and on one occasion (in February 1891) he remarked, cloyingly, to some Gaelic supplicants that 'I love the games you love' (as W.F. Mandle has observed, 'no one had the churlishness to remark that he had been a long time in showing it').[56] This sentimental union was lastingly formalized at the time of Parnell's death when, famously, 2,000 hurlers escorted his coffin from Dublin's City Hall to Glasnevin cemetery. A few months later, in January 1892, a Parnellite MP, William Field, was elected as treasurer of the GAA in a further and more practical obeisance to the Uncrowned King's legacy.

Far from blossoming in the immediate aftermath of Parnell's death, the GAA went into sharp, if temporary, decline. There was thus no simple inverse relationship between the health of parliamentarianism and that of the Association: but nor was there any more direct link between the two movements. The key to the connection between the party and the GAA in fact lay elsewhere, with the Irish Republican Brotherhood. Parnell's party, through the New Departure (1879), had made its peace with Fenianism; and the party contained numerous members of the IRB (including – perhaps – Parnell himself). Michael Cusack, at least initially, took a fairly ecumenical approach to the formulation of the GAA, consulting with a wide variety of opinion (including a Unionist clergyman, the Reverend Maxwell Close) and seeking patrons for the Association who would underline, for nationalists, the respectability and integrity of the Association (Archbishop Croke of Cashel, Parnell and Michael Davitt were eventually selected). But Cusack had also strong Fenian connections; and there is a case for believing that (even though a District Inspector of the RIC, a sports enthusiast, was present at the Thurles meeting) the IRB was significantly involved in the launch of the GAA. Certainly, in 1887 the GAA leadership was annexed by the Brotherhood in what has been described, by Tom Garvin, as 'a spectacular organisational coup'.[57]

The tribulations of the GAA in the early 1890s were a reflection not only of the temporary break-up of the parliamentary party but also of strife within the broad Fenian movement – between old-time Fenians and the neophytes of the Irish National Brotherhood. The resolution of this internecine conflict in July 1900 paved the way for reform within the GAA and for the installation of a new, efficient and heavily Fenian executive in 1901. This fresh regime oversaw the rebuilding of the Association as a trenchantly nationalist organization, which – without losing the support of the clergy – could nurture not only wide enthusiasm for traditional sports but also advanced separatist opinion. The GAA now provided a network and spring-board for militant republicans (five of those executed after the Easter Rising had strong connections with the Association, as did many fighters in the Anglo-Irish war, including Cathal Brugha and Michael Collins). The semi-official organ of the movement, the *Gaelic Athlete*, launched in 1912, offered a further outlet for extreme nationalist sentiment, opposing Redmond's 'despicable imperialism' in 1914 and looking forward in Pearsean terms to a bloody protest against British rule.[58] Members of the GAA were heavily involved in the Irish Volunteers, formed in November 1913.

It would be quite wrong to overlook the presence of a significant Redmondite wing within the GAA. It would also be wrong to overlook the temperate attitudes of numerous IRB men within the leadership of the Association – cautious strategists who believed that any overt militancy would only provoke official suppression. But, in the end, the success of the GAA reflects not so much on its connections with the parliamentary tradition as on its connection with Parnellism. The GAA sought to sustain the inclusiveness and ambiguity that had been one of the hallmarks of Parnellism: it sought to uphold an alliance of Fenianism, agrarianism and the Catholic Church. Redmond's party retained some old Fenian connections, but it had little direct contact with the movement reinvigorated by Tom Clarke in the later Edwardian era. In a sense, then, the GAA practised some of the techniques of Parnellism much more effectively than those who were the ostensible inheritors of the tradition. It united militants and moderates. It harboured aspiring revolutionaries, yet was never banned by the British. It was heavily infiltrated by a secret society, yet enjoyed the patronage of the Church. All this might well be seen as the ultimate expression of the parliamentary craft: but the practitioner evoked is Parnell, and not Redmond.

Some sense of the cultural vibrancy and diversity of the new nationalism should, by now, be evident. This is not to imply that the old nationalism, certainly in its Parnellite formulation, was tainted by any cultural or intellectual poverty. On the contrary, the breadth of Parnellism created some of the same strategic problems that confronted the new nationalists of Edwardian Ireland. The very richness of the two movements hinted at a certain shared diffuseness, or even fragility; and indeed the force of this suggestion was made fully apparent in 1891 and, again, in 1922–3. The architecture of the GAA illustrated a typically Parnellite conjunction of unlikely elements: but the GAA represented only one, albeit important, aspect of the national movement. There were other organizations and individuals who had

Plate 8   Arthur Griffith, *c.*1922.
Source: Hulton Getty.

been touched by Parnell; and of these Arthur Griffith (who had been galvanized by a handshake with the Uncrowned King in 1891) was pre-eminent. No wilting violet, Griffith was also too self-effacing to cast himself as the reincarnation of Parnell, but his strategic analysis bore some striking similarities to that of the dead hero.

Griffith and his politics were rooted in the intellectual ferment of the Home Rule era and the years of the Parnell Split. He was a member of several of the countless local debating societies that provided a forum in the 1880s and 1890s for those young nationalists who aspired to put Ireland, the Empire and the world to rights. Like most other new nationalists (D.P. Moran, as ever, was an exception), Griffith drew admiringly on the work of the Young Irelanders, and especially Davis and Mitchel: the caustic patriotic ironies of Dean Swift were also an influence. He was also in the shadow of a charismatic young Fenian contemporary, William Rooney, whom he joined in the Celtic Literary Society (formed in February 1893): interestingly, Rooney launched the Society with a lecture on Samuel Ferguson, following the example of Yeats, whose career as a critic had been heralded by an essay lauding the Unionist man of letters. Griffith was sympathetic to the GAA. He was also, though a poor speaker of Irish, supportive of the Gaelic League. But he was never a doctrinaire advocate of the language, and he looked to other strategies in his pursuit of national revival.

There are three striking themes within Griffith's political career: journalism; the enunciation of simple, attractive (often ambiguous) national ideals or strategies; and the propagation of umbrella organizations designed to unite the disparate forces of advanced separatism. Griffith, like others labouring in the shadow of the Split, was preoccupied with the need for national unity; and this obsession, rather than some of its symptoms (such as his abstentionist or dual monarchist convictions), provides the key to unravelling his actions and influence. Like many of his literary contemporaries (Yeats, George Russell), Griffith was also on the lookout for a national avatar, a new Parnell: unlike some of his contemporaries, he did not cast himself as the Christ-like saviour of his nation. George Moore, the novelist and playwright, once breezily assured Yeats that 'I am your best advertiser, inside the houses I frequently cry: I am not the Lord, there is one greater than I'.[59] And there is a sense in which Griffith saw himself, with perhaps rather greater sincerity than Moore, as a John the Baptist preparing the way for a national messiah. At the same time, however, the legacy of Parnell suggested a certain restraint: while Griffith was prepared to 'advertise' those with apparently greater gifts of leadership, he sought to create a national movement through (in the description of Brian Maye) 'a "minimum of agreement", operating through a collective body, and not dependent on an individual who must have within himself the possibility of downfall'.[60]

Griffith saw himself, and was seen, first and foremost as a highly gifted if necessarily rebarbative journalist. His most important vehicle was the *United Irishman*, founded in 1899 and named to celebrate the inclusivist and generous patriotic ideals of the body founded in 1791 (but he was not an unquestioning celebrant: he came to believe that Tone had been a dupe of British policy and that the 1798 rising had been a mistake, because both the man and the event had helped to precipitate the end of the Irish parliament). Through the pages of this journal, relaunched as *Sinn Féin* in May 1906, and later ventures (he tried to sustain a daily separatist newspaper between August 1909 and January 1910), Griffith sought an audience for his constitutional prescriptions. Of these the most celebrated are perhaps his call (in 1902) for a policy of parliamentary abstentionism and his series of articles (of early 1904) highlighting the Austro-Hungarian *Ausgleich* of 1867 as a possible model for the Anglo-Irish relationship. Under the influence of the German economist Friedrich List, he called for a stringent tariff policy in order to protect and nurture Irish industry. Through his papers and through pamphlets – most importantly 'The Resurrection of Hungary' (1904) and 'The Sinn Féin Policy' (1906) – Griffith outlined his ideal of an autonomous, economically protected Ireland, bound to Britain only by the institution of the monarchy. In this Griffithite Arcadia a 300-strong council or parliament was defined as the principal focus for national political life.

But, while Griffith passionately defended his particular nostrum for Irish freedom, like many separatists he was more interested in the practical realization of autonomy than in fighting over the details: despite his reputation, he was not so much the inquisitorial theologian of independence as a highly pragmatic thinker who sought to forward the national movement on the basis of a broadly shared 'minimum of agreement'.[61] His practical political initiatives tend to bear out this reading. He was a progenitor of Cumann na nGaedheal, formed in 1900 – during the Boer war – as a focus for a wide variety of literary and other cultural groupings: its first President was John O'Leary, Yeats's mentor and the presiding genius of much cultural nationalist activity in the 1890s. Despite this Fenian patronage, the organization was diffuse in structure and woolly in its ambitions, but at the very least it highlighted the issue of coordination and provided a platform for Griffith (it was at the Cumann na nGaedheal convention of 1902 that he elaborated the abstentionist strategy). A later initiative, the National Council, was launched in 1903, at the time of King Edward VII's visit to Ireland, as a means of drawing together the different types of separatist protest: again, as with Cumann na nGaedheal, the governing principle seems to have been to achieve as wide a confederation as possible on the basis of a 'minimum of agreement'. Building on this very hesitant consensus, Griffith sought to move forward by winning support for a broadly based separatist strategy: it was to the annual convention of the National Council, in November 1905, that he first enunciated the policy that became known – the title came from Máire Butler, a cousin of Edward Carson – as 'Sinn Féin' ('ourselves'). A degree of organizational union and rationalization occurred in the separatist movement between 1905 and 1908: Cumann na nGaedheal united with the northern and Fenian-linked Dungannon Clubs (created by Bulmer Hobson and Denis McCullough) to form, in April 1907, the Sinn Féin League. In September 1908 the Sinn Féin League amalgamated with the National Council to form the organization called, simply, Sinn Féin. A broad measure of unity had been achieved, partly at the behest of Griffith, and between organizations which individually owed much to his inspiration: the basis for union was an ambiguously defined separatism.

But it would be quite wrong, in chronicling Griffith's progress, to overlook some bitter animosities within the separatist tradition: equally, it would be wrong to exaggerate the significance, at this time, of the Sinn Féin movement. Before 1914 the Irish Parliamentary Party had, despite the well-publicized and energetic activities of the separatists, virtually a hegemonic role within the national tradition. Among the separatists, however, there was a certain amount of contemporary whistling in the dark, and later rationalization: this was evident when a Sinn Féin candidate, C.J. Dolan, contested the North Leitrim seat in February 1908 and scored a creditable 1,157 votes as against the 3,103 votes of the Parliamentary Party candidate, F.E. Meehan. From one perspective this was certainly a strong Sinn Féin performance: Griffith's pungent journalism still had only a comparatively small circulation, and his movement had only recently been organized as a political party. This was also Sinn Féin's first electoral outing (there would not be another until February 1917). Moreover, Griffith had defined success for his party as the garnering of 1,000 votes. The Sinn Féin performance, judged by these various yard-sticks, was a modest triumph: Griffith joyfully predicted that 'ten years more and five sixths of Ireland – Catholic and Protestant – will be banded together in national brotherhood and the epitaph for foreign rule in this country will be in the graving'.[62] But this perhaps says more about Griffith's powers as a spin-doctor than as a prophet. For while the North Leitrim result seemed, from the perspective of 1917–18, to be a portent of the final victory, it was – like other auguries – not without ambiguity. It seems probable that the small number of Unionists in the constituency had voted for Sinn Féin rather than the Irish Party: and this, while pleasing to pluralist thinkers like Griffith, underlined the weakness of Sinn Féin's command of mainstream Catholic, nationalist support in the constituency. Moreover, the Sinn Féin candidate was also the former Irish Party MP for the constituency; and it must be supposed that some of his backing was personal rather than ideological: Dolan was not a carpetbagger, like many of the Sinn Féin candidates in 1918, and he had the status that came from having served the county in the House of Commons. Finally, it should be noted that the Irish Party did not simply rely upon its traditional resources – the Church, local farming and business interests – in fighting the contest: some of the toughest opposition to Griffith and to the Sinn Féin machine came from the intellectual stormtroopers of the Irish Party, the Young Ireland Branch of the UIL. Given that the YIBs included not only Tom Kettle but also such Young Turks as Liam Lynch, Cruise O'Brien, Rory O'Connor and Francis Sheehy Skeffington, it might well have been assumed that the future lay with an inclusivist Home Rule movement rather than Sinn Féin. After 1910, with the Irish Party reaching its zenith and with a third Home Rule Bill in the offing, this assumption appeared to be confirmed: Sinn Féin receded to the political margins, and Griffith – like so many other separatists – began to reconcile himself to the Redmondite agenda.

Griffith had sought to create a series of institutional and political focuses for the Irish Ireland movement of the Edwardian period: he had tried to summarize and to popularize the diversity of Irish Irelandism within a single political philosophy and (eventually) a single party – Sinn Féin. But these pretensions, and this territory, did not go unchallenged: as has been noted, the Irish Party's tentacles stretched as far as the national revival and its leaders, while there were many outside the party who took issue with Griffith's prognostication. Although Griffith himself was a member of the IRB until 1910, others from within this tradition saw his monarchist leanings, and his pragmatism, as potentially a dangerous challenge to the republican ideal. There was also an abiding tension between Griffith and the high-priest of Irish Irelandism, D.P. Moran. Moran, editor of the *Leader* between 1900 and his death in 1936, championed a highly ethnocentric nationalism: it was he who coined the phrase 'Irish Ireland', and it was he who presented the most sustained (and the most narrow) version of this creed through *The Philosophy of Irish Ireland* (1905). Moran saw much of the politics of mainstream Irish nationalism as Protestant and unIrish in origin; and he sought a purer form of Irishness through a Gaelic and Catholic cultural revival. Like Griffith, Moran was an advocate of the Irish language and of Irish industry. Unlike Griffith, Moran saw Catholicism and Irishness as essentially indistinguishable (there were admittedly numerous Castle Catholics and West Britons, and a few Protestants, who came close to an Irish spirit, but these were the exceptions that proved the rule). Unlike Griffith, he devoted much of his early journalism to highlighting specifically Catholic interests in the workplace, and especially the discrimination experienced by Catholics at the hands of some Protestant employers.

Moran groused about the misdeeds of the Irish Party; but he was also deeply antagonistic to aspects of the separatist tradition, where one might have expected greater bonds of sympathy. He saw Griffith and Sinn Féin as anti-clericalist (even though Griffith, like Parnell, was generally wary of antagonizing the Catholic Church). He also saw Griffith as dangerously susceptible to foreign intellectual influences. He was a sharp critic of 'The Resurrection of Hungary', and highlighted some of the undoubted problems with Griffith's analogies: exercising a brutal (if somewhat adolescent) propensity for name-calling, he labelled Sinn Féin as 'the Green Hungarian Band'.[63] He was profoundly unimpressed by many (Protestant) patriots who were among the most immediate influences on Griffith's philosophy. In part these various difficulties may have arisen because, as Brian Maye has argued, both Griffith and Moran were competing for the same patriotic audience.[64] But they were also very different types of nationalist: Griffith, born of the cultural revival, was fundamentally political in his ambitions, while Moran defined the Irish nation as, in essence, Catholic, and looked above all else to its cultural and economic revitalization. Griffith stood at the intersection of Young Ireland and the new nationalism; Moran stood at the intersection of O'Connellism and the new nationalism. They each were prepared to open the columns of their respective papers to a wide range of political opinion; but pluralism and pragmatism were more than an editorial strategy for Griffith.

Two other key areas of the social and political life of Edwardian Ireland overlapped with the campaigns and organizations of the new nationalism: feminism, especially suffragism, and labour. Both movements drew upon a wide international range of influences and precedents, but both benefited from the political and intellectual ferment of the national revival: the tendency at this time for Irish feminists and Irish workers to create distinctively local institutions through which to pursue their respective campaigns is one simple example of the way in which Irish Irelandism might touch movements that were not exclusively, or even largely, nationalist. D.P. Moran and Arthur Griffith were both cautious suffragists (in the case of Moran, highly cautious): both, however, were clear that feminism could not stand in the way of the national struggle. And indeed it would be a mistake to posit any unshakeable relationship between the new nationalism, or separatism, and feminism: equally, it would be a mistake to imagine that there was any unshakeable bond between the 'old' nationalism (or indeed Unionism) and anti-feminism. Some leading separatist men, notably the labour leader James Connolly, were prominent feminists; some leading feminist women, notably Hanna Sheehy Skeffington, were prominent separatists. Some women's organizations were affiliated to Sinn Féin or other separatist bodies. But, beyond these necessarily hazy generalizations it would be dangerous to proceed.

It was not the case, for example, that the Irish Party was resolutely opposed to women's rights. It was, however, true that a substantial section of the party (roughly one half) was either opposed to women's suffrage or was neutral on the question: crucially, the anti-suffragists included the leader, Redmond, and Dillon, his deputy. In addition the party's heavies, the Ancient Order of Hibernians (AOH), were associated with violent attacks on suffragist meetings, particularly those of the Irish Women's Franchise League (IWFL, founded in 1908 by, *inter alios*, Hanna Sheehy Skeffington and Margaret Cousins as a more aggressive suffragist body than those already in existence); Sheehy Skeffington claimed that, for the Hibernians, the women of the IWFL 'were a pestilential red herring across the trail of Home Rule'.[65] Cliona Murphy has pointed out the role assumed by some parliamentarians in supporting women's issues: Joseph Biggar, otherwise exploitative of women, took a friendly interest in the suffrage and related questions, while in 1887 even Parnell deigned to present a petition to the Commons on the issue of women's political rights.[66] A younger generation of parliamentarian (Stephen Gwynn, Tom Kettle, Hugh Law, Willie Redmond) raised feminist expectations by a carefully modulated support for the women's cause. But the result was only disappointment, despite the hopes invested by suffragists (foolishly, in the view of some critics) in the Irish Party. Murphy has drawn the overall conclusion that 'Irish M.P.s were either anti-suffragist, ambivalent, or if pro-suffrage, unwilling to risk supporting it'.[67]

The radical nationalists within Sinn Féin were also divided on the suffrage question: some, like Griffith, were welcoming but were basically unexcited by the issue; while others saw suffragism in a more explicitly hostile light and as a diversion from the republican grail. On the other hand, a number of well-known radical nationalist leaders (Connolly, Francis Sheehy Skeffington) were publicly identified with a feminist stance: indeed, by 1914 many of the most prominent advanced nationalists were women (Maud Gonne, Constance Markievicz), albeit not always women interested in suffrage. For some women the Irish Parliamentary Party supplied a limited if adequate forum until its demise in 1918; however, it was evident that for politically active and ambitious women, whether or not they were suffragists, the parliamentary tradition offered little encouragement. Equally, while the issue was not beyond doubt, the intellectually exhilarating environment supplied by radical nationalists seemed to promise these women greater scope than parliamentarianism. Maud Gonne's Inghinidhe na hEireann, founded in 1900 in the wake of a protest against the visit to Dublin of Queen Victoria, was a radical nationalist organization designed by women for women; but its significance within the history of women's political organization arose not because it pursued a determinedly feminist agenda (far from it), but rather because it provided a republican environment acceptable to women. Inghinidhe na hEireann, which was later incorporated within Sinn Féin, was anti-suffragist (though some of its members – like Markievicz – took the opposite line); but at the same time it reflected women's disquiet at the inadequate and unwelcoming political structures supplied by nationalist men. Even after affiliating with Sinn Féin, the Inghinidhe retained its distinct identity.

Cumann na mBan, founded in April 1914 as a women's auxiliary to the Irish Volunteers, reflected a slightly different balance between nationalism and feminism, with the former predominating along with (initially) an exaggerated respect for male sensitivities. Indeed, some feminists within the IWFL and elsewhere criticized Cumann na mBan on the grounds that it operated only as a handmaiden to the male Volunteers, and thus condemned women to a secondary and supporting role. However, it is also easy to forget the essentially radical purpose of Cumann na mBan; and Margaret Ward has argued with some conviction that the women of the movement 'challenged a great many more cultural norms, given the deep-rooted conservatism of Irish society, than did men joining the Volunteers'.[68] Cumann na mBan women were emphatically not parliamentarians, unlike the overwhelming majority of the Volunteers. The force of this is illustrated by the fact that Cumann na mBan voted to embrace the MacNeillite Irish Volunteers after the split of late 1914, rather than the Redmondite mainstream. Some 90 women (60 from Cumann na mBan and 30 from the Irish Citizen Army) fought in Easter Week.

There was an equally ambiguous relationship between the ideologues of the new nationalism and the labour movement. As in their response to the suffrage movement, Griffith and Moran expressed some cautious sympathy for Irish workers, while at the same time holding that the sectional interests of labour should be subordinated to the broader national cause. Both men were sympathetic to the local union movement; both were hostile to British unions and to their Irish organizers. Both were impressed by the depth of poverty in Dublin, and tended therefore to sympathize with the social concerns of labour representatives. But both men were also highly sensitive to the needs of Irish capitalism: the growth and diversification of native industry were central to both the Sinn Féin and the Moranite creed. Both men were, at root, very far from socialism: Moran has been dubbed a 'reactionary moderniser', and bears more than a passing resemblance to the radical conservative ideologues of Edwardian Britain who advocated national efficiency.[69] Griffith, too, reacted conservatively to many social issues: he was too obsessed by the need to reconcile the different forces within advanced nationalism to be swayed by any one sectional case. The complexity of his attitude to labour may be illustrated by his response to the two great socialist leaders of Edwardian Ireland, Jim Larkin and James Connolly: Larkin (born in Liverpool, originally an organizer for an English union, and first and foremost a socialist) he abhorred; but he lauded Connolly (who saw nationalism as a vehicle for progress and as precursor to socialism).

As with the women's movement, therefore, there is no simple equation between the new nationalism and labour (or at least not before 1913–14). Nor, indeed, was there any simple hostility between labour and the old nationalism (or, at any rate, not in its Parnellite heyday). Parnell himself had always sought to create a balanced and inclusivist movement, and had – at the end of his career – identified himself with the urban working classes. Of his colleagues, Michael Davitt had perhaps the strongest and sincerest sympathy for labour. But neither Parnell's apparently pragmatic concerns nor Davitt's highly individualistic socialism found favour within the party or, indeed, in the wider parliamentary movement. Davitt's advocacy of land nationalization was greeted stonily by the substantial farming interest; while his belief that the English working classes would be vital to the liberation of Ireland chimed neither with the convictions of the metropolitan socialists of Belfast nor with the tenets of Connolly, ultimately the most influential of the Dublin labour ideologues. Davitt's colleagues on the Irish benches were often (though not always) able to echo his anti-imperialist sentiments, and were able in particular to endorse his support for the Boers during the South African war; but his social convictions (what Emmet O'Connor has called his Lab–Nat philosophy) marked him out as an oddball within the party – and even Parnell cheerfully remarked that, in the event of Home Rule, he would be gaoled.[70] In part this was because of Davitt's dangerous integrity (he was closer to Parnellism than to anti-Parnellism, and yet endorsed the latter cause; he was closer to the nascent Labour Party than to the Liberals, and yet remained loyal to the Liberal alliance); but he was also dangerously far to the left of the median within the Irish Party.

Davitt had worked in the mills of Lancashire as a child (losing an arm in an accident); but the Irish Party contained few members with this or any kind of working-class background (there were in fact only two elected between 1910 and 1918). While one of these, J.P. Nannetti, claimed in 1906 that 'the Irish parliamentary party were the labour party', its predominant concerns suggested a very different conclusion.[71] For the party had been born out of the struggle between landlord and tenant, and it had been driven by a faith in the relationship between land and the national question: the interests of the rural labouring classes, still less of the urban working class, had not been an intrinsic element of its origins or purpose.

Organized labour found other outlets. The different waves of worker organization that washed through Ireland in the late nineteenth and early twentieth centuries lapped against the Irish Party, but made little impact: indeed, the force and direction of this activity were often inimical to the perceived interests of the party. The Parnell Split had coincided with the brief but hectic heyday of the new unionism (some 30 trade unions were created in Ireland, mostly for the unskilled or semi-skilled, between 1889 and 1891): this activity helps to explain why Parnell was anxious to tap the support of the labour movement. In fact the new unionism, which tended to reinforce the dependence of Irish workers on British labour organization, might well have been reconciled to the constitutional needs (if not the economic interests) of the Irish Party – and it is perfectly possible that Parnell grasped this point. But the mainstream anti-Parnellite lobby, propertied and clericalist, had much less interest than their former master in the urban working class or in its organizational initiatives, and much less need for its endorsement: little wonder that the youthful Connolly should have found himself opposed by the Irish National League of Great Britain at the Edinburgh council elections of November 1894, or that in October 1896 he should have railed against the inadequacies of parliamentarianism in the columns of the *Labour Leader*. And the broader direction of union development – away from the small craft unions and the anglocentric 'new unionism' towards particularist organization and syndicalist aspirations – made the assimilation of the working-class leadership within the Home Rule movement an even more remote eventuality.

All this is not to deny that the Irish Parliamentary Party enjoyed the limited blessing of British Labour (in so far as British Labour members endorsed Home Rule). Nor is it to deny that many working-class Dubliners were supporters of the Irish Party (in so far as they were enfranchised and had few alternatives). But the party did little to address the interests of this body; and in any event the labour movement was being driven by international political and economic influences beyond the reach of Redmond's ample embrace. James Larkin's Irish Transport and General Workers' Union (ITGWU, 1909), a home-grown union with a strong syndicalist tendency, addressed an unskilled or semi-skilled constituency whose interests ran counter to those of the mainstream Home Rule movement, and which was therefore untouched by the parliamentarians: Emmet O'Connor has remarked that 'the formation of the ITGWU marked the beginning of a long and painful decolonisation that . . . modernised the movement, and made it more relevant to native conditions'.[72] Connolly, at this time an organizer for the Socialist Party of Ireland, but later (after July 1911) the ITGWU organizer in Belfast, was not only contemptuous of the Irish Party but had also been seeking (in 1909) some form of accommodation between Irish socialism and Sinn Féin. This was scuppered both by the suspicions of Arthur Griffith (his general regard for Connolly notwithstanding) and by the apparent breakthrough that the parliamentarians achieved on the Home Rule issue in 1910–12; but it foreshadowed the shape of things to come. In addition, Connolly – despite Larkin's syndicalist leanings – was pressing for the creation of an Irish Labour Party, and he succeeded in winning the support of the Irish Trades Union Congress in 1912 (though a formal inauguration had to wait until 1914). This was a reflection of the extent to which organized labour felt that its concerns could best be expressed through independent representation: it was a reflection of the gulf that had opened up not only between British and Irish labour, but also between Irish labour and Redmondism – even with Redmondism in its heyday.

The rapid consolidation of the ITGWU (there were 14,000 members by 1913) was dramatically halted when Connolly and Larkin attempted to bring their gospel to the business empire of the formidable William Martin Murphy. For Murphy also sought security in combination – in the 400-strong Employers' Federation, which in September 1913 agreed to take on the ITGWU by locking out all employees who were members of the new union. The resulting clash was a protracted and painful affair, which brought further impoverishment – indeed starvation – to many of the working men and women who were participants, and which resulted in an effective victory for the employers (or, alternatively, in what Connolly bullishly claimed as 'a drawn battle').[73]

The Lock-out had underlined the distance between the parliamentary tradition and organized labour. Murphy had been a member of Parnell's party as MP for the St Patrick's Division of Dublin City between 1885 and 1892; and although his ardour had subsequently cooled (he used his newspaper, the *Irish Independent*, to harry the Redmondites), he remained – like his fellow Bantryman and ally Tim Healy – 'the enemy within'. Just as they had been deployed against the suffragists, so the Hibernians, the party roughs, were used as strike-breakers during the conflict. Catholic clergy, still frequently seen as allies of the parliamentarians, denounced Larkin's efforts to rescue the starving children of strikers by removing them temporarily to England: this 'deportation scheme' apparently exposed vulnerable youngsters to the Satanic lure of Protestant evangelists, and therefore lost Larkin vital support. The residue of bitterness which accompanied the return to work of early 1914 did not bring any immediate radicalization of Dublin politics. But it did unquestionably contribute to the party's relative weakness in the city, as exposed in September–October 1914, at the time of the split in the Volunteer movement (many Dublin activists supported Eoin MacNeill's dissident grouping rather than the Redmondite National Volunteers). And it did help to produce at least one unnerving election result for the parliamentary apparatchiks – the College Green poll of June 1915, when a Connollyite, Thomas Farren, performed well against an official party nominee.

But the Great Lock-out had a much wider resonance. It spawned a further, significant armed militia to add to the Irish battlefield: the Irish Citizen Army, formed in November 1913 by a northern Protestant Home Ruler, Captain J.R. White, and revived in 1914 by Connolly and by a Protestant working man from inner-city Dublin, Seán O'Casey. It provoked a highly variegated series of reactions from among the new nationalists. Moran, worried by the charges of souperism thrown at Larkin, was condemnatory. Griffith hedged: he was hostile to Larkin and concerned about the health of Irish capitalism, yet also moved by the plight of the workers. But the publicity given in 1913 to the hellish Dublin tenements, and to the degradation of their inhabitants, helped to create a bond between other new nationalists and labour activism. George Russell published an open letter, addressed 'To the Masters of Dublin', in which he condemned 'an oligarchy of four hundred masters [for] deciding openly upon starving one hundred thousand people'.[74] Yeats penned a letter of support to the *Irish Worker*, the organ of Larkin's ITGWU: his great poem, 'September 1913', though written before the Lock-out, 'exploded as a salvo in that battle too'.[75] Pearse was profoundly moved by the plight of the strikers and their families, and declared his sympathies openly in October 1913 through the columns of the Fenian journal, *Irish Freedom*.

Support such as this, combined with the opportunities opened up by the outbreak of war in August 1914, helped to bring an accommodation between the IRB and the labour movement. Connolly and his lieutenant, William O'Brien, met with Pearse and other leading Fenians on 9 September 1914: Griffith, a lapsed Fenian, was also of the company. The purpose of the gathering was to plan for an insurrection. The venue was suggestive: the library of the Gaelic League, in Dublin's Parnell Square. Here, then, was forged a union between the new nationalists and Connollyite socialism which would be finally sanctified within the walls of the General Post Office, in Easter Week, 1916.

The stalling of Home Rule and the outbreak of war helped to stimulate answers to many of the great controversies that had fired the national revival. Many personal or institutional tensions were set aside. Yeats may have maintained the primacy and integrity of his art, but he harnessed his Muse more completely than ever to national political causes: there may still have been a distinction between his own artistic creed and that of more untrammelled nationalist literary figures, but there was scarcely any meaningful difference. Personal tensions between Yeats and Russell, or between Russell and (say) Thomas MacDonagh, poet and rebel, were resolved in the face of great unifying events like the Lock-out or, later, the Rising. The role of Protestants within the national movement was now finally being established, albeit at the margins. The Gaelic League, which had always hovered just inside the closet of cultural nationalism, came out as an overtly political movement at Dundalk in 1915. Tensions within the labour movement had mirrored those within the literary revival: within each there had been a conflict between nationalism and supranational principle – between, on the one hand, perceptions of artistic or socialist principle and, on the other, the duties of the citizen and the national interest. Among both writers and labour activists, these tensions were resolved in 1914 and after along national lines.

The new nationalists were essential in creating and clinching the Irish revolution. Gaelic Leaguers and Gaelic Athletes were prominent among the heroes of 1916 and of the Anglo-Irish war. Connollyite socialists fought alongside neo-Fenians: indeed, many of the Connollyites had now enrolled within the Brotherhood. Politicized women fought throughout the period. The men and women of the Anglo-Irish literary revival commemorated the dead, reflected on the revolutionary achievement, and damned the forces of reaction. The intellectual rage of the new nationalism was therefore channelled directly into military action. But there is, however, a danger in pushing this argument too far. While the prominence of members of the Gaelic League and the GAA within the revolutionary elite is undeniable, there is no direct correlation between involvement within these two organizations and military action. The elaboration of this point must wait until the Anglo-Irish war is addressed more fully and directly later in the book. But it is enough for the moment to sound a note of warning against any automatic or over-simplistic equation between the cultural revival and violent separatism.

Nor is it possible to write the old nationalism out of the history of the new. And, in so far as this is true, it is impossible to write the old nationalism out of the history of the revolution. The parliamentary movement engaged with different aspects of the new nationalism, and often in a constructive manner: there was, for example, no absolute chasm between parliamentarians and the language movement, or (indeed) the GAA. Nor was there any absolute equation between Sinn Féin, the key political focus of the new nationalism, and the progressive forces (feminism, socialism) in Edwardian Irish politics.

In fact the abiding impression of the revival is of the interconnections between ostensibly different forms of new nationalism, and between the new nationalism and the old. Indeed, the vitality of the cultural and national revival is all the more remarkable given the intimacy and smallness of the Irish intellectual elite. Perhaps the crispest warning against any over-simplification comes – appropriately – from within the classrooms of that most elusive cultural and political leader, Pearse. For within Pearse's school, St Enda's, were gathered not only sons of Eoin MacNeill and a daughter of D.P. Moran, but also James Larkin Junior and Denis Gwynn, son of the parliamentarian Stephen Gwynn. The enterprise was blessed with the sympathetic attention not only of Douglas Hyde, but also of Yeats and the Unionist Standish O'Grady. Robin Dudley Edwards, hailed (or damned) as one of the founders of historical revisionism in Ireland, began his educational career in St Enda's in the confused and dark days after Pearse's execution. Out of these classrooms came not only revolutionaries but also careful, sceptical scholars: the brightest of Pearse's protégés (Gywnn) was also the most successful apologist for Redmondism. The diversity, distinction and energy of St Enda's might serve as a metaphor for the broader national revival.

5.3　The Parliamentarians and their Enemies, 1914–18

We've Home Rule now the Statute Book adorning
It's there to be seen by every mother's son
We brush the cobwebs off it every morning
For the constitution movement must go on

Chorus: And on and on and on for ever more
　　　　　　Popular republican doggerel
(quoted by Ernie O'Malley, *On Another Man's Wound*)[76]

In the years of Redmond's chairmanship and Dillon's influence, the Irish Parliamentary Party had been engaged in a zero-sum game, the prize for which was Home Rule. The rules of the match were clear: the party would only play with the Liberals, and it would only play seriously within the arena of the British parliament. Its determination to win involved a ruthless and ultimately dangerous subordination of all other interests to the one all-absorbing goal. The party had refused to play conciliationist politics with Wyndham, and it had flouted Irish electoral opinion in 1909–10 over the issue of the Budget. It had defied its own traditional and safe strategies, reversing its stand on the South African war by endorsing the British military campaign of 1914.

The history of the Irish Party's demise has been so minutely probed that it is easy to lose sight of some of the more fundamental issues. The party had banked much of its political resources on the Liberal alliance: the political manoeuvrings that had produced the Parliament Act and then the Home Rule Bill had given Redmond a reputation for political sagacity which impressed even those, like Patrick Pearse, who were much more 'advanced' in their nationalist convictions. These basic strategies of the party were shaken first of all by the Ulster Unionists, who, while themselves part of a Europe-wide drift into militancy, also helped to reactivate militant nationalism in Ireland: the Unionists helped indirectly to humiliate the parliamentarians and to expose their strategic obfuscation and inadequacy. But the party was shaken even more comprehensively by the war, which created a consensus between the Liberals and Tories and which effectively neutralized the value of the Irish vote. The tacit British national coalition of August 1914 was formalized by the creation of the first coalition government in May 1915. Carson's appointment to the attorney generalship in this ministry has often distracted attention from the more basic and important points – that the gradual crystallization of the Liberal–Conservative wartime alliance replaced the pre-war Liberal–nationalist 'understanding', and that both the Irish Party and Irish issues were now of a massively diminished significance.[77]

This was inevitable, but the party leadership might nevertheless have attempted some damage limitation. The first coalition was still dominated by the Liberals, although there were (for the nationalists) some problematic appointments. As is well known, Carson's transformation from being a patron of illegality in Ulster to a law officer at Westminster bewildered and angered Home Rule opinion. In fact Carson's elevation reflected not so much the importance of Ulster Unionism in general as his personal influence over Tory backbench opinion, and his capacity to create trouble: from an Irish perspective it was easy to forget that Carson was always more than the murderer of Home Rule, as was subsequently illustrated by his resignation over the issue of Serbia and by his mounting prominence as a backbench malcontent in 1915–16. In any case, some of Carson's influence during his brief tenure of office might have been negated had Redmond been prepared to join the coalition. He was invited so to do; indeed, when he declined, Asquith was prepared to extend the invitation to either Dillon or Devlin. But the traditional line of the party had been to refuse such invitations; and the memory of Keogh and Sadleir in the 1850s loomed large even as late as 1915. However, it had also been the traditional line of the party to distance itself from British military enterprises, and yet Redmond and the leadership had broadly recognized the special conditions created by the Great War. That these special conditions might have justified accepting office seems to have occurred at least once to Redmond, for he mentioned, somewhat wistfully, to his colleague Stephen Gwynn that if he had 'been Asquith, and wished to make it as difficult as possible to refuse, I [Redmond] should have offered a seat in the Cabinet without portfolio and without salary'.[78] It is difficult to tell whether such a course of action would have benefited the Irish Party. It might simply have meant that the party would have been directly implicated in the misjudgements and confusion of British government in wartime Ireland. But, since many voters made this connection anyway, it seems possible that something might have been gained by an Irish voice, however reedy, in the government of Ireland.

Another earlier damaging episode has a bearing on the question of Irish membership of the first coalition. Part of the difficulty for Irish members lay in being seen to accept remuneration as ministers of the crown. But in 1911 the Irish Party had accepted, albeit with some qualms, the proposition that MPs should be salaried. There was certainly an important, indeed – for the Irish Party – a crucial distinction between being paid to represent a constituency and being paid to serve as the King's minister. This distinction might have mattered less had the Prime Minister implemented Redmond's own idea of a non-salaried, non-departmental cabinet post, but Asquith did not have the imagination to make such an offer and the Irish did not feel politically free to make the suggestion. Aside from issues of nationalist principle, the unpopularity in Ireland of the official salary which MPs now received was such that it may well have scuppered any chance of Irish cabinet membership. For this Saxon dole appeared to have debased Parnell's proud, independent party and to have turned it into a body of official hirelings: 'it was the surrender', claimed William O'Brien, 'of the very citadel of the Parnell movement'.[79]

Underlying the marginalization of the Irish Party at Westminster was the war; underlying the marginalization of the party in Ireland was its endorsement of the British war effort. On 20 September 1914, speaking at Woodenbridge, Redmond urged the East Wicklow Volunteers, and beyond them the broader Volunteer movement, to 'account for yourselves as men, not only in Ireland itself, but wherever the firing line extends, in defence of right and freedom and religion in this war'.[80] This was unquestionably a political gamble, though perhaps in a different way than is generally interpreted. Redmond knew the political risks involved in any Irish nationalist leader making such a call, but he was elaborating a particular and delicate national case. At the beginning of the war he had offered the Volunteers as a defensive force in Ireland; at Woodenbridge he was extending this offer. His original House of Commons speech was designed to underline not just some form of Irish support for the British war effort, but rather the extent to which Ireland, as a nation on the brink of Home Rule, was capable of assuming her own defence. The Woodenbridge speech, interpreted by separatists as a betrayal of Irish nationality, was in reality the opening gambit in a prolonged effort to create a distinctive, united Irish national fighting force within the international coalition that was the British army.

This strategy failed, and the separatists' view of Redmond's apparent treachery eventually came to be the general nationalist perspective. But this need not have been the case. At one level it was astonishing that a nationalist leader should make such a call, even in the exceptional circumstances of September 1914: as has been noted, the Irish Party had traditionally been ferocious critics of the British army, deploring its imperial conquests and relishing setbacks such as those sustained in the early stages of the South African war. But the relationship between nationalist Ireland and the British army was more complex than the traditional stand of the Irish Party implied. While the Irish Party was damning the suppression of Boer nationality in 1899–1900, some of the most successful 'suppressors' were the soldiers of the Royal Dublin Fusiliers, the Royal Munster Fusiliers and the Connaught Rangers. The Curragh Incident had revealed the depth of Unionist sentiment in the officer corps of the elite cavalry regiments. But this was not the full story: during the Buckingham Palace Conference, when Redmond and Dillon were returning from the negotiations to the Commons, they were recognized by Irish Guardsmen, who 'raised a cheer . . . which ran all along the barrack square'.[81] Even a highly charged and controversial episode such as Bachelor's Walk, while unquestionably illustrating the bloody hostility that could exist between Irish people and British soldiers, is not without its complications: one of the three victims of the King's Own Scottish Borderers was a woman whose son was a soldier in the Royal Dublin Fusiliers.[82]

What was bizarre about the Woodenbridge speech was not, therefore, that Redmond should seek to forge a close relationship between a body of Irish nationalists and the British army – for, in truth, this existed already. What was unusual in Redmond's declaration was rather the direct and open way in which he alluded to a profoundly ambiguous and divisive relationship, which had long been both a source of pride and self-reproach for the nationalist movement. Even this unusually frank declaration might have been politically tolerable had Redmond's broader vision of a distinctive Irish army corps been realized. There were certainly problems after the speech, but (as is well known) the overwhelming majority of the Volunteer movement endorsed Redmond's view: of 170,000 Volunteers, there were only 12,000 dissidents, though – as has been noted – there was a worrying concentration of supporters of Eoin MacNeill in Dublin. And some Redmondite MPs faced difficulties in trying to sell the message of Woodenbridge to their constituents: Paul Bew has detailed the problems faced by Thomas Scanlan, the MP for Sligo, in this regard.[83] In general townspeople, excepting radical labour, responded well to the call, while the farming population remained loyal to their traditional view that soldiering was both socially demeaning and economically suicidal.

In the opinion of moderate nationalists such as Stephen Gwynn, it was the petty bureaucracy of the War Office, in particular the narrow-mindedness of the new Secretary of State Earl Kitchener, which caused the most comprehensive damage to Redmond's vision of an Irish army in France and Flanders.[84] There seems little reason to doubt this view. One issue above the others created controversy and has been a recurrent source of confusion since 1914–15: this relates to the nationalist desire for a distinctive 'Irish Brigade' within the British army. It has been occasionally suggested that the War Office thwarted the idea of an Irish division, or even the idea of Irish regiments, but these notions reflect confusion over both the state of Irish representation in the army and the nature of nationalist aspirations.[85] There were, of course, numerous historic Irish regiments which recruited mainly in the south and west of the country (the Royal Dublin Fusiliers, the Leinster Regiment, the Connaught Rangers, the Royal Munster Fusiliers, the Royal Irish Regiment, South Irish Horse); there were in addition two full divisions of the British First Army – the 10th and the 16th – which were Irish in composition and, indeed, in name. To some extent the confusion of later commentators is understandable, since its origins lie in the confusion generated by contemporaries: Redmond, for example, originally claimed that he wanted an 'Irish Brigade', but in reviving this romantic allusion to the 'Wild Geese' of the eighteenth century, he was in fact selling his followers short: what he sought (and he was eventually forced to change his terminology) was in reality an Irish army corps, for this chimed with the Commonwealth model that he seems to have been following. He also wanted the British government to recognize the National Volunteers, and indeed Asquith expressed the hope that 'the Volunteers will become a permanent, an integral and characteristic part of the defensive forces of the Crown'.[86] But despite the Prime Minister's oleaginous good wishes, no official recognition was forthcoming. Nor was any Irish army corps formed (as it might have been) from the two nominal Irish divisions together with the 36th (Ulster) Division. Moreover, the official recognition granted to the 'loyal' Ulstermen – UVF units were incorporated as distinctive new battalions within the 36th Division – contrasted with the much greater caution shown by the War Office to the 'disloyal' National Volunteers. And irritation and jealousy were sparked by more minor matters such as the divisional badge that the Ulstermen were permitted to wear (and which looked very much like the UVF emblem): while the Ulstermen had their 'dixie-lid' (as the badge was nick-named), there was no distinctive insignia for those National Volunteers who took the King's shilling.

Redmond's strategies were threatened not just by the suspicions and cussedness of the War Office, but also by the direction of the war itself. The absence of 'an Irish Brigade', or some similarly distinctive unit, was a handicap to his efforts, but the protracted and indecisive nature of the conflict was also a tremendous political burden. Redmond had received no tangible political rewards for his gesture of support; but neither did the war deliver any military dividend. There were no resounding victories to stimulate Irish patriotism and to vindicate Redmond's strategies: instead, the Irish soldiers were, at best, involved in momentarily glorious rear-guard actions such as at Etreux in 1914 or in impressive but futile offensives such as Gallipoli in 1915.

Moreover, the heavy death toll on the Western Front created a variety of problems for Redmond. At a personal level, as has been noted, the war claimed his brother and also an ex-colleague, T.M. Kettle. At a political level there were two main difficulties. First, those who answered the recruiting calls of Redmond, Devlin and other Irish Party leaders tended to be 'the pick of the young and keen' among the National Volunteers and their sympathizers.[87] This meant that the Volunteer organization at home tended to grind to a halt. It also meant that, while the National Volunteers were originally much larger than the Irish Volunteers, the latter were effectively enhanced by the disappearance of much of the strength and talent of their rivals. The mounting slaughter in France and Flanders not only ensured that this relative advantage would be maintained, it also created an even more immediate difficulty for the Irish Party. For by early 1916 the heavy death toll had brought the issue of conscription into the political arena. The uniform application of a draft across the United Kingdom would have been disastrous for the Redmondite strategy, both in terms of principle and practice. Conscription represented the negation of Redmond's vision of a distinctive and voluntary Irish army: this, even though part of a larger British whole, would have been an effective affirmation of Irish nationality rather than, as separatists alleged, its antithesis. Moreover, conscription was also a highly unpopular notion in Ireland, where public opinion was generally prepared to accept voluntary enlistment on the advice of democratically elected leaders, but was not prepared to accept coercion by the British government. In January 1916 Redmond spoke strongly against conscription ('rest assured, do not try to drive Ireland'), and for the moment his advice was taken seriously.[88] This successful plea for Ireland's exclusion was also, by its nature, a plea for the special treatment of a distinct national unit: it was, as Stephen Gwynn remarked, 'the high water-line of Redmond's achievement'.[89] Thereafter the parliamentary tide began its relentless ebb.

The vulnerability of the Irish Party will be clear: but, as with contemporary British Liberalism, it would be a mistake to diagnose a terminal condition ignoring the possibilities of remission, and secure in the knowledge of the patient's ultimate death. As with contemporary Liberalism it is possible to trace the cancer within the Irish parliamentary tradition back, perhaps, to the death of Parnell.[90] But Paul Bew's work on the by-elections in Ireland between 1914 and 1916 suggests a different and more intriguing picture of Redmondite strength and weakness. It is useful to be reminded through Bew's analysis that, even though the Irish Party was swept aside by Sinn Féin in December 1918, it was consistently winning by-elections in the months immediately before the 1916 Rising (indeed – though Bew's work does not extend so far – the party was also winning contests in the immediate aftermath of the Rising, until the Roscommon North debacle of February 1917). But it is equally clear from Bew's work that, while the general picture suggests that the party was still in command of the Irish electorate, there were serious weaknesses in its case. In the two Dublin contests that were held in the period, the Irish Party performed in a significantly weaker manner than in the countryside: in the College Green contest of 11 June 1915 Thomas Farren, an associate of James Connolly, came within 629 votes of the successful Irish Party candidate; in Dublin Harbour, in a three-cornered contest between different types of parliamentary nationalist held on 1 October 1915, the candidate closest to Redmond was easily defeated. Outside of Dublin the Irish Party's performance was generally better – though even here radical independents (such as Hamill in North Louth) did well, while significant weaknesses in the UIL machinery were exposed.

The party's difficulties lay to some extent with its organizational base. Machinery, however, could sometimes be repaired: for example an attempt was made to put right the defects in the UIL organization in 1915. But the party leaders also relied increasingly on the AOH, a body which, though well rooted in the north, was of a somewhat recent and superficial growth elsewhere: assisted by an electoral pact with Sinn Féin, the success of the Hibernians in Ulster allowed the party to survive there as a kind of eastern empire after Rome had fallen in 1918. It has been argued, however, that the Hibernians provided the party leadership with 'a false sense of confidence', and that the success of the movement encouraged parliamentarians to neglect popular opinion: in this analysis the Hibernians acted as a praetorian guard, a useful but dangerous set of heavies who separated the leadership from the public rather than providing some form of linkage.[91] It is certainly the case that the very swift flowering of the Hibernian movement was helped by what was arguably an artificial and temporary stimulant (the National Insurance Act of 1911, under which the AOH derived brokerage benefits as a recognized friendly society). Indeed, this connection seems to be typical of the over-confidence of the party in its heyday: just as the parliamentary leaders based their Home Rule strategy on a profoundly unpopular measure (the 'People's Budget' of 1909), so the growth of a key con-stituency organization was based upon a further unpopular welfare reform (the National Insurance Act was endorsed by the party, but condemned by the Church, by the O'Brienites and others as 'totally unfitted and burdensome to Ireland').[92] The massive success of the party between 1910 and 1914 obscured the shakiness of some of these foundations; but when its strategy misfired – when legislative autonomy did not emerge, and indeed when Home Rule finance seemed to have been com-promised by the spread of the British welfare state – the political sacrifices that the party had made earlier now seemed intolerable.

The key difficulty with the Irish Party lay, therefore, in the fact that after 1914 it had little or nothing to offer the Irish electorate beyond a call to join the British army. Indeed, it functioned as a grim mechanism for its own destruction: after Woodenbridge it helped to export some of its best supporters to the slaughter in France and Flanders. But even before 1914 there had been an occasionally suicidal arrogance, or – at best – directionlessness. The party's radical agrarian traditions had to some extent been compromised during the ranch war; and after Birrell's Act of 1909 it could no longer rouse the Irish electorate on the basis of the land question. Its usefulness to the substantial farmers and shopkeepers who were a main-stay of its support was therefore lessened after the last of the great land reforms. Indeed, to some extent, given the party's tactical commitment to the 'People's Budget' and to the Liberals' costly social welfare programme, it became a liability to the Irish rural middle classes. To these and to its other supporters, the party presented a vision of Home Rule that receded and became blurred: the Parnellite version of Home Rule was compromised by concessions on the issue of financial autonomy and by progressive concessions on the Ulster question. The likelihood of Home Rule becoming effective even in a highly qualified form became slighter as Ulster Unionist resistance quickened and as the stalemate on the Western Front became (quite literally) entrenched. The party appeared to be tantalizing its support by promises which it could not, and did not, keep. That the responsibility for this dangerous political tease lay with the British government only served to underline the Irish Party's broader strategic misjudgement.

Moreover, if the party was apparently breaking electoral promises, then there were large sections of Irish society to whom it was promising, and delivering, little or nothing. It was a legion of the excluded who went to war against the British crown and against the Irish parliamentary tradition on Easter Monday, 1916. The Rising was led by those who had largely been beyond the interest or appeal of the parliamentarians – Fenians, socialists, Gaelic Leaguers, GAA members, politicized women, the young – and one of its principal achievements was to expose the compromises and contortions which parliamentarianism had involved: it overturned the artificial political certainties that the Irish Party had for so long exploited. However, it was not immediately clear that the Rising would also (as its authors hoped) overturn the strategies of the party: the Rising was always a likely military failure, but it was by no means a certain political success.

It seems clear that the conspirators – who were concentrated in the Military Council of the IRB – were more anxious that a rising should take place than that it should be successful. Certainly more effort was invested in deceiving the sceptics within both the Irish Volunteer movement and the IRB (including, crucially, the President of the Volunteers, Eoin MacNeill) than in ensuring that the sceptics' forebodings would be proved wrong. This is not to say that the Rising was seen exclusively as a necessary blood sacrifice; but it certainly is the case that the conspirators were primarily interested in framing their declaration of a republic with a credible display of force. The rank and file of the insurgents do not seem to have worried unduly about their military prospects; but even the leaders did not plan meticulously for success. The rising was postponed from 1915 until the spring of 1916 because the outlook for the earlier year was so bleak; but in truth little was done (beyond fiddling with the dates) to ensure that the postponed rising would triumph. Charles Townshend has commented on the curiously hamfisted approach to the issue of weapons: the conspirators were promised German arms but wanted the arrival of these to coincide with the rising rather than precede it.[93] There appear to have been no detailed plans for the distribution of these weapons, once landed; but in the event this scarcely mattered for the Irish and Germans had difficulties of communication and coordination, and the vessel bearing the shipment, the *Aud*, fell into the hands of the Royal Navy. The greatest achievement of the conspirators (and this may well have been their principal concern) was in keeping the news of their activities quiet for so long, and in misleading their quondam allies (MacNeill, Bulmer Hobson) within the Irish Volunteer leadership so comprehensively. But this triumph was also their tragedy, for some leakage was inevitable, and particularly in the hectic lead-up to the insurgency. In the days preceding Easter Sunday (the day originally assigned for the outbreak), those opposed to the revolt discovered the extent to which they had been deceived: there were two angry exchanges between MacNeill and Pearse, and the former sent out an order cancelling all Volunteer activity for the planned day of action. Easter Sunday saw not the comprehensive uprising that had been planned, but rather a fraught meeting of the conspirators at Liberty Hall, the headquarters of Connolly's ITGWU: here it was decided that the revolt would go ahead on the following day even if the confusion of orders and counter-orders threatened an initially poor response. By now even the most sanguine of the leaders can have had little hope of success; and this gloom was crisply expressed by Connolly who, when asked of the rebels' chances, replied 'none whatever'.[94]

Plate 9 Patrick Pearse, *c.*1916.
Source: Hulton Getty.

The military strategy of the insurgents during Easter week is as hard to decipher as the state of their confidence. It is reasonably clear that the key strategists were Connolly, who had served in the British army in Dublin in the 1880s, and Joseph Plunkett, Director of Operations of the Volunteers and a member of the Military Council of the IRB: Plunkett had sketched out plans for street fighting in Dublin as early as 1914. It seems likely that the rebel strategists hoped to impel moderate nationalist opinion towards their stand, although the exact mechanisms by which this end was pursued remain questionable. Plunkett and Seán MacDiarmada, another member of the Military Council, co-wrote the so-called Castle Document, a forged instruction purporting to come from Dublin Castle, and calling for the suppression of the Volunteers and widespread arrests: the Document appeared on 19 April 1916 and seems to have been designed to fire outrage among moderates. A similar guile has been detected elsewhere. In pondering the rebels' decision to house their headquarters in the General Post Office in Sackville Street (a building close

Plate 10   The General Post Office, Dublin, after the Rising.
Source: Private collection.

to the slums of the north side and lacking any special significance), David Fitzpatrick has concluded that the purpose was to provoke 'maximum bloodshed, destruction and coercion, in the hope of resuscitating Irish Anglophobia, and clawing back popular support for the discredited militant programme'.[95] It was certainly the case that the location of the GPO made communication between the rebel commander in Dublin, Connolly, and his lieutenants very difficult: the outlying rebel strong points were at the Four Courts, the South Dublin Union, the Mendicity Institution, Jacob's biscuit factory, Boland's Mill (where Eamon de Valera was in charge) and – closer to the city centre – St Stephen's Green, where a contingent of the Irish Citizen's Army was led by Connolly's deputy, Michael Mallin, and by Constance Markievicz. There was virtually no contact with the few scattered risings outside Dublin city (at Ashbourne, North County Dublin, where Thomas Ashe and Richard Mulcahy inflicted heavy casualties on a superior force of RIC men; at Athenry, County Galway, and at Enniscorthy, County Wexford).

Pearse was overall commander-in-chief of the insurgents and President of the Provisional Government of the Irish Republic, as announced on the steps of the GPO on Easter Monday (24 April). But, although he had been an enthusiastic if over-fussy Director of Military Organization for the Irish Volunteers, his generalship during the Rising mattered much less than that of Connolly: as J.J. Lee has remarked, Pearse was important in military terms not because of his strategic insights, but because he boosted morale, bestowing 'bouquets on his comrades in the manner of a headmaster presiding over a school prize-giving and offering rousing addresses'.[96] If Pearse was over-shadowed as a soldier, then his significance as the ideologue and draftsman of the rebellion was unchallenged. He was the author of the Proclamation that announced the establishment of the Provisional Government (although Connolly and Thomas MacDonagh have also been identified as influences over the content and wording).[97] The strong sense of historical continuity that the Proclamation conveyed, linking 1916 to earlier rebellions, was distinctively (though of course not exclusively) Pearsean: the inspiration provided by the memory and example of Robert Emmet is evident within the document and throughout many of Pearse's reflections on Easter week. The representation of the insurgency as a highly chivalrous military enterprise reflected Pearse's deepest aspirations. On the other hand, the egalitarian vision expressed within the document, as well as its mild feminism (women's suffrage was implicitly endorsed), are generally ascribed to Connolly – or, at any rate, to Connolly's influence over Pearse.[98]

Pearse was also the author of a second manifesto, designed – like the Proclamation – to rouse Dubliners from their apathy and to ensure that the 'new honour' of Ireland would not be besmirched by looting or other discreditable actions.[99] This was published on Easter Tuesday (25 April). There were other communiqués, including one, dated Easter Thursday, where Connolly was singled out for special commendation and where the theme of a restored national honour also loomed large. Interestingly, from the perspective of the debate on Pearse's view of the Rising, this manifesto underlined the extent to which he believed (or claimed to believe) that, had the original plans for a coordinated rising on Easter Sunday not been upset, the Irish

Republic would not only have been honourably proclaimed but also 'enthroned'. As it was, Pearse's literary endeavour on behalf of his republic culminated on Saturday 29 April when, on a cardboard picture backing, the decision of the Provisional Government to seek terms with the British was sadly recorded and promulgated.

The initial popular reaction to the insurgents seems confused: traditional accounts have emphasized a degree of hostility among the Dublin public, although some recent interpretations – most notably by J.J. Lee – have sought to correct this impression.[100] The reason for these conflicts is almost certainly that they reflect the extent to which the Rising was in reality a highly paradoxical event. It was largely a Fenian rising, yet was concealed from elements of the IRB leadership and contravened (at least in the opinion of Bulmer Hobson) the Brotherhood's constitution. It was a separatist rising which was disavowed by many separatists. It was an armed insurrection against British rule, but the victims (there were 450 dead) were often Irish, and indeed the initial casualties inflicted by the rebels were probably Irish nationalists: the first victim was an officer of the Dublin Metropolitan Police and, if the general condition of this force is a guide, almost certainly a Catholic and a Home Ruler. Stephen Gwynn was admittedly no supporter of the Rising, but he did make a point of gathering stories from the Irish soldiers who had been used in its suppression. These men (belonging to the 10th Royal Dublin Fusiliers) confirmed that an early casualty of the rebels' fire was an officer 'so strongly Nationalist in his sympathy as to be almost a Sinn Féiner'; they told Gwynn that there had been no need for scouting activity since 'the old women told us everything'.[101] Many of these 'old women' had sons who were serving Ireland (as they thought) on the Western Front.

By the end of Easter week it seems that the Rising might still be seen as an attack on democratic Irish opinion, and indeed – to an extent – on the Irish people themselves. The suppression of the Rising had involved some scandalous episodes: the murder of Francis Sheehy Skeffington and two journalists by a deranged Irish officer of the British army stands out as amongst the grimmest events of the conflict. Two murders committed by soldiers of the South Staffordshire Regiment also inflamed civilian resentment. But on the whole it seems that the teetering pendulum of popular sympathy probably swung against the insurgents during and immediately after the Rising. It was the mid-term British response, both in political as well as military terms, that helped to win a popular re-evaluation of the conflict. Capital sentences were imposed upon 16 leaders, a retribution which, as J.J. Lee has observed, helped to engender the 'maximum resentment, minimum fear': the conduct of the trials (British military courts imposed the sentences) and the protracted, semi-secret nature of the executions helped to consolidate popular sympathies.[102] Widespread arrests and internment – some 3,500 suspected revolutionary nationalists were detained – again helped to ensure widespread animosity without enlivening much fear or respect. Around 1,500 were released almost immediately, while 1,800 were interned in Britain, but only for at most seven months; 170 of the suspects were tried and convicted by court martial. What this rather crude but not particularly brutal reaction achieved was an active sympathy for militant nationalism where often only a passive interest had existed. Moreover, the government not only provided the

emotional spur for this transformation, it also provided material help: the internment camps (such as Frongoch) served as revolutionary academies, helping to
create valuable contacts and to offer opportunities for political education.

Some constitutional leaders saw the dangers inherent in the actions of the government, and sounded a note of warning. In a famous speech, delivered in the Commons
on 11 May, Dillon passionately denounced the executions and praised the bravery
of the insurgents in provocative terms ('it would have been a damned good thing
for you if your soldiers were able to put up as good a fight as did these men in
Dublin').[103] But all this was a belated and disastrous effort to change tack: in a 'desperate lunge towards neo-Parnellism', Dillon was awkwardly trying to claim the rebels
as his own and to annex some of the popular favour that they had won; he was
trying to lead his party onto a course of more strident opposition.[104] But these were
futile endeavours: his indictment of the Liberal-dominated government was the repudiation of an alliance that he had himself pursued since the death of Parnell, while
his taunting of the British army was in effect the repudiation of a recruiting policy
that his party had endorsed since September 1914. The Easter rebels had exposed
the limitations and inconsistencies of the Irish Party's rhetoric and actions – a party
which celebrated the achievements of earlier insurgents, and which daily compromised the ideals of Irish self-government; the rebels had also exposed the distance
that the party had travelled since the death of Parnell – the extent to which his great
coalition of militant and constitutionalist had degenerated into a party of tough-
talking but sedentary and aging gentlemen. In the very act of purloining the rebels'
sanctity, Dillon underlined the integrity of their case.

The traditional response of the British government to Irish nationalist insurrection had been a mixture of armed suppression and legislative concession; and the
pattern of events in May–June 1916 did not, despite the demands of the Great War,
differ greatly from earlier precedents. Traditionally, this sequence of actions could
not have been better calculated to endorse revolutionary nationalism: it involved
the martyring of insurgents, followed by the legislative enactment of at least part
of their programme. It was a testimony to the failure of the Union, and to the failure of imagination on the part of British ministers, that they were unable to break
the logic of this course of action in 1916. Past parliamentarians had been sufficiently
distant from the British government and sufficiently close to the militants to be
able to benefit from both: the Fenian rising of 1867 had created conditions from
which Isaac Butt had been able to benefit, and the agrarian militants and the Clan
na Gael bombers of the early 1880s had, again, created a political environment within
which Parnellism had been able to flourish. But Redmondism was a purer form of
constitutional nationalism – a movement with little of the blurring into extremism
that had characterized its predecessors: it was the Irish Party without its traditional
militant roots, and therefore without the capacity to benefit from any revolutionary
nationalist initiative.

Having suppressed the Rising and deified its architects, the British government
proceeded to endorse their achievement through a political initiative: at the very least,
therefore, the rebels had been able to achieve what had eluded the parliamentarians

since August 1914 – the reactivation of the national question. In May and June 1916 Lloyd George was commissioned to bridge the gap between the Irish Party and the Ulster Unionists that had been defined at the Buckingham Palace Conference, and indeed as early as March 1914: the gap between the Unionists' call for six-county permanent exclusion from Home Rule, and the nationalists' concession of county option on the basis of a six-year term of temporary exclusion. Redmond moved further to the Unionist position by accepting the exclusion of six northern counties, and this was reluctantly endorsed by a convention of northern nationalists which met on 23 June 1916. The issue of the term of exclusion was deliberately fudged by Lloyd George and would possibly have brought further acrimony, indeed even perhaps a renewed stalemate. But, as it was, the negotiations foundered on the bitter opposition expressed by southern Unionist sympathizers within the coalition ministry. This was the worst of all conceivable outcomes for the Irish Party, and indeed for the fate of the parliamentary tradition. The British initiative had certainly vindicated the rebels' action, but – if it had resulted in an agreement – it is possible that the cause of Home Rule might have been won a last-minute reprieve. Whether a new Home Rule assembly, compromised by concessions on the questions of Ulster and of finance, would have long survived the pressure of republican militants is debatable; but this, though interesting, is a separate issue. On the other hand, if the parliamentarians had trenchantly refused further concession in May–June 1916, they might well have emerged from the negotiations at least in no worse a condition than would otherwise have been the case. But the parliamentarians offered too much in terms of their political credibility, and yet too little to secure a binding agreement. Their sacrifice counted for nothing, indeed was actually damaging, since the negotiation failed. But, worse than that, the party was effectively humiliated by the brusque manner in which the government announced that the Lloyd George initiative was at an end: 'that day', as Stephen Gwynn remarked of 22 July 1916, 'really finished the constitutional party, and overthrew Redmond's power'.[105]

Between 1914 and 1916 it may be said that the Irish Party was becoming increasingly vulnerable; but it would be quite wrong to argue for an irreversible decline. Equally, it might well be argued that the Easter Rising created some of the conditions for the party's demise without actually guaranteeing this finale. The failure of the Lloyd George talks was, however, a defining moment: it underlined the extent to which the Irish Party was a marginal force and its concerns of secondary significance within a British parliament broadly united by the war. The negotiations vindicated armed force: they were, at root, a response to one set of militants (the Easter rebels), and they involved humiliating concessions to others who had threatened militancy (the Ulster Unionists). But the negotiations were also a diversion: they meant that the party 'was muzzled when barking or growling might have done something to redeem its reputation'.[106] After July 1916 the Irish Party was still capable of winning by-elections in Ireland, but only because there was as yet no organized alternative.

This alternative was to be found in Sinn Féin, which was growing against the background of popular political realignment in 1916–17. One of the first tangible expressions of this evolving menace to the parliamentarians came in February 1917 with a by-election in North Roscommon, when Count G.N. Plunkett was returned ahead of the official party candidate: Plunkett, the father of one of the martyrs of the Rising (Joseph), usefully illustrates the rapid radicalization of nationalist opinion, for in the 1890s he had been an unsuccessful parliamentary candidate in the Parnellite interest, and as late as 1914 he had applied – again unsuccessfully – for the post of Under-Secretary in Dublin Castle. But there was other unmistakeable evidence of decline: as Sinn Féin gained momentum, stimulated by the Roscommon victory and by the newly freed militants from Frongoch and Reading, so the Irish Party slowed down to a sclerotic shuffle. The party's organizational base disintegrated: the Hibernians 'melted away', while many local nationalist leaders and organizations simply reinvented themselves as separatists and Sinn Féiners.[107] Some northern nationalists, dismayed by the party's wetness on partition, created a breakaway Irish Nation League, initially reformist but later separatist in its loyalties. The Catholic Church, a generally reliable gauge of political change, wavered in its support for the parliamentarians: in a vital by-election, fought in Longford South in May 1917, Dillon boasted that 'we have the bishop, the great majority of the priests and the mob', but the Sinn Féin candidate had an archbishop and a majority of 32 at the poll. For William Walsh, the Archbishop of Dublin, had solemnly declared on the eve of the contest that 'the cause of Ireland had been sold', a judgement which was 'a decisive factor in the election' and which also 'grossly misrepresented Redmond's whole policy and action'.[108] D.P. Moran thought that the narrowness of the Sinn Féin victory indicated that popular sympathies remained in the balance; but even his unflagging scepticism was overcome by the massive support given to the minor players of the 1916 drama, now released from internment.[109]

After the Longford result deceleration became paralysis: the local party disintegrated, while the leadership voluntarily entombed itself within yet another diverting and exhausting and futile process of negotiation. The idea of the Irish Convention, which was put to the House of Commons by Lloyd George on 21 May 1917, seems to have originated partly with Redmond. This was in itself an interesting testimony to the desperation of the Irish leadership, for it represented a highly belated reversion to the kind of 'conference plus business' strategies which William O'Brien had been advocating (in the end fruitlessly) 15 years before (though in fact O'Brien came to condemn the Convention). Nor was the prognosis for the new Convention reassuring to any but the despairing: the Irish Party was seeking a settlement on the basis of a united Ireland, and yet had now painfully little room for manoeuvre. The Ulster Unionists, on the other hand, were seeking a settlement on the basis of a permanent partition of the island – precisely the form of settlement that the Irish Party was too vulnerable to pursue, even if it had so wished. Essentially, the Irish Party was too weakened by the electoral slaughter of Roscommon, Longford and (in July) Clare East to be able to offer concessions; while the Ulster Unionists were so weakened by the actual slaughter on the Somme and at Messines that they, too, had little to offer. The only party within the nationalist community strong enough to strike a deal – Sinn Féin – chose to remain aloof while the ancient antagonists played out their dreary rituals of abuse.

As always, however, there was the fleeting mirage of success. A potentially valuable rapport was established between Redmond and Sir Alexander McDowell, a Belfast solicitor, who – though a government nominee – was highly respected by both his fellow Ulster Unionists and the Irish Party. Together Redmond and McDowell streamlined the process of negotiation at the Convention, and indeed they might have achieved more had it not been for McDowell's death in early 1918. 'In losing him', observed Stephen Gwynn, a member of the Convention, 'we lost certainly the strongest will in his group, perhaps the strongest in the Convention; and it was a will for settlement'.[110]

There were other dashed hopes. In December 1917 Lord Midleton, the leader of the southern Unionist delegation at the Convention, proposed a historic reconciliation between his community and Home Rule on the basis of a generous but qualified measure of self-government. The contentious issue was the control of customs, which Midleton wanted to see vested in the British government and which the nationalists wanted for the proposed Home Rule administration. By January 1918 Redmond and Midleton had come to an understanding on the basis of a shared authority over customs, with the British empowered to strike rates and the Irish granted rights of collection: this half-way house preserved the principle of a customs union within the British Isles, while giving substantial powers of administration to the new Irish government. But the breakthrough never came, for both men had edged beyond the tolerance of their support. Redmond, who was prepared to move for the acceptance of the revised Midleton scheme, was deserted by influential supporters, including Devlin and the representatives of the Catholic hierarchy. Midleton, on the other hand, had acted without consulting and without the consent of the Ulster Unionists, and indeed he had failed to canvass widely within his own southern Unionist constituency. In the end the Convention delegates took a characteristic but understandable decision to postpone the customs issue for the duration of the war (an echo, here, of Asquith's stratagem of September 1914 with Home Rule); and the delegates also, finally, endorsed a proposal for self-government, tinctured by provisions for the special representation of minority communities. By the time this report was hesitantly accepted (by less than half of the Convention), it was already an anachronism: its proposals were as archaic as the structure that had produced them. It was a tragic but appropriate metaphor that two of the most influential men of goodwill among the delegates – Redmond and McDowell – should have died while the Convention was still haggling and scheming.

Nevertheless, the Convention was a revealing forum. It has been documented many times, yet one of its most striking symmetries has been overlooked.[111] Its single significant achievement was to induce a form of agreement between moderate southern landed Unionists and the vestiges of the Home Rule movement. Redmond, true to his political origins, had come close to fulfilling the complete Parnellite agenda in the last weeks of his life. He had helped to win a comprehensive Land Act, he had helped to guide a Home Rule measure onto the statute books (if not into operation); and, crucially, in 1917–18 he had helped to bind, as his master had sought before him, the southern gentry to the idea of Irish self-government. Redmond's closeness to greatness is striking; his tragedy lay in the minute but crucial space separating him from the enactment of the deals which he had so carefully won.

The Irish Convention was never likely to resuscitate the constitutional tradition, and the surprise is rather that it should have held out so many tantalizing prospects for a settlement. By the spring of 1918, when the Convention broke up, the Irish Party was left in a fragmentary and compromised state: it had split on the issue of the Midleton initiative and over the final report; and it had been bound into yet another failed British scheme at precisely the moment when such an association was undesirable. For on 21 March 1918 the German army launched its last great offensive of the war, and for some weeks it looked possible that the stalemate that had long characterized the Western Front would be blown away by a dramatic Allied retreat, and possible defeat. In these circumstances the British government, never particularly tender towards Irish nationalism, was unlikely to proceed with any sensitivity. This was all the more certain given that, with the death of Redmond on 6 March, Dillon took over the leadership of what remained of the constitutional tradition. For though the gratitude of the British government amounted to no more than the proverbial gratitude of the Hapsburgs, Redmond was widely respected by ministers and backbenchers: it has been suggested, with some truth, that – even allowing for the German offensive – the government might well have been restrained by him from its disastrous strategies of April 1918.[112] As it was, Dillon proved to be no more an influence on British policy than on Irish popular opinion.

In fact the German offensive damaged the Irish Party in several respects. First, many National Volunteers who had joined the British army were among the heavy casualties sustained on 21 March and in the weeks afterwards: the 6th Connaught Rangers, for example, which contained Volunteers recruited from Catholic West Belfast, was severely bloodied on the chaotic first day of the offensive. But the mounting losses also drove the British government into a panic over the supply of troops, and this led in turn to the spectre of conscription for Ireland. The rest of the United Kingdom had been subject to conscription since 1916, but then no nationalist regarded Ireland as anything other than a distinct nation on the brink of some form of legislative independence: this indeed was the founding principle on which even the Redmondites based their approach to the war. On 10 April 1918 Lloyd George proposed, through the Military Service Bill, that the government should be empowered to extend conscription into Ireland, were the need to arise. This was an enabling bill rather than an actual measure of conscription; but, given the dire condition of the British army, the distinction between theory and practice seemed slight. There is no question that ministers grasped the unpopularity of this proposal (they had been told often enough by Redmond); but equally there is no question that their imaginations were gripped less by the threat of Irish disturbances than by the threat of imminent defeat in the war, and the probable disintegration not just of the Union but of the entire United Kingdom. Indeed, Lloyd George undertook as a sweetener to couple the draft with the immediate enactment of Home Rule. All this of course confirmed the extent to which Redmond's vision of a voluntary Irish army, which united Irish and Ulster Volunteers and which fought alongside other imperial troops, was as dead as its author. Dillon and the Irish Party, their morale already enfeebled, endorsed Sinn Féin strategy by walking out of the Commons and by associating themselves with their rivals in the Mansion House Conference of 18 April; here Eamon de Valera drew up a national pledge against the enforcement of conscription and hinted (as did the Ulster Covenant of 1912) at extreme measures of resistance. This pledge was signed by tens of thousands at church doors on 21 April, and endorsed by the Irish Trades Union Congress through a one-day general strike on 23 April. But it was Sinn Féin who derived the popular credit for the initiative. An official swoop on the leadership of the party on the night of 17–18 May helped to underline its patriotic credentials and created a momentum which carried Arthur Griffith to the top of the poll in East Cavan on 20 June. The Irish Party, defeated yet again on home territory (and the party was strong in south Ulster), stood meekly by, broken by recurrent humiliations and now wearing the ill-fitting livery of the republican movement.

By the general election of December 1918 the country was ripe for an electoral revolution (though by no means ripe for a guerrilla war). The discreet, comparatively propertied electorate that had sustained the Irish Party from 1884–5 (there were only 700,000 voters as late as 1910) was replaced under the Representation of the People Act: at the 1918 election in Ireland there were over 2 million voters. This in itself need not have implied change: the Parliamentary Party, which had flourished in the 1870s and the early 1880s under a franchise created in 1850, had successfully met the challenge of the 'fourth' Reform Act. But in 1918 the new electorate had new separatist preferences. The party that had returned 73 supporters in 1910 was left with six in 1918; of these only one – Redmond's son, Major William Archer Redmond – survived the Sinn Féin deluge in the south and west, and even then by only around 480 votes in a poll of over 9,000. Otherwise the party was routed. Sinn Féin won under 48 per cent of the total Irish vote, but it won 65 per cent of the vote in the 26 counties of what would become the Irish Free State. There was some regional differentiation, most noticeable in the contrast between Ulster and the rest of the island: in the north an electoral pact with Sinn Féin gave an artificial boost to the Irish Party, though it also derived strength from the survival of the AOH organization. Elsewhere the Sinn Féin tide was blocked more effectively in the east of the country than in the west: rural Ireland, which vigorously opposed the war, was more separatist than the towns, where large numbers of young men joined the British army (though, on the other hand, an alternative urban challenge to Sinn Féin – from the Labour Party – did not materialize). This effect may have been enhanced slightly by the opposition of Protestants to Sinn Féin: in the Dublin City and County constituencies and in seats such as East Wicklow (where there were concentrations of Protestants) the Irish Party vote was respectable, as indeed was that of the Unionists (who actually won the new Rathmines constituency). In the west of Ireland, rural and overwhelmingly Catholic, and especially in west and central Munster, there were many unopposed Sinn Féin candidates: there were in total 25 Sinn Féin walkovers, with entire counties such as Clare, Cork and Kerry offering no opposition.

Even allowing for these regional and religious distinctions, it would seem futile to argue that there was any marked survival of the parliamentary tradition in the aftermath of the 1918 contest. The comprehensiveness of the Irish Party's rout, combined with its partial submission to the tenets of Sinn Féin, would appear to confirm this perception. But in fact the issue of continuity hinges upon a question of definition. What died in 1918 was certainly not Parnellism, but rather Redmond's interpretation of Parnellism: as George Boyce has argued, 'the Party's problem in 1918 was not that Parnellism had lost its appeal, but that the Party had ceased to convince the people that they stood for Parnellism'.[113] The extent to which the party had developed in 1910–16 away from its earlier traditions is a measure of the risk that Redmond was taking with Asquith's government: Redmond had tried to crown a political career characterized by profound caution with an impetuous gamble on the Empire in September 1914. His instincts had not been entirely wrong (the Empire after all had eventually won through), but he had insufficient political capital to see through the game of carnage.

The truth was perhaps that Parnell's legacy was so expansive and ambiguous that Redmond was as much a Parnellite in 1918, when he struck a deal with the southern Unionists, as he had been in 1888, when he had been gaoled for his outspoken agrarian principles. It is unquestionably true that, just as the Irish Party ceded political initiative to Sinn Féin, so Sinn Féin annexed some of the most valuable Irish Party assets: Sinn Féin, then, by 1918 appeared in the popular mind to be the upholders of the Parnellite tradition, rather than the parliamentarians who had sold their birthright to the Saxon government. Sinn Féin retained much of Parnell's ambiguity: just as the Chief had endorsed Home Rule after toying with a more advanced separatism, so Sinn Féin's goal, while ostensibly a republic, was in fact highly ambiguous. Only at the Sinn Féin ard-fheis of October 1917 was the ultimate purpose of the party settled, and only then in a comparatively hazy manner (a republic was declared to be the first aim, but it was also emphasized that once a republic had been won the future of Irish government would be decided by the people). Sinn Féin had the same opaque stand on political violence that had characterized classic Parnellism: neither advocated violence, but each was prepared to accept that opportunities might arise where purely political action might be inadequate.

There were other parallels. Although Parnell was highly suspicious of any independent abstentionist initiative within the Irish Party of the 1880s, he bequeathed a passion for a centralized parliamentary machine to Sinn Féin. After 1891 the Irish Party was a comparatively localized body, despite the preferences of both William O'Brien and Dillon: it was, as Tom Garvin has remarked, 'dominated by territorially-based "satraps"'.[114] But Sinn Féin, by contrast, reactivated the Parnellite preference for machine politics, highly disciplined and highly centralized. De Valera, who bears some of the marks of the Uncrowned King's political style, specifically claimed that he and Sinn Féin were the true followers of Parnell. The almost Saxon interest in parliamentary form and procedure that characterized the inauguration of Dáil Éireann in January 1919 may be interpreted as a further ironic testimony to Parnell's abiding influence.

De Valera, charismatic and authoritarian, reconstituted some of Parnell's political chemistry; Redmond, uncharismatic and malleable, clearly found the experiment beyond his powers. Indeed, in the final analysis, just as the early success of the Irish Party was to some extent Parnell's personal achievement, so its demise was the work of Redmond: this, at any rate, is the theme that pervades even the work of Redmondite apologists. Parnell and de Valera were 'chiefs' to their followers, while Redmond was always the respectable but profoundly unromantic 'chairman': 'he could persuade, but he could not compel', as Stephen Gwynn sadly remarked.[115] William O'Brien, ever caustic but not without insight, went further: 'the best defence of Mr Redmond's leadership really is that he never was the leader'.[116]

There were other defects of leadership. Parnell looked as if he were detached, but in reality possessed an ever-vigilant political intelligence; Redmond betrayed the unwary by the appearance of accessibility. Redmond seems in fact to have been a more remote leader than Parnell, relying exclusively on a narrow 'inner cabinet' and being highly suspicious of young talent: Parnell, by contrast, drew around him a protective circle of comparative youngsters, who represented the most active and alert political talent in the broader nationalist community.[117] While the best example of his coercion of local nationalism (the effort to impose O'Shea on Galway in 1886) is also amongst the worst examples of his judgement, Parnell created a party which, broadly, held the imagination of the Irish electorate until the eve of independence. Redmond, by contrast, permitted stagnation, and was both neglectful of new talent and tolerant of inadequacy. Parnell looked and sounded fanatical, but was in fact an unrelenting pragmatist; Redmond looked and sounded pragmatic, but oscillated between uncertainty and the single-minded pursuit of phantoms. Parnell sacrificed the unity of his party at the altar of his leadership; Redmond (arguably) sacrificed the survival of the party at the altar of its unity. Redmond's tragedy, therefore, was that he bore the scars of Parnell's failings. This gentle, honourable man compromised his friendships and principles in order to preserve the Irish Party for its strategic opening; and, single-mindedly chasing the phantom of Home Rule, he then compromised and broke the party itself.

5.4   Making and Unmaking Unionism, 1853–1921

The history of Unionism in Ireland is a history of simplification, of retreat and retrenchment. Through much of the nineteenth century Unionism – defined very broadly as a belief in the constitutional connection between Britain and Ireland – was the normative condition of Irish politics. Unionism was a luxuriant intellectual and cultural growth, which entwined itself around mainstream Liberal and Tory politics and which pollinated even those more popular movements that have been seen exclusively within the history of nationalist development and progression: O'Connellite repeal and Parnellite Home Rule were, stripped of their patriotic ebullience, campaigns for a more workable relationship with Britain – for a more refined Union – rather than for absolute separation.

Even when the definition is tightened and when Unionism is seen in a more conventional light (as the movement upholding the Act of Union), its ideological grip upon a wide and diverse section of Irish society, whether northern or southern, was still astonishing. Unionism linked southern landed capital with the world of northern Presbyterian embourgeoisement: it bound commercial magnates with Orange labourers. Unionism commanded a working-class constituency in late Victorian Dublin no less than in Belfast: it ruled in the southern suburbs of the national capital (Rathmines returned a Unionist to the Commons as late as 1918) no less than in the southern suburbs of its northern rival. Unionism linked financial with intellectual muscle: the movement found unembarrassed advocates among the luminaries of both Trinity College Dublin and Queen's College Belfast – this, moreover, at a time when, as the *Northern Whig* remarked in 1914, there were 'giants among the professors'.[118] And yet this luxuriant diversity was swiftly pruned down to a northern core, very largely middle class in its leadership and unadorned by the intellectual foliage of its mid- and late Victorian predecessor: the stolid and mostly undifferentiated bourgeois ministers seated around James Craig's cabinet table were merely the remnants of a once more varied and sophisticated political culture. In an island where this vibrancy is for the most part remembered only through fossilized remains, and where Unionism is seen as alien and marginal, it is instructive to recount not just the processes of retreat, but also the extent to which the movement once occupied a central role within Irish political life.

The issue of definition has already been broached. Defined in institutional terms, Unionism was essentially an amalgam of Irish Toryism, Orangeism and the Church of Ireland. Defined in social terms, Unionism was essentially an amalgam of the Irish landed interest with the northern Presbyterian bourgeoisie: if nationalism drew strength from Catholic embourgeoisement in the nineteenth century, then there was a parallel northern Protestant development. There was, of course, much more to Unionism than these several building blocks, and in particular with the passage of time new forces, new organizations and a new equilibrium emerged within the movement; but these three institutions and two social groupings were arguably the key constituents of the Unionist conglomerate, at least so far as the mid- to late Victorian period was concerned.

The strength of Unionism, certainly in terms of money and social influence, lay in the consensus between landlordism and northern commerce. The Unionism of these classes was (by and large) unflinching, yet it was by no means preordained. The political roots of the northern Presbyterian middle classes lay partly in the urban radicalism that produced the United Irishmen in Belfast in 1791; and while (as J.R.B. McMinn has argued) the integrity of this radicalism should not be exaggerated, it survived in a fragmentary fashion well into the twentieth century.[119] However, the predominant tendency within Victorian Presbyterianism was Unionist, and much analytical skill has been devoted to explaining why this should have been so. On the whole, the more starkly the contrast between the Presbyterian rebels of '98 and the Presbyterian rebels of 1913–14 is portrayed, the more difficult the problem of deciphering their political evolution becomes; but it is now generally accepted that the radicalism of the men and women of the 1790s should not be exaggerated any more than the conservatism of the Unionists of the Home Rule era. The continuities – anti-Catholicism, anti-episcopalianism – are no less impressive for having been long obscured; while the complexity of the community's evolution has also been steadily unravelled, and in particular through the work of Peter Gibbon.[120] Broadly, it has been argued that the embourgeoisement of northern Presbyterianism brought with it an intensifying commitment to the Union. Belfast industry grew after 1801, a success that was attributed unhesitatingly to the Union ('look at Belfast and be a repealer if you can', was Henry Cooke's famous appeal); but, no less important than the extent of this industrial growth was its nature – semi-detached from the rest of the Irish economy, and export-oriented.[121] The northern Presbyterian middle classes bought into Union and (to a lesser extent) Empire partly because this is where their economic interests lay; but it was also the case that their radicalism had always been circumscribed and that the essentially Catholic concerns of nationalism in the nineteenth century held out little appeal to Presbyterian emotions, to say nothing of the community's perceived self-interest.

At first glance the union between these Presbyterian business magnates and Irish landlordism might seem bizarre, given the historic sectarian and economic antagonism between the two groups. Some of the ways in which the animosity between the Church of Ireland and Presbyterians was being broken down have already been described in an earlier chapter: in particular, the emergence of a shared religious identity and vocabulary – supplied by evangelicalism – deserves re-emphasis. However, throughout the years leading up to the land purchase legislation of 1903 and (to a lesser extent) 1909, tensions remained between the Church of Ireland elite and some elements of Presbyterianism within Ulster, particularly, of course, the tenant interest. Moreover, if the unity of the emergent Unionism should not be exaggerated, then other aspects of the complicated political chemistry of Victorian loyalism should not be taken for granted. Just as the political evolution of Presbyterianism did not follow any predictable trajectory, so the political tenets of Irish landlordism only seem conventional with the benefit of hindsight. The Unionism of the 'British garrison' might well be assumed, yet – as W.E. Vaughan has strikingly argued – Irish landlords were in ways much worse off under the Union than might have been the case under some form of self-government. After the Famine, and with the long period of Liberal dominance, Irish landed influence over British government was decisively reduced: 'Irish landlords did not control, or even perhaps influence the British state after 1846 . . . [they] had some influence in parliament but it was a power to resist rather than to innovate'.[122] Moreover, Irish landed capital was of diminishing political and economic significance within the context of the Victorian industrial economy, to say nothing of the developing overseas Empire: landlords would – short of summary expropriation – have been a much more telling force within any self-governing Irish polity. Indeed, in those few moments when landlords overcame their fear of violent nationalism or their distaste for an expansionist Catholicism, the logic of an Irish patriotism became irrefutable (as evidenced, for example, by the limited Tory and landed support for the Home Government

Association, or indeed the residual landed presence within the Home Rule Party of 1874 and 1880). But for the most part landlords were happier to accept the Union and an incremental surrender rather than risk an Irish parliament and the possibility (however remote) of a more comprehensive and immediate disaster. Their accession to the cause meant that Unionism was upheld by both the commercial capital of Belfast and the rental income of almost the entire island of Ireland. Little wonder, then, that a minority cause should have demonstrated such powers of resilience and survival.

Of the three institutions that were identified earlier in the chapter as crucial within the early development of Unionism, perhaps the single most significant was the Irish Conservative Party. Irish Toryism supplied much of the organizational infrastructure around which Unionism was constructed; and it supplied trained advocates to the loyalist cause. As has been earlier observed, Conservatism was the unsung success story of mid-Victorian politics, profiting from the tightly regulated electorate created under the Irish Franchise Act (1850) and from a well-regimented party organization (as evidenced by the Central Conservative Society, created in 1853); indeed, as Theo Hoppen has observed, the modernization of Conservative organization in Ireland occurred well ahead of similar initiatives within the English or Scots parties.[123] Nor was this Conservative success exclusively a northern phenomenon: on the contrary, throughout the country a combination of a disproportionately Protestant electorate, landed influence and a well-oiled organizational machine ensured regular Tory victories in such (from the late nineteenth-century perspective) unlikely territory as County Sligo. Moreover, although the cause suffered a succession of legislative reverses – the disestablishment of the Church of Ireland in 1869 (of which more later), the passage of the Ballot Act in 1872 and the Corrupt Practices Act in 1883 – there were compensations. Unlike the Liberals, who remained tied to the farming and textile interests (and even then only in an incomplete fashion), the Tories attracted new talent, both among the young and from new and influential professional and commercial interests: an army of young lawyers, fired with righteousness, fought the battle for loyalty in the revision courts of the 1850s and 1860s. In addition a rich populist tradition upheld the values of the cause, both in Ulster and in other parts of the island: William Johnston of Ballykilbeg, elected as an independent MP for Belfast in 1868, was soon accommodated within Conservatism and articulated a populist sectarianism that was identifiable elsewhere (such as in the fulminations of the Reverend Tresham Gregg, the hero of Dublin working-class Protestants). The challenge supplied by Johnston, and by the Home Rule and Liberal parties in the 1870s, kept up the need for organizational revision, and this was especially marked in the north where in 1880, the year of the great Liberal revival, an Ulster Constitutional Union was founded – and where in 1883, the year of the Home Rule 'invasion' of Ulster, an Ulster Constitutional Club opened its doors to the Belfast commercial elite. Both would soon prove to be organizational pivots for the Ulster Unionist movement.

Conservatism was a predominant influence within emergent Unionism, both in an ideological and an institutional sense. But it would be wrong to dismiss the impact of Irish Liberalism, even though it is conventionally assumed that nationalism annexed the vestigial Liberal tradition. Certainly the Home Rule movement acquired Liberal parliamentary constituencies, most spectacularly at the general election of 1874 when some 56 Liberal seats fell to supporters of Isaac Butt: but the moribund party rallied in Ulster in 1880, revived momentarily by the oxygen of the land crisis, only to fall victim to the polarization wrought by the Home Rule issue in 1885–6. Still, if the Home Rule Party inherited Liberal seats as well as the favour of Catholic voters, then Unionism inherited both many Liberal activists and some of the ideological trappings of the effectively defunct party: a meeting of Ulster Liberals held on 19 March 1886 declared its support for the Union, and from this there grew an uneasy alliance with Conservatism. What this meant was not so much a massive electoral accession as the (highly tentative) recruitment of Presbyterian leaders and activists as well as some popular farming support: it introduced a measure of social reformism into Unionism, in particular with regard to landed issues, but it also heightened tensions within the movement over policy as well as patronage. The enlistment of the Liberal Unionists also tended to dilute the strongly Orange flavour of the Unionist alliance, since many of the most influential of the new recruits, while no great friends to Catholicism, were at the same time intensely suspicious of all forms of religious chauvinism.

It would also be quite wrong, however, to interpret the broad Liberal Unionist tradition as exclusively enlightened. On the contrary, Liberal Unionism not only embraced a social radicalism (as articulated most passionately by T.W. Russell), but also a sterner Whig tradition which mixed a passionate sense of Irishness with an unflinching respect for the revolutionary settlement of 1688 as well as a boundless faith in the powers and abilities of the landed elite. Edward Saunderson, the first leader of the Irish Unionist Parliamentary Party (1886–1906) – indeed, arguably the first leader of Irish Unionism – seemed to be the epitome of Orange Toryism, but in reality he had migrated from a longstanding family tradition of Whiggery (he had sat as a Liberal MP for Cavan between 1865 and 1874) and had joined the Orange Order only in 1882, when he was 45. This ideological journey was much shorter than might otherwise be supposed.

Saunderson was a passionate Anglican, and indeed the Church of Ireland represented another key element within the Unionist compound. Once again the truth of this point may be expressed both in an organizational and in an emotional or spiritual sense. The Church of Ireland, indeed the evangelical tradition within broader Irish Protestantism, supplied a spiritual self-confidence, a missionary zeal and a rhetorical tone to Conservatives, and later to Unionists. Many Unionists learned an oratorical style and passion either through listening to evangelical ministers or – after disestablishment – through participating in the councils of the Church of Ireland. Certainly Edward Saunderson, who was an extremely diffident parliamentary speaker in the mid- and late 1860s, seems to have acquired a confidence and a passion through contributing to debates within the Church of Ireland committee devoted to the work of prayer book revision (1871–3). Other leading Ulster Unionists (such as Fred Crawford) gained speaking and other semi-political skills within the Church and its associated organizations.

Plate 11   Colonel Edward Saunderson, September 1906.
Source: Private collection.

But perhaps the greatest, and certainly the most direct, contribution of the Church of Ireland to the evolution of organized Unionism came, paradoxically, through its defeat and humiliation in 1868–9 over disestablishment. Disestablishment was W.E. Gladstone's initiative, and it was simultaneously the keystone of a broader project promising 'justice' for Ireland as well as part of a highly astute electoral strategy: as Vincent Comerford has wryly observed, 'Gladstone had a well publicised and sincere conscience about such matters [as the Church of Ireland] but his conscience never ran ahead of his pragmatic political practice'.[124] The issue of disestablishment united Irish Catholics with some Irish Presbyterians and brought success to the Liberals throughout Ireland: 66 Irish Liberals were returned at the general election of 1868, including several seats in the relatively unpromising Tory heartland of Ulster. The calls of the dying Henry Cooke for Protestant unity on the basis of the Church establishment went unheeded, and the patriarch of Presbyterian Conservatism went to his eternal reward on 13 December 1868 secure in the hope of salvation, but much less confident concerning the temporal outlook. As *The Times* observed in November 1868, 'the political attachment between the episcopalian and presbyterian laity, which was rooted chiefly in the Orange system, and carefully cherished by the conservative leaders, had been cleft by the church question and shorn of its strength'.[125]

In fact there was much less real cause for Irish loyalist concern than the psephological evidence seemed to suggest. It is certainly true that the Ulster election results of 1868 undermine any overly emphatic suggestion that Cooke had converted his church to Toryism. On the other hand, the results do not illustrate any unflinching Presbyterian commitment to the Liberal Party: they are remarkable rather for the extent to which they reveal a comprehensive Catholic Gladstonianism. This united Catholic endorsement, combined with the more tentative approval of Irish Presbyterians, gave Gladstone a mandate to proceed on the question of disestablishment; and in March 1869 an Irish Church Bill was duly introduced into the Commons. The measure offered little to substantiate the more lurid fears of its Tory opponents: in its final form it created an Irish Church Temporalities Commission, which had charge of approximately half of the property of the former Church establishment (around £8 million). Of the remaining millions, some compensation was earmarked both for the Presbyterians, who were to lose their official subsidy, the regium donum, and for the Catholics, who were to lose the parliamentary grant to the Maynooth seminary: the residue (some £7 million) was set aside for charitable work of different kinds. All church buildings still in use were to remain in Anglican hands, while disused sites were to be handed over to the Board of Public Works. There was thus no sweeping expropriation (except in a strict technical sense, and in the rhetoric of the measure's opponents); nor did the Irish Church Act announce (as many Catholics and some Presbyterians fondly hoped) the demise of the Church of Ireland. Indeed, though the Act is conventionally seen as a measure of democratization which heralded the unravelling of the Union, there is a strong case to be made for exactly the reverse proposition. At the very least disestablishment 'can with equal justice be seen as a new beginning for the Union'.[126]

In some respects the Irish Church Act acted not as a spanner in the works of the Union, but rather as a mechanical refinement that prepared the constitutional jalopy for future mileage. The Church of Ireland was removed from the focus of a damaging political controversy and forced to come to terms with demographic realities. Disestablishment brought with it not just the ending of the somewhat fitful protection supplied by the constitution, but also a measure of democratization: an uncertain external source of support was replaced therefore by a more fundamental internal restructuring, with a new copper-fastening of the ties binding the clergy and laity. The new synodal structure of the Church helped to create a stronger (if perhaps more defensive) sense of confessional identity. Moreover, the termination of the establishment, though supported by many Presbyterians, removed a source of division between the two main Irish Protestant traditions, and therefore prepared the way for the inclusivist 'Protestant' identity that underlay the early successes of Unionism. Disestablishment bolstered Unionism in even more direct and tangible ways: the cause of the threatened Church stimulated the creation of several protest organizations – the Central Protestant Defence Association, the Ulster Protestant Defence Association – which in a modest form looked forward to the organizational spree of 1885–6. In addition many of the most prominent defenders of the establishment (the third Earl of Erne, Viscount Crichton, Lord Claud Hamilton) would soon move into the last ditch of the Union: many of these advocates of Church and Union shared a social base in the landed elite of the 'outer' counties of Ulster (Tyrone, Fermanagh, Cavan), and were disproportionately significant in formulating the ideological first principles of Irish Unionism. Disestablishment underpinned the evangelical identity of these men and taught them the limits of what British politics might deliver for their cause.

One of the key resources in Protestant society exploited by territorial dynasties such as the Hamiltons, the Crichtons or (eventually) the Saundersons was the Orange Order. Even though many Irish loyalists in the mid-1880s (such as Saunderson) sought to promote a non-sectarian Unionism, in reality the organizational foundation supplied by Orangeism seemed to be both crucial for future growth and a barrier to wider Catholic participation. This tension between the ideal of a secular Unionism and the utility of Orange organization has characterized the movement since its origins in the early and mid-1880s. At this time the Order provided the only credible basis for loyalist opposition to both the Land League and the National League, since the alternatives (such as the Ulster Constitutional Union) were either party-based or regional. Orangeism served to unite members of the Church of Ireland with the increasing number of Presbyterians who saw the Order as being a necessary, if sometimes unlovely, remedy to the greater evil of an expansionist Catholicism. Although dissolved in 1836, the Order was reconstituted in 1845–6 with the Earl of Enniskillen (another of the south Ulster populist magnates) as Grand Master: in general, however, the reputation of the Order for rowdiness and its alleged association with the Duke of Cumberland's Ruritanian ambitions towards the English throne meant that, with one or two prominent exceptions, the gentry held aloof from enrolment. One of the exceptions who demonstrates this rule is William Johnston of Ballykilbeg, the owner of a small and encumbered estate in Lecale, County Down: Johnston's efforts to overthrow the Party Processions Act (1850) won him a short spell in Downpatrick gaol (in March–April 1868), massive popular favour (he was returned as an independent MP for Belfast in November 1868), and the utter contempt of his landed peers. The social appeal of the Order was thus, despite its wide confessional and geographical spread, highly limited, at least until the challenge of the Land League helped the northern gentry to overcome their squeamishness.

The significance of the Orange Order in terms of the ideological and institutional groundwork for Unionism can hardly be overstated. When, in 1879–80, the Land League began to make inroads into Ulster, and even among Protestant farmers, it was the Order that supplied the predominant loyalist response: in the autumn of 1880 a series of Orange counter-demonstrations was held, designed to coincide with League meetings and to proclaim the Order's faith in the necessity for reform. This articulation of a cross-class identity of interest would soon emerge as a fundamental tenet of the Unionist creed. Moreover, the Orange campaign against the League brought to the forefront numerous landed leaders (E.M. Archdale, Viscount Castlereagh, Viscount Crichton, Lord Hill-Trevor, Somerset Maxwell, Edward Saunderson) who lent the Order both an enhanced social respectability and high-political connections and experience (Lord Crichton, for example, as has been mentioned, had been a leader of the campaign to save the Church of Ireland from disestablishment). Again, when the Land League was replaced by the National League in October 1882, it was the Order that governed and supplied the northern response. Timothy Healy's 'invasion' of Ulster was met by Orange counter-demonstrations, including one controversial affair at Rosslea, County Fermanagh, on 16 October 1883 when an Orange leader, Lord Rossmore, seemed bent on a violent confrontation with the Leaguers. The first efforts at popular Unionist organization, in 1885–6, were certainly influenced by the new Orange leaders and their inclusivist social message: but the organizational roots of the Irish Loyal and Patriotic Union (May 1885) or the Loyal Irish Union (August 1885) extended far beyond Orangeism. On the other hand, it was a coterie of Orange MPs, and pre-eminently Edward Saunderson, who successfully agitated for the creation of a distinct Irish Unionist Parliamentary Party in January–February 1886. Several of the originators of this new party had been associated either with the Orange campaign against the League, or with the struggle against disestablishment.

So far an emphasis has been placed on the social and institutional origins of Unionism, at least within the 20 or so years before the first Home Rule Bill. The following 30 or so years – from the defeat of the Home Rule Bill on 8 June 1886 through to the eve of the Battle of the Somme, 1 July 1916 – may be regarded as the apogee of the Unionist movement, at least in so far as it successfully maintained its central objective and sustained a form of organizational unity and harmony. For this period the central interpretative theme is unquestionably the localization of the movement, a motor force which was fuelled by several interconnected but subsidiary developments. The defining relationships of the period serve to illustrate the importance of the drift towards a more localized Unionism: the relationship between landed and middle-class power within the movement; the changing bond between Ulster and southern Unionism and between Ulster Unionism and British Toryism; the changing balance between the parliamentary and militant traditions within the movement. The unravelling of these different themes helps to unveil not merely the logic of the partition settlement of 1920–1, but also the pattern of later Unionist failures within the confines of that settlement.

The successes of Unionism in this, its Antonine age, are not hard to locate. With Irish Unionist help Home Rule was defeated in June 1886 and again in September 1893; with this help the Conservatives were in power with a Unionist agenda for most of the 20 years preceding 1906. The challenge of Parnellism was seen off, while the relatively conciliatory public face of John Redmond reflected not simply his own temperament, but also the strength of his opponents. The Ulster Unionist stand against the third Home Rule Bill, in 1912–14, was – judged from the institutional and technical perspective – a resounding success, even if Asquith used the cover of the First World War to nudge the bill onto the statute books.

Nor are some of the basic explanations for these successes difficult to find. Irish Unionism for much of the period before the war was a comparatively united movement, whether socially, regionally or in terms of its bond with British allies. Broadly speaking, the movement – though highly fissile – contained dissent, even if there was momentary turmoil in the ranks and occasional embarrassment. After 1913, however, there was a very rapid disintegration, a collapse which reflected both the pressures brought about by the partition question and the changing conditions created by the war, but which also highlighted older fault-lines within the move- ment. Until the eve of the First World War there was always the potential for disaster, but on the whole this was staved off. Late Victorian and Edwardian Unionism was a formidable if unlikely combination of landed and commercial capital, of the southern gentry and Belfast industrialists, of small-town Orange brokers as well as metropolitan Tories and imperialists. The narrative of the disintegration of Unionism after 1913–14 is the story of how this soaring electoral architecture eventually ceased to defy the gravity of democratic politics.

One of the keystones of Unionism, as has been argued, was the alliance between landed and commercial capital. Between the mid-1880s, when the institutions of Unionism were laid down, and 1914, the balance of social forces within the leader- ship of the movement was decisively altered: indeed, the balance of power between land, commerce and the professions shifted within Ireland and Britain as a whole. In 1885–6 Irish landed politicians were of great importance to the formation of independent loyalist bodies, both within and beyond the House of Commons: the Irish Loyal and Patriotic Union and its northern counterpart, the Ulster Loyalist Union (January 1886), were each largely the result of landed initiative, while the Irish Unionist Parliamentary Party was predominantly landed in the 1880s, as were its progenitors (Saunderson, Lord Claud Hamilton). This is not to deny the sig- nificance of business leaders or commercial capital even at this formative stage: various Belfast magnates – J.P. Corry (Mid Armagh), William Ewart (North Belfast), H.L. Mulholland (North Derry) – had already infiltrated the ranks of the parlia- mentary party with the general election of 1886. But even with massive urban demon- strations of Unionist conviction, such as Lord Randolph Churchill's visit to Belfast on 22 February 1886, or the great Ulster Convention of 17 June 1892, landlords played a significant part: the committee of senior Unionists who guided the Convention into existence was still predominantly landed and was chaired by Lord Arthur Hill, the uncle of one of the greatest Irish proprietors of the age, the sixth Marquess of Downshire. Irish squires such as Saunderson had a remarkable influence over sections of the Conservative leadership throughout the 1890s, and in particular over Lord Salisbury, the party leader: Saunderson and his allies acted as a brake upon the reformist initiatives of constructive Unionist ideologues like Gerald Balfour and Horace Plunkett. Irish landlordism continued to lurk within all the upper ranks of

Plate 12 The Ulster Unionist Convention Building, June 1892.
Source: Public Record Office of Northern Ireland.

British politics: at the cabinet level (St John Brodrick, the eighth Duke of Devonshire, Lord George Hamilton, the fifth Marquess of Lansdowne were all both ministers and Irish proprietors), within the Lords (where there were around 144 peers with Irish interests in the Home Rule era) and within the Commons (where there was a more variable but – as late as the 1890s – still substantial Irish landed interest).

But the overall drift within Unionist politics, as indeed more broadly, was towards landed decline. The landed command of the parliamentary party very swiftly collapsed after 1900, having held relatively steady throughout the 1890s: by the general election of 1918 only one landed proprietor was returned to the Commons in the Irish Unionist cause. The new representative institutions of Ulster Unionism which were emerging after 1904, though they retained a landed presence, were principally agencies for the commercial and professional interests of the Belfast middle classes. The Ulster Unionist Council (UUC), which was created in 1904–5, was in some ways a rejection of the landlord-dominated and high-political focus of late Victorian Unionism; and while it gave a representation to landlords – about a third of the UUC standing committee were proprietors in 1910 – this was always a minority representation. The leadership of Ulster Unionism at the time of the third Home Rule Bill contained landed elements (the Londonderry and Abercorn families remained prominent), but again as a marginal and in some ways merely a symbolic phenomenon. In the 'outer' areas of Ulster landlords like Basil Brooke (Fermanagh) or Lord Farnham and Oliver Nugent (Cavan) retained a primacy, active in recruitment to the Ulster Volunteer Force (January 1913) and in some cases to the Ulster Special Constabulary (1920): it might be speculated that just as the landed proprietors of these counties were disproportionately significant forces in the origins of organized Unionism, so their ascendancy was preserved longer here than elsewhere. It might be further conjectured that the serious nature of the challenge to loyalist culture in southern and western Ulster invoked a social conservatism and a continued acceptance of deference, which were more marked than in areas with a more complete Unionist dominance.

How is the broad pattern of landed retreat to be explained? Landlordism was on the wane throughout Ireland, Britain and continental Europe, the victim of falling property values, heightened competition from north American and antipodean agriculture, and a halting political democratization. In Ireland the rise of the farming interest in the years after the Famine, and its political mobilization after the agricultural crisis of the later 1870s, meant that Irish landlordism was very soon on the defensive, both at home and even at Westminster: indeed it is arguable that this retreat began earlier, and was more protracted, the result in part of disengaged managerial policies as well as an inefficient rent structure. A succession of measures (the Acts of 1870, 1881) altered the law of tenure in ways favourable to the farmer lobby, but the most comprehensive blows to the landed position came – ironically – from the very policy which was designed as a rescue mechanism and which was embodied in a succession of Acts from 1885 through to 1909: land purchase. Land purchase levered the proprietors out of their estates, compensating them generally in the form of land stock: it accelerated a process of marginalization which had been developing since the Famine, and indeed – arguably – from even earlier. As W.E. Vaughan has remarked, 'land purchase made no provision for the recruitment of landed families: land purchase bonds did not tie families to a particular locality, and their sale did not bring new families in'.[127] Irish landlords were therefore the victims of a modest democratization of capital: they were in addition the victims of the land agitation, the First World War, the Anglo-Irish and the civil wars, and of the mildly unfriendly policies of the new Free State. This landed retreat provoked few tears among the northern Protestant democracy, and in a sense it helped to resolve simmering social tensions within the broader Irish Unionist movement. But the price of internal political ease was an external political catastrophe: for the landlords had brought not merely irritating condescension and narrow economic interests to Unionism, but also capital, political skills and contacts, and social influence. Their passage simultaneously altered the character of the movement as well as its resources: a proportionately more localized and bourgeois Unionism was in part the consequence of the landed retreat behind the walls of the demesne and from thence to the south of England or the colonies. But this localized, middle-class and democratic Unionism was also weaker than in the past, both culturally and materially.

These shifts within the social typology of the Unionist command have an importance beyond the obvious: they are linked to the issue of regional differentiation within the Unionism movement, as well as to the question of the relationship between Unionism and British politics. Unionism began as a movement that encompassed the entire island of Ireland, albeit in a highly uneven manner. In some ways southern Unionism educated its northern partners: perhaps the earliest example of effective Liberal–Tory cooperation on the issue of the Union occurred in Rathmines in March 1885, well in advance of similar developments within Ulster. Also, the first effective Unionist missionary organization was created in Dublin, in May 1885, in the shape of the Irish Loyal and Patriotic Union: Ulster Unionists, though very much alive to the challenge of Parnellism, were much slower in giving organizational shape to their apprehensions. Indeed, it is tempting to broaden this point and to question whether certainly Dublin Unionism might not in fact have been, for all its cussedness and occasional regression, intellectually more vibrant and more proactive than its Belfast counterpart.

The richness of Dublin Unionist culture is easy to overlook, given its defeat and reinvention within independent Ireland, but the interlayering of different social classes and networks, of churches and clubs, was (even allowing for the relatively small size of the community) impressive in its complexity. A thriving working-class and lower-middle-class loyalism in Dublin, of which only the merest vestiges remain, gave birth to a talent such as Seán O'Casey: indeed O'Casey, though clearly unique in terms of his literary gifts, might conceivably serve as an illustration of the forces of political and social accommodation as well as upward mobility that helped to dissipate the community from which he sprung. But there was also a Pooteresque world of clerks and shopkeepers who lived in the primly respectable townships south of the capital, and whose existence might easily be forgotten were it not for the evidence of church records and the admission books of Orange lodges. Harder to miss is Dublin's Unionist bourgeoisie, whose eastward longings are perpetuated in the street names of Blackrock, Dalkey and Dún Laoghaire: many commercial and professional figures spent their days in the city, only to retreat to Rathmines or Rathgar or (for the more prosperous) to a coastal villa in the evening (Edward Carson's father, for example, had lived in Rathgar while pursuing his work as an architect in the city centre). At the top of the pyramid were the haute bourgeoisie – figures such as Sir Maurice Dockrell of Monkstown (who represented Rathmines in the House of Commons between 1918 and 1922) and Andrew Jameson of Howth, a director of the Bank of Ireland and chairman of John Jameson Ltd. Also in this august sphere were déclassé squires such as Horace Plunkett of Foxrock (MP for South Dublin between 1892 and 1900) and Bryan Ricco Cooper of 'Khyber Pass' villa, Dalkey, and Markree, Sligo (who represented South Dublin both as a Unionist MP in 1910 and later as a deputy within Dáil Éireann).

In fact, even if one were to examine only the world of Dublin Toryism, a scarcely less complex picture might emerge: a world that united the self-regarding sophis-ticates of Trinity College with the rougher trade of the Dublin City and County Workingmen's Club; a world that combined the urbane if treacherous circle around Lord Justice Fitzgibbon at Howth with the Orange readership of Lindsay Crawford's paper, *The Irish Protestant*. Dublin Conservative organization had always been luxuriant, and a succession of initiatives from the Irish Protestant Conservative Society (1831) through the Metropolitan Conservative Society (1836) and the Central Conservative Society (1853) underlined the vitality of the party's strategists: indeed, as K.T. Hoppen has observed, 'the first great centre of organised working class Protestantism was Dublin, not Belfast'.[128] Trinity College supplied an intellectual force to these partisan impulses, with its long tradition of Conservative thought (repre-sented variously in the careers of such very different Tories as Gerald Fitzgibbon, Edward Gibson (Lord Ashbourne), William Johnston and William Moore, and also in the work and thought of a renegade Orangeman like Isaac Butt or a lifelong nation-alist like John Redmond). Trinity provided a home to two of the greatest conser-vative thinkers of the time, the historian W.E.H. Lecky (strictly speaking a Liberal Unionist) and the literary critic Edward Dowden: both men were also prominent advocates of the Union.

Outside Dublin and Ulster, the pattern of Unionist activity grew rather more faint. The focus of Unionism in many localities was inevitably the Big House, together with the networks of aristocrats and squireens who dominated rural Protestant society in the south and west. Some farming communities, in west Cork and in the northern midlands, contained Protestants and Unionists, but these tended to be both politically and socially vulnerable (both were targeted by the IRA during the Anglo-Irish war).[129] There were some signs of Unionist life elsewhere, but the evidence was often ambiguous: Galway City, for example, returned a Unionist MP to the Commons in 1900 in the shape of a popular Catholic gentleman, Michael Morris; but, when Morris inherited the family peerage in the following year, the pleasing aberration of a loyalist Galway was rectified. In other major towns there were small Unionist electorates, but these were rarely given a chance of declaring their faith: in no-hope divisions like Cork City or Limerick City the electoral battle was generally left to rival nationalists, even though there were sizeable Unionist minorities in both boroughs. Cork Unionists last fielded a candidate in 1891, when – despite the crisis within Parnellism, and despite the blessing of having a candidate named Patrick Sarsfield – the party amassed only 1,100 votes in a poll of just under 7,000.

In some ways the apparent strengths of southern Unionism – its cultural diversity, as well as its metropolitan vitality – acted instead as a cancer, which accelerated the demise of the movement and the surrender of initiative to the North. For diversity implied difference, and vitality brought with it the energy to pursue differences into sometimes disastrous divisions. One of the best examples of this comes with the Dublin elections of 1900, when two sitting Unionist MPs – Horace Plunkett in South County Dublin and J.H.M. Campbell in St Stephen's Green – were ousted, and very largely because of the actions of fellow Unionists: Unionist abstentionism helped to unseat Campbell, while the intervention of F.E. Ball, an independent Unionist candidate, in South Dublin brought to an end Plunkett's parliamentary ambitions. It is dangerously easy to oversimplify the issues that provoked this self-immolation, but ideological and personal tensions were certainly important: Plunkett, for example, was disliked because of his neglect of the constituency, because of his overly energetic reformism, because of his centrism and moderation, and – above all – because, though a great patriot, he was also an insufferable prig. Right to the end of its existence southern Unionism displayed this tension between an accommodationist strategy, represented in the 1890s by Plunkett and after 1917 by Lord Midleton, and the hardline irreconcilables, represented in the 1890s by the group around Lord Ardilaun, and after 1918–19 by John Walsh and the vestigial Irish Unionist Alliance (IUA). These divisions were self-wounding in 1900; but – as will become clear – by the final years of the Union they were nothing less than suicidal. It is sometimes argued that the marginalization of southern Unionism after 1920 occurred because of northern self-interest: but the internal state of the southern movement also provides clues and explanations.[130]

Was this marginalization avoidable? In the 1880s and 1890s Irish Unionism was to all intents and purposes a genuinely Irish phenomenon: southern Unionist organization was well funded and vibrant, if sometimes low-key, while Ulster Unionism was more haphazard in its mobilization and more expensive to maintain. Southern Unionist missionaries from the Irish Unionist Alliance maintained northern contacts in this period, supplying cash and other resources: for example, an influential young southern Unionist intellectual, C.L. Falkiner, stood as a parliamentary candidate in South Armagh in 1892, and performed creditably for his cause. Other southern Unionists were exported to the North in search of safe seats and opportunities for evangelism: Godfrey Fetherstonhaugh migrated from his home territory in Dublin and Mayo to serve the electors of North Fermanagh, while – as is well known – Edward Carson volunteered to lead Ulster Unionism in 1912–14, and eventually cemented this connection by moving from his Dublin University seat to the rather harsher environment of Duncairn, Belfast. Other prominent southern

Unionists, such as J.H.M. Campbell of Milltown, Dublin, were closely identified
with the northern struggle against the third Home Rule Bill. At an organizational
level, Ulster and southern Unionists for long cooperated within the ranks of the
Irish Unionist Parliamentary Party, the Joint Committee of the Unionist Associations
of Ireland (founded in 1908 as an all-Ireland proselytizing organization), and even
within what seemed like definitively northern bodies (such as the Orange Order or
the Ulster Unionist Council).

There were, however, at least three strong centrifugal forces pulling apart this
tentative all-Ireland Unionism. First, as has been argued, the rather fragile condition of southern Unionism in itself militated against a settled uniform movement.
In some ways it is an oversimplification to see Ulster Unionism and southern Unionism
in binary terms, given the highly complicated regional political relationships within
the movement: but it is nonetheless true that, while some branches of southern
Unionism maintained friendly links with Belfast, the increasingly fragmented condition of the movement meant that Ulster Unionists, like the British or indeed Sinn
Féin, tended to discount its credibility and importance. But there were other aspects
of this disintegration. The decline of Irish landlordism, which has already been chronicled, was also by implication the decline of southern Unionism, given the very strong
landed nature of the community outside of Dublin. The financial and physical retreat
of this class helped to exacerbate tensions between an embattled landed lobby and
an often more conciliatory urban Unionism; at a more fundamental level this retreat
ultimately robbed Unionism of both financial as well as intellectual capital.

But an equally complex problem for southern Unionists lay with the gradual
popularization and localization of the movement in the North. The heyday of parliamentary Unionism – roughly the 20 years between 1886 and 1905 – permitted
southerners to exercise a disproportionate influence over their northern counterparts, since southern Unionism possessed exaggerated parliamentary and financial
resources. But, with the defeat of the second Home Rule Bill in 1893, this parliamentary focus was being challenged within the North by various interest groups
who argued in unison that the rather disengaged Unionism of the 1880s and 1890s
was no longer adequate for the needs of the movement. This case was presented
by labour candidates and by populist sectarians in Belfast, by farmers under the
leadership of the wayward but brilliant T.W. Russell, and – briefly between 1898
and 1900 – by dissident Presbyterians in eastern Ulster. Each of these groupings
had a distinct sectional case, but they all were united by the conviction that the
Irish Unionist parliamentary leadership was failing to represent its broad constituency.
By far the most serious of these challengers was Russell, who cobbled together an
alliance of thrusting farmers, Presbyterian malcontents and some tactically minded
Catholics, and who, behind the call for compulsory land purchase, captured the
Unionist constituencies of East Down (February 1902) and North Fermanagh
(March 1903), and came within 850 votes of seizing South Antrim (traditionally
one of the safest Unionist seats in Ireland) in February 1903.

These challenges, and in particular Russellism, were occurring at a time when the
parliamentary influence of Unionism was apparently exhausted and when ambitious

Plate 13   Sir Edward Carson, *c.*1910.
Source: Public Record Office of Northern Ireland.

Tory ministers like Gerald Balfour and George Wyndham were pursuing their revisionist course, unworried by the burden of loyalist dissent: indeed, it seemed that
Wyndham was reinterpreting Unionism as a devolutionist creed, a philosophical
contortion that unnerved even his front-bench allies. This combination of local as
well as parliamentary humiliation forced the Ulster Unionist leadership into a series
of strategic initiatives, of which the most important was the creation of a popular
representative forum in Belfast, the Ulster Unionist Council (March 1905). The UUC
provided some (highly limited) representation to southern Unionists, but it was in

practice a coordinating mechanism for the North rather than for Ireland as a whole. Communication between Ulster Unionism and Dublin did not abruptly cease in the aftermath of the UUC: and indeed the leaders of the movement – Walter Long (1906–10) and Carson (1910–21) – for long remained bound to southern Unionism, at least through family and constituency ties. Moreover, cooperation continued at other levels of the loyalist hierarchy (in the Orange Order, for example, or the Joint Committee of the Unionist Associations of Ireland). But while it would be wrong to portray the creation of the UUC as effecting an immediate, dramatic change in the relationship between the two Unionisms, it would be equally misleading to ignore the importance of this development. For Ulster Unionism had taken a hesitant but still vital step towards the creation of a distinctive northern movement; and indeed it might well be contended further that the UUC represented not merely an eye-catching regional initiative, but also a prototype for the Unionist parliament that came into being in 1921, and which governed Northern Ireland for 51 years. At the very least the UUC, and the parallel constituency reforms of the mid- and late Edwardian period, helped to lay the groundwork for the mass mobilization of Ulster Unionism that occurred in 1912–14. Viewed in this light, the Council represented the institutionalization of a growing chasm within Irish Unionism.

If, given the vestiges of cooperation which remained in the later Edwardian period, there lingered any doubt about the regional unity of Unionism, this was further dispelled between 1911 and 1914 when the movement once again went to war against Home Rule. By the time of the third Home Rule Bill Unionism was to all intents and purposes an Ulster phenomenon: southerners still played a prominent role (Carson and J.H.M. Campbell are obvious examples of this), but only within the context of the northern movement. Thus, some of the most famous images of Unionist resistance to Home Rule portray southern leaders (such as at the signing of the Covenant at Belfast City Hall in September 1912), but they are invariably acting as advocates for, or adjuncts to, the northern cause. Southern Unionism resorted to the low-key agitation which had been apparently successful in the past (county meetings, invitations to English and Scots voters to see Irish 'realities', evangelism in Britain); there were also isolated examples of efforts to mimic the more militant tendency within Ulster Unionism. Kingstown and District Unionist Club attempted in a half-hearted manner to emulate the military discipline of their northern counterparts by organizing drilling practice; but these bourgeois rebels proved themselves to be more bourgeois than rebellious, continually fretting about the possible repercussions of their action and soon abandoning their thoughts of military glory in favour of a relatively cushioned ringside seat for the Irish revolution.

In fact the indecision of the Kingstown loyalists reflected the broader condition of southern Unionism. There is a discernible pattern in southern Unionist action, which to some extent is also perceptible within the more recent convolutions of Ulster Unionism. Southern Unionists were divided throughout most of the Home Rule era, but often it was the most rigidly conservative elements that were the most vocal, or the most conspicuous, elements of the broad partnership. This combination of stridency and division, coupled with the very severe external challenges that the movement continually confronted, meant that there was a predictable sequence to southern Unionist politics: tough-minded, even reactionary, protest was often followed by an astonishingly swift, and even gratuitous, collapse. Many southern Unionist leaders advocated a hardline resistance to the third Home Rule Bill, and many associated themselves with the Ulsterized Unionism of the time, believing that this held the key to a successful campaign, and that a revitalized Union, rather than partition, would be the prize. Nevertheless, as Carson and the Liberals edged towards a deal on the exclusion from Home Rule of the six northeastern counties, so the strain on the southern Unionists grew: already by the autumn of 1913 there was a degree of frustration and hostility between the southern leadership and Carson, who privately complained that the southerners had not been 'prepared to run any risks . . . it is very difficult to ascertain what the South and West want us to do as they only talk in generalities'.[131] The crystallization of the Ulster Unionist case into a demand for the permanent exclusion of the six counties was complete by the spring of 1914, and effectively reduced southern Unionists to the role of anxious bystanders.

The final years of the movement, which may now be conveniently dealt with, were also characterized by this overlayering of division, anger and a cancerous demoralization. Rocked by the looming threat of partition, and educated in a tradition of political entrenchment, southern Unionists oscillated between an affectionate embrace of Redmondism at the outbreak of the war, when the nationalist leader promised support for the British war effort, and the sabotaging of the Lloyd George negotiations of May–July 1916 – a Pyrrhic victory which helped to destroy Redmond, and which bought five more years of Union at the cost of effective political marginalization. Southern Unionists attempted to broker a deal with the Redmondites through the Irish Convention (July 1917–April 1918); but the result, while embodying a historic reconciliation, was marred by rank-and-file opposition within both traditions, and was in any case overshadowed by the conscription crisis and by Sinn Féin's growing strength. Subsequent divisions within southern Unionism, institutionalized by the split between the Irish Unionist Alliance, led after 1919 by John Walsh, and Lord Midleton's Anti-Partition League (APL), effectively immobilized the movement. Midleton had some minor influence over the details of the Government of Ireland Act (1920), and was a useful go-between for the government and Sinn Féin in the weeks preceding the truce of July 1921; again, he and his followers had some slight input into the shaping of the Irish Free State Constitution Act (1922).

But in truth southern Unionism was already dead by 1919, certainly in an institutional sense, broken by the strength of its opponents and by the constraints of its own traditions. The smallness and heterogeneity of the movement had made for cultural interest, even sophistication, but had been at the same time an immense political burden. The relative wealth of the community had offered some compensation, and had acted as a life-support machine both for relations with the North as well as the Union as a whole. But the retreat of landlordism, and the relative diminution of landed capital, had ultimately served to flick the switch on this support mechanism. The devastation visited on the community by the First World War,

and by the 'Tan' and civil wars, have been seen as crucial factors in the marginalization of southern Unionism: but there is also a counter-argument which,
while acknowledging the reality of this devastation, highlights broader contexts.
W.E. Vaughan was doubtless coat-trailing in claiming that 'the loss of [gentry] sons
during the First World War was the mere speeding up of what usually happened
on the hunting-field', but his core conviction that 'the gentry's depletion after 1914
was to some extent a continuation of what had always happened to landed families' has to be taken seriously.[132] In more narrowly political and strategic terms,
it is difficult to resist the suspicion that a divided leadership, staffed by arrogant
liberals and blinkered reactionaries, did little to negotiate terms for its people;
certainly internal differences invariably defied resolution, producing schism and
weakness. Lord Midleton, by no means incapable or immoderate, refused to disarm opposition within the IUA to his strategies, and preferred to leave the Alliance
in 1919 in order to form the APL, a body which he also eventually left, in 1922 over
a disagreement concerning the Free State senate. A prevailing tendency within the
movement to use its waning strength to garrison untenable positions brought
inevitable failure and demoralization. Southern Unionism failed as dramatically as
it did partly because its political culture did not develop in step with its social retreat.

The overwhelmingly northern nature of Unionism in 1911–14 had undoubtedly
speeded the southerners along this path towards isolation and defensiveness, division and defeat. The gradual democratization of Irish politics, the relative decline
of the landed interest and the concomitant strengthening of the business and professional classes, all facilitated the rise of Ulster Unionism within the broader Irish
alliance. As has been chronicled, the mounting challenges supplied by local politics in the North, as well as the mounting frustrations of parliamentary life, each
encouraged the belated but sweeping elaboration of Ulster Unionist organization.
A luxuriant northern popular political culture both reflected and encouraged the
mass mobilization of the Ulster Protestant community behind the cause of Union.
In addition, by 1910 – probably for the very first time – a systematic policy of
militancy was being planned in conjunction with more conventional constitutional
strategies by the Unionist leadership.

Before the issue of militancy is considered, one particularly striking aspect of this
mass mobilization in the North demands attention – namely, the growing involvement of northern women within the institutions of Unionism. The role of women
within the propagation of Unionism has often either been overlooked, or – where
it has received attention – judged merely within a formal and institutional context.
The importance of women in promoting loyalist and Unionist conviction within
the home, the role of voluntary and recreational organizations in consolidating wom-
en's Unionism, have still received insufficient scholarly notice. Some early women
Unionists, primarily Isabella Tod, who founded the North of Ireland Women's Suffrage
Committee in 1872 and who organized a women's protest against the first Home
Rule Bill, have fared rather better (Tod has been the subject of at least two biographical essays): successive marchionesses of Londonderry have also received their
due.[133] Some Unionist men who were sympathetic to women's political concerns

have also been studied (though – as with William Johnston of Ballykilbeg – rarely from the standpoint of their feminism). All this is to say that women's Unionism before 1912 was significant, even if in scholarly terms it remains submerged beneath apparently more considerable issues. The third Home Rule crisis, however, coinciding as it did with the crescendo of suffragist activity throughout the United Kingdom, brought an empowerment of Unionist women: women created for themselves, or were given, wider opportunities than before for involvement in Unionist politics, while the formerly dismissive Unionist high command was forced to reconsider its patriarchal attitudes. The most significant expressions of this new women's Unionism came with the Ulster Women's Unionist Council (UWUC), created in 1911, and the women's Covenant, signed (as with the men's Covenant) *en masse* in September 1912. There were, however, other significant developments: a Unionist Women's Franchise Association flourished at this time, claiming just under 800 members in 1913; and Carson (himself an anti-suffragist) declared that women would be enfranchised by the Ulster Provisional Government (the executive that was to be established by the Unionists in the event of Home Rule).[134] Deprived of a formal role within high politics, some women (notably Theresa Lady Londonderry) contrived to carve out an individual role and influence in defiance of conventional restraints. It would, of course, be wrong to pursue this argument for empowerment and politicization beyond the available evidence. There were obvious boundaries within which these Unionist women operated: the UWUC (like Cumann na mBan in its first weeks) tended to work to a male agenda and to be governed by women who sometimes owed their position to the eminence of their husbands. Equally, the role of women within the Ulster Volunteer Force – as nurses, secretaries, despatchers – was sometimes seen as subsidiary to that of the men. Some nationalist women, certainly, were suspicious of Carson's promises of enfranchisement: Hanna Sheehy Skeffington said that 'I profoundly distrust Sir E. Carson throughout, in spite of his apparent concession to Ulsterwomen'.[135] Sheehy Skeffington was also unimpressed by the role of women within the UVF. But, while such critics had undoubtedly a case to argue, and while the restraints upon women's Unionism are unmistakeable, it is easy to lose sight of the genuine liberation that had occurred within the North in 1912–14. As with nationalist politics and the Irish Free State, this first wave of feminism made little impression upon the patriarchal Northern Irish state: as in the south, where nationalist women were often nationalists first and feminists second, northern women were often more concerned about the Union than about gender. But, equally, it would be wrong to interpret the women's Unionism of 1912 with an exclusively paternalist hindsight.

Ulster Unionist militancy in 1912–14, to which women contributed so extensively, was rooted in a variety of shifting political relationships. First, the militancy was in part an expression of the looser bond with the south, since southern Unionists – for all their bluster – tended, as a vulnerable minority and as property owners (for the most part), to shy away from threat or violence: the heroes of Kingstown Unionist Club were the exception that illustrates the broader rule. Second, Ulster Unionist militancy was an expression of a deeply flawed relationship with British

Conservatism, a relationship that had come close to divorce under the Chief Secretaryship of George Wyndham (1900–5) and which had scarcely undergone any significant improvement since Wyndham's resignation in March 1905. Lastly, this militancy reflected increased fear of both Home Rule as well as Rome Rule, partly because of worsening sectarian relations in the later Edwardian era and partly because, with the threatened emasculation of the House of Lords, the nationalist millennium looked to be at hand.

The first evidence of Ulster Unionist militancy is discernible in November 1910, when the UUC established a secret defence committee with a view to approaching foreign arms dealers. By mid-December 1910 sample weapons were already before the committee, while in March 1911 substantial sums of money were voted for the purpose of large-scale acquisitions: by the early summer of 1911 at least 2,000 weapons had already been bought and imported for the Ulster Unionists. This arming was accompanied by a training effort: already in December 1910 the first attempts to teach Orange activists 'simple movements' were being made, and in April 1911 a body of Tyrone Orangemen created a widespread impression of martial efficiency during a Unionist mass meeting held at Craigavon, the home of James Craig. The preoccupation with arms was made public in September 1911, at another Craigavon demonstration: the menu cards for Craig's lunch party on this occasion bore crossed rifles and the motto, 'the arming of Ulster'.[136]

These early efforts towards an armed response were much less conspicuous than later initiatives such as the creation of the Ulster Volunteer Force (formally launched in January 1913), or the Larne gun-running (of 24–5 April 1914). But they were an essential starting point for this subsequent activity. In addition they illustrate the extent to which Ulster Unionist militancy was not simply a gradualist response to the mounting challenge of the Parliament Act and the third Home Rule Bill, but predated both these measures and reflected instead a series of more complicated political relationships and attitudes.

Nevertheless, the most famous aspects of Ulster Unionist militancy were unquestionably the formalization of the popular paramilitary craze that swept Unionist Ulster in 1911–12 into the Ulster Volunteer Force. This body was organized along the lines of the British army, with local platoons and battalions, and a county regimental structure: its structure reflected not only the experiences of many of its Irish officers and men in the service of the crown, but also the influence of the numerous English officers who were recruited to the Ulster Unionist cause, including the commander, General Sir George Richardson, and Captain Wilfrid Spender. The UVF expanded very rapidly and by late 1913 was claiming a membership of 100,000: the true total may have fallen somewhat short of this boast, but probably not by much. The purpose of the UVF was in reality more complex than appearances might have suggested: it has been sometimes (and persuasively) argued that the creation of the Force reflected the desire of Unionist political leaders to exercise greater control over the militants within their movement.[137]

It is also sometimes suggested that the UVF first imported the gun into Irish politics.[138] The validity of this argument, like many political debating points, depends upon perspective. It is unquestionably true that the UVF was a substantial influence over militant separatism, and that it also stimulated the creation of a rival nationalist body, the Irish Volunteers (November 1913). It is also true that, whatever the doubts about the legality of the UVF drilling activity, the importation of weapons that occurred after the official ban of December 1913 was unambiguously illegal. But the militant tradition in Irish politics did not begin with the UVF, and the relationship between this Force and militant separatism was not one-way. The UVF was in some ways a lineal descendant of Fenianism: like the Fenians in the 1860s, the UVF was part of a broader craze for volunteering and militarism; like the Fenians the UVF was passionately interested in morale-boosting displays of martial vigour. As with Fenianism, membership of the UVF may be regarded as a recreational passion as much as a coherent endorsement of civil war. Both the Fenians and the UVF were arguably much less important as military phenomena than in terms of popular culture and mass politicization; both bodies made earnest efforts to acquire arms, and both staggered towards rebellion – in the case of the Fenian movement rather further and more bloodily than the UVF.

The complexity of the Unionist leadership's attitudes towards the UVF and the broader issue of militancy is underlined by an examination of the issue of arms. The forces impelling the Unionists towards a civil conflict should not be underestimated: a disproportionately large number of the Unionist leaders had been inured to violence in the South African war, while parliamentary politics, even under the late Conservative government, had held out ever-weakening attractions. There were thus many hawks in the loyalist aviary, but this is very far from saying that there was a consistent or homogeneous policy of militancy. On the contrary, while there were relatively uncomplicated belligerents like Fred Crawford represented in the high command of the movement, there were also those like Lord Londonderry, or even Carson, who associated themselves with militant defiance while privately expressing qualms or seeking to apply moderation. It is probably accurate to see popular Unionist militancy as a kind of Frankenstein's monster, called into life by Carson and Craig, but threatening to defy the authority of its creators. Certainly Carson blessed Unionist militancy through his speeches and through his presence at various martial displays; but in private he advised against pushing the make-believe aggression of the UVF into the realm of reality. On at least two occasions – in December 1912 and in May 1913 – Carson argued against the general arming of the Volunteers; and it was only comparatively late in the crisis, on 20–1 January 1914, that he finally succumbed to the pressure of the hawks, and indeed to the logic of his own strategies, by accepting the need for a major gun-running coup. This was the hesitant beginning of the Buchanesque adventure that culminated in the landing of some 25,000 rifles and 3 million rounds of ammunition at Larne and other Ulster seaside towns on the night of 24–5 April 1914.[139]

The Larne gun-running was one of the defining episodes in the Unionist epic – a moment when audacity and good fortune bolstered the honour of the movement and its prospects of success. In truth, however, the issues surrounding the affair were more complicated than this, and the fall-out was no less problematic. Judged from the military perspective, the gun-running only partly solved the problem of arming the UVF, since the force was perhaps 90,000 strong and the Larne episode brought the loyalist arsenal to a strength of around 40,000 rifles: that is to say, there was not even one rifle available for every two Volunteers. There were three different types of weapon in the Larne cache alone, to say nothing of the multiplicity of arms already in loyalist hands: this, in the authoritative verdict of Charles Townshend, would have created a 'logistical nightmare' for the Unionist hawks.[140] In addition, the amount of ammunition available was scarcely sufficient to train the UVF, let alone conduct the 'stand-up fight' which its strategists dreamed of conducting. The Volunteers had the arms and the local knowledge necessary for a successful guerrilla conflict, but this was precisely the form of warfare which (partly because of its association with the Boers) was most distasteful to the loyalist high command.

Larne not only failed to solve the military problems of the UVF (indeed, to judge it in narrowly military terms would probably be a mistake): in some ways it also rendered a political solution to the Ulster crisis more difficult to attain. For most of the period between 1912 and 1914 loyalist militancy had been closely regulated by the political leadership of the movement, and it had been interwoven with its constitutional strategies. Indeed, though paramilitarism was the most conspicuous aspect of Unionist endeavour in these years, and the aspect which was most celebrated by the Unionists themselves, it is arguable that for some of the key leaders – notably Carson – militancy was subservient to the process of negotiation. More prosaic, but possibly more significant than coups such as Larne, was the steady process of debate within Westminster, and between leading Unionists and Liberal ministers. The Irish Unionist Parliamentary Party had unquestionably been relegated as a result of local initiatives such as the Ulster Unionist Council or the Ulster Provisional Government (planned between 1911 and 1913 and constituted in September 1913): but the party fought the Home Rule Bill with tenacity through each parliamentary circuit, and it remained the chief point of contact between Unionism and the ideologues of Home Rule. Carson negotiated in private with Asquith in December 1913 and January 1914: indeed it is arguable that the rumours of this diplomacy, combined with its ultimate failure, nudged Carson towards his decision to sanction the gun-running.

The Liberal government subsequently moved a little further than Asquith had been prepared to do in January 1914: in March Lloyd George pursued the possibility that those Ulster counties with Unionist majorities might vote themselves out of the Home Rule polity for a six-year respite. But Carson, famously, did not want 'a sentence of death with a stay of execution for six years'; and in any case the Curragh Incident intervened to redirect loyalist energies away from parliamentary negotiation and back to military preparations.[141] The decision of 58 cavalry officers at the Curragh camp, Kildare, to refuse to participate in any offensive (as opposed to policing) action against the Ulster Unionists was interpreted by nationalists as broader evidence of the British army's partisanship; it was seen by Unionists, on the other hand, as the culmination of a plot to suppress the movement against Home Rule.

It is unlikely whether, given Carson's attitude, anything further could have come of the Lloyd George initiative, but the Curragh affair, which apparently exposed the bad faith of Liberal ministers, ensured the final dissipation of Unionist patience: only a significant gesture of appeasement from Asquith could have diverted popular Unionism from the descent into violence. A final effort to hammer home an agreement – the Buckingham Palace Conference of 21–4 July 1914 – brought simply a restatement of positions, with the Ulster Unionists reiterating without enthusiasm their demand for the permanent exclusion of the six northeastern counties and the nationalists and Liberals reluctantly offering a combination of county plebiscites and temporary exclusion.

The Larne gun-running had made it more difficult for the Unionist leadership to accept anything less than a six-county and permanent partition scheme – even assuming that they would otherwise have been willing to retreat. If, as is arguable, the Ulster Unionist command had sought to condition the parliamentary process with the implied threat of force, then this strategy was, by July 1914, demonstrably a failure: the Home Rule Bill was still being nudged towards the statute books, while the concessions offered by the Liberal government were deemed to be too feeble to be worth the effort of debate. Indeed, the constitutional dimension to Ulster Unionist endeavour had already been discredited by the years of (from the perspective of popular loyalism) fruitless diplomacy culminating in the failure of the Asquith talks and the further revelations of ministerial perfidy elicited during the aftermath of the Curragh Incident. Thus, if Carson had raised loyalist militancy with a view to strengthening his advocacy, then by the spring of 1914 it was he who was the servant of the militants: in April 1914 he privately admitted to Horace Plunkett his inability to control his own forces; in May 1914 his tentative interest in federalist solutions to the challenge of Irish government was briskly rejected by the Ulster Unionist press. Militancy had been created as a means to an end, but it was now threatening to become (in every sense) the end of Unionism itself.

Nevertheless, these years of resistance to Home Rule have been judged within the Unionist tradition to be a period of unsullied success: indeed, it is possible to go further and argue that the character of Ulster Unionist political behaviour at this time has left an indelible and damaging impression, not just on the historical sensitivities of contemporary Unionists, but also on their strategic thinking. At one level, it is not hard to understand this reverence for the men and women of the 1912–16 era: the story has acquired the trappings of a Norse saga, with heroes who faced down monstrous, superior forces, and who ultimately sacrificed themselves in the cause of honour on the battlefields of France and Flanders. Equally, it is hard to escape the contribution of these men and women to the formulation of a long-term strategy for Ulster Unionism – a strategy that was maintained through the negotiations of 1916, the Irish Convention of 1917–18, and during the evolution of the Government of Ireland Bill in 1919–20. These northerners have assumed a mythic stature for contemporary Unionists, as the selfless patriots who created Northern Ireland.

And yet – though it might seem superfluous to say so – the problems in their achievement should not be overlooked. This is not just a matter of pointing to the contested nature of the Northern Ireland state, and ascribing blame. Judged even within the terms of the broader Irish Unionist tradition, the northern Unionists of 1912–14 took decisions that not only had a lasting influence within their community, but also wrought lasting damage. The decision to fight Home Rule on the basis of exclusion seems originally to have been taken as a means of separating Liberal pragmatists from nationalist fundamentalists, and thereby wrecking the bill: but it seems clear that the self-interest of the Belfast commercial elite propelled the choice from a merely strategic gambit into a more proactive campaign goal. Perhaps this was a necessary compromise between Unionism and broader democratic principles; perhaps it was merely an acceleration of deeply rooted trends within Irish society and politics. But it also necessarily involved the reduction of a diverse and complex community down to its northeastern core, and the amputation of some of the most culturally sophisticated and politically interesting members of the wider Irish Unionist family.

Exclusion may have seemed like practical politics, but it inflicted wounds on northern nationalists, and also less obviously and perhaps more insidiously on Irish Unionism itself. A combination of exclusion and militancy, though still celebrated within contemporary Ulster Unionism, in fact separated northerners from their southern allies and educated the movement into a highly dangerous form of brinkmanship to which it still occasionally clings. In reality the militant strategy was highly flawed and brought with it the probability of defeat – glorious, perhaps, but certainly bloody and comprehensive. Moreover, the tactic of brinkmanship, while it was arguably forced onto the Ulster Unionists by the Liberal government, involved the gradual eradication of constitutional diplomacy and a resort to armed threat: this in turn led Ulster Unionism to the edge of the abyss. In July 1914 Unionist strategic thinking combined with Liberal prevarication meant that loyalism was faced with the choice of a humiliating climb-down, or political and military destruction at the hands of the Liberal government and the British army. After 1969 Unionist strategies, influenced by the apparent successes of the Home Rule era, produced the same political choices: defeat or annihilation.

The definition of the Ulster Unionist case that was being offered at the Buckingham Palace Conference in July 1914 remained largely fixed until the establishment of the Northern Ireland state in 1920–1. However, although Carson and Craig had been bargaining for a six-county exclusion agreement from late 1913, the mandate to conclude a deal on these terms was given by the UUC only in June 1916. The occasion for this decision was the Lloyd George initiative of May–July 1916, designed to address the crisis in Irish government created by the insurgents of the Easter Rising: Lloyd George's preferred strategy was an immediate enactment of Home Rule, with the exclusion of the six northeastern counties on what looked like a permanent basis to the Ulster Unionists, but at the same time looked like a merely temporary arrangement to nationalists. The debate on this initiative was effectively the first time that the UUC in Belfast had a chance to address the implications of the strategy which its leaders had been pursuing for almost three years. The results were, predictably, far from harmonious, with much distress in evidence concerning the impending desertion of the Unionists of Cavan, Donegal and Monaghan, and indeed the broader southern Unionist community. Delegates saw partition as a betrayal of pledges laid down in the Ulster Covenant of September 1912: some saw a grant of Home Rule as being, in the circumstances, a sop to traitors. The full flow of Carson's advocacy was required to turn opinion towards a more pragmatic stance; and even then there remained an irreducible core of last-ditchers – such as Somerset Saunderson of Cavan – who suspected that treachery and poltroonery were rife in the northern leadership. Indeed, had these ditchers possessed greater political weight, they might well have profited from the eventual collapse of the Lloyd George scheme (at the hands of southern Unionist sympathizers within the cabinet): there were certainly hints that Saunderson was exploiting the affair in a bid to recover his father's position as leader.[142] As it was, Carson was wounded, but not overthrown.

The Lloyd George negotiations supplied the first indisputable evidence that the historic Unionist alliance was fragmenting, and that the price of Belfast leadership during the third Home Rule crisis was the salvation of eastern Ulster alone. The chasm between Ulster Unionism and southern Unionism was already evident in 1913–14, if not before; but because the Home Rule crisis was not brought to any definable resolution in 1914 the implications of these divisions were never fully worked out, and the forms of unity – if not the substance – remained in place. To the extent that the Lloyd George initiative also ended inconclusively, then a superficial unity between Ulster and southern Unionism continued to be possible, and was still claimed; but in reality the attitude of Carson, combined with the unanimous (if doubt-ridden) vote of the UUC, meant that exclusion was no longer a matter of gamesmanship but was a democratically endorsed tenet of the Ulster movement. The actions of southern Unionists within the cabinet in scuppering the initiative underlined the divergence between the two Unionisms, and this was confirmed (if confirmation were needed) by the proceedings of the Irish Convention in the following year.

The Convention, which has been explored elsewhere in the volume, was designed to divert the energies of the Irish parties and to clothe Lloyd George's constitutional nakedness before the USA, and in particular before Irish America. In the context of Unionism, it helped to supply an institutional and ideological cementing of regional divisions within the movement: the Convention, which met from July 1917 until April 1918, had 90 delegates and included representatives, not from Irish Unionism as a whole, but rather from both the northern and southern movements. Indeed, the very distinctive styles of the two delegations exemplified at a micropolitical level broader divisions within the Irish Unionist movement: the southern Unionists acted, in the famous verdict of R.B. McDowell, with 'the self-confidence bred by generations of governing', combining a free-booting lack of responsibility to the broader movement with the sober paternalism of the self-righteous but well-intentioned Viscount Midleton.[143] The Ulster Unionists, by way of contrast, were led by a sober Scots businessman, H.T. Barrie, and were much less flamboyant, both personally as well as intellectually: they were well regimented and reported back to an advisory committee of the UUC. The northerners were working within a limited brief

– opposition to Home Rule and, if appropriate, exclusion of the six counties: but even had this not been the case, they lacked the freedom of manoeuvre of the southern Unionists, who weaved and dodged unhindered by the watchful eye of any external authority. Nor were these distinctions purely organizational or cultural: a combination of the freedom enjoyed by the southerners with the arrogance of Midleton allowed them to move towards striking a deal with the representatives of the Irish Parliamentary Party at the Convention. While the Ulster Unionists looked on aghast, the southern Unionists accepted a moderate Home Rule proposal as being the mildest of the unpalatable choices available to them. This helped not only to formalize the ideological split within Irish Unionism, but also to divide and over-turn southern Unionism itself – for the Midletonites, with characteristic courage and tactlessness, had moved out ahead of mainstream opinion within the body of the Irish Unionist Alliance. The Convention, which seemed at one point to be so close to squaring the circle of Irish politics, instead helped to divert and destroy the Irish Party and to divide and truncate Irish Unionism: its proceedings, no less than its failure, helped to elevate extremism at the expense of the centre-ground in Irish political life.

If the Convention formalized the divide between southern and Ulster Unionism, then the Government of Ireland Bill helped to formalize a divide within Ulster Unionism itself. With the failure of the Convention in April 1918, and the end of the war in November, the government returned to the issue of Irish self-government, forming a cabinet committee in October 1919 under the chairmanship of the southern Unionist sympathizer Walter Long. Long, who had helped to scupper the Lloyd George détente of 1916, had been battered by the war and in particular by the loss of his son, a youthful and highly decorated Brigadier General, who was killed in action in 1917: like many other Tories, the bitter experience of military conflict had helped to soften the rigidities of Long's politics, and this former apostle of an all-Ireland Unionism was by 1919–20 prepared to countenance a nine-county partition scheme. The debates within Long's committee between the advocates of six-county partition and the advocates of a nine-county proposal were eventually resolved in favour of the former: they prefigured similar, if more emotive, discussions within the ranks of the UUC. The fruits of Long's deliberations were published in February 1920 as the Government of Ireland Bill, an ingenious combination of Home Rule as well as Unionist principles, which proposed a six-county Northern Ireland, complete with a Home Rule executive and parliament, and a 26-county Southern Ireland, endowed with similar constitutional trappings.

If the Lloyd George debacle of 1916 had foreshadowed the split between Ulster and southern Unionism that occurred in 1917–18, then the same fraught process of negotiation looked forward to the fracturing of Ulster Unionism that occurred between March and May 1920. Both aspects of the disintegration of Irish Unionism involved considerable internal acrimony. The Government of Ireland Bill was debated by the Ulster Unionist Council on 10 March 1920, and again on 27 May, with a majority favouring acceptance of the measure: but there was a consider-able dissenting minority (comprising 80 delegates out of 390 in May), whom the

Belfast-based leadership of the movement made minimal efforts to appease. These Unionists of Cavan, Donegal and Monaghan had been willing to acquiesce in the six-county scheme touted in 1916; but a combination of the mounting tension and defensiveness created by the Anglo-Irish war as well as somewhat brusque handling by the Unionists of eastern Ulster meant that the debates that occurred in the spring of 1920 were considerably more bitter. The Unionists of southern and western Ulster were consigned to the purported darkness of Rome Rule in May 1920 with as little compunction as was applied to the southern Unionists in 1913–14, when six-county exclusion was first seriously advocated in the North.

The enactment of the Government of Ireland Bill in December 1920 looked forward to the creation of the Northern Ireland parliament in May–June 1921, and it represented the final triumph of an exclusivist Unionism over the more generous and diverse alternatives which had been current since the mid-1880s, but which had been killed off as straggling liabilities during the great retreat of the movement after 1912. A once widely (if often thinly) spread movement had effectively withdrawn to the north-east of the island; a socially and culturally diversified movement had been simplified, stripped of the advocacy of Trinity intellectuals and the more tangible support of southern land and Dublin commerce. Perhaps the advocates of an all-Ireland Unionism were fighting history, seeking to dilute a relentlessly self-confident nationalism, and to sustain a gentry class that had been inching a retreat since the eighteenth century. Or perhaps these advocates were seeking to reverse the fundamental development of Ulster Unionism towards particularism and prominence.

The problem with Ulster Unionism may have been, as its most acerbic nationalist critics allege, that its supremacist impulse meant that it could not function outside of a Unionist state: but in truth the competitive supremacism of Unionists and nationalists make this allegation hard to substantiate.[144] Maybe, modifying this point, the fate of an all-Ireland Unionism was sealed by the notorious unwillingness of Ulster Unionists to accept compromise. But in reality the most striking feature of Ulster Unionism in the years after 1912 was not its rigidity, but rather the nature of its flexibility: the leaders of the movement, based in Belfast and eastern Ulster, wanted no part of a self-governing Ireland and they were willing to sacrifice territory, partners and principles in order to protect their own loyalist Arcadia. The death of Irish Unionism came about not because of the Ulster Unionists' inflexibility, but rather because they were too willing to flex in certain directions.

Or perhaps an all-Ireland Unionism died because Ulster Unionists were too faithful to the leadership of their messianic Carson. Carson's career and leadership combined bumptiousness with diffidence, and an icy sobriety with a violent flirtatiousness. Like later Ulster Unionist leaders, Carson led his army to the precipice, only to find good reason to retreat; like later leaders, Carson was intolerant of compromise – except when the compromise was (as was often the case) his own construction. He was appalled by Midleton's efforts to save the skin of southern Unionism; but he unblushingly advocated a strategy that was designed to rescue the north-east for the Union. In truth, the difference between Carson's political tastes and those of

Midleton was the difference between a short, sharp charge of Unionism, and a larger, if more diluted, draught of loyalty.

Like the Ulster Unionist culture that he embraced, Carson was contemptuous of trimming and indecision, and he increasingly detected both among the southern Unionist community from which he was sprung, but which he increasingly spurned. Like Ulster Unionism, Carson masked an underlying insecurity with a braggadocio. Carson, the apparently unflappable braggart of the courts, was in reality uncertain of his abilities and of his health, and nervous about high office. Ulster Unionists, by extension, apparently one of the most unyielding strains of Irish political culture, were pledged to die in the last ditch of the Union: but in the end they shied away from the opportunity to protect their friends in an all-Ireland context, and turned down the chance to play a significant, perhaps even a commanding, role within an all-Ireland polity. Rejecting the chance to walk into the new Ireland of the nationalist visionaries, northern Unionists accepted the amputation of southern loyalism and limped instead into the diminished safety of their Ulster. Little wonder, then, that Carson was accepted so readily in the North – for he was in truth the personification of the strengths and weaknesses of the movement that he came to command.

5.5   Other Men's Wounds: The Troubles, 1919–21

Impatient for the coming fight
And as we watch the dawning light
Here in the silence of the night
We'll chant the soldier's song.[145]

Few Irish political movements – no matter how persuasive their assertions to the contrary – preserved a clear distinction between parliamentary and militant activity. This was most obviously true of the Ulster Unionists, whose campaign against the third Home Rule deliberately combined constitutional and paramilitary strategies – but even the Redmondites had repeatedly endorsed political violence, exploiting the cult of the Fenians of 1867 and attempting to muscle in on the celebrity of the Fenians of 1916: the parliamentary and paramilitary frontier had in any case already been thoroughly blurred through Redmond's annexation of the Irish Volunteer movement. Many ostensibly constitutional nationalists (and Unionists) were opposed not to the principle of violence, but rather to its practicality: many ostensibly constitutional nationalists, and Unionists, were, given the comparatively small scale of Irish politics and society, inextricably linked, however distantly, to political militancy. A fundamental ambivalence towards violence was therefore a much more thoroughly established characteristic of Irish politics than the superficial niceties might otherwise suggest.

In this limited sense Sinn Féin was little different to those nationalist umbrella organizations that had preceded it. The party was not formally in favour of violent revolution, and in 1918 it did not seek any popular mandate for a military overthrow of British rule. Indeed, the party's origins were neither revolutionary nor even republican, but rather cultural and quirkily monarchist. The chief influence over the early evolution of Sinn Féin was Arthur Griffith, who (as mentioned in an earlier section) was a thorough-going by-product of the Gaelic revival. Griffith was an enthusiastic cultural and economic nationalist, a founder of the Celtic Literary Society (1893) and also of the generously defined, if somewhat directionless, Cumann na nGaedheal (1900). He was perhaps the most thoughtful and wide-ranging prophet of separatism, borrowing from European constitutional and economic models to weave a nationalist philosophy which in 1905 was dubbed (by a cousin of Carson, ironically) the 'Sinn Féin' policy. Sinn Féin, as defined by Griffith, implied parliamentary abstentionism and autarky, both of which he linked to a constitutional settlement on the Austro-Hungarian model (that is, a dual monarchy for Britain and Ireland that would arch over separate governments and parliaments). This patiently elaborated separatist creed found an organizational clothing, first through the Sinn Féin League, created from several existing nationalist bodies in 1907, and later, with a further amalgamation, through a new party, dubbed 'Sinn Féin', *tout court*.

There was no sudden electoral endorsement, however. Before 1916 Sinn Féin was too weak to pose any serious threat to the Home Rule Party, even when (as in 1908–10) the parliamentarians looked to be stumbling: for most of this time it did not even try to compete electorally with the Irish Party. Sinn Féin's victory lay not initially at the polls, but rather in establishing a high level of brand recognition as the market leader in separatist politics: in fact Sinn Féin and advanced separatism became inextricably linked in the popular imagination, to the extent that the Easter Rising was speedily identified as the work of Sinn Féin, even though there was no formal connection between the rebels and the party. With the popular beatification of the rebels, Sinn Féin found itself on an electoral roll. The party was the preferred destination of the veterans of 1916 (indeed, they had little alternative in terms of available electoral resources); and the release of prisoners at the end of 1916 inaugurated a period of intense reorganization which culminated at the ard-fheis of October 1917. There the bond between the insurgents and Sinn Féin was solemnized with the election of the surviving commandant of the Rising, Eamon de Valera, as President of the party. This marriage contract involved not merely the curtailment of Griffith's authority within his own movement, but also the relegation of his constitutional views: Sinn Féin was now committed to the achievement of a republic, although the party was also now bound to a popular referendum on the future of Irish government once independence from Britain had been won. The party was also now committed to the enfranchisement of women over the age of 21, even though Griffith's track record as a feminist had been weak, to say the least. Within a month of the ard-fheis there was a further highly charged development: the Irish Volunteers undertook a reorganization, which involved the creation of a Dublin GHQ as well as the nomination of de Valera as the President of the movement. Griffith's non-violent political party had lost its innocence: it had been radicalized, popularized and – now, in November 1917 – bound with militant separatism.

Yet the formality of these initiatives could not occlude the chaotic sub-structure of Irish politics. Despite new alliances and refinements, politics remained overwhelmingly local in orientation, riven by family loyalties and personalities. A new facade, Sinn Féin, might be applied to an ancient core, but the fundamentals remained largely unchanged: if Home Rule, as George Boyce has quipped, was the Irish for independence, then Sinn Féin's republic was simply another definition of the same goal.[146] Moreover, the attitude of the old, pre-1914 Home Rule Party to violence was not far removed from that of the Sinn Féiners: the attainment of legitimate political goals by physical force might not be desirable or practicable, but equally violence was not out of the question. Even with the apparent radicalization of Irish electoral politics in 1918, some of the old ambiguities remained. Although there was an apparent affinity between Sinn Féin and the Irish Republican Army (as the Volunteers took to calling themselves in 1919), the party was often embarrassed by the war against British rule: for example, the opening shots of the conflict – the killing of two RIC men at Soloheadbeg, Tipperary, in January 1919 – alarmed many Sinn Féiners. Towards the end of the war, in May 1921, the assassination of 'two Dublin Anglo-Irishmen' provoked condemnation from the Sinn Féin leadership.[147] Peter Hart has emphasized the (at best) equivocal statistical relationship between Sinn Féin membership and IRA activity, arguing that 'political mobilisation was thus neither a sufficient nor a necessary condition for sustained IRA operations'.[148] Indeed, it was only in April 1921 that Sinn Féin, through Dáil Éireann, accepted full responsibility for the IRA campaign.

It would therefore be a mistake to see the Irish campaign as a broadly based, united effort, even though many separatists, viewing the 'troubles' of 1919–21 from the perspective of the civil war of 1922–3, adopted precisely this sentimental view. Sinn Féin was a loose coalition, as even a cursory examination of its organizational or constitutional development underlines; and the assembly which it formed in January 1919 – Dáil Éireann – was in some ways a distraction from the efforts of the militant separatists of the IRA. The Soloheadbeg ambush was not simply unpopular with many Sinn Féiners, it also was an expression of militant republican frustration with the party's political initiatives. The IRA campaign, once begun, certainly helped to create a superficial unity of purpose amongst the separatists (just as the Sinn Féin constitution of 1917 had created the semblance of a shared political agenda). Attacks on the crown forces might be unpopular to begin with, but whatever response the Castle offered was likely to be much more unpopular: official repression invariably created massive popular resentment, while more relaxed or conciliatory gestures were frequently either exploited or taken as evidence of weakness (as the British commander-in-chief, Sir Neville Macready, lamented, 'whatever we do, we are sure to be wrong').[149] But the price for this tentative separatist coalition would only become clear once the focus for unity – the Castle administration – was removed. Indeed, it is arguable that the full cost of the revolutionary nationalist campaign in 1919–21 was obscured by the civil war, and is only now being slowly and painfully calculated.

The IRA campaign was necessarily limited in both scope and ambition: there were two main geographical focuses – in Dublin and south and central Munster – while a third and more minor offensive was conducted in south Ulster in 1920–1 (Tom Garvin has calculated that, allowing for population, Cavan was the most active county of Ireland during the IRA campaign, followed by Tipperary and Cork – although his mathematics have been disputed by Peter Hart).[150] Cities and large towns played a crucial part in the revolution: Hart has argued, on the basis of his work on Cork, that the IRA thrived in relatively urbanized territory.[151] Even within the rural areas there were other, topographical, features of the IRA campaign: in otherwise strongly militant counties such as Kerry there was sometimes a distinction between the lowlands, where farmers tended to be both more prosperous and politically inert, and the glens, where physical force republicanism was much better rooted. On the other hand, judged within a national context, there was no automatic correlation between poor, mountainous land and IRA activity: indeed, if anything the broader pattern suggests the opposite conclusion. Given the dimensions of this base, few IRA commanders thought that a complete military victory over the British was attainable, and indeed many seem to have come to the view that survival was as much as might be expected.

There was much that was, at least superficially, novel about the campaign: a well-defined hierarchy of command was in place by the spring of 1921, with a headquarters in Dublin and both a divisional and brigade organization. But, inevitably, the view from Dublin was not always that from the hills of Tipperary, or the bogland of Cavan: in a sense Richard Mulcahy, the IRA chief of staff, was seeking to impose at least the semblance of a British-style military structure in the same way that the leaders of Sinn Féin had sought to create a British-style parliamentary assembly in the shape of the Dáil. But, while Mulcahy certainly achieved much on the basis of a comparatively limited bureaucracy and arsenal, his emphasis on centralization, on planning and on written communication ran contrary to some of the more spontaneous and independent impulses at the local level. The system of written reports, for example, though essential for a strategic overview, was always open to sabotage by the crown forces (Mulcahy's headquarters was successfully raided by the British in March 1921, with damaging consequences to the IRA campaign); and military convention, in the form of the command structure, sometimes had to give way to local family loyalties (as in the case of Clare, where three brigades were created in order to accommodate three rival clans). Personal and factional tensions pervaded the IRA hierarchy, from the local level (where, as in East Waterford, there might be two competing and mutually antagonistic brigade structures) to the highest level (where there might be damaging personal animosities – such as between Mulcahy and his nominal boss, the Dáil Minister of Defence, Cathal Brugha). The IRA campaign as a whole therefore evinces a tension between a modernist and professional view of guerrilla warfare and a more traditionalist and local (but by no means ineffective) exposition of rebel action.

Charles Townshend has identified three broad phases of the guerrilla offensive: the first of these, from 1918 through to the winter of 1919–20, involved comparatively small-scale attacks on the police, with the destruction of minor outposts and the killing of numerous individual officers.[152] This period included not only the ambush at Soloheadbeg, but also the assassination, on 23 June 1919, of District Inspector Michael Hunt of the RIC at Thurles, Tipperary (defined by Townshend as 'unmistakably the first blow in a methodical campaign of terrorism') as well as the first killing (in July 1919) of a member of the detective division of the Dublin Metropolitan Police.[153] This phase was followed in early 1920 by larger-scale assaults on police barracks: 16 occupied barracks were razed in the first half of the year. Lastly, following this analysis came the formation of the 'active service units', better known as the IRA flying columns. These came into operation in the late summer of 1920, sometimes – as with the Kilmichael ambush of 28 November 1920, or that at Headfort, Kerry, in March 1921 – with (from the republican perspective) spectacularly successful results: 18 auxiliary policemen were killed at Kilmichael, while nine British soldiers died at Headfort.

Through the course of the IRA campaign there was unquestionably a drift towards a greater degree of professionalization, a greater concentration of resources and ever-larger operations. While the IRA operations of 1919 were generally small-scale efforts, by the later stages of the war considerable bodies of volunteers were being gathered for particular enterprises: the British were pleased to learn, on the basis of information garnered during the raid on Mulcahy's office, that the IRA command was urging large attacks as small ambushes had been a failure.[154] Although the number of active IRA may have been as low as 2,000 in 1921, around 120 men were gathered for Collins's attack on the intelligence and other British officers on 'Bloody Sunday', 21 November 1920; some 150 volunteers were recruited for the Headfort ambush. In 1921 de Valera seems to have been exerting pressure on the IRA command for more conventional, large-scale operations, and to have been concerned by international unrest at the sledge-hammer ambushes on small British police and military patrols. His influence seems to have lain behind the disastrous IRA attack on the Customs House in May 1921, when some 70 of the Dublin No. 1 Brigade were lost, captured or killed by the forces of the crown.

However, if there were strategic refinements within the IRA's offensive, then there were also marked continuities. The IRA command, scarred by the history of earlier rebel failures in 1798 and 1867, had an abiding interest in intelligence work and persistently emphasized its importance to the local brigades. Michael Collins, as the IRA director of intelligence, assumed a legendary status during the two and a half years of the 'troubles', penetrating different aspects of Castle government as well as ruthlessly targeting spies and informers of all kinds. Members of the detective or 'G' division of the Dublin Metropolitan Police were picked off one by one, culminating in the assassination of 'the last really capable head of the division', Assistant Commissioner W.C. Redmond, in January 1920: after Redmond's death the division withered into insignificance.[155] The assassination of 14 British officers on 'Bloody Sunday' was the most sensational counter-intelligence coup of the war, even though only perhaps 11 of those killed were actually agents (one of Collins's victims, a Captain MacCormack of the Veterinary Corps, was a second cousin of Michael Davitt and had been sent to Ireland in order to buy mules for the British army): it seems likely that one of the IRA 'Squad' engaged in this operation was Seán Lemass, the future Taoiseach. The killing of an elderly woman, Mrs Lindsay of Cork, proved to be a much more damaging and controversial episode for the IRA than 'Bloody Sunday'. Mrs Lindsay, who was in her seventies, warned the British authorities of an impending IRA ambush and was subsequently shot by republicans as an informer. Her death caused a certain amount of embarrassment and recrimination within the IRA command, but it illustrates sharply the ruthless punishment meted out to those deemed guilty of treachery to the republican cause.

The 'Bloody Sunday' killings were both a practical exercise in counter-intelligence and a grim *coup de théâtre*. Indeed, the republican concern for the secret world of intelligence was complemented by an unflagging concern for appearances – by an interest in spectacular military operations as well as in publicity generally. Erskine Childers, ironically a distinguished British ex-serviceman, was a brilliant propagandist for the republican cause, and his particular creation, the *Irish Bulletin*, a news-sheet, 'excelled in portraying an exchange of shots as battle, the sniping of a police barrack as an assault, or the breaking of windows by the Crown Forces as the sacking of a town' (so successful was this that the British attempted a fake).[156] But there was often little need for hyperbole. From the beginning of the war one of the focuses of the IRA campaign was on the assassination of high-profile British military and political personnel. There were numerous attempts on the life of the lord lieutenant, Viscount French, culminating in the unsuccessful ambush at Ashtown, on the edge of Phoenix Park, on 19 December 1919. Efforts were made to kill Major General Sir Peter Strickland, the British commander of the troubled 6th Division, stationed in the martial law area of Munster. On 26 June 1920 the North Cork IRA seized Brigadier General Lucas, the British officer commanding the 16th Brigade, while he and two fellow officers were on a fishing trip: this, for the British, humiliating episode was partly (but only partly) mitigated by Lucas's later escape from his IRA captors. Other IRA efforts were better rewarded: the killing of Assistant Commissioner Redmond in January 1920 has already been noted. The RIC Divisional Commissioner for Munster was killed on 20 January 1921 at Tureengarriffe Glen in Kerry, while Colonel Commandant T. Cumming, the British military governor of Kerry, was shot in an ambush at Clonbanin, Cork, on 5 March 1921. But the most sensational of these IRA assassinations came after the war had ended, on 22 June 1922, when the ultra-loyalist Field Marshal Sir Henry Wilson was shot by two IRA men on the doorstep of his London home. Wilson was acting as a military advisor to the new Northern Ireland government; but his death, coming after the conclusion of his real period of influence (he had recently retired as Chief of the Imperial General Staff), suggests an older tradition of vendetta rather than a coda to the politically useful killings of 1919–21.[157]

The young men and women who were contributing to the IRA campaign defy easy categorization. Some of the regional characteristics of the war have already been highlighted (the proliferation of activity in Dublin, south and central Munster, and parts of south Ulster). However, there was no clear social profile to militant republicanism: Tom Garvin has suggested that 'its centre of social gravity seems to have been among the small-town and rural "lower middle class" of post-Parnell Ireland', though there was also some support from both those with greater wealth and the more impoverished.[158] In general, however, it seems that the really poor of the Irish countryside were not active in the IRA, while the most prosperous also held aloof (and indeed may have been resentful of republican billets and imposts). Joost Augusteijn has observed the role of middling farmers within the IRA while tracing a progressive dip in the social eminence of those recruited to the movement.[159] Peter Hart has identified a marked lack of paternal influence in a significant number of the Cork Volunteers whose careers are known.[160]

The educational attainments of the militants seem high, in keeping with the rather austere intellectual character of the 1916 rebels. In particular Hart has been able to correlate IRA militancy with the influence of the uncompromising educational regime of the Christian Brothers (a similar suggestion has been applied to the impact of the CBS structure within the Northern Ireland of the post-1945 era): 'in teaching patriotism the brothers created gunmen'.[161] Numerous conspicuous IRA men had a university education, including Ernie O'Malley, who graduated from a divisional command in 1921 to minor literary celebrity through his *On Another Man's Wound* (1936); Kevin Barry, one of the most celebrated republican martyrs of the war, was enrolled at University College Dublin at the time of his execution by the British (on 1 November 1920). In 1921 the 17-year-old Seán MacBride, a student at University College Dublin, was posted by the IRA command to work for the cause in County Wicklow. More broadly, it seems that, while no simple correlation can be made between areas of IRA activity and concentrations of Gaelic League or GAA strength, the gunmen were influenced both 'by the programmatic patriotism of their teachers and by the cultural revivalists of Edwardian Ireland'.[162]

On the other hand, service with the British army also appears as a common characteristic of the IRA (and indeed, given the large numbers of Irishmen who served during the First World War, and given the long tradition of Irish military service to the British crown, this should come as no surprise): accepting the King's shilling did not always imply endorsing the actions of the King's ministers in Ireland (as the mutiny of the Connaught Rangers in India in July 1920 readily demonstrated). Tom Barry, the architect of the Kilmichael ambush, was a veteran of the British campaign in Mesopotamia; Tom 'Trigger' Morris, a leading IRA man in south Derry, had been decorated by the British for his war service and promoted to the rank of major. One of the assassins of Sir Henry Wilson, Joseph O'Sullivan, was both an officer in the London battalion of the IRA and a disabled veteran of the British army. Others, not themselves veterans, had an unexpectedly complicated attitude to the British forces: Ernie O'Malley had a brother, Frank, who served in the Royal Dublin Fusiliers, and infused the pages of *On Another Man's Wound* with a grudging admiration for 'the enemy'.[163]

O'Malley thought that women republicans were more splenetic than their male counterparts, and more uncompromising in their attitude towards violence: this, he thought, was a result of their (at best) auxiliary role within the struggle.[164] There were some 3,000 women in Cumann na mBan during the Anglo-Irish war, many of whom supported flying columns and other forms of IRA activity. Tom Barry in Cork acknowledged the vital help supplied by some 500 or so local women in keeping the IRA campaign on course: this involved essential (if often unspectacular) labour, supplying food and clothing to Volunteers on active service or on the run.[165] The wounded received nursing care from women republicans. Women were also actively involved in propaganda and intelligence activities, scouting, carrying information or disseminating the IRA's spin on events: they were crucial to the success of the *Irish Bulletin*. Six women were elected to the second Dáil in May 1921. At the time of the truce some 40 republican women were in prison as a consequence of their work for the cause.

If the volunteers of the IRA defy any easy categorization, then the extent of their military (as distinct from their political) success is almost equally difficult to judge. The Neil Jordan film of Michael Collins's life, together with celebratory war memoirs by veterans such as Tom Barry and Ernie O'Malley, and indeed numerous local historical analyses of the conflict, all offer an uncomplicated picture of republican victory: this tends to be confirmed by the defensiveness, or indeed the embarrassed silence, of those who served in the crown forces. By the time that the British offered a truce, in July 1921, the IRA had scored a number of remarkable victories, but many of these (such as the Kilmichael ambush, or even individual high-profile killings) had comparatively little military (again, as distinct from political) significance. The IRA achievements in the intelligence war, and in particular the assassinations carried out on 21 November 1920, unquestionably did damage to the British military cause. On the other hand, some IRA leaders – especially those who came to support the Anglo-Irish Treaty of December 1921 – affirmed that the strongest reason for accepting a settlement was that the IRA had not the capacity to sustain the conflict. Collins's remark to the British Chief Secretary for Ireland, Hamar Greenwood, that 'we could not have lasted another three weeks' was perhaps a final fusillade in the psychological warfare of which he was a master; but there seems also to have been some conviction behind his hyperbole.[166] British pressure on the Dáil administration meant that by April 1921 the Sinn Féin courts (which were flourishing between June 1919 and August 1920) had been thoroughly crushed. By the spring and early summer of 1921 the British had gained the upper hand in Dublin, with striking military successes (such as the Customs House debacle) and achievements in the field of intelligence (Mulcahy seems to have been forced into considering another 'Bloody Sunday' coup at the time of the truce). Arrests and arms seizures by the crown forces appear to have severely undermined the IRA's capacity (by the spring of 1921 5,500 volunteers out of a total strength of perhaps 7,500 were in British custody). There were some signs of renewed IRA effort: there was certainly a massive increase in republican activity between May 1921 and the truce, and batches of the new Thompson sub-machine gun were arriving in Ireland from the United States at this time. It was also the case that the position of the IRA in Munster was more favourable than that of their embattled comrades-in-arms in Dublin: Tom Barry of the West Cork IRA thought that his men could go on for another five years;

Ernie O'Malley wondered 'why had the truce been ordered', given the IRA gains in his 2nd Southern Division (north Munster).[167] But the Dublin command clearly had a better overall view of the republican struggle than any local, even divisional, commander; and, while the British successes in Dublin possibly exaggerated the pessimism of the rebel GHQ, it was also the case that, as Mulcahy observed, no provincial victory would be worth having 'if Dublin is lost in a military sense'.[168] Despite regional successes, therefore, it was clear to the IRA command that the military tide was turning; and certainly Collins was convinced that a prolongation of the war would produce only an Irish defeat.

On the other hand, the political achievement of the IRA was remarkable: following in the footsteps of the Fenians of 1867, they had levered political concessions from a British government which would almost certainly have otherwise proved unrelenting. The terms offered to the Irish in the summer of 1921, and which were eventually embodied in the Treaty of December 1921, amounted to full dominion status, and therefore went far beyond the Home Rule measures of 1914 and 1920. Roy Foster has asked whether 'the bloody catalogue of assassination and war from 1919–21 was necessary in order to negotiate thus far'; Ronan Fanning has replied by pointing out that 'there is no shred of evidence to suggest that the British would have moved beyond the niggardliness of the Home Rule proposals . . . if they had not wished to end the Anglo-Irish war'.[169] Both, ostensibly conflicting, views have merit. The IRA had indeed extorted a much more generous definition of Irish legislative independence from the British government than was on offer even as late as December 1920: but, equally, the cost was high and, in terms of the lives lost, it was borne principally by the Irish people – the RIC and DMP men shot by the IRA, the IRA volunteers killed by the British, the civilians, arbitrary victims and 'spies', caught in the cross-fire of this bloodily intimate conflict. But the IRA's political success, great as it was, was also based upon an evasion – an evasion of the Ulster question: the IRA did not, indeed it could not, address the problem of Ulster Unionist opposition any more effectively than their constitutionalist predecessors. In fact they did not have to make the effort: the dominion status offered to the Irish in 1921 was only available because the British government had partly rid itself of the Ulster problem through the creation of Northern Ireland. Sinn Féin and the IRA won their independence, but in a war which scarcely touched Ulster at all; they won their independence by, to all intents and purposes, accepting the reality of partition. This the Home Rulers of 1914, rooted much more deeply in northern Catholic support, had been unable to do: they bore the burden of negotiating a deal on partition in a way which the IRA of 1921 was spared. Had a settlement on the Ulster question been successfully brokered in 1912 (a by no means fantastic speculation), there is every possibility that Irish autonomy would have speedily developed to the point reached in 1921.[170] Viewed from this perspective, therefore, the IRA's particular success lay in exploiting both the new reality of partition and a much older, and growing, British desire for disengagement.

Aside from the political achievement of the fighting men and women of the IRA, it may also be emphasized that the Dáil government, though frequently disrupted, and certainly under severe pressure by 1921, did go some way to wresting power from the British administration well before the signing of the Treaty. Recent scholarship (by Tom Garvin, Mary Kotsonouris and Arthur Mitchell) has laid stress on the achievements of the Dáil government, and particularly in the judicial and local government fields. If, as is sometimes argued, the Parnellites and the Catholic Church in the late nineteenth century came close to forging a state within a state, then this accolade might be applied with no less confidence to the administration of the Dáil: Mitchell, for example, has written of the Dáil 'counter-state'. Although, as has been noted, the court system established under the authority of the Dáil was under pressure from the British by 1921, it had established a wide popularity and effectiveness in 1919–20. Equally, the Dáil Department of Local Government, headed by W.T. Cosgrave, had won the allegiance of many of the local councils outside of the north-east; and it had speedily emasculated its official rival, the Local Government Board of the Castle regime. The Dáil government created a National Land Bank and land tribunals. It was not just, then, that IRA men fought their way into the government of Ireland: a parallel constitutional and democratically mandated assault was launched by the officials and members of the Dáil. It was a comparatively unspectacular thrust; but, equally, there is an argument for believing that the government of Ireland had – at least in part – been popularly reconstituted well before the official hand-over of power by the British.

Some attention may now be directed to the campaign waged by the crown forces between 1919 and 1921. The predominant characteristics of the political management of the British cause were (at least to begin with) relative disinterest and confusion. In the aftermath of the holocaust on the Western Front, much British effort was invested in the international and imperial arenas, in terms of both the diplomatic round and military commitment (such as in the campaigns in support of the White Russians and in Iraq and Afghanistan). Moreover, the development of labour unrest after the war was a major concern for British political and military leaders, and even ultra-loyalist army officers such as Sir Henry Wilson seem to have been as much preoccupied with the Red menace as with the Green. These centrifugal tendencies were reinforced by the divided nature of the government: Lloyd George's coalition bound enthusiastic Unionists with committed Home Rulers, and entrusted the conduct of Irish business to a relatively inexperienced Canadian Liberal, Hamar Greenwood. On the whole these divisions and diversions meant that there was comparatively little coherent political management of the British campaign, and this abdication became all the more glaring as the war developed and as martial law was imposed over large stretches of Munster.

However, it was not just that the IRA was shooting its way into the purview of the British cabinet: the problem of Irish government was thrust onto British attention in 1919–20 much more directly as a result of Liberal draftsmanship than of republican marksmanship. The Home Rule Act of 1914 had been suspended for the duration of the Great War, and with the signing of the treaties of Versailles (in 1919) and Sèvres (in 1920) it could no longer be disguised that the conflict had formally ended and that an Irish parliament would have to be instituted. The proposed settlement that emerged was the product both of a wartime shift in British attitudes and (to a limited extent) the changing pattern of Irish politics. The Government of Ireland Bill, introduced into the House of Commons in February 1920, envisaged the creation of two Irish states, each endowed with a Home Rule executive and parliament: a proposed Irish Council, embodying representatives from the two Irish assemblies, was intended to serve as a machine for future Irish unity and to divert attention from the solidity of the partition arrangements. In fact the drafters of the legislation need not have wasted their ingenuity: the principal opponents of a fixed partition arrangement, the Irish Party, were no longer a serious parliamentary force, while the new standard-bearers of popular nationalism, Sinn Féin, were trenchant but much less coherent anti-partitionists, and in any case were concentrating their energies within Dáil Éireann. The Bill was therefore an indirect by-product of Sinn Féin abstentionism; but it also reflected the wartime disintegration of the 'Ulsteria' which had inflamed Conservative passions in 1912–14. The dual Home Rule settlement expressed the Tories' cooler Unionism, as it did the Ulster loyalists' renewed wariness for their *soi-disant* allies. But only in the most limited sense was the measure a response to the developing war in Ireland.

The detachment of British ministers reflected alternative, competing political demands as well as the hazy conviction that the IRA represented merely another reincarnation of Irish criminality. But the limitations of these metropolitan attitudes were not offset by any particular rigour within the British political and military command in Dublin. The Castle administration had traditionally been highly diffuse, and has generally been treated as a quagmire of bureaucratic confusion and political reaction. In fact, as Lawrence McBride has trenchantly argued, the Castle was 'greened' between 1892 and 1922 – reoriented from its Unionist and Protestant character in the nineteenth century towards a relatively more Catholic and nationalist nature.[171] However, this did little to alleviate the problems of the British government during the war against the IRA (paradoxically, the closest contact between the Castle and Irish popular opinion may have come with the intelligence leaks that Collins so effectively tapped); and in addition much administrative confusion remained. An attempt to cut a way through the bureaucratic undergrowth was made by an investigative committee from London in the early summer of 1920; but, while this grafted some much-needed intelligence and liberalism onto the highest rank of the Castle bureaucracy, it also tended to exacerbate the apparent directionlessness of the British administration. Liberal-minded civil servants were pulling in one consensual direction; angry soldiers were pulling towards full-scale repression. As Charles Townshend has remarked, 'by the summer of 1920 the threads of British policy had become so complex that lines are hard to distinguish'.[172]

If this confusion was evident in the relationship between the administration and the military, then it was equally clear within the military structure itself. Presiding over the British army in Ireland was Sir Neville Macready, whose attitude to the division of authority beneath him has been well described as 'one of sardonic resignation'. Macready had some experience of Ireland (as GOC in Belfast in 1914); he had also policing experience (he was Commissioner of the Metropolitan Police between 1918 and 1920) and some degree of political nous. But he hated Ireland ('I loathe the country'), and his policing experience provided little qualification for the guerrilla war that was developing in 1919: he was carping and passive and highly pessimistic.[173] He refused command of the RIC, and thereby avoided both a further professional burden and the opportunity to create a coordinated security command structure. Instead the role of 'police advisor' (later 'police chief') fell in May 1920 to Major General Sir Henry Tudor, who oversaw an administrative reform of the RIC as well as the creation of its new auxiliary division (in July 1920). Tudor inherited a further initiative to bolster the police – the recruitment of British ex-servicemen, which had begun earlier in the year: on 2 February 1920 'a musician and ex-soldier', Henry Batten, became the first of these new recruits, and thereby gained the distinction of being the first 'Black and Tan' to venture to Ireland.[174]

Tudor oversaw in a genial and brutal manner a highly lax, if expansive, policing empire. He tolerated (as indeed did some of his political masters, including Lloyd George) an unofficial system of reprisals which gave rise to some of the more controversial and bloody episodes in the war: an early example of this form of unofficial reprisal came with the 'sacking' of Balbriggan, Dublin, on 20 September 1920, when over 50 buildings were destroyed and two civilians killed after the shooting of a popular RIC officer. But Balbriggan was followed, in late November and December 1920, by two even more sombre episodes: the Croke Park killings (21 November) and the burning of part of the centre of Cork city (on the night of 11 December), both actions being undertaken by the temporary cadets of the auxiliary force. The 'burning of Cork' presents few problems of interpretation: a body of auxiliaries, enraged by an IRA ambush, set alight a large section of Patrick Street as well as the City Hall and the Carnegie Library. Four days later an auxiliary cadet compounded local outrage by killing a 70-year-old priest together with a young man at Dunmanway, Cork. These two grim events excited not only popular animosities but also tensions between the different arms of the British security forces (General Strickland, the military governor of the martial law area in Munster, expelled the auxiliaries from Cork after the conflagration).

The precise origins of the Croke Park killings are less clear: there is (inevitably) conflict between official and republican versions of the affair. What may have begun as an attempt to locate the IRA gunmen responsible for the killing of the British intelligence officers earlier in the day degenerated into a gunbattle: 12 civilians were killed, and many more were injured either by gunfire or in the panic that followed. It is certain that the auxiliaries fired into the grandstand at the stadium. It is probably fair to judge that any attempt to 'lift' IRA men during a match at the Park was madness. It is possible that, under the cover of a search operation, the auxiliaries were bent on indiscriminate revenge.

If it is hard to define the membership of the IRA, then there are even greater difficulties with the crown forces. This is partly because the literature on the British security apparatus, though growing, remains slight; but it is also the case that the crown forces were so diverse than any generalization must inevitably fail. The RIC and DMP were essentially Irish and Catholic bodies, and were characterized by mild nationalist sympathies; the Black and Tans and auxiliaries, on the other hand, were British forces, and were each recruited from different social groupings. The plight of the conventional RIC, easy targets for assassination, is poignant: as the war escalated they were increasingly ostracized from their communities, and their families – even police widows – were subject to petty humiliations and intimidation. The auxiliaries, who drew heavily from the officer cadre of the Great War, were probably the least disciplined of the crown forces and seem to have been characterized by hard-living: they were given to drunkenness and to occasional brutality as well as reckless bravery (many of their IRA enemies later commented on their willingness to fight to the last). For many Ireland provided recreation and adventure: there is plenty of evidence to suggest that they underestimated the commitment and skill of their opponents. These attitudes, combined with the sporadic nature of the war, gave rise to an astounding insouciance: Brigadier General Lucas was captured while on a fishing trip; an auxiliary stationed at Macroom later recalled that he had organized several recreational trips through 'bandit country'; the victims of the Kilmichael ambush appear to have been rutted in a fixed patrol route.[175] The shadow of the carnage on the Western Front seems to have fallen over these men, who lived hard and died hard.

In military terms the Anglo-Irish war was a learning experience for both sides: paradoxically, just as the IRA was drifting towards larger units and more formal structures, so the crown forces were drifting towards some small-scale initiatives and informality. The British intelligence network, successfully disrupted by the IRA in the early stages of the war, was painstakingly reconstructed and seems to have been delivering valuable materials in Dublin and Cork city (and indeed elsewhere) by 1921. If 'Bloody Sunday' had underlined the value of effective intelligence to the British, then the dangers of fixed patrols were highlighted by the IRA success at Kilmichael: by early 1921 there seems to have been a concerted effort by some of the crown forces to pursue a more flexible policing operation. There were echoes of the IRA flying columns in the roving foot patrols and concealed observation units which the formidable Essex Regiment in south Cork and the 26th Brigade in Dublin were adopting in the spring of 1921.

But, even if the military balance was shifting in favour of the British, then this was coming too late and at too high a price for the London government. In addition, British military successes were obscured both by a determined IRA offensive in May and June of 1921 and by the Sinn Féin landslide in the elections of May 1921 (held in fulfilment of the terms of the Government of Ireland Act). The militarist lobby in the cabinet had been significantly weakened by the resignation of Andrew Bonar Law, the Conservative leader and an ultra-Unionist, in March. Some influential soldiers (Macready and Wilson) held, or affected to hold, a highly pessimistic view of the military situation; those less remote from the conflict tended to be more upbeat – but they also tended to be more distant from the decision-making process. Even some of those soldiers and politicians who were relatively optimistic about the state of the British campaign (such as Winston Churchill) thought that there was a case for negotiating from a position of strength. Tentative contact between the Castle and Sinn Féin, which had been initiated briefly in late 1920, was resumed in June 1921; and in July the combatants agreed on a truce as a necessary preliminary to a process of negotiation.

5.6   Trucileers, Staters and Irregulars

At noon on Monday 11 July 1921, a truce came into operation between the IRA and the crown forces. Tom Barry of the West Cork IRA, initially bewildered, soon came to see that 'the forcing of the enemy to offer such terms was a signal victory in itself'. For Barry, looking back after the civil war, the months following the ceasefire comprised 'the longest and most brilliant Summer in living memory' – much as veterans of the Great War came to project their pain and nostalgia in looking back on the bitterly glorious summer of 1914: the truce served as the triumphant climax to his 'determinedly myopic' *Guerrilla Days in Ireland* (1949).[176] For Ernie O'Malley, another – more lyrical – chronicler of what he called 'the scrap', the truce was source of similar, but in this case unresolved, confusion: 'What did it mean?' O'Malley and his men, confident of escalating their campaign against the British, found themselves 'bewildered' by the 'bald message' from Richard Mulcahy that announced the truce.[177]

What indeed did it mean? The swiftness with which the British swung from pursuing their 'small war' against the 'murder gangs' of the IRA towards arbitration astonished contemporaries and has intrigued historians: it has also served to inspire later generations of militant republican. Tom Barry's belief that the truce represented a 'signal victory' for the IRA was widely held. Nor was it at all unrealistic, given that the British government had been caught in a political ambush, pinned down by the fire of domestic liberal criticism and international hostility: this macropolitical Kilmichael was the IRA's great strategic victory. Nevertheless, to view the truce exclusively in such terms is (as has been mentioned already) to simplify a highly complicated military and political situation: such a perspective also makes it extremely hard to disentangle the politics of the Treaty negotiations, as well as the Treaty document itself (this, of course, was precisely the problem of perception that republicans faced).

A crucial, but often forgotten, analogy was supplied to the British by their experience in South Africa. The parallels with Ireland were superficially convincing: an aggressive guerrilla force had inflicted large-scale casualties on the British army in 1899–1902 before being finally overwhelmed. The Boers, former antagonists, had been further disarmed by the generosity of the peace settlement: they had chosen to maintain the formally despised imperial linkage through a new dominion, the Union of South Africa, and they had fought loyally alongside British troops at Delville Wood and other of the killing fields of the Western Front. The British had certainly not broken the IRA, but there was evidence that they had turned the military campaign around in the course of 1921; and, with the problem of the Ulster Unionists apparently resolved through the settlement of 1920, there was no obvious reason why British statecraft could not make a loyal dominion out of the unpromising materials supplied by Ireland – in much the same way as had been achieved with an equally unpromising situation in South Africa. General Jan Smuts was an important influence behind the diplomacy that produced the truce; and very shortly the British press was drawing comparisons between the Boer military leaders and the leading Irish commanders. Ernie O'Malley observed ruefully that Collins was being hailed by the British press as 'the Irish de Wet'.[178]

There was initially plenty of evidence to confirm the view that a combination of military advantage and political open-handedness would achieve the same results in the Ireland of 1921 as in the South Africa of 1902. Eamon de Valera was accorded the title of 'President of the Irish Republic' by the second Dáil in August 1921, but in settling the terms for a negotiation between the British and Irish leadership, he did not lay any particular stress on his republican aspirations, nor did he rule out the possibility of an association between Ireland and the Empire. Indeed, the agreed formula for talks ('ascertaining how the association of Ireland with the community of nations known as the British Empire may best be reconciled with Irish national aspirations') focused on the relationship between Ireland and the Empire rather than on the republican 'aspirations' of (some) Irish leaders.[179] Michael Collins was later to remark, with a characteristically cool insight, that the surrender of the republic had occurred not with the Treaty signed in December 1921 but 'with the acceptance of the invitation': the Irish had not initially insisted on republican status, nor indeed would the British have been prepared to accept such a precondition.[180] The location of the talks, 10 Downing Street, involved the Irish shuttling back and forth to the imperial capital and underlined the imbalance of power which determined the proceedings. The Irish negotiators arrived in London on 11 October 1921, burdened by the terms of the impending diplomacy, by the relative weakness of their military position, and by varied definitions of the 'national aspiration': they had to cope with the consequences of earlier constitutional fudges within Sinn Féin (such as the constitution of 1917); they had to make sense of the wanna-be politics of ambitious young revolutionaries who believed that they had brought the British Empire to its knees.

The Irish team was headed by Griffith and comprised Collins, Robert Barton, Gavan Duffy and Eamon Duggan. The strongly republican Erskine Childers served in the Irish secretariat. The delegation was granted full plenipotentiary powers by the Dáil, but de Valera (characteristically) insisted that Dublin be apprised of developments and consulted before the conclusion of any agreement: the President seems to have been keeping his options open, anxious to have ultimate control over the negotiation without incurring any of the unpopularity that might accrue from failure or from a problematic deal. The likelihood of failure, or even of a humiliating climb-down, was great: the starting point for the Irish was an independent unitary nation, loosely bound to the Empire, but accepting the crown only as head of the Empire: there was, at least for de Valera (whose vision of an 'external association' between Ireland and the Empire lay behind the Irish pitch), no question that the English King would be recognized as the source of sovereign authority in

Ireland. The British, on the other hand, sought to apply a modified form of dominion status to Ireland, granting wide autonomy but retaining the King as a nominal head of state, and demanding an oath of fidelity to the crown. In addition the British saw any Irish settlement in fundamentally partitionist terms: given the strong Conservative presence in the coalition government, there would be nothing approaching the 'coercion' of Ulster Unionism.

The Irish to some extent became victims of their own aspirations; Lloyd George, to some extent, successfully turned his weaknesses (especially his dependence on Unionist partners) into bargaining counters. Although isolated and unrepresentative Sinn Féiners (such as Father O'Flanagan) had sought to come to terms with the problem of Ulster Unionism, in general the movement had been no more focused than had the Irish Parliamentary Party (and with similarly embarrassing results). The Irish negotiators started out by insisting on the unity of the national territory, and they followed the de Valera line by arguing that their tolerance of any form of imperial association represented a painful concession to the minority Unionist interest. But such an attitude spoke more eloquently about the integrity of national politics than about the realities of Ulster Unionist dissent, or of partition. Just as the Irish Parliamentary Party had been forced into retreat in 1914 and 1916, so Griffith and the Sinn Féin team slipped back from the front line of unitary nationalism towards a more easily defended position. In 1914 and 1916 the Redmondites had reconciled themselves to partition by clinging to the device of a temporary settlement; and in 1921 the Sinn Féin team retraced much the same ground, seizing on a mechanism supplied by Lloyd George – a Boundary Commission – as proof that the division of the country would be merely a transient evil. The commission, one of the more startling examples of Lloyd George's ingenuity, was sold to the Irish as a means of pruning the territory of Northern Ireland, and of rendering the new polity unviable; but the price that they had to pay for this salve was a promise not to break the talks on the issue of Ulster.

For Sinn Féin this was a much more expensive undertaking than might at first be seen. De Valera had been insistent (and – from a narrow, tactical perspective – rightly) that if the talks were to fail, then the breaking-point should be partition: this was an issue around which Sinn Féiners of all types might be rallied, and there was a fair prospect that international, even imperial, opinion might be sympathetic. But with the loss of the Orange card (generally speaking, the ace of trumps for those seeking nationalist unity), the Irish leaders were left with a much more vulnerable hand. The great remaining issue for the negotiators, and therefore the only alternative breaking-point, lay with the relationship between Ireland and the Empire. Here, remarkably, the most bitterly contested areas were the symbols and rituals of British 'dominion', rather than the practicalities of independence: the Sinn Féin team, for example, speedily acceded to British demands for naval facilities around the Irish coast, and the sub-committees of the negotiation rapidly disposed of other apparently fraught issues. But, even though the British were effectively conceding Irish independence, in the form of a modified dominion status, the viability of this offer depended upon the mode of presentation. Tom Garvin, following the German political scientist Leo Kohn, has emphasized the extent to which the British were actually conceding the substance of republican institutions to Sinn Féin; but the trappings of the British offer – a governor general, representing the crown, an oath of fidelity to the King – diverted the gaze of both monarchists in the United Kingdom and many Irish separatists away from the breadth of the concession.[181] In a clash between two emotive and fundamentalist political creeds – Irish republicanism and British imperialism – each was more concerned about symbols than about substance: British Tories, who had squirmed over Home Rule in 1912, accepted Irish independence in 1921 because it was defined in superficially imperial terms; equally, many Irish separatists, who might have accepted Home Rule in 1912, were not now prepared to accept any grant of independence which fell short of the republic for which Pearse and Connolly had laid down their lives.

Herein lay the difficulty of the Irish negotiators. Those elements of the British offer that were necessary to reconcile Unionists and imperialists to Irish independence were also the aspects that were hardest for republicans to swallow. Tom Garvin has defined this paradox with characteristic verve: 'the symbols of monarchy in the [evolving] treaty, there to comfort English opinion and to deceive it as to the status of the new polity, actually succeeded in deceiving much of Sinn Féin and the IRA'.[182] Of these symbols, unquestionably the most painful and controversial lay in the oath of allegiance to the British crown. For the British government it was politically crucial that former 'murderers' be seen to take an oath of fealty to the King: the obeisance of the treacherous Irish would underline the extent to which some sort of recognizable victory had been achieved in 1921. In addition the oath and the other vestigial trappings of monarchy were central to the definition of dominion status: no British politician, and particularly the Unionists, would tolerate any explicit form of republican settlement, and in fact – given the attitude of the other dominions – they did not have to make the effort. For those sympathetic to the Irish cause in the Empire, the Sinn Féin quest for legislative independence was a recognizable and broadly familiar aspiration – but republicanism was at this stage an alien and much less accessible creed.

For many separatists, the republic was an almost religious passion: in politics, as in religion, there was one true, narrow path to freedom, but there were also many blind alleys and many treacherous siren voices. In addition, for many separatists, fired by millenarian zeal, the republic was close at hand – foretold Isaiah-like by the United Irishmen of the 1790s, formally established by Pearse, and realized by his disciples during the 'troubles' of 1919–21. That what was widely interpreted as a British climb-down in July 1921 should lead to anything other than the consummation of this republic was unthinkable: that a successful revolution might turn the country on its head and yet leave the genially philistine King George V as head of state was a blasphemous speculation. Oaths had traditionally played a significant part in the politics of Irish separatism: recruitment to the succession of revolutionary secret societies, including the Irish Republican Brotherhood, was by a solemn oath, and the members of the second Dáil swore to bear 'true faith and allegiance' to the Irish Republic.[183] That these same deputies might be required to perjure and dishonour themselves through an oath of fealty to the English King was indeed an extremely grim prospect.

De Valera's solution to the problem of the oath was designed to minimize the offence to republican sensitivities – but its cool treatment of the monarchy and of the Empire did not appease the British: the oath-taker, in de Valera's formulation, would swear 'true faith and allegiance to the constitution of the Irish Free State, to the Treaty of Association and to recognise the King of Great Britain as head of the Associated States'.[184] This clearly complemented de Valera's plans for an Ireland 'externally associated' with the 'associated states' of the Commonwealth – and, as such, it was swiftly repudiated by the British negotiators. Their alternative went some slight way to recognize Irish qualms – 'true faith and allegiance' was sworn in the first instance to the Irish constitution, and not to the King; moreover, the declaration of fidelity to George V was defined as being 'in virtue of the common citizenship of Ireland with Great Britain and her adherence to and membership of the group of nations forming the British Commonwealth of Nations'. In other dominions, as Alan Ward has pointed out, the oath of allegiance was sworn to the King personally.[185] But the British oath was essentially a reformulation of their arguments and their requirements rather than a major concession to Irish susceptibilities. In any case, the mixture of Irish self-determination and monarchy was not unpalatable to at least one, and arguably the most important, of the Irish negotiating team – Arthur Griffith, whose separatist faith had for long admitted the possibility of a shared monarch. Others for whom the English crown remained hateful nevertheless saw the constitutional reality beyond the gawdy monarchical trappings: and on 6 December 1921 a deal was struck with the British on the basis of their oath (bound into article four of the new Treaty), partition (masked by a Boundary Commission), and various concessions on the issue of security. The very title of the proposed new polity – Saorstát Éireann, or the Irish Free State – was a skilful exploitation of a linguistic ambiguity, and satisfied British imperialists (who were familiar with the Orange Free State province in the Union of South Africa) as well as (some) Irish separatists (for whom 'saorstát' was close enough to republic): as Tom Garvin has wryly pointed out, those TDs of the first Dáil who in 1919 swore allegiance to the republic in Irish were actually pledging themselves to the 'saorstát'.[186]

Thus, the ambiguities of British constitutional law and the ambiguities of Irish separatist conviction had apparently been able to accommodate an agreement between the two ancient national antagonists (neither 'dominion status' nor the ultimate purpose of Sinn Féin had ever been defined beyond question). The Irish cabinet accepted the Treaty on 8 December (by four votes to three), and on 7 January 1922 so too did Dáil Éireann (by 64 votes to 57). The six women deputies – Mary MacSwiney, Ada English, Margaret Pearse, Constance Markievicz, Kathleen Clarke and Kate O'Callaghan – were all in the republican camp: 'I have seen the star', proclaimed Markievicz in a biblical allusion, 'and am not going to follow a flashing will o' the wisp'.[187] President de Valera, whose favoured device, external association, had been so comprehensively rejected, sought a vote of confidence, which he lost by a close margin (60 votes against, 58 votes for): he was replaced by Griffith, who undertook the task of reconstructing the Dáil ministry. This, rather than the change of government in 1932, was – as Alan Ward has remarked – 'the first peaceful transfer of power in modern Ireland'.[188] And it was followed in January 1922 by an equally remarkable event – the surrender of Dublin Castle by the outgoing British authorities to Michael Collins, who only six months earlier might have occupied a prison cell on death row rather than the viceroy's throne room.

But the apparently smooth pro-Treaty victory was accompanied by tensions and bitterness which cut to the quick of Irish separatist politics. Majorities had been recorded for the Treaty both in the cabinet and in the Dáil – but narrow majorities, secured only after hours and (in the case of the Dáil) weeks of impassioned debate. The distance between the republican aspiration and the reality of the Treaty was wide (though in fact much less wide than appearances implied); and the chasm could only – for some – be explained by the duplicity of the British, or Irish cravenness ('the British government selected its men', remarked the republican Brugha, in a damning allusion to the signatories of the Treaty). Indeed in December 1921 and January 1922, much time was devoted to disentangling the terms under which the 'plenipotentiaries' had been appointed: they had not referred the Treaty back to Dublin, but under the Dáil terms of appointment they had not been required so to do – it was only as a result of de Valera's later stipulations that such an approach was required (and in any case on 6 December 1921 the President could not have been reached in Dublin since he was in his home territory of Limerick). Behind these attacks lay the conviction that, had the Irish team resisted, a unitary republic might have emerged, if not from the smoke-filled cabinet room at 10 Downing Street then from the smoke of gunfire. Indeed, the Treaty has provided a tantalizing counter-factual problem for commentators since the 1920s: but the balance of probabilities does not favour the republican case. Lloyd George threatened war in the event of a breakdown; and the Irish signatories were (despite Brugha's contempt) well placed to judge whether such threats were merely the bluster of a defeated giant. The British retained a capacity to fight a war, and were now perhaps better able to do so (at least in the sense that some of their political problems might have dissolved had the Irish broken on the question of dominion status). Collins was downbeat about the prospects for the IRA – and the evidence on the whole confirms his attitude. Although the ranks of the IRA were swollen with recent recruits – what K.T. Hoppen has called the *Märzveilchen* of the truce – there were problems of discipline and of security: there was also the perennial shortage of ammunition and other supplies.[189] Pro-Treatyites (predictably, perhaps) concentrated on these issues during the debates on the Treaty.

It has frequently been remarked that the distance between the two antagonists, the supporters and opponents of the Treaty, was so slight as to make the later civil war virtually inexplicable: it was the difference between supporting a *de facto* and a *de jure* republic.[190] But the importance of symbols and of detail in the early 1920s is hard to miss: the British, for example, offered sweeping concessions to the emissaries of the Dáil, yet they would not formally recognize that assembly (the Treaty had to be ratified by the southern MPs elected in May 1921 under the terms of the

Government of Ireland Act). The Irish, for their part, while undertaking to be 'faithful' to George V, happily obliterated his image on the first postage stamps of the new regime (these bore the legend 'Provisional Government of Ireland' or 'Irish Free State, 1922' franked boldly over the King's portrait). More serious, from the British perspective, was the Irish attempt to draft a constitution which exploited some of the ambiguities of the Treaty and which enshrined the sweeping practical freedoms of dominion status rather than the more restricted formal, legal definitions: the Treaty had explicitly mentioned that the Irish should follow 'the law, practice and constitutional usage of Canada' – but the 'practice' and 'usage' of the Canadian constitution was in fact much less restrained than 'the law'.[191] This attempt to evade the hateful symbolism of monarchy and of British authority – and to unite the separating forces of the revolution – met with a predictable veto from the London government on 27 May 1922.

Again, if little apparently separated the parties, then there were systematic efforts towards a reconciliation: the draft constitution of the Irish Free State embodied one such effort. After the resignation of de Valera in January 1922 there was some (albeit cautious) goodwill: the pro-Treatyites were respectful, while the retiring President pledged that he and his allies 'will be there with you against any outside enemy at any time', an unmistakeable allusion to the campaign against the British and to the possibility of its renewal. In addition (as F.S.L. Lyons has noticed) de Valera promised that the anti-Treatyites would not 'interfere' with the new government 'except when we find that you are going to do something that will definitely injure the Irish nation' – a rider that would have had less significance had it not been for de Valera's legalistic turn of mind, and the very sensitive views of his supporters concerning 'injury' to the Irish nation.[192] Within the new government there were some who were desperately keen to ensure that the passive goodwill which de Valera seemed to be offering was not in any way flaunted: of these 'centrists' Michael Collins was by far the most significant. Collins was chair of the drafting committee for the new constitution and appointed all but one of his remaining colleagues. Thus, although he attended only two of the drafting sessions (giving the broad sweep of his views, while subcontracting the detail), his influence on the proposed constitution was immense: in particular he believed that, by writing out the crown, there was a strong possibility that de Valera and his supporters might be reconciled to the pro-Treaty majority. In addition he was keen to avoid the consolidation of tensions by further, precipitate votes on the Treaty: he and de Valera agreed that no such vote should be taken at the Sinn Féin ard-fheis of February 1922. It was also agreed to postpone an election in order to create space for the reconciliation process. Much more controversially, on 20 May 1922, Collins and de Valera agreed to avoid a direct electoral confrontation: this pact proposed in effect that the election should pass uncontested, with a National Coalition Panel, comprising the existing number of Treaty supporters and opponents, being rubber-stamped by voters at the polls. But the success of this daring enterprise depended on the British accepting the draft constitution (for de Valera and his allies would not act within a monarchical framework); and the British, as has been noted, were mortified by what they saw (with some justification) as a radical revision of the Treaty agreement. By the time the election was held, on 16 June 1922, Collins had already repudiated the pact, and there was a bitter, if somewhat confused, race: only 37 of the 142 seats were uncontested, and it has been estimated that 78 per cent of the poll was pro-Treaty.[193] Certainly the election, in an admittedly imperfect manner, emphasized the broad popular support for the Treaty, and for the Irishmen who had signed it.

Yet there was an ominous bass line underlying the lyrical soprano of these conciliatory efforts. Although a majority of the IRA and IRB leadership were supportive of the Treaty, it soon became clear that a majority of the rank and file of both bodies clung to the republican ideal. On 12 January 1922 a number of senior IRA officers wrote to the Dáil Minister of Defence, Richard Mulcahy, demanding that an Army Convention be held in order to reaffirm military allegiance to the republic: this was scarcely even a veiled threat to the new government, yet Mulcahy – short of calling on the British (of course an unthinkable stratagem) – had no means of resisting this pressure. He therefore accepted that the Convention be held within two months, and turned immediately to the task of raising a National Army in order to counter-balance the looming threat of a republican military coup. By the time that the Convention was to take place (in March), Mulcahy felt strong enough to execute a U-turn, banning the Convention which he had initially agreed to call. But the Convention went ahead, a well-publicized focus for republican defiance, and indeed threatened treachery: in an explicit challenge to the Provisional Government, the delegates elected an executive of 16 IRA officers, which looked very much like a military junta, and indeed scarcely bothered to deny its ambitions in that direction ('you can take it that way, if you like' was the famous reply of one of the Army executive, Rory O'Connor, to a journalist enquiring about the threat of an armed dictatorship).[194]

The Convention was not the first showdown between the republicans and the Provisional Government, but it was the most dangerous and one of the best-publicized acts of defiance. There had been earlier clashes between the 'irregular' IRA, as the anti-Treatyite military were coming to be called, and the 'national' forces of the Provisional Government: one such dispute occurred at Limerick in late February, but – again – Mulcahy was not yet prepared to fight what he still considered to be an unequal struggle (his antipathy for potentially disastrous heroics, born in the struggle against the crown forces, served him well). But the Army Convention helped to realize these unresolved threats and challenges: on 14 April O'Connor and other members of the new IRA executive seized the historic centre of the Irish judiciary, the Four Courts in Dublin, as well as numerous other important buildings in the capital. The extent to which these men saw themselves as retracing the footsteps of the 1916 insurgents could scarcely have been more marked if they had seized the General Post Office itself: like the Easter rebels, the Irregular leaders concentrated on occupying symbolically significant buildings, and indeed gravitated towards, if not the GPO, then at least O'Connell Street as one of the focuses of their action. Like the men and women of 1916, it might be remarked of the Irregulars that the politics of their militarism were well judged: the seizure of key buildings in the national capital represented a humiliating and well-publicized blow to official pride. But, equally, it might be said that the military execution of their political aspirations was appallingly mishandled. The extent to which the Irregulars were victims of their own past and their own illusions was underlined by these actions: for, unlike the 1916 insurgents, the rebels of 1922 had actually a fair chance of winning a military showdown – provided that they were able to liberate themselves from the legacy of glorious republican military failure and the traditional strategy of committing large numbers of troops to fixed (and ultimately indefensible) positions. But, in the decisive first months of the conflict, they proved themselves unable to perform this leap of imagination.

As has been noticed, the seizure of the Four Courts did not in itself represent the beginning of the civil war between the Provisional Government and the Irregulars. There remained the possibility that another bloody Irish civil war, which had already begun in early 1922 – that between Unionists and nationalists in the new Northern Ireland – would provide a spur to the unity of the IRA. There was also the possibility that the continuing efforts of Collins to woo de Valera back into the political process might succeed. But by May–June 1922 de Valera was increasingly marginalized from the republican militants, and it is not at all clear whether his cooperation would have dispelled the threat of military conflict. The plight of northern nationalists possibly delayed the onset of civil war: Collins was unflaggingly sensitive to the urgency as well as to the political opportunities of their position ('we have the bloody Treaty', he allegedly exclaimed, '. . . and I don't know whether they'll take it or not in Dublin, but we can always march on the North').[195] But the northern question, though important, did not in fact resolve the fundamental differences that were beginning to lever apart the supporters and opponents of the Treaty. There remained a third possibility: that British intervention against the Irregulars might permit a reconstruction of national unity around its traditional focus. The assassination of the retired British Field Marshal and active Ulster Unionist Sir Henry Wilson on 22 June 1922 may have been ordered by Collins, and it may indeed have been a joint operation between him and the Four Courts command (there is inconclusive evidence pointing to Collins's involvement, and – rather less certainly – to the involvement of the Irregular leaders).[196] The British, whose alarm at the Four Courts defiance had for long been mounting, chose to lay the blame in the republican camp (though they can scarcely have been persuaded by Collins's disavowals), and on 23 June they began to formulate plans for a military reprisal in Dublin. Once again, however, Macready's lachrymose passivity stood him in good stead, for – having helped to draw up the British offensive – he soon developed what Michael Hopkinson has termed 'military cold feet'.[197] Macready fended off the order to attack, which came on 24 June, and (as his self-congratulatory memoirs affirm) thereby averted the likelihood both of a further British embroilment in Ireland and a reunified Irish response.[198] The British, thwarted in the short term, applied an ever-intensifying political pressure on the Provisional Government, threatening the reoccupation of Ireland in the event of the republican challenge being left unanswered; and this (rather than any later stimulus) appears to have goaded an extremely reluctant Irish cabinet into action on 26 June. The interception and arrest of a republican raiding party in Dublin by national troops on 27 June seems to have been designed as a warning shot or, indeed, as a provocation; and, when the Four Courts replied with the kidnapping by Ernie O'Malley of the popular Free State general J.J. ('Ginger') O'Connell, the Provisional Government was supplied with a pretext for an assault on the republican positions in Dublin. The bombardment of the Four Courts began on 28 June in a tragi-comic manner (the Free State troops were unfamiliar with heavy artillery, and shelled sporadically and inaccurately); but this initial hesitation would soon be resolved into the unadulterated tragedy of the Irish civil war.

Who were the contending parties? The political leadership of the Free State army was of course supplied by the Provisional Government (which, with the enactment of the Irish Free State constitution in December 1922, subsequently became the Executive Council of the new dominion). Michael Collins, stepping down from his ministerial duties, became commander in chief of the government forces in July 1922 and represented a critical link between the Treatyite politicians and their military. Mulcahy, who was both Minister of Defence as well as the army's chief of staff, represented a similarly important point of contact: when Collins was killed in the Béal na mBláth ambush in August 1922, Mulcahy took over as the commander of the national forces. It would be wrong to imply, however, that the relationship between the civil and military authorities of the new government was absolutely unblemished (a minor crisis would soon emerge in 1924): but certainly by comparison with the republicans, the Free State cause admirably preserved the ascendancy of democratically elected politicians. Mulcahy, who might well have been tempted to exploit his extremely powerful military position, instead adhered strictly to the rule of law and was alert to the need for a speedy reconstruction of civil authority as the Free State forces pushed westwards.

The army over which these men had ultimate authority was a hastily constructed composite force, comprising veterans of the struggle against the British as well as Irish veterans of the British campaigns of the First World War: in addition there was a large recruitment among young urban men who (as Garvin has noted) would in earlier times have naturally gravitated towards the disbanded Irish regiments of the crown (such as the Connaught Rangers, the Royal Munster Fusiliers and the Royal Dublin Fusiliers).[199] There was a particular irony here, given that another of the building blocks of the new national army was Collins's Squad, one of the British army's most ruthless opponents in the Dublin of 1920–1. But perhaps the most crucial military resource that the Free State forces possessed was the support of the people: although there was a granite core of republican commitment, most Irish people supported the Treaty and most hailed the Free State campaign as a liberation. In addition the blessing provided by the hierarchy of the Catholic Church in October 1922 was welcome (even though there was some episcopal hesitation when – in December – the government began a programme of summary executions).

In general the forces of the Free State were the forces not just of the newly established order, but also of the vestigial *ancien régime*. The supporters of the Treaty

Plate 14   Michael Collins and Richard Mulcahy, *c.*1922.
Source: Public Record Office of Northern Ireland.

included the urban middle classes, the industrial working class and the larger farmers (a positive correlation has been noted between farm valuation and Free State
sympathies).[200] Protestants and ex-Unionists were also strongly in favour of the Treaty
(though there were some striking exceptions such as Erskine Childers). The career
of Bryan Ricco Cooper, a Sligo landlord, is worth mentioning, if only because it

illustrates the rather hurried political education which many southern Unionists underwent in the revolutionary era: Cooper was a Unionist MP for South County Dublin in 1910, a British military censor during the Anglo-Irish war, and an independent TD in Dáil Éireann until 1927, when he joined the Free State party, Cumann na nGaedheal.

Though, in superficial terms, so little separated the national forces and the Irregulars, and though (as Collins never forgot) many of these new enemies had so recently been united in the small but bloody war of 1919–21, there were important distinctions – as any comparison of the Free State and republican camps immediately highlights. With the republicans the military command was all-important: de Valera tried to recapture some initiative in March 1922 with the creation of a popular anti-Treaty party, the Cumann na Poblachta – but it is hard to question Michael Hopkinson's verdict that 'the period between the Treaty and the end of the Civil War represented Eamon de Valera's political nadir'.[201] The once revered national leader was treated at best off-handedly, even by his ostensible military allies: he was appointed as President and Chief Executive of the 'republic' by an Army Executive meeting, which was held on 16–17 October 1922, but this was in reality a belated and rather arbitrary military initiative. De Valera assumed a marginally greater significance in the calculations of the Irregular commanders when – in early 1923 – there were various proposals for a truce: but the suspicion, indeed contempt, with which these commanders viewed all 'politicians' may be gauged by the fact that during an Army Executive meeting in March 1923, their nominal President was initially refused admission (when he was at last granted access, it was without voting rights). After the civil war had ended, de Valera clawed back some of his former prestige within the republican movement by contriving to get himself arrested by the Free State authorities (August 1923): but the year which he spent in gaol, while it helped to restore his fame, also meant that his practical influence was still limited.

The IRA commanders who effectively controlled both the political and military aspects of the republican campaign in 1922–3 included many of the most celebrated gunmen of the former 'troubles': indeed, it is probably true that at all levels, except GHQ, the best of the fighting men reaffirmed their faith in the republic rather than in the pusillanimous alternative brokered by the faint-hearted in London. Perhaps this wealth of military talent gave rise to a certain profligacy (as evidenced in the 1916-style fascination with unlikely defensive positions and in the truly reckless bravery of men such as Brugha, killed on 5 July 1922 as he attempted to shoot his way to freedom). Perhaps, too, it was natural that the most ferocious of those who fought the British should also be those with the most imperturbable republican faith: certainly the legendary figures of the IRA in Munster – Tom Barry, Dan Breen, Liam Lynch, Ernie O'Malley – came down against the Treaty. But it was precisely the qualities of tenacity and unbending zeal which, while they had been so inspiring and awesome in 1919–21, now distanced these demigods from a war-weary and unzealously patriotic Irish public. And, though the republicans had abundant supplies of courage and talent, their opponents found compensation in a plentiful supply of weaponry (courtesy of the British), ammunition, and of recruits.

Women activists tended to be republican. Women deputies voted with de Valera in January 1922. A Cumann na mBan convention, held on 5 February 1922, over-whelmingly endorsed the anti-Treaty position (the vote was 63 for the settlement, and 419 against): indeed, it has been suggested that this rejection of the Treaty 'em-bodied some feminist understanding of its implications'.[202] But the relationship between republicanism and feminism was always complex, and in so far as the anti-Treaty line was inherited by the patriarchs of Fianna Fáil, then mainstream republicanism scarcely represented a more secure liberation for women than the Free State. In addition, not all women activists were republican: women supporters of the Treaty created their own breakaway organization, Cumann na Saoirse. However, women certainly contributed extensively to the republican cause during the civil war, as they had done in the struggle against the crown forces: 'the women were the impla-cable and irrational upholders of death and destruction' observed the choleric Free State polemicist, P.S. O'Hegarty.[203] Aside from formal military activity, a Women's Prisoners' Defence League was formed, which – driven by the unflagging energies of Hanna Sheehy Skeffington – raised money in the United States for republican internees. Women themselves were gaoled in large numbers: some 400 were confined by the Free State authorities during the civil war. These prisoners continued their campaign in the cell-blocks, and were harrying the government until the eve of the ceasefire: one of the last controversial episodes of the war was the riot in April 1923 by women republicans imprisoned in the North Dublin Union.

If there were distinctions of gender, then there were also economic distinctions between the Free Staters and republican activists. In general, as has been noted, there was a correlation between property and enthusiasm for the Treaty. There were, however, some ascendancy figures (such as Robert Barton, at any rate after second thoughts) who came to support the republican cause; and there were also – by way of contrast – some poorer elements in Irish society who were pro-Treaty, such as industrial workers who depended upon the British trade connection. It has been suggested that a good deal of residual agrarian radicalism was bound into the anti-Treaty position, and this is corroborated by the intensity of the civil war in western areas which had been in arms during the land war, but relatively quiescent during the struggle of 1919–21.[204]

Tom Garvin has defined the ideological differences between the republicans and the Free Staters in terms of the distinction between an ethnic and civic national-ism; and he has made a very persuasive case.[205] The division of 1922, he has argued, was certainly about the way in which an independent Irish republic might be attained (the difference between the deferred gratification of the Free Staters as opposed to the instant gratification demanded by republicans); but – more than this – it was about the goal of the national struggle. The division was between 'a national moral community . . . [as opposed to] a nation-state of citizens whose individual moral state was, subject to minimal legal restraints, a private rather than a public matter'.[206] Garvin has laid some emphasis upon the severe moralism of the republican cause, and indeed he has traced parallels between this and non-conformist puritanism as well as to the settler puritanism of the new colonies of the British Empire. There was also a quasi-religious content to republicanism, a reflection, perhaps, of the severe Catholicism with which many of these young men and women had been brought up: a strictly moral and mystical view of politics was often expressed in biblical language. Garvin has also noted a rise in religious vocations in 1923, a phenomenon which may simply have been a Christian reaction to troubled times, but which may also be seen as complementing the secular convictions of those married to the republic.[207]

In certain respects the bitter campaign that was fought in 1922–3 was an automatic extension of the struggle against the British. The main areas of unrest in 1919–21 – Dublin and Munster – were also focuses of the civil war, although in the latter there was conflict in western areas which had been relatively untouched by the Anglo-Irish 'troubles'. However, the initial stage of the civil war – lasting about two months – involved large-scale operations of a kind virtually unknown during 1919–21 (discounting exceptional confrontations such as at the Customs House): the Free State forces directly engaged the Irregulars in large numbers and steadily drove them from the cities and large towns. Liam Lynch, the Irregular commander in chief, hoped to be able to hold a line from Limerick to Waterford, but this idea was soon exploded as the national army advanced to the south and west: Limerick city fell to the Free State general, Eoin O'Duffy, on 21 July, while Waterford fell at around the same time to General J.T. Prout. On 8 August 1922, Cork was taken by the Free State troops under Emmet Dalton, who had briskly side-stepped the problem of outlying republican resistance by adopting the expedient of a sea-borne attack from the rear. Thereafter the war developed into the guerrilla-style conflict which had been of such central importance in 1919–21: its course followed in outline the pattern of the South African war of 1899–1902, which also began with major confrontations and ended in a diminuendo of ambushes and skirmishes.

It was here, in the protracted guerrilla phase, that the parallels with the earlier 'troubles' were perhaps more marked than before. The strategies of the Provisional Government, faced with an Irregular campaign broadly similar to that of the 'old' IRA, reacted in much the same way as the British government had done. Collins was killed in an Irregular ambush in August 1922, displaying the same reckless bravery in familiar but dangerous territory that had characterized earlier, similarly ill-fated RIC officers: his last letters record a concern for the restoration of civil government and for the seizure of republican bank assets which echo earlier British preoccupations.[208] Nor was the Provisional Government, despite its widespread popular acceptability, any more able than the British regime to cope with the challenge of insurgency within the parameters of the normal criminal law: just as the British had passed a draconian Restoration of Order in Ireland Act in 1920, instituting 'a form of statutory martial law', so too the Provisional Government was compelled, on 27 September 1922, to vote for a Special Powers resolution which granted wide discretionary authority to its military forces. As Charles Townshend has remarked, 'the sad irony by which the new state was reduced to the same political bankruptcy as the former British state in countering violent political change left an indelible mark on Irish history'.[209]

In addition the Provisional Government formulated a version of the British system of official and unofficial reprisals, and pursued (with an enhanced vigour) a policy of executions. The first of these occurred on 17 November, but it was widely suspected that this was merely a prologue to the main event – the killing of the republican Minister of Propaganda, Erskine Childers, who had been captured on 10 November: the suspicions proved correct, and Childers faced a firing squad on 24 November. The assassination by the republicans of a pro-Treaty deputy, Seán Hales, on 7 December 1922 marked the start of what was intended to be a series of revenge attacks on senior Free State ministers and TDs, orchestrated by an angry but hesitant Liam Lynch. But the response of the Provisional Government was swift and bloody: four leading republicans (Rory O'Connor, Liam Mellowes, Joe McKelvey and Dick Barrett), chosen as representatives of the four provinces, were shot on the morning following the death of Hales. It was a terrible action, which unsettled even the supporters of the Provisional Government. But as a crude deterrent, it appears to have fulfilled the cabinet's expectations: there were no further attempts to carry out Lynch's reprisals order, and in addition there is much evidence to illustrate the demoralizing effects which the deaths of these leaders had upon the broader republican struggle. In all 77 republicans were executed by the government, including some who – in a tragic irony – had slipped out of Northern Ireland, evading possible internment, only to find themselves facing a Free State firing squad in Donegal.

But, in addition to these grim but publicly acknowledged events, there ran an undercurrent of unofficial killings, which were sometimes specific acts of revenge, but occasionally reflected simply a murderous partisanship. Into this latter category fall (arguably) the Kerry killings of March 1923. Here the Free State troops, who included members of Collins's old 'Squad', were unpopular and there were allegations that republican prisoners had been tortured: on 6 March, in what the republicans claimed as an act of retaliation, five Free State soldiers were killed at Knocknagoshel by a mine explosion. The Free State commander, Paddy Daly, replied to this by ordering that republican prisoners be used to clear their own mines, and from his instruction there developed some of the most grisly killings of the war. As with many bloody encounters during the Anglo-Irish war, it may always prove impossible to disentangle conflicting accounts and perceptions – but the uncontested outlines are sombre enough. On 7 March eight republican prisoners were killed at Ballyseedy, having been tied together (it was alleged) before a nearby mine was detonated by their Free State captors. On 8 March four republican prisoners were killed in a mine explosion near Killarney. On 12 March at Cahirciveen five further prisoners died under similar circumstances (although here it was also alleged that the prisoners had first been shot).[210] The impact of these tragic episodes was reinforced by the numerous executions which the Free State military authorities carried out in this, the smouldering fag-end of the civil war.

When the determined Irregular commander Liam Lynch was killed on 10 April 1923, the end came into view: his replacement, the more pragmatic and downbeat Frank Aiken, was an architect of the ensuing ceasefire (agreed at a joint meeting of the Army Executive and the republican government on 14 May and published on

24 May). The killings continued on a sporadic basis: Noel Lemass, brother of the prominent republican and future Fianna Fáil Taoiseach, Seán, was killed in July and his body ignominiously dumped in the Wicklow mountains. One of the last of the killings related to the war, and one of the most sensational, came as late as July 1927, when Kevin O'Higgins was shot on his way to mass: O'Higgins was Vice-President of the Executive Council and was an ardent Treatyite. Yet it also seems to be the case that, despite his image as the hard man of the Cosgrave administration, he had only been reluctantly converted to some of the brutal initiatives which so angered republicans: for example, he had been hard to persuade over the execution of Barrett, McKelvey, Mellowes and O'Connor in December 1922. It also seems that his own killing was a spontaneous act of republican vengeance rather than a carefully planned assassination.

O'Higgins's death raises the broader issue of the personal, political and financial cost of the war. The total death toll still remains a matter for some conjecture. This may seem surprising, but given the chaotic condition of parts of the campaign, and given the traumatic impact of this fratricidal conflict, the uncertainty becomes more explicable: many Irish people dealt with this, as they had dealt with earlier psychological assaults, with the weapon of silence. The civil war provided a rationale for the party organization of the new state, and the loyalties that were formed and dissolved during the brief, bloody months of the conflict shaped political networks and dynamics for several generations. But though the war had a long-lasting public significance, in private – paradoxically – a silence often masked the reality of broken families and horrific bloodshed. Some calculations place the total death toll at around 4,000 or 5,000, but this has been reckoned as 'too high': nevertheless, perhaps as many as 800 Free State troops were killed, alongside much heavier republican casualties.[211] The Free State government executed 77 republicans in different locations – from County Kerry to Mountjoy Gaol, Dublin, and, in the north, Drumboe Castle, Donegal.

The personal and political impact of this slaughter is also hard to calculate. It is difficult, even, to construct a vision of Ireland making the counter-factual assumption that Collins or O'Higgins had escaped their assassins: both were very young men (Collins was 32 at the time of his death, O'Higgins died at the age of 35), and both might have developed in unexpected ways. But, broadly, the death of Collins robbed northern nationalists of their best friend in the Provisional Government, and robbed the republicans of one of their best friends in the enemy high command: his death, which occurred when he seems to have been probing the chances of a settlement, possibly made for a more protracted and bloody conflict. Certainly the Provisional Government had now both the political means and the opportunity to pursue the republicans with bloody war. The broader consequences of O'Higgins's death are equally, indeed more, elusive: it is possible that his monarchical speculations and committed stand within the structure of the Commonwealth might have created the conditions for some form of Irish unity. But this was always a long shot, and O'Higgins had little command over popular opinion. His death certainly robbed the Free State of an exciting and sophisticated political talent, which might conceivably have produced workable solutions to otherwise intractable constitutional problems. But whether the electorate would have given this talent political space is quite another matter.

The deaths of many leading republicans – from Brugha, in the early days of the war, through to Lynch, in its closing weeks – had also wider implications. As with Collins and O'Higgins, these republicans were generally young men (Erskine Childers, who was shot at the age of 52, may be regarded as the senior of these martyrs); as with Collins and O'Higgins it is difficult to be certain about future political education and development. But in general the dead included some of the most inspirational, as well as some of the most politically entrenched, of the republicans; and it seems possible that their departure, indeed the broader Irregular defeat, created more space for pragmatic lieutenants. It is certainly true that the death of (for example) Lynch created a vacuum at the head of the republican movement which only de Valera could effectively fill. Perhaps the deaths of these determined and idealistic young men, who believed that they could teach the Irish electorate but who were not prepared to be taught, helped to smooth the transition from the *ancien régime* to a settled democratic polity.

Did the civil war avert the possibility of a war of unification between North and South? It is certain, as has been mentioned, that Collins was concerned about partition and about the situation of northern Catholics caught within an, at best, unfriendly and Unionist-controlled territory. On the other hand, he and other Free State leaders also believed in the transient nature of the partition settlement, and invested their hopes in the impending Boundary Commission. In addition the certainty of massive British military action to protect the North, and the possibility of humiliating British incursions into Free State territory, may have carried weight: there were eight battalions of the British army stationed in the North at this time, and they could easily have been reinforced. The Northern Ireland government had also, by mid-1922, a formidable range of military or paramilitary resources at its own disposal: the Royal Ulster Constabulary was only 1,000 strong, but the Ulster Special Constabulary (which was based on the pre-war UVF) had around 20,000 members. The likelihood is that the diplomatic pipeline between Belfast and Dublin might have been much icier without the civil war than was actually the case; but it is equally likely that this political plumbing, though frozen, would not have actually broken.

Beyond the personal tragedies of the civil war lay an enormous material cost: indeed, for many Irish people the principal burden of the war *was* material. For many the cost was counted in terms of burned homes and businesses, stolen money and vehicles, and – in the case of a few (such as the centrist landlord and reformer, Sir Horace Plunkett) – permanent exile. It has been calculated that the war cost the Free State government £17 million, with an additional £30 million paid out in different forms of compensation.[212] But behind these bare statistics lay many personal as well as cultural and artistic tragedies: the wrecking of many architectural gems, the looting or destruction of many national treasures (most significantly, the historic archives stored in the Public Record Office). Churchill pronounced that 'the

archives of the Four Courts may be scattered, but the title deeds of Ireland are safe':
but this was the rhetoric of the politician rather than the anguish of the scholar.[213]

The new Free State therefore entered into its infancy with shattered illusions,
and a combined burden of personal tragedy as well as financial and cultural loss.
Perhaps the greatest political casualty lay with the loss of unity and confidence and
moral certainty which had characterized the national struggle against the British:
the British might be (and sometimes were) blamed for the political entanglement
that had precipitated the conflict, and they might be blamed for supplying arms,
but it was Irishmen who pulled the triggers and fired the shells. The response of
many Irish people to this trauma lay in silence (including even de Valera); and
it is only with the passing of the civil war veterans, and indeed with that of their
children, that the dead of 1922–3 have found a voice.

6

'THREE QUARTERS OF A NATION ONCE AGAIN': INDEPENDENT IRELAND

6.1 Saorstát Éireann, 1922–32

> *I turned my back*
> *On the vision I had shaped*
> *And to this road before me*
> *I turned my face*
> > Patrick Pearse, 'Renunciation'[1]

There are parallels between the dreams of legislative independence envisioned by the patriots of the early 1780s and those which comforted the separatists of the early 1920s: there are some parallels between the 18 years of Grattan's parliament and the 18-year span binding the Treaty and the outbreak of the Second World War. In each period an uncharismatic but gifted political elite sought to enact a constitutional settlement which fell short of absolute independence; in each period an elite sought to tie down constitutional ambiguities and to expand upon Ireland's legal freedoms. Ireland in the 1790s was buffeted by economic and political squalls which had their origin partly in continental Europe and in the United States; the Ireland of the late 1920s and early 1930s was challenged by political movements and economic crises which, again, had been born in Europe and North America. Much of Irish politics and society in the 1780s and 1790s had been vitally shaped by the American war of independence; much of Ireland in the 1920s and 1930s still bore the sombre imprint of the Great War. The experiment of legislative independence ended in the context of British military conquest in 1798–9 and a still unstable international arena; the fragile newly independent Irish Free State might well have ended in the military turmoil of 1939–45.

But the creators of the new Ireland, while sharing some of the limitations of the patriots of the 1780s, possessed a grander political vision. Even here, though, in the realm of political ideology, there were strong linkages, as Jeffrey Prager has skilfully argued (Prager has defined the political divisions between Free Staters and republicans in the 1920s in terms of a cultural and intellectual tension between an 'Irish-Enlightenment' tradition, rooted in the 1790s, and a 'Gaelic-Romantic' tradition of more recent vintage).[2] The state-builders of the 1920s were committed to the idea of an efficient and inclusivist parliamentary democracy, and they were prepared to face down military challenges as well as educate their 'slightly constitutional' republican opponents in pursuing this grail. If, in the context of the civil war and in the experience of other newly independent ex-colonies, this quest seemed hopelessly ambitious, then from the start the Free State ministers possessed a number of indispensable tools. They inherited from the British an administrative system which, while it was unwieldy and contained at the highest levels a disproportionate number of 'anti-national' mandarins, had also recently been overhauled (in 1920), and had been progressively expanded and popularized since the late nineteenth century. The Ministers and Secretaries Act of 1924 refined the existing structure into 11 major departments, but the overwhelming majority of civil servants were retained: more than 98 per cent of the old British administration in Ireland transferred to the service of the Irish Free State in April 1922. These administrators would become a focus of republican resentment, both for their perceived political influence as well as for their apparently cushioned lifestyle; but they provided an essential element of continuity in the transition between British and Irish rule. In addition the British bequeathed to the new regime a model of policing which, while it was modified in certain crucial and visible respects (arms, uniforms), was incorporated into the new Garda Síochána (1922): indeed, remarkably, the Dublin Metropolitan Police, which had been the popular and inefficient agency of the crown in the capital, survived until 1925, when it was amalgamated wholesale into the Gardaí. The limited nature of the Irish revolution, and the curious mixture of intimacy and antipathy which characterized the relationship between the new rulers and the departing British, meant that the Irish Free State emerged with an unusually large number of relics from the *ancien régime*.

The new governing party was Cumann na nGaedheal, formed in 1923 out of a variety of pro-Treaty forces. Even though it had sprung from a bloody civil war, Cumann na nGaedheal retained much of the mind-set of earlier, hegemonic nationalist parties, preoccupied by the Anglo-Irish relationship, sensitive about outside perceptions of the national cause, and cavalier towards local political evangelism. Its mission seemed to involve not a narrow and ruthless consolidation of its military and political victory in 1923, but rather the incorporation of a highly disparate political culture within the institutions of the new state. As will become clear, the government was prepared to sacrifice its own party interests in its attempt to construct political life on the foundations of the Treaty and the constitution of 1922. This meant wooing both the ex-Unionists of the south and west of Ireland as well as the republicans who had been pursued so mercilessly in 1922–3. On the whole Cumann na nGaedheal found it easier to appeal to the influential but unthreatening Unionist community; but by 1927 the party was also able to compel the participation of the main republican party, Fianna Fáil (1926), within the structures of the hated Free State. By this time Cumann na nGaedheal had seen off a military challenge from its own forces, resolved (in however unsatisfactory a fashion) the question of the boundary with Northern Ireland, and established the economy of the new Ireland in a sound if unimaginative fashion. But in truth these achievements were won only to be bequeathed to Fianna Fáil: it is hard to escape the impression that Cumann na nGaedheal had performed as a warm-up routine for the republicans of 1932. The state-builders of Cumann na nGaedheal offered the Irish people structures, not symbols, and an international dignity at the price of petty domestic humiliations. Cumann na nGaedheal ministers like Kevin O'Higgins would establish themselves with ease within the rarefied world of international diplomacy, while neglecting both local party organization and local sensibilities.

This strategy of incorporation began, arguably, with the former Unionists of southern Ireland. The system of proportional representation, which was bound into the Irish Free State constitution of 1922, was designed in part to ensure some voice in the Dáil for the scattered ex-Unionists of the new polity. In addition the new upper house of the parliament, the Seánad, or Senate, provided balm for the comfort of the ex-Unionists: Unionist hopes of guaranteed representation within the house, as well as a power of veto over Dáil legislation, were swiftly broken, but there was some recognition of their case. As a temporary placatory measure 30 out of a total of 60 senators were to be appointed by the President of the Executive Council 'with special regard to the providing of representation for groups or parties not then adequately represented in Dáil Éireann', and William Cosgrave proceeded to appoint 16 former Unionists of different descriptions.[3] The first chairman of the Senate was Lord Glenavy, a former lieutenant to Carson and one of the most prodigious supplicants for patronage in the history of the Unionist movement: his son, Gordon Campbell, also emerged as a prominent supporter of the new Free State administration, and indeed held the critical appointment of secretary to the department of industry and commerce. Generally, the 'troubles' of 1919–21 and the civil war wrought havoc especially within the vulnerable Unionist communities of southern Ulster and south Munster, where there were numerous killings and expropriations: there was a significant decline in the southern Protestant population, which occurred between the censuses of 1911 and 1926 – not all of which can be accounted for by the Great War. But for those who emerged, dazed, into the relatively more settled conditions of the mid-1920s, the Irish Free State offered a home: a home where there were some restrictions and some threats, where some territory was out of bounds, but a home nonetheless.

The Cumann na nGaedheal government had won the tentative loyalty of the ex-Unionists, first to the new dispensation, and eventually to the party itself: after 1927 a number of prominent ex-Unionist figures (the Dockrells, Bryan Ricco Cooper, the Jamesons) identified themselves with the Cosgrave administration. This was a not unmixed blessing for the government. On the one hand, the adherence of Unionist capital and Unionist votes represented a welcome addition of strength as well as a tentative but vital step towards new forms of political dialogue, and away from the essentially sectarian politics of the Home Rule era; on the other hand, the resonant unpopularity of Unionism within the Irish Free State meant that republicans could argue convincingly that Cumann na nGaedheal was the tool of 'imperialists' and 'freemasons'. Not the least of the Cosgrave government's achievements in state-building was its willingness – without unduly compromising its commitment to popular sovereignty – to ride out this challenge and to seek the incorporation of former enemies not just within nationalism, but beyond as well.

The assimilation of the ex-Unionists was important in terms of political symbolism as well as in some practical, but undramatic, ways. Winning the adherence of the army to the civil authorities of the Free State was a much more treacherous undertaking, and one which threatened to overturn the constitution itself. The National Army had a strength in June 1923 of almost 50,000, representing both an enormous burden on the finances of the new state as well as a potential challenge to civil government. Although it might have been expected that victory in the civil war would have unified and elated the army, in reality its condition was more problematic. There were tensions between the IRB-dominated (and pro-Treaty) Army Council and other senior elements within the officer cadre; and there were also tensions between those who had served in the British army – generally First World War veterans – and those soldiers whose patriotism was apparently less sullied (a record of service to the crown was generally a source of suspicion in the spy-obsessed, conspiratorially minded Ireland of the early 1920s). In addition the army, having successfully fulfilled its purpose, was to be reduced to a strength of around 35,000; and on 2 November 1923 another series of cuts was announced, designed to bring numbers down further, to around 20,000.

Tensions had been evident from late 1922, when several of the veterans from Michael Collins's 'Squad' established a ginger group, the Irish Republican Army Organization (IRAO), within the ranks of the National Army. The IRAO saw themselves as the particular military guardians of Collins's legacy, and indeed in June 1923, just after the republicans had 'dumped' their weapons, the organization formally petitioned the government to make 'a genuine effort . . . to keep absolutely to the forefront the ideals and objects for which the late commander-in-chief [Collins] gave his life'.[4] In reality, as Ronan Fanning has argued, the issues related not just to grand questions of strategy or to the memory of the fallen hero, but also to sectional jealousies and personal concerns among the petitioning officers.[5] As the pressure of the demobilization intensified and caught up with the officers of the IRAO, so their desperation, or boldness, grew; and on 6 March 1924 the ringleaders – General Liam Tobin and Colonel Charlie Dalton – demanded an end to the lay-offs as well as the sacking of the Army Council as a precondition for talks with the government on the future of the Treaty settlement. This was accompanied by reports of acts of mutiny in different army barracks, and of the theft of weapons from military stores. On 18 March the leaders of this incipient mutiny gathered at Devlin's Hotel in Rutland Street, Dublin; but the army command, true at least to Collins's faith in intelligence work, tapped a telephone exchange, discovered the details of the conspiracy and was able to suppress it with little difficulty.

The fall-out from this complex and resonant episode highlights the inter-twining of several issues. The mutineers were defying the authority of the government, but so, too, were the officers who had suppressed the revolt: the military action of 18 March took place without any authorization from Mulcahy or any of his ministerial colleagues, and indeed it ran counter to a deal which the government had earlier struck with the mutineers, granting them until 20 March to surrender. The casualties from the episode, therefore, included both mutineers as well as over-zealous government loyalists: Mulcahy, as responsible minister, resigned, along with the three senior army officers who comprised the Council of Defence. The Minister for Industry and Commerce, Joe McGrath, who had been the mutineers' single ally on the Executive Council, had resigned as early as 7 March. In total almost 100 officers, mostly holding the rank of captain or commandant, lost their commissions as a consequence of the affair. But the government, and principally the ruthless and brilliant Kevin O'Higgins, had demonstrated a breathtaking confidence in enforcing the principles of democratic civilian government: it had, after all, disciplined the very officers who – acting on their own initiative – had been defending its immediate interests (this masochistic regard for political principle was the defining feature of the Cumann na nGaedheal record). There were other benefits from the episode: as Prager has argued, 'the mutiny illustrated the remarkable increase in the strength of the parliamentary structures and in the government's ability to respond to political challenge'.[6] Not that there can have been much doubt after the civil war – but it was also the case that the government's actions in 1924 underlined its unyielding commitment to the construction of a democratic state. Indeed here, as with so much else of the Cumann na nGaedheal record, it was patently clear that some of the Free State ministers were at least as steely in their idealism as the most unyielding of their republican opponents.

It has been argued that the Cumann na nGaedheal government was distinguished more by its regard for democratic structures than for popular symbols; it has been argued, too, that its 'last major effort to develop a symbolically significant political program' lay with its investment in the Boundary Commission of 1924–5.[7] The northern policy of Sinn Féin and of Cumann na nGaedheal had been riddled with paradoxes from the start, and the symbols and structures which the parties generated were utterly at variance. Sinn Féin had emphasized the essential integrity of the Irish nation, yet in September 1920 had instituted a boycott of Belfast industry and commerce as an act of solidarity with the beleaguered Catholics of the North. Michael Collins had deployed the IRA in the North in 1922 with a view to protecting Catholic interests and destabilizing the Unionist state: for Collins and for later Sinn Féin and Cumann na nGaedheal leaders, 'our people' were, in a northern context, the nationalist people, while the Unionists were – in private and in practice, if not in separatist theology – the defining 'others'. The civil war and the death of Collins had undermined the northern IRA offensive and had given rise to a more pacific and gradualist approach to reunification, outlined first by Ernest Blythe in August 1922. But, despite Blythe's insistence that even economic sanctions might prove counter-productive, pin-pricking assaults on partition and on the Belfast

government continued: in April 1923, remarkably, the Free State authorities established a chain of customs posts along the boundary with Northern Ireland, thereby
– as Ronan Fanning has observed – 'giving it a permanence and physical appearance it had not had previously'.[8] Free State policy towards Northern Ireland was
thus a self-defeating mixture of consensual rhetoric, petty coercion and an increasingly passive sympathy with Ulster Catholics: the symbolism suggested a commitment to an inclusivist unitary state, but the programme of action riled northern
Unionists without bringing much benefit to northern nationalists. But perhaps the
supreme paradox of the reunification strategy was that Dublin sought an end to
partition through consolidating the structures and attitudes that maintained it. When
– as in early 1922 – the Belfast government was politically vulnerable and open to
moderate concession on the constitutional question, the Dublin ministry, sensing
blood, ruthlessly applied the principle of northern subordination to any cross-
border deal. When – in early 1923 – the northern government was economically
vulnerable, the Dublin ministry sought to reinforce the economic divide between
the two territories. Reunification was admittedly never likely in the early 1920s: but
there were certainly junctures when perhaps critical cross-border institutions
might have been put in place. These passed unattended, partly because of the Free
State government's untenable claims of absolute supremacy over its northern
counterpart. Cumann na nGaedheal's unconvincing efforts to incorporate northern Protestants failed, therefore, because the price of this incorporation might well
have racked the southern state, and partly because these northern Protestants were
not, and never had been, central to the vision of Ireland embraced either by the
party or by its republican opponents.

By 1925 this position had been reluctantly abandoned, but by then partition had
been consolidated and the political and financial position of the Belfast government
was comparatively strong. If the Anglo-Irish Treaty was the central tenet of the
Cumann na nGaedheal political creed, then article 12 – which made provision for
a Boundary Commission – was central to their stand on the partition question and
reunification. This, combined with a variety of other pressures, may explain the
party's initial reluctance to explore other more effective, if also more circuitous, routes
around the border issue. Cumann na nGaedheal had fought a civil war in defence
of the letter of the Treaty, and the party leadership continued – even after May 1923
– to be harassed by a strong republican movement in the country as well as by those
pro-Treatyites who, like Collins, had some sympathy with the republican aspiration.
Just as the party adhered to the other articles of the Treaty, so it would not be lured
away from its commitment to a Boundary Commission as a vehicle for progress
towards reunification: for example, a British initiative in February 1924, which proposed limited ministerial and parliamentary cooperation between Belfast and Dublin
for a prescribed period, met with a swift rejection and renewed calls for the establishment of the commission. But, as is well known, the Boundary Commission –
when it came – proved in many ways less satisfactory than some of the deals that
had been put on the table by London ministers – and even, remarkably, by Belfast –
earlier, between 1922 and 1924 (the Belfast view of the Commission is reconstructed

later in the book). The Commission, chaired by a South African judge, Richard Feetham, and manned by Eoin MacNeill (for the Free State) and by J.R. Fisher (coopted by the British on behalf of the truculent Belfast administration), produced a plan which, when leaked to the press in November 1925, caused outrage in Dublin. For the deeply grounded nationalist expectation that any boundary revision would apply a mortal wound to Northern Ireland was exposed (as some in Dublin had suspected all along) as a fantasy: indeed, not only was it clear that Northern Ireland would emerge largely undiminished, it was also likely that there would be a minor exchange of border areas in which the Free State would unquestionably come off best – but which would also involve the cession of southern territory to Belfast. In the event the Commission was not given time to deliver a formal report: MacNeill, the embarrassed southern representative, resigned, and his former colleagues hurried to strike a deal with the British and with the Ulster Unionists on the basis of the suppression of the draft report. The Irish border was left untouched and the British (as usual) showed themselves to be happy to pay for the temporary, if strategic, amity between Belfast and Dublin: the authority of the Northern Ireland government was enhanced by a minor revision of the Government of Ireland Act, and the Irish Free State's liability for a portion of the United Kingdom war debt – a liability confirmed by the treaty of 1921 – was waived. Each of these concessions in fact underlined the vitality of partition rather than the reverse; and, indeed, this was entirely appropriate, for, whatever the rhetoric, the effective actions of both the northern *and* the southern government had been tending in this direction.

It has been argued that the Boundary Commission debacle left the Cumann na nGaedheal government 'symbolically bankrupt'.[9] Certainly, the central potent, if uninspiring, symbol of the party – the Treaty – was further diminished. Indeed, the failure of the Boundary Commission was a failure for the Treaty settlement, and it was a humiliation for those who, like Collins, believed that the Treaty had brought 'the freedom' to achieve more: this was the first great test of the Treaty as a vehicle for national aspirations, and it was an embarrassing failure. In terms of popular symbolism, the government was therefore left denuded. In practical terms, there was much dissension within the ranks of Cumann na nGaedheal: three deputies broke away from the party to form their own grouping, Clann Éireann, a parliamentary mutiny which, in the wake of the Army Mutiny of the previous year, the government could ill afford. But in truth the short-term fall-out might have been much worse. The government had handled with skill the political dimensions of the crisis of November–December 1925, limiting the damage by swift action and by levering minor but useful concessions from the British. The desertion of the deputies might also have been much more problematic, had it not been for the fact that the main parliamentary opposition to the government – supplied by Sinn Féin – was still adhering to its policy of abstentionism. Indeed, the debacle coincided with a mounting schism within the ranks of Sinn Féin – a split which came to a head in May 1926, when Eamon de Valera and his revisionist supporters left the party to form Fianna Fáil: this meant that the government was spared some of the extra-parliamentary difficulties which the suppression of the Commission might well have created. At the same time, however, there could be no mistaking that partition had been anything other than entrenched; nor – from the perspective of late 1925 – did it seem that 'the freedom to achieve freedom' was other than a euphemism for a divided nation and the shackles of imperial power.

It was not that Cumann na nGaedheal failed to make the Treaty work in terms of the consolidation of Irish sovereignty. On the contrary, Free State ministers, in particular O'Higgins, were able with the support of other Commonwealth countries, notably South Africa and Canada, to elaborate the dominion status that had been granted in 1921: at the Imperial Conference of 1926 O'Higgins worked with the Canadians and South Africans to establish the co-equality of the dominions with Great Britain; and in 1931, with the Statute of Westminster (where again Irish influence was evident) the legislative authority of the British parliament over the dominions was effectively abolished. Equally, the Treaty was tested and arguably extended through the independent foreign policy of the Free State, and the establishment of missions at Washington in 1924 (where Timothy Smiddy was minister), and – in 1929 – at Paris and Berlin (a brilliant young lawyer and Celticist, Daniel Binchy, was appointed at the age of 29 as the first Irish minister to Germany). But, impressive though these diplomatic triumphs were, they did not permit the Cumann na nGaedheal ministers to claim the high ground of nationalist morality and integrity. On the contrary, the crowning glory of the party's diplomatic offensive within the Commonwealth – the Statute of Westminster – came too late, and was in any case an insufficiently dramatic national achievement to be of any electoral use. This apparently legalistic victory paled beside the ongoing humiliation of partition: it provided a somewhat shrill battle-cry when compared with the republican credentials trumpeted by the new Fianna Fáil.

Nevertheless, Cumann na nGaedheal's true failure was not so much that it did not play the green ace as that it held aloof from the electoral card school. A good case has been made by Richard Dunphy for believing that the party's failure extended far beyond its perceived loss of nationalist initiative to Fianna Fáil.[10] Cumann na nGaedheal had won widespread, if sometimes grudging, loyalty to the institutions of the new state, and had concentrated on developing these institutions; but it had scarcely bothered to stimulate any more narrow, partisan loyalty. In other words, and paradoxically, the party had successfully attained its grail, but had failed utterly to stimulate any excitement for the missionary quest.

Part of the reason for this failure was that the party had no exclusive constituency, and, furthermore, never felt the need to acquire any. Cumann na nGaedheal was the party of law and order, and it was associated with the classes who depended upon law and order: the large farmers, major commercial and professional interests. In addition, it was the party that seemed most capable of sustaining good relations with the British: it therefore could appeal to ex-Unionist sentiment as well as to the interests of those who profited from commercial ties with Britain. But, taken together, these groups scarcely constituted a popular constituency, and indeed, as the issues that had recruited a majority for the Treaty in 1922–3 fell into the background, so too the strength of Cumann na nGaedheal dissolved. Even in 1923, in the immediate aftermath of the civil war, there had been a strong republican vote (anti-Treaty Sinn Féin won 44 seats to Cumann na nGaedheal's 63), and in June 1927 the infant Fianna Fáil, which proclaimed itself as 'the republican party', came within three seats (with 44 deputies) of the Cumann na nGaedheal total (47). The assassination of Kevin O'Higgins in July 1927 permitted his party to consolidate some of its support on the basis of the law and order question; but, even then, when a second general election was held in that year, in September, Cumann na nGaedheal emerged with a lead of only 10 seats over Fianna Fáil (67 as opposed to 57 for 'the republican party').

It was not just that Fianna Fáil was able to tap an electoral core which was unreconciled to the Free State: it was rather that the party was able to reconstruct the political chemistry of Parnellism by combining nationalist fundamentalism with a carefully tailored social and economic appeal. Cumann na nGaedheal, by contrast, was almost Redmondite in terms of its apparent tolerance of the vestigial British connection, its uncharismatic political loftiness, and its distance from crucial sections of the Irish electorate. The force of this distinction may easily be demonstrated by turning to the social and economic programmes of the two parties. Cumann na nGaedheal's economic policy has often been noted for its lack of adventure – but of course this was scarcely surprising, given that these 'most conservative revolutionaries' (in O'Higgins's famous description) were anxious to avoid dangerous experiments which might jeopardize the stability and the international credit of the new state.[11] Three key committees of inquiry determined the broad outlines of the party's economic strategy – those examining fiscal policy (1923), agriculture (1924) and banking (1927) – and, as Mary Daly has noted, their reports upheld the status quo: 'Ireland would maintain financial links with sterling, produce food for Britain, and retain a free-trade industrial sector'.[12] The government remained strongly committed to the grazier interest and to the cattle trade, and it did little to aid industrial development – except indirectly through its programme of electrification (the Shannon hydro-electric scheme was begun in 1925 and led to the establishment of the Electricity Supply Board in 1927). The Hogan Land Act of 1923, which was amended in 1925, finished off the work of the earlier British land purchase measures by transferring the remaining property in landlords' hands to the possession of the tenant farmers. The Agricultural Credit Act of 1927 was designed to offer a degree of protection to indebted farmers, and came six years in advance of Fianna Fáil's parallel Industrial Credit Company (of 1933). All in all, however, the government had little appeal for the small producers of the country, whether agricultural or industrial. It wooed the middle classes by lowering personal taxation, but offset some of the electoral utility of this device by pruning the salaries of those in the public service. It offered little to the urban and rural labouring classes, except lower wages and an impecunious old age: its policies did nothing to encourage labour-intensive tillage farming or industrial employment, while – in one of the most notorious penny-pinching exercises of the era – it reduced old age pensions by 10 per cent.

Fianna Fáil not only benefited from this electoral wrist-slashing, it was rescued from its own suicidal abstentionist politics through the actions of the Cumann na nGaedheal government. Fianna Fáil was prepared to participate in the institutions of the Free State (this had precipitated the original split with Sinn Féin in 1925–6), but only on the (for Cumann na nGaedheal) impossible condition that a central feature of the Treaty settlement, the oath of allegiance, be removed. However, the assassination of O'Higgins stimulated the government into introducing an Electoral Amendment Bill in July 1927, which demanded that all candidates for the Dáil pledge their willingness, if elected, to take the oath of allegiance to the Free State con-stitution and the British crown. This has been widely seen as an act of political self-sacrifice in the interests of the democratic political culture of the newly inde-pendent state ('the decision by Cumann na nGaedheal leaders to sacrifice their own popularity for democratic order probably knows few parallels in other nations'): it certainly had the effect of compelling the Fianna Fáil deputies, albeit with much begrudgery and equivocation, to enter the Dáil after the general election of September 1927.[13]

The Electoral Amendment initiative has been seen as an act of political suicide by the Treatyites, partly because of the popular nationalist credentials of Fianna Fáil, but also because the party had constructed both an organization and a socio-economic programme designed for mass appeal. The party was able to attract republicans who were disillusioned with the dead-end politics of Sinn Féin: it built swiftly and securely upon the foundations of the 'troubles', exploiting the charisma of local IRA heroes, tapping into the networks of republican ex-prisoners and com-mandeering the loyalties of those who had sworn their allegiance to the republic. Fianna Fáil was therefore from the start symbolically charged as well as highly disciplined, combining republican mystique as well as a military formality: 'organ-isational success was immediate and impressive', with by 1927 a local base of 1,000 cumainn and an effective propagandist weekly, the *Nation* (a title which in itself evoked the heady idealism of Young Ireland, and the contrast with the sullied and worldly O'Connellite movement).[14]

But Fianna Fáil was much more than a republican veterans' organization. Repub-licans were certainly a core constituency, but – unlike Cumann na nGaedheal – the party was able to remain loyal to its civil war origins, while simultaneously tran-scending them. For Fianna Fáil developed a broad social as well as symbolic appeal which (not unlike the Conservative hegemony in Britain from 1979 to 1997) brought an electoral ascendancy in the 1930s and 1940s and ensured that the party has for long remained the largest and most formidable political 'movement' in Ireland. Fianna Fáil appeared at the start to be sensitive to the needs of women: its first executive (in 1926–7) included Kathleen Clarke, Linda Kearns, Dorothy Macardle, Constance Markievicz, Margaret Pearse and Hanna Sheehy Skeffington. Seán Lemass, one of the party's founders, appeared to be particularly supportive, combining an appreciation of the role and the political potential of women with an admiration for leading women republicans such as Markievicz. If these appearances very quickly proved to be deceptive (Lemass would soon emerge as the author of the hated

Conditions of Employment Act), then at least Fianna Fáil momentarily put up a front – in contradistinction to the patriarchs of Cumann na nGaedheal.

Fianna Fáil was the party of the small producer, promising tariff protection to nascent industry as well as action on the land annuities question for the small farmers: Cumann na nGaedheal, by contrast, appeared to favour the small export-oriented and (in Fianna Fáil eyes) pro-British classes, as well as the grazier interests. Fianna Fáil promised jobs and a cure to emigration; Cumann na nGaedheal presided over high unemployment and the leeching away of the country's population. Fianna Fáil conjured up a vision of an over-powerful and overfed bureaucratic elite, which it promised to cull; Cumann na Gaedheal by contrast seemed to be the mouthpiece for insensitive, even anti-national civil servants, and to be simultaneously oppressing the poorest beneficiaries of state support. Without being socialist, Fianna Fáil ate into the support of the Labour Party; without being violently republican, the party provided an alternative to the IRA regrouping of the later 1920s. Without being markedly more Catholic than Cumann na nGaedheal, the party was able by the early 1930s to credibly defend Catholic sectarian interests; without being strong on law and order, the party was able to pose as a force for stability in Irish society. In other words, by 1932 Fianna Fáil was offering something to workers and to capitalists, to small farmers and to the urban petite bourgeoisie. It had reinvented the republican tradition as both a superior and an accessible caste among the untouchables of the Free State.

While Fianna Fáil focused obsessively on electoral domination, Cumann na nGaedheal pursued an equally unyielding commitment to the consolidation of the state, and indeed the nation: the two processes – Fianna Fáil's partisan successes and Cumann na nGaedheal's national achievement – were of course intimately connected, and indeed some final observations need to be directed towards this paradoxical relationship. Like many recent US Presidents, Cumann na nGaedheal had sought to compensate for domestic failure or, at best, blandness with international success and spectacle. But the party's tragedy was that its long-term investment in foreign and commonwealth relations only really bore marketable fruit when it was too late: the Statute of Westminster, the product of years of work within the imperial conference circuit, came only in 1931; while the close Irish association with the League of Nations blossomed fully only in 1932, just in time for Eamon de Valera to take on the Presidency of the Council of the League. In addition the party had done nothing to disconnect the fate of the Irish economy from that of the British; and, when the American and British economies went into free-fall after 1929, so the Irish followed. It is of course difficult to see how the Cumann na nGaedheal government could have fully insulated the Irish economy from the general downturn of the late 1920s; but it is unquestionably true that Fianna Fáil's economic nationalism – its protectionist ideas as well as its pump-priming and other interventionist proposals – presented a favourable contrast to Cumann na nGaedheal's defeatist austerity.

Cumann na nGaedheal had established the credibility of the new Irish state within the international community and had defined its financial probity in terms that were appreciated both by local business interests and by the British. But the price for this exercise in statecraft – the price of applause in London and Geneva – was the electoral disillusionment of those teachers, gardaí and taxpayers whose incomes were cut through the supplementary budget of 1931, as well as the disillusionment of those smallholders who saw their land annuity payments drain out of the country at a time of mounting economic difficulty. There were other areas where this tension between state-craft and partisanship was all too painfully evident. Cumann na nGaedheal was strongly associated with the Catholic Church, and Cosgrave in particular was a highly devout man who was strongly influenced by the hierarchy in all matters touching public morality: in 1923 the Church had in effect dictated the policy of the government with regard to the sensitive issue of divorce. Clearly this influence had a bearing on sectarian relations within the state; but, while leading Protestant intellectuals (such as Yeats) decried what they saw as clericalism, most Protestants in the south of Ireland probably thought little differently about the issues of divorce and contraception and censorship to the majority of their Catholic compatriots. What has been described as the Catholic triumphalism of the new state was therefore possibly much less important for southern Protestants than the recognition of their interests through the Senate and through the presence of the Ulster Protestant, Ernest Blythe (from Lisburn, County Antrim), in the Executive Council (indeed, the symbolic significance of Blythe's ascent to the Vice-Presidency of the Council in 1927 is easily overlooked). Without compromising its Catholic orthodoxy or integrity, the government made a number of limited but – in electoral terms – expensive gestures towards the southern minority which helped to reconcile these (for the most part) ex-Unionists. Indeed, it is scarcely an exaggeration to suggest that Cumann na nGaedheal was expanding the traditional definition of the Irish nation by winning the allegiance of these former opponents.

Equally, such gestures of reconciliation created opportunities for the government's ambitious electoral rival. As the economic climate worsened, so the almost traditional sectarian bitterness within the area of local government patronage intensified. Some ultra-Catholics renewed their opposition to the appointment of Protestants as dispensary doctors (this was a suppurating issue which dated back at least to the mid-Edwardian era). But it was the case of Letitia Dunbar-Harrison which focused sectarian passions and which proved the greatest test of the Cumann na nGaedheal government's resolve to defend its national achievement. Dunbar-Harrison was sufficiently gifted to win in 1930 an open competition for the post of county librarian in Mayo: she was also a Protestant, a Trinity graduate and anglophone. The library committee of Mayo county council, backed by the council itself, refused to confirm the appointment; and they were supported by the local Catholic clergy and by Fianna Fáil. There was little electoral mileage for Cumann na nGaedheal in championing Dunbar-Harrison against such a formidable local coalition; but the government recognized that, for the southern minority as well as for international opinion, the integrity of its commitment to an inclusivist state was under trial. It therefore resisted the opposition, dissolved the county council and maintained Dunbar-Harrison in post. Cumann na nGaedheal had held on to the moral high ground (if the morality of the case is to be judged in terms of a meritocratic appointments policy); but while it preserved its integrity, Fianna Fáil garnered the votes.

In another, final key area the government's determination to guard and consolidate the state proved to be electorally counter-productive, and indeed very nearly self-defeating. One of Cumann na nGaedheal's chief claims on the electorate was its record in having established law and order within the Irish Free State after the turmoil of the revolutionary era. But this record came under threat between 1929 and 1931 with an escalation of IRA violence, and the launching in 1931 of Saor Éire, a leftist (or, in the Department of Justice's judgement, 'frankly communistic') political initiative emanating from the IRA army convention.[15] The 'communistic' aspirations of the IRA aside, there were ominous echoes of the struggle against the British: two men were shot as 'spies', one of whom was killed; a Garda barracks in County Galway was bombed (a – for the South – late example of a republican tradition dating back to 1867), and detectives as well as uniformed gardaí were denounced as 'social pariahs' (in a manner reminiscent of the verbal attacks on RIC men). The government responded with the Constitution (Amendment No. 17) Bill, a measure which has been deemed, with some justification, to be 'really a Public Safety Bill of a most ferocious kind': the measure banned 12 organizations, including the IRA and Saor Éire, and it instituted military tribunals in order to circumvent the intimidation of jurors and witnesses (a state witness had been killed by the IRA in February 1929).[16] For the government, nearing the end of its term of office, the emergence of what it deemed a 'red scare' might well have proved to be an electoral blessing in its campaign to ward off the challenge from Fianna Fáil. But in reality the new military tribunals were widely condemned; and the prosecution of the Fianna Fáil organ, the *Irish Press*, backfired, serving only to highlight the government's apparent heavy-handedness and its opponents' case.

Fianna Fáil's line was – by way of contrast – both electorally more shrewd as well as apparently more compassionate. In the highly schizoid political culture which was common to both parts of Ireland, it was possible for voters to – as Jeffrey Prager has remarked – 'culturally applaud' militant republicanism, while withholding electoral support.[17] Fianna Fáil, through its still active, if discreet, links with militant republicanism, was able to associate itself with the ideals and motivations of the 'green' left, while avoiding any more damaging connection. The party was therefore able to exploit the popular understanding or tacit approval of radical republican activity, while publicly distancing itself from violence and from the sins of 'Bolshevism'. Once again, the Cumann na nGaedheal government lacked this potent symbolism; and even though it argued that it was defending the achievements of independence (and indeed saw itself in this light), ministers offered nothing of more immediate relevance to Irish voters. The election of February 1932 was fought by the government with the weapon of a red conspiracy; but Fianna Fáil replied by conjuring up an unholy trinity of Cumann na nGaedheal, Unionism and freemasonry. These were more familiar and more potent demons; and it was therefore the 'orange scare' rather than the 'red scare' which seems to have had the greatest electoral force. But above all, of course, Fianna Fáil provided more than spectral threats: it offered a skilfully tailored and apposite social programme to which the government had no effective response. And on 16 February 1932, with the end of the campaign, Fianna Fáil's choice of lures as well as threats was thoroughly vindicated.

6.2   Manifest Destiny: De Valera's Ireland, 1932–48

With the change of government in 1932 came a change not merely of party, but also of style and of substance. The workaday offerings and aspirations of Cumann na nGaedheal were dispelled, to be replaced by the republican mystique of Fianna Fáil and the quirky charisma of its leader, Eamon de Valera. De Valera was Parnell to Cosgrave's Justin McCarthy, a 'chief' rather than a 'chairman'. Indeed, Tim Pat Coogan has recorded that in later years, as President of Ireland, de Valera graciously absolved an intimate official from the need to append 'Your excellency' to every sentence of conversation: 'you need just call me Chief'.[18] This self-appointed guardian of the national conscience was deemed (by T.K. Whitaker, no less) not to be Irish 'in his manner': he could exercise a frosty charm, and seems to have relented a

Plate 15   Eamon de Valera.
Source: Hulton Getty.

little in conversing in Irish or with scientific or scholarly acquaintances. But on the whole his intensity of purpose, both personal and political, combined with a highly calculating intelligence to create a rather formidable personality. This was bolstered both by his political and military *cursus honorum* (he was the senior surviving officer of the Easter Rising, and Pearse's direct successor as President of the Republic), and indeed by the quiet passion of his religious faith: Maurice Moynihan, the long-time secretary to the government, described 'his thought as being primarily political and Catholic'.[19] Even in the early 1930s the new President of the Executive Council had a sure sense of his own dignity and destiny, and seems to have actively cultivated the veneration surrounding him. His penchant for dramatic clothing – black cloaks and wide-brimmed hats – emphasized a slight but useful detachment from ordinary Irish people. His speaking voice, never mellifluous, had an almost oracular quality: Liam Skinner, writing in 1946, drew a pointed contrast between the public utterances of the latterday 'Chief' and the 'high-sounding words and gripping phrases cultivated by the old Irish Parliamentary Party'.[20] For Skinner, too, the Chief's charisma was reinforced by his mixture of asceticism and high-voltage intellectual attainments: de Valera sacrificed himself for his people as their leader, and when he had had time to spare – largely, evidently, during his earlier periods in gaol – 'Einstein became his companion, and an occasional game of chess with jailers and comrades his relaxation'.[21] Indeed, de Valera's knowledge of relativity became one of the defining features of his apparent intellectual ascendancy: his son would boast that the great physicist himself had declared that 'Dev' was one of only nine people in the world who had a thorough grasp of the theory.[22] Such was the stuff of the legend: it is hard to imagine a similar claim being made for Cosgrave, and harder still to imagine his son, the laconic Liam Cosgrave, making the attempt.

It is easy to highlight the technical political skills both of de Valera and his party; and it is dangerously easy to highlight their constitutional agenda to the detriment of other issues. The ambience of the Fianna Fáil movement was certainly rife with civil war passions and a defensive national pride; the movement was also unusually authoritarian, and ridden with clientilism. However, the party had a social conscience, and – even though its relationship with the Church was always complex – it had a commitment to holy charity and some interest in the corporatist thought fashionable among Catholic political ideologues in the 1930s. It has been argued with justice that 'possibly no aspect of Fianna Fáil's programme explains the breadth and solidarity of the party's popular support better than the social welfare reforms which it introduced when first in office' – even though these tend to be overshadowed by de Valera's apparently all-consuming passion for national sovereignty.[23] The first Fianna Fáil budget, outlined in May 1932, raised spending on welfare, bringing a greater investment in housing, unemployment benefit and old age pensions: an additional 250,000 pounds was allocated to the elderly during the first Fianna Fáil cabinet, a sum which outraged the Department of Finance and which would have scarified the Cumann na nGaedheal ministers. A large-scale building and slum-clearance programme brought the construction or renovation of 132,000 homes in the first ten years of Fianna Fáil power. The sustained nature of this investment indicates the long-term nature of the party's commitment: this was not a welfarism which waxed and waned according to the electoral calendar.

Fianna Fáil had been returned to power in 1932, dependent upon the votes of Labour Party deputies; and it was undoubtedly the case that Labour priced its support in terms of welfare expansion. But Fianna Fáil was reelected in January 1933, this time with a majority of one over a combination of all the other Dáil parties. The votes of Labour deputies were unquestionably useful for the government, yet it was also true that the programme of welfare reform often had little connection with Labour pressure and, indeed, came to be an electoral embarrassment for them (in so far as Fianna Fáil appeared to have all the ideas). For Fianna Fáil had stolen the Labour Party's agenda, expanding the application of unemployment assistance through a measure of 1933, legislating for workmen's compensation in 1934 and for widows' and orphans' pensions in 1935 (a measure which, according to Seán T. O'Kelly, had no more to do with Labour 'than the King of Bulgaria').[24] Seán Lemass, the exciting and unconventional Minister for Industry and Commerce, sponsored a Conditions of Employment Act in 1936, a sweeping measure which affected working hours, holidays, rest rooms within the work-place, and which regulated areas of abuse such as piecework and the employment of young people or children: it was also, however, a measure which reflected widespread concern at the high level of male unemployment and which (under its controversial section 16) empowered the government to regulate the number of women working within industry. Lemass enacted a Shops Bill, designed to improve the often Victorian working terms and conditions of the army of shop workers. A Wages Board, a blasphemy in the eyes of the liberal economists of Finance and the new Fine Gael party (1933), was established in 1938.

It would of course be wrong to infer from these initiatives that the Ireland of the 1930s was a veritable workers' paradise, or that Fianna Fáil was simply the Irish for socialism. On the contrary, if the party was concerned about the living and working conditions of the poor, and if – in the assessment of Richard Dunphy – it thereby created an army of dependent supporters, then it was also acutely concerned about the health of the native capitalist class – and this, allied with the party's national pride, fed a protectionist zeal and brought high prices and comparatively modest increases in the standard of living.[25] There was always an underlying ideological spin to economic planning (for Fianna Fáil, to paraphrase Horace Plunkett, political economy was always spelt with a capital 'p' and a small 'e'): but the ideological priorities (despite the later ruminations of senior Fianna Fáil ministers) were not socialist. A combination of the great depression, which was hitting both Britain and Ireland severely by the early 1930s, as well as an ideological inheritance from Griffith and from the early Sinn Féin movement, led Fianna Fáil to what has been called its protectionist 'spree' during its first years in power. As with so much else of the Fianna Fáil record, its 'spree' was in fact made possible by structures established under Cumann na nGaedheal, and indeed the new government has been seen (by John Horgan) as inaugurating 'more a change of pace than a change of policy': in 1931 the Cosgrave government had passed the Customs Duties (Provisional

ᵗ, which enabled it to impose emergency import tariffs.[26] But the
﹍₅ used only once by Cosgrave, and in total, in 1931, only 68 articles
﹍₄ble to import tariffs. By 1937, after five years of Fianna Fáil government,
﹍ᵢₑ tariff net had been widened to take in 288 articles, with just under 2,000 other
articles being restricted through the application of a quota system. Some types of
import were completely banned. In addition, Control of Manufactures legislation
was passed in 1932 and 1934 to prevent non-Irish companies cutting through
this protectionist trap by disguising their control of Irish businesses. By 1936 the
average level of impost was 35 per cent, as compared with the level of 9 per cent
sustained in 1931 under the departing Cumann na nGaedheal administration.

There were some positive features of this strategy, both in terms of the growth
of the heavily protected Irish industries and with regard to what Mary Daly,
writing in the early 1990s, has called 'the first sustained growth in industrial
employment for a century at a rate not yet surpassed'.[27] Moreover, there was an efflorescence of the semi-state (or what Lemass preferred to call the 'state-sponsored')
sector, and many new bodies were created – following the Cumann na nGaedheal
initiatives of the 1920s – to develop and manage particular critical areas of the economy: the Irish Sugar Company was founded in 1933, as was a 'state merchant bank',
the Industrial Credit Company; the national air line, Aer Lingus, followed in 1936.
But recent scholarship has tended to stress the limited impact of these initiatives,
in terms of both their relatively modest scale and what Daly had judged 'their
non-competing status vis-à-vis private business'.[28] Moreover, bigger government and
protection brought high levels of personal and corporate taxation, and an indirect
tax structure that was amongst the most oppressive anywhere in the world. Offering
meaningful comment on changes in the quality of life in the Ireland of the 1930s
is equally difficult: but it is certainly the case that Fine Gael was able to attack the
government on the issue of living standards as early as 1933–4, while the level of
emigration, temporarily depressed because of the bleak economic prospects in Britain
and the USA in the early 1930s, rose with the improvement of the host economies.
Fianna Fáil's quest for a thoroughgoing autarky had ended by 1938 amidst the sham-
bles of high prices (especially for vital raw materials), bloated uncompetitive
industries (the 'rats who could not race', in Joe Lee's memorable indictment), and
a still endemic poverty.[29]

Underlying Fianna Fáil industrial strategy was the Sinn Féin impulse towards
an economic liberation from Britain: import duties were, almost by definition, directed
towards this end, since the overwhelming bulk of Irish imports came from Britain.
Within the arena of agricultural policy this mixture of politics and economic strategy is even more unmistakable. The abiding argument against stringent industrial
protection had always been the threat of retaliatory levies on Irish agricultural exports,
and indeed the prophecies of the free-trade jeremiahs were broadly fulfilled, if
in a much more complicated way than had been envisioned. The immediate cause
of the trade war, or – more grandiloquently – 'the economic war' between Ireland
and Britain was not Fianna Fáil's dream of a self-sufficient and protected Ireland,
but rather the party's dream of an Ireland untrammelled by what it perceived as

degrading linkages with the former imperial power. One of the many continuities linking British rule and independent Ireland had been the payment, by Irish farmers, of the annuities on their land purchase agreements: these monies, which represented a form of repayment on a British-supplied mortgage deal, were garnered by the Treasury in London until 1922, and continued to be collected and transmitted under the Cumann na nGaedheal administration. Indeed, the annuity payments were guaranteed to the British by two agreements (signed by the Cosgrave government in 1923 and 1926); but de Valera rejected the moral and legal force of both these deals, and all the more emphatically since neither had been ratified by the Dáil. The annuity payments were therefore withheld from the British (even though they were still collected by the Irish government from the farmers). Efforts at diplomacy failed; and the British acted swiftly to recover the outstanding sums by imposing a 20 per cent import duty on a wide range of Irish goods, including cattle. With the Irish retaliation (duties on numerous British raw materials) the basic structures of the 'economic' war were in place – though, as Ronan Fanning has pointed out, the political nature of the conflict was plain to all.[30] For de Valera the issue of the annuities was tied up with the quest for sovereignty; for the British, the Irish default was looked upon as the repudiation of long-standing agreements – and it also provided the pretext for a campaign which, it was hoped in Whitehall, would undermine the Fianna Fáil administration in favour of Cumann na nGaedheal.

It has been said that Fianna Fáil used 'the screen of the economic war' to implement some political and economic goals of a more fundamental nature.[31] The party cast itself originally as the champion of the small farmer, and it envisioned an Ireland widely populated by smallholders, who would eke a modest living primarily from tillage. Viewed in this light, the British assault on the cattle trade, while surprising in its swiftness and brutality, was not without some political utility. De Valera's government was prepared to bolster some agricultural exports, but live cattle exports, though half-heartedly subsidized, were not among the government's economic or indeed ideological priorities. While the cattle trade reeled from the impact of the British attack, the government did as much as it could to promote Irish tillage: a guaranteed price was promised for Irish wheat, while tremendous efforts were expended to develop the sugar-beet industry. Barley was protected for the benefit of the brewing industry. The land annuities, which were still being levied by the government though not transmitted, were halved and used for rate relief: this in turn was directed particularly at smallholders and at tillage farmers.

But there was no return on this investment. There was no massive conversion from the failing livestock trade to tillage, and indeed the principal movement occurred within the tillage sector, from unsubsidized crops to those carrying government support. Moreover, though the government had no love for the graziers, their centrality to the Irish economy was underlined as the cattle trade collapsed between 1932 and 1935, and as the knock-on effects were felt within the broader economy: the graziers may have been unloved and unlovely, but their trade helped to pay for the industrialization drive which was another central feature of the Fianna Fáil agenda. In brief, Fianna Fáil's efforts to boost rural employment were incompatible with its strategy for industrial employment, and this inconsistency was recognized by the government's willingness to come to terms with the British, first of all through the Coal–Cattle Pact of January 1935. This modest deal involved raising the import quota on British coal, and the British reciprocating with Irish cattle. It was hardly an overbrimming testimony to mutual goodwill, but it represented the first tentative step towards the comprehensive agreement struck in 1938 (and which will be reviewed shortly).

But the main focus of the attempted disengagement from Britain was not economic; and the populist appeal of the first Fianna Fáil governments was certainly not confined to its protectionist mission. For de Valera the Fianna Fáil accession to power in 1932, confirmed in the election of January 1933, provided the opportunity to continue the civil war by other means: indeed, there is a satisfying symmetry and symbolism in the fact that, even though the republicans 'dumped' their weapons in May 1923, apprehensive Fianna Fáilers, including Eamon and Vivion de Valera, entered the Dáil in March 1932 armed with revolvers (de Valera's grim expression on the eve of his empowerment was apparently to be explained by his lack of faith in his son's marksmanship).[32] As has been elaborated, the party was now much more than a haven for recusant republicans: nevertheless, the anti-Treatyite agenda was central to the purpose of the new Fianna Fáil government. A little over a month after assuming power – on 23 April 1932 – de Valera introduced the Constitutional Amendment (Removal of Oath) Bill, a measure which sliced through the Gordian knot that had choked Irish party politics between 1922 and 1927. The Senate, still largely pro-Treaty in its sympathies, and with a vestigial ex-Unionist presence, used its powers to delay the bill; but, in the context of de Valera's remarkable political tenacity, it was a forlorn hope, and the measure passed into law in 1933. Indeed, the government's hands were strengthened by the Fianna Fáil electoral victory of January 1933, a contest which spelt the end not only for the oath, but also for the Senate itself. This chamber, viewed by de Valera as an integral part of the alien imposition of December 1921, and also as a practical obstacle to his own authority, survived only until May 1936: its expiry stimulated little grief in the broader Irish electorate, but it had been an important focus for ex-Unionist sentiment, and to that extent had been a useful if minor tool in the programme of national reconciliation tacitly pursued by Cumann na nGaedheal. But there was little electoral advantage in appeasing 'Orangemen' and 'Freemasons'; and, given the bitterness of the revolutionary struggle, it is scarcely surprising that the Fianna Fáil of the 1930s should have been short on consensual gestures. The surprise is rather that their predecessors should have done so much towards expanding the embrace of the Irish nation.

Nor does the Fianna Fáil assault on the office of governor general pose any significant interpretative problem. At one level, the governor general was a creation of the Treaty agreement, and was therefore *ipso facto* an outrage to party sentiment. The governor was also, of course, the representative of the British crown, and – even though his functions were largely ceremonial – he represented an offence to the broader republican movement. Setting aside republican principle and civil war passion, the office of governor general looked like a continuation of the viceroyalty, which throughout the later nineteenth and early twentieth centuries had seemed to many nationalists to be the epitome of British excess and abandon (the reign of Earl Spencer – the 'Duke of Sodom and Gomorrah' – in the early 1880s, and the Crown Jewels affair of 1908, episodes spiced with revelations concerning the sexual and financial proclivities of the viceregal court, appeared to confirm long-standing suspicions). The gubernatorial reigns of T.M. Healy (1922–8) and of James McNeill (1928–32) provided little by way of grand larceny or gay 'outing' to fire the prurient imagination, but there remained the lingering fear that the governor generalship involved 'the inevitable re-creating of the old sham Court, gathering round it all the hovering sycophants and certain social types alien to the National life of the country'.[33] Moreover, if it seems rather improbable that the 'Heliotropolis' of the 1920s (as the Dublin wags dubbed T.M. Healy's official residence), together with its septuagenarian occupant, constituted much of a distraction from 'National realities', it should not be forgotten that both Healy and McNeill were heavily implicated with the Cumann na nGaedheal administration and provided their office with a partisan taint. Healy was the veteran of the Land League era who had been most accessible to the Sinn Féin elite, but part of the reason for this was that he was connected by marriage to Kevin O'Higgins; James McNeill had been the Irish High Commissioner in London, but in addition he had served in the Indian Civil Service (and was therefore embroiled in British imperialism) and was the brother of Eoin MacNeill, who had been a Cumann na nGaedheal minister. In fact McNeill responded in a proper and dignified manner to the new Fianna Fáil government, even upturning protocol by journeying to the Dáil in order to confirm the new ministers in office. But such tokens of sensitivity did nothing to divert de Valera from his purpose in downgrading and marginalizing the governor generalship. After a series of humiliating affronts, McNeill was forced into resignation with effect from 1 November 1932: his successor, Dónal Ó Buachalla, lived as a private citizen, surrendering some of his powers to the Executive Council and obediently falling on his court sword in 1937 when, with the new constitution, his office was abolished. The idea of appointing a plain man as governor general had probably arisen from the inventive legal genius of (ironically) a British signatory of the Treaty, Lord Birkenhead, but it had also been prefigured in the satirical imagination of the journalist F. Frankfort Moore, whose comic creation, *The Viceroy Muldoon* (1893), in some ways resembles Governor General Buckley.

This meticulous demolition of the constitution of 1922 involved as well a re-excavation of the idea of external association, which had been buried since the civil war: in effect, de Valera, with a breathtaking self-confidence, and with only the scantiest acknowledgement of the Cumann na nGaedheal achievement, was reaffirming his main constitutional strategies of 1921 (Deirdre McMahon has, however, warned against any overly simplistic equation between 1921 and the 1930s).[34] This meant dismantling the Treatyite shrine, even though it had served Irish national aspirations pretty well; but it also meant the painstaking installation of the old deity, external association, whose effectiveness was still untested and unknown. This latter task began in 1935, with the passage of two measures – the Irish Nationality and Citizenship Act and the Aliens Act – which established and defined Irish citizenship and, in doing so, classed British subjects as 'aliens'. A decision was taken in June 1936 to promulgate a new constitution; and – as an interim measure – the Constitution (Amendment No. 27) Act was hurriedly passed on 11 December in order to excise from the existing constitution all references to the crown. A second bill was approved on the following day, the Executive Authority (External Relations) Act, which in clumsy language recognized that the King was head of the Commonwealth and might act on behalf of the Free State for as long as it was a member nation. The proximate cause of this legislative flurry, Edward VIII, seemed (unusually for the House of Windsor) to have some sympathy with Irish national aspirations: his long-standing embroilment with Wallis Simpson and his departure on 10 December may well have simultaneously robbed the Irish of a benign monarch while making possible the emergent republic. But the abdication crisis was certainly not the sole inspiration behind this legislation, in so far as many of its objectives had been mooted much earlier in the year: the abdication did mean, however, that the Irish government could accomplish the most difficult part of its reform agenda well ahead of schedule, and without the breakdown of the slowly improving Anglo-Irish relationship.

The British accepted these repudiations of the Treaty, partly because in late 1936 and early 1937 they did not want to pursue an international quarrel on the still sensitive question of the monarchy. But it was also the case that they had little choice but to acquiesce, given the ambiguities of the 1921 settlement as well as the developing nature of the Commonwealth. Lionel Curtis, one of the secretaries of the British delegation at the time of the Treaty, hailed the agreement as 'one of the greatest achievements in the history of the Empire' and Lloyd George promised action if its terms were broken – but in reality, as many recognized at the time, it was impossible that the Treaty should remain a static formula, and it became therefore well-nigh impossible to judge what constituted a breach of terms.[35] In particular the ever-expanding definition of the dominion status contained within the Treaty meant that the Irish could – paradoxically – alter its substance without contravening their obligations. In addition the British had from the start denied that the Treaty was an international agreement, and had therefore deprived themselves of the protection of international law: the Irish, by way of contrast, had a double protection in the international registration of the Treaty as well as in the highly sensitive Commonwealth audience for the Anglo-Irish relationship. All this meant that the Treaty, a characteristically ambiguous and ingenious achievement of imperial diplomacy, could be simultaneously upheld and overturned, and honoured in the breach. More specifically, as Alan Ward has observed, 'this appeared to mean that the Irish could whittle away the link with the Crown because no one knew where the breaking point lay'.[36] Like Alice's Cheshire cat, the Treaty faded away, leaving only a taunting smile – the memory of British complacency at what had been 'one of the greatest achievements in the history of the Empire'.

The first steps towards the new constitution had already been taken by the time Edward lugubriously broadcast his farewell to the British public from Fort Belvedere.

The single-minded nature of de Valera's quest for sovereignty, and the fervour of his desire to prove the viability of 'external association', or a version of it, have already been highlighted. But, within clear limitations, the new constitution that was published in 1937 was the outcome of a series of compromises. The new Ireland, or Éire, was to be a republic in all but name, with a President as head of state, a Taoiseach (or Prime Minister) and cabinet, and a bicameral legislature. The self-denying refusal to embrace the republic was explained by de Valera as a concession to Ulster Unionist feeling – a recognition of the loyalty felt by the northern community towards the British crown. But this is only really acceptable either as a feint or as an expression of the immense gulf separating de Valera from the northerners whom he affected to conciliate: articles two and three of the new constitution laid claim to the territory of Northern Ireland (despite the opposition of influential figures like J.J. McElligott of the Department of Finance), and the special position allotted to the Roman Catholic church (article 44) and to Catholic social teaching was certainly not calculated as a harbinger for a settled, reunified Ireland. In reality, de Valera did not want to compromise his vision of a Gaelic, Catholic, rural nation, and he therefore did little to promote the unity to which he paid lip-service. There was no Irish republic in 1937 either because de Valera thought northern Unionist sympathy could be bought on bargain-basement terms, or (much more likely) because the straitened economic climate of the late 1930s provided too bleak a backdrop for the final act in an 800-year struggle.

Even the apparently unambiguous deference to the authority of the Roman Catholic Church was the outcome of a protracted negotiation between different interested parties. Early drafts of the constitution had affirmed that 'the true religion is that established by Our Divine Lord Jesus Christ Himself' and that 'the Church of Christ is the Catholic Church' – the logical inference being that Catholicism alone represented 'true religion'.[37] But, while this was the formula endorsed by Cardinal MacRory, the Roman Catholic Archbishop of Armagh, other senior figures within the hierarchy (such as Archbishop Byrne of Dublin) were more accommodating. Moreover, the Vatican was prepared to turn a blind eye to an assertion of Catholicism which was less than triumphalist, and perhaps even less than strict orthodoxy might have required (Cardinal Pacelli genially told an alarmed Joseph Walshe, secretary of the Department of External Affairs, and an exceptionally devout Catholic, that the government might be guilty of heresy in its suggested approach).[38] The mixed attitude of the hierarchy, combined with the apparent indifference of Rome, provided de Valera with some space to negotiate with the Protestant churches and to avoid an affirmation of Catholic identity which would cause outright offence to the spectrum of Irish Christianity. In particular de Valera seems to have been impressed by the intellectually distinguished and flinty Church of Ireland Archbishop of Dublin, John Allen Fitzgerald Gregg, who insisted that the formal title of the Catholic Church be applied in the constitution ('the Holy Catholic Apostolic and Roman church'), thereby preserving the claims of his own communion to be 'catholic'.[39] One last aspect of this article 44 deserves emphasis: this was the specific recognition of the Jewish congregations in Ireland, a constitutional blessing which may not in practice have amounted to much, but which in the context of the rabid anti-semitism of the time was a more liberal proceeding than might have been expected. Indeed, as has frequently been noted, the entire constitution reflected an uneasy accommodation between Catholicism and liberalism – a blend, as Richard Dunphy has remarked, 'of cultural and moral authoritarianism and political liberalism'.[40]

The constitution guaranteed freedom of conscience and 'the free practice and profession of religion', but only 'subject to public order and morality': this qualification may well have been intended to address the issue of public preaching by, in particular, evangelical Protestants – an issue which had for long simmered, occasionally blazing into life when such preachers had inspired a backlash among those to whom they purported to preach 'the Word'. Otherwise, the constitution embodied the gamut of Catholic social teaching, emphasizing the centrality of the family within society, prohibiting divorce and locating women firmly within the home: Mrs Tom Clarke's feminist critique of the constitution won short shrift at the Fianna Fáil ard-fheis of 1937. Efforts by Hanna Sheehy Skeffington and the Women Graduates' Association to obtain the deletion of the most offensively anti-feminist articles (40, 41 and 45) produced a stir in Dublin, but not beyond: some minor and grudging amendments ensued. A Women's Social and Progressive League was created in November 1937 to carry on the campaign, but it won little support at the general elections of 1938 and 1943. The constitution also defined the highly limited role of the state, upheld private property and affirmed a preference for 'private initiative in industry and commerce'. Yet, if all this reflected Catholic social teaching (and, more specifically, the influence of de Valera's friend, Father (later Archbishop) John Charles McQuaid), it should be emphasized that the values which were propagated chimed with the convictions of much of Irish Protestantism. Secularized middle-class Protestants along with Catholic liberals may have had qualms about the intrusive nature of the constitution, but in practice it did not so much impose as reflect a shared value system.[41]

In terms of the relationship with Britain, the constitution defined a bold compromise between separatist principle and political practicalities: it was a macro-political essay in keeping options open. Ireland might be associated with the Commonwealth for some purposes, but not for others: the British King, now George VI, might fulfil certain diplomatic functions for the Irish government without having any internal role, however nominal, and – emphatically – without being head of state. The Anglo-Irish Agreement of April 1938 addressed some of the older and – for the Irish – more problematic ambiguities in the relationship with Britain, completing the work of the constitution in overturning the Treaty of 1921. But while substantial British concessions in 1938 – the evacuation of the Treaty ports (at Berehaven, Cobh and Lough Swilly), the resolution of the land annuities dispute on bargain-basement terms (the Irish paid 10 million pounds as a final settlement), and the effective lifting of duties on Irish imports – bought a certain amount of cautious personal goodwill between de Valera and the British Prime Minister Neville Chamberlain, they did not purchase any broader cross-channel reconciliation: instead, Irish resentments focused ever more sharply on the issue of partition, while the British (who tended to treat Anglo-Irish relations as an irritating diversion from the European floor-show) turned from mollifying the Taoiseach to the more intricate task of appeasing the Führer.

De Valera eventually came to regard the settlement of 1938 as his greatest political achievement, and historians on the whole have concurred (Theo Hoppen has described the deal on land as – for the Irish – 'the bargain of the century').[42] Seán T. O'Kelly, de Valera's Tánaiste, or Deputy Prime Minister, expressed one prevailing ministerial view in his 'John Bull' speech when he declared: 'look at the last agreement that we made. Why we won all round us. We whipped him [John Bull] right, left and centre, and with God's help, we will do the same again when opportunity arises'.[43] The explanations for the Fianna Fáil diplomatic coup are varied, but are not hard to find. The British, unsettled by the development of German and Italian ambitions and fearful of the strategic consequences of having an unfriendly Irish neighbour, were determined to have an agreement, even though the price might be high. The Anglo-Irish Agreement was clearly viewed by Chamberlain not simply within its own terms, but very firmly within the international context and as part of a series of interlocking diplomatic settlements forged between Britain and Italy and Germany. In addition, although the British government was dominated by the Conservative Party, the ultra-Unionist leaders of the Home Rule era had all but passed away: indeed, there was a powerful vestigial Liberal influence within government, represented by the Chancellor of the Exchequer, Sir John Simon, and by the Permanent Under-Secretary of the Treasury, Sir Warren Fisher, both of whom had been educated as Gladstonians, and both of whom accepted the moral debts owed by Britain to Ireland ('it is too often forgotten by us English that our record over the larger part of the period has been outrageous', opined Fisher in January 1938; and later in the same month he affirmed that 'the Irish are historically on incontestable ground in their view of England as an oppressor').[44] These rats in the skull of British diplomacy, allied with a certain amount of confusion and wishful thinking about Irish strategy, helped to create opportunities for Irish gain which a relatively weak bargaining position might not otherwise have provided. In addition the ailing and erratic Prime Minister of Northern Ireland, James Craig (from 1927 Lord Craigavon), was prepared to defy his Stormont ministerial colleagues by unilaterally accepting an unattractive Anglo-Irish trade agreement (whether he was motivated by the promise of British compensation or by Chamberlain's appeals about the international situation, or – as Sir Wilfrid Spender, the Northern Ireland cabinet secretary grimly believed – by the hospitality of Mrs Annie Chamberlain, is unclear).[45] The British were under no illusions that their settlement with the Irish had been bought on other than difficult terms: Neville Chamberlain prophesied that 'I shall be accused of having weakly given way when Éire was in the hollow of my hand', and indeed the accusations came – not immediately, it is true, but when, during and after the Second World War, British opinion sought the 'guilty men' responsible for appeasement.[46] In 1938, however, Chamberlain believed that 'we [British ministers] have only given up the small things (paper rights and revenues which would not last) for the big things – the ending of a long quarrel, the beginning of better relations between North and South Ireland, and the cooperation of the South with us in trade and defence': he believed that the trauma of the Austro-German Anschluss would reinforce the popular perception 'that there is no time for keeping open old sores'.[47] Few British (except the small group around Winston Churchill) were unduly worried by the 'small things' surrendered in 1938, whether the land annuities or the Treaty ports (which were generally regarded as run-down and obsolete, and hard to defend in the case of Irish opposition). On the other hand, Chamberlain's conviction that 'small' tactical concessions might allay historic grievances was as ill-founded in the Irish case as it was elsewhere in his diplomatic endeavours. De Valera, while he was able to win a general election in June 1938 partly as a result of the trophies brought back from Chamberlain, continued to profess himself aggrieved by partition. And while Chamberlain thought that he was completing his father's and brother's work in defining a just Anglo-Irish relationship, the truth was that the Agreement of 1938 was seen in Ireland not so much as the ending of a long quarrel as the ending of a brief and – for the British – unsuccessful round in an ongoing contest.

Where the British were hampered by internal division and were highly sensitive to a range of external diplomatic and economic factors, de Valera was the overwhelmingly dominant influence within Irish strategy, and he professed himself (and indeed probably was) ready to sacrifice economic well-being in what he saw as the wider national interest. He was also helped, in terms of both his Anglo-Irish diplomacy and broader external affairs, not just by his own dominance within Fianna Fáil but also by the lack of a coherent opposition (one further explanation of British tractability is that they had all but given up hope of a Treatyite electoral revival). In order to demonstrate this point, it is necessary to return once again to the early and mid-1930s and to the state of Cumann na nGaedheal after their electoral humiliations in 1932 and 1933. Cumann na nGaedheal had existed only to govern, and out of power it seemed directionless and desperate: the party leadership flirted with paramilitarism and with the trappings of fascism, and eventually agreed to submerge itself within a broader anti-republican alliance. Having lost control of state power, and increasingly harassed by a resurgent IRA, the more militant supporters of the late government formed themselves into the Army Comrades' Association (ACA) in February 1932. By January 1933 the ACA was claiming a membership of over 30,000 and had adopted the blue shirt as its uniform: by the summer of 1933 the Association had been reborn as the National Guard, and had acquired its own charismatic, if erratic, duce in the shape of Eoin O'Duffy, a former Free State general. It is an eloquent testimony to the confusion and demoralization of the pro-Treatyite tradition that in September 1933, when Cumann na nGaedheal, the National Guard and the Centre Party of James Dillon and Frank MacDermot came together as the Fine Gael, or United Ireland Party, O'Duffy rather than Cosgrave or any of the other ministerial veterans was selected as the overall leader. However, these rather extreme efforts to provide Cumann na nGaedheal with an increased popular leverage backfired: the fascist trappings supplied by O'Duffy were an inadequate substitute for a broader socio-economic base or programme, and in fact were counter-productive in the sense that they scared off some of the middle-class property owners who had been natural Cumann na nGaedheal voters. As de Valera distanced himself from the IRA (which was banned in June 1936), accommodated himself with the Irish business elite and took up the role of international statesman, so it seemed that Fine Gael were the fashion victims of Irish politics: momentarily modish, perhaps, but soon faintly ridiculous. In fact O'Duffy's fondness for outrageous rhetoric and elaborate uniforms was more O'Connellite than Hitlerian: his march on Dublin, planned for August 1933, was swiftly abandoned after government intervention, and was therefore closer to Clontarf in 1843 than Rome in 1922 or Munich in 1923. The death of a young Blueshirt, Michael Lynch, in August 1934 might in different circumstances have provided a Horst Wessel to the movement (and perhaps even lyrical inspiration to its most celebrated literary sympathizer, W.B. Yeats), but in fact the movement was already in decline by this stage, and in September O'Duffy was ousted with comparatively little difficulty from the leadership of Fine Gael and replaced by the unflagging Cosgrave. In 1935 O'Duffy and his supporters founded the National Corporate Party; and in the following year the Blueshirts were formally wound up, with O'Duffy and 700 volunteers departing for Spain and a brief and inglorious campaign on behalf of Franco. But the damage inflicted on the Fine Gael tradition was lasting. Even though (as Cumann na nGaedheal) it was the party which had defended the ostensibly secular constitution of 1922 and defined the role of Ireland within the League of Nations, it was also defensively Catholic and – now – corporatist: it was therefore divided over the issue of sanctions on Italy in 1935, and over the Spanish civil war in 1936. Moreover, the workable if tepid relationship between Cumann na nGaedheal and Unionism was dramatically chilled by O'Duffy's periodic declarations of war on the North. Those who had supported Cumann na nGaedheal as the party of stability had to reassess this support in the light of Blueshirt aggression: those who had opposed de Valera on the grounds that he was a herald of revolution had, by the mid-1930s, to come to terms with a more workaday and politically acceptable reality. By the time of the elections of 1937 and 1938 Fine Gael had not yet outlived its association with the excesses of O'Duffy and the Blueshirts: nor had the party sought out new constituencies and a new purpose. Support for the Treaty was now an anachronism, a sentimental rather than a practical political choice, since the last vestiges of the Treaty had disappeared in 1938. Political initiative as well as the middle-ground of Irish politics had fallen to de Valera; and he would reap the electoral rewards for the following ten years.

Nowhere was de Valera's moral authority and his command of the political centre more starkly revealed than with the issue of Ireland's neutrality during the Second World War. Here was the true test of Irish self-determination, and more specifically of the doctrine of external association – for if external association meant anything, then it offered the Irish the chance to buck the trend of mainstream Commonwealth opinion by remaining neutral when Britain and its dominions were at war. Yet the pressures on the Irish government were intense, and especially between 1939 and 1941, when a German invasion of Britain and Ireland seemed to threaten, when the Battle of the Atlantic between Allied shipping and the German submarine packs was developing, and before the accession of American strength to the Allied cause. De Valera explained the Irish position partly in terms of the ongoing affront represented by partition: in the past he had scuppered the prospects of Anglo-Irish defence cooperation with this weapon, and on 10 May 1940 he led the British representative in Ireland, Sir John Maffey, to believe that Irish military engagement 'would probably be the consequence' of reunification.[48] And indeed the British – with the fall of France in June 1940, the sole survivor of the western combatants – were prepared to consider paying over Northern Ireland as the price of an all-Ireland military effort. In June 1940 the unflagging Malcolm MacDonald, together with Neville Chamberlain, put forward a tentative proposal for Irish unity, and (as in 1938) began the politically fraught task of edging towards de Valera's stated position. Despite these efforts, however, the Fianna Fáil cabinet rejected the deal on 4 July on the grounds that the British were demanding immediate Irish engagement and offering only the future and hazy prospect of reunification: de Valera 'mentioned that when he was a child it was customary for two boys swopping treasures to insist on "equal holds" – that each should have a firm grip on what he was to receive before he loosened his grip on that with which he was parting. The offer . . . did not give "equal holds" '.[49] But the truth behind this homely metaphor seems to have been, as John Bowman has remarked, 'that no British offer, other than the establishment of a guaranteed, united, neutral Ireland would have had any serious appeal to the Fianna Fáil cabinet'.[50] Partition represented, despite the rhetoric on the subject, a secondary concern for the Irish, just as it had done in December 1921; and just as it had done in 1921, it was also both a bargaining counter and a breaking-point.

In fact the MacDonald–Chamberlain initiative of June 1940 represented the high-water mark of British tractability and was stimulated by the desperate conviction that Ireland represented a vital strategic asset. But of course precisely the same circumstances which made the British anxious to trade on partition made the Fianna Fáil government aware that the goal of a united Ireland might be bought at too high a price: both sides were frightened by German success, and the Irish in particular calculated on the possibility that their neighbours might be beaten. In addition any deal on reunification was subject to the approval of the government of Northern Ireland, and while some Ulster Unionist ministers (including the rising star, Basil Brooke) were willing to countenance tighter cross-border ties in the interests of the war effort, it was clear to Dublin that any substantive progress towards union involved some very difficult manoeuvres. It is easy to imagine ways in which the chances of an agreed union might have been improved in June 1940, but it takes a very great leap of imagination to envisage a deal actually being clinched: if Lemass had had greater influence in the Fianna Fáil cabinet, and Frank Aiken less, if Brooke had achieved power in Northern Ireland in the threatening circumstances of 1940 rather than (for the Allies) the comparatively more favourable context of 1943, then perhaps some form of agreement might have been visible on the horizon. It is also possible to suggest that, by rejecting the MacDonald–Chamberlain détente, de Valera may have played too safe a political hand, when the chance of the jackpot was at its height. It is difficult to see how else he might have acted, however:

the bottom line was that neutrality was an extremely popular policy (even with southern Protestants) upon which Fianna Fáil was consolidating i leadership of Éire; while in Northern Ireland the war had served to bolst for the Union and British patriotism. As in 1914–18, therefore, the in European war in Ireland was centrifugal rather than centripetal, with the acceleration of the political forces that maintained partition; as in 1914–18, however, there was an initial moment when the war also seemed to have dramatically upset the natural tensions within Irish politics.

But the moment of unity passed. With the Battle of Britain (August–October 1940) the threat of German invasion receded, and with the resignation and death of Chamberlain at the end of 1940 the single most sympathetic presence (so far as the Irish were concerned) within the British government disappeared. The enforced goodwill of June 1940 speedily evaporated, to be replaced in December with sanctions on Irish trade, and in May 1941 with a row on the issue of extending conscription to Northern Ireland. The Japanese attack on Pearl Harbor in December 1941 was the occasion for Churchill's 'nation once again' telegram to de Valera – but the allusion was rhetorical rather than substantive, and reflected not just Churchillian bombast but also the extent to which mainstream British political opinion had moved on since June 1940.[51] For as the war developed reunification became barred, not just by northern Protestants but also by hitherto ambivalent British voters: the 'nation once again' telegram might, in June 1940, have represented a serious offer, but it did not – and could not – do so in December 1941.

Much has been written on the subject of Irish neutrality during the Second World War. In part this reflects a still active sensitivity concerning the apparent ambiguities in the Irish response to the horrors of national socialism and fascism: but yet again other European neutrals (such as Sweden or Spain) have addressed their wartime record with greater equanimity than the Irish or, alternatively (as in the case of Switzerland), have only recently been forced by outside pressures to confront the moral difficulties of their stand. The Irish historiographical response to neutrality has been intricate and defensive because Irish neutrality was a highly complicated political strategy, which was rooted in a concern for national unity and sovereignty, and which reflected a traditionally ambiguous response to Britain's European wars. Neutrality accommodated all but the most fanatical republicans, and was treated as holy writ by senior ministerial anglophobes such as Frank Aiken; neutrality was equally acceptable to many southern Irish Protestants, mindful perhaps of the devastating impact of the First World War on their community. On the other hand, neutrality did little to undermine the tradition of Irish service in the forces of the crown, and perhaps 50,000 Irishmen and women were recruited to the British armed forces, including recipients of the Victoria Cross like Leading Seaman James Joseph Magennis of Belfast, and the unsung recipients of the Military Cross (such as the Mullingar doctor, Captain K.F. Patton of the Royal Army Medical Corps) or of the Military Medal (such as Sergeant E. Maher of the Irish Guards, from Bandon). In addition, the Irish government increasingly defined neutrality in a pro-Allied manner, permitting the use of Lough Foyle for Allied naval craft and of a corridor of land in South Donegal for the British flying boats stationed in Lough Erne. Other valuable concessions were offered in the areas of military intelligence, meteorological information and prisoners of war (Allied service personnel who found themselves in Éire could expect a speedy repatriation, while their German counterparts – possibly the more fortunate – were destined for a spartan but safe period of internment). This slant grew more marked as the likelihood of an Allied victory increased, but there were other explanations: Dublin's acquiescence in certain Allied infringements of its neutrality may have been as much enforced as voluntary (policing air space would have been a problem, for example, given the limits of the air corps and the – at best – 'half-armed' nature of Irish neutrality). But it also seems to be the case that, while most Irish people endorsed neutrality, there was a broad sympathy for the Allied cause: massive recruitment to the British army was compatible with popular support for de Valera in his tough handling of both the USA (as with the American note affair of February–March 1944, when Washington pressed for the expulsion of Axis ministers from Dublin) and the British (as with de Valera's famous radio address of 16 May 1945, quietly repudiating Churchill's earlier broadcast complaints about Irish 'frolics' with the Axis powers).[52] Indeed, de Valera's adroit treatment of the American note affair, an interlay of public defiance and private conciliation, illustrates his skill in simultaneously coping with Irish patriotic sensitivities as well as macro-political realities: his reward was a ringing popular endorsement in the general election of May 1944.

But, while de Valera preserved Ireland from the European military conflagration, his political ingenuity did not extend to fending off some of the more sweeping ideological and practical consequences of the war. As in much of the rest of Europe the war brought to Ireland more elaborate government (despite Fianna Fáil's old suspicions of fat-cat civil servants), and a leftward surge in terms of economic planning, social welfare and even (despite the heroic conservatism of the Irish electorate) in terms of voter preferences. The paradox of neutrality was that, because it involved the wholesale export of Irish people to the British army and the British workplace, so it tended to strengthen Irish susceptibility to British social and economic trends; and once the influence of the intensely conservative Seán MacEntee had temporarily waned within government (as was arguably the case after his 'serious demotion' from the Finance portfolio in 1939), and that of Lemass had begun to consolidate, so Ireland began to follow the British lead in terms of long-term economic planning and welfare reform.[53] De Valera may have been seeking to 'stifle Lemass in the interests of cabinet unity and caution' through the cabinet committee on emergency problems (May 1940) and the committee on economic planning (November 1942), but it is Lemass's interest in Beveridge and even in Keynesianism that shines (sometimes rather faintly, admittedly) through many of the government's wartime initiatives.[54] MacEntee's Wages Standstill Order (1941) and the Trade Union Act (1941), though limp alternatives to the draconian proposals that this uncompromising northerner had originally advocated, were still severe when set aside the initiatives that would shortly be pursued by Lemass. Lemass, who followed MacEntee as Minister of Industry and Commerce from August 1941, was by no means an unqualified friend of the proletariat, and particularly not of the relatively advantaged members of the amalgamated unions: nor was he willing to hand back to the labour movement the gains that had been won under his predecessor. However, his Trade Union Act (1942) 'was of symbolic importance in restoring a consensual style to labour-state relations', even though it did little to mitigate the severities of MacEntee's original legislation.[55] Lemass also oversaw the relaxation of wage restrictions for the very poor and increases in unemployment benefit: he was a supporter of free food and free fuel for the poor (1941–2) and of a non-means-tested children's allowance (1944), a piece of 'Beveridgeism' that was viewed by MacEntee as a communistic heresy calculated to demoralize the faithful. Lemass's appointment as Tánaiste in 1945 strengthened his position within the cabinet (and also his claims over the succession to de Valera), and gave more weight to his reformist objectives: a new Industrial Relations Act (1946), based on a measure of agreement between the union movement and the employers, made provision for a labour court and appeared (however momentarily) to herald a new era of industrial tranquillity. In December 1946, in the first major overhaul of the administrative structure created in 1924, the new departments of social welfare and health were created with Lemass's support and blessing.

If a concern for full employment and for social welfare mimicked British domestic preoccupations, then there were some shuffling movements within the electorate which – if only in a small way – resembled the seismic rifts within British and continental European politics in the post-war years. There was a modest, if temporary, upsurge in the fortunes of the highly fissile Irish Labour Party: in August 1942 Labour became the biggest electoral force in Dublin, capturing the lord mayoralty, and in the general election of June 1943 the party won just under 16 per cent of the vote and 17 seats in the Dáil. Bitter internal divisions, which produced a breakaway National Labour Party under the talented but authoritarian William O'Brien, hamstrung this electoral sprint and allowed Fianna Fáil an unremarkably comfortable win in the election of 1944. But the social and economic problems that had fostered the momentary Labour revival did not go away, even if the party itself had fractured so readily. A rising cost of living (between 1937 and 1945 industrial wages rose by 30 per cent, while prices rose by 74 per cent), rationing and shortages combined with the relative weakening of some traditionally 'respectable' professions such as teaching to create an upsurge of industrial unrest in 1946–7: the Irish National Teachers' Organization strike of 1946 was a particular embarrassment since it won the endorsement of Archbishop McQuaid and gave rise to episodes such as the Croke Park protest of September 1946, when demonstrating teachers invaded the pitch in the interval of the All-Ireland football final and were roughly beaten back by the Guards. In addition to problems within the area of labour relations, the government – and even the hitherto largely sacrosanct de Valera family – were afflicted with a series of 'sleaze' controversies which damaged the preferred party image of self-denial and national self-sacrifice: the most potent of these controversies related to the sale of the Locke distillery, Kilbeggan, and gave rise in November 1947 to a judicial investigation.

Shortages, strikes and allegations of graft fed into mounting popular electoral resentment. Hitherto Fianna Fáil had relied not only upon its own organizational tentacles and carefully modulated appeal but also upon the shambolic nature of the opposition: Labour, as has been noted, split asunder in 1943, while Fine Gael remained largely bereft of imagination and leadership, the 'somnambulist of Irish politics', in Theo Hoppen's striking description.[56] In 1946, however, an alternative to these rather jaded forces emerged in the shape of Seán MacBride's Clann na Poblachta. The Clann offered a radical social programme which seemed to be in tune with electoral feeling throughout western Europe – though crucially it did so in a thoroughly safe, unthreatening manner, sculpting its proposals around the traditional framework of Catholic social teaching. But the new party not only appeared to be able to cut through the problems that were befuddling the government, it also boasted an apparently more genuine and effective social conscience and a more uncompromising republican integrity: in other words, the Clann threatened to steal the traditional electoral garb of Fianna Fáil. The Clann bound together the economically disaffected (such as many teachers), impatient republicans (the Fianna Fáil record on partition was blustering but ineffectual) and radical youngsters (such as Dr Noel Browne) who were unlikely to find much comfort within the existing party structure: its Catholic reformism and lurking republican militancy seemed to unite the O'Connellite and United Irish traditions within Irish nationalism. In particular there was an overlap between the Clann and the well-organized support networks for the republican prisoners (one of whom, Seán McCaughey, had died while on hunger strike in 1946): there are some faint parallels between this political chemistry and the support for the Fenian prisoners of the late 1860s which carried into the Home Rule movement. Two by-election victories for the Clann in the Fianna Fáil heartland in October 1947, following local government triumphs in June, simultaneously announced the arrival of a new force in Irish politics and scared de Valera into calling a general election for February 1948, despite his Dáil majority and the prospect of a further year in office.

This characteristically nifty piece of electoral timing, along with Seán MacEntee's loaded constituency revision of 1947, helped to contain the threat represented by MacBride and the Clann. The election of 1948 removed the Fianna Fáil majority, but the party still captured just under 42 per cent of the vote and 67 seats in the new Dáil. Clann na Poblachta, on the other hand, was to some extent a victim of de Valera's strategic shrewdness, as well as MacEntee's unscrupulousness: the newcomers won only ten seats, as opposed to the 19 which – with a popular vote of 175,000 – they might have expected to claim. But the Clann was also damaged by its over-brimming confidence, since part of the explanation for its relatively poor showing rested with an extended electoral machine and an army of under-resourced candidates. This mixture of over-confidence and gaucheness proved to be damaging in yet another respect: rather than consolidate its unity and its roots, the party made a lurch for office in the bizarre coalition which was the first Inter-Party government. United only by a suspicion of de Valera, and certainly not by any shared ideological conviction or political vision, the Inter-Party government bound the Clann

with Fine Gael, Labour, the farmers' party (Clann na Talmhan) and numerous straggling independents: it is hard to fault Roy Foster's judgement that 'the combination of Fine Gael's Mulcahy and McGilligan with hitherto intransigent republicans
was as surprising as any rapprochement since that of Charles James Fox and Lord
North'.[57] On the other hand, neither Fox nor North had graduated from University
College Dublin into the intimacy of the Irish bar – a professional trajectory which
was traced both by the new Taoiseach, John Aloysius Costello of Fine Gael, and his
ostensibly very different Minister for External Affairs, Seán MacBride. Nor had the
eighteenth-century 'odd couple' shared a schooling at Mount St Benedict's, the exclusive academy in Wexford which claimed both MacBride, the former IRA Chief of
Staff (1936–8), and James Dillon, the new Minister for Agriculture and a co-founder
of the National Centre Party (1932), among its alumni. It was also therefore the case
that 'the [new] government functioned as well as it did more because of inter-locking
family, educational and temperamental affinities among its more important members than because of anything as mundane as agreement over aims and policies'.[58]

The fall of the Fianna Fáil government in February 1948 marked the end of a
16-year period of rule by de Valera – an unrivalled personal record and a party
achievement matched only by the Fianna Fáil reign from 1957 to 1973. In these
years between 1932 and 1948 Fianna Fáil had achieved a virtual hegemonic status,
appealing materially to the small producers of the country and emotionally to the
working classes: the party satisfied national pride by appearing to score off the British
in the 1930s, and provided a focus for national unity during the 'Emergency' years.
Fianna Fáil came quickly to be seen as reliable by Irish business, while – especially
given the populist leanings of Seán Lemass – it was simultaneously able to forge
a working relationship with the union movement. It advertised one or two token
Protestants (such as Erskine Childers) without compromising its assertively Catholic
identity: it broadcast its concern for northern Catholics while privately treating them
as political pawns in a bigger game. Fianna Fáil satisfied republicans by sounding
off on the partition question; but here again it did not rock the already leaky vessel
of Anglo-Irish relations by converting rhetoric into sustained action. Equally, in the
electoral sphere, though Fianna Fáil had originally endorsed the claims of the small
farmers, a declining and therefore expendable interest group, it offered little practical assistance when in power; and the farmers duly realigned themselves behind
a new party, Clann na Talmhan (1938).

The formation of the first Inter-Party government signalled perhaps the end of
Fianna Fáil's hegemony, but certainly not the end of the party's dominance over
the Irish electorate. It had lost its virtual monopoly over republicanism and social
reformism; it had been seen to spar with the Church and with powerful interest
groups such as the teachers. The party had appeared to lose its direction and
dynamism. But, in the end, all these were perhaps the natural consequences of such
a lengthy command of government. Clann na Poblachta achieved its limited success
precisely because it appeared to be a reversion to the purer Fianna Fáil of 1932, the
Fianna Fáil unsullied by office: its success was therefore a vindication of the Fianna
Fáil tradition. That the newcomers responded so badly to the pressures of power

and were soon bitterly divided was a further mute testimony to the achievement of their predecessors. For if (as it seemed) the Clann had inherited the O'Connellite–Christian Democratic tradition within Irish politics, then there could be little doubt that the Great Dan's cuteness had fallen to de Valera alone. Yeats was perhaps never further off the mark when he judged that de Valera 'will fail through not having enough human life as to judge the human life in others'.[59]

What is remarkable, therefore, is not that Fianna Fáil should have been ousted in 1948 but that this defeat should have been so long in coming, and so narrow when it came. For Fianna Fáil was above all a romance, spiced with republican chiliasm, cultural ideals, social reformism and personal loyalties forged through war or (equally emotive and equally binding) through patronage. If there was always a leap of faith involved in reconciling the party's rhetoric with its achievements, then – such was the charisma of de Valera and the siren call of his movement – the faithful were always to hand. These political acrobatics brought inevitable casualties, however: the IRA men executed by Fianna Fáil for attempting to put the party's history and trumpeted ideals into action; the farmers who dared to believe that de Valera was the reincarnation of Parnell; and the northerners of both main traditions who took the party's stand on partition at face value, and adjusted their fears and ambitions accordingly. But in February 1948, despite strikes and shortages and rising prices, and despite the international isolation of the country, there were still many Irish voters (42 per cent of the total, in fact) who were prepared to judge Fianna Fáil on the basis of its creed rather than its record. This is the true measure of the party's success and of its leader's stature.

6.3   Towards a Redefinition of the National Ideal, 1948–58

These years, from the fall of the Fianna Fáil government in 1948 through to the resignation of de Valera from the Taoiseach's office in 1959, represented the heyday of an Irish Butskellism – in the sense at least that it was an era characterized by an unrelenting party warfare but also by minimal ideological and policy distinctions. Disagreements (as over the utility of the new Industrial Development Authority) seem to have been exaggerated beyond the conventions of manufactured controversy. Indeed, the unpredictable, apparently combustible first coalition seemed – even though its brittle links were forged through an antipathy to de Valera – to be chiefly concerned with proving to the Irish people that it was another Fianna Fáil, albeit one endowed with a French accent and youthful flair and bereft of its rival's military discipline. The Inter-Party government was anxious to yield nothing in terms of either Catholic or republican orthodoxy to its outgoing opponents; and the most striking features of its tenure of power (1948–51) bore the stamp of the Fianna Fáil legacy.

The new Minister for Finance, a talented lawyer named Patrick McGilligan, pursued an expansionist policy which, while it certainly outraged some of the more conventional economic thinkers on the Fianna Fáil frontbench (such as Aiken and

MacEntee), nevertheless chimed with the ideas being mulled over in private by Seán Lemass (his public attitudes – as Bew and Patterson and, more recently, John Horgan have remarked – were much more bland).[60] Both Lemass and McGilligan were Keynesians, albeit of a fairly gentle hue: Lemass had been an early (if relatively ineffectual) evangelist for both Keynes and Beveridge within the Fianna Fáil wartime cabinet, while McGilligan became, in the words of Joe Lee, 'an intellectual as well as a political convert to the potential of a moderate Keynesianism in Irish circumstances'.[61] This, at any rate, was the message conveyed by the McGilligan budget of 1950, a modestly expansionist measure which represented a liberation from the austere, revenue-centred approach of the past. McGilligan's defence of his strategy against the troglodytes of Finance might well have been privately recited by Lemass: 'we value the production of national expenditure in terms of (1) social stability (2) expanding national income (3) efficient operation of government services, in that order of importance'. (On the other hand, those who remembered McGilligan in an earlier incarnation – as Cumann na nGaedheal Minister for Industry – may have been less than convinced: he was then intoning that 'people may have to die in this country and die through starvation').[62]

The creation of the Industrial Development Authority (IDA, 1949), a particular enthusiasm of the politically omnivorous Seán MacBride (the Inter-Party Minister for External Affairs), also echoed some of the concerns expressed by Lemass when at Industry and Commerce. The IDA was intended to encourage new industry and the expansion of existing industries, and in addition was briefed to investigate the effects of protection on the Irish economy. Although it was initially the victim of some vicious sibling rivalry from Finance and of some tactical grousing from Lemass, the IDA survived and thrived: it has been rightly described as the Inter-Party version of Lemass's Industrial Efficiency Bill (a measure that proposed an Industrial Efficiency Bureau similar in some of its powers to the IDA).[63]

MacBride proved himself to be a follower not merely of Lemass, but also of his old 'Chief', de Valera: the Inter-Party government veered little from the foreign policy guidelines laid down by their Fianna Fáil predecessors. There were, however, some intriguing differences of emphasis. Fianna Fáil, the republican party, had resolutely held back from a final excision of the monarchy, even though the constitution of the country was widely acknowledged as republican in form: the reasons for this self-denial have already been outlined, and probably relate more to de Valera's acute sense of political timing than his professed concern for the monarchist sympathies of northern Unionists. The new Taoiseach, John Costello, had represented the Cumann na nGaedheal government at a succession of imperial conferences in the 1920s and early 1930s; but he was a firm opponent of de Valera's External Relations Act, and he recognized the cogency of Fianna Fáil's claims to be better patriots than their Fine Gael rivals. He also saw an opportunity to undercut the IRA by an inexpensive (indeed, perhaps even politically profitable) gesture. In addition he was under general (though evidently not immediate) pressure from MacBride, an even more strident opponent of de Valera's legislation than himself, and an even more ardent republican than was commonly found in the Fianna Fáil hierarchy. Costello therefore took the apparently outrageous step (for a Fine Gael Taoiseach) of announcing his government's plans to remove the legislation of 1936, with its attendant ambiguities, and to establish an Irish republic. The announcement was made abruptly at Ottawa on 7 September 1948, and has since been the subject of an unflagging controversy. On the whole it seems that, while the issue may have been previously discussed within the Inter-Party cabinet, no detailed plan of action was agreed. MacBride, for example, though strongly republican, was not pressing for immediate action on the External Relations Act, and indeed had not even made its repeal a condition of entering the government: Costello's announcement was conveyed to him while he was dining with the British representative in Ireland, John Maffey, Lord Rugby, and seems to have taken him by surprise. Whether or not the rookie Taoiseach had committed a diplomatic gaffe remains open to question: although he was in some respects a gauche successor to de Valera, he had experience on the international stage and was too skilled a lawyer to be easily tempted into indiscretion or pique. In addition, as has been mentioned, there were good tactical reasons for acting as Costello did: he was thereby able to play the republican ace before either de Valera or MacBride, and to underline the patriotic credentials of his own party (as distinct from the coalition as a whole). Though the Irish people were deeply unexcited by the formal establishment of the republic in April 1949, this should not divert attention from the long-term party political utility of Costello's initiative.

Elsewhere in the realm of foreign affairs the Inter-Party government ventured little from the paths of righteousness explored by Fianna Fáil. Indeed it is arguable that, as with the issue of the republic, the new government acted in a more rigidly orthodox Fianna Fáil manner than had the de Valera government itself. The new government was certainly anxious to underline its Catholic orthodoxy: its ministers therefore telegraphed Pope Pius XII at the conclusion of their first meeting, pledging 'devotion to your August Person, as well as our firm resolve to be guided in all our work by the teaching of Christ' (this has been described as 'the most effusively Catholic message ever sent by any Government of the Irish state').[64] The government also facilitated the efforts of the Irish Catholic hierarchy to aid the Christian Democrats of Italy in their apocalyptic struggle against the godless reds of Italian communism. Indeed, despite the radical dimension to Clann na Poblachta and the revolutionary pedigree of its leader, MacBride, the Inter-Party government was resolutely pro-western in its sympathies. MacBride was an enthusiastic Europeanist, supporting the Council of Europe (1949) as a bulwark against communism and sponsoring the proposed membership of right-wing clericalist dictatorships such as Franco's Spain and Salazar's Portugal. Just as de Valera had been prepared to consider trading defence concessions for progress on the issue of partition, so MacBride attempted early in 1949 to abandon neutrality and join NATO in return for American support on the issue of the border. But the Irish offer was refused (Britain was too valuable a cold war partner for the Americans), even though the seriousness of MacBride's intentions seem clear. Nor were the Americans much more forthcoming over the issue of Marshall Aid: Irish hopes for massive grant support were disappointed, although substantial loans were made available by the Federal government. Apparently so much like his 'Chief', MacBride was more concerned about the republic than about political practicalities, and much more concerned about partition than about neutrality: de Valera, on the other hand, rarely made the mistake of allowing rigid principle to stand in the way of the exercise of power.

The crispest illustration of these truths, and of much else, came with the 'mother and child' debacle of 1951: here MacBride, through personal obtuseness as well as uncomplicated religious conviction, helped to create a political crisis out of problems which the smoother diplomats of Fianna Fáil might well have defused or at least handed on. And indeed the origins of the 'mother and child' affair lay with an inheritance from the previous Fianna Fáil administration. The Fianna Fáil Minister for Health and Social Welfare, Dr Jim Ryan, enacted a measure in 1947 that was designed to tackle the problem of infectious diseases within the community and also to limit the risks for expectant or recent mothers as well as children up to the age of 16. The Ryan Health Act provoked some considerable resentment from both the Catholic hierarchy and the Irish medical profession: the Church saw threats to its social teaching, and indeed to its broader educational function, while those doctors who (in the memorable indictment of Joe Lee) 'worshipped at the altar of Croesus while demurely wrapped in the robes of Hippocrates' saw a threat to their income in the shape of 'socialized medicine'.[65] But, since the Fianna Fáil government fell in February 1948, it was left to the Inter-Party ministers to face down the formidable union of scalpel and crozier which Dr Ryan had inadvertently helped to forge.

In the late summer of 1950 the crusading but temperamental Minister for Health, Dr Noel Browne, moved to implement the 'mother and child' proposals of the Ryan Act: his plans were leaked in the *Sunday Independent* in September and stimulated a lengthy rebuttal from the hierarchy in the following weeks. After this preliminary skirmish, there followed a phoney war of some months before hostilities were resumed in March 1951. But the short, sharp conflict that emerged was fought not between the Irish government and the hierarchy, or between ministers and doctors, but rather between, on the one hand, an alliance of the government, the Church and the medical profession and, on the other hand, the embattled Noel Browne. No Inter-Party minister, including Browne, proposed to act in defiance of the Church's verdict on the morality of the 'mother and child' proposals: the rights of the Church to intervene in legislation affecting Catholic welfare and morals were not in dispute. What was questionable (at least in Browne's eyes) was the precise nature of the Church's attitude: Browne chose to argue to his colleagues – in defiance of the evidence – that the bishops were not opposed to his proposals and were in fact open to negotiation. Throughout the controversy Browne made some hamfisted efforts at intrigue (he tried unsuccessfully, for example, to represent his plans as approved government policy and thereby to widen his quarrel with the hierarchy into a genuine Church–state clash); but he was outclassed in terms of strategic ability by Costello. Nor did the hierarchy help Browne's case: despite his affected optimism, the bishops remained resolutely opposed to 'socialized medicine' (confirming their attitude on 4 April 1951) and the Inter-Party ministers followed happily in the episcopal wake. Browne was now thoroughly isolated from the Church and from his government colleagues – including his own party leader, MacBride; and on 10 April the Clann na Poblachta boss demanded and won his errant minister's resignation. Falling, Browne helped to bring down the Inter-Party edifice with him: embarrassed by the Health Minister's loud departure (Browne published the correspondence relating to the affair in the *Irish Times*), and weakened by the desertion of three independent deputies over a separate issue, the first Inter-Party government fell in May 1951. The 'mother and child' episode, coming on top of a succession of other ministerial humiliations (including the 'Battle of Baltinglass', where the Minister for Posts and Telegraphs was exposed to the country dishing out patronage in a more than usually overt and insensitive manner), had put paid to Ireland's first experiment in coalition government.

The 'mother and child' affair illustrates a number of home truths – and not always expected truths – about the first Inter-Party government. Costello was perhaps only reiterating the values of the old Cumann na nGaedheal tradition when he declared during the affair that 'I am an Irishman second; I am a Catholic first'.[66] But though the relegation of national identity behind religious conviction may not be especially surprising, the emphatic publication of this priority is of greater interest, given that the Costello government was associated with the most determined effort to address the issue of partition since the early 1920s. Moreover, while Costello's very public expression of his faith echoed similar pronouncements from de Valera and other Fianna Fáil frontbenchers, Fianna Fáil on the whole showed themselves to be more effective – equally respectful, but more assertive – in dealing with the hierarchy. The 'mother and child' controversy also provoked the most unambiguous assertion of the Church's views on this key area of social policy, and the most explicit – though polite – rebuke to government for venturing into areas where it was argued that the family, informed and guided by the clergy, should be autonomous. Again, this is scarcely surprising, except when viewed in the light of the shifts of emphasis within Catholic social teaching in the 1960s: what is more important, again, is not the fact of this dialogue between ministers and bishops, but that the Church's views should be expressed so emphatically and – because of Browne's leaks – so publicly: as Conor Cruise O'Brien has remarked, 'the episode was atypical in its blatancy'.[67] This is to be contrasted with the more discreet and more dexterous handling of a related issue (the Health Act of 1953) by de Valera and the incoming Fianna Fáil government. The near-unanimous ministerial acquiescence with the Church's line is also, superficially, surprising, given the nuances within a complicated coalition: but then religious fidelity crossed the boundaries of party, with the Labour Tánaiste, Willie Norton, as loyal a member of the Knights of Columbanus as long-standing Fine Gaelers such as Richard Mulcahy (Minister for Education) or Seán MacEoin (Minister for Justice). Seán MacBride, it will be remembered, defined the social radicalism of Clann na Poblachta within the formal bounds of Catholic teaching; and indeed one of the central thrusts of his project was the alignment of Catholicism and republicanism. Outside government, as Kieran Allen has observed, even the Irish Trades Union Congress (somewhat less Catholic in its ethos than the rival Congress of Irish Unions) backed away from any endorsement of Browne.[68] Thus the 'mother and child' affair, far from being a crisis in Church–state relations, highlights the solidity of the consensus on social and religious values within the Ireland of the early 1950s. The affair says as much about the political power of an influential professional lobby, the Irish Medical Association – 'the most successful trade union of all', in the verdict of Desmond Williams – as about the authority of the Church; and it says as much about the energy, the obtuseness and the bloody-mindedness of Noel Browne as it does about the energy, the obtuseness and the bloody-mindedness of Archbishop John Charles McQuaid.[69]

As has been mentioned, the new Fianna Fáil administration, returned in the general election of 30 May 1951, defused the 'mother and child' issue with a characteristic combination of briskness and menace. Jim Ryan (who returned to the Health and Social Welfare portfolio) promoted a new Health Act (1953) which, while it has been understandably deemed a 'sideshow compared to the fundamental question of the management of the economy', is nevertheless not without interest.[70] Ryan proposed to proceed along the general lines traced by Browne (whose support, along with that of another left-wing deputy, Peadar Cowan, was important to the survival of the Fianna Fáil government); like Browne – though possibly with greater reason – he seems to have thought that he had episcopal support when he introduced his bill into the Dáil on 26 February 1953. As with Browne, this was not in fact the case – and it seemed as if the coalition between the hierarchy and the Irish Medical Association would be reactivated: more worryingly, the bishops proposed to announce their opposition (and therefore entrench their position) through a letter to the press, to be published on 19 April. It was at this stage that de Valera intervened, mobilizing the moral and political self-righteousness which the British and other political opponents had found so formidable: in this case de Valera, by sounding out a theological advisor to Pius XII, Cardinal Michael Browne, was able to inform the Irish bishops that their position was not in absolute accord with current thinking at the Vatican. Having threatened to separate the Irish hierarchy from Rome, de Valera and Ryan proceeded to negotiate an agreement with the bishops, which in turn meant that the episcopal alliance with the Irish Medical Association was now broken. There were certainly concessions to the hierarchy's case: but the most recent commentators accept that, while the bishops were given enough to save face, the compromise that was struck favoured the government.[71] Much of the Browne–Ryan scheme had been salvaged (even though Browne himself saw the agreement as an example of Rome Rule): here again – Browne's discontent notwithstanding – the continuities between the administrations are striking.

However, the differences between de Valera's handling of the issue and that of Costello are no less instructive: de Valera, a respectful and faithful son of the Church, nevertheless treated the bishops at least partly in political terms – as an influential force in Irish society who could not be ignored, and whose support was important, but who certainly could be outplayed or, indeed, faced down. Costello, by way of contrast, following in the Cosgrave tradition and lacking the spiritual and political self-confidence of the 'Chief', tended towards a more submissive approach to the hierarchy. For Costello, the views of the bishops were holy writ rather than a bargaining position.

But on the whole, as ever, it is the continuities between Fianna Fáil and the Inter-Party team which impress. In part each had to deal with the same apparently endemic problems in Irish society – high levels of unemployment and devastatingly high levels of emigration. In addition, both the Fianna Fáil government of 1951–4 and its successor, the second Inter-Party government (1954–7), struggled with balance of payments deficits. On the whole each political tradition responded in a similar manner to these challenges, combining a moderate social reformism with an orthodox approach to budgetary management. Seán MacEntee, whose fortunes were – briefly – on the rise in the 1951–4 government, was Fianna Fáil Minister for Finance and presented a viciously deflationary first budget in 1952: the centre-piece was a hike in the standard rate of income tax by one shilling (or 5 per cent). MacEntee saw himself (or affected to see himself) as righting the misdeeds of the voluptuaries in the previous Inter-Party administration, and he was therefore anxious to present corrective measures as speedily as possible (so as to deflect the blame): no less a commentator than T.K. Whitaker endorsed this thinking. But, faultless though MacEntee's political sense may have been (at least in the short term), it is now generally accepted that his economic timing may have been badly misjudged and that he was hitting the fragile Irish economy with a deflationary salvo at precisely the moment when the balance of payments was improving.[72] In any event, MacEntee certainly compounded, if he did not create, the slump of the mid-1950s, pursuing the same broad deflationary policies in 1953–4 even when the evidence suggested that they were not warranted. He thereby helped to crush local consumer demand and to undermine the manufacturing base of the still protected Irish economy. The MacEntee strategy produced minimal levels of economic growth, and even a measure of industrial contraction: it helped to consolidate an environment unsuited to export achievement and entrepreneurial risk-taking.

Nor was the main Inter-Party response to the problems of the economy any more imaginative (at least in the first instance). Costello, who returned as Taoiseach at the general election of May 1954, inherited a still fragile economy, characterized by some cosmetic improvements and some apparently irreducible problems (such as the growing figures for emigration). The new Minister for Finance, Gerard Sweetman, pursued the same broad strategies as MacEntee (the intellectually more adventurous McGilligan, aged 65 and apparently in poor health – in fact he lived until he was 90 – chose to serve as attorney general rather than return to Finance). But MacEntee's strategies had addressed symptoms rather than the disease itself, and a series of devastating announcements in 1955–6 suggested that the country was being bled of its people as well as its capital. The balance of payments crisis reappeared, with a deficit of £35 million in 1955; more worrying, the census of 1956 revealed that, even after 35 years of independence, the Irish population was at an all-time low. Sweetman's instinctive response to this statistical pummelling was to apply more taxes (he did so between March and July 1956). But (as MacEntee had found) this was a politically very dangerous strategy: it had provoked, for MacEntee, unrest even in the normally submissive civil service as well as carefully orchestrated and embarrassing militancy from the Dublin Unemployed Association; it threatened, for Sweetman, to alienate the Inter-Party government's working-class support – and this at a time when the labour movement was progressing towards a reunification after the split of 1943–4 (unity was eventually completed in 1959 in the shape of the ICTU). In addition Lemass, still the most populist of the Fianna Fáil leaders, was outlining a programme for the creation of 100,000 jobs over five years, based upon hikes in public expenditure and external investment and drawing upon the Italian Vanoni Plan of 1954: this was the substance of his famous (though somewhat ambiguous, even 'intellectually incoherent') 'Clery's' speech of October 1955.[73] The Inter-Party government was therefore goaded by political and economic pressures into traversing some underexplored outreaches of economic policy: a Capital Investment Advisory Committee was formed in 1955 in order to scrutinize public investment and to seek more productive means of deploying capital. Willie Norton, the Tánaiste, began pressing openly for foreign investment in 1955–6, while Costello incorporated this cry into a sweeping economic revitalization plan, published in October 1956. Costello's initiative combined the familiar with the more daring: it called for agricultural research and expansion, tax breaks for exporters, grants for new plant, an advisory committee on capital investment, as well as foreign capital. It signalled a breakdown of the cross-party consensus on economic management; it represented a striking modification of the traditional tenets of Irish economic nationalism. But, since the government collapsed early in 1957, the Costello plan was in effect still-born; and it fell to Fianna Fáil – united, ironically, around the old war cries of an economic nationalism – to elaborate a radical solution to the social and economic crises of post-war Ireland.

In other respects the second Inter-Party government looked very much like a continuation of the first. With Browne on the opposition back benches, the government was able to represent more directly the interests of its professional base. Dr T.F. O'Higgins, the Minister for Health, bowed to the pressure of the medical lobby through modifications to the Ryan Health Act of 1953: although the original Browne–Ryan proposals might, with the aid of a rose-tinted lens, have looked like the beginnings of a widely embracing free health service, in fact the second Inter-Party government successfully and lastingly bolstered the private sector through the creation of the Voluntary Health Insurance Board. If the government respected the interests of the professions, then it continued to be deferential towards the Church: Costello was not prepared to defy doctors and bishops either in 1951 or (at any rate in the short term) when returned to power in 1954. The Taoiseach tacitly endorsed Archbishop McQuaid's opposition to sporting ties between Ireland and communist countries, withholding any form of official recognition when the Yugoslav and Irish football teams played a match in October 1955. However, it should also be said that Costello seems to have learned from de Valera, and from his experience of submitting to McQuaid: appointments to the censorship board (which included a Protestant) and to the directorship of the Arts Council (Seán Ó Faoláin) in 1956 emphatically did not meet with the approval of the archbishop.

In the realm of foreign affairs the new Minister, Liam Cosgrave, built on the achievements of the first Inter-Party administration, and indeed of his father's government, in consolidating Irish participation in the international arena. Cosgrave served as chairman of the Committee of Ministers of the Council of Europe in 1955 (Irish membership had been negotiated by MacBride); and also in 1955 Cosgrave led Ireland into the United Nations, an event that had been delayed for some years owing partly to the opposition of the Soviet Union. In these ways the second Inter-Party administration continued to elaborate the European themes originally essayed by MacBride and the first Inter-Party government; and it sought to establish a significant presence on the larger stage, within the United Nations, just as W.T. Cosgrave and the Cumann na nGaedheal government had achieved prominence for Ireland at the League of Nations.

And yet, with the second Inter-Party government in 1957, just as with Cumann na nGaedheal in 1932, Ireland's international standing mattered much less with voters than their standard of living and day-to-day economic matters. The renewed IRA campaign – Operation Harvest (1956) – against the Northern Ireland government also revived republican and anti-partitionist sympathies which Fine Gael, despite Costello's Ottawa pronouncement and his commitment to reunification, was ill-equipped to exploit. The proximate cause of the fall of the government was MacBride's withdrawal of Clann na Poblachta support (the party had three strategically crucial seats in the Dáil): the Clann leader complained about Costello's clamp-down against the IRA and the lack of any long-term economic strategy. And, broadly, these were the dominant issues of the election contest, which was fought out in March 1957 and which produced a dramatic victory for Fianna Fáil (with 77 seats, as opposed to Fine Gael's 40). The IRA campaign seems to have stimulated traditional republican feeling, which helps a little to explain the Fianna Fáil victory as well as the return of four Sinn Féin deputies. But the fundamental issue was the economy and the unpopularity – as well as the comparative inefficacy – of Sweetman's austerity programme.

Much scholarship has concentrated on examining the relative decline of Fianna Fáil in the ten years between 1948 and 1957 – a decade sandwiched between two 16-year periods of uninterrupted electoral triumph. The complete and lasting nature of the victory of 1957 might seem to suggest that the party had at last hit upon a persuasive manifesto with which to reconstruct its support. In fact, it is all too easy to see the election of 1957 as unequivocally a turning point both for Fianna Fáil and, indeed, the country as a whole. Most scholars agree that the 1957 result was less a victory for Fianna Fáil than a defeat for the Inter-Party ministers and for their discredited record of economic management: Joe Lee has drawn parallels with the election of 1944, where Fianna Fáil won 76 seats out of 138 and yet was out of office within four years.[74] The reality was that Fianna Fáil entered the 1957 contest without any agreed economic programme: as Bew and Patterson have argued, 'the election result showed that the two major coalition partners had lost many more votes than Fianna Fáil had gained, and demonstrated that divisions in Fianna Fáil were no compensation for the perceived incapacity of the coalition to deal with the disastrous economic conditions'.[75]

The election of 1957 was important because it gave Fianna Fáil a breathing space – a chance to restructure its electoral appeal and to re-establish its hold over Irish voters. In the 1930s, as Kieran Allen has argued, Fianna Fáil was able to hold together its support by offering native manufacturers tariff protection and working people a modest reformism; in the 1940s the party was able to muster support on national grounds, and with the benefit of a broken and disoriented labour movement.[76] But the slump of the post-war era had restricted what the party could offer to its support; and though de Valera returned to the question of partition in the late 1940s, both out of principle and as a result of limited alternative options, patriotic drumbeating could never completely divert the Irish electorate from the issues of jobs, emigration and declining standards of living. The pendulum swings of Irish politics in the years between 1948 and 1957 highlighted voter dissatisfaction with each of the parties in power, and underlined the extent to which none of the parties was able successfully to address the key problems of the economy.

The election of 1957 brought most of the failed Fianna Fáil leadership team back into office, and to this extent the party might well have looked forward only to a further prolongation of economic turmoil and a correspondingly brief period in power. But, beneath the apparently dead wood encrusting the heroes of 1922–3, there were signs of rebirth. Seán MacEntee, the architect of the party's austerity programme, had been discredited by the election defeat of 1954 and had never fully recovered ground: in a remarkable demotion (for the otherwise comparatively static Fianna Fáil frontbench), MacEntee was moved by de Valera from the Finance portfolio to Health and Social Welfare. This humiliation served to emphasize the ascendancy of MacEntee's old rival, Lemass, who once again held the office of Tánaiste, and who now – for the first time – looked like the unbeatable successor to the aging 'Chief' (though, when the time came, there was in fact a tussle between Lemass and Frank Aiken). Lemass's newly consolidated strength had other connotations, however. The Tánaiste had always been careful not to stray too far away from the economic nationalist creed of his colleagues, at least in terms of his public pronouncements. But since the Second World War Lemass had been interested in the possibilities of greater state involvement in the Irish economy, together with an improved relationship with the unions: he had looked forward to the possibility that the old economic doctrines might be refined along Keynesian lines. There was some tactical camouflaging of these opinions, when necessary, but the outlines of Lemass's intellectual and political development were clear enough. In 1953 he had spoken in favour of foreign investment in the country, a turnaround from the pretty determined efforts he had made in the 1930s to gaelicize Irish business: in January 1954 he asked the IDA to review the effects of the long-standing protectionist policies of successive Irish governments. Lemass's progress from what Joe Lee has called 'the age of faith to the age of reason' was gradual and was accompanied by much trimming and apparent recantation.[77] But its significance is unmistakeable, because Lemass's own prominence within Fianna Fáil was, by the late 1950s, assured. Moreover, the importance of Lemass's development was enhanced because an intellectually self-confident and skilful young civil servant – T.K. Whitaker, from 1956 the Secretary of the Department of Finance – was making roughly the same philosophical trek. This concord between minister and bureaucrat would shortly have the most profound consequences for both the Irish economy and the balance of Irish politics: both Fianna Fáil and Ireland were to be rescued from what looked in 1957 like the edge of the abyss.

6.4   The Age of Lemass, 1957–73

If Mr de Valera is the architect of modern Ireland, then Mr Lemass is indisputably the engineer, the contractor and the foreman rolled into one . . .

Irish Times, 25 July 1953

Is there a faultline in Irish history, marked by the return of the Fianna Fáil government in 1957? If there is, what is its nature and completeness? The geological strata on either side of the apparent divide are evidently related: the economic policies which Lemass and the new Minister of Finance, Dr James Ryan, pursued had been foreshadowed by a variety of initiatives or ideas launched by earlier administrations. The fossil remains are similar: underperforming veterans of the civil war and the 'troubles' occupied much of the Fianna Fáil frontbench, both in opposition and in government. The bedrock is evidently the same in composition: a conglomerate of a passive republicanism, populist conservative values and an intense commitment to the interests of the Irish bourgeoisie.

Debate on these issues tends, inevitably, to have a strong ideological flavour, with leftist historians emphasizing the long-term continuities in elite strategy, and those of a more centrist or conservative disposition tending to highlight divergence and disjunction. Inevitably, too, the evidence is ambiguous. There were indeed, for example, continuities in the personnel of the Fianna Fáil leadership: de Valera remained Taoiseach for the moment (he resigned in June 1959 in order to take up the Presidency), while most of the earlier stalwarts returned to ministerial prominence. On the other hand there were some small but telling changes: MacEntee, the 'high-Tory' of the party, was demoted, his place at Finance taken by Jim Ryan, an ally of Lemass; Gerry Boland, strongly republican and now aging (72 in 1957), was dropped from office; some youngsters were introduced into the cabinet (Neil Blaney, aged 35, went to Posts and Telegraphs, and Kevin Boland, aged 40, went to Defence: Jack Lynch, also aged 40, had already junior ministerial experience in the 1951–4 Fianna Fáil government, and now acquired cabinet rank as Minister for the Gaeltacht). Lemass, reappointed as Tánaiste, had a greater than ever influence, partly because of the eclipse of leadership rivals but also because de Valera was aging (75 in 1957) and ailing, both physically and politically: from late 1958 until retiring as Taoiseach in June 1959 he was buffeted by allegations of impropriety concerning shares in the party newspaper, the *Irish Press*.

Lemass was no radical, nor was he a thoroughgoing modernist: he was too astute a party politician to venture far from the median, and particularly when the demands of opposition imposed the need for old-fashioned patriotic rhetoric. On the other hand, if he was a convinced nationalist, then he was also a pragmatist who saw the health of the nation primarily in material rather than in spiritual terms: he differed from de Valera, therefore, in the direction but not in the solidity of his nationalism. Lemass may not have been an innovative thinker, but he was certainly the most prominent of the Fianna Fáilers who were looking with interest at the social and economic ideas of those in other parties, and indeed in other countries. As has frequently been said, Lemass bridged the old and the new. He had fought alongside Pearse in the General Post Office and had served (so it would seem) in Collins's 'Squad' on Bloody Sunday, 21 November 1920: but he had the good taste to be discreet about his patriotic achievement and to trade on his ministerial achievements rather than on his prowess as a teenage fighter.[78] He had, in addition, the moral courage to develop and expand his nationalist vision.

Lemass is, with T.K. Whitaker, the Secretary of the Department of Finance, the figure most closely associated with the rapid economic growth of the early and mid-1960s, and the concomitant political and social changes. And yet, even though the names of Lemass and Whitaker are often interlinked, it was the coalition Minister for Finance, Gerard Sweetman, who had been the critical patron of Whitaker, appointing him to the secretaryship at the age of 40, in 1956. It was Jim Ryan who encouraged Whitaker in the elaboration of his ideas; and it was Ryan who sponsored Whitaker's paper on Economic Development (first outlined as 'Has Ireland a Future?' in December 1957) before the Fianna Fáil cabinet: the full-blown plan was published in May 1958. In addition Lemass, though an easy convert to Whitaker's line of argument, was not an unquestioning disciple: Whitaker tended towards a doctrinaire economic liberalism, while Lemass always remained sensitive to the politics of political economy. He was, however, a keen patron of the Programme for Economic Expansion, a modified and expanded version of Whitaker's earlier papers and a document that came to represent the holy gospel of the Lemass years.

The Programme, which was published in December 1958, has traditionally been seen as the blueprint for the rapid process of modernization that occurred in Irish society and in the Irish economy over the following decade: it has been seen as the document heralding the age of enlightenment within Irish economic thought and practice. It should be said at once that it has also long been recognized that Whitaker's Plan and the related Programme reflected not only the Secretary's own gradual intellectual reorientation but also the long-term gestation of Keynesian ideas within Irish politics and also the civil service.[79] Indeed, the Programme has to be viewed at least partly in the context of the political and intellectual life of the bureaucracy: aside from its many other connotations, the Programme represented 'the snatching by the Department of Finance of the initiative in planning' at a time when it seemed that this initiative might fall into other hands.[80] The Programme highlighted the need for a shift away from protectionist policies, a move that had already been cautiously investigated and adumbrated in the early 1950s: it called for a five-year investment programme, with an emphasis on economically productive expenditure, and a target growth rate of 2 per cent each year. As with Costello's plans of 1956, there was also an emphasis on the gearing of agriculture towards the export market. Equally, as with the initiatives of the second Inter-Party administration, there was a recognition that growth could not be achieved in the absence of substantial foreign capital: the Industrial Development (Encouragement of External Investment) Act of 1958 was the tangible expression of this insight. Whitaker and Lemass therefore owed debts to earlier administrations: but while they were not the earliest government team to shift away from an emphasis on budgetary equilibrium, they were arguably the first to shift towards an economically productive dis-equilibrium. Nor were they the earliest to recognize the importance of foreign investment and export-led growth (the IDA had, after all, been founded in 1949, and an Export Profits Tax Relief measure had been enacted in 1956): but they were the first to combine these ideas with both intellectual rigour and political self-confidence. Earlier administrations had been much more sensitive about the leftist connotations of economic planning; and in the event earlier administrations did not have the political opportunities provided by the Fianna Fáil electoral roller-coaster which ran from 1957 until 1973.

If there has been some scholarly debate about the balance between continuity and change within the Whitaker–Lemass 'revolution', then there has also been some dispute – or at least difference of emphasis – about the relationship between planning and results. What is not in question is that Ireland, in common with elsewhere, experienced remarkable rates of growth: the gross national product rose at an average rate of 4.5 per cent for each of the years between 1959 and 1963. Nor is there any question that growth helped to stimulate social change, perhaps the most important aspect being a dramatic fall in the numbers of emigrants and a parallel rise in the total population of the country: in each year of the period 1956–61 an average of 43,000 Irish people were emigrating, while only 11,000 emigrated in each year of the span 1966–71. But how far was the Whitaker initiative responsible for this social and economic turnaround, and how far did 'the comparatively modest hibernian boomlet' merely reflect a natural and predictable upturn in the business cycle or, indeed, wider international economic improvements?[81] The scale of growth, while unremarkable by international standards, was certainly unusual within the context of recent Irish economic history, and was therefore more than might normally have been expected from a conventional recovery. The nature of Irish growth was also striking: traditional agricultural exports were important, but manufacturing was of increasing significance, and in particular burgeoning new sectors of Irish industry. It would be unrealistic to detach any discussion of these improvements from the global context, or indeed from the initiatives taken by earlier administrations and dating back to the late 1940s: in particular it would be unfair to discount the efforts of Costello's second government, even if this coalition had collapsed before the fruit of its labours had fully matured. Lemass and Whitaker built on earlier achievements, and Fianna Fáil had the good fortune to be in office at the time of an international economic upswing. But it seems clear that the Irish fall-out from this global activity might well have been much more modest had it not been for the Programme for Economic Expansion.

Socialist historians have occasionally asked why the Programme did not create more problems for Fianna Fáil, and more broadly in Irish society, than in fact was the case.[82] To some extent the answers to this issue should already be clear. The Programme was novel, even revolutionary, but not in obvious ways: it was new, not in its ideas but rather in terms of the political consensus (between government and civil service) upon which it was founded and also in terms of the care with which it was explained to the Irish public. It was novel in so far as it provided the right combination of (albeit familiar) ideas at an appropriate moment both in terms of Irish politics (a stable Fianna Fáil administration was in power with 78 Dáil seats) and of the international economy (which was booming). Still, Fianna Fáil's electoral strength rested partly on its support of native industry, and in particular upon its protectionist policies – precisely the areas identified by the Programme as needing attention and reform. But Lemass and Whitaker were not proposing an immediate abandonment of the tariff strategy, nor were they proposing to smother native industry by favouring more efficient foreign counterparts. On the contrary, tariffs might still be applied for the protection of sapling Irish industries, while the ending of protection was seen in highly gradualist terms. Moreover, foreign capital was seen by Lemass primarily as a means of boosting exports, and not as a way of edging out native industries from their privileged position in the Irish market place. Fianna Fáil was therefore not so much abandoning its economic nationalist convictions as modernizing them and rendering them workable: the party pulled off a remarkable display of two-timing, simultaneously courting foreign business while reassuring Irish entrepreneurs of its undying affection.

Again, socialist historians have tended to see the Programme for Economic Expansion in terms of Fianna Fáil's need to retain electoral control of the Irish working classes.[83] It has been argued that the party's electoral strategies had foundered in the 1950s, having been buffeted by the squalls of the Irish economy: Fianna Fáil had therefore little or nothing to offer either its business or its working-class support. By way of contrast, in the 1930s the party had been able to deliver modest social reform to its working-class constituency while promising protection to its entrepreneurial support and a robust nationalism to everyone: in the 1940s, during the war, the party's patriotic credentials, combined with a divided opposition, meant that Fianna Fáil could still thrive, even though the economic context was becoming progressively more threatening. The initiative of 1958 has been seen as a way of squaring the circle of capitalist politics, by reconciling bourgeois and working-class electoral support. A revamping of the Irish economy meant not just the possibility of gain for the business classes (provided that the new foreign investors were not set in competition with their Irish counterparts for the home market): it also meant the possibility of advance, in terms of employment and social welfare, for ordinary Irish voters. And, indeed, Lemass – in keeping with the substance of his political ideas from the 1940s – saw the Programme for Economic Expansion as working within a corporatist framework: in November 1961 he sponsored an Employer–Labour Conference, and in June 1963 he was invited for the first time (bizarrely, given the rightward thrust of Fianna Fáil) to address the annual conference of the Irish Transport and General Workers' Union. In 1963 Lemass set up the National Industrial and Economic Council, representing government, employers and labour, with a view to harmonizing industrial relations and informing debate about the broader development of the Irish economy. In fact, despite these initiatives, the rapid economic growth of the early 1960s was accompanied by severe labour unrest, and particularly in 1962–3. But the broader party aim – of balancing the political support of the working and business classes – was triumphantly sustained for 16 years: the business elite demonstrated its loyalty to the party through subscriptions to Taca (the aptly named Fianna Fáil fund-raising body), while the workers repaid growing opportunities for employment and a more generous welfare provision with their votes.

The most serious political challenge to Lemass's delicately balanced social partnership came, ironically, not from working-class protest or the desertion of the business interest but from within the Fianna Fáil cabinet, through the resignation in 1964 of P.J. Smith, the Minister for Agriculture. Smith, who, in the (somewhat ambiguous) verdict of Liam Skinner in 1946, allowed 'nothing to restrict his close and constant touch with the people he represents', was an agrarian republican from Cavan who articulated the farmers' belief that Fianna Fáil had surrendered to the labour movement.[84] The resignation was the first to have been sustained by a Fianna Fáil government on a matter of policy, and it was instantly the subject of a damage-limitation exercise, involving even President de Valera. But despite some tactical obfuscation from the party managers, and despite Smith's own relative (perhaps enforced) discretion, the issues were clear enough: the belief among some rural Fianna Fáilers that the unions were gaining the upper hand, and the simultaneous conviction that farming incomes were coming under challenge. The Smith affair, muted though it was, highlighted both the political difficulties inherent in Lemass's very urban strategies and a glaring defeat in another key area of policy – the Irish government's failure to win admission to the European Economic Community (EEC), and its consequent inability to lead restless farmers to the over-brimming trough of the Common Agricultural Policy.

The snub experienced by the Irish in 1962 at the hands of the EEC, and in particular the French, was mitigated by the fact that the British received similar treatment: it was, however, an expensive setback, and one which Lemass – who of course recognized clearly the benefits that would flow from membership – laboured hard to correct. On the whole, however, this was the only major failure sustained by Fianna Fáil within the realm of foreign policy. As with the Programme for Economic Expansion, so with foreign affairs, some of the groundwork for later achievement was laid by earlier administrations: as with the economy, it was the good fortune, or perhaps the good electoral housekeeping, of Fianna Fáil to survive in office long enough to reap the benefits of long-term diplomatic labour. Ireland had been admitted to the United Nations in 1955 under the second Inter-Party government, and in July 1956 John Costello, as Taoiseach, enunciated the principles governing the Irish presence in New York (non-alignment and – characteristically – the maintenance of 'Christian civilization').[85] It was Frank Aiken, however, who, as Fianna Fáil Minister for External Affairs (1957–69), put these principles into action and who, with, as Joe Lee delicately puts it, the 'cerebral support' of some brilliant civil servants, in effect reconstructed Irish foreign policy after the false starts and diplomatic set-backs of the immediate post-war era.[86] Ireland's commitment to the UN was expressed materially through involvement in seven out of 12 peace-keeping missions in the period 1955–70: in November 1960 ten Irish soldiers were killed at Niemba, in the Congo, in one of the most bloody episodes of this international activity. The independence of Irish foreign policy was underlined by Aiken's decision, taken in 1957, to support the idea of discussing China's membership of the UN: this created horror at the State Department and within Irish America, and involved some later back-tracking, but was nonetheless an interesting signal of the mixture of cussedness and idealism that would characterize Aiken's track record at Iveagh House. Generally, however, Lemass's consensual instincts in terms of social partnership were applied, through Aiken, within Irish foreign affairs (even if – according to Brian Lenihan – the Taoiseach regarded Aiken as 'a fool'): relations with the United States and with the British were improved after the troughs plumbed in the late 1940s and early 1950s.[87] The China episode notwithstanding, and despite some uncharitable pri-vate assessments of the Fianna Fáil cabinet, the State Department applauded Lemass's efforts to modernize Ireland and to make the country more open, both politically and economically: this judgement was made all the more easily after John F. Kennedy, of Boston Irish descent and a Catholic, assumed the Presidency of the USA in 1960. Kennedy's visit to Ireland in June 1963, which was an emotionally intense occasion for both guest and hosts, set the seal on the restoration of relations between the two countries.

Equally, the strained Anglo-Irish relationship of the 1930s and 1940s was reworked by Lemass and Aiken along more businesslike and less emotive lines: a trade agree-ment was forged between the two countries in April 1960, a herald of the more comprehensive Anglo-Irish Free Trade Agreement of December 1965. This deal, a highly characteristic piece of Lemass diplomacy, gave the Irish immediate tariff-free access to the British market, while calling for the gradual elimination of Irish duties on British imports: a free trade area was to be in place by 1975. Irish exporters were given an immediate boost, while home producers were given time to adjust to the demands of the market place: the agreement conveyed some immediate advantages on the Irish while being simultaneously a modest but useful piece of national rec-onciliation, as well as a valuable preparation for membership of the EEC. Republicans affected to see a restoration of the Act of Union and a betrayal of 1916; but the focus of Lemass's vision had shifted from the General Post Office towards Brussels.

In 1966, with the fiftieth anniversary of the Easter Rising, it was by no means easy to look beyond the parapets of the GPO; nor was it altogether clear whether mystical republicanism had in fact been thoroughly overtaken by the new materi-alist nationalism and the new pragmatism of Lemass. The links between the cele-bration of the birth of the republic, and therefore of militant nationalism, and the resurgence of violence in Northern Ireland in 1968–9 are complicated but real: it would, however, be quite wrong to argue for any straightforward connection. A younger and unblooded generation of republican was certainly made aware of the magnificent seven who had signed the Proclamation of the Republic, of their stand against the odds and of their ultimate self-sacrifice on behalf of the Irish people. For these young men and women nationalist protest on the streets of Northern Ireland and the rapid regrowth of violent republicanism could not fail to recall the stand made by the generation who had fought in 1916 and throughout the 'Tan' war. Paradoxically, many of those in the Fianna Fáil leadership who had in fact been 'out' in 1916 or who had fought in the flying columns, and who therefore had nothing to prove, were taking a more relaxed line on the partition question and on the subject of relations with Ulster Unionism. De Valera, as the most senior surviving figure associated with the Easter Rising, occupied centre-stage in 1966 and spoke reverentially of his comrades-in-arms: but he was also softening towards the North, and indeed the growing complexity of popular attitudes towards the 1916 legacy was reflected in the fact that the 'Chief' only just scraped home to Áras an Uachtaráin when he stood for re-election in June 1966 (and this despite the formidable assistance supplied by the young Charles J. Haughey). Tim Pat Coogan recounts an anecdote of President de Valera in his later years entertaining members of the Barton-Childers clan, the leading Protestant republican connection: de Valera told the party that Erskine Childers, the martyred patriarch of the family, had written a letter before facing the firing squad in which he had argued that the greatest challenge for republicanism would come from Northern Ireland, and that Ulster Unionists 'were a special people with special fears and ideals which needed to be understood and allowed for'. De Valera reportedly told the gathering that he 'deeply regretted' not having accepted this counsel.[88] This quiet admission was far removed from the extravagance of the anti-partition 'world tour' of 1948.

De Valera's shift towards a more consensual approach to Unionism and partition may well have been partly stimulated not just by uncomfortable memories such as the Childers's letter, but also by the example of Lemass. The integrity of Lemass's nationalism was unquestionable (Joe Lee has suggested that the apparently relaxed Lemass 'took Irish nationalist rhetoric very seriously', and this is confirmed by John Horgan's study): he was perfectly prepared to echo the anti-partitionist polemic of the party when occasion demanded (such as in the 1948–51 period).[89] However, on the whole Lemass took the same functionalist line with Northern Ireland that he applied to so much else. While the IRA campaign in the North was petering out in the 1960s, Lemass delivered a number of speeches in which he acknowledged both the strength of Ulster Unionist sentiment and the need for substantial change in the South as an inescapable prelude to any reunification. These were not in themselves especially remarkable insights: but, in the context of a longer and highly damaging tradition of threat, Lemass's conciliation signalled the beginnings of a shift not just within the Fianna Fáil leadership but within Irish society as a whole. Moreover, these soft words (and even the political vocabulary of Fianna Fáil was changing, with 'Northern Ireland' replacing the more defiant 'Six Counties') were backed up by actions: urged on by Whitaker (who had been born in Rostrevor, County Down, before partition), Lemass opened up communication with his northern counterpart, Terence O'Neill, and journeyed to Belfast in January 1965.[90] This encounter (which is discussed at greater length in the following chapter) can scarcely have looked

Plate 16   Seán Lemass and Terence O'Neill, Stormont, Belfast, January 1965.
Source: Public Record Office of Northern Ireland.

like a meeting of hearts and minds: O'Neill was from a landed and military background, was highly anglicized and – if his speeches and autobiography are a guide – was also gratingly patronizing in manner. But appearances were deceptive: in fact both O'Neill and Lemass were laconic technocrats who were each rather distant from their respective parties, temperamentally as well as ideologically. The meeting went well: O'Neill travelled to Dublin in February in order to reciprocate Lemass's gesture and to sustain the momentum that had been achieved. Again, an exchange visit between two chief executives, whose governments were separated by only 100 or so miles, might not appear an especially bold adventure, but this was the first occasion of its kind since W.T. Cosgrave and Sir James Craig had met in the 1920s. Moreover, the visit had been preceded by 40 years of anti-partitionist rhetoric and action from Dublin, sometimes of a determinedly petty kind: nor at any time were the Belfast ministers prepared to be outdone in terms of cussedness.

When Lemass retired in November 1966 his northern initiative, and indeed other aspects of his policy, were only half-formed. The visits to Belfast had resulted in some cautious reappraisal of attitudes and some tentative progress towards cross-border economic cooperation; but all this was dissipated with the onset of street violence in Northern Ireland in 1968–9. Another casualty of the hardening of attitudes in the later 1960s was Lemass's drive for substantial constitutional change: his cross-party committee on the constitution, which began its work in 1966 and reported in 1967, urged that the territorial claim on Northern Ireland be recast in more emollient language, and that divorce be available to those Irish people whose religious faith accommodated such matters. But with the threat of civil war in the North, and the wave of popular sympathy for Catholic victims of the communal violence, with the revival of hardline republicanism in certain sections of the Fianna Fáil leadership, the time was scarcely ripe for the enactment of Lemass's vision. A referendum, held in 1972, approved one of the constitutional committee's recom-mendations – the deletion of the section defining the special position of the Catholic Church. But, predictably, it had proved easier to modernize the Irish econ-omy than to achieve a modernization of the national soul.

Jack Lynch succeeded Lemass as party leader and Taoiseach, and inherited not only a process of northern détente that was becoming unworkable, given the rapidly changing conditions within Northern Ireland, but also an economic policy which – as with the efforts towards the North – had once looked highly promising but was no longer delivering the expected results. Lemass's impeccable political judge-ment had held up, therefore, even with regard to the timing of his departure: he left only 18 months after a ringing electoral endorsement (Fianna Fáil won 72 seats in April 1965), and with his various strategies either blossoming or at least bud-ding. Lemass may have been motivated by health worries (he had heart trouble which would shortly – in May 1971 – kill him); he may also have been sensitive to the needs and ambitions of a younger generation, given that de Valera had only been wrested from the levers of power – in tears and in the context of the *Irish Press* shares scan-dal – at the age of 77. De Valera had self-evidently outstayed his welcome as Taoiseach, compromising his reputation of the 1930s and 1940s by presiding over the lack-lustre Fianna Fáil government of 1951–4 and by threatening an equally uninspired performance when returned to power in 1957. By way of contrast, Lemass left office on a high (at least so far as the Irish public could tell), the victor of two successive general elections (October 1961 and April 1965) and the architect of policies that were transforming the country and its foreign relations. It is interesting to specu-late how Lemass would have responded to the political and economic challenges of the later 1960s and early 1970s, and whether his performance would have bur-nished or occluded his reputation. It is unlikely that Lemass's attitude towards Northern Ireland would have differed significantly from that of his successor: it is just pos-sible that his record as a fighter might have provided him with some more leeway than was available to Lynch, and it is also possible – given the conciliatory nature of his comments when in retirement – that he might have been able to play a more constructive and emollient role than Lynch. In terms of the economy, however, it is hard to see how Lemass would have responded differently to the relative slow-down of the later 1960s, or how he could have overcome the crises of the early 1970s, given that these were largely external in origin. On the whole, therefore, Lemass timed his departure to coincide with a peak in national morale; and this in itself helps to explain why his name is redolent of the good times and why his reputation continues to stand so high.

In reality Lynch inherited problems that had been gestating under the Lemass regime. The second Programme for Economic Expansion, which had been launched in 1964, was soon proving to be inadequate and was ditched in 1967: the growth rate of the Irish GNP was beginning to slow by the later 1960s, and unemployment was beginning an apparently unstoppable rise. The Lemass reforms had barely touched agriculture: growth rates had remained low within this sector even during the boom years of the early 1960s. Even before Lemass's retirement it was clear that Irish agriculture was set to create both political and economic problems for the government: despite the hopes of Whitaker's first Programme, and indeed of Costello's initiative of 1956, agriculture was not modernized, nor was it the vanguard of the national economic revival. Irish farmers remained wedded to traditional techniques and outmoded economic goals. Shut out from the markets of the EEC, the farmers endured poor working conditions and comparatively low prices until, in the autumn of 1966, their representative organization, the National Farmers' Association, was driven into public protest.

Nor had Lynch inherited an industrial elysium. Despite Lemass's corporatist strategies, and despite plentiful channels of communication between labour, the employers and government, industrial unrest continued to plague the Irish economy: grassroots protest and breakaway unions dispelled any cosy dreams of social partnership. The building workers' strike of 1964 had helped to precipitate potentially the most severe political crisis of the Lemass years – the resignation of Paddy Smith from the Ministry of Agriculture – and politically challenging strikes continued under Lynch. But the most serious threat to Irish industry and the economy came from the spiralling inflation of the late 1960s, driven by economically unrealistic national wage settlements and – after 1973 – by an international crisis stimulated by the hike in the price of oil. Moreover, the rapid rise in wages sustained during these years was accompanied by high levels of unemployment, so that the normal regulatory mechanisms of the economy were failing to function. The growing economic promiscuity of these years was underlined by the decision of George Colley, Fianna Fáil Minister for Finance (1970–3), to permit a deficit to creep into his current budget of 1972 – a grim augury of the free-spending times to come, and a very different approach to public borrowing from that sustained under Lemass.

Still, if Lemass's record provided few clues about dealing with the economic slowdown of the later 1960s, then it was scarcely any more helpful in relation to the main political difficulty faced by Lynch: Northern Ireland. Indeed, it is arguable that Lemass laid down problems both in terms of the economy and Northern Ireland which came to fruition under Lynch: Lemass's conciliatory approach to the unions in the early 1960s may well have helped to foster unrealistic expectations within the labour movement; while his conciliation of Stormont – however imaginative – may have made life more difficult for Lynch in 1968–70, given that Ulster Unionism, under pressure from the civil rights movement, was shifting to the right at this

Plate 17 Charles Haughey, *c*.1970.
Source: Victor Patterson/Linenhall Library.

time. On the whole Lynch accepted Lemass's rhetoric about peaceful reunification, sometimes edging into asperity or (as in August 1969) into menace. But as northern Catholics came under increasing pressure from the Northern Ireland security forces (the RUC and USC), and eventually from the British army, a cadre within the Fianna Fáil leadership saw Lynch's generally mild language as an abdication of responsibility: while he faffed around at the United Nations, seeking support for a peace-keeping force, other party elders sought more direct and militant action.

The full history of the arms affair of 1969–70 is still, despite several books on the subject, unclear.[91] It is certainly the case that several Fianna Fáil ministers – Charles Haughey (Finance), Neil Blaney (Agriculture) and Kevin Boland (Local Government) – were out of sympathy with the Taoiseach, either as a result of a genuine fellow-feeling with their northern co-religionists (Blaney was a Donegal Catholic and Haughey had close family ties with South Derry), or through political ambition (Haughey in particular may have sensed weakness in Lynch's early handling of the northern crisis). It is also clear that Lynch, and many other senior figures in the Dáil, came to believe that there had been a conspiracy, the tentacles of which had stretched within the Fianna Fáil cabinet, to use official channels to buy and supply arms to northern nationalists. Once apprised of these allegations, Lynch moved to crush what was in effect a challenge to his own leadership: Haughey and Blaney were both sacked from the government on 6 May 1970, and Boland followed shortly afterwards, resigning in a display of sympathy with his fallen comrades. Haughey and Blaney were subsequently charged with conspiracy to import arms. But Lynch's troubles were far from over – for the case against Blaney was dismissed on 2 July and Haughey was acquitted on 23 October after a 14-day trial. The subsequent fallout was highly revealing. Despite a generalized sympathy for northern nationalists, Fianna Fáil was always more concerned about internal discipline than about the partition question; and Lynch was able to orchestrate acclamations from the republican elders of the party, such as Frank Aiken, as well as win a vote of confidence among Fianna Fáil deputies. There was noisy support for Boland and Blaney at the party ard-fheis, held in February 1971; but, again, the party's natural sense of hierarchy overcame its visceral republicanism and Lynch was able to win endorsement for his moderate line. If those who had been implicated in the arms affair thought that Northern Ireland provided the materials for a leadership challenge, then these events provided instead a political education: the affair underlined the extent to which Fianna Fáil had inherited not merely the moderation of Lemass, but also the genial hypocrisy of de Valera, who in his prime had roused his followers against partition but who had never been prepared to enact his principles. As Tim Pat Coogan has gruffly commented, de Valera was 'an arch-practitioner of the general philosophy of never putting off until tomorrow what could safely be deferred much longer': the same maxim might well be applied to Fianna Fáil's stand against partition.[92]

But, though de Valera's shadow was hard to escape, and though he seemed unstoppable (he remained President until 1973 and died – aged 93 – in 1975), this was in truth the age of Lemass. Even the Lynch years (1966–73) represented a low-voltage continuation of the governing principles that had been laid down by the Lemass governments – and this should scarcely come as a surprise, given the genial passivity of the new leader, and given the continuities in the Fianna Fáil frontbench (Lynch was something of a protégé, chosen by Lemass in 1959 to take over his beloved Ministry for Industry and Commerce, while Lynch's Minister for Finance between 1966 and 1970, Charles Haughey, was Lemass's son-in-law: other frontbenchers were Lemass nominees, the beneficiaries of his sustained efforts to rejuvenate the party leadership). As has been argued, Lynch inherited Lemass's emphasis on economic planning and his moves towards a more conciliatory stand on Northern Ireland; as has been argued, in the absence of Lemass's political savvy, these bequests proved to be fraught with difficulty. But there were other aspects of this shared inheritance that would prove, if not less contentious, then at least more workable as policies and less ambiguous as blessings.

A sustained commitment to educational reform and expansion characterized the 16 years of the Fianna Fáil reign. Comprehensive schools were created in 1963; and in September 1966, shortly before Lemass's retirement, his rumbustious Minister for Education, Donogh O'Malley, announced during a speech to the National Union of Journalists that free secondary education would be established ('the most celebrated example of policy-making by publicity', as Brian Farrell has termed this episode).[93] Community schools were created in 1970, as was the first polytechnic-style National Institute for Higher Education (NIHE) at Limerick: the NIHE at Dublin was to follow in 1976, founded when the Cosgrave coalition government was in office. O'Malley was a graduate of University College Galway; and this fact, combined with his irreverent genius, may help to explain his proposal to unite Trinity College Dublin (founded in 1592) and University College Dublin (1908), by far the biggest constituent of the National University of Ireland. However, even O'Malley's very considerable energy and skill were no match for the clout wielded by each of these venerable institutions. His – viewed from a passionless perspective – entirely logical proposition was an example of Lemass's functionalism and his fixation on performance carried to a politically illogical extreme.

Donogh O'Malley's nephew and political heir was Desmond O'Malley, an equally gifted and courageous figure and a rising star within the Fianna Fáil of the 1970s. Des O'Malley was appointed by Lynch as Minister for Justice in 1970, succeeding Micheál Ó Moráin, whose incapacity had done much to exacerbate the seriousness of the arms affair. It was the younger O'Malley who inherited the Fianna Fáil tradition of toughness towards the threat of the IRA, although he had little of the compromising political baggage of earlier exponents of this tradition. O'Malley re-established the Special Criminal Court in May 1972, a tribunal which had civil judges but no jury: this initiative was followed in November 1972 by the Offences against the State (Amendment) Bill, which authorized the conviction of suspects charged with membership of an illegal organization on the basis of the testimony of a senior garda officer. These actions, much more than the antics of the alleged arms conspirators, represented the true Fianna Fáil: dirigiste, hard-nosed against any hint of challenge, and effective in its thrusts because knowledgeable about its targets.

Another Fianna Fáil strategy from the late 1950s was revived in October 1968, when Lynch attempted to persuade the Irish electorate to abandon proportional representation in favour of a first-past-the-post system: this was an unapologetic effort to enshrine the party's electoral hegemony (the parallels with James Craig's earlier gamesmanship on behalf of the Ulster Unionists are irresistible). De Valera and Lemass had attempted a slightly more insidious version of this stunt in June 1959, when the poll for the Presidency was combined with a referendum on proportional representation. Then the Irish electorate had chosen the Fianna Fáil candidate for office, de Valera, but not the party's recommended voting mechanism. In 1968 Fianna Fáil's renewed efforts towards electoral 'reform' proved fruitless, when the country once again voted overwhelmingly to retain PR. On this occasion voters showed the same subtlety that they had displayed in 1959: then they had chosen the party's man but not its policy, while in 1968 they rejected the policy while preparing to endorse the party (Fianna Fáil won an impressive 75 seats in the general election of June 1969). Irish voters in the 1960s were thus highly enthusiastic about Fianna Fáil; but they were much less excited by its determined efforts to create, in effect, a one-party state. They endorsed Fianna Fáil in the general elections of 1957, 1961, 1965 and 1969, and in the Presidential contests of 1959 and 1966, but they reserved the right to change their mind.

Ireland's application for membership of the EEC was an additional legacy of the Lemass years, which – like PR – might have functioned as an electoral prop to the party and which was unresolved at the time of Lemass's resignation. With the retirement of General de Gaulle from the French Presidency in April 1969, the chief political obstacle to Irish and British membership of the Community disappeared; and in May 1972 the Irish people overwhelmingly approved the idea of the country's admission (83 per cent of a high poll voted 'yes' to membership). Ireland formally joined the EEC in 1973, an act which brought to completion many of Lemass's ambitions and strategies dating back to the 1950s. Membership of the Community had eluded Lemass in 1961, and this failure had professedly represented one of the most bitter disappointments of his career: admission to the Common Agricultural Policy would certainly have dissolved much of the farmer protest that plagued Fianna Fáil in these years, while the prospect of generous economic subsidies more than offset any perceived threat to national sovereignty. Lemass, however, had long retired before the Irish application for membership of the Community was reactivated; and he did not even live to see the negotiations and referendum that delivered the prize for which he had long worked and schemed.

In fact, when Irish membership of the Community was formally ratified, on 1 January 1973, Fianna Fáil itself was at the end of its 16-year electoral reign: a general election, held in February 1973, ousted the party and produced an electoral coalition, led by Liam Cosgrave and Fine Gael. Historians are naturally wary of over-rigid categorization, or indeed of overdramatization, but there are grounds for arguing that, just as the Programme for Economic Expansion and the accession of Lemass as Taoiseach inaugurated a new period in Irish political life, so the early 1970s, with the death of Lemass, the referendum on EEC membership and the oil crisis, brought that period to an end. These years between the late 1950s and 1973 were, arguably, the era of Lemass.

The changes wrought in this era were unmistakeable. Economic growth soared in the early and mid-1960s, stimulating employment and applying a brake to the emigration figures. The importance of the media expanded: Radio Telefís Éireann began broadcasting in December 1961, immersing Irish viewers (as Ronan Fanning has argued) in a culture which was 'essentially Anglo-American or mid-Atlantic'.[94] The censorship of literature, so active even in the 1950s, was relaxed under the regime of Brian Lenihan, Fianna Fáil Minister for Justice; the censorship of films went the same way. Popular social and political attitudes became markedly more relaxed following – sometimes pre-empting – the greater accessibility of outside ideas and influences. The dance hall has been seen as the central symbol of the new Ireland of the 1960s: an expression of perceptibly greater social freedom, greater affluence and leisure time, as well as the agency for a whole range of new American and British cultural influences. There is certainly a pleasing irony in the fact that de Valera, following the guidance of the hierarchy, should have legislated against dance halls in the early 1930s; while in the 1960s Albert Reynolds, following the advice of his accountants, should have found a fortune in these same 'dens' – and that he should have thereby launched a political career which took him to the leadership of Fianna Fáil and, indeed, of the nation itself.

If the diversity of social and political change is impressive, what is its significance? It is scarcely an exaggeration to suggest that these years saw a turnaround in certain fundamental aspects of national life. For virtually the first time since the Famine the decline of the Irish population was halted. The broader importance of this is easy to overlook: while emigration remained a deeply ingrained and sometimes tragic feature of Irish life, the modest growth of the Irish population registered in the 1960s and 1970s began to undermine the lurking fears of national extinction, and may indeed have contributed to the perceptibly more relaxed nationalism of the Republic of Ireland in these years and after. John Horgan has identified an upsurge in national self-confidence, the weakening of 'the old slave spirit', as one of the principal legacies of the Lemass years.[95] This broaches the issue of ideological change: mainstream Irish nationalism shifted remarkably in this era, both in terms of its social agenda and its constitutional expression. Paul Bew and Henry Patterson have gone so far as to suggest that 'the social ideal of Irish nationalism, which sustained it through many great struggles, has disintegrated and has been replaced by something new'.[96] While the shift away from the old nationalist shibboleths of the small farm and local, tariff-protected industry had long been prefigured, it was only in the late 1950s and 1960s that the new ideals became coherently enshrined in economic policy and in legislation: foreign investment, a free market, efficient enterprise. The spiritual nationalism of the revolutionary era was replaced by a more materialist ideology, still assertively Irish but promising tangible comforts rather than an empty stomach and an ascetic conviction of moral superiority.

This was an era of internationalization, therefore, whether culturally, economically or ideologically. In the 1920s and 1930s Ireland had been bound into the British Commonwealth and the League of Nations, playing a prominent role in each. Wartime neutrality, the rejection of the Commonwealth in 1948–9 and the initial failure to gain admission to the new United Nations all tended to heighten Ireland's isolation, and also – arguably – to focus attention on the suffocating Anglo-Irish relationship. The Irish entry into the UN in 1955, and the elaboration of the Irish role in New York through the efforts of Aiken and Lemass, helped to restore the country's international prestige and to divert national energies from counter-productive quarrels with the British and over partition. The increasingly sharp focus on Europe, prefigured under Seán MacBride and the first Inter-Party government, fulfilled much the same function within Irish nationalism, softening asperities and quietening any defensiveness. The prospect of entry to the EC, first mooted in 1961, created real hopes of economic support as well as the further development of national dignity.

But, if the significance of these changes is impressive, to what extent was Seán Lemass the architect of this modern Ireland, and to what extent was it created by a broader globalization of markets and mores? This is an extension of a question posed earlier concerning the relationship between planning and economic growth: on the whole, the answers are the same, too. Just as the upturn in the international economy would in all probability have percolated through the tariff walls of the Irish economy regardless of the Programme for Economic Expansion, so some of the broader social and political consequences of growth might well have occurred without ministerial intervention. Still, it is unquestionable that, just as Lemass and Whitaker facilitated the expansion of the Irish economy, so Lemass took decisions – and sometimes politically courageous decisions – which eased the modernization processes in Irish politics and society. The decision to scale down tariff protection might seem inevitable, and was probably inevitable, given the state of the Irish economy in the 1950s: but even if one accepts the socialist argument that Lemass was merely rejigging his party's defence of native capitalism, then it is equally true that the Programme for Economic Expansion looked very much like the abandonment of a key area of Fianna Fáil support as well as the repudiation of a policy which had its roots in Sinn Féin dogma. Enacting the Programme was therefore a politically risky enterprise, requiring some considerable tactical subtlety.

Television was gently subversive of many traditional Irish attitudes and convictions: but then (as Rob Savage has demonstrated), the form of state-run commercial service that emerged in the early 1960s owed much to the vision of the Lemass government (which might well have felt compelled to accept the proposal, sponsored by the cultural body Gael-Linn, for a predominantly Irish-language service).[97] Equally, Lemass might well have chosen politically expedient but short-term strategies with regard to constitutional change and partition: instead he pioneered constitutional reform proposals which were spiked with difficulty in terms of nationalist politics, but which demonstrated magnanimity in relation to the southern Protestant minority and to Ulster Unionists. Moreover, he overrode the opposition or (at best) prevarication of some of his colleagues in journeying to Belfast to meet Terence O'Neill, and thereby to bestow informal recognition on what for Fianna Fáil had been the unrecognizable horror of the partition settlement.

If experimenting with ideas ahead of their time is the definition of a visionary, then Lemass had vision. If taking calculated risks in the broader interests of social justice is a definition of statesmanship, then Lemass was a statesman without being anything other than an effective patriot. If the combination of vision, statesmanship and survival skills is the hallmark of political greatness, then Lemass was a great politician and a great executive. Lemass had the imagination to generate ideas, and the intelligence to know when they had failed; he had the physical courage to fight the enemies of his youth, and the moral courage to embrace some apparent enemies in later life. He was never tested by the Northern Ireland crisis, or by the economic collapse of the early and mid-1970s; but then he had the judgement and the confidence to retire when he was on a high. This gruff Stakhanovite helped to pull de Valera's comely maidens and athletic youths out of the emigrant boats; and he helped to convert the cold comfort of small farms into the greater consolation supplied by a stronger mixed economy. He failed in much: his vision of a social partnership vanished with the acceleration of industrial unrest in the 1960s; his confidence in economic planning was perhaps misplaced; and his overture towards the North, while brave, proved largely futile. Nevertheless, it is arguable that even here, in the debris of his northern policy, there were suggestive clues for those who were prepared to look. For if partition were to be peacefully refined or overturned, then it was not through outrageous hyperbole, mock indignation, lavish condescension or offensive rebukes. Lemass set out to woo Unionists by persuasion, and to kill Unionism by kindness: and who is to say that, given a more favourable climate, he and his political heirs might not have succeeded?

7

Northern Ireland, 1920–72: Specials, Peelers and Provos

the battle here is for some sort of ascendancy ... somebody has got to capture ascendancy here, and each one gains support by coming forward as the champion of some sort of ascendancy. I am not very happy about the future.

Lord Londonderry, 1928[1]

The history of Northern Ireland since 1920 reads like a compressed version of the story of Ireland in the eighteenth and nineteenth centuries – and indeed there are those who gain comfort from a seemingly inevitable dénouement. The ascendancy parliament which served the interests of the Anglican elite until 1800 was reborn as a Protestant parliament for a Protestant people in 1921: the exclusivism and obtuseness of College Green, Dublin, became the exclusivism and obtuseness of College Square, Belfast. The popular Catholic mobilization of 1798 became the popular Catholic mobilization of 1968: each was tinctured by cautious liberal Protestant endorsement, and each brought fears of collapse and the imposition of a form of direct rule from London. Terence O'Neill has played Earl Fitzwilliam, thrusting cosmetic change onto a distrustful ruling elite and raising expectations among the excluded. The history of the Union, from 1800 to 1921, may be seen in miniature through the story of the government of Northern Ireland from 1972: initially sporadic efforts to defuse Catholic nationalism have gathered pace until the whole form of government has acquired, certainly in the judgement of one commentator, a 'green tinge'.[2] The elaborate challenge of killing Home Rule by kindness in the 1890s has given way to the task of killing revolutionary nationalism by kindness in the 1990s, a self-evidently more ambitious undertaking.

Northern Ireland was established between 1920 and 1925, a technical achievement of some distinction (as Bryan Follis has argued); but the new state was founded on the defeat of the IRA in the North, and not on the firmer clay of political consensus.[3] This might well have proved difficult, if not impossible, to locate, but the effort was not made until the late 1960s, when the evidence of constitutional subsidence was already overwhelming. Northern Ireland has been described, in the well-worn quip of R.J. Lawrence, as 'not a half-way house, but a lean-to whose stability depended on the ties that bound it to Britain'.[4] In the event this stability was undermined by nationalist sappers as well as the constitutional engineers of Unionism, whose skills lay with jerry-building and with siege architecture rather than any more intricate or permanent construction.

The constitution of Northern Ireland was defined by the Government of Ireland Act (1920) and by subsequent amending measures such as the Irish Free State Act of 1922. It is still sometimes argued within a populist nationalist tradition that the Government of Ireland Act was an act of desperation committed by the British government in order to retain some last foothold in Ireland. In reality, as Follis, Ward and other commentators have recognized, the measure was marked not so much by a desire for dominion as a desire for disengagement: it reflected not so much an archaic Unionism as the rather more fashionable tenets of 'Home Rule all round'.[5] The Government of Ireland Act in fact imposed a Gladstonian settlement in Ireland, the crucial distinction from earlier Home Rule Bills being that the measure brought with it a partitioning of the six northeastern counties from the rest of the island. Each of the two new territories was granted a Home Rule administration, complete with an executive, a bicameral legislature and separate judiciaries. Each was bound to the other by a Council of Ireland, uniting 20 members from the two new parliaments and endowed with limited legislative powers as well as the right to vote to create a single parliament for a unitary state. In the event neither the Council nor the Home Rule administration planned for Dublin ever came into operation. The logic of mainstream Irish political development had for long pointed in other directions, just as the unspoken logic of the increasingly particularist and defensive Unionism was fulfilled in the unlikely form of the new Belfast parliament. When elections for this assembly were held in May 1921, Unionists won 40 out of the 52 available seats: the professional and commercial classes of eastern Ulster, who were the major beneficiaries from this contest, had at last won a tangible political expression of their regional political domination, as well as a belated reward for their systematic ditching of allies in the south and west and in 'outer' Ulster since 1913.

Presiding over the new state and its constitutional trappings was the Prime Minister, James Craig (created Viscount Craigavon in 1927). Craig's earlier career, though in many ways distinguished, was scarcely an adequate preparation for the demands and frustrations of his new role; and indeed, it is arguable that the skills and achievements that brought Craig to prominence in the first place were carried into his premiership and defined its limitations. Craig was formed by a variety of forces, in part by the South African war but also by the Unionist campaign to see off the challenge of Russellism in the years between 1900 and 1905: Craig's Home Secretary, Richard Dawson Bates, a solicitor and apparatchik of somewhat limited intellectual calibre, and the despair both of his friends and his many enemies, may have been retained at least partly because he, too, was a hardened veteran of the campaign to halt the electoral advance of T.W. Russell. Both Craig and Bates, moulded in the crises of early Edwardian loyalism, were profoundly impressed by the need for Unionist unity, and indeed with some justification: there is little doubt that the more unified hardline Unionism created in eastern Ulster between 1913 and 1921 by the rejection of outlying allies enabled Craig to present an apparently unmoveable bloc of support to both the British government and the authorities in the emergent Irish Free State. One of the overriding priorities of the Craig government, and indeed of later administrations, was the maintenance of Protestant electoral unity (Terence O'Neill's economic modernization has convincingly been depicted as a latterday variation of this political reflex): but it became increasingly clear that while this defensiveness could give rise to some constructive initiatives, it was essentially a diversion from the task of achieving a thoroughgoing stability within Northern Ireland.[6]

Craig's wartime experiences in South Africa and with the Ulster Division, and his successes in fighting Russell and Redmond, made him a brilliantly cussed defender of Northern Ireland in the early 1920s. His parliamentary and executive experience – he had been an MP at Westminster (1906–21), Parliamentary Secretary to the Ministry of Pensions (1918–20) and Financial Secretary to the Admiralty (1920–1) – gave him an entrée to the most elevated levels of British politics and was widely thought to be preparation for a more senior ministerial appointment. But all this did not qualify him to address some of the more lasting and more fundamental problems of government in the region. His government responded well to the military and external political challenges faced by the new state: but the demands of achieving long-term stability within a divided society as well as long-term prosperity within an area of rapid economic decline proved to be beyond the intellectual or imaginative capacity of the new regime. Home Rule was Gladstone's inspiration; and it would have required a Gladstonian intellect and Gladstonian subtlety to disentangle the problems of administering Home Rule within the new Northern Ireland. These were evidently not at hand.

In the military sphere Craig's government quelled sporadic IRA violence in 1921 and a more concerted offensive in the early spring of 1922. The chief instrument of the regime's counter-insurgency campaign was the Ulster Special Constabulary (USC), launched in October 1920 by Craig and the new Assistant Secretary for Ulster, Sir Ernest Clark: Clark, admired by Unionists as the 'mid-wife' of their state, 'did not so much establish the Special Constabulary as create it'.[7] There were three categories of Special Constable – A (full-timers), B (part-timers) and C (emergency men) – but only the B 'Specials' survived the demobilization of the mid-1920s. As a whole the USC enjoyed a mixed reputation. There is little doubt that, locally recruited and exclusively loyalist, the force was an effective weapon against the IRA: it was therefore lauded by Unionists and rigorously defended by the new Northern Ireland government. For northern republicans the USC was a dangerous and ruthless enemy; and for northern nationalists of all kinds the force was an intrusive and sometimes a repressive presence in their everyday lives. Although there is no clear evidence of any grand strategy of harassment, the USC were certainly implicated in some highly controversial episodes. It is possible that USC men were guilty of the McMahon murders – the killing of four members of this Catholic family together with one of their employees on the night of 23 March 1922. It is certain that a USC patrol was responsible for the killing of three Catholic youths in Cushendall, County Antrim, in June 1922, although the circumstances of the deaths were (and are) disputed.

Aside from the USC, the Craig government also came to rely upon legislative deterrents, and in particular the draconian Civil Authorities (Special Powers) Act, passed in April 1922, at the height of what was in effect a civil war within Northern Ireland. The Special Powers Act, as it came to be known, was an adaptation of the Restoration of Order in Ireland Act (1920) passed by an embattled British government, and it granted the Minister of Home Affairs the right 'to take all such steps and issue all such orders as may be necessary for preserving the peace and maintaining order'.[8] An (ill-fated) effort to hammer out a formula for peace and reconciliation, launched on 31 March 1922 by Craig and Michael Collins, delayed the implementation of the measure; but as the pressure applied by the IRA offensive continued unabated, the northern government was forced into action. The specific catalyst was the killing by the IRA of the Unionist MP for West Belfast, W.J. Twaddell, on 22 May 1922: Twaddell was shot on his way to his outfitter's shop in Lower Garfield Street, Belfast, by a gang of five, one of whom (a Michael Pratley) was later convicted and hanged. Twaddell was a prominent Belfast loyalist; and though he was only one of 14 victims of murder on the weekend of 21–2 May, his death created widespread consternation among Unionists and forced the northern government into using their newly acquired 'special powers'. A string of decrees followed: the proscription of the IRA, the internment of 500 suspects, and a province-wide curfew between 11 p.m. and 5 a.m. Flogging was extensively used as a 'special punishment'. These penalties fell heavily on the nationalist minority within Northern Ireland, and particularly heavily – as with similar legislation in the South – on the republican community. But for the Craig administration a cowed and demoralized minority was a small price to pay – and a price willingly paid – for the military defeat of the IRA within the confines of the new state.

The third leg of the tripod upon which northern security policy rested was the regular police force, the Royal Irish Constabulary (until May 1922) and later the Royal Ulster Constabulary. The main law-enforcement agency of the crown had been the Royal Irish Constabulary (RIC), severely buffeted during the Anglo-Irish war and one of the chief institutional victims of the Treaty of December 1921. Under the Constabulary (Ireland) Act (1922) the RIC was to be disbanded by the end of March 1922, although the peculiar circumstances of Northern Ireland meant that the force there was granted a stay of execution until the end of May. It was therefore the RIC which, together with the 'Specials', bore the brunt of the IRA campaign in 1922, and from this a number of consequences flowed. First, the role of the RIC in defending the new Northern Ireland meant that Craig's ministers were all the more inclined to retain its substance in the aftermath of disbandment. The new Royal Ulster Constabulary (RUC), foreshadowed by an official report published on 31 March 1922 and launched under the terms of the Constabulary (Northern

Ireland) Act (1922), closely followed the model of its parent and predecessor. The existing strength of the old RIC in the six counties was deemed adequate, augmented only by a new headquarters staff. Of the planned total of 3,000 officers, one-third were to be Catholic; and it was hoped that many of these, and indeed a high proportion of the force as a whole, would be recruited from among RIC veterans. The district and county organization of the new force, its rank structure and central organization, its armed nature, all reflected its immediate parentage and all bucked the normal practice of British police organization. The second main consequence of the comparatively late birth of the RUC, and of its relative unimportance in the context of the civil strife of 1922, was that it was not embroiled in the more controversial aspects of the war against the IRA, and therefore carried no specific and immediate moral stigma for many nationalists. It remained an overwhelmingly Protestant force (the Catholic quota was never filled), and indeed there were strong Orange influences: it remained a key agency of the Northern Irish state and therefore of partition. But until 1968–9 the RUC enjoyed some grudging degree of acceptance among northern nationalists, if not republicans – in much the same way, in fact, that the old RIC had been tolerated by many Home Rulers in the relatively calm years before the Anglo-Irish struggle.

The last major episode of the IRA offensive against partition and the Northern Ireland government came in the south-west of the new territory, in a triangle of land defined by Pettigo, on the Fermanagh–Donegal border, Belleek and Lower Lough Erne. This salient of northern territory was occupied by republican Irregulars, supported – seemingly – by the troops of the Free State authorities, who garrisoned Pettigo and commanded Belleek from the vantage point of an old fort overlooking the town. Local Unionist efforts to dislodge these forces failed miserably (indeed, the IRA captured a Lancia armoured car from the Specials); but Craig prevailed upon the British colonial secretary, Winston Churchill, to use British military force to repel the intruders, with the result that Pettigo was retaken on 4 June and Belleek on 8 June 1922. A British garrison occupied the Belleek fort – which was in Free State territory – until August 1924, when tensions had relaxed and the border was apparently more secure.

By the summer of 1922 the civil war in the south and west of Ireland was beginning to divert many Ulster republicans from the campaign against the Belfast government. This redirection, however, was not so much a 'cause' of the IRA defeat in the North as its consequence. The USC, containing many hardened veterans of the First World War, was a sometimes ruthless antagonist of the northern republican movement, while the Special Powers Act ensured that neither the Specials nor their political masters would ever be unduly constrained by libertarian niceties. It was widely accepted by Ulster Unionists that Craig had won a military victory; and this perception, allied with memories of his earlier achievements (in 1912–14), ensured that for the following 18 years he sustained a genial ascendancy over the Unionist electorate.

Less dramatic than the 'liberation' of the Pettigo triangle, or the subjugation of the IRA in Belfast and elsewhere, was the achievement of the Craig administration in establishing the institutions of the northern government and in fending off political challenges, particularly at the time of the Treaty negotiations and during the sessions of the Boundary Commission. The inauguration of the Northern Ireland parliament in June 1921, involving as it did a plea from King George V to 'all Irishmen to pause, to stretch out the hand of forbearance and conciliation, to forgive and forget', very nearly proved to be both a baptism and a funeral for partition, for the King's carefully formulated address was a public overture to Sinn Féin, which led to the truce of 9 July and sustained pressure on Craig to come to terms with Eamon de Valera. Craig faced some of the same external pressures in the summer and autumn of 1921 that David Trimble would encounter in the summer and autumn of 1997, though Craig was operating from a position of rather greater (if by no means complete) political security. Suspicious about the truce, as later Unionists would be suspicious of the IRA ceasefires of 1994 and 1997, Craig refused to meet de Valera unless the President 'accepted the principle of Ulster's independent rights, and that he gave a written statement to that effect'.[9] This, predictably, was not forthcoming and Craig concentrated instead on building up the institutions of the new northern state as a defensive resource – a kind of bureaucratic Derry's walls behind which Unionists might shelter free from Lundyite Tories or rebel 'Shinners'. Pressure from Unionist sympathizers within the governing coalition meant that Lloyd George could not browbeat Craig with as much violence as he might otherwise have wanted; and indeed this backbench pressure seems to have driven Lloyd George into accepting the transfer of administrative services from London to the fledgling government in Belfast. Lloyd George had hitherto dragged his feet on this issue, but eventually gave way on 5 November 1921, with the result that at the end of the month the titular government of Northern Ireland found itself endowed for the first time with executive functions.

A hitherto unremarked aspect of this proceeding was the timing: on 5 November, the day that Lloyd George agreed to the transfer of services, he summoned Craig to London in a renewed effort to sell the idea of an all-Ireland state. Later, on 10 November, the British Prime Minister tried to persuade the Northern Ireland government to accept subordination to the future dominion parliament in Dublin. Craig, who had been expecting the British government to insist upon the implementation of the Government of Ireland Act, replied by demanding dominion status for Northern Ireland. But by this stage Lloyd George, hampered by the threat of divisions within his coalition support, was relaxing his grip on the northern government: on 25 November he affirmed to Craig that, unless there was agreement, there would be no infringement of the rights of the Belfast regime. This was not so much a concession as a recognition of political realities which the Prime Minister himself had helped to forge. Lloyd George had simultaneously cajoled and empowered the Ulster Unionists, bolstering the northern government at the same time as he was demanding its subjugation. These bizarrely dissonant overtures may have embodied Lloyd George's faith in the ultimate triumph of Craig's cussedness. Alternatively, it might be argued that the inconsistencies in the Prime Minister's tactics with Northern Ireland chimed with inconsistencies in his backbench support and among his ministerial lieutenants, as well as with the complicated nature of his fundamental political sympathies.

Craig, therefore, had no direct input into the 'Articles of Agreement', or Treaty, signed by the British and Irish representatives on 6 December 1921. But his influence within that document was unmissable: the Treaty, the masterpiece of Lloyd George's political artifice, simultaneously recognized the unity of Ireland as well as the reality of the Northern Irish state. Northern Ireland was given the right to opt out of the new dominion, the Irish Free State; but if it chose this course, its territory would be automatically subject to the scrutiny of a Boundary Commission. Even this device, which in 1921–2 was so hateful to Craig and his supporters, in fact originated in the fertile (if defensive) political intelligence of the northern leader: Craig had conjured up the notion of a Commission in December 1919, when the Government of Ireland Bill was gestating at Westminster (as the normally urbane Nicholas Mansergh has querulously remarked, 'did no one [in 1921] see fit to remind him of its origins?').[10] No one did, however, and the Craig government formally rejected the Treaty, upbraiding the British government for its bad faith in threatening the borders of Northern Ireland. If the origins of the Commission idea had been forgotten, then the idea of a highly limited boundary revision had not – and it was with this salve that Lloyd George sought to assuage Ulster Unionist tempers in December 1921.

Nevertheless, the looming threat of the Commission was clearly a destabilizing force within the new Northern Ireland, and for this reason Craig sought to strike an alternative agreement with the strong man of the new Dublin government, Michael Collins. It was a forlorn hope, however, since while Craig and Collins each shared a dislike of the Commission, their agreement stretched no further: Craig saw the proposed body as a source of instability, while Collins wanted more direct and immediate ways of overturning the northern state. A series of meetings between the two men produced a preliminary agreement on 31 January 1922, by which the Commission was to be replaced by direct negotiations between the northern authorities and the Irish Free State; but this deal soon broke down in a welter of confusion and recrimination. Much the same fate befell the more celebrated Craig–Collins pact of 30 March, whose confident rhetoric was not matched by any sustained good faith or competence on the part of its signatories. Well before Collins's assassination on 22 August 1922, this agreement had also collapsed: it had been nullified by the rapid development of the political scene, as each side in the North greedily snatched after an ultimate victory and as the authorities in the South were diverted into a bloody civil war. From the wreckage of sectarian conflict and civil war, the Boundary Commission re-emerged in 1923 (like Churchill's steeples of Fermanagh and Tyrone) as one of the remaining constants in Irish politics.

In some ways the civil war had in fact reinforced the significance of the Commission. Collins's death had removed from the Provisional Government one of the chief hawks of its northern policy and had opened the way to a more cautious approach to the issue of partition. Ernest Blythe, an Ulster Protestant and one of Collins's ministerial colleagues, composed a memorandum in early August 1922 in which he ventured some tacit criticisms of the Big Fellow's emotional but unsophisticated handling of the northern challenge. Blythe's call for a more constructive and gradualist approach to the quest for Irish unity became a convenient orthodoxy for the Provisional Government and for its Cumann na nGaedheal successor: his more pacific strategies also incidentally elevated the importance of the Boundary Commission as a means of addressing in a strictly legal and constitutional manner the wrongs of partition. The Commission idea was also reactivated by the formal creation of the Irish Free State in December 1922 and by the northern government's immediate decision to opt out: under the terms of the Treaty this endorsement of partition brought with it a need to scrutinize the border, and a need, therefore, for a scrutinizing authority.

The Boundary Commission was a major test of Craig's leadership, for, as in December 1921, he was under pressure from the British political establishment, including indeed King George V, to reach a deal with the Dublin government; at the same time his backbench supporters in the Belfast parliament, often limited in their political vision, were vehemently opposed to any initiative on the border, even if (as was suggested) the northern spokesperson on the proposed Commission were Carson himself. Craig was, as ever, more politically imaginative than his support, and saw advantages in reaching a settlement with the new and comparatively emollient leader of the Free State, W.T. Cosgrave (his easy personal relationship with Cosgrave may have helped). He was prepared to tolerate a Commission, on the understanding that its brief would be confined to minor rectifications of the border; he was also interested in the idea of Carson as the Northern Ireland representative on the body. But the backbench furore which greeted the suggestion of Carson's appointment, involving blasphemous reflections on the great man's loyalty, demonstrated the extent of the political risks involved; and Craig therefore backed down, committing his government to a policy of non-recognition. When the Boundary Commission eventually saw the light of day, in October 1924, it contained no official representative of the northern government: Richard Feetham, a South African judge, chaired, Professor Eoin MacNeill, an Ulsterman and a Cumann na nGaedheal minister, spoke for the Irish Free State, while J.R. Fisher, a barrister and former editor of the Liberal Unionist *Northern Whig*, was appointed by the British government as an unofficial guardian of Ulster Unionist interests.

The first meetings of the new Commission were held on 5–6 November 1924, and it gathered and reviewed evidence until the summer of 1925: its report was complete by 17 October 1925, and apparently leaked to the *Morning Post* for the edition published on 7 November. Each side had high expectations of the result, but from the start the Irish Free State authorities were at a disadvantage. Feetham, the chairperson, in the absence of other guidelines, acted according to his legal experience and conducted the proceedings of the Commission in the light of his reading of article 12 of the Treaty: this meant in practice that only minor rectifications of the boundary were under consideration, and not the wholesale transfer of territory envisaged by the more ambitious nationalist commentators. Feetham, a liberal and honourable man, was inevitably dubbed 'cheat 'em' by an outraged Free

State establishment.[11] But the problem, for Dublin, lay not only with the legalistic approach of the Commission chairperson: the Irish representative, Professor Eoin MacNeill, was chosen because he was both a minister and an Ulster Catholic, and not because of his powers of advocacy or any ruthless partisanship. He had been an object of suspicion for some nationalists since his countermanding order to the Irish Volunteers on the eve of the Easter Rising; and his high-minded, judicial approach to his role as a commissioner engendered wider anger and resentment. Doubtless this would have been even more emphatic had the private verdict of J.R. Fisher, the unofficial Ulster Unionist representative, been known: 'I will say – before friends and enemies – that my two colleagues [Feetham and MacNeill] were perfectly loyal and straightforward and Ulster had fair play throughout'.[12] MacNeill, however, was hampered not only by his own honest political limitations, but also by the burden of unrealistic public expectations, fostered by Collins through his territorial demands of February 1922 and by the expansive claims of the North Eastern Boundary Bureau, a Free State propaganda agency headed by Kevin O'Shiel. Indeed, to some extent a similar burden was carried by J.R. Fisher, who believed that a limited exchange of land was inevitable, but who feared the 'non-sense about "not an inch"' which was being written and spoken by leading Ulster Unionists, and in particular by the northern Minister of Home Affairs, 'that ass' Dawson Bates.[13]

The world of early Irish historical scholarship is not always tranquil; but on the whole Fisher, an experienced barrister and journalist, was trained in a rather harder school of knocks than Eoin MacNeill. Fisher's advocacy, combined with MacNeill's hesitation and with the limited brief defined by Feetham, meant that the Commission proposed only a minor boundary change, with each side ceding and acquiring territory. Even so, this still involved a net gain of some 130,000 acres by the Irish Free State, as well as around 24,000 new citizens. But the reality of these acquisitions was obscured by some relatively small-scale transfers to Northern Ireland and by the overall modesty of the scheme in relation to previous demands. A furore grew in Dublin, fanned by the leaks in the *Morning Post*, which engulfed MacNeill and brought his resignation: the Cosgrave government moved rapidly to distance itself from the Commission. An agreement signed between Cosgrave, Craig and the British Prime Minister, Stanley Baldwin, on 3 December 1925 brought the suppression of the Commission report and the confirmation of the existing boundary. Some minor financial concessions were given to Cosgrave, while Craig's executive authority was further enhanced: the powers allotted to the putative Council of Ireland by the Government of Ireland Act, and hitherto retained by London, were now delegated to the Belfast administration. At the close of 1925 'Carson's Ulster' seemed secure, its territory having been successfully defended against military as well as political challenge. Only the more subtle or sceptical observers (of whom Fisher was one) could see that, had the Commission report stood, 'it would have been a legal and permanent decision from which there was no appeal' and that 'the present is merely a political compromise, and the "settlement" can and certainly will be reopened'.[14]

Whether through luck or its own resourcefulness, the Craig government had dealt successfully with the various (and formidable) challenges of the early 1920s. While it would be wrong to underestimate the seriousness of this technical achievement, there is also a sense in which Craig's survival is unsurprising. The Ulster Unionists, after all, had been trained in the arts of defensive combat from the time of the first Home Rule crisis, in 1885–6; and they had acquired a more direct military education in 1913–14 and, bloodily, in the First World War. They had shown some administrative skill in creating popular political organization in 1912–14, and in forging the institutions of the new Northern Ireland state in 1921–2. But in truth the popular organization of Ulster Unionism owed much to nationalist precedents and its success only underlined the vigorous partisanship of the new northern leadership. Moreover, the task of state-building fell more heavily on the shoulders of senior civil servants like Sir Ernest Clark than upon the Unionist command. Few Unionists had ministerial experience within the British government; and those few (like Craig) had had generally little opportunity for intricate constructive achievement. Yet this was precisely what was demanded in Northern Ireland in the more settled constitutional conditions of the mid-1920s: the creation of institutions to heal community divisions, the creation of opportunities for vital economic growth. But nothing in the ideology or in the practical experience of the Ulster Unionist movement suggested that these challenges might be addressed with any lasting success.

The Boundary Commission affair had been a triumph of sorts for Craig, even if right-wing Unionists, lulled by belligerent rhetoric, saw few signs of victory, and if more subtle and liberal commentators saw the omens of disaster in the hastily patched-up agreement of 3 December 1925. But for northern Catholics the collapse of the Commission was already a disaster, since much of the community's political self-confidence had been vested in the hope of a major cession of territory to the Irish Free State. The apparent if tacit acceptance of the existing border by the Free State government meant that the community had to square up to the reality of partition: the reality, however, was unpleasant. Catholics suffered disproportionately in the sectarian hysteria that swept across the North in the years between 1920 and 1922: 58 per cent of those killed in Belfast in the period were Catholic, a statistic which is all the more compelling when it is remembered that Catholics numbered only around a third of the city's population. Taut sectarian tensions in Belfast in July 1920, wound up by the IRA campaign and by inflammatory rhetoric from Carson (among other leading Unionists), brought the violent expulsion of Catholic workers from the shipyards, engineering firms and mills of the city. On this occasion the assassination of Colonel G.B. Smyth, a divisional commissioner of the RIC and a northern Protestant, in Cork seems to have acted as the immediate source of the tsunami of loyalist fury; and in the following month a second IRA assassination prompted further aggression against the local Catholic community: the killing of District Inspector O.R. Swanzy of the RIC on the steps of Lisburn Cathedral.

Northern Catholics believed that the very high casualties that they sustained, together with the evictions and expulsions, represented a concerted loyalist pogrom.[15] Even with the benefit of hindsight the evidence for this is ambiguous: Protestant casualties were not insignificant, and IRA offensive action in predominantly Protestant towns (such as, in fact, Belfast or Lisburn) continued unabated through much of the period 1920–2. But it is not hard to see why an embattled and suffering minority community should have sensed a conspiracy; nor is it hard to see the significance that this perception of a 'pogrom' subsequently acquired for northern Catholics. Fear of further persecution, allied with some more tactical calculations, persuaded the Ulster nationalist leadership to boycott many of the agencies of the new Northern Ireland state. Nationalist MPs did not take their seats in the Belfast parliament until 1926 and after; nationalists on the whole stayed clear of the RUC; and the community's leaders refused to participate in official reviews of the local government boundaries (the Leech Commission, 1922–3) and of education (the Lynn Committee, 1921–2). The predominantly nationalist county councils in Tyrone and Fermanagh refused to recognize the new Belfast parliament (Tyrone later amended this position in December 1921 into short-term recognition); and nationalist teachers, encouraged by Collins, refused to sanction partition by taking their salaries from the Belfast Ministry of Education (they were paid instead, for a time, by Dublin). This strategy owed something to a mixture of fear and hatred; but it was also based partly on the belief that non-recognition would strengthen the hand of the new Irish government in its effort to deal with the border issue. In fact after the death of Collins in August 1922, and indeed before, this effort had amounted to comparatively little – and even the little that was done tended to be reflexive and counter-productive. The collapse of the Boundary Commission confirmed that the most northern nationalists could hope for from Dublin was sympathy, and not even this could be guaranteed.

Were there any circumstances under which the plight of northern nationalists might have been alleviated in the early and mid-1920s? Some aspects of their condition seem irreducible: they were always likely to be entangled in a difficult, competitive relationship with their Unionist neighbours, even in the context of a united Ireland. They were always likely to be the victims of the sectarianism endemic in the region, and especially within certain sections of Unionism. On the other hand, it is just possible (with the luxury of hindsight) to conceive certain circumstances in which the position of northern Catholics might have been strengthened. The community was badly divided in the years after 1916, with a strong core of support for the charismatic Joseph Devlin and the parliamentary tradition in the east of Ulster, and mounting support for Sinn Féin in the west: one important cause of this tension was the parliamentary party's grudging but clear acceptance of temporary six-county partition in 1916, a concession which in fact did little to facilitate a settlement and was to prove costly at the polls. The Devlinite and Sinn Féin movements patched up their quarrel in order to fight the northern general election of May 1921; but only in May 1928, with the establishment of the National League of the North, was a form of organizational unity created (and even then the level of Sinn Féin participation was low, despite the presence of Cahir Healy as a joint secretary of the new body). These divisions were disastrous. They prevented coherent northern nationalist pressure on the Dublin and London governments, and even upon the new regime in Belfast. In a national context, the survival of a strong parliamentary tradition in the North was bizarre; and it did not help the task of mutual understanding between the Northern Ireland minority and their *soi-disant* protectors among Sinn Féin in Dublin. In addition these divisions must be related to the policy of abstentionism, a strategy which, while it was founded partly in a mixture of fear and calculation, was also desirable from the point of view of maintaining some semblance of unity. But while the abstentionist harness may have kept northern nationalists moving in broadly the same direction, it was arguably the wrong direction, for it meant that there was no Catholic representation at the formative stage of many of the institutions that were to dominate the Northern Ireland state.

The division and disengagement of Catholics are also crucial in understanding Craig's attitudes. There can be little doubt that, had Craig shown greater magnanimity in the late 1920s and 1930s towards the minority within Northern Ireland, then both the condition of that community and, indeed, the broader stability of the partition state would have been improved. But Craig's record in certain crucial respects was unimpressive, to say the least. The abolition of proportional representation for local government contests in 1922, combined with the activities of the Leech Commission in redrawing council boundaries, significantly impaired nationalist representation at a local level: Craig seems to have approved of gerrymandering, at any rate as a short-term expedient. These initiatives were followed in 1929 by the abolition of proportional representation in parliamentary contests, a move which damaged nationalist confidence further (though in fact it reflected the Prime Minister's preoccupation with the threat of Unionist dissidents rather than any proactive desire to suppress Catholic rights). Yet, Craig, who had spent part of his life outside of the swamp of northern sectarian politics, was not without some more generous and imaginative impulses. His problem was that until 1922 he confronted an IRA which in the North was punching beyond its weight; he was also sandwiched between a defensive and embittered cabinet and a popular Unionism whose Protestant fury, never far beneath the surface, was inflamed by a succession of high-profile IRA killings and by the well-publicized reports in the Belfast press of the plight of southern loyalists in the years up to 1923. As the effective victor in the North of the war against republicanism, Craig had probably sufficient political weight to move (if only tentatively) towards some form of reconciliation with the northern minority. After 1925 there was also arguably sufficient political confidence within the Unionist movement to facilitate such an initiative. But by this stage the level of Catholic demoralization was such that there was no sustained pressure to affect significant changes within the new polity. And the bitterness of the conflict in the early 1920s remained: many Unionists felt that they had played a desperate zero-sum game, and had miraculously won. There were thus problems, but there were also glimmers of opportunity: it is a reflection on Craig's imagination and on his personal ascendancy that he could conceivably have pursued these glimmers; and it is a reflection on his excessive caution and his abiding concern for Unionist unity – rooted in the Russellite years – that he preferred to remain in the darkness.

In the end, however, the Unionist leaders shared the limitations of their community as well as the broader sectarian impulses within Irish society, both North and South. In few parts of Europe were the inter-war years characterized by a marked liberalization of popular attitudes – and the new Northern Ireland conformed to the broader pattern of intolerance. Perhaps it is unreasonable to impose alien standards of public virtue or achievement on these men and women: but it should be remembered that, judged even by the more limited gauge of their own self-interest and the stability of the community they sought to preserve, they emerge as wanting. The Cumann na nGaedheal leadership in Dublin, an appropriate source of comparison, pursued their enemies with the same, indeed a greater ruthlessness than the Unionists; but they also sought to bring these enemies into public life, and towards this end gambled recklessly with the constitutional settlement that they had so bloodily defended in 1922–3. Neither in addressing the aspirations or civil rights of the Catholic minority, nor in squaring up to other economic problems within the new Northern Ireland, did the Unionist leadership display anything like the same political courage as their southern counterparts. Both with the question of community relations and economic retreat, there were broader structural restraints on what might be achieved: it would have taken an exceptionally gifted and bold Unionist leader to hold out a hand of partnership to northern nationalists; and it would have taken an exceptional leader to disentangle the shroud that was smothering the Northern Ireland economy. Exceptional gifts and exceptional moral courage were, however, in rather short supply in the Belfast government of the inter-war years.

Just as in the field of community relations, so with the economy Craig and his ministers alleviated symptoms without worrying about the underlying political pathology. Just as in the field of community relations, so with the economy Craig inherited a body politic that was so disease-ridden as to be well-nigh incurable. The Government of Ireland Act, the basis for the Northern Ireland constitution, reserved to the United Kingdom parliament all aspects of trade and commerce as well as almost every aspect of taxation: the Belfast administration could impose new forms of tax, but most of the important existing forms (including income tax, corporation tax and customs and excise) were controlled by London. This meant effectively that few of the levers of economic policy were in the hands of the Ulster Unionist government. This would have mattered less had the provincial economy been blossoming, but, as will become clear, this was emphatically not the case. Moreover, the financial relationship between Belfast and London, as defined by the Government of Ireland Act, soon created an intolerable burden for the Northern Ireland administration: the calculations were done at a time of relative (if transient) prosperity in the North, and without taking account of the speedy post-war collapse of Belfast industry (there are ghostly echoes here of the problematic economic formulae laid down by the Act of Union in 1801, based upon a flourishing wartime economy and heedless of the possibility of a later downturn). Under the Act of 1920 the new Northern Ireland government was expected to pay the cost of both its own activities in the province and those of (what was known as) the imperial government: there was, in addition, an 'imperial contribution' to be made to London, a sum originally fixed at £7.92 million. This tribute was painfully high, and, given that its collection was to be a priority, a first charge, pain speedily developed into agony. Within three years of its foundation, the Northern Ireland government – having seen off the gunmen of the IRA – very nearly fell victim to the actuaries of the British Exchequer.

Craig's cabinet, and the Ulster Unionist parliamentary party as a whole, reflected some of the broader strengths and weaknesses of the northern business class. Ministers were adept at haggling over details, in winning grand 'luck pennies' from the Treasury, but rather less skilled when it came to developing imaginative economic strategies. It should be re-emphasized, however, that the constitution of Northern Ireland gave little scope for imaginative planning, even assuming that this would have been within the ideological grasp of Ulster Unionism (which, until the 1960s, it was not): nor should the difficulties imposed by an on the whole unfriendly southern neighbour (such as during the trade war), and a scarcely less hostile British Treasury, be underestimated. These were the constraints within which the Craig government had to operate, and perhaps the best that can be said for its achievement is that it gamely tried to tinker with this configuration of problems to create a little more space for economic growth. But the government's economic ambitions (such as they were) were always subservient to its constitutional defensiveness; and the fundamental and generally unspoken problem was that Northern Ireland had not been created with a view to its economic health – in fact, rather the reverse. It was not that the new state was 'uneconomic': the problem instead was that Northern Ireland could not operate with British standards of social and welfare services and, at the same time, British levels of taxation. Lowering welfare standards would have turned 'loyal Ulstermen' into second-class Britons and would have underlined the poverty (real as well as ideological) of Unionism; raising taxation would – at a time when the Irish Free State tax regime was relatively liberal – have been tantamount to weakening the border by penny increments. Unionist governments were therefore caught in an economic-cum-constitutional quandary: they could win greater freedom from London at the cost of a generally lower standard of living. Alternatively, they could accept the relative powerlessness imposed by the modified Government of Ireland Act, and with it British doles and, in the context of the regional economy, an artificially high standard of living. This meant, of course, that the Unionist regime was dependent upon the support and sanction of London. Either course of action threatened the sanctity of partition. Unionists found themselves caught in the elaborate Home Rule harness constructed by Gladstone; and in the end perhaps the most that they could be expected to do was to rattle the gilded chains that kept them in place.

At first, the chains seemed more real than the gilding. By 1924 the financial formula binding Belfast to London was beginning to choke the nascent Unionist government. However, this hold was slackened in 1924–5 by the intervention of the Colwyn Committee, which in two reports decreed that the imperial contribution should be a final and therefore fluctuating charge on the revenue of Northern Ireland rather than a priority: this verdict was, of course, acclaimed by Craig and by his Minister of Finance, H.M. Pollock. The Belfast government also won concessions from London in the vital area of unemployment insurance: levels of unemployment in Northern Ireland were much higher on average than in Britain, with the result that the strain on insurance provision was intolerably great. In 1926 and again in 1936, Unionist ministers won reinsurance agreements which, while they did not solve all the financial problems arising out of high unemployment, did 'enable Northern Ireland to keep benefits and contributions at British rates without being waterlogged by debt'.[16] In 1938, as part of the deal which ended the Anglo-Irish trade war, James Craig (to the annoyance of his lieutenants, who thought that he had sold out too cheaply) wrested a number of minor concessions from the government of Neville Chamberlain: some agricultural subsidies would be paid to northern farmers by London; some arrangements were put in place to enable London to bail out the Belfast government in times of budgetary deficit; and the issue of unemployment insurance was revisited once more. Earlier deals had permitted the Belfast government to overdraw the insurance fund to the tune of £1 million, and at the same time to continue to win subventions from London: with any deficit exceeding £1 million the British government could intervene and possibly revise its support. This credit limit was now removed, and the threat of unfriendly (indeed potentially disastrous) British intervention in times of economic distress and political vulnerability was also diminished.

Unemployment was thus one of the main reasons why the Unionist begging bowl was so often in action at Whitehall. Craig and his ministers had to adapt to the very changed and more threatening economic environment of the inter-war years; and in so far as the staple industries of the North entered into a seemingly terminal decline in this period, it might be argued that the degree of adaptation was comparatively modest. As has been mentioned, ministers certainly strove to deal with some of the symptoms of the problem, and particularly the high demands made upon social welfare provision. But even here it sometimes took an exceptional pressure to stimulate official action. Widespread civil unrest spread among the 76,000 unemployed in the summer of 1932, precipitated by cuts in relief and orchestrated by the Unemployed Workers' Committee: conflict between the RUC and the supporters of the Committee descended in October 1932 into ferocious riots during which Catholics and Protestants banded together (however momentarily), their sectarian resentments swamped by a shared sense of poverty and injustice. The government collapsed to this pressure, and on 14 October authorized a massive increase in relief provision (some £330,000). Despite their fears, the proletarian millennium had not in fact arrived: the working-class unity of the autumn of 1932 was only one and, in the event, an exceptional expression of shared hardship. More frequently the deep social resentments of the era, and the intense competition for the little employment that was available, were expressed within conventional sectarian forms. The poor of each community bolstered their morale and self-esteem through occasions such as the Eucharistic Congress (1932) or George V's Silver Jubilee (1935), and each gave rise to violent sectarian passions: in 1935 riots claimed the lives of eight Protestants and five Catholics and brought the expulsion of 430 Catholic and 64 Protestant families from their homes.

Sectarianism underlay some of these crimes; but there also seems to have been a correlation between economic distress and the violent expression of sectarian resentment. Throughout the inter-war years there was little evidence to suggest that poverty was anything other than ascendant, given the unflaggingly high levels of unemployment (27 per cent between 1931 and 1939, a period of gradual recovery within the British economy). The peak number of unemployed was reached at the time of the Jubilee riots, in the summer of 1935, when just under 102,000 were out of work; but, as Patrick Buckland points out, the relative position was actually worse in 1938, when, though 92,000 were on the dole, the unemployment rate stood at 29.5 per cent, as compared with an average of 12.8 per cent for the rest of the United Kingdom.[17] Other survey evidence revealed grim levels of deprivation in working-class Belfast: folk-memories – of bare-footed children, humiliating economies, slums and squalor – corroborate in an anecdotal form the 'blue-book' findings of investigative teams from the Presbyterian and Methodist churches. Poverty and pawnbroking flourished together, the pawn shops of the city packed with second-hand coats and shoes, wedding rings and the campaign medals of the First World War. Poverty and disease spread together, with tuberculosis and pneumonia claiming many victims: the sanatoria of the pre-war era, now converted to other uses, serve as a reminder of these devastating plagues.

The underlying cause of this misery was the decline of the regional economy. The Northern Ireland government, hampered by its constitutional position as well as by its own ideological limitations, took some action and achieved some minor successes; but the scale of the disaster was bigger than the competence or imagination of those in authority. As has been mentioned, the northern government was relatively successful in winning concessions from Whitehall, which was, as always, willing to be persuaded that Irish political questions could be dissolved by cash. But the core problem – the structural obsolescence of much of the Northern Irish economy – could not be resolved by the relatively small and haphazard subventions from London. It may be emphasized immediately that northern agriculture, which, fostered by both British and local legislation, flourished in the inter-war years, should be excepted from the overall picture of economic decay: agriculture, always a regional strength, maintained a high quality of production and preserved its competitive advantage – even over the South. Elsewhere the picture could scarcely have been bleaker: the traditional stalwarts of Belfast industry – shipbuilding and related forms of engineering – suffered from the glut created in the First World War and in its immediate aftermath. Linen, which dominated the industrial base of the Belfast hinterland, was comparatively expensive to produce and was threatened by cheaper rivals, by new synthetic fibres and by the tariffs levied in the United States, hitherto a key customer for this and other traditional Irish products. Just under 60 per cent of the workforce was located in these declining sectors of the economy:

only 6 per cent found employment in new areas. Industry as a whole was organized on a rather disparate basis, with a proliferation of small, often family-run businesses that maintained both their independence and impossibly high production costs: it suffered from a lack of raw materials such as coal or iron, not a problem in the boom years of the late nineteenth century when the competitive margin was wider, but of greater seriousness when rivals were pulling ahead. It is possible that this apparently rather diffuse picture was, in fact, more coherent than appearances might otherwise suggest: the comparatively small nature of the business elite in the North gave rise to interlocking directorships and familial ties. But the difficulties facing dynamic management or an interventionist administration were clear enough; and in any event dynamism was not a particular feature of executives whose style had been set in the late Victorian glory days of the region and who complacently awaited the end of what was assumed to be a momentary recession. Moreover, intervention came only slowly to a government whose Minister of Finance (Pollock) had been born in 1852 and who remained determinedly mid-Victorian in outlook until his retirement in 1937.

Nevertheless, the northern government made some efforts towards addressing these difficulties. It sought to alleviate the problem of raw materials by subsidizing the production of coal at Sir Samuel Kelly's mine in south-east Tyrone: but the Coalisland seams proved (despite expert assurances) to be too expensive to exploit. It sought, too, to follow British precedents by passing Loans Guarantee Acts, beginning in 1922: these were essentially a form of dole and involved the underwriting of some of the Belfast shipyards' activities at a time of severe retraction within the industry. New Industries (Development) Acts, passed in 1932 and 1937, shadowy precursors of more determined efforts in the 1960s, sought to bring outside investment into Northern Ireland and to achieve as well some level of diversification. But the new endeavours that helped to revive the British economy in the mid- and late 1930s – the production of electrical goods and of motor cars – on the whole did not yield to the blandishments of the Belfast government. Only 27 firms were operating under the new industries legislation by 1939, and of these only the Short and Harland aircraft plant (1937) absorbed significant numbers of workers. Again, the issue of the North's perceived remoteness, its lack of raw materials and its lack of an appropriately skilled workforce all weighed against the possibility of serious external investment. It is also entirely possible, despite later O'Neillite rhetoric, which lauded the advantages of accessible devolved government, that the constitutional status of Northern Ireland deterred nervous investors. Devolved government meant, at one level, that the British government subcontracted political responsibility while retaining effective political control: Northern Ireland industry was Craig's problem, even though much of the environment within which that industry operated had been created by the United Kingdom parliament. The relative political insignificance of Belfast was reflected in the refusal of the imperial government to protect linen, even though English textiles were nurtured under a wall of tariffs: moreover, the constitutional defensiveness of the Unionists meant that, as with the linen issue, they were often unwilling to risk a breach with the

London government for fear that the Union might be further jeopardized. The political remoteness of Northern Ireland was also underlined by the relative dearth of official contracts that found their way to the 'Imperial Province': English ministers preferred to pursue their own party interests in awarding defence orders or other forms of government business. Nor, of course, were English ministers happy to see investment in Northern Ireland which might have reaped political dividends within their own constituencies. It was only where British political and economic interests and those of the Unionist government coincided – as in the area of agricultural production – that the advantages of devolved administration became apparent. In other words, it was only by dotting the 'i's and crossing the 't's of language formulated in London that Unionist ministers could communicate effectively with local business and advocate its needs and concerns.

The First World War had dislocated the familiar patterns of regional industry in the North; and it took a similar cataclysm to bring some relief from the long-term consequences of the earlier disaster. The demand for ships and for linen had been steadily increasing in the years immediately before the onset of the Second World War in September 1939, though it took some considerable time before the benefits of this were felt by the unemployed. Indeed, the contagion of joblessness raged on: by November 1940, over one year into the war, there were still 72,000 northerners on the dole. Thereafter, as the scale of production was ratcheted up to meet the despairing demands of the Ministry of Supply in London, unemployment fell rapidly, reaching an all-time low in 1944. Wartime orders brought a level of business that had been unimaginable for almost 20 years; bomb devastation created the opportunity to build new, modern works; cool scrutiny from London highlighted antiquated styles of management and outmoded methods of production. There was short-term pain: the German attacks on Belfast in April and May 1941 flattened not only industrial plant but also many working-class residential areas. On a more microscopic level, the reorganization of parts of Belfast industry by Whitehall brought mortification to the gimcrack magnates of Ulster's middle management. Wartime demands also brought stress to a workforce accustomed to massive differentials between skilled and unskilled labour, and to a market dominated by unemployment or, at best, underemployment.

Between 1941 and 1945 the level of strike action in Northern Ireland was between three and four times greater than the average in Britain (523 strike days for every 1,000 workers as opposed to 153 strike days 'across the water'). It is comparatively easy to highlight the immediate origins of much of this industrial action: the most damaging strike of the war came in February 1944, when 1,200 shipyard workers demanded a pay rise and were supported by a wide section of Belfast labour. It is also possible to identify some broader features of the workers' experience that rendered the pressures of wartime production unusually great (such as earlier wage structures and unemployment levels). However, there is an apparent contradiction between the supposed super-loyalism of Protestant Ulster and many features of the community's attitude towards the war: comparatively high levels of labour protest, comparatively low levels of recruitment to the armed forces. The burden of the earlier Great War weighed heavily on Northern Ireland: all too vivid memories of the carnage at the Somme and Passchendaele were poor recruiting sergeants for the British army in 1939–40. But it was also the case that, given the more recent and lasting experience of poverty, the supposed pay-off for this sacrifice – the creation of a Unionist government in Northern Ireland – looked like a rather poor exchange for the lives of the fallen. Belfast was not, in fact, a home fit for heroes; in April–May 1941 it looked as if the city was rather a mortuary fit for heroes. Quite simply, the record of the Unionist government in protecting and nourishing its citizens was not likely to inspire any particular acts of heroism, whether on the battlefield or on the shopfloor.

If the war facilitated a belated but vital overhaul of Belfast industry, then it brought devastation and rebirth to Ulster Unionism. In 1940 the Unionist leadership was aging and weary: Craig had been in office for almost 20 years, as had several of his senior lieutenants (John Andrews, John Milne Barbour, Richard Dawson Bates); the average age of this cadre in 1940 was over 68 years. The onset of war brought further complications to an already formidably difficult political position. With the fall of France, a panicky London government toyed with the idea of harrying the North into a unified Ireland, which in turn would join in fighting the Germans. Eamon de Valera and a memorably emphatic Frank Aiken put paid to this initiative, and relieved the northerners of the burden of apparent disloyalty to the beleaguered imperial cause.[18] But other compelling issues appeared in the Stormont in-trays: civil defence had been a British preoccupation since at least 1937, and British legislative initiatives and broader debates were thus forced onto apparently reluctant Belfast ministers (air-raid precautions first appeared on a Stormont cabinet agenda in October 1937). The lethargy of the Unionist government over this vital concern has been much emphasized and chimes with other apparent evidence of a sclerotic disregard for the lives under its charge: the record of Unionist ministers is, at least superficially, astounding. In fact, a closer and cooler scrutiny (by no means an easy task, given the 1,100 dead of 1941) suggests that the sins of the government were as unexceptional as its virtues. Aging ministers like Craig, who had been schooled in the South African war, found it hard to believe that remote Belfast would ever prove to be a target for German bombers – and this (with the benefit of hindsight) alarmingly outdated judgement was in fact initially confirmed by the War Office. In addition, even assuming that there had been a political will, the enfeebled resources of the Stormont Ministry of Finance did not permit much action: Unionist ministers squabbled with their London counterparts about the responsibility for civil defence expenditure, each trying to pass the buck on to the other. When the nightmare came, on 15 April 1941, ministers met the following day to review the damage, and two weeks later met again, armed with draft legislation designed to protect the homeless and evacuees. The less devastating raid of 4 May (which still brought 191 deaths) produced within ten days a lengthy cabinet meeting which decided on a further range of initiatives for evacuees and those remaining in Belfast. Some two months after the main raid, ministers began – amongst other concerns – to fret about the political symbols of the state: the Stormont parliament building and the iconic Carson statue. Of course all of this was too little, too late: it could not resurrect the 1,100 dead, nor comfort the bereaved and the wounded. But it was a lack of imagination and a lack of moral courage, the endemic vices of the Unionist high command, which characterized ministers, rather than callousness or hauteur.

The devastation caused by the air-raids, and the flustered and sometimes quirky nature of the government's response, appeared to confirm the widely held view that the regime was incompetent – that it was locked into patterns of thought and action that were inappropriate to the demands of war. But the raids merely fanned an existing discontent, which had already brought the resignation of two junior ministers (Warnock and Gordon) from the government in May–June 1940. Inertia on the civil defence question, the still high and, in the context of a supposedly full-throttle wartime economy, embarrassing levels of unemployment, and the related failings of the Ministry of Commerce were pressing issues for the departing ministers. However, Craig's increasingly eccentric and disengaged leadership did not inspire confidence either; and in particular his expansive (but misleading) boasts about the level of preparedness were sometimes greeted with ill-concealed derision. Craig's death in November 1940 might have alleviated this pressure had there been a full-scale reconstruction of the government: but instead there was merely a reshuffling of duties among the gerontocrats at Stormont. John Andrews, aged 69, became Prime Minister; Milne Barbour, aged 72, was – astonishingly – promoted from Commerce, where he was under fire, to Finance; and Dawson Bates, aged 64, remained at Home Affairs. The retention of Bates and the promotion of Milne Barbour were disastrous mistakes for the new Prime Minister. The demands of gearing Belfast industry to the war had fallen on the Ministry of Commerce, where Milne Barbour was perceived to have been 'wrong, inept and palsied': the implementation of civil defence precautions fell partly on Home Affairs, where Bates (certainly in the opinion of the head of the civil service, Spender) was plodding out of his depth.[19] Craig had earlier endeavoured to protect his flagging Minister of Home Affairs, fobbing off calls for an enquiry into air-raid precautionary measures (which might in turn have exposed Bates's unpreparedness): he appears to have felt a sentimental commitment to the old sectarian warrior, who had helped to see off the republican challenge in 1921–2. With the accession of a new Prime Minister Bates might usefully have been dropped from the government – but again, apparently, sentimental considerations came into play (Bates was ailing and impecunious). Andrews's decision to retain already discredited ministers came only months before the German air-raids, and undoubtedly paved the way for his own downfall in May 1943. In the end the central issue was much as it had been in 1940, when discontent first began to fester: the apparent inadequacy of ministers to meet the challenges of war.

The crisis which engulfed Andrews in the late spring of 1943 had been a long time in gestation, but it was an eloquent testimony to the atrophied nature of the higher ranks of Unionist politics that so little was done to avert the final coup. It is also striking that the leadership within such an intimate political forum as Stormont should have remained so determinedly out of touch with the concerns of its support: but then there has been a deeply embedded tendency among Unionist commanders to pursue unpopular or incoherent policies, banking on the ultimate tractability of the faithful (Edward Saunderson, Terence O'Neill and James Molyneaux conform to this broad pattern). Even the remorselessly populist Craig, lulled by 20 years in office and trusting in the intricate webs of patronage which he had woven over this time, seems to have come to believe in his own untouchability. Just as the marginalization of Saunderson in 1905–6 brought a rejuvenation of the Unionist command, so too in 1943 the toppling of Andrews brought to an end the geriatric politics with which he had been associated. The new Prime Minister was Sir Basil Brooke, hailed as a youthful dynamo (he was in fact just under 55 at the time of his appointment). With Brooke, who had remained impassive during the coup, came some of the 'young' turks who had been responsible for its orchestration: Maynard Sinclair, the new Minister of Finance (aged 47 in 1943), Edmond Warnock, the new Minister for Home Affairs (aged 54), and Brian Magennis, who was appointed as Minister for Labour in 1945 when he was only 44. These men, fired with righteous anger at the failings of their elders and bubbling with ideas about the future direction of Unionism, were reminiscent of their Edwardian counterparts – the young men of the loyalist 'radical right' who, dissatisfied with the leadership of Saunderson, mobilized the party in its assault on Russellism and ultimately against the third Home Rule Bill. In addition the men of 1943 came to power at – for them – a highly auspicious time: while labour relations remained strained, unemployment was rapidly falling, a reflection of the more efficient mobilization of the North within the wartime British economy. More important, the course of the war was beginning to turn in favour of the British and their allies: the contribution of Northern Ireland to the broader effort was beginning to gather force, with the development of naval and air facilities, the landing of US troops and the use of the province during the preparations for D-Day. Brooke and his disciples had thus not only overcome their enemies within the party; they were also being seen to play a part within the broader triumph of the Allied cause. By May 1945, confidence soaring, these young men seemed to have inherited the earth: it would take ten years before it became clear that their legacy was in fact a sectarian swamp.

The Second World War created the opportunity for Brooke's premature accession; and the legacy of the war, political and economic, ensured that Brooke and his chosen lieutenants for long remained in office. At first, however, there were jitters: the new Labour government of Clement Attlee was elected on a programme of sweeping welfare reform, and was untested on the constitutional question. Moreover, the Northern Ireland parliamentary election of June 1945, while of course confirming Brooke in office, brought the second lowest tally of Unionist MPs in the history of the state (only 33). There were also fears concerning unemployment – that the boom conditions of the Second World War would be as transient as those of the Great War, and would be followed by the same poverty and relative instability. For these reasons there were serious debates within Unionism about the future of Northern Ireland, and in particular whether alternatives should be pursued to the existing form of devolution: the question of dominion status was raised (a conventional ultra-Unionist response to serious external threat). More remarkably, the possibility of reintegration within Westminster was discussed, the argument being that an elaborate welfare system in Britain would create a chasm between London and Belfast, and possibly endanger the partition settlement itself. The core problem for the governing party was thus similar to that faced by Craig in the 1920s and 1930s – that of maintaining the integrity of the Unionist class alliance. And in the end a (temporary) solution to this challenge was found not in fancy constitutional experiments, but rather in accepting further British doles and therefore further British influence.

In 1946 it was agreed that there should be a parity of social services in Northern Ireland and Britain, a deal made possible because the British government was willing to pay for its implementation. It was later decided that the unemployment funds of Britain and Northern Ireland should be amalgamated with effect from July 1948: in 1949 further fine-tuning occurred, when the British undertook to pay 80 per cent of any excess social service costs that might arise out of the perennially depressed condition of the northern economy. Despite earlier fears of socialism and centralization, the Unionist Party happily accepted a torrent of British social and welfare legislation, lulled by the conviction that they had struck a deal which offered fabulous riches in return for a minimal outlay. These new benefits promised to bolster the partition settlement by tranquillizing possibly restless Protestant voters. In addition, the superior welfare structure in place in Northern Ireland might well have the effect of killing northern nationalism by kindness (some Unionist backbenchers were of course disgusted to see 'disloyalists' being blessed with the natural rewards of loyalty). There was certainly a minor political cost to be borne in terms of heightened British scrutiny and interference; but, since this had come anyway, given the exigencies of war, and – particularly in the context of the cold war – was probably desirable, there were few Unionist complaints. Moreover, the Labour government, conscious of the northern record during the war, was comparatively well disposed towards Ulster Unionism; and indeed it composed the most solid legislative endorsement of the Stormont regime ever on offer – the Ireland Act (1949). This affirmed that Northern Ireland would only cease to be a part of the United Kingdom if the devolved parliament so decided: the Act was Attlee's clipped response to the formal inauguration of an Irish republic by John A. Costello on Easter Monday, 18 April 1949.

Bew, Gibbon and Patterson have remarked that 'by committing itself to welfarism and step-by-step the Unionist bourgeoisie was redefining its dependence on the Protestant working class and the British state in potentially dangerous ways'.[20] Further potential dangers, both tactical as well as long term, arose from the benefits which this new welfarism might bestow on northern Catholics. Colonel Hall-Thompson's Education Act (1947), an extension of the earlier British measure (the Butler Act of 1944), sought to increase capital funding for voluntary schools (by and large Catholic institutions), while reinforcing the non-denominational character of the state schools (which were effectively Protestant). Catholics sought to achieve greater state support while preserving the independence of their schools; while Protestants were inflamed by what they saw as the old crime of official support for denominational education. At the same time, however, many of these same critics were alarmed by the creeping secularization of the state institutions and by their regression from an emphatically Protestant character. In the event, by a combination of good groundwork and dogged determination, Hall-Thompson guided his measure into law; but only two years later he was tripped up by Protestant protest at a further proposal designed to benefit the voluntary (Catholic) sector, and was compelled into resignation. Hall-Thompson represented the comparatively more liberal Unionism which the accession of Brooke (his sectarian outbursts in the early 1930s notwithstanding) appeared to promote in 1943. But the modest wartime consensus speedily disintegrated, the victim of a Protestant evangelical revival, as well as the renaissance in the South of a recidivistic nationalism. The generation of Unionist elected in the late 1940s, and particularly in the election of 1949, received their political education at a time of relative loyalist confidence as well as southern braggadocio; and though sometimes bright (as with Brian Faulkner), they were not at this time open to even tentatively consensual gestures. The relative liberals within the Unionist cabinet found themselves outgunned by populist evangelical Protestants: Hall-Thompson, for example, was driven from office largely through the intervention in debate of Ivan Neill, a prominent Baptist. Others of Hall-Thompson's stamp fell as the Protestant character of the regime was increasingly reinforced: Brian Magennis, George B. Hanna and Walter Topping each ventured to defy Protestant opinion at different times (particularly over the marching question), and each suffered as a result. Public Order legislation in 1951, the Flags and Emblems Act (1954) and an unwillingness, or inability, to ban the more provocative Orange parades, such as at the Longstone in South Down, all signalled a marked collapse before populist Protestant pressure. Welfarism and an emphatic Protestantism: these, then, were the formidable resources with which the Brooke government sought to sustain its control over the Unionist electorate, and thereby over Northern Ireland.

There was as yet no coherent nationalist opposition to this ascendancy: indeed, to a certain extent – and certainly in the short term – the republican movement played into the hands of the regime. Nationalists had for long been debilitated, not only by the restrictive political rules devised by the state but also by their own divisions; and it was with a view to rectifying this, and focusing energies, that the Anti-Partition League was launched in Dungannon, County Tyrone, in November 1945. The timing was propitious, at least in domestic Irish terms, for within seven months Seán MacBride had launched Clann na Poblachta and was poised to challenge Fianna Fáil for possession of the grail of republican purity: MacBride and de Valera therefore became locked into a contest from which northern nationalists and the Anti-Partition League were able – at least in the short term – to profit. But, while the plight of these northerners and the evils of partition were momentarily at the top of the Irish domestic agenda, within Northern Ireland, and indeed further afield, the effort expended was, arguably, counter-productive. Brooke's government, basking in the afterglow of the Allied victory, still occupied some moral high ground in London and Washington; and the qualified loyalist sympathies of the Attlee government combined with the strategic importance of the British at this formative stage of the cold war meant that Stormont ministers did not have to try very hard to be loved. In fact the Anti-Partition League's own tactics, and the broader controversies of southern politics at this time, helped to disarm some of its effectiveness: the national 'chapel-gate' collection of 31 January 1949, designed to raise funds for the Stormont election of 10 February, appeared to underline the clerical nature of the League and served to mitigate some of its criticisms of Unionist sectarianism. Moreover, the 'mother and child' controversy which raged in 1950–1 was, despite its complexities, easily interpreted by Unionists as evidence of southern irredentism and was used to deflect the onslaught of the League.

Poor election results in 1949 and 1953, the result in part of effective Unionist mobilization, appeared to underline the hopelessness of constitutional strategies. Violent republicans, who had not been completely demobilized during the League initiative, were quick to seize their opportunity. The freelance militancy of Liam Kelly, a Pomeroy man who had been expelled from the IRA, caught the imagination of demoralized republicans in the west; and in 1953 Kelly was elected to Stormont for Mid Tyrone on an abstentionist ticket. In addition, the return of two Republican members at the Westminster election of 1955 seemed to highlight a broader degree of electoral endorsement for a militant initiative. There had already been preparatory arms raids (including one spectacularly successful endeavour at Gough Barracks, Armagh, in June 1954); and the full offensive came in December 1956 with Operation Harvest. This provided further martyrs to both causes (12 IRA volunteers and six policemen were killed); but it was a military failure and – at least in the short term – a political humiliation as well. The reasons for this are not hard to locate: both governments dealt vigorously with the militants – both used internment, and indeed Seán Lemass was (as ever) willing to throw off the burden of history and use the military tribunals which his Free State opponents had created almost 30 years before. Northern Catholics did not support the campaign, perhaps because it scarcely touched some areas (such as Belfast), or perhaps because of a general demoralization: it is also possible that better welfare provision in the North, and a higher standard of living for the employed, may have temporarily disrupted traditional allegiances. The Unionist government was therefore able to claim a comparatively easily won victory even before the formal cessation of hostilities (in February 1962).

Yet it would be quite wrong to dismiss the overall importance of Operation Harvest. The campaign brought 600 'incidents', from murder to minor public order offences; it brought the mobilization of hundreds of IRA men and thousands of police. But more important, the campaign heightened the defensiveness of all aspects of Unionism, and tended to reinforce the already influential populist and sectarian tendencies within the movement. There had been tensions between modestly liberal Unionist ministers and populist Protestantism even before 1956 (there was, in fact, a history of interaction between a popular sectarian loyalism and a more centrist leadership dating back at least to the mid-nineteenth century). Brooke's strength (he was raised to the peerage in 1952 as Viscount Brookeborough), like that of Craig, was that he had populist prejudices and knew how to resolve these tensions and impose a form of unity within his movement; his critical weakness, again as with Craig, was that he was never prepared to work towards the substance of unity within his state. Into this political chinashop in 1963 stepped the bullish Terence O'Neill, a leader who was certainly interested in the forms of a broader consensus, but who in the end improved on his predecessors only in so far as he brought a personal rather than a sectarian paranoia into Stormont Castle.

In the short term it was not, in fact, the challenge of the IRA that threatened to destabilize Unionism, but rather the economic condition of the state. There has long been scholarly argument concerning the relationship between economic development in Northern Ireland and state power, with some historians emphasizing the role of new multinational capital in importing new standards into the hitherto comparatively static northern political arena.[21] The nominal liberalism of Terence O'Neill has sometimes been linked to the demands of multinational investment. It has for long been recognized, however, that the weakness of the Brookeborough regime in its latter years and the reorientation pursued by O'Neill were not so much the result of external pressures, whether from multinational industries or the IRA, as of the internal pressure created by unemployment and the Northern Ireland Labour Party (NILP). To an extent, the Northern Irish state and its Unionist masters were in fact the victims of some limited economic success: agriculture sustained a steady growth throughout the post-war era, but increased efficiency was often bought through mechanization and the lay-off of unwanted labour. Other areas of growth brought long-term political problems, though not necessarily of the kind identified by commentators in the 1970s: some forms of economic growth, though encouraging, did not make a serious impression upon the labour market. The expansion of the civil service in the post-war era brought massive employment opportunities, but these for a variety of reasons – informal discrimination, anti-partitionist sensitivities, residual Catholic educational disadvantage – fell disproportionately to Protestants and therefore served in the long term to enhance nationalist alienation from the state. Between 1945 and 1962 45,000 jobs were created by various new industries tempted into Northern Ireland by a panoply of preferential grants and loans: but this could only dent the unemployment figures, which were sustained by a steady annual increase in the population of around 15,000 and by the uneven decline of the traditional industries. Here the Brookeborough government struggled to protect its own, both in terms of the traditional local Unionist business class and the Protestant workforce; but it was an expensive and – in the face of global economic pressures – a futile task, a kind of protracted and mild 'Black Friday'. Some plea in mitigation might be made on the basis that the declining industries did not sink smoothly, but instead tended to rally confusingly before plummeting headlong into the abyss. Linen had enjoyed a rebirth during the Second World War and was in demand during the Korean conflict of 1950–3: thereafter the industry went into freefall, with the government spending £4 million in the period 1956–61 in order to support mills which shed 10,000 workers in the same period. Shipbuilding pursued a more gentle, if still unmistakeable, downward trajectory, with massive lay-offs in the early 1960s despite a previous decade of relative strength. Some of the threatening political combinations of the 1930s began to re-emerge: a protest meeting of 12,000 workers paraded to the Belfast City Hall in August 1962, where they were addressed by NILP politicians as well as nationalists and representatives of the Irish Labour Party. The NILP vote soared, reaching 26 per cent at the Stormont election held in May 1962. Government-sponsored reports into the economy offered only political capital to its enemies: the Isles and Cuthbert *Economic Survey of Northern Ireland* (1957) argued that devolved government was a hindrance to economic development rather than (as was so often boasted) an asset; Sir Robert Hall's *Report of the Joint Working Party on the Economy of Northern Ireland* (1962) provided a bleak assessment of its subject and condemned the government's efforts to sustain moribund traditional industries.

In March 1963 the 75-year-old Brookeborough found himself threatened by the unemployment crisis, by subdued though unmistakeable official criticisms, and by the possibility that Unionism might fracture under the pressure applied by the NILP. Welfarism had only served to bolster working-class Protestant expectations and morale; populist sectarian gestures had preserved a cosmetic unity at the expense of demoting or marginalizing some of the more fertile talents within the Unionist high command. In the end it was a telling measure of the limited significance of Operation Harvest that it should have coincided with an upsurge in support for the labour movement and with pressures on Brookeborough to make way for new leadership. It was paradoxical that, within a year of the formal cessation of the IRA campaign, one of the lasting hate-figures for republicanism should have been overthrown; and it was a startling reflection of the psychological weaknesses of the Unionist command, as well as of the apparent irrelevance of Operation Harvest, that Terence O'Neill should have emerged as the new Prime Minister rather than the chief ministerial adversary of the IRA, Brian Faulkner. In the event, however, it seems that – despite questions of rhetoric and style – both men were chiefly concerned to preserve the Protestant electoral coalition that kept Unionism in power: the difference between the two was simply that Faulkner had greater skill.

It is tempting to see O'Neillism as an elaborate confidence trick (and indeed some commentators, such as David Gordon, have happily succumbed to the temptation).[22] Certainly gestural politics were an essential feature of the O'Neillite project: in fact the Prime Minister's very name, which hinted at Gaelic kingship (and which was therefore a useful asset in addressing a broader Irish constituency), concealed his direct descent from the Chichesters, the aggressive planter clan of the seventeenth century. This apparently quintessential northerner – from a mixture of planter and Gaelic stock – had in fact spent most of his early life in London and further afield, and spoke in a nasal drawl which owed little to the more emphatic cadences of his adopted Ahoghill. O'Neill's political credentials were equally ambiguous: he was the son and grand-nephew of undistinguished and taciturn Ulster Unionist MPs, but a much more looming presence in his early life was the Liberal statesman, the Marquess of Crewe, who was his maternal grandfather (he once teased nationalist MPs by proclaiming that he was 'a Home Ruler').[23] Not quite a northerner, not quite a Unionist, not quite a planter – O'Neill might have served as the embodiment of a new consensual politics in Northern Ireland: this indeed was his expectation. But these ambiguities were appreciated only by a minority constituency in Northern Ireland: certainly most Unionists were attuned to a much less demanding and more blatant political style. And, in any event, O'Neill's consensuality ultimately appeared to be as ambiguous as his personal and political heritage.

Is it possible, then, to define O'Neillism in terms of conventional Irish political traditions? In part O'Neill may be seen within the context of the strengths and limitations of the constructive Unionist tradition. Like the late nineteenth-century proponents of this gospel, O'Neill seems to have regarded popular nationalism as (to borrow Feargal Cochrane's description) a 'behavioural problem' rather than as a deep-rooted political conviction.[24] As with his late nineteenth-century precursors, O'Neill prided himself upon a vigorously rational approach to the challenges of Irish government; as with these precursors, this rationality was confounded by the visceral sectarianism and emotionalism of a political culture apparently untouched by the Enlightenment. Like the Balfour brothers and George Wyndham, O'Neill seems to have believed that economic progress would dispel political hatred and sectarianism: his infamous (and still astonishing) remark that 'if you treat Roman Catholics with due consideration and kindness, they will live like Protestants in spite of the authoritative nature of their Church' was at one level simply an unusually crude expression of Balfourian conviction.[25]

O'Neill may also, helpfully, be seen within the traditions of paternalistic landlordism. Although assessments of O'Neill's sincerity and of his political sophistication vary – he has been described by one provocative commentator as 'the most reactionary of all the Unionist Prime Ministers' – the most recent analyses of his rule have tended towards generosity.[26] Like an improving or paternalistic squire, O'Neill administered along apparently rational, scientific lines, placing an excessive faith upon the benefits of planning and upon a coterie of expert advisors. The distinction between the well-crafted and generous public speeches drafted for the Prime Minister by bright senior civil servants (such as Ken Bloomfield) and his own highly ill-judged autobiography reveals the extent to which the light of O'Neillism benefited from being filtered through other lenses. Recent work suggests that behind the bland exterior lay a relatively high-voltage intellect: but O'Neill's brightness was all too frequently eclipsed by a grating condescension and occasional sectarian gaffes.[27] He seems to have felt a paternalistic concern for his charges, the people of Northern Ireland. Equally, and like earlier paternalist squires, he was ill at ease away from the comfort of the Big House and of 'civilized' company. His occasional descents into the community – visits to factories or to schools – could be painfully stilted and often revealed the extent of his distance from ordinary people. Like earlier squires, he believed implicitly that he worked from a superior wisdom, and he was flabbergasted when his charges chose their own recidivistic patterns of thought. One of the fundamental paradoxes, indeed tragedies, with O'Neill was that he combined a defensiveness, even a paranoia, at Stormont with an alarming measure of innocence in the popular arena. He was the flawed ingénu of northern politics.

The main philosophical elision with O'Neillism came with the relationship between economic and political modernization. O'Neill believed that the economic problems of Northern Ireland were susceptible to rational management, and he argued, in turn, that enhanced prosperity would undermine the 'irrationality' of much of northern politics (especially nationalist politics). Some of the groundwork for the revolution in economic planning that occurred in the 1960s had been laid by the Brookeborough administration; but on the whole Brookeborough (in so far as he was interested in economic detail) was nervous about planning and was only coaxed into exceptional measures (such as commissioning the Isles and Cuthbert and the Hall reports) by exceptional pressures. O'Neill, on the other hand, made a virtue out of the necessities of the Brookeborough regime, and enthusiastically looked beyond his cabinet table and backbenches for expert guidance. In August 1963 he and his rival, Brian Faulkner, oversaw the creation of an Economic Council, designed to unite trade unionist and industrialist and – like its southern counterparts – to provide informed advice to the government. Later, in October 1963, O'Neill commissioned a distinguished Ulster-born academic, Tom Wilson, to devise an economic blueprint along the lines of the Whitaker Programme. This was ready by the end of 1964 and resulted in the creation of a Ministry of Development under the direction of the wayward but gifted William Craig. Wilson advocated, too, the extension of existing schemes to attract new business into Northern Ireland (much as Whitaker had built upon similar earlier initiatives within the Republic): he also called for designated areas of growth, endorsed an earlier official proposal (contained in Sir Robert Matthew's *Belfast Regional Survey and Plan*) to create a new city in North Armagh, and outlined ambitious ideas for the improvement of the economic infrastructure of Northern Ireland (new motorways, new educational and housing resources). Subsidiary reports (by Benson on rail transport, and by Lockwood on a new university) supplied the detail which Wilson's panoramic approach eschewed.

These efforts were complemented by a succession of initiatives within the realm of community relations. The pontificate of John XXIII had prepared the way for some mild thawing in the attitude of liberal Unionists towards the Roman Catholic hierarchy; and when Pope John died, in June 1963, the government of Northern Ireland was able (in defiance of earlier practice) to send its condolences to Rome. O'Neill provided his own eulogy of the dead pontiff, a gesture which, again, was unprecedented. Later rhetoric and (to a lesser extent) later actions built upon this tentative generosity: in April 1964 O'Neill visited a Catholic school in Ballymoney, County Antrim, the first northern Prime Minister to flirt with the Scarlet Woman in this daring way (in fact O'Neill's predecessors, particularly in their later years, did not deign to visit schools of any description). However, while O'Neill's spin-doctors interpreted the visit as a landmark in community relations, there were ambiguities: the school serviced the relatively inert nationalist population of Ballymoney rather than a more aggressively republican constituency; and the venerable priest who chaired the Board of Governors had served as an army chaplain in the First World War rather than as a mouthpiece for the contemporary Sinn Féin movement. It was thus a particular and passive form of northern Catholicism that O'Neill was keen to bless.

But the most celebrated of these cross-community gestures came in January 1965 with the visit to Stormont of Seán Lemass. The auspices were not encouraging. There had been no similar meeting since the 1920s, and the arrangements for the event nearly foundered upon a typing error (a government secretary in Dublin had addressed a key letter to 'Stormont Castle, Dublin', while an irrepressibly patriotic official of An Post had scrawled 'try Belfast, Ireland'): doubtless O'Neill's Paisleyite opponents, alert to the signs and portents of treachery, would have perceived a more ominous significance in this, as indeed in the fact (noted by T.K. Whitaker) that the wine served for the visit was Châteauneuf-du-Pape.[28] O'Neill seems to have been principally concerned to greet his visitor in an inoffensive manner ('welcome to Ulster' and 'welcome to Northern Ireland' were deemed to be too provocative); but his earnest efforts to learn the language of nationality ('welcome to the North') were wasted, since the Taoiseach maintained a characteristically grim silence.[29] But the visit was a success: the two men empathized with each other's political difficulties in the sanctuary of the Stormont Castle lavatory, and return expeditions were planned. O'Neill, an ascendancy figure and a veteran of the Irish Guards, may have had apparently very little in common with Lemass, the hatter's son who had been 'out' in 1916 and who had fought with Collins's 'Squad': but both were laconic technocrats who were pursuing broadly similar policies in their respective territories. Both men were patriots, by their own lights; but where Lemass's economic drive successfully harmonized with national self-confidence, the northern variations on the Whitaker theme only accentuated a sectarian cacophony. In part this was because O'Neill had less political nous than Lemass. But, at a more fundamental level, it was also the case that, as in the past, economic growth and rapid social change tended to overturn the carefully plotted sectarian frontiers of Ulster society.

With the implementation of the Wilson report came the unravelling of O'Neill's millenarian vision for Ulster and for Unionism. The creation of new dwellings – the goal was 64,000 units in five years – helped to open up long-standing Catholic dissatisfaction with the allocation of public housing. Debates about the rationalization of transport – the Wilson report called for four new motorways – highlighted regional grievances, and in particular the anger widely felt in Derry with the axing of a rail connection to Belfast. Again, the proposal for a new university, allocated by the Lockwood Committee to the predominantly Unionist town of Coleraine, outraged the mainly nationalist Derry, which had a long-standing tradition of tertiary-level education (in the form of Magee College). The proposal for a new town evoked similar suspicions and resentment: the site chosen, in North Armagh, was also in a predominantly Unionist locality, and the name chosen for the new venture – Craigavon – underlined its evidently partisan origins. The drive for investment certainly brought in new business, but mostly to the eastern part of Northern Ireland where the Unionist population was concentrated.

The accuracy of these furious and wide-ranging suspicions varied. There was serious discrimination against Catholics in the field of public housing. There does seem to have been a remarkable collusion between some Derry Unionists and Stormont ministers over the allocation of the new university to Coleraine. The name of the new city was a thoughtless provocation (Bill Craig seems to have been responsible). On the other hand, Unionists found it hard to grasp that, given the divisions in the North, they could not commemorate their heroes in the manner favoured by their counterparts in Dublin: from this (limited) perspective the new town of Craigavon or the proposed 'Carson' bridge over the Lagan were as unremarkable as Connolly or Pearse railway stations in Dublin, or the Collins barracks, or (for that matter) O'Connell Street. Nor was there apparently any systematic effort to favour the east in terms of investment: on the contrary, O'Neill's strategies of killing nationalism by kindness by no means precluded investment in western Ulster. But the bulk of the population of Northern Ireland was in the east; and in addition ministers (such as Brian Faulkner) claimed that they sometimes found it impossible, even wielding special financial inducements, to persuade outside investors to locate their businesses in the west, away from the eastern ferry ports and British markets.[30]

The Wilson report embodied the O'Neillite vision of economic modernization: but, as has been outlined, there was no corresponding political pay-off. Instead, and paradoxically, economic modernization tended to stimulate political recidivism. Indeed, the paradox is perhaps more apparent than real, for there were plenty of precedents available which might have served to highlight the implications of O'Neill's economic ambitions. The rapid industrial growth of Belfast in the nineteenth century had altered denominational balances and frontiers, and created political fault-lines which would remain active in some cases for over a century. The growth of the linen trade in south Ulster in the late eighteenth century, and indeed the broader growth of the Irish agrarian economy after *c.*1740, helped to destabilize existing political relationships and institutions and to create the turmoil of the 1790s. Equally, the economic planning of the 1960s, designed to copper-fasten Unionist rule, instead contributed to its demise. Unionists became the victims of their own success (or at least of British subvention): the now clearly terminal decline of the traditional industries was mitigated by highly successful (if also highly expensive) job creation elsewhere; an impressive annual industrial growth rate of 5.7 per cent was recorded through the 1960s. But the location of this investment, disparities amongst the beneficiaries and the simultaneous loosening of sectarian frontiers created resentments and fed into social disorder. It is an ironic but not wholly unreasonable reflection that, having struggled for 40 years to devise effective business incentives and a beneficial economic relationship with London, Unionist ministers should have hit upon a formula which also brought their own immolation.

There is, of course, no simple or exclusive relationship between the Northern Ireland economy in the 1960s and the eruption of violence in 1968–9. Indeed, it is now clear that past analyses have posited too crude a connection between economic modernism and political change. In the most deterministic hypothesis, the relative liberalism of O'Neillite politics has been linked to the increasing predominance of international investment within Northern Ireland: liberalization and internation-alization have been seen as developing hand in hand. This view has been effectively challenged (by Bew, Gibbon and Patterson): it has been pointed out that the new capital seeping into northern industry was not a uniform quantity – that it was not all 'international', nor was it uniformly detrimental to local capital. Moreover, the lavish inducements offered by Stormont helped to smother any qualms that metropolitan investors might have harboured concerning the regime (not that there were many): as Bew, Gibbon and Patterson have quipped, 'with eggs like this, few recipients were interested in the colour of the goose'.[31]

On the other hand, it is easy to miss some fundamental truths lurking behind this persiflage. While it would be wrong to exaggerate the reports of the death of local (that is to say, generally Unionist) capital, and while it would be equally wrong to exaggerate the uniformity or the hegemony of international capital, it was also clearly the case that the overall significance of Unionist business was declining. This shift provoked a political crisis both for Unionism and indeed for Northern Ireland, just as the very swift retreat of the Unionist landed elite after the 1880s sent shock waves through Edwardian Unionism and brought a comprehensive reorganization of the movement in 1905. The shipyards and linen firms had been effectively Unionist preserves and – as has been mentioned – these were precisely the areas of the local economy that were in freefall. Earlier Unionist governments had attempted to shore up linen and shipbuilding as key political and economic supports of the regime: but these efforts, though determined, had little long-term impact in the context of overwhelming international pressures. From the 1930s on there had been a sneaking recognition that alternative employment opportunities would have to be created, and that the traditional configuration of Unionist politics and Unionist business would have to be reconstructed (just as in 1904–5). The industrial development programme associated with O'Neill and with Faulkner was simply a more thoroughgoing version of earlier initiatives: in addition, it was also the most complete recognition by a Unionist government that its economic sub-structure had collapsed. Viewed from this perspective, the inter-relationship between O'Neillite modernization and the overturning of the Unionist government becomes easier to understand.

But there were, of course, more direct explanations for the collapse of Stormont. If the economic growth of the 1960s heightened instability, then this was partly because growth coincided with other social and intellectual shifts within the northern com-munity (and indeed beyond). The slow but inexorable rise of the Catholic middle class since 1947 has been much discussed; and on the whole, while it would be wrong to overemphasize the degree or the speed of upward social mobility, it is clear that the consolidation of an articulate, educated nationalist elite helps (at least in part) to explain the impact of the civil rights movement. The O'Neillite economic pro-gramme served (inadvertently) to highlight broad issues of social justice; but just as its roots lay with earlier Unionist governments, so too the complicated political

fall-out associated with the project had in fact begun long before 1963. The provision of free and universal secondary education which came in 1947 brought
disproportionate benefits to the poorest sections of the northern community, and
in particular Catholics. The expansion of free university education in the 1960s
was equally important as a means of nurturing the abilities of those who had been
hitherto excluded, empowering the disadvantaged and liberating the ghettoized.
Again, it would be wrong to exaggerate the speed or the comprehensiveness of these
developments – but the general trends are clear. Protestant and Unionist predominance in the educational sphere, and therefore in the learned professions, would
hereafter be challenged; Protestant and Unionist predominance within northern
political debate, underpinned by comparative educational advantage, would soon
be eloquently and forcefully overturned. There are faint parallels here with the
consolidation of Catholic strength in the South before 1921: just as the social
resentments of the Catholic middle classes (articulated bitterly by the likes of
D.P. Moran) fed into revolutionary sentiment in the years before independence,
so similarly thwarted ambitions among northern Catholics fanned the flames of
protest and rebellion after 1968–9.

Perhaps the most remarkable of the many astonishing features of Northern Irish
politics in the 1960s was the comprehensive mobilization of Catholic political
opinion that had occurred by 1968–9 – a mobilization that was facilitated by some
of the developments already outlined, and which, in turn, created a political base
both for a new, socially alert nationalism (the SDLP, formed in 1970) and a more
socially committed republican movement. Both liberal reformist politics as well
as (more surprisingly, perhaps) traditional republicanism flourished in the 1960s:
indeed, as Bob Purdie has argued, the two success stories were interrelated.[32]
The republican movement had emerged from the ending of its Border Campaign
(Operation Harvest) in 1962 in a remarkably phlegmatic and positive mood: it set
about analysing and addressing the causes of failure, and in particular it was
concerned by the distance between the movement and the everyday grievances and
aspirations of ordinary nationalists. It is clear that republicans saw the issue of Catholic
civil rights as a means of forwarding their political objectives in the aftermath of
the failed Border Campaign; it is equally clear that for the moment violent strategies
were laid aside. The intellectual driving force behind these insights were the Wolfe
Tone societies, created in 1964 out of the movement to commemorate the bicenten-
ary of the revolutionary hero's birth (this anniversary had fallen in the previous year):
as one of their founders, Roy Johnston, remarked, they were 'a Fabian Society to
the Republican Movement'.[33] These bodies, born out of one commemoration,
received a tremendous fillip from another: the fiftieth anniversary of the Easter Rising,
which gave rise to numerous impressive parades and related events, underlined the
widespread popular reverence for the militant creators of the Irish revolution. In
the afterglow of the anniversary, on 13–14 August 1966, the Wolfe Tone societies
met in conference at Maghera, County Londonderry, and it was decided – on the
initiative of the Dublin society – to pursue a civil rights agitation with a view to
re-energizing the national struggle: the emphasis was on constitutionality, although,

Attitudes
Values

c... YOU H...

...lance included Cathal Goulding, the commander-in-chief of
...e result of this endeavour was a conference on civil rights,
...er 1966; and this in turn gave rise to the Northern Ireland
...NICRA), formally inaugurated on 9 April 1967.

...s were influential in moulding the civil rights agenda, this
...as some Unionist ministers (like Bill Craig) evidently
...s merely a sophisticated ruse, a libertarian camouflage for
...the contrary, the strategic insights and the relative success
...y possible because of widespread Catholic frustration as
...itiatives. Republicans helped to focus these resentments, as
...forts of Terence O'Neill; but their origins stretched back to
...ern state, and indeed before. Some aspects of the condition
...have already been explored: there was, however, a variety of
...aftermath of the Second World War that tended to inflame
...reate opportunities for their expression. Some mention has
...ng educational possibilities: but there were other issues. After
...id growth in the state, and thus in the civil service: but bureau-
...land, and in particular its upper echelons, remained determinedly
...after 1945 there were several minor but highly charged British
...but the Northern Ireland government would not follow the
...es pursued at Westminster. Until 1969 there was a restrictive local
...hise in Northern Ireland, characterized by the exclusion of those
...es and by the multiple votes enjoyed by certain businessmen:
...e Protestants were disfranchised by this antique arrangement
...hough the proportion of Catholics was greater; and Protestants
...than Catholics from the business vote. In addition local govern-
...es, many of which had been defined by the Leech Commission in
...d Unionists, sometimes outrageously so – as in the case of Omagh
...or Londonderry Corporation ('where a supplementary gerrymander
...nsouciance was accomplished in 1936').[34] With the public housing
...ost-war period, these local councillors came to possess an enhanced
...llocations, and in several Unionist local authorities west of the Bann
there was a marked effort to exclude Catholic families from the new provision: this
discrimination was partly rooted in a fervent desire to protect the sometimes
artificially crafted majorities which sustained the local Unionist administration.

It was the issue of housing that originally galvanized protestors. The first
significant flash-point was Dungannon, where, as in so much else of Northern Ireland,
the local government boundaries had been drafted in 1922 in the context of
nationalist abstention. The result was a solid Unionist majority in a town that was
in fact equally divided between the two communities: following the pattern of much
of the rest of western Ulster, these Unionist councillors looked after their own in
the allocation of public housing. In 1963, fired by the example of the civil rights
movement in the USA, a young Catholic woman, Patricia McCluskey, together
with her husband Conn, created a Homeless Citizens' League in the town; and this

successfully attracted public and ministerial attention to the injustices that were being committed. The League represented a particular constituency – young Catholic married couples – and the organization that it spawned, the Campaign for Social Justice in Northern Ireland (January 1964), retained an educated, middle-class Catholic appeal (these were the 'middle-class, middle-of-the-road do-gooders' who so irritated radicals like Bernadette Devlin).[35] The Campaign for Social Justice (or CSJ), while still very much concerned with the housing question, extended its brief to include a wide variety of issues relating to actual or perceived discrimination: it published a newsletter and five pamphlets, the last of which – *The Plain Truth* – was an expansive condemnation of Unionist misrule. In addition it had a powerful ally in Britain, in the shape of the Campaign for Democracy in Ulster (CDU), whose membership included many Labour MPs and which was deeply committed to the improvement of civil rights across Northern Ireland: the CDU was launched in June 1965 at the House of Commons, with 20 MPs in attendance and 60 MPs acting as sponsors.

The importance of the CSJ is hard to miss. The very respectability that so angered Devlin lent credibility to the Campaign's message: here were no revolutionaries concealing anarchy underneath the cloak of libertarianism. For this reason, the Campaign had an enthusiastic following in Britain, and in particular within the Labour Party. Moreover, like earlier successful agitators, the leaders of the CSJ mobilized popular resentments around a single central issue – housing. This had an immediate appeal, since it affected a fundamental aspect of daily life: but it was also an issue that fed into a deep tradition of concern for landed property, dating back to the Parnellite agitations of the nineteenth century. And just as the Land League had been able to capitalize upon well-publicized, aggressively conducted evictions, so the CSJ campaign benefited from the press attention given to the eviction of homeless squatters. But the Campaign also tapped the O'Connellite legacy: its Catholic orthodoxy (the very title of the CSJ movement echoed the social teaching of the Church), its exclusively Catholic leadership and abiding concern for Catholic civil rights all recalled the dimensions of O'Connellism. Like O'Connell, the CSJ was willing to subordinate the national question to workaday issues of equality. In all these ways, the CSJ was an essential precursor to the Northern Ireland Civil Rights Association: and, indeed, the Campaign was represented, along with the Wolfe Tone societies, the labour movement and the Ulster Liberals, in the committee which, on 9 April 1967, ushered NICRA into existence. The new Association thus embodied an amalgam of middle-class Catholic constitutionalists, republicans, socialists and liberal Protestants: it was a formidable combination, reminiscent in some ways of the Sinn Féin alliance forged in 1917. And, like Sinn Féin, for a brief period (in 1968–9) NICRA swept all before it.

The initial phase of NICRA's development – from April 1967 until the summer of 1968 – has been described as 'a period of general ineffectuality'.[36] The Association had defined its purpose in general libertarian terms rather than in relation to specific Catholic grievances; and on the whole this almost disengaged high-mindedness characterized the Association's early activity. The change came in the spring of 1968, when, influenced heavily by the strategies of Martin Luther King, NICRA reviewed its achievement and took the 'fateful' decision to launch a series of popular protest marches.[37] The first of these occurred in Dungannon on 24 August and received the support both of the CSJ and local republicans. Though there were minor skirmishes between some protestors and the police, on the whole the day was judged to have been a success. In fact the portents of disaster were already evident.

The issue of protest or traditional marches within the North has had a controversial history, dating back at least to the 1840s; and, while there have been local variants, on the whole the pattern has changed little. Marches have often involved an 'invasion' of opponents' territory and have therefore been seen as a provocation; demonstrations often provoked counter-demonstrations and forced the police either to ban both protests (this was the loyalist strategy in the early 1880s, and again in 1968), or to act as arbiters. Banned demonstrations might be used as an opportunity to defy or discredit the authorities, or to tempt the police or army into public acts of oppression. The problem for NICRA was that, while some older and cooler leaders (such as Betty Sinclair) had a clear perception of this relationship between marching and sectarian passion, many within the Association saw that gradualist or quietist strategies had achieved nothing. Furthermore, assessments of the Dungannon episode tended to be overshadowed by the publicity won, the generally festive nature of the occasion, and the consolidation of the links between NICRA and its satellite organizations. But, ominously, the marchers had not been allowed to proceed along their intended route, and there had been anger as a result and some attempts to rush the police lines. In addition, the march had been counterbalanced by a significant loyalist demonstration held on the same day. The potential for a clash with either the police or loyalists had in fact been averted, although the safety margin was painfully slim.

Dungannon opened the way for a succession of marches which achieved worldwide publicity for the issue of civil rights – but the cost of this high-profile advertising was high. The demonstration at Derry on 5 October has generally been seen as a turning point in the history of the Northern Ireland crisis: here, as at Dungannon, NICRA was keen to identify itself with local protest, in this case emanating from one of the key Catholic popular bodies in the city, the Derry Housing Action Committee (DHAC). Here, as at Dungannon, a loyalist counter-demonstration was arranged to coincide with the NICRA-DHAC march; and, as at Dungannon, the police intervened, this time to ban both parades. But the march went ahead, and brought the protestors into confrontation with the police: the result was mayhem, with television images of baton-wielding policemen apparently illustrating the broader oppressiveness of the regime, and hence underlining the credibility of the NICRA case. British sympathies were engaged: it looked as if Prague or Paris or the American South had come to the backdoor of the United Kingdom. In Tralee, County Kerry, Seán O'Callaghan, a future Provisional activist and Garda informer, watched a news broadcast and was 'totally shocked by the naked hatred and violence of some of the police'.[38] At home in Northern Ireland the movement won converts amongst those Catholics who had been unsure about confrontational protest strategies, and who had hitherto suspended judgement about the RUC: by the last months of 1968 NICRA was beginning to fulfil its potential as a vehicle for mass mobilization.

Further violent confrontation followed, at Armagh and at Dungannon. But the most controversial of these episodes came on New Year's Day 1969, when a radical and largely student-led affiliate of NICRA – the People's Democracy (PD) – started out on its 'Long March' from Belfast to Derry in order to highlight continuing civil rights grievances. This venture unilaterally brought to an end a period of truce, and it seems in fact to have been designed as a conscious effort both to subvert any accommodation with O'Neillite Unionism and to divert popular energies more directly against the state: 'what we really wanted to do', Bernadette Devlin – who was on the march – claimed, 'was to pull the carpet off the floor to show the dirt that was under it so that we could sweep it up'.[39] The route of the march took the PD activists through loyalist areas, and eventually to Burntollet bridge, near Derry, where it was ambushed by Protestant extremists, including off-duty members of the Ulster Special Constabulary: 'a traditional street-fight carried back into the countryside; a violent marker to the limits of modernisation'.[40] If the intention was indeed to undermine the northern state and its security apparatus, then this goal was broadly achieved. On the other hand, the cost of this victory involved popular Catholic outrage at the new evidence of the state's oppressiveness; and Protestant horror at what liberals saw as the PD's revolutionary extremism, and at what hardliners saw as 'enemy' incursions into traditional loyalist territory. By the spring of 1969 both the PD and, indeed, NICRA were venturing into a more radical stand, and were becoming progressively marginalized: one of the reasons for this, ironically, was that the focus of publicity was moving onto the splintering Unionist government and party. But their legacy, and that of the police aggression at Derry on 5 October and after, would be long felt in the sectarian polarization and inter-communal violence that was already beginning to spawn throughout the North.

The radicals of People's Democracy were not the only 'wild men' screaming through the key-hole of Terence O'Neill's study.[41] In some ways the most threatening of those outside the sanctuary of the Unionist high command were the militant Protestants. It was in fact a grim tribute to O'Neill's political cack-handedness that he should have presided over both a unification of the (very disparate) nationalist forces within Northern Ireland and the disintegration of his own Unionist alliance. Traditionally, Unionist Prime Ministers had been much more concerned about the threat of disruption within their own 'natural' – Protestant – constituency than about the political challenge posed by northern nationalism (even though there was anxiety and gerrymandering at the level of local government). O'Neill was, like his predecessors, very much alive to the possibility of Protestant defections, and indeed his economic initiatives have generally been seen in the light of the challenge from the partitionist Northern Ireland Labour Party: he saw this 'stealing of the NILP clothes' as a significant political success.[42] However, it had been the achievement of Craig and Brookeborough to suppress other forms of Protestant dissent, and notably from within the realms of religious fundamentalism or ultra-loyalism: there were occasional independents from these traditions (such as ex-District Inspector Nixon), but on the whole the vigorously populist nature of Craig's party (a style inherited and cultivated by his natural heir, Brookeborough) combined with some electoral dodges (such as the abandonment of proportional representation in 1929) kept the ultras at bay. Indeed, the party strategists would have had to look back as far as the early Edwardian period to find evidence of a widespread, populist Protestant challenge: this had been supplied by Tom Sloan, Lindsay Crawford and the Independent Orange Order, who (like some working-class Protestant militants in the 1990s) combined a certain constitutional flair with an uncompromising religious faith. The Edwardian Independents were, at least in part, a reaction to the challenge of reforming Conservative governments as well as an expression of distrust in conventional Unionism: they supplied some of the charisma, some of the boldness and some of the religious certainty which the main Unionist leaders seemed to lack. In response, the Unionist Party had shifted to the right, and away from the tentative endorsement that it had supplied to reforming Tory ministers such as George Wyndham; in addition, by 1910 it had found a supremely charismatic leader in the shape of Edward Carson. The Independents found it difficult to respond to these moves, and all the more so given the re-emergence of the Home Rule threat between 1910 and 1914. But something of their achievement was recaptured 50 years later in the career of the Reverend Ian Paisley.

Paisley represented a number of constituencies untouched by O'Neillite Unionism as well as (needless to say) the civil rights mobilization. He had strong family roots in Tyrone and Armagh, both counties with long histories of bloody sectarian rivalry, and both far removed from the metropolitan Unionism promoted by O'Neill. In addition, Paisley was deeply connected with the evangelical Protestant tradition: he followed his father into the Christian ministry and was blessed at his first Sunday Service by the Reverend W.P. Nicholson, the patriarch of anti-modernism amongst northern evangelicals. Although he was educated by the ultra-Calvinist Covenanters and was popular among some 'conventional' Presbyterians, Paisley ultimately founded his own church, the Free Presbyterians, in 1951. But his diatribes against ecumenicism, against romanizing influences within Protestantism and against the Scarlet Woman herself found favour within a wide evangelical constituency in the North, which stretched beyond the confines of his own communion. Here again was a community scarcely understood, let alone addressed, by the modernist rhetoric of O'Neill. When Paisley's evangelical certainties were combined with a populist political flair – the elders of Unionism were, famously, the 'fur-coat brigade' – the result was a resurrection of the Sloanite radicalism that had caused so much damage to the Unionist Party in the early and mid-Edwardian era.[43] Paisleyism was the answer of working-class urban Protestants, lower-middle-class farmers and all types of evangelical to O'Neill's patrician and secular vision. But Paisleyism not only supplied the needs of certain types of evangelical and socially disadvantaged Protestant: it also answered the need of those radical protestors within the PD and elsewhere who, at the end of 1968, feared that O'Neill and the Unionists would compromise their way into safety. Paisley's fundamentalist pressure on the Ulster Unionist Party, combined with the defiant tactics of the PD movement, ensured that there would be no accessible middle-ground.

Paisley sought legitimacy and dominance within both the evangelical and the Unionist traditions of the North: he saw himself as the heir not only of W.P. Nicholson but also, more questionably, of Carson and Craig. He guarded his people against religious heresy: he protested against the public acts of mourning for the death of Pope John XXIII in June 1963, and in June 1966 he and supporters abused Lord Erskine, the Governor of Northern Ireland, and the dignitaries of the 'trimming' Presbyterian Church on the steps of the General Assembly (this disturbance occasioned his first spell in gaol). Vigilant against any romanizing tendency, he also policed the Unionist state for evidence of concessions to Dublin: at the general election of 1964, he protested against the flying of the Irish tricolour by republicans in West Belfast, and in 1966 he was involved with the formation of an Ulster Constitution Defence Committee (a 12-strong committee known, inevitably, as 'the twelve disciples'), to which was linked a shady paramilitary body, the Ulster Protestant Volunteers.[44] In 1968 and 1969 he resurrected the old Orange tactic of the early 1880s by organizing loyalist demonstrations to coincide with Catholic protest: his counterpoint to the NICRA campaign helped to over-stretch the police and, together with civil rights militancy, accelerated the spiralling descent into general civil unrest. The most conspicuous of these counter-demonstrations was held on 30 November 1968 at Armagh, after which Paisley was again gaoled and his status as the martyr-king of ultra-loyalism was reaffirmed.

The dilemma faced by O'Neill in the months preceding his resignation in April 1969 was unique, although certain aspects were familiar enough. Previous Unionist Prime Ministers or leaders had faced populist Protestant dissent or angry Catholic protest; previous leaders had come under pressure from London and, less frighteningly, from Dublin. Colonel Saunderson (or rather his lieutenants) had seen off the challenge provided by T.H. Sloan and the Independent Orangemen of the Edwardian era. Craig and his cabinet had dealt with IRA violence in 1920–2 and had suppressed various forms of internal Unionist dissent (from temperance advocates, ultra-loyalists and others); Brookeborough had pursued similar opponents and, until the growth of the NILP vote between 1958 and 1962, had achieved similar success. Occasional British threats (such as in 1940) were also ridden out by Unionist governments. What was unique about O'Neill's situation was both the extent of Catholic mobilization that had occurred in 1968–9 and the conjunction of problems that he faced: civil rights anger, Protestant protest, threatened intervention from London and the renewed hostility of Dublin. There are very inexact parallels with the early 1930s, and in particular the poor law riots of 1932, when the Catholic and Protestant poor united in virtual rebellion: but the hungry and malnourished make poor revolutionaries, and had few allies. O'Neill's political plight also recalls that of George Wyndham between 1903 and 1905. Wyndham, like O'Neill, had found himself momentarily hailed as a bridge-builder (with the success of his Land Act of 1903), but, like O'Neill, he also found that the life-span of centrists in

Irish politics could be alarmingly short. Like O'Neill, Wyndham was perceived by hardline Ulster Unionists as well as party colleagues to have taken his constructive policies to indefensible limits; and, like O'Neill, Wyndham soon found himself facing a coalition of those who had earlier professed their admiration. Extreme Ulster Unionists saw in both men evidence of treachery; militant nationalists saw both as guileful agents of an alien and sectarian government.

The collapse of the O'Neill government and the melt-down within Unionist politics were disconcertingly swift. Initially, the auspices were good: on 22 November 1968 the Prime Minister offered protestors a five-point reform programme covering the fair allocation of public housing, the appointment of an ombudsman, the reform of local government, the abolition of Londonderry Corporation and the modification of the Special Powers Act (1922). Many Unionists were sceptical, and the Paisleyites were fired by what was seen as a concession to militant pressure: the civil rights campaigners and nationalists were cautious, some being prepared to accept O'Neill's goodwill while others – as events demonstrated – saw only a mixture of weakness and begrudgery. But O'Neill's famous broadcast call for a breathing space (his 'Ulster at the Crossroads' speech of 9 December) won widespread support outside the ranks of the Paisleyites and the increasingly influential militant wing of the civil rights movement.[45] The 'Long March' of 1 January 1969 came about partly because the PD leaders scented blood (though it was their own that was shed at Burntollet); and the divided Unionist showing at the crucial general election of 24 February 1969 on the whole confirmed this analysis. O'Neill had hoped to translate the apparent success of his call for moderation into votes, and he evidently believed that he could recapture the Unionist Party for reform. But, while his supporters polled well, the principal feature of the contest was the fissure opening up not merely within the broad Unionist movement (Paisley's Protestant Unionists performed creditably), but within the Ulster Unionist Party itself: O'Neill's supporters won 27 seats, but his opponents within the party won ten and there were in addition two Unionists whose attitude was ambiguous. There was thus no indisputable mandate. Indeed, in so far as the election revealed the developing collapse of Unionism, there appeared to be an expanding vacuum within northern politics; and this served to stimulate further street protest. O'Neill's inevitable resignation (on 28 April 1969) did little to correct this impression; nor did the choice of his successor, Major James Chichester-Clark, who, gentrified and well meaning, was arguably not up to the job.

Perhaps this says more about the job than about Chichester-Clark (though his general air of amiable vacuity or deep puzzlement did not inspire confidence). He inherited a difficult public order situation, which worsened during the marching season (July–August) in 1969: the devastating riots that followed the annual Apprentice Boys' demonstration in Derry on 12 August spread to Belfast (where some 1500 Catholic and 300 Protestant families fled their homes), and forced the new Prime Minister to request the support of the British army. This was a humiliation, and it underlined the failure of the Stormont administration to deal with either the political or the policing challenges of the popular uprising that was occurring: the decision added a military dimension to the complete financial dependence of the regime on London, and thus paved the way for direct rule. The political vulnerability of the Northern Ireland government was further underlined by the determined way in which Harold Wilson overrode Unionist objections and forced reform onto the police services (the RUC was disarmed and reorganized and the USC was disbanded). This was not just a case of urging unpopular but necessary policies on foot-dragging reactionaries; it was also a matter of insensitive presentation: Wilson unilaterally pronounced the fate of the USC in a television interview, impelling Chichester-Clark into denials which he was shortly obliged to retract. This genial humiliation of the Stormont 'Tories' did nothing to mitigate nationalist unrest, and served in fact to drive loyalist voters into the ranks of Paisleyism.

Indeed, Chichester-Clark presided over not merely a minor civil war on the streets of Belfast and Derry, but also the collapse and redefinition of the traditional party divisions within Northern Ireland. In parallel with the rapidly escalating civil unrest, there were comprehensive changes in northern party organization: but these did not so much mitigate the traditional divisions as reinvent them, formalizing political shifts that had occurred within Unionism and nationalism over the preceding years. In fact arguably, the break-up of traditional Unionism, with some supporters drifting into the Alliance or Democratic Unionist Parties, or the paramilitaries, reflected tensions within the movement that had been implicit (if suppressed) since the 1880s. O'Neillite Unionists and other moderates combined to create the Alliance Party in April 1970 (a relatively early convert was O'Neill's flamboyant cousin and an ex-minister, Phelim O'Neill). The developing success of Ian Paisley's Protestant Unionists at the expense of the old Unionist Party continued throughout 1970 (there were two Stormont by-election successes and – a bigger coup – victory for Paisley himself in the North Antrim Westminster constituency): this trend was cemented by the formation of the Democratic Unionist Party in September 1971, six months after Chichester-Clark's resignation. Many younger nationalists and moderate civil rights protestors found a home in the Social Democratic and Labour Party (founded in August 1970). In addition the hard men and women of the loyalist and republican housing estates were reorganizing along more militant lines: the Provisionals emerged in December 1969 as a reaction against socialist 'trimming' within the traditional IRA and by 1971 had acquired an offensive capability; while different forms of loyalist vigilantism coalesced in the Ulster Defence Association, formed in September 1971.

The immediate cause of Chichester-Clark's departure, in March 1971, was a spate of killing, which culminated in the deaths of three young Royal Highland Fusiliers, lured from a pub at Ligoniel, in Belfast. Just as earlier Unionist ministers had journeyed to London in search of cash subventions, so now Chichester-Clark petitioned for a substantial security initiative: this was not forthcoming, and the Prime Minister (who had been threatening to depart since January) resigned. His successor was Brian Faulkner, one of the most intellectually acute and ambitious Unionists to have emerged in the Stormont years: he was in a different class of ability (and indeed volubility) to most of his parliamentary colleagues, and this in fact was his problem. He had been passed over for the leadership when his abilities might have been usefully deployed for the broader community, both in 1963 and again in 1971: the intellectually inert Unionist parliamentary party preferred gentlemen, and Faulkner was never quite one of these. This aside, there are obvious parallels between Faulkner and David Trimble in the 1990s: both men were associated with a hardline Unionism, and both had some credibility with the ultras in their movement. Both, however, were highly subtle tacticians, who sought to move Unionism on from its deeply rooted zero-sum gamesmanship: both were frequently seen as over-clever by their own backwoodsmen, who were determined to die in the last ditch, and all too frequently did so.

Faulkner's approach to the challenge of government was essentially Balfourian: he combined a coercive security policy with a number of more emollient initiatives. He combined his premiership with Home Affairs so as to retain personal control over law and order; and he recruited a former NILP leader, David Bleakley, as his Minister for Community Relations. In October 1971 he appointed G.B. Newe as a Minister of State for Minority Affairs – the first Catholic to hold office within a Northern Ireland government since the formation of the state (and, indeed, the last under the Stormont dispensation). Besides these (albeit striking) gestures, Faulkner also offered the minority a role within the committee structure of the parliament, promising two out of the four available committee chairs to its representatives. But the security situation overwhelmed these efforts: two men were shot dead in Derry by the army on 9 July 1971 and the SDLP demanded an enquiry as the price for its continued cooperation. However, this formed no part of Faulkner's Balfourian vision (indeed, he had resigned from the O'Neill cabinet in January 1969 over the timing of the Cameron Commission, designed to investigate the origins of the civil unrest): no enquiry was forthcoming. As violence intensified, an even more controversial episode ensued: the introduction of internment without trial on 9 August. This was applied exclusively to nationalist areas and was accompanied by heavy-handed interrogation techniques: the result was massive alienation among the minority, and mounting enthusiasm for the PIRA. Internment also underpinned the SDLP's boycott of Stormont, and therefore destroyed Faulkner's very tentative move towards power-sharing.

One of Faulkner's main sources of strength at this time was the support supplied by the Heath government, but this was decidedly negotiable, and indeed was clearly flagging as it emerged that internment was not a quick-fix solution to the security crisis. The shooting, by soldiers of the Parachute Regiment, of 13 people in Derry on 'Bloody Sunday', 30 January 1972, served to underline the apparent collapse of Faulkner's security strategies and the need for the London government to assume control. A transfer of responsibility was proposed, along with other initiatives, on 22 March. Since acquiescence implied an admission of failure, this was, in effect, an invitation to resign: and on 24 March, left with little alternative, Faulkner and his ministers meekly did so. There would be no replacement. After the end of March the parliament and government of Northern Ireland were prorogued, and their powers transferred to Westminster and to a secretary of state.

This was, of course, a thoroughly Unionist gesture, bringing Northern Ireland into line with the arrangements for Scotland and Wales. But for the crowd of 100,000 or so loyalists who assembled at Stormont on 28 March, there was no ambiguity in the defeat that had been sustained.

Why did Stormont fail? The question might well appear redundant, given the preceding narrative. In terms of proximate causes, Stormont failed because it was no longer compatible with the exigencies of British policy, and because it showed no signs of being able to cope with street violence and organized terror. In the longer term, it had been unable to represent any other than Unionist opinion, and had been at best grudging towards Catholic aspirations. But there is a danger in approaching the debacle of 22–4 March 1972 in too deterministic a fashion. Though there had certainly been contingency planning, the prorogation of Stormont was not the culmination of any deeply laid British policy: indeed, it has been frequently pointed out that the evidence for a coherent policy is hard to find. Nor, while the subsequent government of Northern Ireland unquestionably benefited by its demise, was the cryonic suspension of Stormont necessarily the best or the most obvious strategy for the British to pursue in the spring of 1972.

In fact the fate of Stormont really only assumes a deafening historical resonance if one accepts the rhetoric of O'Neillite Unionism at face value. Just as legislative independence in 1782 rendered the Union of 1801 all the more emphatic, so the increasingly devolutionist nature of Ulster Unionism meant that the suspension of Stormont seemed all the more dramatic. This is a commentary not just on the ideological development of Unionism, but also on its tactical successes. In reality Stormont was an extended form of local government, with tightly circumscribed powers and much pomp and circumstance: its elaborate structures concealed its real lack of power in such areas as taxation or foreign relations or the army. In reality the governing power within Stormont, Unionism, was not the monolithic popular movement of its own delusions and nationalist fears, but rather a highly fissile alliance which repeatedly showed signs of fragmenting. The truth was that the Ulster Unionist leadership showed very considerable tactical skill in sustaining the complicated alliance that held them in power; but in winning the battles for Protestant unity, they lost the war for their constitution. Their success lay in the fact that they clutched onto power for so long, and preserved the fiction that Stormont mattered; their failure lay not only in Catholic alienation, but also in the fact that, given the limited nature of their parliament, there was so very little at stake.

THE TWO IRELANDS, 1973–98

8.1 The Republic, 1973–98

Much of Irish public life from the early 1970s through to the mid-1990s, and indeed beyond, was profoundly influenced by three broad conditions: the oil crises of 1973 and 1979, membership of the European Economic Community (achieved in 1973), and the simmering, occasionally boiling, turmoil within Northern Ireland. It would be wrong to be over-deterministic in pursuing this case; and it would be wrong to neglect internal Irish explanations for changes in Irish public and private life. But the shock-waves from several international developments can clearly be discerned throughout the Ireland of the late twentieth century.

It has been argued with conviction that the oil crises of the 1970s – the quadrupling of the price of oil in 1973, and the further price hikes of 1979 – did not so much create devastation in the Irish economy as exacerbate an already grim situation. There were certainly already inflationary pressures within the Irish economy before the first oil crisis had an impact: the economic growth of the 1960s had stimulated an appetite for hefty wage claims, which continued despite the slow-down of the later part of the decade and the early 1970s. Moreover, the economic growth of the Lemass years had not created full employment in Ireland, for the creation of jobs in new areas was offset by the decline of traditional industries: the level of unemployment in the early 1970s was around 8 per cent. Even before the oil crisis, the Fianna Fáil Minister of Finance, George Colley, had decided to break a fundamental convention of Irish public finance in drawing up his plans for 1972 – by failing to balance the current budget of the state and permitting a projected current account deficit of around 1.3 per cent of GNP. The oil crisis smashed through the already shaky edifice of the Irish economy like a demolition ball. The projected deficits in 1972 and 1973 (1.3 per cent and 1.5 per cent, respectively) were in fact well above the real figures (0.2 per cent and 0.4 per cent); but what little comfort might have been gleaned from this was overturned in 1974 and 1975. By 1974 the current deficit had reached £92 million, or 3.1 per cent of GNP; and in 1975, the nadir of Irish public finance, this deficit had swollen to just under £259 million, or close to 7 per cent of GNP. Some modest degree of stabilization occurred after 1975–6, together with efforts to bring the current account deficit under control; but this only served to encourage some (with the benefit of hindsight) ludicrously optimistic projections of growth and, with these, another relapse into deficit finance. The general idea, as defined by the Fianna Fáil Minister for Economic Development, Martin O'Donoghue, and by the Minister of Finance, Colley, was to prime the pump of the economy through public spending. But the pump was primed indiscriminately: local business did not respond to the challenge, and unemployment levels remained high. There was certainly a consumer boom; but it was foreign industry and the import sector which were the beneficiaries. Those who were employed contrived in effect to sustain the numbers of jobless, by seeking enormous wage hikes (peaking at some 20.5 per cent in 1980) and then spending their ill-gotten gains on foreign imports. But once again, as in 1973, it was oil which converted a dangerous situation within the public finances into cataclysm: the oil crisis of 1979 added a crucial external dimension to the home-grown inflationary pressures. By 1979 the Irish balance of payments deficit was 10.1 per cent of GNP; and, though there was a slight recovery in 1980, this figure slipped to 12.5 per cent in 1981. By December 1992 the accumulated debt of the state had reached £12 billion.

It is hard to envisage what the state of the Irish economy might have been without the crises of 1973 and 1979. It is clear that there were some home-grown problems, especially in the area of wage inflation. It also seems clear that the management of the public finances was tinctured with a degree of, at worst, political opportunism, or, at best, unfettered risk-taking. In 1972, with a general election pending, George Colley took the decision to plunge into a current deficit: as Joe Lee has remarked, 'a bastardised Keynesianism provided a convenient facade to give respectability to the most opportunistic impulses'.[1] The general election of 1977, where – as Gemma Hussey has argued – the politics of the auction house reigned supreme, provided a further outlet for this 'bastardised Keynesianism'.[2] But it also has to be recognized that the gambling addicts in Irish government (especially among Lynch's lieutenants within Fianna Fáil) lost out as badly as they did because of the international context. In any event it was probably a misjudgement for Colley to play with deficit financing in 1972, or for him and O'Donoghue to revive the wager in 1978: but while they can be blamed for recklessness, their analysis had admittedly some contemporary logic. It was their misfortune, or rather the nation's misfortune, that they did not factor into their calculations the impact of two profound international crises.

It is scarcely an exaggeration to suggest that the economic crisis of the 1970s helped to shape some of the fundamental features of Irish politics not just at the time, but for much of the next 20 years. The disastrous handling of the country's economy by successive ministers of finance (Richie Ryan and George Colley seem to be the most culpable of the 'guilty men') involved the accumulation of massive debts, and thus a permanently enfeebled budgetary condition. Careful management by the different FitzGerald and Haughey governments in the 1980s went some way to clawing back budgetary strength (FitzGerald boasted that when he left office in 1987 the ratio of debt to GNP was half that in 1981); but the country was still highly susceptible to an international downturn, such as occurred with the stock market tumbles of the late 1980s, or the currency crisis of 1992.[3] The ministers of the 1970s mortgaged the future of the country at first for narrowly partisan reasons, but ultimately in order to avert national bankruptcy. It was their successors in the 1980s, and indeed after, who paid the price for this mixture of mis-judgement and reck-lessness and misplaced party loyalty. The cost involved the modification of certain fundamental attitudes and institutions within Irish political life.

There is – at the very least – a coincidence between the economic crises of the Irish state in the 1970s and 1980s and a degree of political destabilization. The electoral history of Ireland until 1972 was the history of Fianna Fáil's political hegemony: of the 50 years since independence, Fianna Fáil had been in office, untram-melled by coalition partners, for 34 years. The economic turmoil of the post-war period, especially in the 1950s, helped to encourage support for alternatives to Fianna Fáil and the construction of relatively weak coalition governments in 1948 and again in 1954. Yet in the 25 years between 1948 and 1973 there were only six changes of government; while in the 25 years between 1973 and 1998 there were 12 such changes (including major reconstructions that have involved a new Taoiseach or the accep-tance of coalition partners by the governing party). In 1989, for the first time in its history, Fianna Fáil went into coalition and, all the more remarkably given the traditionally stern attitude of the party towards rebels or traitors, accepted the six Progressive Democrat deputies as partners in government (the PDs had been formed in 1985 essentially as a neo-liberal breakaway from Fianna Fáil). Between 1989 and 2008, except for very brief transitional periods, Fianna Fáil was not able to govern without the support of other parties, whether Labour or the Progressive Democrats or (after 2007) the Greens.

Clearly the economic condition of the country is not in itself sufficient to explain all this ministerial turmoil since 1973. But the crises of the 1970s, and the legacy of debt and fiscal instability which they bequeathed, have certainly been a consid-erable influence on the fate of successive Irish governments. The Fine Gael–Labour government of Liam Cosgrave (1973–7) was defeated at the general election of 1977 partly because voters were unimpressed by its belated fiscal rectitude, and partly because they were sweet-talked by the lavish promises of public spending offered by Jack Lynch and Fianna Fáil. However, the apparent inability of Fianna Fáil to cope with the mounting deficits of the early 1980s brought swift disillusionment, as did the turnaround within the party from the up-beat promises of the 1977 elec-tion campaign to the portentous broadcast in January 1980 by Charles Haughey, as Taoiseach, on the dire economic state of the nation. Garret FitzGerald's first govern-ment – the minority Fine Gael–Labour administration (June 1981–February 1982) – fell because it could not get its cost-cutting budget past the Dáil; and indeed voters in the general election of February 1982 were also unimpressed by the outgoing government's money-raising initiatives, and in particular its proposal to extend VAT to children's clothing and footwear. Equally, FitzGerald's second administration (a reformulated Fine Gael–Labour coalition) started to come apart at the end of 1986 as a result of swingeing cuts in public spending which the Labour ministers were not prepared to stomach. Nor was the public persuaded by what even FitzGerald conceded was 'an uncompromising budget'; and Charles Haughey and Fianna Fáil were returned to power at the general election of 1987.[4]

There were, of course, other factors which helped to decide the fate of Irish governments in these years. Scandal dogged the career of the charismatic Charlie Haughey, and several of his administrations were associated with what he himself described famously as 'bizarre happenings', 'unprecedented situations' and events that were 'grotesque and unbelievable': from these euphemisms the former Labour minister Conor Cruise O'Brien coined the acronym 'GUBU', which he applied in ironic and pejorative fashion to what he saw as the misdeeds of the Fianna Fáil government of February to November 1982.[5] The 'unprecedented situations' of 1982 included both the discovery of a murder suspect in the flat of the attorney general and the Dowra affair (when a garda, related by marriage to the Minister for Justice, was charged with assault but walked free because the RUC had helpfully detained a key prosecution witness). Underlying these public eruptions were rumours of official phone-taps on two journalists (Bruce Arnold and Geraldine Kennedy) who were thought to have had contacts with some of Haughey's ministerial opponents. Taken in connection with the Dowra episode, these rumours seemed to suggest that ministers were interfering dangerously with the Garda and using state security mechanisms for personal or partisan advantage: they served of course to further discredit the administration (even though the full history of the phone-tapping was not fully aired until the results of an enquiry were published in January 1984). Haughey's later career remained controversial. In the autumn of 1991 a number of stories emerged which (as Gemma Hussey has tactfully commented) 'cast possible doubts on the probity of government appointees to State boards, or indicated failure of control and accountability by those entrusted with running State companies'.[6] These coincided with the opening months of a judicial investigation into possible political favouritism and malpractice in the beef industry, and created a widespread impression of corruption within the political and economic elite of the country. One of the immediate casualties of this public concern was Haughey, who – having served as Taoiseach since 1987 and having survived numerous challenges from within his party – was at last ousted in February 1992.

Economic pressures, together with other international influences, had an ideological impact within Irish politics. Coping with debt meant tax increases and reduced public spending. The middle classes suffered, especially those who were taxed at source: so did those poor whose quality of life depended upon welfare provision and other forms of state expenditure. Unemployment levels remained very high throughout the 1980s and early 1990s, with some 300,000 (or 21 per cent of the workforce) still jobless in 1993. These different features of the Irish economy, combined with other pressures, were associated with an apparent growth in class politics in the 1980s. As has been mentioned, the Progressive Democrats were formed in December 1985 as a party which advocated the neo-liberal economic strategies favoured by right-wing administrations in the United Kingdom and the United States. To some extent their function and support were undermined by the increasingly stern fiscal rectitude of the two main parties, and particularly of Fianna Fáil: but the Progressive Democrats (though highly vulnerable and sometimes disoriented) remained an influential force in Irish politics throughout the 1990s. The party won 11.9 per cent of the vote and 14 seats in 1987, and joined the government in July 1989 in order to keep Fianna Fáil on the paths of fiscal righteousness. In 1992, as a result of some effective gamesmanship as well as the quirks of the electoral system, the party captured ten seats on only 4.7 per cent of the vote.

If the PDs seemed to represent the growth of a radical conservative challenge, then there was also some consolidation of support in the late 1980s for the parties of the left. The Workers' Party (WP) gained seven seats in 1989, though – partly as a result of a split within WP ranks in February 1992 – the showing of its main successor, the Democratic Left, in the general election of 1992 was poor (only four seats). On the other hand, the main party of the left, Labour, strengthened its representation from 16 seats in 1989 to a remarkable 33 seats in 1992, a result that reflected widespread social and economic concerns, but also unquestionably the personal popularity of the new Labour-backed President of Ireland, Mary Robinson, as well as of the party leader, Dick Spring.

The economic crisis of the late 1980s was rooted in the legacy of debt from earlier years, as well as in the collapse of the international stock markets that occurred in 1987 and after. These pressures brought not only the creation of a radical conservative party in the form of the Progressive Democrats, but also some realignments within the mainstream Fianna Fáil and Fine Gael traditions. In the late 1980s Fianna Fáil abandoned some of the political opportunism that had characterized its handling of the economy in the 1970s, and came increasingly to accept the neoliberal disciplines that were being practised in other troubled economies. Equally, Fine Gael had moved from its social democratic emphases in the 1960s to occupy a broadly similar position to Fianna Fáil regarding the management of the Irish economy. This was crisply illustrated when FitzGerald, conceding defeat in the 1987 general election, promised his support for the incoming minority Fianna Fáil government – provided that it applied the rigorous budgetary constraints that he deemed necessary. This approach was confirmed when Alan Dukes, who succeeded FitzGerald as Fine Gael leader in March 1987, enunciated the Tallaght strategy – a strategy of supporting Fianna Fáil in its pursuit of spending cuts and economic growth. The Tallaght doctrine remained in place until 1990, when in the light of gradual economic recovery as well as the flagging popularity of the party, Fine Gael dumped both Dukes and his experiment in constructive opposition. But FitzGerald for one saw a victory of sorts for his party in the fact that Fianna Fáil had accepted the stringent cost-cutting strategies advocated by Fine Gael in 1987, and had deployed them in the budgets of 1988 and 1989.

Yet the fact that there was so much shared ground in Irish politics in the 1980s was obscured by the apparently very different personalities and styles of the two main party leaders of the period: Haughey and FitzGerald. Each man dominated his party for well over a decade. FitzGerald inherited the leadership of Fine Gael from the gruff old Free Stater, Liam Cosgrave, after his party's election defeat in 1977: he was Taoiseach in the minority Fine Gael–Labour administration of June 1981 to February 1982, and in the coalition that survived from December 1982 to February 1987. Haughey's pre-eminence covered a similar, if slightly longer, period. In December 1979 he fought off a strong challenge from George Colley to succeed Jack Lynch both as Fianna Fáil party leader and Taoiseach. He led a reconstructed Fianna Fáil government until June 1981, and again between February and November 1982. He clung onto power within a minority Fianna Fáil administration between February 1987 and 1989, when he was compelled to accept the PDs as partners: he survived at the head of this coalition until January 1992.

The two leaders presented an apparently sharp contrast. Haughey has been described (by Joe Lee) as a kind of renaissance potentate: Dermot Keogh has lauded him as 'a political fixer and good ward politician'.[7] Both assessments emphasize Haughey as boss: both stress the theme of clientilism. Haughey looked and sounded like a leader: his appearance hinted at a reptilian menace, and he was curt or laconic. In public he was often highly cautious; in private he could be genially abusive or, sometimes, ungenially abusive. He had great charm; but equally his anger sent a frisson of terror among those ministers or civil servants who were deemed to have erred. He conducted cabinets as a chief rather than as a chairman; and business was transacted briskly and without philosophical exegesis. He had a feel for populist politics, and a feel, too, for eye-catching policy initiatives. His roots were in the republican wing of his party, and with the arms trial affair of 1970 he seemed to have made a personal sacrifice for the holy cause. But, like Parnell, Haughey had the great gift of seeming like a visionary without ever presenting any coherent vision to his people. Like Parnell, Haughey was a technician of power; like Parnell, he was something of a tragic hero – an immensely gifted man, finally brought down by fatal weaknesses.

FitzGerald, by contrast, was (at least for the spin-doctors) Garret the Good: with his shock of untidy, wavy hair and his generally smiling countenance, he seemed unthreatening and approachable. His earlier career as an academic economist, combined with his evident mental dexterity, meant that he was often (and sympathetically) viewed as a kindly, if slightly batty, professor. His cabinet meetings were lengthy and discursive: FitzGerald was interested in ideas, and he tended to reward those whom he regarded as bright (his memoirs often record judgements on the intellectual equipment of colleagues). It is difficult to envisage the Fianna Fáil leadership (which contained some unquestionably gifted figures – not least Haughey himself) making as many concessions to brain power in the matter of patronage as did FitzGerald. He was talkative (the sobriquet 'Garrulous FitzGerald' gained currency), and he probably made more gaffes than Haughey.[8] He was as rooted in the Treatyite tradition as was Haughey in republicanism: but FitzGerald's visionary zeal came from his social democratic principles, which he had advocated since the 1960s, rather than from the skirmishes of the civil war or the conflict with the British or Ulster Unionists. On the whole (and paradoxically), Haughey may well be judged as a more pragmatic politician than FitzGerald: both men shared a desire to rectify the economy and to seek an accommodation with the British over Northern Ireland, but it was FitzGerald who pursued these objects with an unblinking ferocity. It is hard to escape the impression that Haughey's principal object was the pursuit of power.

And yet, setting aside these differences of style and emphasis, the degree of alignment between these two leaders and their respective parties that had been achieved by the late 1980s (if not before) perhaps hints at some more fundamental congruities within Irish political culture. Both men benefited from the strong family links that they had with the revolutionary elite of 1916–21: Haughey's father, Seán, was second-in-command of the Northern Division of the IRA, and his father-in-law was Seán Lemass; FitzGerald's father, Desmond, was 'out' in 1916 and was later Minister of Foreign Affairs in the executive council of the Irish Free State. Each man had a family connection with Northern Ireland: Haughey's roots were in the republican village of Swatragh, County Londonderry, while FitzGerald's mother was a Presbyterian nationalist from Belfast. Both Haughey and FitzGerald attended University College Dublin, the intellectual forcing house of the Irish political elite. Each, though populist, was strongly anti-communist. Both came to prominence within their respective parties very much as technocrats and modernizers. Each had an appropriate degree of political ruthlessness: in 1981, on becoming Taoiseach, FitzGerald cut a scythe through the Fine Gael elders, passing over many of Cosgrave's former ministers in selecting his own team for government. Both were wilful rulers: Conor Cruise O'Brien has observed that FitzGerald 'lived in the sunny confidence that he was invariably acting for the common good, which . . . often coincided with his own good'.[9] Though each man had connections in the North, and though FitzGerald has emphasized his ties with northern Unionism, in truth many of these connections seem to have had little fundamental (as opposed to symbolic) value: both men were basically as detached from the visceral realities of northern politics as most of the political elite in Dublin. Both cared about the North, sometimes passionately; but, for example, FitzGerald's apparently good lines of communication with Ulster Unionism seem to have given him little insight into that movement's likely actions and reactions. The cerebral and generous social democrat seems to have been liked by northern Unionists – for whom he must have seemed generous but also untouchably exotic. It was unfortunate that Haughey was evidently too tainted by the arms trial to be trusted by Unionism: for Fianna Fáilers – populist, localist, clientilist, partisan – were in some respects on a closer wavelength to Ulster Unionists than the Fine Gael leadership. On the other hand, if even a tentative détente was out of the question in the Haughey era, some of the very real potential for meaningful communication between Fianna Fáil and Ulster Unionism was realized in the late 1990s under Bertie Ahern and David Trimble.

A further key determinant of the shape of Irish politics and society in the last quarter of the twentieth century was the recruitment of Ireland to the EEC in 1973. Once again, just as the oil crises of the 1970s and the fragile condition of the Irish economy in the 1970s and 1980s had broad implications for the government of the country, as well as day-to-day life, so, too, much sprang from Ireland's involvement in Europe. And again, just as it would be an overly blunt argument which ascribed political and social change simply and solely to economic development, so, too, it would be wrong to exaggerate the consequences of membership of the EEC, or European Union. On the other hand, Ireland's close relationship with its European partners has been seen both as a consequence and a cause of some fundamental political and social shifts in the domestic scene.

Ireland's interest in membership of the EEC was rooted in the crisis of confidence that afflicted the country in the post-war era, and especially in the troubled 1950s: it was rooted in the ideological shifts which culminated in the work of Whitaker and Lemass, and which involved a movement away from the old culturally xeno-phobic and economically protectionist verities of the Sinn Féin tradition. Some euphoric celebrants of Ireland's European identity have sought a more ancient lineage, looking back to the long history of Irish patriotic, military, commercial or ecclesiastical involvement in continental Europe and seeing membership of the Community as a seamless extension of these traditions. In more immediate and prosaic terms, membership was logical and attractive because it promised the Ireland of the early 1960s, and especially Irish agriculture, immediate cash benefits (the Common Agricultural Policy was formulated in 1963): membership also chimed with the wider economic as well as political vision of Lemass (his scaling down of tariffs and his 'technocratic' approach to partition). But Ireland's initial applica-tion (in 1963) was turned down, as was that of the British: both were stymied by French suspicions that, in recruiting these two nations, the Community would have been ushering an American Trojan horse into the fortress of European civilization. General de Gaulle's retirement from the French Presidency in 1969 removed one of the key opponents of Irish and British membership: negotiations were duly revived, and culminated in a referendum, held on 10 May 1972, which overwhelmingly approved Ireland's admission (83 per cent voted 'yes' in a 71 per cent turnout of the electorate). Irish membership was formalized on 1 January 1973. It was unfor-tunate that Lemass, who was the architect of the original Irish application, and for whom membership had been a fundamental goal, had died scarcely 18 months before the realization of his dream.

At one level, the impact of the European Union on Ireland is not hard to calcu-late. Subventions from Brussels to Ireland through the medium of the Regional and other funds totalled £14 billion in the period from 1973 to 1991. Access to the Common Agricultural Policy, with its subsidy mechanisms, brought enormous benefits to Irish farmers, whose income doubled in the first five years of Irish membership: £10.3 billion of the £14 billion given to Ireland by Europe before 1991 went to the agricultural sector. Nor should it be forgotten that, although there was a great growth and diversification of the economy in the later 1990s, at the beginning of the decade Ireland still depended 'to an almost unnerving extent' upon agriculture, with just under a quarter of total export value coming from this sector.[10] It is unquestion-ably the case that these direct subventions mitigated the impact of the economic crises of the 1970s and 1980s and helped to sustain Irish living standards: it might even be ventured (at the risk of exaggeration) that this investment helped to bolster the state itself at a time when it was being buffeted by numerous destabilizing currents.

Membership of the EEC also underpinned the attractiveness of Ireland to American investors. As a relatively low-wage economy (at least until the mid-1990s), Ireland served as a useful location for American firms seeking entry to other European markets. It should be emphasized, however, that this has not been a sustained or, indeed, an unmixed blessing. The accession of other relatively poor countries to the Community – Greece, Portugal and Spain – undermined the attractiveness of Ireland. Moreover, many of the new industries that found an Irish home in the 1970s and 1980s 'were typically satellites carrying out a few of the stages in a more complicated manufacturing process'.[11] Profits were in most cases repatriated. New jobs were created, but, as has been noted, unemployment remained high because of the withering of traditional areas of manufacturing employment. Equally, however, it would be a mistake to ignore the significance of these investment trends. It can only be assumed that, whatever the liabilities, Ireland was better with these companies than without them: they may not have represented a long-term source of strength to the country, but they did provide much-needed employment. Moreover, this influx of foreign, especially American, capital in the 1970s and 1980s also had a profound impact on the overall pattern of Ireland's trading relationships: the historic commercial intimacy between Ireland and Britain was gradually being replaced by a more diverse web of economic partners.

Membership of the EEC and of the European Union has also had a direct impact on civil rights, and in particular the issue of women's rights. Again, it would be wrong to imagine that there was no movement on these issues before 1973 and that the process of change flowed simply and wholly from Brussels. Many of the legislative barriers on women's rights which had been enacted in the 1920s (the prohibition of divorce, the ban on contraception) remained in place in the 1960s: as late as 1965 a wife might be totally disinherited by her husband. There was, however, some movement in the early 1970s with the establishment of the Commission on the Status of Women (1970), with its far-reaching report (published in December 1972), and with the emergence thereafter of a Council for the Status of Women. Acknowledging these home-grown developments, it has also been the case that EEC membership has forced the pace on a variety of social issues, and particularly women's rights in the workplace and the home. Occasionally, as with the European Equal Pay Directive of 1975, Irish governments have initially sought to resist the pressure for reform. However, here a combination of domestic protest and external admonition produced an Employment Equality Act, and with it an Employment Equality Agency (1977). Gemma Hussey, reverting to a somewhat problematic metaphor, has described the EEC's intervention within the field of women's rights as being 'like a knight on a white charger': Europe has guaranteed to Irish women equal pay and equal opportunity in the workplace, and has (through a directive signed in October 1992) confirmed a statutory right to maternity leave and other benefits.[12] It would be wrong to pretend that these legal requirements have changed mind-sets, any more than, for example, Catholic emancipation in 1829 created an immediate and effective religious equality. Nor would it be entirely reasonable to see Brussels as the ultimate source of this liberalization, given the international mobilization of women from at least the 1960s, and given some limited movement by Irish governments before 1973. The extent to which Irish women have been responsible for their own empowerment also should not be missed: Mary Robinson, President of Ireland (1990–7), was a beneficiary of the enlivened political aspirations of Irish women, and served in turn as a beacon to the women's movement. But, as with some of the economic issues examined, it may be fairly argued that Europe has been the proximate source of benefits for many women; and that, without European intervention, progress towards full sexual equality might well have come, but more slowly and more painfully than in fact has been the case.

Europe has brought profound change, not only in the Irish economy and with the rights of Irish women and Irish workers generally, but also in less tangible matters. It is arguable that Europe has wrought some changes in the political culture of the country. Before 1932 the energy and skills of Irish diplomats had won a disproportionately great influence for the Irish Free State within the Commonwealth: until 1939 the same persistence and dexterity was applied within the League of Nations. Irish membership of the United Nations came relatively late (in December 1955): but here again the country quickly established itself as one of the most influential of the smaller nations, prominent amongst the non-aligned and a relatively great contributor to UN peace-keeping and aid programmes. Since 1973 the same feat has been repeated within the EEC. Although the Irish public has sometimes taken a genially piratical attitude to Brussels, many of their politicians and civil servants have impressed their European peers by sharp negotiating skills and by a general intellectual quality. Garret FitzGerald is worth mentioning in this context, and – even allowing for some understandable self-aggrandizement – it is clear from his autobiography that he established a peculiarly effective rapport with European leaders both as Minister for Foreign Affairs (1973–7) and as Taoiseach (1982–7): he seems, for example, to have been influential in nudging Jacques Delors towards the Presidency of the European Commission and – as an evident trade-off – to have persuaded Delors to appoint an Irishman, Peter Sutherland, to the strategically vital Commissionership for Competition.[13] The Irish Presidencies of the European Council (in 1975, 1979, 1984, 1990) were widely judged to have been successful; and indeed in 1998, a new recruit to the European Union, Austria, turned to their Irish partners for detailed guidance concerning the conduct of the Presidency and the strategic role of the smaller nations within the EU. Ireland, it was clear by the later 1990s, was punching above its weight as a champion of the small European nations.

Europe provided a new forum and a new direction for Irish political ambition. It permitted Irish politicians and civil servants to work on equal terms with their counterparts from bigger and more powerful European states. There has been a mutual learning process. But on the whole, the success of the European experience has reinforced national self-confidence; and it contributed in the 1990s – along with furious economic growth, and the international recognition won by figures like Séamus Heaney or Mary Robinson – to a reaffirmation of Irish identity.

Part of this cultural and political affirmation has sprung from the maturing of Ireland's relationship with Britain, historically the country's most intimate and embittered tie. Membership of the EEC, or European Union, has decisively changed the nature of this relationship. In 1973, even allowing for the years of economic growth and diversification under Lemass, Britain remained overwhelmingly the single most important Irish export market. The difference in per capita GDP between the two countries emphasized the relative poverty of the Irish. Disparities in power and wealth, combined with intimate cultural and economic bonds, made for a political relationship charged with British condescension and Irish defensiveness. Shared membership of the Community brought some oxygen into this fetid atmosphere: Ireland's economic links with Britain have grown more tenuous, while at the same time Irish interests within the European Union have often brought a strategic unity with the British. Ireland joined the European Monetary System in 1979, well ahead of Britain, and thereby broke a connection with sterling that dated back to 1826. Irish trade with continental Europe has grown at the expense of the connection with Britain: in 1973 56 per cent of Irish exports went to Britain, while in 1991 the comparable figure was 32 per cent. Irish exports to continental Europe grew from 17.6 per cent to 42 per cent in the same period. Massive, if patchy, economic growth in Ireland, aided by subventions from Europe, has brought a turnaround in the per capita wealth of the two countries: Irish GDP per head overtook that of the British in 1997. At the same time, and partly as a consequence of this process of economic release and equalization, the political relationship between Ireland and Britain inside the European Union has improved: Irish civil servants and ministers who had no particular reason to deal with their British counterparts before 1973 found, because of the mechanisms of the Community, that they were now frequently thrown together. This has brought a keener degree of mutual understanding and sympathy than hitherto, though it would be useless to pretend that suspicions do not linger (FitzGerald tells in his memoirs of a pantomimic incident at the Stuttgart European Council meeting of 1983, when he was alarmed to discover a British diplomat lurking outside his rooms: the Briton was evidently looking for a whiskey bottle rather than secret intelligence).[14] However, FitzGerald provides evidence not just of lingering tensions, but also of some fundamental strategic congruities between the British and Irish stands inside Europe: in 1976 he spelt out an aspect of this to the British Foreign Secretary, Tony Crosland, arguing that Irish interests lay in an equilibrium between the three major powers of the EEC, and that a more active British role suited the Irish since it mitigated the threat of Franco-German domination.[15] Close British and Irish communication, stimulated largely by European contacts, lay behind the radical initiative on Northern Ireland which began tentatively in 1981 and which culminated in the Anglo-Irish Agreement (November 1985).

This leads naturally to a consideration of the third of the key influences on the modern Irish state mentioned earlier: the crisis in Northern Ireland. Violence in the North has ricocheted into the Republic. There have been several high-profile assassinations, including that of the Fine Gael Senator Billy Fox by the IRA on 11 March 1974 (Senator Fox was the first member of the Oireachtas to be killed since Kevin O'Higgins in 1927): the British ambassador to Ireland, Christopher Ewart-Biggs, was killed by an IRA landmine at Sandyford, County Dublin, on 21 July 1976. The IRA also assassinated Earl Mountbatten of Burma (at Mullaghmore, County Sligo, on 27 August 1979). The Ulster Volunteer Force detonated a series of bombs in Dublin and Monaghan, killing a total of 33 people and injuring over 100: 17 May 1974 has the grim distinction of being the bloodiest day in the history of the Irish troubles. Several gardaí have been killed by the IRA over the years since 1969, often during or after bank raids: in one such bloody episode in July 1980 two gardaí were shot dead at Ballaghadereen, County Roscommon.

The impact of this sporadic, but painful and bloody, overspill from the North in terms of the Irish economy is harder to calculate than the casualty lists. It is probable that some potential investors have been deterred by the prospect of political instability. It is clear that the tourist trade has been stifled, if not suffocated; and it is equally clear that the cost of enhanced security measures in the 1970s and 1980s imposed an unwonted burden on an already stretched public purse.

Tough security legislation has also impinged upon civil liberties. The re-establishment of the Special Criminal Court by Desmond O'Malley in May 1972 brought juryless trials back into the judicial process. The Offences against the State (Amendment) Act of December 1972 allowed the summary conviction (on the word of a senior garda) of those suspected of belonging to illegal organizations. After the assassination of Christopher Ewart-Biggs the Fine Gael-led coalition government promoted an Emergency Powers Bill, which permitted the detention for seven days of those suspected of crimes under the Offences Against the State Act. The impact of this measure was in fact more far-reaching than could have been imagined by its authors, or indeed the killers of Ewart-Biggs, though it usefully illustrates the knock-on effects of terror. The President of Ireland, Cearbhall Ó Dálaigh, a distinguished lawyer, exercised his right to refer the bill to the Supreme Court in order to test its constitutionality: the Court duly confirmed the legality of the measure. But the Minister of Defence, Patrick Donegan, was angered by what he saw as academic quibbling in the face of a national emergency, and condemned Ó Dálaigh as 'a thundering disgrace'. The Taoiseach, Liam Cosgrave, stood by his minister; and Ó Dálaigh resigned on 23 October 1976 'in order to protect the dignity and independence of the Presidency'.[16] True to his Free State roots, Cosgrave acted selflessly and in the interests of national stability, and turned to a respected Fianna Fáiler, Patrick Hillery, as an agreed successor to Ó Dálaigh (an irredeemably sceptical observer might indeed see a subtle piece of partisanship here, as with earlier acts of Treatyite statesmanship, but such scepticism would probably be misplaced). Hillery was duly inaugurated as President on 3 December 1976.

Northern violence has also supplied some painful lessons in practical politics. Mainstream nationalist conviction in the Republic has been shifting at least from the era of Lemass, with his 'technocratic' and economistic approach to the challenge of partition. The war in Northern Ireland reinforced this modernization of the centre-ground, albeit at a terrible cost. Loyalist violence underlined the existence of a ferocious and armed section of northern Unionist opinion which could not easily be accommodated by the traditional advocates of Irish unity in the South. The popularity of fundamentalist Protestants like the Reverend Ian Paisley among Unionists posed problems for those in the South who sought a liberal and secular Ireland. Equally, the growth of militant republicanism exposed some of the elisions and evasions within traditional anti-partitionist thought. Many constitutional nationalists in the Republic revered the heroes of the struggle of 1916–21; many were sympathetic towards the ideal of reunification as well as towards the embattled nationalists of Northern Ireland. But, at least from their own perspective, the gunmen from the nationalist ghettoes of the North were continuing the anti-imperialist struggle begun in 1916, and which was so central to the official mythology of the Irish state: these gunmen were, again in their own estimation, merely trying to realize the legitimate aspirations of the Irish constitution as well as of mainstream southern opinion.

In this way militant republicanism applied pressure to the ideological imperatives of southern politics. This is not to say that the Provisional IRA was primarily responsible for initiating change within mainstream southern nationalist thought: but it is to say that pressures from the North helped to expose or to reinforce certain ideological shifts which had their origins at the very least in the Lemass years. Lemass's creative redefinition of anti-partitionist strategy to some extent laid the foundations for the goals pursued in 1973, at the time of Sunningdale, and in 1984–5 with the New Ireland Forum and the Anglo-Irish Agreement. The challenge of violence in the North provided the context for the initiatives of these years, but their intellectual origins were deeply rooted within the processes of modernization in the Irish state. The Sunningdale Agreement, signed in December 1973 by the British and Irish governments together with the main constitutional parties in Northern Ireland, created a Council of Ireland with 'executive and harmonising functions and a consultative role' which was designed to unite ministers and parliamentarians from Belfast and Dublin: provision was made for cross-border security coordination. Significantly, under the terms of article five, the Irish government 'fully and solemnly declared that there could be no change in the status of Northern Ireland until a majority of the people of Northern Ireland desired a change in that status'.[17] This was seen by the Ulster Unionist leader Brian Faulkner as a significant modification of the official Irish approach to partition; and indeed it may also be seen as the logical corollary of the strategies being pursued by Lemass less then ten years before. The practical significance of the Agreement was of course undermined both by a legal challenge from the republican Kevin Boland and, more decisively, by the Ulster Workers' Council strike of May 1974. But its significance in terms of the development of mainstream southern attitudes towards partition should not be missed.

It was developments in the North which again, in the early 1980s, precipitated a further effort to establish a generous and consensual approach to Northern Ireland, which at the same time remained essentially nationalist in its construction. This was the New Ireland Forum, which was promoted by Garret FitzGerald as Taoiseach and which met in Dublin Castle between May 1983 and May 1984. The context was the hunger strikes by PIRA prisoners in Belfast in the summer of 1981 and the consequent hardening of the Sinn Féin vote in Northern Ireland: FitzGerald was

Plate 18   Liam Cosgrave, Brian Faulkner, and ministers from the Belfast Executive and the Dublin coalition government, Hillsborough, February 1974.
Source: Victor Patterson/Linenhall Library.

seeking to rally constitutional nationalism in both the North and the South behind an agreed statement of conviction which, in turn, might be used as a basis for negotiation with the British. Much of the final report, especially its historical section (which seems to have embarrassed FitzGerald), was a reiteration of traditional patriotic verities: but it also contained the first broadly based nationalist recognition of the complexities, and the Britishness, of Ulster Unionist identity. The ultimate thrust of FitzGerald's strategies was towards the achievement of a form of joint British–Irish authority within Northern Ireland, which could bolster constitutional nationalism there and divert support from Sinn Féin. The Anglo-Irish Agreement, signed at Hillsborough in November 1985, bore the imprint of FitzGerald's analysis, even though the deal that was struck in fact fell short of joint authority: it embodied a half-way house between the loose consultative procedures that were in place between 1980 and 1985 and FitzGerald's more ambitious goals. Once again, an Anglo-Irish Agreement affirmed that 'any change in the status of Northern Ireland would only come about with the consent of the majority of the people of Northern Ireland' (article 1a); though the Hillsborough deal seemed to inch a little further than this by recognizing 'that the present wish of a majority of the people of Northern Ireland is for no change in the status of Northern Ireland' (article 1b).[18] This was seen by Unionists (who largely opposed the Agreement) as simply a statement of reality; but in truth even limpid statements of reality have not always come naturally to the main political traditions on the island.

The Anglo-Irish Agreement did not uniformly live up to the expectations of those on the Irish side who had helped in its construction. The Agreement did not, in fact, undermine support for Sinn Féin, as FitzGerald had hoped and predicted; it did, however, bolster constitutional politics, though again not quite in the manner which had been expected. Bew, Patterson and Teague have argued that not only did the Agreement fail to marginalize Sinn Féin, in some senses it helped to bolster republicanism.[19] Sinn Féin had already peaked before the signing of the Agreement in November 1985, while in certain key areas it subsequently actually gained ground: in (for example) the pivotal West Belfast constituency, Protestants – who in some cases had offered tactical votes to the SDLP – now returned to Unionism, thereby permitting the seat to fall to Gerry Adams, the Sinn Féin leader. The Agreement demonstrated to nationalists of all hues that the British government was willing to circumvent Unionist opposition in the pursuit of a deal: it encouraged the call that the British should set aside the Unionist 'veto' and become 'persuaders for unity'.[20] It demonstrated, in a general sense, that there were gains to be made through the exploration of constitutional avenues. The Agreement encouraged, though it certainly did not satisfy, northern nationalist expectations: it has been argued that, in conjunction with the evident disarray of the Unionists, it fuelled a nationalist maximalism, as evidenced by the cautious détente between Adams and John Hume, the leader of the SDLP, which began in 1988. Sinn Féin leaders seem to have begun to think in terms of a broad patriotic front of constitutional nationalists, militant republicans and Irish Americans which, given British hesitation and Unionist demoralization, could press forward to an ultimate victory.

The failure of the constitutional parties to reach a deal, combined with the possibilities opened up by the Hume–Adams initiative, drove both the Irish and British governments towards a settlement which incorporated not just the contentious middle-ground of Ulster politics, but also the militant periphery. This redirection was spurred on by the failure of the inter-party talks sponsored by the successive Secretaries of State for Northern Ireland, Peter Brooke (1989–92) and Sir Patrick Mayhew (1992–7): with the collapse of the Brooke–Mayhew process in late 1992, Hume returned in 1993 to his still highly controversial dialogue with Adams. To some extent, however, this initiative was simultaneously gagged as well as kidnapped by the Irish and British governments: in late 1993 the two administrations agreed that (in the words of Albert Reynolds, Taoiseach between 1992 and 1994) 'Hume/Adams was being declared dead in order to keep it alive'.[21] Squabbling between the constitutional parties, face-to-face dialogue between the leaders of the two main nationalist traditions in the North, some tentative communication between the British and republicans – these were the contexts against which the Downing Street Declaration was affirmed by Reynolds and John Major (British Prime Minister, 1990–7) in December 1993: this looked forward to an inclusivist talks process for all those who 'permanently' rejected armed force. For their part the British formally disavowed any 'selfish strategic or economic interest in Northern Ireland' and promised to act as facilitators for an agreement which might 'embrace the totality of relationships'.[22] This stance, and particularly the crucial fourth paragraph of the Declaration, contained some concessions to the language, if not always the substance, of the Hume–Adams dialogue (it has been said that the Irish and British were 'negotiating around a highly diluted version' of the agreement reached between Hume and Adams).[23] The Irish government, for its part, now moved beyond the affirmations of the Anglo-Irish Agreement in its bid to assuage Unionist sensitivities: Reynolds ruled out the imposition of a united Ireland against the wishes of a majority in Northern Ireland, repeating the assurances given by Irish governments (though, significantly, not Fianna Fáil-led governments) in 1973 and in 1985. But he also undertook – as part of a broader talks process – to examine those aspects of life in the Republic which offended Unionists or otherwise fell short of his government's pluralist vision. In this context, he underlined that contentious aspects of the Irish constitution might be altered as part of a broader settlement in Northern Ireland. Such alterations had been mooted at both Sunningdale and in the run-up to Hillsborough, but the obstacles had seemed overwhelming, and the issue had not been pursued.

Privately, Reynolds threatened that, if the Declaration as a whole did not bring a permanent IRA ceasefire, he would proceed hand in hand with Major and leave the republicans behind.[24] This tough-minded approach may have been one of the clinching forces behind the announcement by the Provisionals, on 31 August 1994, of a complete cessation of hostilities. Moreover, the 'green-tinted' Frameworks Documents, published in February 1995, seems to have been designed in part to give further encouragement to those nervous doves within the republican movement. Three strands for discussion between the Northern Irish parties were defined, including a proposed North–South body with apparently sweeping powers ('a bureaucratic fantasia designed to appeal to [the] Sinn Féin leadership').[25]

There were subsequent setbacks. The first IRA ceasefire ended in February 1996, with the detonation of a bomb in Canary Wharf, London. Elections in May 1996 for a constitutional Forum underlined the political polarization of Northern Ireland, and produced a bear-pit. Changes in administration in both London (with the election of Tony Blair and Labour in May 1997) and Dublin (with a succession of Taoisigh – Reynolds, Bruton, Ahern – in the period between 1994 and 1997) brought some distinct alterations of emphasis, and much relearning. But much of the delicate pattern of a settlement was in fact already either in place or being put in place in 1996–7. The accession of Bertie Ahern, in charge of a Fianna Fáil–Progressive Democrat coalition, brought to the Taoiseach's office a man renowned for his steely affability as well as his diplomatic skills: the structure of his coalition was helpful in that it represented both mainstream republican feeling and neo-liberals who were relatively 'soft' on Ulster Unionism. The Irish had repeatedly confirmed the importance of majority consent within Northern Ireland before any reunification could take place: there were now promises of constitutional revision. On the other hand, the Labour victory in Britain might have caused the Ulster Unionists to bolt: but in fact the electoral landslide was helpful to the prospects for a settlement in that Unionist backbenchers – and therefore Unionist passivity – could no longer decide the fate and direction of government (as had been apparently the case, certainly from the nationalist viewpoint, in the last years of the vulnerable Major administration). Blair's massive majority gave him an authority to pursue a settlement, while his broadly Unionist sympathies were a comfort to those in Glengall Street not blinded by sectarian fears concerning his Anglo-Catholicism or the Roman Catholicism of his wife. The British had repeatedly acknowledged their lack of any 'selfish' interest in Northern Ireland, and they had explicitly acknowledged the legitimacy and dignity of nationalist aspirations. John Hume had remained committed to the involvement of his Sinn Féin rivals in any final settlement. The Sinn Féin leadership (as opposed to some other sections of the republican movement) seems throughout to have remained interested in the idea of peace. The Ulster Unionists had recently (September 1995) acquired as leader David Trimble, a high-voltage pragmatist whose combination of public defiance and private realism had Carsonite overtones. The loyalist militants, with the significant exception of the Loyalist Volunteer Force, had maintained a (sometimes shaky) ceasefire since October 1994, and indeed had produced a political leadership distinguished not only by (some) criminal records but also by a relatively generous and imaginative strategic analysis.

The document which the Irish government signed at Stormont on 10 April 1998 incorporated some significant changes in mainstream nationalist thought over the preceding 30 years. The government had certainly won concessions from both the British and the Ulster Unionists: the Unionist signatories, for example, had now formally abandoned a crude majoritarianism and had accepted the reality of cross-border institutions. The British had recognized that 'it is for the people of Ireland alone' to decide on the issue of unification: they had earlier – from the time of Peter Brooke's Whitbread speech of November 1990 – disavowed any 'selfish strategic or economic interest in Ireland'.[26] On the other hand, the Good Friday Agreement acknowledged (as did the Anglo-Irish Agreement) that a majority in Northern Ireland wanted the maintenance of the Union: more than this, the deal explicitly underlined for the first time the legitimacy of this Unionist position. The Agreement bound the Irish government to initiate some highly charged revisions in the constitution of 1937. It tied the government into a new British–Irish Council, meeting in different formats at least twice a year in order to pursue cooperation across a range of mutual interests. A new British–Irish Inter-governmental Conference was created to replace the precursor institutions created in the 1980s. The Irish government was now formally committed (as was the new Northern Ireland Assembly and Executive) to a sweeping review of human rights issues within their respective jurisdictions; and the government reaffirmed an intention 'to take further active steps to demonstrate its respect for the different traditions in the island of Ireland'.[27]

Northern Ireland had changed dramatically since 1969, and the Irish government had had a role in pursuing much of this change. But the process was reciprocal, for Ireland as a whole was in flux and some at least of the change may be traced back to the northern crisis. The fundamental nationalist ideal remained in place in 1998:

the goal of a sovereign unitary state. Most nationalists believed still in the integrity of a single Irish nation. But nationalism had now accommodated itself philosophically as well as practically to partition, and to the legitimacy of the Unionist aspiration and tradition. The once central and uncomplicated notion of Irish self-determination had been redefined to allow for the self-determination of northerners within a Northern Irish state. Notions of the primacy of a Gaelic, Catholic Irishness had long gone: the Agreement of 1998 paid special attention to the role of the Irish language within Northern Ireland, but this was as part of a pluralist rather than a supremacist vision. Catholic identity within nationalism remained vitally important; but the special constitutional position of the Roman Catholic Church within the Irish state had long since been overturned (in May 1972), while formerly stringent legislation on a variety of matters affecting the Church's social teaching (marriage, divorce, contraception, abortion) had been relaxed. The publicity given to a number of paedophile priests had a profound impact on the Church's standing; less shocking, but still disturbing, was the exposure of the stern and sometimes abusive record of the Christian Brothers within Irish schools. Liberal Catholics were sometimes worried by the Church's ban on women priests. All these issues fed the currents of secularization – or, at any rate, the processes by which the long dominant, nineteenth-century, definition of Irish Catholicism has been overturned. But there remained the possibility, as Fintan O'Toole argued, 'that the [redefined] Irish Church . . . will look remarkably like what it was in 1800 – a focus for a relaxed but deep spirituality in which the broad culture rather than the devotional and behavioural rules is what matters'.[28]

The emphasis had once been on territorial imperatives. The constitution of 1937 had been not only Catholic but also territorial in its thrusts. The emphasis had once been on civic duty rather than on civil rights. Republicans in 1921–2 had argued that the Irish people, in supporting a 26-county Free State, had not the right to be wrong. Nationalists until the 1970s had often argued that Irish people – Unionists – had not the right to be British. The Agreement of 1998 gave formal expression to a more pluralist nationalism, where diversity was respected, and indeed celebrated. 'In keeping with our principles', Bertie Ahern declared in February 1995, 'it is the people of Ireland who are sovereign, not the State': but 'our principles' had evidently not been shared by his republican father, or indeed – until lately – by his own party.[29]

8.2 Northern Ireland, 1973–98

So far war and peace in Northern Ireland have been examined exclusively in the context of southern economic and political concerns. But the internal dynamics of the northern crisis remain to be examined. And the resolution of this crisis – even allowing for the encouragement and admonition of the Irish and British governments – may not be fully understood without evaluating the role of the northern parties and their respective leaders. Northern Ireland, the Good Friday and St. Andrews Agreements provide a suitably Whiggish dénouement to the volume: three themes

– the war and its protagonists, the constitutional parties and their respective leaders, and the efforts towards a settlement – light the way to the happy 'ending' traditionally called for in histories of Ireland.

Some of the origins of the conflict in Northern Ireland have been considered in an earlier chapter. The story of the war itself is still first and foremost the story of its many victims. It is an essential starting point (though in fact one that is not always chosen) for any broader discussion of Northern Ireland, not least because the peaks and troughs of violence determined the birth, growth and (often) the death of political dialogue. Political initiatives were often rooted, or fostered by, the intensification of violence (such as in 1972, or in the early 1980s, or early 1990s): but the mounting casualty lists simultaneously increased the need for a settlement while reducing the likelihood of agreement. Intense violence provoked instability, which in turn stimulated political initiative; but the growing numbers of victims within each community tended to reinforce both the loyalist and republican stake in an ultimate victory. This was perhaps particularly true for the Unionists who, surrendering a position of supremacy within the old Stormont parliament, were most inclined to see political movement as a sell-out to violence – and who were therefore most inclined to look to (British) military strategies and a (British) military victory. But republicans, too, were interested in victory (in the form of the expulsion of their enemies), and seem to have felt periodically – especially in the early 1970s – that this was within their grasp.

Leading the republican offensive on the partition settlement and upon British rule in Ireland was the Provisional IRA (PIRA), formed in December 1969 when the republican movement as a whole was inching towards more emollient – or, depending on the viewpoint, more collaborationist – policies. The Provisionals armed and recruited rapidly in 1970–1, their fortunes boosted by the hamfisted application of internment in August 1971 and by the widespread resentments that this aroused: the 'Bloody Sunday' killings in Derry in January 1972 also fired popular nationalist anger and the popularity of the PIRA. Weapons and cash came from a variety of sources: sympathizers in the South were disproportionately useful in the early months, but later supplies were independently obtained in eastern Europe (particularly Czechoslovakia) and in the United States. American financial support has always been important for the republican movement, whether during the Anglo-Irish war (1919–21) or during the 'Long War' (1969–97): there has also been a drip-feed of American arms (as with the smuggling of Thompson sub-machine guns in 1921). Libyan arms supplies were (oddly, given the importance of Irish America) vital, especially in the mid-1980s: four major shipments are believed to have been landed in Ireland in 1985–6, while a fifth – carried in the *Eksund* – was intercepted by the French in October 1987.

The purpose of this cash and weaponry was to fight for British withdrawal and for the reunification of Ireland: these were the irreducible republican goals, although there was some modulation of emphasis and of strategic design over the years. The political party linked to the PIRA, Provisional Sinn Féin (formed in 1970 after a split with 'official' Sinn Féin), advocated at first a phased British departure from the North, together with the establishment of regional assemblies in each of the four provinces of Ireland: this was the 'Éire Nua' policy, promulgated in March 1972.[30] The party also remained abstentionist, true to the traditional republican disdain for the 'flawed' institutions of the partition settlement. However, significant strategic changes were effected in 1981–2, when the federalist agenda of the party was abandoned and when there was a move towards a more active political engagement. At the party's ard-fheis of 1981, a dual policy of electoral and military struggle was enunciated, with the director of publicity, Danny Morrison, asking 'will anyone here object if, with a ballot paper in this hand and an Armalite in this hand, we take power in Ireland?'.[31] The party used hunger-striking PIRA prisoners as election candidates in 1981, and achieved a boost in popular support: Bobby Sands was elected as MP for Fermanagh-South Tyrone in April 1981. The deaths of ten of the hunger strikers (seven of whom were Provisionals) in the summer of 1981 galvanized further nationalist support for Sinn Féin and helped the party to win 10 per cent of the popular vote at the Assembly elections held in October 1982. At the general election of 1983 Gerry Adams, one of the party's most influential strategists, was returned as MP for West Belfast, defeating the veteran nationalist Gerry Fitt.

Adams, a highly acute political intelligence, seems to have come to accept that more could be done to further republican demands through constitutional channels than through the war of attrition being fought by the Provisionals. Towards this end he sought to engage John Hume of the SDLP in dialogue, first in 1988 and again in 1993, partly with a view to exploring the common ground within the nationalist family and producing a shared statement of nationalist principles (this emerged as the Hume–Adams declaration of April 1993). Adams also seems to have been a major influence behind the IRA ceasefires in 1994 and 1997: he was, with his colleague Martin McGuinness, the leading negotiator for the republican movement in the talks that produced the Good Friday Agreement. With McGuinness, he was responsible for the major reassessment of republican tactics which fed into the Agreement; and he was responsible, too, for successfully selling this revisionist analysis to his party and the wider movement.

But, aside from these increasingly important political initiatives, the central thrust of the republican movement between 1969 and 1997 was towards the violent removal of the British presence from Ireland. The central features of this campaign were bomb attacks on major military and economic targets, together with the assassination of individual soldiers, policemen or others deemed to have been inculpated in British rule. Many of these episodes remain highly sensitive and highly controversial, and in the cross-fire of charge and counter-charge it is sometimes difficult to distinguish motive from result, and conscious intention from accidental outcome. However, in the early 1970s there seems to have been a sharp push to overturn the northern state by a concerted fusillade of bombing, shooting and – in some cases – street protest: bombs in Belfast on 21 July 1972 ('Bloody Friday') claimed 11 victims, while ten days later in the sleepy village of Claudy, County Londonderry, eight more were killed in explosions. But it was soon grasped that local victims and local incidents had a relatively slight impact on British ministers; and it was also grasped

– certainly by the later 1970s – that there could be no swift and concerted charge to a final victory. Indiscriminate bomb attacks on local civilians were therefore curbed, although they by no means disappeared: the fire bombing of the La Mon Hotel in February 1978, with 16 dead, was perhaps a late example of a tactic pursued with greater vigour in earlier years, while the Enniskillen bomb (8 November 1987) killed 11 people and seems to have been sectarian in motivation (both bombs may, or may not, have been detonated accidentally and thus prematurely). Other republican assaults on perceived military targets have sometimes claimed many civilian casualties; the INLA attack on the Droppin' Well pub at Ballykelly, County Londonderry, in December 1982 killed 12 soldiers and five civilians and injured 66; while the explosion at the Shankill Road fish shop in October 1993 was designed as a PIRA thrust against the UFF, but instead killed nine local shoppers and one of the bombers. It is unclear whether the Omagh bomb of 15 August 1998, planted by dissident republicans, was intended as an assault on property or human life: 29 died in the single bloodiest episode of the 30 years of violence.

Attacks such as these provoked loyalist counter-assaults on the nationalist population, while having little visible impact on the government. Bombing missions in England, therefore, emerged early on in the 'war' as a strategic imperative: one of the most bloody and controversial of these came in Birmingham in November 1974, when 21 people died in bomb blasts (six men were wrongfully convicted of the crime, and released only in 1991). There has also been a sustained preference for 'spectaculars' – the bombing of high-profile targets in England such as the Household Cavalry barracks, Knightsbridge (in July 1982, in an episode reminiscent of an attack in May 1921 on George V's mounted escort) or the Canary Wharf complex (on 9 February 1996).

Attacks on policemen had been central to the republican struggle of 1919–21, and remained so in the 1970s and thereafter. Attacks on prominent Unionists were relatively uncommon in the early 1920s (W.J. Twaddell, a Stormont MP shot in May 1922, was a grim exception), but were pursued with greater vigour in the 1970s and 1980s: John Taylor, a junior minister at Stormont and a rising star of Unionism, was seriously wounded by Official IRA gunmen in February 1972; Robert Bradford, Unionist MP for South Belfast, was shot dead by the Provisionals in November 1981; Edgar Graham, widely tipped as a future Unionist leader, was shot dead, also by the Provisionals, in December 1983. Equally, the assassination of prominent members of the British establishment had been a goal in 1919–21, which was occasionally (though in fact not often) pressed home: the lord lieutenant, Lord French, was targeted on several occasions, but escaped; while Field Marshal Sir Henry Wilson was gunned down in 1922. The republican assassins of the 'Long War' had a more grimly successful career than their heroes from the struggle for independence: Airey Neave, the Conservative spokesperson on Northern Ireland, was killed by an INLA bomb in March 1979, while Earl Mountbatten, a senior member of the British royal family, was killed by the Provisionals in August 1979. Plans were laid for the assassination, in July 1983, of Prince Charles and Princess Diana at the Dominion Theatre, London. A bomb attack on the Grand Hotel, Brighton,

Plate 19   The aftermath of the Omagh bombing, August 1998.
Source: Popperfoto/Reuters.

in October 1984 during the Conservative Party conference very nearly eliminated the British cabinet. By this time, the hopes of the early 1970s (encouraged by the rapid overthrow of Stormont in March 1972) for a speedy victory had long been set aside, and republicans had settled down for a long war of attrition.

Facing the Provisionals was militant loyalism, organized into the Ulster Volunteer Force (UVF, formed in 1966) and the Ulster Defence Association (UDA, launched in September 1971): linked with these larger bodies were the smaller and more aggressive Red Hand Commandos (1972) and the Ulster Freedom Fighters (UFF, 1973). As with the PIRA, these bodies were armed from a variety of sources, both within Ireland and beyond. Some weapons came from sympathizers within the crown forces or from raids on crown installations: in March 1988 three men (two former soldiers in the Ulster Defence Regiment, a regular component of the British army) were convicted of participating in a UDA arms raid on a military camp in Coleraine, County Londonderry. Weapons for both the UDA and the UVF appear to have been stockpiled in Scotland and occasionally imported into Northern Ireland. In 1988 a conspiracy to import arms for the UVF from Canada was scuppered by the authorities. A highly controversial figure, Brian Nelson, a double agent working for both the UDA and the British army, seems to have forged a connection between loyalists and South African arms dealers.

The core political purpose of this arsenal was to sustain a fight for the Union, although – as exasperation with British policy mounted – this goal was in fact negotiable. Some of the ideologues within the UDA seem to have been interested in the idea of an autonomous Northern Ireland, and indeed in November 1974 a delegation arrived in Libya intent on sounding out the Gaddafi regime about possible aid in the event of independence. In 1978 the UDA established the New Ulster Political Research Group, which advocated negotiated independence and an American-style constitution: the Ulster Loyalist Democratic Party (later the Ulster Democratic Party or UDP) was founded in 1981 to evangelize a determinedly sceptical electorate (Unionist voters for long remained suspicious of parties with close paramilitary connections). The Anglo-Irish Agreement of 1985 and its aftermath hinted at the political bankruptcy of mainstream Unionism and created opportunities for some of the more unconventional thinkers within paramilitary loyalism. With the Ulster Unionists and Democratic Unionists beginning to descend into mutual recrimination as the campaign against the Agreement flagged, John McMichael of the UDA recognized a political opportunity and launched a blueprint for devolved government (*Common Sense: An Agreed Process*). McMichael had already created a stir among Unionists by suggesting in 1986 that Sinn Féin should be represented at any peace talks that might be held; and he underlined the extent to which he was trying to reposition the UDA by arguing in *Common Sense* that Northern Ireland should have a cross-community government based upon a 78-member Assembly, elected by proportional representation. The language of the document was progressive and consensual (although mounting accusations from mainstream Unionists that the UDA was selling out meant that its blueprint was defended in increasingly traditionalist terms). McMichael was assassinated by the Provisionals in December 1987 (acting in collusion with a leading loyalist racketeer), and the loyalist paramilitaries moved swiftly away from philosophical speculation towards a sectarian offensive in the early 1990s. But McMichael's combination of militancy and pragmatism was reinvigorated by his son Gary, working through the UDP, and by David Ervine of the Progressive Unionists (a party associated with the UVF). Both represent distinctive military organizations within loyalism; and each offers an individual spin on the future of Northern Ireland government. But both seem to be indebted to John McMichael's realistic approach to the challenge of Sinn Féin, as well as to his quirkily consensual vision.

It would be utterly wrong, however, to judge loyalist paramilitarism exclusively, or even mainly, on the basis of *Common Sense*: Feargal Cochrane has recently, and rightly, tried to dampen some of the more euphoric assessments of McMichael's blueprint.[32] The UVF and the terror group associated with the UDA, the UFF, were generally more adept with guns and bombs than with policy initiatives; and generally more interested in killing Catholics than in planning to share power with them. The bombing of targets in the South has been a strategy pursued intermittently by the UVF: the Dublin and Monaghan explosions of 17 May 1974 brought a total of 33 deaths and marked the worst day of violence in the bloody history of the 'Long War'. Leading republicans have also been frequently targeted: Máire Drumm, the Vice-President of Sinn Féin and one of the most prominent northern republicans, was shot dead – possibly by the UVF – in October 1976; Dr Miriam Daly, a lecturer at Queen's University and a senior republican activist, was shot dead in June 1980; Bernadette Devlin-McAliskey was wounded by loyalist gunmen in February 1981; Gerry Adams was the victim of a UFF assassination bid in March 1984. Sinn Féin workers and councillors were targeted by the UFF, especially in the early 1990s: Sheena Campbell, a Queen's law student and Sinn Féin parliamentary candidate, was killed by loyalists in October 1992. Both the UVF and the UFF have pursued a more nakedly sectarian agenda than the PIRA, targeting Catholics on an indiscriminate basis: in February 1992 five Catholics were shot dead in a bookmaker's office on the Ormeau Road, Belfast; four Catholic workmen were shot dead by the UFF at Castlerock, County Londonderry, in March 1993; in October 1993 seven people – six Catholics and one Protestant – were killed by the UFF in the Rising Sun bar at Greysteel, County Londonderry; in June 1994 the UVF shot dead six Catholics in a pub at Loughinisland, County Down.

It has always been the republican contention that loyalist paramilitaries have had close connections with the crown forces in Northern Ireland: the Ulster Defence Regiment (UDR, 1970–92), the Royal Ulster Constabulary (RUC, founded in 1922), the British army and the various agencies of British secret intelligence. In some ways these arguments evoke memories of the alleged collusion between the USC and loyalist death squads in Belfast in 1922, and in particular the allegations surrounding the highly controversial police officer, District Inspector J.W. Nixon. The latter-day accusations focused in particular on the locally recruited forces, the UDR and RUC, and came to a head in the late 1980s, a time of mounting loyalist violence, when official files on republican suspects fell into the possession of loyalist paramilitaries: suspicions mounted that loyalist assassinations were being conducted on the basis of the information supplied through these materials. Some light was thrown on this murky affair by the work of an official investigation, the Stevens Inquiry, although in some ways this served to raise more suspicions than it allayed. The RUC was cleared by the Inquiry, but ten UDR soldiers were charged with complicity in the affair. In addition, numerous UDA activists were arrested and one, Tommy Lyttle, was convicted on a charge of possessing materials likely to be of use to terrorists. But, as Steve Bruce has observed, the 'result of the Stevens Inquiry was double-edged': the Inquiry uncovered the existence of an army spy within the ranks of the paramilitary UDA, Brian Nelson, who was subsequently convicted of conspiracy to murder.[33] This simultaneously raised broader republican suspicions while persuading a murderous element within the UDA that it could now act untrammelled by British spies.

Both the RUC and the UDR were the front-line troops of the British government in its fight against militant republicanism. The RUC was handicapped from the beginning of the 'troubles' by its unlovely reputation with nationalists, a reputation which hardened in 1968–9 when the force responded aggressively and with evident partiality when facing the challenge of popular protest and civil disorder. Part of the problem lay with the close official relationship between the police and Unionist government: part of the problem lay, too, in the overwhelmingly Protestant membership and ethos within the RUC. It was also the case that the force was ill-equipped, not just in terms of its political awareness or sensitivities but also in terms of numbers and training: in 1970 there were only 3,500 RUC officers, where in 1991 there were roughly 8,500 officers supported by a reserve force of 5,000 men and women. A report into policing by Lord Hunt in 1969 effected some changes and a remodelling of the force along British lines; but in a sense, while well-intentioned and progressive, the Hunt report was based on the same philosophy that underlay Mrs Thatcher's remark that Northern Ireland was 'part of the United Kingdom – as much as my constituency'. The pre-eminent tradition within the RUC remained not the British 'Dixon of Dock Green' model, but rather the essentially paramilitary legacy of the old Royal Irish Constabulary.

The RUC have been seen as both victims and aggressors in the 'Long War', and it will take time and further evidence to judge accurately where the balance lies. It was involved in some highly controversial procedures: interrogation techniques in 1971 at the Castlereagh holding centre in Belfast aroused widespread concern and were judged by the European Court of Human Rights to have been 'inhuman and degrading' (while not amounting to 'torture'). The killing of six unarmed Catholic men (including some PIRA suspects) in Armagh in 1982 gave rise to suspicions of a 'shoot to kill' policy. An inquiry into the affair stimulated further controversy, for allegations of obstruction were made by the investigating officer, John Stalker: moreover, Stalker was later replaced under somewhat suspicious circumstances. His report was completed by Colin Sampson, Chief Constable of West Yorkshire, and remains unpublished. Inquests into the deaths of the six men were abandoned in September 1994, because the results of the Stalker–Sampson investigation had not been made available to the coroner. There have been other highly charged issues. The use of plastic bullets in riot control by the police has brought serious injury, and some fatalities. More generally, allegations of harassment and of heavy-handedness were made by republicans (but not only republicans) throughout the 'troubles':

'SS: RUC' was one of the few chants or slogans in Belfast which knew no sectarian frontier.

Membership of the RUC was voluntary and, in the context of a depressed local economy, was relatively well paid. On the other hand, the officers of the RUC (like the RIC men of 1919–21) were local and accessible, and as such they bore the brunt of the republican military campaign. Off-duty officers were easy targets, and many were shot in their homes or killed by booby-traps fixed to their cars: the families of officers sometimes fell victim to these assaults, and occasionally under grim circumstances. Minor police stations were abandoned (again, as in 1919–20), and the larger barracks were elaborately fortified (the siege architecture of the 'Long War' demands investigation): but PIRA mortars were capable of breaching these defences, sometimes, as in February 1985, when nine RUC officers were killed in their barracks at Newry, County Down, with devastating results. Nor were the heavily armoured vehicles used by both the police and army proof against the massive land-mines or roadside bombs favoured by the Provisionals: in July 1990 three RUC men were blown up while driving near Armagh; a nun, Sister Catherine Dunne, who was travelling in a car behind the policemen, also died in the explosion.

The RUC has been supported in its counter-insurgency effort by the British army, and in particular by the locally recruited UDR. The army was brought onto the streets of Belfast and Derry in August 1969 after the police had conceded that they were outnumbered and exhausted. British soldiers were at first welcomed by some nationalists, but the honeymoon ended abruptly in 1971–2. In March 1971 three young Royal Highland Fusiliers were lured from a pub in Ligoniel, Belfast, and subsequently shot by the Provisionals. The shooting of two men in Derry by the army in July 1971 provoked a major political crisis, for the Northern Ireland government refused to authorize an enquiry and the SDLP withdrew in protest from the Stormont parliament. The 'Bloody Sunday' killings of January 1972, when 13 Catholic men were shot dead by the army in Derry, focused nationalist hatred of what was increasingly seen as an aggressive occupying force; and recruitment to the Provisionals spiralled. 'Bloody Sunday' also set in motion an official review of security operations in Northern Ireland, which brought the Unionist government into conflict with Westminster and which led ultimately to the prorogation of, for republicans, the hated Stormont regime.

As Northern Ireland came close to anarchy in the early 1970s, the numbers of British soldiers were dramatically increased: the garrison in 1969 and before had been 2,000, but by July 1972 there were some 21,000 troops in the province. In the later 1970s the government pursued a policy of 'Ulsterization' through which the RUC (and the local UDR) were given a primacy in the policing of Northern Ireland: this helped to bring a simultaneous expansion in the RUC and a reduction in the level of troop deployment. Periods of crisis brought military reinforcement: the unrest surrounding the two loyalist strikes (in 1974 and 1977) and in the aftermath of the Anglo-Irish Agreement necessitated the strengthening of the garrison. Periods of crisis also tended to bring the deployment of the army's special forces, and primarily the Special Air Service (SAS): the SAS were introduced into Northern

Ireland in 1976 after an intensification of the Provisionals' campaign in the border area. An upsurge in violence in the later 1980s brought further and controversial SAS action: in May 1987 at Loughgall, County Armagh, SAS soldiers killed eight PIRA volunteers during a raid on a police barracks; and in March 1988 in Gibraltar they shot dead three Provisionals who were allegedly on reconnaissance duty.

The discussion has focused thus far on the military protagonists of the 'Long War': some mention has also been made of those political parties and leaders who have had strong links with the armed struggle against British imperialism or, alternatively, 'pan-nationalism'. One of the central political themes of the period has been the gradual integration of each of these armed forces, or rather their political representatives, within the political process, whether as active players (in the case of Sinn Féin, the Progressive Unionists and the Ulster Democratic Party), or items on a reform agenda (the RUC). As has been observed, Sinn Féin made energetic moves at the time of the hunger strikes to harness popular nationalist anger to their own electoral strategy; equally, there were some signs of serious political thought and re-direction in the UDA in 1986–7. On the other hand, the persistent failure of the main constitutional parties – the SDLP, the DUP and the Ulster Unionists – to reach an accommodation among themselves was driving the British government first towards side-stepping these cussed 'moderates' (during the run-up to the Anglo-Irish Agreement), and later – after 1992 – towards broadening the forum for debate to include the paramilitaries. This was clearly a politically adventurous hike; but, setting aside the difficulties of principle and emotion, it was logical in so far as the constitutionalists in the Unionist and nationalist movements had always been fearful of being out-manoeuvred by the militants, and had therefore often taken up highly defensive positions. And it was also the case that there were signs of rational, even innovative, political thought among the hardliners which were not always evident within the constitutional mainstream. Nevertheless, it would be a mistake to exaggerate the importance of the militants at the expense of the constitutionalists, without whom no lasting settlement would have been conceivable. And it is therefore on the main constitutional parties and their leaders that the final focus of this chapter rests.

John Hume was leader of the SDLP between 1979 and 2001 and has been widely regarded as one of the main shapers of the political agenda in Northern Ireland from the early 1970s. He has also helped to sustain the constitutional nationalist tradition in the North at a time when, beset by the pressures supplied by the PIRA and sometimes by the Unionists and the British, the SDLP might well have followed Redmondism into political oblivion. Indeed, it is hard to escape the impression that the shadow of the general election of 1918 has fallen heavily on the SDLP; and it is easy to imagine that the fate of the Irish Parliamentary Party has been emblazoned on the walls of the party like a scriptural text warning of the judgement that befalls the sinful. Both Hume and Redmond were strict constitutionalists who, in a broader interest, sometimes had to negotiate with the militants. Both had a vision which transcended their respective parties: Redmond saw a Home Rule Ireland as proudly taking its place within the British Empire, while Hume has seen Northern Ireland within the broader context of a Europe of the regions. Both men achieved a personal international celebrity and dignity, which aided their respective causes. Both were able to draw upon their individual circumstances to look in a friendly fashion towards Unionists. But beyond this point the comparisons cease to work. Redmond was the quintessential Irish parliamentarian who, despite his Parnellite ancestry, was left behind by the swift radicalization of Irish popular politics. Some, at least, of his affinities lay with the Big House; and he was essentially conservative in his outlook. Hume, on the other hand, has been fundamentally in tune with the drift of popular nationalist politics and he has frequently taken decisions on this account which, in the light of his consensual instincts, have alienated or surprised not just Unionists but also more friendly observers in Dublin. Highly energetic, he has hustled on behalf of Derry and the wider northern economy in Europe and North America. A parliamentarian, he has never been content at Westminster; and though enthusiastic about the European parliament, he has never allowed Strasbourg to divert him from his essentially local preoccupations. Moreover Hume, though he has focused almost exclusively on winning a particular form of constitutional settlement, is generally thought to be leftist in his wider orientation. His roots remain with his people in the Bogside of Derry.

The pre-history of Hume's party has been outlined in an earlier chapter. The origins of the party were as a non-sectarian, left-of-centre body, which combined a consensual nationalism with a wide variety of progressive social policies: the party, and indeed Hume's individual prominence, owed much to the successful mobilization of the civil rights campaign in the late 1960s. Critics – notably Gerry Fitt, the first leader of the party – argued that the SDLP soon moved away from its socialist ideals towards a more conventionally nationalist stance (and indeed, Fitt resigned from the leadership in 1979 holding to this conviction). Although Hume and others have rejected the Fitt critique and are irked by the 'mainly Catholic' label frequently applied by journalists to the party, it is clear that the SDLP has relied almost exclusively upon Catholic and nationalist votes. However, while individual SDLP leaders have subscribed to the ideal of a unitary state, the party as a whole has frequently declared against an immediate British withdrawal from Northern Ireland, on the pragmatic grounds that anarchy might well ensue: the party's conference of 1978 did, however, accept that an eventual British withdrawal was 'desirable and inevitable'.[34] Setting aside such aspirations, the immediate goal of the party over many years has been a constitution distinguished by a power-sharing administration and by strong cross-border institutions where nationalist ideals and practical concerns would be guaranteed by the influence of the Irish government.

There have been some variations in this formula. In 1972, with the imposition of direct rule, the party called for a form of joint British–Irish authority in Northern Ireland and a timetable for reunification. It was a major participant in the Sunningdale Agreement (December 1973), which offered a power-sharing executive and a Council of Ireland; and its members held four seats in the new government (where Fitt was Deputy Chief Executive, and where Hume had responsibility for Commerce). But the collapse of the Executive in May 1974 at the hands of the Ulster Workers' Council was a major blow to the party's morale; and in the later 1970s, in the face of integrationist pressures from London, it became more assertively and defensively nationalist. The PIRA (and INLA) hunger strikes in 1981, and the concomitant surge in support for Sinn Féin, threatened to overturn the SDLP's command of northern Catholic opinion; and in this context it acquired a strengthened leverage in Dublin and, indirectly, in London. The New Ireland Forum (May 1983–May 1984), a broadly based constitutional nationalist conference, reflected Hume's desire for an agreed nationalist agenda (even if the direction of the Forum, and its report, owed much to the dexterous management of Garret FitzGerald). One of the three political options blessed by the Forum was for joint authority in Northern Ireland (a resurrection of the SDLP's stand in 1972); and it was this which provided both a focus for FitzGerald's diplomacy with the British and, indeed, in the opinion of Bew, Patterson and Teague, the intellectual rationale for the deal eventually struck between the two governments (the Anglo-Irish Agreement, or AIA, of November 1985).[35] The Agreement created a permanent Intergovernmental Conference wherein Irish ministers could contribute their views on the administration of Northern Ireland: there was, in addition, a secretariat for the Conference, based at Maryfield, near Belfast. The impact of the Agreement on Unionists will be considered shortly; but for the SDLP it was a godsend, in so far as it helped to cap Sinn Féin's electoral support and because it was in some ways a 'greener' interim settlement than had been previously thought possible: it offered a strong Irish dimension in the administration of Northern Ireland, without a counterbalancing Unionist-dominated executive and assembly. As Feargal Cochrane has observed, the SDLP clung in the late 1980s to the Agreement 'as a "banker" position which was unlikely to be improved through talks with a moribund unionist leadership'.[36]

It was not intended that the AIA should create a static mechanism, still less a permanent settlement. However, it bolstered Hume and the SDLP and encouraged a 'maximalist' thrust, which came to a head in the party's proposal of June 1992 when it argued that the government of Northern Ireland should be vested in a six-member commission (three of whom would be elected locally by proportional representation, with the other three being appointed by the British and Irish governments and the European Union): the new commission would be supported by a North–South council of ministers. This striking proposal reflected the SDLP's confidence in the 'banker' position supplied by the AIA: it also reflected the relative weakness of the party's opponents, the Unionists; and it embodied Hume's vision of a Northern Ireland subsumed within the European Union. But of course it also represented a hardening of the party's position, since in the past it had argued that an all-Ireland council would be accompanied by a purely northern executive, which even allowing for power-sharing and proportional representation would contain a preponderant Unionist element. The idea found little favour in London, or indeed in Dublin: it was also sharply rejected by Unionists, who were beginning slowly to regroup after years of division and marginalization, and by militant loyalists, who were asserting themselves through a bloody offensive in 1992–3. Still, a reconsideration of the initiative sheds some intriguing light on the ambitious strategic thinking of Hume and the SDLP in the early 1990s.

An ultimately more important thrust in these years came with the dialogue between Hume and Gerry Adams, and later between other members of their respective parties. This began, at any rate in a serious and intensive fashion, in 1988, and was resumed in 1993, in the aftermath of the failure of the Mayhew talks process. This initiative (which was fraught with difficulty for Hume, not least as a result of anger within elements of his own party) was again linked to his analysis of the impact of the AIA: it rested on his belief that the British were moving towards a position of neutrality on the northern question, and that the Unionists were now crippled by internal division and recrimination. Republican violence was mounting in the late 1980s; but it was also clear that Adams and Sinn Féin were increasingly interested in the possibility of a political strategy. The Hume–Adams détente culminated in a joint statement in April 1993: later, in October, Hume handed to Albert Reynolds and Dick Spring an agreed document which evidently proposed that the British should become 'persuaders for unity'. But the significance of the Hume–Adams dialogue lay perhaps less with its immediate and tangible results than with its indirect impact. It helped to bring Adams and Sinn Féin into the political process, and thus to prepare the way for the PIRA ceasefire in August 1994. It also stimulated the British and Irish governments into action, for, though both were dissatisfied

Plate 20   John Hume and David Trimble with Bono from U2, Belfast, May 1998.
Source: Popperfoto/Reuters.

with the October document, it seems clear that the influential Downing Street Declaration of December 1993 owed something to the earlier initiative. In this way the Hume–Adams process, though highly skewed, can be seen as one of the points of origin for the Good Friday Agreement of April 1998. It may well be the case that the Hume–Adams declaration will come to have a significance within the history of Irish nationalism, and indeed the wider history of Ireland, no less conspicuous than the New Departure of 1879.[37]

Hume's deputy, Séamus Mallon, once quipped that the Good Friday Agreement amounts to 'Sunningdale for slow learners'. From this perspective, the slowest of the slow learners have been the Democratic Unionists and their leader between 1971 and 2008, Dr Ian Paisley (though Paisley would presumably argue that the learning curve that began with Sunningdale ascends towards a united Ireland). Some of Paisley's personal origins and political lineage have been traced in an earlier chapter, and need not be rehearsed at length once again: he appealed to an evangelical and popular Protestant constituency desperately afraid of Satan, Rome, Dublin, London and propertied Unionism (in roughly that order of priority). Garret FitzGerald has rightly observed that the hallmark of Unionist politics is fear; and this applies with particular force to the Paisleyite tradition where anger and bitter rhetoric reflect profound anxieties about ungodliness, the machinations of the Catholic Church, the wiles of Irish and British diplomats, and the weak-kneed trimming of secularized Unionists.[38] The potency of Paisley's personal appeal is undisputed and remains – after virtually 40 years – astonishingly consistent. He regularly topped the poll at the elections for the European parliament held in the Northern Ireland constituency: in the contests of 1994 and 1999 Hume and he ran a close race for the prime position, but Hume was twice beaten into second place (albeit by a margin of only 0.3 per cent of the poll). Frequently results like this have constituted a thorn in the flesh of official Unionism, whose leaders have been either genially punctured by the Big Man, or (sometimes) whipped off the political stage. The basic electoral problem of the party for long remained, however, its inability to permanently transcend the Ulster Unionists: the style of the party was presidential, and prominent and charismatic figures polled well, but only once before 2005 (in the 1981 council elections) was the whole party able to outpace its main Unionist rival. This meant that Paisley and the DUP were able to function as thought police within the Unionist family; but it also meant that they were only able belatedly to achieve command of Unionism, and of Northern Ireland. Put another way, Paisley and the DUP had sufficient strength to wreck the ambitions of their rivals, but for years were not strong enough to impose their own vision within the North. Partly on this basis, and also because of his uncompromisingly localist agenda, some critics of Paisley (Enoch Powell, David Trimble, David Ervine) have seen him as one of the most formidable enemies of the wider Unionist cause.

The core policy of the DUP is support for the Union: at the time of its foundation in 1971, one of its leaders insisted that the party would be 'right wing in the sense of being strong on the Constitution, but to the left on social policies'.[39] The party has shown some progressive tendencies on some social issues, but equally its fierce evangelical Protestant ethos has shone through on questions such as abortion or reform of the law relating to homosexuality (the party launched its memorable 'Save Ulster from Sodomy' campaign in 1982, at a time of belated legal reform). The party has been strongly against the European Union, where Paisley saw the hand of the Vatican at work: as has been noted, this has not prevented him consistently topping the poll in local elections for the Strasbourg parliament. The party was also strongly opposed to formal political connections between Northern Ireland and the Republic, seeing these as merely unification by increments.

The Unionist principles of the party have never been in doubt, though the proposed application of this Unionism has changed somewhat over the years. In 1971–2 Paisley seemed to take up an integrationist stand, and happily predicted the toppling of the Stormont government. Later experiments with devolved government have also caused problems for Paisley and the DUP, even though they eventually accommodated themselves to the principle of devolution. He and his party were strongly opposed to the Sunningdale Agreement (December 1973), and to the power-sharing Executive: this stand was based on an abhorrence for the Council of Ireland idea, as well as for the prescriptive power-sharing arrangement. He was the predominant figure within the Unionist coalition (the United Ulster Unionist Council), which was formed in January 1974 to campaign against Sunningdale; and he was an active supporter of the Ulster Workers' Council strike which brought down the Executive in May 1974. The creation of the British–Irish Intergovernmental Council through the Anglo-Irish Agreement of November 1985 was also an anathema to Paisley; and he overshadowed the determinedly unflamboyant Ulster Unionist leader, James Molyneaux, in the united loyalist campaign to topple the Agreement. The ultimate collapse of this campaign (David Trimble has talked about tactical successes but a strategic failure) seems to have brought some electoral damage to Paisley.[40] And this political pressure, combined with growing tensions between the DUP and their temporary allies, the Ulster Unionists, led to a markedly more bitter rejection of the Downing Street Declaration (December 1993) than that offered by Molyneaux. Though both parties shared a hostility to the Framework Documents (January 1995), Paisley and the DUP were recognizably more emphatic than the modulated negativism of the Ulster Unionists. Paisley's boycott of the talks of 1997–8 which produced the Good Friday Agreement was based on his unwillingness to negotiate with Sinn Féin; and his rejection of the Agreement recalled the DUP approach to Sunningdale in so far as cross-border institutions remained a central problem. But the contentiousness of the Agreement, for Paisley, stretched beyond that of Sunningdale in that it broached the issue of prisoner releases and a Sinn Féin presence in government. The Good Friday deal was thus, for Paisley, not so much 'Sunningdale for slow learners' as a completely different and altogether more fraught curriculum.

Teaching this curriculum to loyalists in 1998 was the crisply Gradgrindian David Trimble, leader of the Ulster Unionists. The political legacy which Trimble inherited in 1995 from his predecessor, James Molyneaux, was unenviable – a party racked by division, by distrust of its perceived allies and demoralization. Memories of the party's travail in the early 1970s remained all too alive and resonant in the later 1990s. The legacy of the AIA and of the failed united loyalist campaign of opposition (1985–8) was one of broken Unionist confidence and internal recrimination. Long-term trends within the political and social structure of Northern Ireland, and of the island as a whole, tended to reinforce this pervasive sense of doom.

The Ulster Unionists had traditionally been not only the biggest party within Northern Ireland, but also the power-wielders within the provincial government and parliament at Stormont. The stand of the party in the Home Rule era, at any rate until 1913, had been integrationist: it had supported the idea of the constitutional union between Britain and Ireland unsullied by any partitionist notions, still less by the idea of a parliament for Unionist Ulster. The party's acceptance of the Government of Ireland Act (1920) brought some philosophical readjustments; and the practice of uninterrupted power within Northern Ireland between 1920 and 1972 turned its integrationists into devolutionists. There were thus two utterly different, and venerable, strains of thought on the party's fundamental concern: the nature of the relationship with Britain. There was, in addition, a wealth of social and cultural diversity among the Ulster Unionists, despite the common, but overly simplistic, view of the party as a monolith: as Feargal Cochrane has quipped, 'far from singing from the same hymn sheet, many [Unionists] do not actually believe in the same God'.[41]

Stormont came to matter to the Ulster Unionists not because it exercised wide powers (for it did not possess wide powers in many key areas), but because it provided excessive ministerial and senatorial dignity and a very considerable influence over all forms of local patronage. Stormont was an ego-trip for Unionists; and it bolstered a self-confident and highly provincial political culture. The removal of Stormont in 1972 damaged this self-regarding Unionist provincialism and flagged the beginning of the party's retreat from its local ascendancy. But this period (between 1972 and 1974) was more broadly decisive in forging Unionist beliefs and strategies. The summary removal of the Stormont parliament by Edward Heath's Conservative government after a dispute with Faulkner over security strategy underlined the vulnerability of Unionists to the whims of British policy: and it underlined the capacity for 'treachery' even from the traditional Tory allies of the Unionists at Westminster. Faulkner attempted to relaunch a devolved government in Northern Ireland through a deal struck at Stormont in November 1973 between the local parties and through the Sunningdale agreement of December 1973 (which applied a cross-border dimension to the internal arrangements); but this was rejected by his own party in January 1974, and later by Unionist workers and paramilitaries, whose combined action in May 1974 served to topple the experiment. Faulkner tried to rally his supporters through creating the Unionist Party of Northern Ireland (or UPNI) in September 1974; but in essence his political influence had been abruptly terminated and his formal retirement from politics (at the age of only 55) followed swiftly in 1976. His political scalp was claimed by Paisley, the most vocal of his opponents; and like other trophies of war it has served as a warning – in this case to those Unionist leaders who have been tempted to stray from the paths of orthodoxy.

Faulkner has been compared to Trimble.[42] There is some interest in the comparison, although it serves to highlight as many contrasts between the two men and their positions as it does similarities. The similarities, of course, are striking: both men sought to tie their party to a deal which provided a devolved government with a power-sharing arrangement and with a cross-border dimension. Both have been intellectually impressive performers, in terms of expounding and defending their political and strategic vision. Both men were rooted in the right wing of the party and moved swiftly towards more pragmatic positions. Both men faced opposition from within the ranks of their own party, as well as from other forms of hardline Unionism: both have been hate-figures for Ian Paisley. But in some ways Faulkner faced a more striking challenge than that encountered by Trimble (though it would of course be foolish to underestimate the latter's difficulties). Faulkner had the task of selling an institutionalized power-sharing arrangement as well as intricate cross-border bodies to a party which had only just – scarcely two years earlier – recovered from the surrender of its local parliament. Moreover, this hustling was taking place against the backdrop of intense paramilitary violence. And Faulkner was given little outside aid in terms of selling the deal to his followers: on the contrary, despite his warm personal relationship with Liam Cosgrave, events in the Republic served to undermine his sales pitch rather than the reverse. It is hard to imagine who, if anyone, in contemporary British politics could have profitably come to Faulkner's aid in early 1974.

The second crucial formative influence on the Ulster Unionist Party was the Anglo-Irish Agreement (1985). Some of the background to this measure has already been highlighted in an earlier chapter, but the Ulster Unionist dimension remains in the shade. The collapse of the Sunningdale settlement in May 1974 gave a temporary boost to militant, majoritarian Unionism, but in a sense this was disastrous for the Unionist tradition, and indeed for the wider Irish political arena. For the Ulster Unionist Party had been taught that popular loyalist mobilization could serve as a substitute for difficult or dangerous concessions; and its leaders had been taught that the articulation of a simple Unionist faith was an easier and – in the short term – a more popular strategy than complicated and potentially disastrous cross-party dialogue. Out of the wreckage of Sunningdale sprang a number of unhelpful consequences: the 'greening' of the SDLP and an upsurge in paramilitary violence (in 1975–6). But perhaps the chief of these was an Ulster Unionist Party characterized by a political minimalism (or, alternatively, 'masterly inactivity'), as well as by a tendency towards sporadic all-out gambles on the strength of popular loyalist protest.[43] Ulster Unionism shifted towards a low-key integrationist stand, and particularly under the leadership of James Molyneaux (1979–95). The poverty of this erratic minimalism was exposed in the run-up to the AIA, when the Ulster Unionists (who had relied on their access to the decision-makers at Westminster) were utterly disoriented by the rapid evolution of British policy: the Unionists seem to have been deliberately kept in the dark, but it was certainly also the case (as Trimble later conceded) that they 'did not work hard enough, and did not have their finger on the pulse of the British government to an adequate extent'.[44]

The interpretation which the Ulster Unionists placed on the AIA was, at least in the short term, the least challenging of those available: the Agreement was the latest exemplar of British treachery in a tradition which dated back beyond 1972 to the attempts at a sell-out in 1940 and 1921. Their response to the Agreement also followed a familiar and undemanding logic: the Unionist parties joined, as they had done in 1974 (or indeed at the time of the third Home Rule Bill), to organize days of action and coordinated election campaigns. A mass demonstration at Belfast City Hall on 23 November 1985 recalled the Ulster Day protest at the same location in September 1912. The Unionists forced a series of by-elections in Northern Ireland in January 1986 and fought on a united rejectionist platform (just as they had fought two general elections in 1974 in opposition to Sunningdale). A variant strain of protest was developed in the local councils, where the Unionists sought to create disruption through a strategy of adjournment. But the campaign against the AIA, though fought according to successful earlier formulae, was – from the perspective of its leaders – a disaster which had profound repercussions. The impressive day of protest in November 1985 led nowhere: the by-elections were characterized by an element of farce and brought the loss of a seat in Newry and Armagh to the SDLP. The local council adjournment tactic was characterized from the start by confusion and division. Street protests were dealt with efficiently by the RUC, and soon faded away (although for a time police families living in loyalist areas became the victims of intimidation and violence). The campaign as a whole rapidly lost momentum; and by 1988 it had stalled. Firmness from the Thatcher government, and from the police, provide part of the explanation for the failure. But it was also the case that the demonstrators lacked any clear target (beyond the drab and well-guarded offices of the Anglo-Irish secretariat at Maryfield, County Down); and their Ulster Unionist and Democratic Unionist leaders were soon bitterly divided over strategy. Molyneaux was predictably much more cautious and much more pacific in his leanings than some of the Democratic Unionists (though even Paisley had become renowned – as the 'Grand Old Duke of York' – for ineffectual posturing).[45] But the Ulster Unionist leader also lacked a radical alternative vision to the AIA; and, given that the Agreement offered so little tangible focus for its opponents, the absence of an attractive substitute was possibly of disproportionate significance in the campaign's ultimate collapse.

Molyneaux clung to his integrationist Unionism, a strategy which suited the quietists among the Protestant middle classes but which offered little appeal to the DUP and popular loyalism, and still less – needless to say – to the SDLP (some of whom, led by Hume, turned to Gerry Adams and Sinn Féin in 1988). Unionists for long stuck cussedly to the principle that the AIA would have to be suspended before they would engage in further debate: predictably, this masochistic stand was at last set aside in order to permit 'talks about talks' in early 1990. But the problem was not simply that Molyneaux lacked 'the vision thing', or that Unionists had once again backed themselves into a tactical dead-end in order to demonstrate the intensity of their convictions. It was also the case that the AIA had reinforced the ambitions of Hume and the SDLP, and that some limited Ulster Unionist movement went unrewarded (Ulster Unionists defied loyalist convention by journeying to Dublin to debate with Irish ministers during the course of the Brooke–Mayhew talks in 1992; and on 9 November 1992 they delivered a discussion document containing some progressive suggestions). But the Brooke–Mayhew initiative failed to bring the constitutional parties together in agreement, and the dialogue between Hume and Sinn Féin was resumed in 1993 to explore the possibilities for progress which had evidently been lacking in the broad middle-ground of northern politics. As has been chronicled, the Hume–Adams process led indirectly to a re-energized British–Irish détente, expressed in the Downing Street Declaration (November 1993) and the Framework Documents (February 1995). The political configuration bore, for some Ulster Unionists, some resemblance to the early and mid-1980s, when an Irish-driven initiative had marginalized Unionists and produced a green-tinged document. Molyneaux, his minimalist style and integrationist convictions had managed to survive the humiliation of 1985: all three were jettisoned in the aftermath of the Framework Documents. In September 1995 the Ulster Unionists acquired as their leader David Trimble, a choleric and energetic devolutionist.

It is too early to offer lapidary judgements on Trimble's vision, still less of his political achievement (after 2007 he left Ulster Unionism, and reinvented himself as a Conservative peer). However, it seems fair (on the basis of the available evidence) to argue that, much more directly than his predecessors, he tried to address the causes and symptoms of decline within his own party and within the wider movement. In terms of political strategy, it seems that, bucking Unionist tradition, he was prepared to make careful judgements on the fundamental requirements of his party, and then to haggle and trade over non-essentials. Trimble was a pragmatist who was not afraid of Faustian deals: his Unionist opponents, on the other hand, were conviction politicians who preserved their consciences at the expense of their political standing, and who perhaps misread the 'not an inch' traditions of their own movement.

It seems that the legacy of 1972 and of 1985 – of the suspension of Stormont and of the AIA – weighed heavily: Trimble was keen to recognize that in the past Unionist tardiness and negativism had led inexorably towards marginalization and humiliation. Thus in June 1996, when a multi-party talks process once again staggered into life, he accepted as chairperson George Mitchell, a former United States senator and majority leader who happened to have Irish Catholic family connections: other Unionist party leaders were appalled, but Trimble made a judgement on the basis of Mitchell's professionalism. In 1997, when the talks were relaunched and when Sinn Féin was admitted for the first time, Trimble's Ulster Unionists together with the representatives of the loyalist paramilitaries dithered, but eventually joined the process (this despite the comparatively recent restoration of the Provisionals' ceasefire). Again, other Unionist leaders offered a more traditional response, boycotting the new and (as it transpired) crucial round of negotiations.

The broken self-confidence of his community was a recurrent theme in Trimble's interviews; and it seems that much of his work was directed towards empowering Unionists through a restored local assembly and executive. These local institutions re-emerged as a central component of the Good Friday Agreement of April 1998: a 108-strong legislative assembly, together with a ministerial council. The import-ance of what the Ulster Unionists saw as British identity in Ireland was further enhanced through the creation of a British–Irish council. There was, of course, a price to be paid for these trophies. A significant cross-border dimension was con-tained within the Agreement, focusing on a North–South ministerial council: this echoed the proposals of the Sunningdale deal (although in fact Sunningdale also called for an all-Ireland Consultative Assembly, whereas the Good Friday Agreement only alluded to the future possibility of such a body). More painful, but essential to hardline republicans and loyalists, was the call for the accelerated release of pris-oners belonging to paramilitary bodies on ceasefire. Brian Faulkner never had to sell the issue of prisoner releases to suburban Unionism, and yet still failed. But Faulkner did not benefit from a prolonged paramilitary ceasefire, and he was ham-pered rather than supported by British and Irish ministers. Trimble, on the other hand, was assisted by the sensitive attitudes of Irish ministers, and in particular by the likeable Bertie Ahern; and he benefited from the super-charge of charisma supplied by Tony Blair and Bill Clinton. Whether this political arsenal was enough to bolster Unionist confidence and stave off the defeat inflicted on Faulkner for long remained unclear; but Paisley, the scourge of trimmers, and as enthusiastic an opponent of heresy as any Jesuit inquisitor, certainly promised to deliver to his followers 'the death of Trimbleism' and nothing less than the 'hide' of Tony Blair.

In 1997 Feargal Cochrane suggested that 'where David Trimble can lead the Unionist community rather than where he can follow them will be his ultimate test as leader of the Ulster Unionist party'.[46] By the summer of 1998 Trimble had (just about) passed the initial tests of his leadership – the referendum on the Agreement and the elections to the new Assembly: he had skilfully masked decisive leadership with the traditional rhetoric (and sometimes the traditional gestures) of his movement. However, the Good Friday venture proved to be not merely the ultimate test of Trimble's leadership, but also – given the recent history of decline and demoralization – the ultimate test of his people. Paul Bew said provocatively of the Agreement that 'the Unionists have won – they just don't know it'.[47] If this was in any way true, then it should have been remembered that Ulster Unionism was always capable of plucking defeat from the jaws of victory.

Ireland in the New Millennium

Paisley praises Sinn Féin over power sharing.
Headline, *Belfast Telegraph,*
19 November 2009

9.1   The Republic, 1998–2008

In 1999 the Irish GNP was growing at 8.5 per cent per year. By July 2000 unemployment had fallen to 4.4 per cent (having stood at 17 per cent in the mid-1980s). Irish per capita GDP had now, in a well-publicized epiphany bristling with post-colonial significance, overtaken that of its neighbour, and the former governing power, the United Kingdom.

Much scholarly ink has been expended upon understanding and explaining this bewilderingly rapid turn-about. As a starting point it should be observed that, since American investment was disproportionately significant, various long-standing factors such as the cultural affinity between the two countries, and Ireland's anglophone workforce, have to be acknowledged. The consolidation of educational standards since the 1960s, when free secondary-level schooling and university expansion were forwarded by Donough O'Malley and others, is also relevant (though it would be wrong to overlook the country's continuing relatively poor showing in the European league table of literacy attainment). And, as always in modern Ireland, there were the two rival gravitational pulls of (in a binary popularized by the PD politician, Mary Harney) 'Boston and Berlin', or – in the rival formulation of R.F. Foster – Pittsburgh and Paris.[1] Of course an essential part of Ireland's success lay in the fact that it was neither 'Boston' nor 'Berlin', but rather (in some ways much more than Britain) a conduit between the two: or, putting it another way, the Celtic Tiger was Janus-faced, looking both to North America and to continental

Europe. As was noted earlier in the book, Ireland's membership of the EEC, achieved in 1973, but fought for since at least 1961, allied with its accession to the European Monetary System in 1979, brought a range of benefits for external investors, particularly Americans, including an increasingly unified European market place, an exchange rate mechanism (or ERM), and (at least in principle) relatively stable exchange rates. Membership of the EEC (later European Community and later still European Union) also brought access to the riches of the European funds for structural and regional development. But, while European Union sponsorship of this kind was certainly relevant to this economic acceleration, the Single Market was probably still more important.

However, Ireland's membership of the EU, and its cultural and political affinities with both continental Europe and North America, were not enough in themselves to explain the exponential growth of the 1990s and the new millennium. Though (inevitably) there has been some scholarly debate on the issue, it seems fair to acknowledge the role of the IDA in offering grants, tax breaks and in identifying corporate winners – such as Intel, IBM, Dell, Kodak, Hewlett-Packard, Microsoft and so forth. The notion of a meaningful 'social partnership' is also relevant, while heavily contested, and particularly by scholars of the left; but at the very least relatively quiescent industrial relations may be seen as playing a role in the 'Tiger' economy of the nineties and the new millennium.[2]

However, it has been rightly said that 'the more euphoric accounts of the Republic's economic miracle need to be deflated'.[3] For example GDP in Ireland was markedly greater than GNP because of the strength of foreign – particularly American – investments, and because foreign companies allocated their profits within Ireland to take advantage of low rates of corporation tax: around one quarter of Ireland's GDP in 2000 arose from the profits of foreign-owned businesses in Ireland.[4] Tranquil industrial relations may have reflected not only the efforts at social partnership within Ireland, but also a society where (in the 1980s and after) trade union membership was falling rapidly, a retreat associated at first with relative poverty and unemployment, but also later with the vigorously union-free, or actively anti-union, policies of several of the new corporations investing in Ireland. But above all, aside from issues of causation, the economic growth of the era magnified the disparities within Irish society – creating an ever greater chasm between those trapped within the sink estates of outer Dublin, and those luxuriously embedded within the expensive property market of (in particular) the city's southern townships.

The global collapse in the value of information technology and other high-tech companies in 2000–1 – the bursting of the 'dot.com bubble' – hit Ireland with some force, given that much of the country's new employment and growth in the 1990s had been generated by businesses within this sector. The peak of the boom occurred in 2000, and thereafter the fall was precipitate: in 2000 the rate of growth of GNP stood at 9.5 per cent, where by 2001 the rate had fallen to 3.9 per cent. But predictions of the death of the Celtic Tiger were premature (Maurice O'Connell, the governor of the Central Bank affirmed in 2001 that 'the era of the Celtic Tiger is over'), insofar as GNP growth rates recovered somewhat, reaching 6.5 per cent in 2006.[5] A boom within the construction industry and house prices absorbed much of the temporary strain created by the 'dot.com bubble', and fuelled the ongoing economic consolidation which was a feature of the first seven years of the new millennium. Even in the sharpest year of the downturn – 2001–2 – unemployment did not exceed 4 per cent, and (viewing the period 2000–7) peaked at 4.6 per cent in 2003. House price inflation peaked at just below 30 per cent in 1998, and – setting aside 2001, the year of downturn (4.4 per cent) – did not fall below 8.6 per cent in the years before the abyss which opened up in 2007 and afterwards.

These, with the arguable exception of 2001–2, generally settled years of economic growth were associated with a sustained period of net immigration, a trend which effectively reversed the country's long-term condition as a net exporter of its people. The 1996 census, when the population of the Republic of Ireland was recorded as being 3,626,087, has been seen as one key starting point for assessing the rapid demographic developments of the 'Tiger' era: it documented a country which still bore the imprint of the economic turmoil of the 1980s, when labour markets were receding and emigration was spiralling – a country which was still ethnically homogeneous. By the time of the census of 2006, however, the population of the Republic had risen to 4,239,848: just under 420,000 people (or around 10 per cent of the total) were not Irish nationals. In the period between 1995 and 2004 an astonishing 486,300 people moved to Ireland, while 263,800 left the country, giving a net immigration of 222,500. In the period 2000–5 40 per cent of those settling in Ireland were return migrants, but it is clear that immigration in this era was not only about the inflow of Irish people, but also, indeed primarily, about the economic migration of other Europeans, and of asylum seekers from further afield (with the latter numbering around 10,000 a year in the early years of the new millennium). The wider implications of the 'new' Irish of the 'Tiger' era are still unclear, not least insofar as the economic growth which helped to sustain immigration had dramatically stalled by 2007–8. But certainly before then it appeared that the definitions of 'Irishness' which had held sway for much of the nineteenth and twentieth centuries – Catholic, Gaelic, emigrant, nobly impoverished – were beginning to falter. As the island began slowly to diversify in ethnic, cultural and religious terms, a case began to emerge for a 'hyphenated' Irishness, with Anglo-Irish perhaps now being complemented by Chinese-Irish, Nigerian-Irish, Polish-Irish, Romanian-Irish, along the lines of the rich variety of hyphenated American identities.[6]

Economic growth was also associated with political stability, with Fianna Fáil in coalition with the Progressive Democrats and (after the general election of 2007) the Greens. Bertie Ahern ('Drumcondra. That's where I'm from. And it's who I am.') was the dominant figure within Irish politics and government between his election as Taoiseach in 1997 and his resignation from office in 2008 – a record in office not seen since the prime ministerial reign of Éamon de Valera between 1932 and 1948.[7] Like Trimble in the North, Ahern was still a young man when he retired from office: as with Trimble, it is too early to offer lapidary assessments of Ahern's years in office. His critics (who have naturally grown in number since the Irish economy went into freefall in 2008–9) allege that it was simply his dumb luck to

Plate 21 Bertie Ahern, Taoiseach of Ireland (1997–2008).
Source: © Niall Carson/PA Wire.

have been in office while the Celtic Tiger was still active and energetic. Some of these, such as the historian John A. Murphy, accuse him of having wasted the opportunities created by the spectacular growth in the Irish nation's prosperity: insufficient proportions of the wealth generated in the good times (it is said) were directed to the critical task of improving the country's economic infrastructure and welfare provision.[8] Still others suggest that Ahern's reputation for political shrewdness has been a misreading of an ingrained indecisiveness. His folksy and accessible style was in some ways an Irish version of President George W. Bush's performance in the United States: Ahern gave the world 'Bertiespeak' – a slippery and sometimes opaque mode of delivery and response (in haranguing his fellow Fianna Fáil parliamentarians in December 2003, he famously warned against party 'kebabs' [cabals])[9]. Above all, however, his opponents have pointed to the allegations of sleaze surrounding Fianna Fáil in the 1990s, and touching Ahern: in September 2007 he gave four days of sometimes convoluted and stumbling evidence to the Mahon Tribunal (the 'Tribunal of Enquiry into Certain Planning Matters and Payments'), where various disbursements made by Irish businessmen in the 1990s to both him and his party were pursued and dissected by counsel. Two further days of evidence were provided by Ahern to the Tribunal in December 2007. For all of the apparent consensuality and likeability, Ahern seemed inextricably linked to a Haugheyite world of signed blank cheques, clientilism and complicated and overly intimate connections with the nation's small community of rich businessmen.

There is, however, a case to be made for the defence, and Ahern himself (writing with the UCD historian, Richard Aldous) has begun the task.[10] Though there were certainly troughs of popularity (as with the local and European elections of 2004), Ahern led his party into government after three successive general election victories (in 1997, 2002 and 2007), the first national leader so to do since 1944. Aside from the broadly successful economic record (until the days of reckoning in 2008), the Ahern governments had much success in the realm of international relations. In October 2000 Ireland was elected to a seat on the Security Council of the United Nations. Again, while there were some wobbles in the Irish relationship with the European Union (as with the popular rejection of the Treaty of Nice in June 2001), these were overcome, and Ahern's leadership of Ireland's presidency of the European Commission in 2004 was a significant personal, and indeed national, achievement: a new draft European constitution was agreed, ten new member states were admitted to the Union, and there was an improvement in relations between the Union and the USA.[11] In general Ahern and his governments held the balance between two of the key centres of Irish diplomatic effort – Brussels and Washington – with some skill: America and Europe were the driving forces behind Irish economic growth, and Ahern acknowledged the significance of the former through (for example) flexing Irish neutrality by permitting the refuelling of American military aircraft at Shannon airport during the Iraq War. The third focus of Irish diplomacy involved London, and Northern Ireland, and here Ahern worked energetically towards the sequence of agreements – on Good Friday in 1998, and at St Andrews in 2006 – which were the bedrock upon which a settlement was shakily constructed. Tony Blair's advisor on Ireland, Jonathan Powell, whose memoir of the 'peace process' in Northern Ireland is at present the fullest record available, unequivocally saw Ahern as central to the success of the lengthy diplomatizing: 'there would have been no agreement in Northern Ireland if it had not been for his unadorned common sense'.[12] Ahern was also invaluable because 'he did not carry the complexes of the past . . . [and because] he was prepared to override his system by rejecting traditional Irish positions and to take political risks in order to achieve peace'.[13] Lest it be assumed, however, that personal and political relationships on the island were miraculously transformed at this time, or indeed that Ahern's affability was boundless, it is worth noting Powell's memory that, at one meeting, David Trimble 'came across as appallingly rude to Bertie, who came within an ace of hitting him'.[14]

Moreover, if one hallmark of a consummate politician is choosing the correct moment to depart, then Ahern's timing defined his strategic skill.[15] 'Bertie' left office in May 2008, with the Irish economy beginning to tremble, but not yet (at least demonstrably) to fall, and with his many other achievements, particularly over Northern Ireland and Europe, still strongly in place. It was his shrewd but luckless Minister of Finance, Brian Cowen, who inherited not only the swiftly unravelling mess of the Irish economy, in particular the receding property market, but also an increasingly problematic relationship with Europe, and the growing threat posed by dissident republicans to the institutions of government in Northern Ireland.

Where, then, did it all go wrong in 2008? Did it 'all' go wrong? Much of the crisis in the Ireland of 2008–9 arose from the simultaneous detonation of several complex historical legacies. The Report of the Commission to Inquire into Child Abuse, published in May 2009, sought to lance a long-term suppurating sore within Irish society: the Ryan Report (it was named after its author, Mr Justice Sean Ryan) chronicled at length the grim history of the physical, sexual and psychological abuse of large numbers of Irish children, and particularly within 60 industrial and reformatory schools run by Catholic orders under the supervision of the Department of Education.[16] There was much pain, not least at what were seen by the victims as sometimes inadequate official and Church responses; but of course the Report also effectively exposed a post-revolutionary consensus which largely accepted the authority of the Church and the preeminence of Catholic identity. The rejection by Irish voters of the Treaty of Lisbon in a referendum in June 2008 seems to have been stimulated not only by confusion over the contents of the measure, but also by concerns over the security of Irish autonomy and neutrality. A modified Treaty was accepted at a referendum in October 2009 by the voters, now persuaded that the greatest threat to Ireland, her history and values, lay in economic melt-down, and not in the European Union. The economic freefall of 2008–9 was (as Irish and British politicians repeatedly asserted) part of a global phenomenon; but the severity of its impact upon Ireland was widely acknowledged to rest partly with an overdependence on property markets, and with the historic Irish fetishization of landed property. The low-key dissident republican threat on the island, and particularly in the North, was a throwback to earlier theologies of nationalism and revolution, and occasionally (as in March 2009, with the killings of two British soldiers and an officer of the PSNI) exploded bloodily; but the relatively small scale of the threat (judged in the first decade of the new millennium) suggested that mainstream republicanism had indeed outgrown its earlier intellectual cladding. Superficially, then, Irish history was fighting back; but the evidence suggested that the new Ireland was still securely in place.

9.2 Northern Ireland, 1998–2008

In 1998 an historic agreement had been formulated, but Northern Ireland remained a cockpit for paramilitarism, both private and state, and still lacked any form of shared devolved government. Many of the most contentious issues within the North (policing, paramilitary disarmament) had either been postponed or left open-ended: each of the parties to the Agreement was painfully aware that, in the context of a military stalemate, the 'winners' of the Long War might be determined, at least in popular perception, through marginal gains or failures in the enactment of peace. Each of the (in the main, historically literate) parties to the Agreement was painfully aware of the opportunities and pitfalls created by the last great settlement between militant Irish separatism and the British state, the Treaty of December 1921.[17]

The Agreement inaugurated, therefore, not any period of easy executive harmony, but rather an interlude of staccato politics – swift bursts of ministerial cooperation, followed by breakdown and recrimination. Thus, from June 1998 until December 1999 the Unionist leader, David Trimble, refused to sanction any shared administration that included Sinn Féin until the issue of the IRA's arsenal was settled. In the autumn of 1999, with the intervention of Senator George Mitchell, Trimble finally agreed to support the formation of an executive, but only on the understanding that republicans committed themselves on the decommissioning issue by January 2000. The publication of the Patten report on policing in September 1999 complicated Trimble's position further, given the perceived assault on the RUC, a force which (though profoundly alien to republicans) had been strongly supported amongst the Protestant middle classes who formed the electoral backbone of the Ulster Unionists (Patten formed the basis for the Police [Northern Ireland] Act of 2000, which brought the renaming of the RUC as the Police Service of Northern Ireland). The Northern Ireland Executive was indeed launched in December 1999, an historic episode which (given the denouement) is easy to overlook; but in the absence of movement on decommissioning it survived for only two months, and (in February) was suspended by Peter Mandelson, the new Secretary of State for Northern Ireland. Some limited progress on the arms issue permitted the restoration of the Executive in May 2000; but, once this was achieved, the forward inching on arms stalled once again. Only in October 2001 (in the aftermath of 9/11 and of the arrests of Irish republicans in Colombia) did the actual process of decommissioning begin.

Away from the choreography of high politics, Protestant opinion was shuffling away from the Belfast Agreement, and from the Ulster Unionist Party, and rendering Trimble's position acutely vulnerable. One particularly ugly symbol of working-class Protestant 'alienation' (to use the euphemistic vocabulary applied at the time) was the blockading of a Catholic school, Holy Cross Primary, at a complex sectarian interface in North Belfast in 2001–2: images of harassed and frightened schoolchildren, broadcast globally, appeared to vindicate the most negative characterizations of Unionist political behaviour and of the sincerity of political reconciliation in Northern Ireland. The growing failure of Trimble's support meant, indeed, that when the devolved government was restored (yet again) in November 2001, it was only as a consequence of a makeshift constitutional expedient: three members of the Alliance Party and one member of the Women's Coalition in the Assembly redesignated themselves as 'unionist' in order to ensure the embattled Trimble's election as First Minister. The republican infiltration of Castlereagh PSNI station in March 2002, and allegations of a republican 'spy-ring' at Stormont, which came to a head with a PSNI raid on Sinn Féin's Assembly offices on 4 October 2002, further undermined Trimble's ability to address popular Unionist disquiet with the operation of the Agreement. Shortly afterwards, on 15 October, the executive and assembly were, in effect, prorogued for the duration.

The Castlereagh episode and the alleged Stormont spy ring simultaneously evoked the intelligence struggle of 1919–21, and underlined the vital role, for both sides in the 'Long War', of espionage: these were also years which began to see revelations concerning the use of intelligence in the 'Long War'. It was now argued, for example, that (in relation to the early stages of the Peace Process) 'only the impact of serious intelligence work' could explain the British willingness to gamble on the apparently exiguous evidence of republican flexibility at a time when the Provisionals' violence was worsening.[18] After the signing of the Agreement, some sense of the scale of this 'serious intelligence work' began to become hazily apparent. In 2003 Freddie 'Stakeknife' Scappaticci, who had served as an IRA enforcer, was exposed as a long-term British agent: in 2004 Denis Donaldson, a leading figure within Sinn Féin, was also unveiled as an informant to the security forces (and subsequently killed). Further allegations were made which implicated other senior figures within the republican movement. Numerous scholars have emphasized the continuing importance of British intelligence work; and it certainly seems to be the case that this work limited the IRA's offensive capacity, and thus indirectly strengthened the hands of those republican leaders who were moving towards positions of greater pragmatism than hitherto.

However, the direct pressure on republicans to move on the issue of decommissioning came, not as a result of British intelligence, still less from Trimble, but rather from a combination of international embarrassment and local threats to the Sinn Féin vote. The theft, by elements associated with the IRA, of £26 million from the headquarters of the Northern Bank in central Belfast in December 2004 was a major source of discomfiture within the leadership of Sinn Féin. Even more politically problematic (because it directly affected the foundations of the republican community) was the murder on 30 January, in Belfast, of a working-class Catholic, Robert McCartney, by a group which included IRA officers: McCartney's sisters, who had hitherto been supporters of Sinn Féin, were able to generate an international campaign of condemnation, which focused on the ongoing activities of the IRA, and which took the women to the White House on St Patrick's Day 2005, where they were guests of President Bush (Gerry Adams and Martin McGuinness were pointedly excluded from the guest list).[19] The United Kingdom general election of May 2005 provided some tepid comfort to the republican leadership, insofar as the Sinn Féin vote held up (at 24.3 per cent and five Westminster seats); but, equally, they had not delivered the much-desired knock-out blow to the SDLP, and (moreover) their constitutionalist rivals secured three seats, and thus retained a significant voice on Northern Irish matters in the House of Commons. The Northern Bank robbery, the McCartney murder, and (for the more chipper republicans) the lukewarm election results, helped to deliver what Blair and Trimble had not been able to achieve through argument or persuasion: a major advance on decommissioning. On 28 July 2005 the IRA announced (in the manner of the republicans of 1923) that the fighting should end, and that arms be 'dumped': unlike the republicans of the civil war era, volunteers were urged now to 'assist the development of purely political and democratic programmes through exclusively peaceful means'. By late September General John de Chastelain, Chair of the Independent International Commission on Decommissioning, was able to confirm that he, his staff and two independent witnesses, had observed the destruction of 'the totality of the arsenal of the IRA'. What had been intended to happen in 2000, only came now, in the autumn of 2005.

Why had it all taken so long? Two factors are worth stressing above others. Beneath the carefully disciplined, well rehearsed and politically sophisticated leadership of the republican movement existed a vigorous local or gangland culture which could be influenced but not always fully governed. Moreover, as has been said, the caution of republicans, indeed of all parties to the process, was rooted in historical memory, and in the need to sell not merely the communitarian but rather the sectional (indeed sectarian) gains offered by the Agreement. Whatever else the Agreement delivered, it could not be interpreted by any of the parties as defeat: whatever else it delivered, it could not be allowed to precipitate division.

By now, in 2005, Trimble's extensive political ingenuity and fair measure of luck were each exhausted. The May general election was a devastating failure for the Ulster Unionists, who retained only one MP – Sylvia Hermon in North Down: Trimble himself was defeated in his Upper Bann seat by the relatively unknown and inexperienced DUP politician, David Simpson. The election defeat effectively spelt the end for Trimble's leadership of the wider unionist project, which was now inherited by the DUP (a situation indeed anticipated in the polls in November 2003, when the DUP overtook the UUP for the first time in the elections for the Northern Ireland Assembly). The DUP now had to lead and advance the unionist cause, in the context of the Agreement and its institutions, having maintained a (more or less) unrelenting campaign of opposition to it and to its Lundyite perpetrators.

The motivations of the DUP in 2005–6 were complex. There can be no question of the depth of political and (sometimes) religious animosity which shaped the party's opposition to Sinn Féin and the wider republican movement. The traditional competition with the UUP had clearly become institutionalized, despite the similarity of interests and outlook of many of their respective supporters. Personal opposition to Trimble was also a factor for the DUP, insofar as (in the pungent assessment of Gerry Adams), 'he treats everyone like shite': the leaders of the party had condemned Trimble for dealing with 'Sinn Féin-IRA', and had repeatedly alleged that, in his subtle diplomatizing, Trimble had 'sold' Ulster. Well before 2005, however, there was some evidence that the DUP's opposition to the Agreement was becoming negotiable, at least at the margins.

Forward movement still presented some difficulties. The DUP had indeed an electoral mandate based upon the repudiation of the Agreement and its architects. But, beyond this, certainly before 2002–3, the party had little leverage over the British government, still less on those international parties (such as the Americans) interested in 'peace in Ireland'. In addition any forward movement was necessarily going to involve talking to those same 'terrorists', whom the DUP leadership had so consistently reviled and condemned. Against this, however, was some layering within the party's motivations. Some of the leadership were, or were thought to be, hungry for office, its rewards and trappings: the Irish Department of Foreign Affairs and the US State Department were excited by contact with the DUP from the summer of 2002, which suggested that the ostensibly flinty Paisleyites might be more malleable than hitherto thought.[20] Though there was a mixture of 'little Ulster' particularists and UK integrationists within the party, the latter were having to come to terms with the fact that new Secretary of State (from May 2005), Peter Hain, was – seemingly deliberately – seeking to define 'direct rule' in ever more unappetizing ways (over issues such as domestic rates, water charges and educational reform). In April 2006, in the prelude to the St Andrews Agreement, Tony Blair delivered a speech at Navan, County Armagh, where he alluded to the 'serious political issues facing people in Northern Ireland, like water charges and education reform, and decisions on these issues should be taken by Northern Ireland politicians, not by Westminster'.[21] Moreover, while the DUP had, at a high political level, blasted against cooperation with Sinn Féin, ostentatiously refusing to sit at the same cabinet table as Sinn Féin ministers for meetings of the Executive, and for long retaining their ban on shared media events, in reality matters were, or were becoming, more complex. The longstanding refusal of DUP spokespersons to sit in the same television studios as their Sinn Féin counterparts was quietly abandoned in 2005. But, as Christopher Farrington has underlined, the DUP had in fact worked for years with Sinn Féin and other republicans within the environment of local government. Close and wise observers of the DUP in 2005–6, therefore, saw a greater possibility of engagement between it and republicanism than was superficially apparent.[22]

In this respect, the personality of Ian Paisley is also worth revisiting. Although Paisley had been associated with vocal and belligerent stands on the constitutional (and other) questions, he had a well-established reputation for being mightier in his vocalizing than in action. Paisley's threatened paramilitarism at the time of the Anglo-Irish Agreement in 1985, and indeed his earlier leadership of unionism, had been characterized by a willingness to totter on the brink, without actually proceeding further. Paisley's age, ill health, and (paradoxically, perhaps) his religious convictions are also relevant to understanding the chemistry of the evolving rapport between the DUP and republicanism after 2005–6. He had been hospitalized in the summer of 2004, and had come near to death in August of that year: among other close observers, Jonathan Powell saw a change of attitude in the aftermath of this episode – 'all [Paisley's] negativism had switched to a driving desire to conclude the Northern Ireland question before he died'.[23] There can be little doubt, on the basis of the available evidence, that Paisley's otherwise surprising evolution after 2005 towards the St Andrews Agreement in 2006 has been rooted, at least in part, in issues of religious faith and spirituality. Religious faith underpinned the cautious mutual respect shared between Paisley and Bertie Ahern: 'I respected . . . his real Christian faith', recalled Ahern, a devout Catholic, 'religion always played a big part in our

Plate 22   Ian Paisley, First Minister of Northern Ireland, and Martin McGuinness, Deputy First Minister, as the 'Chuckle Brothers'.
Source: © Bebeto Matthews/AP/PA Photos.

discussions'.[24] His relationship with Tony Blair is of course, the classic expression of this shared religiosity: a critical aspect of the prelude to the St Andrews Agreement was the increasingly frequent private meetings between Blair and Paisley, some of which have been recorded by Powell: 'there would be lots of laughter from behind the closed door to the [prime ministerial] den, and when I went in I would often find little religious tracts left behind for Leo'.[25] In December 2006, in the aftermath of the Agreement, Blair 'called Paisley from the King David Hotel in Jerusalem, looking out at the Mount of Olives, and after a discussion of the biblical scene, . . . suggested some language Paisley could use to indicate that he was sympathetic to the Sinn Féin wish for a conditional timetable for the devolution of justice'.[26] Gladstone, with his interest in classical and biblical geography and landscape, and with his real sense of the role of Providence in the settlement of the British–Irish relationship, would have fully understood this kind of communication.[27]

It has been said that (in essence) the St Andrews Agreement, negotiated between the contending parties in October 2006, signalled the DUP's willingness to accept a shared government, and a willingness on the part of Sinn Féin to accept the police force and the criminal justice system. Gerry Adams and the Sinn Féin leadership were now impressed by the (increasingly attainable) prize of an executive shared with their most trenchant constitutional enemy of almost 40 years, Paisleyite Unionism, together with the devolution to Stormont (and thus to Irishmen and women) of powers over justice. For their part, the DUP scented power, and thought that they could sell the idea of a wholly reformed Agreement, together with republican acceptance of policing, to their core support. Each was bolstered by the Assembly elections of March 2007, which confirmed the ascendancy of the DUP and Sinn Féin within their respective communities: both the Ulster Unionists and the SDLP, once unassailable, were comprehensively defeated. On the basis of this crucial mandate, the leaderships of the DUP and Sinn Féin met (for the first time) on 26 March 2007; and from this came the first iconic image of Paisley and Adams in something approaching a cooperative mode (and facilitated by the use of a diamond- – as opposed to circular- or square- – shaped table, requisitioned for the delicate purpose by a bright spark within the NIO).[28] With the nomination, on 8 May, of Ian Paisley and Martin McGuinness as First and Deputy First Minister came the phenomenon of the 'Chuckle Brothers': images of the two former enemies laughing at each other's jokes became a more potent and persuasive symbol of the solidity of peace than the best and most expensive efforts of the spin doctors and advertising agencies.

Was peace solidly established? On 12 May 2007 Sinn Féin took its places on the Policing Board of Northern Ireland, the supervisory authority for the PSNI. Subsequently some progress was made towards the achievement of the devolution of policing and justice powers to Stormont: this had been agreed at St Andrews, but still remained only partly resolved in the autumn of 2009, when Gordon Brown, now British Prime Minister, was able to construct a relatively generous financial package to facilitate the process. When Ian Paisley retired, in the early summer of 2008, the succession, both to the leadership of the DUP and the office of First Minister, passed smoothly to his long-time lieutenant, Peter Robinson. Robinson, who was of the same 'Troubles' generation as Adams and McGuinness, had been MP for East Belfast since 1979, and Deputy Leader of the DUP from 1980: a machine politician, endowed with less charm and charisma than Paisley, he nevertheless established (at least by 2009) an intermittently effective partnership with McGuinness, who remained Deputy First Minister. It was said that the Chuckle Brothers had metamorphosed into the more familiar Brothers Grim; but, while Robinson and McGuinness's working relationship certainly lacked the personal warmth which seemed occasionally to suffuse that connecting the latter with Paisley, there could be no doubt of the potential strength of their bond in 2008–9. When an officer of the PSNI, together with two British soldiers, were killed by dissident republicans in March 2009, McGuinness and Robinson stood side-by-side before the world's press, united in their calls for communal solidarity and support for the police. It was a sombre occasion and a sombre image, even more telling as a symbol of change than the ministerial cavortings of the previous year.

It would be quite wrong, however, to overlook the difficulties. The Real IRA (who claimed responsibility for the soldiers' deaths) together with the Continuity IRA (who claimed that they had killed the policeman), were both break-away movements from the Provisionals, and retained the potential to recreate the bloodily familiar paramilitary strategies of the 1970s and 1980s. Within Unionism, the paramilitaries remained broadly quiescent, and in June 2009 the UVF finally decommissioned its weaponry; but a significant Unionist electoral challenge to the Agreements remained. This was mounted by Jim Allister, a prominent QC, who had left the DUP in March 2007, at the time of the party leadership's meeting with their counterparts in Sinn Féin: in June 2009 Allister, standing as the Traditional Unionist Voice candidate in the European elections, snatched over 13 per cent of the first preference votes, almost exactly the proportion by which the DUP vote had fallen from 2004. Such challenges were potentially given further force when, in January 2010, Robinson and his wife, Iris, became mired in a complex financial and sexual scandal arising from Iris's affair with the 19-year-old Kirk McCambley.

Plate 23   United in support for the PSNI: Robinson, Orde, McGuinness at Stormont, 10 March 2009.
Source: Arthur Allison/Pacemaker Press International.

There were thus some intractable military and electoral inheritances from the years of the Troubles. No less difficult were the spatial and historical legacies: the Brothers Grim had inherited (and indeed had helped to shape) a Northern Ireland at peace, but one where communities often remained physically separated according to religious affiliation, where Catholics and Protestants attended different churches, were educated in different schools, subscribed to different histories, even of the recent past, lived in different areas, and were buried in separate cemeteries.[29] The truly remarkable achievement of the years between the Good Friday and St Andrews Agreements was the relatively peaceful and equitable division of power within Northern Ireland. But it remained to be seen whether this would prefigure a mutually respectful sharing of the Province.

9.3   The End of Irish History?

At the beginning of this work it was suggested that the period from the 1790s through to the millennium represented a discrete phase in the history of Ireland. Some parallels between the end of the eighteenth century and the end of the twentieth century were outlined; and in particular the role of two great international crises – the French revolution and the collapse of the Soviet Union – on Irish affairs was addressed. But this comparison is charged with significance; and some of its implications have at last to be unravelled.

In 1989, against the backdrop of chaos in eastern Europe, Francis Fukuyama wrote of the end of history – the end of the great conflict between capitalism and communism, and the emergence of a settled order based on democratic government and the free market.[30] Fukuyama's confident predictions of the ultimate global triumph of the American way were quickly found to be wanting (the persistence of religious fundamentalism in the Middle East, the 'war on terror', the tenacity of communism in China, and Russia's problems with the free market were not part of his millenarian dream).[31] But the conviction persists in certain scholarly quarters that we are living in a post-historical age – an age when history is losing its former grand narratives and pre-eminent themes.

The late eighteenth century in Ireland, as in much of Europe, marked the end of one age and the beginning of another, with the spread of liberal progressive values, the consolidation of nationalism and the pursuit of the nation state. As in much of the rest of Europe, the late twentieth century and after has also been marked in Ireland by some radical social and political transformations. The collapse of the communist eastern bloc has precipitated a profound realignment in Europe as a whole, with the emergence of a powerful united Germany, the relative diminution of Great Britain (no longer a necessary ally of the United States in its apocalyptic struggle with Marxism), and the acceleration of the drive towards European unity. In some senses, the conventional themes of European history no longer apply with the same force: the confrontation between western and eastern blocs, the antagonism between France and Germany, Protestant and Catholic rivalries within states and between states. Churchill's iron curtain, once a grim but inescapable feature of the European outlook, has gone. Indeed, if (as seems possible) Turkey is eventually admitted to the European Union, then the curtain may be draped across the Middle East rather than from Lubeck to Trieste. European history may, indeed, have 'ended'.

This broader international upheaval has had profound consequences for Ireland and its immediate neighbours. The weakening of Britain's role within American strategy has created opportunities for both the Irish government and Irish Americans. It has also vindicated John Hume's strategy of cultivating external arbiters in order to create pressure on the British government and upon Ulster Unionism. The relatively rapid evolution of a settlement in Northern Ireland through the 1990s and after has owed much to the enhancement of Irish influence within American policy. The boost that has been given since 1989 to the European Union and to the movement for unity has also enhanced Ireland's international standing. For the European Union has helped to level out the political and economic differences between its members; and Ireland has not only profited from these processes but has also emerged as one of the most influential of the smaller nations, and as an energetic and persistent negotiating force.

Some of the dramatic changes in Ireland are traceable to particular momentous events within the international arena. Others are rooted in longer processes of change, dating back to the era of Lemass and beyond. The relaxation of traditional economic and cultural barriers in the 1960s, with the spread of television and other conduits for subversive ideas and approaches, marked a sea change in Irish life. Economic growth in the 1960s and in the 1990s brought relative prosperity and new opportunities. Startling initiatives in terms of the relationship with Britain and Northern Ireland marked the beginning of processes which were strengthened after 1973, when Ireland and Britain found themselves thrust together within the structures of the EEC.

The results of these many shifts and pressures were felt to the full only in the 1990s: the different lines of development bisected in this decade and produced some intriguing patterns and configurations. Even allowing for the freefall after 2008, the traditional notion of Irish poverty has had to be revised: annual growth figures in the later 1990s exceeded 12 per cent. The traditional enmity of Ireland and Britain has been set aside in a welter of mutual admiration and self-denial. The traditional denial of Unionism has been appraised and found wanting. Traditional religious attitudes have changed as scandals have rocked the Catholic Church: vocations and mass attendance have fallen. Popular attitudes towards divorce have changed: Ireland was led between 1997 and 2008 by Bertie Ahern, a man separated from his wife. A traditionally patriarchal country has now had two women Presidents, one of whom – Mary Robinson – came to epitomize the new self-confident and progressive Ireland of the 1990s.

Within Northern Ireland there have been no less profound changes. A bloody civil conflict has markedly cooled, and may (or may not) have ended for good. There has been much rhetoric about mutual tolerance and parity of esteem: and there are some signs that this rhetoric may have a real significance. Militant republicanism has modified its traditional stand on the institutions of partition:

Unionists have accepted that cross-border bodies have a role in the government of Northern Ireland.

Within this rapidly shifting scene the obvious historical analogies begin to break down. Gerry Adams becomes not so much the ideological heir of Liam Lynch, the republican military leader in the civil war, still less of Eamon de Valera, but rather of Michael Collins: Neil Jordan's 1996 film of Collins seems to make this point implicitly. John Hume becomes not so much a Parnell or a Redmond as a Daniel O'Connell or an Arthur Griffith, fighting a protracted, constitutional – and broadly successful – battle for his vision of Ireland. And what of David Trimble? The comparison with Carson might be made, but scarcely works on either personal or strategic grounds. Carson was personally clubbable and a political integrationist: he was acutely concerned for the unity of his movement. But Trimble, an angry and remote Irish Protestant, has fought for his own version of a Home Rule assembly. He has, through his actions, broken his party in two: by 2005 he had been driven out of Irish political life by opponents who accepted and developed the substance of his political achievement.

The familiar contours have shifted, almost beyond recognition. Is this the end of Irish history?

NOTES

1 Introduction

1 Michael Longley, dedicatory lines from *An Exploded View: Poems, 1968–72* (London, 1973).
2 See R.F. Foster, *The Story of Ireland: An Inaugural Lecture Delivered before the University of Oxford on 1 December 1994* (Oxford, 1995).
3 J.C. Beckett, *The Making of Modern Ireland, 1603–1923* (London, 1966), p. 252; Thomas Bartlett, *Theobald Wolfe Tone* (Dublin, 1997), p. 5.
4 Brendan Bradshaw, 'Nationalism and Historical Scholarship in Modern Ireland', *Irish Historical Studies*, xxvi, 104 (Nov. 1989), pp. 329–51.
5 R.F. Foster, *Modern Ireland, 1600–1972* (London, 1988), p. 596.
6 An idea often mooted, but see Georg G. Iggers, *Historiography in the Twentieth Century: From Scientific Objectivity to the Postmodern Challenge* (Hanover and London, 1997), pp. 145–7. For the Famine see (for example) Cormac Ó Gráda, *A New Economic History of Ireland, 1780–1939* (Oxford, 1994), pp. 173–8.
7 James Connolly, *Labour in Irish History* (1910), reprinted in *Labour in Ireland* (Dublin, n.d.), p. 9.
8 Michael Farrell, *Northern Ireland: The Orange State* (London, 1976), p. 12.
9 Richard Kearney, *Postnationalist Ireland: Politics, Culture, Philosophy* (London, 1997), p. 64.
10 Quoted by Iggers, *Historiography in the Twentieth Century*, p. 145.

2 The Birth of Modern Irish Politics, 1790–8

1 Stewart Parker, *Northern Star*, in *Three Plays for Ireland* (Birmingham, 1989), p. 65.
2 I.R. McBride, *Scripture Politics: Ulster Presbyterians and Irish Radicalism in the Late Eighteenth Century* (Oxford, 1998), pp. 9–10.
3 Charles Ross, *Correspondence of Charles, First Marquess of Cornwallis*, 3 vols (London, 1859), ii, p. 441. Edith Mary Johnston, *Great Britain and Ireland, 1760–1800* (Edinburgh, 1963), p. 44.

4   See Nancy Curtin, *The United Irishmen: Popular Politics in Ulster and Dublin, 1791–1798* (Oxford, 1994).

5   A.P.W. Malcomson, *John Foster: The Politics of the Anglo-Irish Ascendancy* (Oxford, 1978), ch. 5; A.P.W. Malcomson, ' "The Parliamentary Traffic of this Country" ', in Thomas Bartlett and D.W. Hayton (eds), *Penal Era and Golden Age: Essays in Irish History, 1690–1800* (Belfast, 1979), pp. 137–61.

6   Theresa M. O'Connor, 'The Conflict between Flood and Grattan, 1782–3', in H.A. Cronne, T.W. Moody and D.B. Quinn (eds), *Essays in British and Irish History in Honour of James Eadie Todd* (London, 1949), p. 182.

7   Cormac Ó Gráda, *A New Economic History of Ireland, 1780–1939* (Oxford, 1994), pp. 3–5.

8   David W. Miller, 'The Armagh Troubles, 1784–95', in Samuel Clark and James S. Donnelly Jr (eds), *Irish Peasants: Violence and Political Unrest, 1780–1914* (Manchester, 1983), pp. 155–91. See also David W. Miller (ed.), *Peep o'Day Boys and Defenders: Selected Documents on the County Armagh Disturbances, 1784–96* (Belfast, 1990).

9   Thomas Bartlett, *The Fall and Rise of the Irish Nation: The Catholic Question, 1690–1830* (Dublin, 1992), pp. 268–9, 311.

10 Ibid., pp. 322–3.

11 Curtin, *United Irishmen*, p. 177.

12 David Dickson, *New Foundations: Ireland, 1660–1800* (Dublin, 1987), p. 89.

13 Eamon O'Flaherty, 'Irish Catholics and the French Revolution', in Hugh Gough and David Dickson (eds), *Ireland and the French Revolution* (Dublin, 1990), pp. 64–5.

14 Bartlett, *Irish Nation*, pp. 144–5.

15 O'Flaherty, 'Irish Catholics', p. 63.

16 Bartlett, *Irish Nation*, pp. 144–5.

17 Dickson, *New Foundations*, p. 184.

18 See Marianne Elliott, *Wolfe Tone: Prophet of Irish Independence* (New Haven and London, 1989).

19 Curtin, *United Irishmen*, pp. 151–2.

20 See Curtin, *United Irishmen*.

21 Allan Blackstock, ' "A Dangerous Species of Ally": Orangeism and the Irish Yeomanry', *Irish Historical Studies*, xxx, 119 (May 1997), pp. 393–405. See also Allan Blackstock, *An Ascendancy Army: The Irish Yeomanry, 1796–1834* (Dublin, 1998).

22 McBride, *Scripture Politics*, p. 13.

23 Curtin, *United Irishmen*, p. 276.

24 Kevin Whelan, 'Politicisation in County Wexford and the Origins of the 1798 Rebellion', in Gough and Dickson (eds), *Ireland and the French Revolution*, pp. 156–78.

25 J.C. Beckett, *The Making of Modern Ireland, 1603–1923* (London, 1966), p. 267.

26 Whelan, 'Politicisation in County Wexford', pp. 156–78.

27 Jean-Paul Bertaud, 'Forgotten Soldiers: The Expedition of General Humbert to Ireland in 1798', in Gough and Dickson (eds), *Ireland and the French Revolution*, pp. 222–3; see also Marianne Elliott, *Partners in Revolution: The United Irishmen and France* (New Haven and London, 1982), pp. 214–40.

28 John Whyte, 'Interpretations of the Northern Ireland Problem: A Reappraisal', *Economic and Social Review*, ix, 4 (July 1978), p. 278.

29 Beckett, *Making of Modern Ireland*, p. 270. See also Ann C. Kavanaugh, *John Fitzgibbon, Earl of Clare: Protestant Reaction and English Authority in Late Eighteenth Century Ireland* (Dublin, 1997).

30 Beckett, *Making of Modern Ireland*, pp. 273–4.

3 Disuniting Kingdoms, Emancipating Catholics, 1799–1850

1 Séamus Heaney, 'Act of Union', *Selected Poems* (London, 1975), p. 125.

2 For a wide-ranging examination of the theme of union see: James Kelly, 'The Origins of the Act of Union: An Examination of Unionist Opinion in Britain and Ireland, 1650–1800', *Irish Historical Studies*, xxv (May 1987), pp. 236–63. See also G.C. Bolton, *The Passing of the Irish Act of Union* (Oxford, 1966).

3 R.B. McDowell, *Ireland in the Age of Imperialism and Revolution, 1760–1801* (Oxford, 1979), pp. 678–9.

4 Ibid., pp. 694–5.

5 Ibid., p. 699.

6 Cormac Ó Gráda, *Ireland: A New Economic History, 1780–1939* (Oxford, 1994), p. 44.

7 Ibid., p. 46.

8 Quoted in Thomas Bartlett, *The Fall and Rise of the Irish Nation: The Catholic Question, 1690–1830* (Dublin, 1992), p. 310.

9 Earl Stanhope, *Life of the Right Honourable William Pitt*, 4 vols (London, 1862), iii, p. 281.

10 Quoted in Oliver MacDonagh, *O'Connell: The Life of Daniel O'Connell, 1775–1847* (London, 1991), p. 161.

11 Bartlett, *Irish Nation*, p. 294.

12 MacDonagh, *O'Connell*, p. 160.

13 Ibid., p. 212.

14 Ibid., p. 495.

15 Quoted several times by Duffy but see (for example) Sir Charles Gavan Duffy, *Thomas Davis: The Memoirs of an Irish Patriot, 1840–1846* (London, 1890), p. 297.

16 Quoted in MacDonagh, *O'Connell*, p. 216.

17 Ibid., p. 273.

18 R.F. Foster, *Modern Ireland, 1600–1972* (London, 1988), p. 300.

19 Bartlett, *Irish Nation*, p. 337; MacDonagh, *O'Connell*, p. 218.

20 Bartlett, *Irish Nation*, p. 337.

21 Fergus O'Ferrall, *Catholic Emancipation: Daniel O'Connell and the Birth of Irish Democracy, 1820–30* (Dublin, 1985), p. 133.

22 Ibid., p. 155.

23 Quoted in MacDonagh, *O'Connell*, p. 233.

24 O'Ferrall, *Catholic Emancipation*, p. 188.

25 Ibid., p. 200.

26 Ibid., pp. 202–3.

27 MacDonagh, *O'Connell*, p. 379.

28 Ibid., p. 319.

29 Ibid., pp. 102–3.

30 Ibid., p. 380.

31 Quoted in ibid., p. 403.

32 Ibid., p. 459.

33 Ibid., p. 416.

34 Ibid., p. 418.

35 Angus Macintyre, *The Liberator: Daniel O'Connell and the Irish Party, 1830–1847* (London, 1965), p. 259.

36   Elie Halevy's phrase, quoted by Macintyre in ibid., pp. 259–60.

37   MacDonagh, *O'Connell*, p. 451. See also Macintyre, *The Liberator*, pp. 219ff.

38   R. Barry O'Brien, *Dublin Castle and the Irish People*, 2nd edition (London, 1912), p. 48.

39   MacDonagh, *O'Connell*, p. 409.

40   O'Brien, *Dublin Castle*, p. 9.

41   MacDonagh, *O'Connell*, p. 480.

42   Quoted by MacDonagh in ibid., pp. 485–6.

43   Ibid., p. 483.

44   Ibid., p. 516.

45   Quoted in Duffy, *Thomas Davis*, pp. 185–6.

46   Denis Gwynn, 'Young Ireland', in Michael Tierney (ed.), *Daniel O'Connell: Nine Centenary Essays* (Dublin, 1949), p. 179.

47   Quoted in Duffy, *Thomas Davis*, p. 186.

48   R. Finlay Holmes, *Henry Cooke* (Belfast, 1981), p. 181.

49   Manus O'Neill, 'John Mitchel', in M.J. MacManus (ed.), *Thomas Davis and Young Ireland, 1845–1945* (Dublin, 1945), p. 44. For the women poets see L.M. O'Toole, 'The Women Writers of "The Nation"', in ibid., pp. 119–22. See also Brigitte Anton, 'Northern Voices: Ulsterwomen in the Young Ireland Movement', in Janice Holmes and Diane Urquhart (eds), *Coming into the Light: The Work, Politics and Religion of Women in Ulster, 1840–1940* (Belfast, 1994), pp. 60–92.

50   MacDonagh, *O'Connell*, p. 380.

51   Donal Kerr, *Peel, Priests and Politics: Sir Robert Peel's Administration and the Roman Catholic Church in Ireland, 1841–6* (Oxford, 1982), p. 112.

52   Ibid., p. 121.

53   Ibid., p. 83.

54   MacDonagh, *O'Connell*, p. 542.

55   Kerr, *Peel, Priests and Politics*, p. 289.

56   Ibid., p. 342.

57   MacDonagh, *O'Connell*, p. 552.

58   Kerr, *Peel, Priests and Politics*, p. 351.

59   Ibid., p. 342.

60   D. George Boyce, *Nationalism in Ireland*, 2nd edition (London, 1991), pp. 159, 167.

61   Ibid., p. 161.

62   Ibid.

63   Ibid., pp. 167–8. See also Padraic Fallon, 'The Poetry of Thomas Davis', in MacManus (ed.), *Thomas Davis*, pp. 24–7.

64   Macdonagh, *O'Connell*, p. 540.

65   Ibid., pp. 590–1, 595.

66   Quoted many times but see, for example, Denis Gwynn, 'Young Ireland', p. 172.

67   Tierney (ed.), *Daniel O'Connell*; MacManus (ed.), *Thomas Davis*. See also Gwynn, 'Young Ireland', p. 171. For Connolly on O'Connell see James Connolly, *Labour in Irish History* (Dublin, 1910), reprinted in *Labour in Irish History* (Dublin, n.d.), p. 116 ('A Chapter of Horrors: Daniel O'Connell and the Working Class'). For a sense of Griffith's ambiguous relationship with O'Connell, see Brian Maye, *Arthur Griffith* (Dublin, 1997), pp. 64, 86, 136, 162.

68   Michael Tierney, 'Repeal of the Union', in Tierney (ed.), *Daniel O'Connell*, p. 170.

69 Pierre Joannon, 'O'Connell, Montalembert, and the Birth of Christian Democracy in France', in Maurice R. O'Connell (ed.), *Daniel O'Connell: Political Pioneer* (Dublin, 1991), p. 107.

70 Geraldine Grogan, 'O'Connell's Impact on the Organisation and Development of German Political Catholicism', in ibid., p. 120. See also Grogan, *The Noblest Agitator: Daniel O'Connell and the German Catholic Movement, 1830–1850* (Dublin, 1991).

71 Peter Alter, 'O'Connell and German Politics', in O'Connell (ed.), *Daniel O'Connell: Political Pioneer*, pp. 117–18.

72 T. Desmond Williams, 'O'Connell's Impact on Europe', in Kevin B. Nowlan and Maurice R. O'Connell (eds), *Daniel O'Connell: Portrait of a Radical* (Belfast, 1984), p. 100.

73 Brian Girvin, 'Making Nations: O'Connell, Religion and the Creation of Political Identity', in O'Connell (ed.), *Daniel O'Connell: Political Pioneer*, p. 21.

74 Richard Hayward (arranger), 'The Boys of Sandy Row', in *Orange Standard: Containing Eighteen Selected Songs* (Glasgow, n.d.).

75 Tom Garvin, 'O'Connell and the Making of Irish Political Culture', in O'Connell (ed.), *Daniel O'Connell: Political Pioneer*, p. 9.

76 Especially K. Theodore Hoppen, *Elections, Politics and Society in Ireland, 1832–1885* (Oxford, 1984).

77 Ian d'Alton, *Protestant Society and Politics in Cork, 1812–1844* (Cork, 1980), pp. 138ff.

78 Hoppen, *Elections, Politics and Society*, p. 280.

79 Garvin, 'O'Connell and the Making of Irish Political Culture', p. 9; Hoppen, *Elections, Politics and Society*, p. 281.

80 Ian Budge and Cornelius O'Leary, *Belfast: Approach to Crisis: A Study of Belfast Politics, 1613–1970* (London, 1973).

81 Hoppen, *Elections, Politics and Society*, p. 284.

82 Ibid., pp. 284–7.

83 Ibid., p. 323. For Orangeism and popular Protestantism in the 1830s and 1840s see also Hereward Senior, *Orangeism in Ireland and Britain, 1795–1836* (London, 1966), and Jacqueline Hill, 'The Protestant Response to Repeal: The Case of the Dublin Working Class', in F.S.L. Lyons and R.A.J. Hawkins (eds), *Ireland Under the Union: Varieties of Tension* (Oxford, 1980), pp. 35–68.

84 Holmes, *Henry Cooke*, p. 115.

85 Ibid.

86 Ibid., p. 118.

87 Ibid., p. 148.

88 McBride, *Scripture Politics*, p. 216.

89 R. Finlay Holmes, *Our Irish Presbyterian Heritage* (Belfast, 1985), pp. 95–141. Holmes emphasizes that the liberal tradition within the Church remained significant.

90 David Hempton and Myrtle Hill, *Evangelical Protestantism in Ulster Society, 1740–1890* (London, 1992), pp. 77–8.

4 The Ascendancy of the Land Question, 1845–91

1 Charles Dickens, *Little Dorrit*, Collins Classics edition (London, 1972), ch. 10, p. 108.

2 Among important recent works on the famine see: Mary E. Daly, *The Famine in Ireland* (Dublin, 1986); Peter Gray, *The Irish Famine: New Horizons* (London, 1995); Donal

Kerr, *'A Nation of Beggars?' Priests, People and Politics in Famine Ireland, 1846–1852* (Oxford, 1994); Christine Kinealy, *This Great Calamity: The Irish Famine, 1845–52* (Dublin, 1994); Christine Kinealy, *A Death-Dealing Famine: The Great Hunger in Ireland* (London, 1997); Joel Mokyr, *Why Ireland Starved: A Quantitative and Analytical History of the Irish Economy, 1800–1850*, 2nd edition (London, 1985); Cormac Ó Gráda, *A New Economic History of Ireland, 1780–1939* (Oxford, 1994), ch. 8; Cormac Ó Gráda, *The Great Irish Famine* (Dublin, 1989). An important regional perspective (correcting the general neglect of the north in the literature) is provided in Christine Kinealy and Trevor Parkhill (eds), *The Famine in Ulster: The Regional Impact* (Belfast, 1997). See Mary Daly, 'Historians and the Famine: A Beleaguered Species?', *Irish Historical Studies*, xxx, 120 (Nov. 1997), pp. 591–601, for a review of recent literature.

3   James Connolly, *Labour in Irish History* (1910), reprinted in *Labour in Ireland* (Dublin, n.d.), p. 135; Daly, *Famine in Ireland*, pp. 98–105; Ó Gráda, *New Economic History*, pp. 178–87.

4   Thomas P. O'Neill, 'The Organisation and Administration of Relief, 1845–52', in R. Dudley Edwards and T. Desmond Williams (eds), *The Great Famine: Studies in Irish History, 1845–52* (Dublin, 1956), p. 215.

5   Ibid., p. 222.

6   Dickens, *Little Dorrit*, ch. 10.

7   O'Neill, 'Organisation and Administration of Relief', p. 223.

8   Ibid., p. 228.

9   Ibid., pp. 232, 258–9; Kinealy, *This Great Calamity*, pp. 350–1.

10 R.F. Foster, *Modern Ireland, 1600–1972* (London, 1988), p. 326.

11 Ó Gráda, *New Economic History*, p. 197.

12 Ibid., p. 198.

13 D. George Boyce, *Nineteenth Century Ireland: The Search for Stability* (Dublin, 1990), p. 123.

14 See the discussion in Desmond Bowen, *Souperism: Myth or Reality?* (Cork, 1970).

15 Daly, *Famine in Ireland*, pp. 89–92.

16 Ó Gráda, *New Economic History*, p. 198.

17 Ibid., pp. 173–8, esp. p. 176; Ó Gráda, *The Great Irish Famine*, pp. 9–10. See also Kinealy, *A Death-Dealing Famine*, pp. 10–11.

18 Kinealy, *This Great Calamity*, p. 350.

19 Mokyr, *Why Ireland Starved*, p. 292.

20 Kevin B. Nowlan, 'The Political Background', in Edwards and Williams (eds), *Great Famine*, pp. 178–9.

21 Despite some revisionist endeavours, Trevelyan remains an essentially bleak, moralistic and providentialist figure in the literature. See, for example, Gray, *Irish Famine*, p. 49; part of Trevelyan's apologia, *The Irish Crisis* (1848), is reproduced in ibid., pp. 153–4.

22 Kinealy, *This Great Calamity*, p. 353.

23 Ó Gráda, *The Great Irish Famine*, p. 72.

24 Ó Gráda, *New Economic History*, p. 191.

25 Sir William MacArthur, 'Medical History of the Famine', in Edwards and Williams (eds), *Great Famine*, p. 315; Kinealy, *This Great Calamity*, pp. 351–2.

26 Ó Gráda, *New Economic History*, p. 176.

27 Oliver MacDonagh, 'Irish Emigration to the United States of America and the British Colonies during the Famine', in Edwards and Williams (eds), *Great Famine*, p. 329.

28 Daly, *Famine in Ireland*, p. 121.

29 Ó Gráda, *New Economic History*, pp. 118–21, 205–8.

30 Daly, *Famine in Ireland*, p. 119.

31 W.F. Adams, *Ireland and Irish Emigration to the New World from 1815 to the Famine* (New Haven, 1932). For an accessible bibliographical survey of this theme see David Fitzpatrick, *Irish Emigration, 1801–1921* (Dundalk, 1984).

32 MacDonagh, 'Irish Emigration', p. 320; Kinealy, *This Great Calamity*, p. 303.

33 MacDonagh, 'Irish Emigration', p. 331.

34 Daly, *Famine in Ireland*, p. 121.

35 Brian Ó Cuív, 'Irish Language and Literature, 1845–1921', in W.E. Vaughan (ed.), *A New History of Ireland VI: Ireland Under the Union II: 1870–1921* (Oxford, 1996), p. 385.

36 See Seán Connolly, *Priests and People in Pre-Famine Ireland, 1780–1845* (Dublin, 1982). For an accessible bibliographical survey of the theme see Seán Connolly, *Religion and Society in Nineteenth Century Ireland* (Dundalk, 1985).

37 MacDonagh, 'Irish Emigration', pp. 329–31.

38 See, for example, Nowlan, 'Political Background', p. 172.

39 Quoted often, but see F.H. O'Donnell, *A History of the Irish Parliamentary Party*, 2 vols (London, 1910), i, p. 10.

40 Paul Bew, *Land and the National Question, 1858–82* (Dublin, 1979), pp. 34–5; Joseph Lee, *The Modernisation of Irish Society, 1848–1918* (Dublin, 1973), p. 39.

41 J.H. Whyte, *The Independent Irish Party, 1850–59* (Oxford, 1958), p. 6.

42 Gavan Duffy provided a chronicle of the League's activities: Charles Gavan Duffy, *The League of North and South: An Episode in Irish History, 1850–1854* (London, 1886).

43 Kerr, *'A Nation of Beggars?'*, pp. 241–81, esp. p. 244.

44 Whyte, *Independent Irish Party*, p. 63.

45 K. Theodore Hoppen, *Elections, Politics and Society in Ireland, 1832–1885* (Oxford, 1984), p. 44; see also pp. 480–1, where he discusses the regional mobilization of the Tenant League.

46 Whyte, *Independent Irish Party*, p. 82. Aside from Whyte's classic study of the party, see also Steven R. Knowlton, *Popular Politics and the Irish Catholic Church: The Rise and Fall of the Independent Irish Party, 1850–59* (New York and London, 1991).

47 Hoppen, *Elections, Politics and Society*, p. 44; Whyte, *Independent Irish Party*, pp. 124–41, 175–6.

48 R.V. Comerford, *The Fenians in Context: Irish Politics and Society, 1848–1882* (Dublin, 1985), p. 142.

49 Foster, *Modern Ireland*, p. 384.

50 Whyte, *Independent Irish Party*, p. v.

51 Foster, *Modern Ireland*, p. 393. The key authority on early Fenianism is R.V. Comerford. See Comerford, *Charles J. Kickham: A Study in Irish Nationalism and Literature* (Dublin, 1979); Comerford, 'Patriotism as Pastime: The Appeal of Fenianism in the mid-1860s', *Irish Historical Studies*, xxii, 87 (Mar. 1981), pp. 239–50; Comerford, *Fenians in Context*.

52 Quoted by T.D. Williams, 'Devoy and Rossa', in T.W. Moody (ed.), *The Fenian Movement* (Cork, 1968), p. 94.

53 Hoppen, *Elections, Politics and Society*, p. 350; Comerford, *Fenians in Context*, pp. 111–12.

54 Comerford, *Fenians in Context*, p. 112.

55 Ibid., pp. 78–9.

56 T.W. Moody, 'The Fenian Movement in Irish History', in Moody (ed.), *Fenian Movement*, p. 103.

57 See Patrick Maume, 'Parnell and the IRB Oath', *Irish Historical Studies*, xxix, 115 (May 1995), pp. 363–70.

58 D. George Boyce, *Nationalism in Ireland*, 2nd edition (London, 1991), p. 177; Boyce, *Nineteenth Century Ireland*, p. 141.

59 Desmond Ryan, 'John O'Mahony', in Moody (ed.), *Fenian Movement*, p. 64; E.R.R. Green, 'Kickham and O'Leary', in ibid., p. 88.

60 Comerford, *Fenians in Context*, p. 240.

61 Ibid., p. 136.

62 Ibid., p. 128.

63 Ibid., pp. 136–7.

64 The point is made by Tom Garvin, *Nationalist Revolutionaries in Ireland, 1858–1928* (Oxford, 1987), p. 35.

65 Charles Townshend, *Political Violence in Ireland: Government and Resistance since 1848* (Oxford, 1983), p. 35 and pp. 24–38.

66 Shin-ichi Takagami, 'The Fenian Rising in Dublin, March 1867', *Irish Historical Studies*, xxix, 115 (May 1995), p. 362.

67 Desmond Bowen, *Paul Cullen and the Shaping of Modern Irish Catholicism* (Dublin, 1983), pp. 219–20, 268–72.

68 Quoted in ibid., p. 268.

69 Bew, *Land and the National Question*, p. 45.

70 David Thornley, *Isaac Butt and Home Rule* (London, 1964), pp. 68–9.

71 Ibid., p. 68.

72 Comerford, *Fenians in Context*, pp. 152–3.

73 Often quoted but see ibid., p. 152.

74 Ibid., p. 203.

75 Ibid., p. 205.

76 Quoted in O'Donnell, *Irish Parliamentary Party*, i, p. 358, n. 1.

77 Hoppen, *Elections, Politics and Society*, pp. 465, 468, 479.

78 O'Donnell, *Irish Parliamentary Party*, i, p. 10.

79 Comerford, *Fenians in Context*, p. 188.

80 Hoppen, *Elections, Politics and Society*, p. 274.

81 Ibid., p. 275.

82 O'Donnell, *Irish Parliamentary Party*, i, pp. 59–60.

83 Thornley, *Butt*, p. 227.

84 Ibid., p. 167.

85 Ibid., p. 255.

86 Ibid., p. 383.

87 O'Donnell, *Irish Parliamentary Party*, i, p. 188.

88 F.S.L. Lyons, *Charles Stewart Parnell* (London, 1977), p. 60.

89 O'Donnell, *Irish Parliamentary Party*, i, p. 214.

90 Dr William Carroll to John Devoy, 16 Nov. 1879, in William O'Brien and Desmond Ryan (eds), *Devoy's Post-Bag, 1871–1928*, 2 vols (Dublin, 1948–53), i, p. 280.

91 Lyons, *Parnell*, p. 75.

92 Ibid., p. 80.

93   Bew, *Land and the National Question*, p. 45.

94   Lyons, *Parnell*, p. 89.

95   Quoted in Jane McL. Cote, *Fanny and Anna Parnell: Ireland's Patriot Sisters* (London, 1991), p. 260.

96   R. Barry O'Brien, *The Life of Charles Stewart Parnell*, 2 vols (London, 1898), i, p. 229; ii, p. 61. The literature on Parnell and Parnellism is considerable; aside from the volumes already mentioned in the notes, see two useful collections: Donal McCartney (ed.), *Parnell: The Politics of Power* (Dublin, 1991); D. George Boyce and Alan O'Day (eds), *Parnell in Perspective* (London, 1991); and Alan O'Day, *Charles Stewart Parnell* (Dublin, 1999).

97   Defined by Frank Callanan, *The Parnell Split, 1890–91* (Cork, 1992), p. 2. See O'Day, *Parnell*, p. 47 for a further, refined periodization.

98   O'Brien, *Parnell*, i, p. 90.

99   Ibid., i, p. 103.

100   Paul Bew, *C.S. Parnell* (Dublin, 1980), p. 33.

101   Ibid.; Bew, *Land and the National Question*, p. 143. For a more admiring view see Callanan, *Parnell Split*, and O'Day, *Parnell*.

102   Alvin Jackson, *Colonel Edward Saunderson: Land and Loyalty in Victorian Ireland* (Oxford, 1995), p. 97.

103   O'Brien, *Parnell*, i, pp. 236–7; Lyons, *Parnell*, p. 134.

104   Lyons, *Parnell*, p. 165.

105   O'Brien, *Parnell*, ii, p. 29.

106   Lyons, *Parnell*, p. 173.

107   Margaret Ward, *Unmanageable Revolutionaries: Women and Irish Nationalism*, 2nd edition (London, 1989), pp. 4–39. See also Cote, *Fanny and Anna Parnell*.

108   O'Donnell, *Irish Parliamentary Party*, i, p. 457; Ward, *Unmanageable Revolutionaries*, p. 37.

109   Lyons, *Parnell*, p. 204.

110   Margaret O'Callaghan, *British High Politics and a Nationalist Ireland: Criminality, Land and the Law under Forster and Balfour* (Cork, 1994), p. 93.

111   Bew, *Parnell*, p. 59.

112   O'Brien, *Parnell*, ii, p. 32.

113   Lyons, *Parnell*, p. 233.

114   Ward, *Unmanageable Revolutionaries*, p. 33.

115   O'Donnell, *Irish Parliamentary Party*, ii, p. 39.

116   Lyons, *Parnell*, p. 257. The classic account of the party in the 1880s remains C.C. O'Brien, *Parnell and his Party, 1880–90* (Oxford, 1957).

117   Maume, 'Parnell and the IRB Oath', p. 370.

118   See Tom Garvin, *The Evolution of Irish Nationalist Politics* (Dublin, 1981).

119   O'Brien, *Parnell*, i, pp. 171–2.

120   Lyons, *Parnell*, p. 71.

121   Ibid., p. 258.

122   Ibid., pp. 260–1.

123   Ibid., p. 285.

124   Although for a different view see ibid., p. 298.

125   Bew, *Parnell*, p. 74.

126   K. Theodore Hoppen, *Ireland since 1800: Conflict and Conformity* (London, 1989), p. 122. James Loughlin emphasizes the importance of land purchase in Gladstone's Home

Rule project: Loughlin, *Gladstone, Home Rule and the Ulster Question, 1882–1893* (Dublin, 1986).

127 Alan O'Day, *Parnell and the First Home Rule Episode, 1884–87* (Dublin, 1986), p. 106.

128 Vernon Bogdanor, *Devolution* (Oxford, 1979), pp. 10–41. See also Alan J. Ward, *The Irish Constitutional Tradition: Responsible Government and Modern Ireland, 1782–1992* (Dublin, 1994), pp. 50–70.

129 O'Day, *Parnell and the First Home Rule Episode*, p. 150.

130 Lyons, *Parnell*, p. 331.

131 Ibid., p. 348.

132 For example by Boyce, *Nationalism in Ireland*, p. 223.

133 O'Callaghan, *British High Politics and a Nationalist Ireland*, p. 93; Maume, 'Parnell and the IRB Oath', p. 370.

134 Bew, *Parnell*, p. 112.

135 O'Brien, *Parnell*, ii, p. 159.

136 Lyons, *Parnell*, p. 366.

137 F.S.L. Lyons, *Ireland since the Famine*, 2nd edition (London, 1973), p. 188.

138 Laurence M. Geary, *The Plan of Campaign, 1886–1891* (Cork, 1986), p. 141.

139 L.P. Curtis, *Coercion and Conciliation in Ireland, 1880–1892: A Study in Conservative Unionism* (Princeton, 1963), pp. 186–7.

140 Geary, *Plan of Campaign, passim.*

141 Lyons, *Parnell*, p. 369.

142 Ibid., p. 437.

143 Ibid.

144 Ibid., p. 444.

145 The best analysis of Parnellite politics in 1890–1 is offered in Callanan, *Parnell Split*. See also F.S.L. Lyons, *The Fall of Parnell, 1890–91* (London, 1960), and Frank Callanan, *T.M. Healy* (Cork, 1996).

146 See Christopher Oldstone-Moore, 'The Fall of Parnell: Hugh Price Hughes and the Nonconformist Conscience', *Éire-Ireland* (Fall, 1996).

147 The point is made by Callanan, *Parnell Split*, p. 156.

148 Ibid., p. 3.

149 Boyce, *Nationalism in Ireland*, p. 223.

150 Callanan, *Parnell Split*, p. 5.

151 Bew, *Parnell*, p. 142. Callanan (*Parnell Split*) is unpersuaded by this point.

152 James Bryce, *Studies in Contemporary Biography* (London, 1903), p. 236; Callanan, *Parnell Split*, pp. 3, 69–72.

153 Callanan, *Parnell Split*, p. 154.

154 Bew, *Parnell*, p. 133.

155 Callanan, *Parnell Split*, p. 177; Lyons, *Parnell*, p. 625.

5 Greening the Red, White and Blue: The End of the Union, 1891–1921

1 Healy's politics at the time of the Split are excavated in Frank Callanan, *T.M. Healy* (Cork, 1996), pp. 257–404. See also F.S.L. Lyons, *The Irish Parliamentary Party, 1890–1910* (London, 1951), and Paul Bew, *Conflict and Conciliation in Ireland, 1890–1910:*

Parnellites and Agrarian Radicals (Oxford, 1987), p. 121. A survey of the literature on Irish politics in the years 1891–1918 may be found in Alan O'Day, 'Review Article: Politics after Parnell', *Irish Historical Studies*, xxx, 120 (Nov. 1997), pp. 602–10.

2   Bew, *Conflict and Conciliation*, p. 21.

3   William O'Brien, *An Olive Branch in Ireland, and its History* (London, 1910), p. 266.

4   Quoted by O'Brien in ibid., p. 288.

5   See Frank Callanan, *T.M. Healy* (Cork, 1996), p. 429.

6   See Callanan, *Healy, passim.*

7   Lyons, *Irish Parliamentary Party*, pp. 51–2.

8   Bew, *Conflict and Conciliation*, p. 36. The UIL and other land agitations are discussed incisively in Philip Bull, *Land, Politics and Nationalism: A Study of the Irish Land Question* (Dublin, 1996).

9   O'Brien, *Olive Branch*, pp. 326–7.

10 This is the argument pursued by Andrew Gailey in *Ireland and the Death of Kindness: The Experience of Constructive Unionism, 1890–1905* (Cork, 1987).

11 Bew, *Conflict and Conciliation*, p. 32.

12 Ibid.

13 O'Brien, *Olive Branch*, p. 169. See also, among contemporary statements, Lord Dunraven, *The Crisis in Ireland: An Account of the Present Condition of Ireland and Suggestions towards Reform* (Dublin, 1905); Lord Dunraven, *The Outlook in Ireland: The Case for Devolution and Conciliation* (Dublin, 1907). There is also a very extensive modern literature on this episode: see, for example, Bew, *Conflict and Conciliation*; Bull, *Land, Politics and Nationalism*; Gailey, *Ireland and the Death of Kindness*.

14 O'Brien, *Olive Branch*, p. 135.

15 Bew, *Conflict and Conciliation*, p. 122.

16 O'Brien, *Olive Branch*, p. 250.

17 Bew, *Conflict and Conciliation*, pp. 117–18.

18 Bull, *Land, Politics and Nationalism*, pp. 190–1.

19 This case is elaborated in Alvin Jackson, *The Ulster Party: Irish Unionists in the House of Commons, 1884–1911* (Oxford, 1989), pp. 253–60.

20 O'Brien, *Olive Branch*, pp. 426–7.

21 Ibid., p. 393.

22 Bew, *Conflict and Conciliation*, pp. 140ff.

23 Ibid., pp. 205–6.

24 R.G. Mullan, 'The Origins and Passing of the Irish Land Act of 1909', MA thesis (Queen's University, Belfast, 1978), p. 55. See also Alvin Jackson, *Colonel Edward Saunderson: Land and Loyalty in Victorian Ireland* (Oxford, 1995), pp. 202–4.

25 Alan J. Ward, *The Irish Constitutional Tradition: Responsible Government and Modern Ireland, 1782–1992* (Dublin, 1994), p. 78. For the politics of the third Home Rule crisis and the details of the measure, see Patricia Jalland, *The Liberals and Ireland: The Ulster Question in British Politics to 1914* (Brighton, 1980).

26 Alvin Jackson, *Sir Edward Carson* (Dublin, 1993), p. 33.

27 Jalland, *Liberals and Ireland*, p. 191.

28 Ibid., pp. 38–9.

29 Stephen Gwynn, *John Redmond's Last Years* (London, 1919), p. 92.

30 William O'Brien, *The Downfall of Parliamentarianism: A Retrospect for the Accounting Day* (Dublin, 1918), pp. 55–6.

31 R.F. Foster, *W.B. Yeats: A Life. I: The Apprentice Mage* (Oxford, 1997), p. 41.

32 Ibid., *passim*, but see pp. 45, 57.

33 John Hutchinson, *The Dynamics of Cultural Nationalism: The Gaelic Revival and the Creation of the Irish Nation State* (London, 1987).

34 Quoted in Declan Kiberd, *Inventing Ireland: The Literature of the Modern Nation* (London, 1995), p. 423.

35 Quoted in David M. Kiely, *John Millington Synge: A Biography* (Dublin, 1994), pp. 151, 203.

36 Adrian Pimley, 'The Working Class Movement and the Irish Revolution, 1896–1923', in D. George Boyce (ed.), *The Revolution in Ireland, 1879–1923* (London, 1988), p. 195.

37 Foster, *Yeats*, p. 170.

38 F.S.L. Lyons, *Culture and Anarchy in Ireland, 1890–1939* (Oxford, 1979), p. 33.

39 Ruth Dudley Edwards, *Patrick Pearse: The Triumph of Failure* (London, 1977), p. 253.

40 Foster, *Yeats*, p. 43.

41 Ibid., p. 41.

42 Often quoted, usually in Yeats's modified lines; ibid., p. 262.

43 Ibid., p. 321.

44 Ibid., p. 253.

45 Ibid., p. 452.

46 Ibid., p. 330.

47 Brian Ó Cuív, 'Irish Language and Literature, 1845–1921', in W.E. Vaughan (ed.), *A New History of Ireland VI: Ireland Under the Union II: 1870–1921* (Oxford, 1996), p. 397.

48 Much quoted, but see Foster, *Yeats*, pp. 125–6; and also Janet Egleson Dunleavy and Gareth W. Dunleavy, *Douglas Hyde: A Maker of Modern Ireland* (Berkeley, 1991), pp. 182–6.

49 Hutchinson, *Dynamics of Cultural Nationalism*, pp. 188, 307.

50 Dunleavy and Dunleavy, *Hyde*, pp. 327–8; O Cuiv, 'Irish Language and Literature', pp. 411–12.

51 Quoted in Ó Cuív, 'Irish Language and Literature', p. 403.

52 Patrick Maume, *D.P. Moran* (Dublin, 1995), p. 4.

53 Ibid., p. 28.

54 Gwynn, *Redmond's Last Years*, p. 164.

55 W.F. Mandle, *The Gaelic Athletic Association and Irish Nationalist Politics, 1884–1924* (Dublin, 1987), p. 4.

56 Ibid., p. 83.

57 Tom Garvin, *The Evolution of Irish Nationalist Politics* (Dublin, 1981), pp. 86–7.

58 Mandle, *Gaelic Athletic Association*, p. 171.

59 Foster, *Yeats*, p. 199.

60 Brian Maye, *Arthur Griffith* (Dublin, 1997), p. 65.

61 Ibid.

62 Ibid., p. 104.

63 Maume, *Moran*, p. 26.

64 Maye, *Griffith*, p. 62.

65 Margaret Ward, *Hanna Sheehy Skeffington: A Life* (Cork, 1997), p. 53.

66 Cliona Murphy, *The Women's Suffrage Movement and Irish Society in the Early Twentieth Century* (Hemel Hempstead, 1989), pp. 169–70.

67 Ibid., p. 169.

68   Margaret Ward, *Unmanageable Revolutionaries: Women and Irish Nationalism*, 2nd edition (London, 1989), pp. 101–2.

69   Patrick Maume, 'David Patrick Moran', in Seán Connolly (ed.), *The Oxford Companion to Irish History* (Oxford, 1998), p. 368.

70   Emmet O'Connor, *A Labour History of Ireland, 1824–1960* (Dublin, 1992), p. 57.

71   Ibid., p. 60.

72   Ibid., pp. 202–3.

73   Ibid., pp. 88–9.

74   George Russell, 'To the Masters of Dublin' (1913), reprinted in James Connolly, *Labour in Ireland* (Dublin, n.d.), pp. 260–4; Foster, *Yeats*, p. 499.

75   Foster, *Yeats*, p. 499.

76   Quoted in Ernie O'Malley, *On Another Man's Wound* (London, 1936), p. 69. For O'Malley see Richard English, *Ernie O'Malley: IRA Intellectual* (Oxford, 1998).

77   See, for example, Tom Garvin, 'The Rising and Irish Democracy', in Máirín Ní Dhonnchadha and Theo Dorgan (eds), *Revising the Rising* (Derry, 1991), p. 26.

78   Gwynn, *Redmond's Last Years*, p. 192.

79   O'Brien, *Downfall of Parliamentarianism*, pp. 10–12.

80   Quoted often but see Paul Bew, *Ideology and the Irish Question: Ulster Unionism and Irish Nationalism, 1912–1916* (Oxford, 1994), p. 120.

81   Gwynn, *Redmond's Last Years*, pp. 122–3.

82   Ibid., p. 125.

83   Bew, *Ideology and the Irish Question*, pp. 120–1.

84   Gwynn, *Redmond's Last Years*, p. 162.

85   See, for example, Michael Laffan, *The Partition of Ireland, 1911–1925* (Dundalk, 1983), p. 50.

86   Gwynn, *Redmond's Last Years*, pp. 156–7.

87   Ibid., p. 166.

88   Ibid., p. 212.

89   Ibid.

90   Bew, *Ideology and the Irish Question*, pp. 144–51.

91   Garvin, *Evolution of Irish Nationalist Politics*, p. 98.

92   O'Brien, *Downfall of Parliamentarianism*, pp. 12–14.

93   Charles Townshend, *Political Violence in Ireland: Government and Resistance since 1848* (Oxford, 1983), p. 298.

94   Often quoted: see Lyons, *Culture and Anarchy*, p. 97; Ruth Dudley Edwards, *James Connolly* (Dublin, 1981), p. 137.

95   David Fitzpatrick, *The Two Irelands, 1912–1939* (Oxford, 1998), p. 60.

96   J.J. Lee, 'In Search of Patrick Pearse', in Ní Dhonnchadha and Dorgan (eds), *Revising the Rising*, p. 126.

97   The Proclamation was mostly composed by Pearse, with suggestions from others within the Military Council: Dudley Edwards, *Pearse*, pp. 279–80.

98   See, for example, Hanna Sheehy Skeffington's firm views on this ascription: Ward, *Hanna Sheehy Skeffington*, pp. 154–5.

99   Dudley Edwards, *Pearse*, p. 291. See also, on the same theme, Lee, 'In Search of Patrick Pearse', p. 124.

100 J.J. Lee, *Ireland 1912–1985: Politics and Society* (Cambridge, 1989), p. 36.

101 Gwynn, *Redmond's Last Years*, p. 227.

102 J.J. Lee, *The Modernisation of Irish Society, 1848–1918* (Dublin, 1973), p. 156.

103 Quoted often, but see F.S.L. Lyons, *John Dillon: A Biography* (London, 1968), p. 382.

104 D. George Boyce, *Nationalism in Ireland*, 2nd edition (London, 1991), p. 288.

105 Gwynn, *Redmond's Last Years*, p. 239.

106 Ibid., p. 232.

107 Garvin, *Evolution of Irish Nationalist Politics*, p. 98.

108 Lyons, *Dillon*, p. 415; Gwynn, *Redmond's Last Years*, p. 257.

109 Maume, *Moran*, p. 38.

110 Gwynn, *Redmond's Last Years*, p. 308.

111 The fullest exploration of the Irish Convention remains R.B. McDowell, *The Irish Convention, 1917–18* (London, 1970).

112 Gwynn, *Redmond's Last Years*, p. 334.

113 Boyce, *Nationalism in Ireland*, p. 289. For a full discussion of the 1918 election in Ireland, see Garvin, *Evolution of Irish Nationalist Politics*, pp. 118–22.

114 Garvin, *Evolution of Irish Nationalist Politics*, p. 90.

115 Gwynn, *Redmond's Last Years*, pp. 61, 338.

116 O'Brien, *Downfall of Parliamentarianism*, p. 17.

117 Gwynn, *Redmond's Last Years*, p. 60; O'Brien, *Downfall of Parliamentarianism*, p. 20.

118 Quoted by Bew, *Ideology and the Irish Question*, p. 35. The literature on Irish Unionism is extensive: the essential starting points remain Patrick Buckland, *Irish Unionism I: The Anglo-Irish and the New Ireland, 1885–1922* (Dublin, 1972), and Patrick Buckland, *Irish Unionism II: Ulster Unionism and the Origins of Northern Ireland, 1886–1922* (Dublin, 1973). For parliamentary and constituency Unionism see Jackson, *The Ulster Party*.

119 See J.R.B. McMinn, 'Liberalism in North Antrim, 1900–1914', *Irish Historical Studies*, xxiii, 89 (May 1982), pp. 17–29.

120 See Peter Gibbon, *The Origins of Ulster Unionism: The Formation of Popular Protestant Politics and Ideology in Nineteenth Century Ireland* (Manchester, 1975). See also, for example, I.R. McBride, *Scripture Politics: Ulster Presbyterians and Irish Radicalism in the Late Eighteenth Century* (Oxford, 1998), pp. 207–31.

121 R. Finlay Holmes, *Henry Cooke* (Belfast, 1981), p. 148.

122 W.E. Vaughan, *Landlords and Tenants in Mid-Victorian Ireland* (Oxford, 1994), p. 219.

123 K. Theodore Hoppen, *Elections, Politics and Society in Ireland, 1832–1885* (Oxford, 1984), p. 284.

124 R.V. Comerford, 'Gladstone's First Irish Enterprise', in W.E. Vaughan (ed.), *A New History of Ireland V: Ireland Under the Union I: 1801–1870* (Oxford, 1989), p. 441.

125 Quoted in Holmes, *Cooke*, p. 196.

126 Comerford, 'Gladstone's First Irish Enterprise', p. 443.

127 Vaughan, *Landlords and Tenants in Mid-Victorian Ireland*, p. 227.

128 Hoppen, *Elections, Politics and Society*, p. 312.

129 See the study by Peter Hart, *The IRA and its Enemies: Violence and Community in County Cork, 1916–1923* (Oxford, 1998).

130 The most comprehensive published study of southern Unionism remains Buckland, *Irish Unionism I*. See also Buckland, *Irish Unionism II*.

131 Quoted in Jackson, *Carson*, p. 32.

132 Vaughan, *Landlords and Tenants in Mid-Victorian Ireland*, p. 227.

133   By Maria Luddy and Noel Armour. Maria Luddy, 'Isabella M.S. Tod, 1836–1896', in
      Mary Cullen and Maria Luddy (eds), *Women, Power and Consciousness in Nineteenth
      Century Ireland: Eight Biographical Studies* (Dublin, 1995). Noel Armour, 'Isabella Todd
      and Liberal Unionism in Ulster, 1886–96', in Alan Hayes and Diane Urquhart (eds),
      New Perspectives on Irish Women's History (Dublin, n.d.). See, too, Diane Urquhart,
      The Ladies of Londonderry: Women and Political Patronage (London, 2007).

134   Maria Luddy, *Hanna Sheehy Skeffington* (Dublin, 1995), p. 20; Ward, *Hanna Sheehy
      Skeffington*, p. 69. For the UWUC see Nancy Kinghan, *United We Stood: The Story of
      the Ulster Women's Unionist Council, 1911–1974* (Belfast, 1975); Diane Urquhart, ' "The
      Female of the Species is More Deadly than the Male?": The Ulster Women's Unionist
      Council, 1911–40', in Janice Holmes and Diane Urquhart (eds), *Coming into the Light:
      The Work, Politics and Religion of Women in Ulster, 1840–1940* (Belfast, 1994),
      pp. 93–125.

135   Luddy, *Hanna Sheehy Skeffington*, p. 20.

136   Jackson, *The Ulster Party*, pp. 307–19.

137   Townshend, *Political Violence in Ireland*, p. 249.

138   For example in John Hume, *A New Ireland: Politics, Peace and Reconciliation* (Boulder,
      Colo., 1996), p. 73. See also Conor Cruise O'Brien, *My Life and Themes* (Dublin, 1998),
      p. 7.

139   Jackson, *Carson*, pp. 36–8. For the gun-running, see A.T.Q. Stewart, *The Ulster
      Crisis: Resistance to Home Rule, 1912–14* (London, 1967).

140   Townshend, *Political Violence in Ireland*, p. 255.

141   Jackson, *Carson*, p. 33. There is a considerable literature on the Curragh Incident. See,
      for example, Ian Beckett (ed.), *The Army and the Curragh Incident, 1914* (London, 1986).

142   Jackson, *Saunderson*, pp. 230–1.

143   McDowell, *Irish Convention*, p. 127. R.B. McDowell has revisited this theme in his
      Crisis and Decline: The Fate of Southern Unionism (Dublin, 1997), esp. pp. 44–66.

144   See, for example, Lee, *Ireland, 1912–1985*, pp. 2–3, a theme reiterated in (for example)
      ' "Eunuchs of Drumcree?" The Problem is the Opposite', *Sunday Tribune*, 12 July 1998,
      p. 16.

145   Quoted many times but see O'Malley, *On Another Man's Wound*, p. 43.

146   Boyce, *Nationalism in Ireland*, p. 279. For Sinn Féin politics in the period see Michael
      Laffan, 'The Unification of Sinn Féin in 1917', *Irish Historical Studies*, xvii, 67 (March,
      1971), pp. 353–79. See also David Fitzpatrick, *Politics and Irish Life, 1913–21: Provincial
      Experience of War and Revolution* (Dublin, 1977).

147   Charles Townshend, *The British Campaign in Ireland, 1919–1921: The Development
      of Political and Military Policies* (Oxford, 1975), p. 16.

148   Peter Hart, 'The Geography of Revolution in Ireland, 1917–23', *Past and Present*, 155
      (1997), p. 168.

149   Townshend, *British Campaign*, p. 178.

150   Garvin, *Evolution of Irish Nationalist Politics*, p. 122; Hart, 'Geography of Revolution',
      p. 154.

151   Hart, 'Geography of Revolution', pp. 160–2.

152   Townshend, *Political Violence in Ireland*, p. 334.

153   Townshend, *British Campaign*, p. 20.

154   Ibid., p. 177.

155   Ibid., p. 42.

156 Ibid., p. 67.

157 Peter Hart, 'Michael Collins and the Assassination of Sir Henry Wilson', *Irish Historical Studies*, xxviii, 110 (Nov. 1992), pp. 150–70.

158 Garvin, *Evolution of Irish Nationalist Politics*, pp. 123–5.

159 See Joost Augusteijn, *From Public Defiance to Guerrilla Warfare: The Experience of Ordinary Volunteers in the Irish War of Independence, 1916–1921* (Dublin, 1996).

160 Quoted by Tom Garvin, *1922: The Birth of Irish Democracy* (Dublin, 1996) p. 96.

161 Hart, 'Geography of Revolution', p. 171.

162 Ibid., p. 172. For the significance of UCD for O'Malley and other revolutionaries see English, *O'Malley*, pp. 4–5, 29–30, 189–90.

163 The ambiguous relationship between the revolutionaries and British culture is one of the central themes of English, *O'Malley*.

164 Ward, *Unmanageable Revolutionaries*, pp. 144–5.

165 Ibid., p. 144.

166 Quoted many times but see Townshend, *British Campaign*, p. 193.

167 Ibid., pp. 193–4.

168 F.J. Costello, 'The Anglo-Irish War, 1919–21: A Reappraisal', PhD thesis (Boston College, 1992), p. 213.

169 R.F. Foster, *Modern Ireland, 1600–1972* (London, 1988), p. 506; Ronan Fanning, 'Roy Foster's Passion for Moderation', *Sunday Independent*, 13 Nov. 1988.

170 This counter-factual notion is considered by Alvin Jackson, 'British Ireland: What if Home Rule Had Been Enacted in 1912?', in Niall Ferguson (ed.), *Virtual History: Alternatives and Counterfactuals* (London, 1997), pp. 175–227.

171 See Lawrence MacBride, *The Greening of Dublin Castle: The Transformation of Bureaucratic and Judicial Personnel in Dublin Castle in Ireland, 1892–1922* (Washington, 1991).

172 Townshend, *British Campaign*, p. 97.

173 Ibid., p. 20.

174 Ibid., p. 46.

175 James Gleeson, *Bloody Sunday*, paperback edition (London, 1963), p. 69.

176 Tom Barry, *Guerrilla Days in Ireland* (Dublin, 1949): the description of Barry's memoir is provided by Foster, *Modern Ireland*, p. 495.

177 O'Malley, *On Another Man's Wound*, p. 336.

178 Ibid., p. 335.

179 Quoted often: see Nicholas Mansergh, *The Unresolved Question: The Anglo-Irish Settlement and its Undoing, 1912–72* (New Haven and London, 1991), p. 168; Sheila Lawlor, *Britain and Ireland, 1914–23* (Dublin, 1983), p. 109.

180 Tim Pat Coogan, *Michael Collins: A Biography* (London, 1990), pp. 226–7.

181 Garvin, *1922*, p. 51.

182 Ibid.

183 Ibid., p. 132.

184 Ward, *Irish Constitutional Tradition*, p. 175.

185 Ibid., p. 163.

186 Garvin, *1922*, p. 55.

187 Ward, *Unmanageable Revolutionaries*, p. 168.

188 Ward, *Irish Constitutional Tradition*, p. 164.

189 K. Theodore Hoppen, *Ireland since 1800: Conflict and Conformity* (London, 1989), p. 139.

190 Garvin, *1922*, p. 161.

191   Ward, *Irish Constitutional Tradition*, p. 172.
192   Quoted in F.S.L. Lyons, *Ireland since the Famine*, 2nd edition (London, 1973), p. 450.
193   Garvin, *Evolution of Irish Nationalist Politics*, p. 133.
194   Dorothy Macardle, *The Irish Republic*, 4th edition (Dublin, 1951), p. 616. See also
       Maryann Valiulis, *Portrait of a Revolutionary: General Richard Mulcahy and the Founding
       of the Irish Free State* (Dublin, 1992), p. 138.
195   Macardle, *Irish Republic*, p. 678; Garvin, *1922*, pp. 38–9.
196   Michael Hopkinson, *Green against Green: The Irish Civil War* (Dublin, 1988), pp. 112–14;
       Hart, 'Michael Collins and the Assassination of Sir Henry Wilson', favours the view
       that the assassins acted alone.
197   Hopkinson, *Green against Green*, p. 116.
198   Sir Nevil Macready, *Annals of an Active Life*, 2 vols (London, n.d.), ii, p. 654.
199   Garvin, *1922*, p. 115.
200   Ibid., p. 155.
201   Hopkinson, *Green against Green*, p. 70.
202   Ward, *Unmanageable Revolutionaries*, p. 178.
203   Quoted in ibid., p. 177.
204   Garvin, *1922*; Hart, 'Geography of Revolution', p. 163, sounds a strong note of cau-
       tion, however.
205   Garvin, *1922*, p. 143.
206   Ibid., p. 144.
207   Ibid., p. 101.
208   Hopkinson, *Green against Green*, p. 176.
209   Townshend, *Political Violence in Ireland*, p. 373.
210   Hopkinson, *Green against Green*, p. 241; see also Dorothy Macardle, *Tragedies of Kerry,
       1922–23* (Dublin, 1924).
211   Hopkinson, *Green against Green*, pp. 272ff.
212   Ibid.
213   Ibid., p. 126.

6   'Three Quarters of a Nation Once Again': Independent Ireland

1   Padraic H. Pearse, *Collected Works*, 5th edition (Dublin, 1922), p. 325.
2   Jeffrey Prager, *Building Democracy in Ireland: Political Order and Cultural Integration
     in a Newly Independent Nation* (Cambridge, 1986), pp. 16–17. See also the important
     thesis by John Regan in his *The Irish Counter-Revolution 1921–36* (Dublin, 1999).
3   Alan J. Ward, *The Irish Constitutional Tradition: Responsible Government and Modern
     Ireland, 1782–1992* (Dublin, 1994), p. 184.
4   Quoted often, but see Maryann Valiulis, *Portrait of a Revolutionary: General Richard
     Mulcahy and the Founding of the Irish Free State* (Dublin, 1992), pp. 203–4.
5   Ronan Fanning, *Independent Ireland* (Dublin, 1983), p. 51.
6   Prager, *Building Democracy*, p. 126.
7   Ibid., pp. 158–9.
8   Fanning, *Independent Ireland*, p. 86.
9   Prager, *Building Democracy*, pp. 158–9.

10 Argued at length in Richard Dunphy, *The Making of Fianna Fáil Power in Ireland, 1923–1948* (Oxford, 1995).

11 For O'Higgins see Terence de Vere White, *Kevin O'Higgins* (London, 1948).

12 Mary E. Daly, *Industrial Development and Irish National Identity, 1922–1939* (Dublin, 1992), p. 32.

13 Prager, *Building Democracy*, p. 159.

14 Dunphy, *Making of Fianna Fáil Power*, p. 85.

15 See Richard English, *Radicals and the Republic: Socialist Republicanism in the Irish Free State, 1925–1937* (Oxford, 1994), pp. 124ff.

16 F.S.L. Lyons, *Ireland since the Famine*, 2nd edition (London, 1973), p. 503.

17 Prager, *Building Democracy*, p. 193.

18 Tim Pat Coogan, *De Valera: Long Fellow, Long Shadow* (London, 1993), pp. 686, 703.

19 Ibid., p. 698.

20 Liam Skinner, *Politicians by Accident* (Dublin, 1946), p. 5.

21 Ibid., p. 9.

22 Coogan, *De Valera*, p. 75.

23 Dunphy, *Making of Fianna Fáil Power*, p. 177.

24 Ibid., p. 182.

25 Ibid., pp. 177–8.

26 John Horgan, *Seán Lemass: The Enigmatic Patriot* (Dublin, 1997), p. 66.

27 Daly, *Industrial Development and Irish National Identity*, p. 180.

28 Ibid., p. 175.

29 J.J. Lee, 'Continuity and Change in Ireland, 1945–70', in J.J. Lee (ed.), *Ireland 1945–70* (Dublin, 1979), p. 177. For these themes see Cormac Ó Gráda, *A Rocky Road: The Irish Economy since the 1920s* (Manchester, 1997).

30 Fanning, *Independent Ireland*, p. 112.

31 Dunphy, *Making of Fianna Fáil Power*, p. 151.

32 Coogan, *De Valera*, p. 436.

33 Coogan, *De Valera*, pp. 458–9.

34 Deirdre McMahon, *Republicans and Imperialists: Anglo-Irish Relations in the 1930s* (New Haven and London, 1984), p. 287.

35 Ward, *Irish Constitutional Tradition*, p. 233.

36 Ibid., p. 234.

37 Dermot Keogh, *The Vatican, the Bishops and Irish Politics, 1919–1939* (Cambridge, 1986), pp. 236–9; Keogh, *Twentieth Century Ireland: Nation and State* (Dublin, 1994), p. 98.

38 Keogh, *Twentieth Century Ireland*, p. 100; Conor Cruise O'Brien, *My Life and Themes* (Dublin, 1998), p. 99.

39 Ibid.; George Seaver, *John Allen Fitzgerald Gregg: Archbishop* (London and Dublin, 1963), pp. 127–8.

40 Dunphy, *Making of Fianna Fáil Power*, p. 208.

41 On feminist protest against the constitution see Margaret Ward, *Hanna Sheehy Skeffington: A Life* (Cork, 1997), pp. 324–7.

42 K. Theodore Hoppen, *Ireland since 1800: Conflict and Conformity* (London, 1989), p. 212.

43 McMahon, *Republicans and Imperialists*, p. 285n.

44 Ibid., pp. 236, 251.

45 Brian Barton, *Brookeborough: The Making of a Prime Minister* (Belfast, 1988), p. 125.

46 McMahon, *Republicans and Imperialists*, p. 281.

47 Ibid., p. 281.
48 John Bowman, *De Valera and the Ulster Question, 1917–73* (Oxford, 1982), p. 217.
49 Quoted often, but see ibid., p. 236.
50 Ibid., p. 237.
51 Ibid., p. 246.
52 Ibid., p. 256. See also O'Brien, *My Life and Themes*, p. 105.
53 J.J. Lee, *Ireland 1912–1985: Politics and Society* (Cambridge, 1989), p. 237.
54 Dunphy, *Making of Fianna Fáil Power*, p. 229.
55 Horgan, *Lemass*, pp. 122–3; Emmet O'Connor, *A Labour History of Ireland, 1824–1960* (Dublin, 1992), p. 148.
56 Hoppen, *Ireland since 1800*, p. 190.
57 R.F. Foster, *Modern Ireland, 1600–1972* (London, 1988), p. 565.
58 Hoppen, *Ireland since 1800*, p. 191.
59 Coogan, *De Valera*, p. 191.
60 See, for example, Paul Bew and Henry Patterson, *Seán Lemass and the Making of Modern Ireland, 1945–66* (Dublin, 1982), p. 58; Horgan, *Lemass*, passim.
61 Lee, *Ireland 1912–1985*, pp. 312–13.
62 Ibid., p. 313. McGilligan's earlier remarks are often quoted, but see Fanning, *Independent Ireland*, p. 100.
63 Lee, *Ireland 1912–1985*, p. 306.
64 Keogh, *Twentieth Century Ireland*, p. 187; O'Brien, *My Life and Themes*, p. 139.
65 Lee, *Ireland 1912–1985*, p. 315.
66 Keogh, *Twentieth Century Ireland*, p. 208.
67 O'Brien, *My Life and Themes*, p. 155.
68 Kieran Allen, *Fianna Fáil and Irish Labour: 1926 to the Present* (London, 1997), pp. 96–7.
69 Quoted by Lee, *Ireland 1912–1985*, p. 318.
70 Bew and Patterson, *Seán Lemass*, p. 64.
71 The 'mother and child' issue has been reviewed many times. For a starting point see (still) J.H. Whyte, *Church and State in Modern Ireland, 1923–1979*, 2nd edition (Dublin, 1980).
72 See, for example, Lee, *Ireland 1912–1985*, pp. 322–6.
73 Bew and Patterson, *Seán Lemass*, p. 95; Horgan, *Lemass*, p. 164.
74 Lee, *Ireland 1912–1985*, p. 327.
75 Bew and Patterson, *Seán Lemass*, p. 104.
76 Allen, *Fianna Fáil and Irish Labour*, p. 85.
77 Lee, *Ireland 1912–1985*, p. 346.
78 Horgan, *Lemass*, pp. 17–18.
79 For example by Lee, *Ireland 1912–1985*, pp. 341–59.
80 Garret FitzGerald, quoted in ibid., p. 343.
81 Hoppen, *Ireland since 1800*, p. 223.
82 Bew and Patterson, *Seán Lemass*, p. 144.
83 Ibid., p. 168; Allen, *Fianna Fáil and Irish Labour*, p. 108.
84 Skinner, *Politicians by Accident*, p. 291.
85 Keogh, *Twentieth Century Ireland*, p. 234. For an explanation of an apparently similar tactless remark (by Liam Cosgrave) see O'Brien, *My Life and Themes*, p. 183.
86 Lee, *Ireland 1912–1985*, p. 369.

87 Horgan, *Lemass*, p. 193. O'Brien is more eulogistic: see *My Life and Themes*, pp. 161–5.

88 Coogan, *De Valera*, pp. 682–3.

89 Lee, *Ireland 1912–1985*, p. 386.

90 Horgan, *Lemass*, pp. 260–1.

91 See, for example, Kevin Boland, '*We won't stand (idly) by*' (Dublin, 1971); James Kelly, *Orders from the Captain* (Dublin, 1971); Tom Macintyre, *Through the Bridewell Gate: A Diary of the Dublin Arms Trial* (London, 1971). See also Justin O'Brien, *The Arms Trial* (Dublin, 2000).

92 Coogan, *De Valera*, p. 662.

93 Brian Farrell, *Seán Lemass* (Dublin, 1983), p. 106.

94 Fanning, *Independent Ireland*, p. 200.

95 Horgan, *Lemass*, p. 351.

96 Bew and Patterson, *Seán Lemass*, p. 193.

97 Robert J. Savage, *Irish Television: The Political and Social Origins* (Cork, 1996), pp. 206–10.

7 Northern Ireland, 1920–72: Specials, Peelers and Provos

1   Public Record Office of Northern Ireland, R.J. Lynn Papers, D.3480/59/68: Lord Londonderry to Lynn, 9 Jan. 1928.

2   Paul Bew, Peter Gibbon and Henry Patterson, *Northern Ireland, 1921–94: Political Forces and Social Classes* (London, 1995), p. 217.

3   See Bryan Follis, *A State under Siege: The Establishment of Northern Ireland, 1920–1925* (Oxford, 1995), *passim*.

4   Quoted often: see R.J. Lawrence, *The Government of Northern Ireland: Public Finance and Public Services, 1921–64* (Oxford, 1965), p. 61.

5   Alan J. Ward, *The Irish Constitutional Tradition: Responsible Government and Modern Ireland, 1782–1992* (Dublin, 1994), pp. 107–9; Follis, *A State under Siege*, pp. 1–2.

6   By (*inter alia*) Bew, Gibbon and Patterson, *Northern Ireland, 1921–94*, and by David Gordon, *The O'Neill Years: Unionist Politics, 1963–1969* (Belfast, 1989).

7   Follis, *A State under Siege*, p. 14.

8   The measure is discussed at length in Patrick Buckland, *The Factory of Grievances: Devolved Government in Northern Ireland, 1921–39* (Dublin, 1979), pp. 206–20.

9   Follis, *A State under Siege*, pp. 52–6.

10 Nicholas Mansergh, *The Unresolved Question: The Anglo-Irish Settlement and its Undoing, 1912–72* (New Haven and London, 1991), p. 130n.

11 Follis, *A State under Siege*, pp. 163–4, 172–3.

12 Lynn Papers, D.3480/59/58: J.R. Fisher to Lynn, 11 Nov. 1925.

13 An epithet that was applied not infrequently: see Lynn Papers, D.3480/59/58: Fisher to Lynn, 7 Nov. 1925.

14 Lynn Papers, D.3480/59/58: Fisher to Lynn, 8 Dec. 1925.

15 Follis, *A State under Siege*, pp. 93–6, offers a fresh (if inevitably controversial) reading of this sensitive area. Eamon Phoenix, *Northern Nationalism: Nationalist Politics, Partition*

    and the Catholic Minority in Northern Ireland, 1890–1940 (Belfast, 1994), pp. 167–251, is judicious and comprehensive.

16   Buckland, *Factory of Grievances*, p. 93.

17   Ibid., p. 53.

18   'Get this into your head [Frank] MacDermot, there are *no* conditions under which we would abandon neutrality': quoted in John Bowman, *De Valera and the Ulster Question, 1917–73* (Oxford, 1982), p. 237.

19   Brian Barton, *Brookeborough: The Making of a Prime Minister* (Belfast, 1988), pp. 153, 209.

20   Bew, Gibbon and Patterson, *Northern Ireland, 1921–94*, p. 106.

21   There have been important contributions from (*inter alia*) Michael Farrell, *Northern Ireland: The Orange State* (London, 1976), and Paul Bew, Peter Gibbon and Henry Patterson, *The State in Northern Ireland, 1921–1979* (Manchester, 1979).

22   See Gordon, *The O'Neill Years, passim*.

23   Ibid., p. 103.

24   Feargal Cochrane, ' "Meddling at the Crossroad": The Decline and Fall of Terence O'Neill within the Unionist Community', in Richard English and Graham Walker (eds), *Unionism in Modern Ireland: New Perspectives on Politics and Culture* (Dublin, 1996), p. 148.

25   Quoted often: see Gordon, *The O'Neill Years*, p. 161.

26   Ibid., p. 9.

27   See Marc Mulholland, 'The Evolution of Ulster Unionism, 1960–69: Causes and Consequences', PhD thesis (Queen's University, Belfast, 1997).

28   Terence O'Neill, *The Autobiography of Terence O'Neill, Prime Minister of Northern Ireland, 1963–1969* (London, 1972), p. 70; John Horgan, *Seán Lemass: The Enigmatic Patriot* (Dublin, 1997), pp. 276–83.

29   O'Neill, *Autobiography*, p. 72.

30   Brian Faulkner, *Memoirs of a Statesman* (London, 1978), pp. 44–5.

31   Bew, Gibbon and Patterson, *Northern Ireland, 1921–94*, p. 174.

32   See Bob Purdie, *Politics in the Streets: The Origins of the Civil Rights Movement in Northern Ireland* (Belfast, 1990), *passim*.

33   Ibid., p. 123.

34   David Fitzpatrick, *The Two Irelands, 1912–1939* (Oxford, 1998), p. 155.

35   Purdie, *Politics in the Streets*, p. 94.

36   Ibid., p. 133.

37   Ibid., pp. 134–5.

38   Seán O'Callaghan, *The Informer* (London, 1998), p. 22.

39   Purdie, *Politics in the Streets*, p. 216.

40   Charles Townshend, *Political Violence in Ireland: Government and Resistance since 1848* (Oxford, 1983), p. 391.

41   The reference is adapted from Kevin O'Higgins's allusion to the wild men of republicanism.

42   O'Neill, *Autobiography*, p. 75.

43   For the rise of Ian Paisley and his movement see Steve Bruce, *'God Save Ulster!': The Religion and Politics of Paisleyism* (Oxford, 1986).

44   Ibid., p. 78.

45   See Terence O'Neill, *Ulster at the Crossroads* (London, 1969), pp. 140–6.

8 The Two Irelands, 1973–98

1   J.J. Lee, *Ireland 1912–85: Politics and Society* (Cambridge, 1989), p. 467.

2   Gemma Hussey, *Ireland Today: Anatomy of a Changing State* (Dublin, 1993), p. 159.

3   Garret FitzGerald, *All in a Life: An Autobiography* (Dublin, 1991), p. 640.

4   Ibid., p. 641.

5   Often discussed: see ibid., p. 413. See, also, Donald Harman Akenson, *Conor: A Biography of Conor Cruise O'Brien* (Montreal and Kingston, 1994).

6   Hussey, *Ireland Today*, p. 295.

7   Lee, *Ireland 1912–85*, p. 498; Dermot Keogh, *Twentieth Century Ireland: Nation and State* (Dublin, 1994), p. 381.

8   Quoted often but see, for example, the review of FitzGerald, *All in a Life* (Chris Ryder, 'How Thatcher Was Led into a Deal with Dublin'), in *Sunday Telegraph*, 13 Oct. 1991.

9   Conor Cruise O'Brien, *My Life and Themes* (Dublin, 1998), pp. 347–8.

10 Hussey, *Ireland Today*, p. 308.

11 Paul Bew, Ellen Hazelkorn and Henry Patterson, *The Dynamics of Irish Politics* (London, 1989), p. 105 (quoting the Telesis report of 1982).

12 Hussey, *Ireland Today*, p. 422.

13 FitzGerald, *All in a Life*, p. 614.

14 Ibid., p. 471.

15 Ibid., p. 176.

16 Lee, *Ireland 1912–85*, p. 482.

17 Thomas Hennessey, *A History of Northern Ireland, 1920–1996* (Dublin, 1997), p. 221.

18 The Agreement is printed in full in Feargal Cochrane, *Unionist Politics and the Politics of Unionism since the Anglo-Irish Agreement* (Cork, 1997), pp. 397–403.

19 Paul Bew, Henry Patterson and Paul Teague, *Between War and Peace: The Political Future of Northern Ireland* (London, 1997), p. 70.

20 Ibid., pp. 4, 63–70.

21 Ibid., p. 206.

22 Quoted in full in Cochrane, *Unionist Politics*, pp. 404–8.

23 Bew, Patterson and Teague, *Between War and Peace*, p. 207.

24 Ibid., p. 210.

25 Paul Bew and Gordon Gillespie (eds), *The Northern Ireland Peace Process, 1993–1996: A Chronology* (London, 1996), pp. 87–8.

26 Bew, Patterson and Teague, *Between War and Peace*, p. 13.

27 See the copy of the Good Friday Agreement printed for public distribution in Northern Ireland: *The Agreement: Agreement Reached in the Multi-Party Negotiations* (n.p., n.d.), p. 18.

28 Fintan O'Toole, *The Lie of the Land: Irish Identities* (London, 1997), p. 75.

29 The speech is reproduced in full in Bew, Patterson and Teague, *Between War and Peace*, pp. 225–31.

30 Hennessey, *A History of Northern Ireland*, p. 176.

31 The inspiration seems to have been supplied by Malcolm X's controversial allusion to 'ballots and bullets'.

32 Cochrane, *Unionist Politics*, p. 226.

33 Steve Bruce, *The Edge of the Union: The Ulster Loyalist Political Vision* (Oxford, 1994), p. 16.

34 *Irish Times*, 6 Nov. 1978.

35 Bew, Patterson and Teague, *Between War and Peace*, p. 66.

36 Cochrane, *Unionist Politics*, p. 271.

37 See Deaglán de Bréadún, 'The Challenge for New Nationalists', *Irish Times*, 27 June 1998.

38 Quoted in Cochrane, *Unionist Politics*, p. 119.

39 Clifford Smyth, *Ian Paisley: Voice of Protestant Ulster* (Edinburgh, 1986), p. 29.

40 Cochrane, *Unionist Politics*, p. 211.

41 Ibid., p. viii.

42 See, for example, Steven King, 'Trimble is an Unlikely Latter-day Faulkner', *Irish Times*, 9 March 1998.

43 Cochrane, *Unionist Politics*, p. 108.

44 Ibid., p. 129.

45 See Steve Bruce, *'God Save Ulster!': The Religion and Politics of Paisleyism* (Oxford, 1986).

46 Cochrane, *Unionist Politics*, p. 354.

47 Paul Bew, 'The Unionists Have Won – They Just Don't Know It', *Sunday Times*, 17 May 1998.

9   Ireland in the New Millennium

1 R.F. Foster, *Luck and the Irish: A History of Change, 1970–2000* (London, 2007), p. 34.

2 E.g. Kieran Allen, *The Celtic Tiger: The Myth of Social Partnership in Ireland* (Manchester, 2000).

3 Henry Patterson, *Ireland since 1939: The Persistence of Conflict* (Dublin, 2006), p. 287. See also, *inter alia*, Colin Coulter and Steve Coleman (eds.), *The End of Irish History? Critical Approaches to the Celtic Tiger* (Manchester, 2003).

4 Foster, *Luck and the Irish*, p. 10.

5 Foster, *Luck and the Irish*, p. 8.

6 Bryan Fanning, quoted in Henry McDonald, *Colours: Ireland – From Bombs to Boom* (Edinburgh, 2004), p. 112. See also Bryan Fanning (ed.), *Immigration and Social Change in the Republic of Ireland* (Manchester, 2007) and Piaras MacÉinrí and Allen White, 'Immigration into the Republic of Ireland: A Bibliography of Recent Research', *Irish Geography*, 41, 2 (July, 2008), pp. 151–79.

7 Bertie Ahern, *The Autobiography* (London, 2009), p. 340.

8 John A. Murphy, 'Credit Where it Is Due – and not Due', *Irish Independent*, 6 April 2008. See also Diarmaid Ferriter's critique, 'History Will Be Kind to Ahern's Legacy', *Sunday Business Post*, 6 April 2008.

9 Ahern, *Autobiography*, p. 262.

10 E.g. Ahern, *Autobiography*, pp. 208–9.

11 Ahern, *Autobiography*, pp. 268–9.

12 Jonathan Powell, *Great Hatred, Little Room: Making Peace in Northern Ireland* (London, 2008), p. 94.

13 Powell, *Great Hatred, Little Room*, pp. 309–10.

14 Powell, *Great Hatred, Little Room*, p. 103. Compare Ahern's tribute in his *Autobiography*, pp. 266–7.

15 Ahern deals with this argument in his *Autobiography*, p. 341.

16 See e.g. Diarmaid Ferriter, *Occasions of Sin: Sex and Society in Modern Ireland* (London, 2009); James Smith, *Ireland's Magdalen Laundries and the Nation's Architecture of Containment* (Manchester, 2008).

17 Alvin Jackson, *Home Rule: An Irish History* (London, 2003), pp. 322–3.

18 Patterson, *Ireland since 1939*, p. 320.

19 Powell, *Great Hatred, Little Room*, p. 267.

20 Paul Bew, *Ireland: The Politics of Enmity, 1789–2006* (Oxford, 2007), p. 552.

21 Powell, *Great Hatred, Little Room*, p. 277.

22 Christopher Farrington, *Ulster Unionism and the Peace Process in Northern Ireland* (Basingstoke, 2006), p. 186; Eric Kaufmann, *The Orange Order: A Contemporary Northern Irish History* (Oxford, 2007), p. 120.

23 Powell, *Great Hatred, Little Room*, pp. 2, 251.

24 Ahern, *Autobiography*, p. 311.

25 Powell, *Great Hatred, Little Room*, p. 275.

26 Powell, *Great Hatred, Little Room*, p. 296.

27 See David Bebbington, *William Ewart Gladstone: Faith and Politics in Victorian Britain* (Grand Rapids, 1992); David Bebbington, *The Mind of Gladstone: Religion, Homer and Politics* (Oxford, 2004).

28 Powell, *Great Hatred, Little Room*, p. 305.

29 McDonald, *Colours*, pp. 97–9, quoting work by Peter Shirlow.

30 Francis Fukuyama, 'The End of History?', *The National Interest*, 9 (Summer, 1989), pp. 3–18.

31 Richard J. Evans, *In Defence of History* (London, 1997), p. 229.

Chronology

1782	20 March	Fall of the North Ministry.
	27 March	Formation of the Rockingham Ministry.
	4 May	Gardiner's (Catholic) Relief Act.
	21 June	Repeal of the Declaratory Act (1720).
	27 July	Amendment of Poynings' Law through Yelverton's Act.
1783	17 April	Renunciation Act passed by the British parliament.
1784	4 July	Foundation of the (Protestant) Peep o'Day Boys, County Armagh, after a sectarian dispute at Markethill.
	September	Spread of the (Catholic) Defender movement.
1788	5 November	George III's illness provokes Regency Crisis in Britain and (later) in Ireland.
1789	19 February	Irish parliament invites George, Prince of Wales, to assume the regency of Ireland.
	10 March	The recovery of George III.
	20 June	John Fitzgibbon appointed Lord Chancellor of Ireland.
	14 July	Attack on the Bastille, Paris: revolution in France.
1791	February	Catholic Committee petition for civil rights.
	14 October	Foundation of the United Irishmen (Belfast).
	9 November	First meeting of the United Irishmen in Dublin.
1792	18 April	Langrishe's (Catholic) Relief Act.
	14 July	Bastille celebrations in Belfast and elsewhere.
	3–8 December	Catholic Convention meets.
1793	1 February	War declared between England and France.
	9 April	Hobart's Catholic Relief Act; Militia Act.
1794	23 May	Suppression of the Dublin United Irishmen.
1795	4 January	Earl Fitzwilliam appointed lord lieutenant of Ireland: purge of the Castle administration.

	23 February	Fitzwilliam dismissed.
	10 May	United Irishmen reformed as a secret, oath-bound revolutionary organization.
	21 September	Battle of the Diamond, Loughgall, County Armagh: Orange Order established.
1796	22–7 December	Hoche's expedition and the French fleet in Bantry Bay: broken up by storms.
1797	13 March	General Gerard Lake's arms proclamation, Ulster.
1798	8 March	Orange Order meets in Dublin: movement begins to organize on a national basis.
	12 March	Arrest of the Dublin United Irish leadership.
	29 March	Viscount Castlereagh appointed as Chief Secretary.
	23–4 May	Beginning of the Rebellion in Leinster.
	6–13 June	Rebellion in Ulster.
	21 June	Defeat of the Wexford rebels at Vinegar Hill.
	22 August	French landings at Killala, Mayo: Humbert surrenders at Ballinamuck, 8 September.
	3 November	Arrest of Tone: dies by his own hand on 19 November.
1800	21 May	Introduction of the Bill for Union into the Dublin parliament.
	1 August	Act of Union receives the royal assent.
	2 August	Last meeting of the Irish parliament.
1801	1 January	Act of Union effective.
1802	28 January	Death of John Fitzgibbon, Lord Clare.
1803	23 July	Rising in Dublin led by Robert Emmet.
	20 September	Execution of Emmet.
1806	23 January	Death of William Pitt.
1808	15 August	Foundation of the Christian Brothers by Edmund Rice.
	14–15 September	Catholic bishops reject veto proposal.
1812	4 August	Robert Peel appointed Chief Secretary.
1814	30 May	First Peace of Paris.
	1 November	Congress of Vienna opened.
1815	18 June	Battle of Waterloo.
	20 November	Second Peace of Paris.
1820	4 June	Death of Henry Grattan.
1821	20 May	Census taken: population recorded as 6,801,827.
1822	12 August	Death of Robert Stewart, 2nd Marquis of Londonderry (and Chief Secretary of Ireland, 1798–1801).
1823	12 May	Foundation of the Catholic Association.
1824	24 January	Catholic Association inaugurates 'Catholic rent'.
1825	18 May	House of Lords rejects Francis Burdett's Catholic Emancipation Bill.
1826	19–29 June	Waterford election: defeat of Lord George Beresford by emancipationist candidate, Henry Villiers Stuart.

1828	22 January	Duke of Wellington appointed as Prime Minister.
	5 July	Clare election: return of Daniel O'Connell.
	14 August	Foundation of the Brunswick clubs (dedicated to the Protestant constitution).
1829	13 April	Passage of the Catholic Emancipation Act.
1830	4 February	O'Connell takes his seat in the House of Commons.
	22 November	Earl Grey appointed as Prime Minister.
1831	3 March	Start of the tithe war in the midlands.
	18 June	Newtownbarry, County Wexford: tithe war killings.
	9 September	Establishment of the national primary school system.
	12 December	Foundation of the Sisters of Mercy by Catherine McAuley.
		Census results: population recorded as 7,767,401.
1832	7 August	Irish Reform Act passed.
	December	General election, United Kingdom.
1833	14 August	Irish Church Temporalities Act.
1834	22 April	O'Connell introduces a parliamentary debate on repeal.
	30 October	Conservative meeting at Hillsborough, County Down.
	17 December	First steam-powered train in Ireland: Westland Row, Dublin, to Kingstown.
1835	January	General election, United Kingdom.
	18 February	Lichfield House Compact: informal alliance between Whigs, Radicals and O'Connell's followers affirmed.
1836	14 April	Dissolution of the Orange Order.
1837	July–August	General election, United Kingdom.
1838	31 July	Irish Poor Law enacted.
	15 August	Tithe Rent Charge Act passed.
1840	15 April	Establishment of the National Association by O'Connell.
	13 July	National Association relaunched as the Loyal National Repeal Association.
	10 August	Irish Municipal Reform Act.
1841	March	Foundation of the Dublin Protestant Operatives' Association.
	6 June	First reliable census of the population (8,175,124 people recorded).
	July	General election, United Kingdom.
	1 November	O'Connell elected lord mayor of Dublin.
1842	15 October	*Nation* appears for the first time.
1843	15 August	'Monster' repeal meeting held at Tara, County Meath: perhaps 750,000 attend.
	7 October	Repeal meeting at Clontarf (planned for 8 October) cancelled.
1844	10 February	O'Connell convicted of sedition.
1845	14 February	Report of the Devon Commission on land published.

	30 June	Maynooth College Act.
	31 July	Colleges (Ireland) Act: Queen's Colleges established at Belfast, Cork and Galway.
	August	Revival of the Orange Order.
	9 September	Potato blight first reported in Ireland.
	16 September	Death of Thomas Davis.
	9–10 November	British Prime Minister Peel authorizes importation of Indian corn.
1846	26 June	Repeal of the Corn Laws.
	30 June	Peel and the Tory government ousted by the Whigs: Lord John Russell heads the new administration.
	28 July	O'Connellite movement split over the use of physical force.
	15 August	Food depots and public works closed down by Treasury.
	28 August	Poor Employment (Ireland) Act: Treasury loans for relief work.
1847	13 January	Foundation of the Irish Confederation.
	26 February	Destitute Poor (Ireland) Act.
	10 April	Peak of fever epidemic.
	15 May	Death of Daniel O'Connell.
	8 June	Poor Relief (Ireland) Act: some outdoor relief granted.
	August	General election, United Kingdom.
1848	12 February	Foundation of the *United Irishman* by John Mitchel.
	22–4 February	Revolution in France.
	29 July	Rising in Ballingarry, County Tipperary.
1849	12 July	Dolly's Brae, County Down: sectarian battle between ribbonmen and Orangemen.
	28 July	Passage of the Encumbered Estates Act.
	October	Opening of the Queen's Colleges.
	14 October	First tenant protection society established (at Callan, County Kilkenny).
1850	24 February	Paul Cullen consecrated as Archbishop of Armagh.
	12 March	Party Processions Act.
	9 August	Establishment of the Irish Tenant League.
	14 August	Passage of the Irish Reform Act: county electorate trebled.
1851	30 March	Census taken: population recorded as 6,552,385.
1852	July	General election, United Kingdom.
	8–9 September	Tenant League conference in Dublin.
1854	28 March	Crimean War opens.
1856	16 January	Armistice in the Crimea.
1857	March–April	General election, United Kingdom.
1858	17 March	Foundation of the Irish Republican Brotherhood in Dublin.
1859	29 March	First number of the *Irish Times*.

	April	Foundation of the Fenian Brotherhood in the USA.
	May	General election, United Kingdom.
	29 June	Peak of the Ulster (evangelical) revival.
1861	7 April	Census taken: population recorded as 5,798,967.
1862	1 January	Edward Harland and G.W. Wolff enter shipbuilding partnership.
1864	29 December	National Association of Ireland founded.
1865	July	General election, United Kingdom.
1867	11–12 February	Original date for Fenian rising: minor disturbances.
	5 March	Fenian rising: rapidly suppressed.
	20 June	Clan na Gael founded (New York).
	23 November	Execution of the 'Manchester Martyrs'.
	13 December	Fenian bomb at Clerkenwell, London: 12 killed.
1868	29 February	William Johnston of Ballykilbeg gaoled for contravening the Party Processions Act.
	5 March	Protestant Defence Association founded (opposed to Church disestablishment).
	13 July	Irish Reform Act.
	3 August	Foundation of the Amnesty campaign for the Fenian prisoners.
	November	General election, United Kingdom.
1869	26 July	Passage of the Irish Church Act: disestablishment of the Church of Ireland.
1870	19 May	Home Rule movement formed by Isaac Butt.
	1 August	Gladstone's first Irish Land Act.
	1 September	First meeting of the Home Government Association.
1871	2 April	Census taken: population recorded as 5,412,377.
1872	27 June	Repeal of the Party Processions Acts (1850, 1860).
	18 July	Ballot Act establishes secrecy during voting.
1873	8 January	Formation of the Home Rule Confederation of Great Britain.
	12 March	Defeat of Gladstone's Irish University Bill.
	18–21 November	Formation of the Home Rule League (Dublin).
1874	February	General election: 60 Home Rulers returned.
	3 March	Home Rule Parliamentary Party created.
	30 July	Obstruction campaign begins in parliament.
1875	22 April	Charles Stewart Parnell enters House of Commons (MP for Meath).
1876	10 August	IRB Supreme Council withdraws support from the Home Rule movement.
	29 December	Society for the Preservation of the Irish Language established.
1877	31 July	Acceleration of obstructionist strategy by militant Home Rule MPs (including Parnell).
	28 August	Charles Stewart Parnell elected President of the Home Rule Confederation of Great Britain.

1878	16 August	Intermediate Education (Ireland) Act: board for secondary education established.
	24 October	John Devoy (Clan na Gael) proposes 'New Departure' to the Parnellites.
1879	20 April	Launch of the land agitation at Irishtown, County Mayo.
	5 May	Death of Isaac Butt, founder of the Home Rule movement.
	16 August	National Land League of Mayo formed.
	21 October	Irish National Land League formed.
1880	2 January–11 March	Parnell in the USA.
	20 February	Parnell's 'last link' speech, Cincinatti.
	March–April	General election, United Kingdom.
	17 May	Parnell elected Chairman of the Irish Parliamentary Party.
	19 September	Parnell launches the boycott campaign against those defying the Land League (Ennis, County Clare).
	24 October	Formation of the Ladies' Land League (New York).
	12–26 November	50 Orange labourers harvest the crop at Lough Mask, where Captain Boycott is agent to Lord Erne.
	December	Property Defence Association founded by landlords.
1881	4 January	Bessborough report on land.
	31 January	Ladies' Land League launched in Ireland.
	3 April	Census taken: population recorded as 5,174,836.
	22 August	Gladstone's second Land Act: legalization of the 'three fs'.
	15–17 September	Parnell advises Land League to test the new Act.
	13 October	Arrest of Parnell.
	18 October	Land League leaders' 'No Rent' manifesto.
	20 October	Proscription of the Land League.
1882	2 May	Parnell released after the Kilmainham 'treaty' with Gladstone.
	6 May	Phoenix Park, Dublin: the assassinations of Lord Frederick Cavendish and T.H. Burke.
	17 October	Irish National League formed.
1883	11 December	Parnell National Tribute handed over (£38,000 raised).
1884	1 October	Agreement between the Catholic hierarchy and the Irish Party over the representation of Catholic educational claims.
	1 November	Foundation of the Gaelic Athletic Association.
	6 December	Representation of the People Act: Irish electorate increased from 224,000 to 738,000.
1885	21 January	Parnell's 'ne plus ultra' speech.
	1 May	Irish Loyal and Patriotic Union founded.
	25 June	Redistribution of Seats Act reforms constituency divisions.

	14 August	Ashbourne Act: land purchase extended.
	24 November–9 December	General election: Liberal victory, with Parnellites holding 86 seats.
	17 December	Reports of Gladstone's conversion to Home Rule published.
1886	8 January	Ulster Loyalist Anti-Repeal Committee launched.
	25 January	Irish Unionist Parliamentary Party created.
	22 February	Lord Randolph Churchill in Belfast, encouraging loyalists.
	8 April	Introduction of the first Home Rule Bill.
	4 June	Formation of the Ulster Liberal Unionist Association.
	8 June	Defeat of Gladstone's Home Rule Bill.
	1–17 July	General election: Conservative victory.
	July–September	Severe rioting in Belfast: 32 killed.
	23 October	Launch of the Plan of Campaign (agrarian agitation).
1887	7 March	Arthur Balfour appointed as Chief Secretary for Ireland.
	18 April	'Parnellism and Crime': article and letter published in *The Times* linking Parnell to the Phoenix Park murders.
	19 July	Criminal Law and Procedure (Ireland) Act.
	9 September	'Mitchelstown Massacre': three demonstrators killed by RIC.
1888	17 September–	Special Commission of enquiry into the
	22 November 1889	allegations published in *The Times*.
1889	20–2 February	Pigott exposed as the forger of *The Times* letter.
	24 December	O'Shea divorce petition lodged, citing Parnell.
1890	15–17 November	O'Shea divorce hearing.
	24 November	Gladstone reports to Justin McCarthy that Liberal support for Home Rule is threatened by Parnell's continued leadership of the Irish Party.
	25 November	Parnell re-elected as chairman of the Irish Party.
	29 November	Parnell's Manifesto to the Irish People: he denounces the Liberal alliance.
	1–6 December	Debate within the Irish Party: the majority come down in opposition to Parnell.
1891	3 February	Final breakdown of the effort for agreement within the Irish Party.
	5 April	Census taken: population recorded as 4,704,750.
	6 April	ILPU becomes the Irish Unionist Alliance.
	5 August	Land Purchase Act; establishment of the Congested Districts Board.
	6 October	Death of Parnell (Brighton).
	28 December	Irish Literary Society founded in London by W.B. Yeats and others.
1892	17 June	Ulster Unionist Convention, Belfast.
	4–18 July	General election: Liberal victory.

	16 August	Foundation of the National Literary Society.
	29 September	Belfast Labour Party formed (first in Ireland).
	25 November	Douglas Hyde speaks on 'The Necessity for De-Anglicising Ireland'.
1893	13 February	Introduction of the second Home Rule Bill.
	31 July	Formation of the Gaelic League.
	9 September	Rejection of the second Home Rule Bill by the Lords.
1894	18 April	Irish Agricultural Organization Society formed.
	27–8 April	Foundation of the Irish Trades Union Congress.
1895	12–26 July	General election: Conservative victory.
1896	29 May	Foundation of the Irish Socialist Republican Party.
	1 August	Recess Committee report.
	14 August	Gerald Balfour's Land Act.
1898	23 January	Foundation of the United Irish League.
	12 August	Local Government Act.
1899	4 March	*United Irishman* launched by Arthur Griffith.
	8 May	First production of the Irish Literary Theatre.
	9 August	Agriculture and Technical Instruction Act.
	11 October	Outbreak of the South African war.
1900	30 January	Reunification of the Irish Parliamentary Party.
	6 February	John Redmond elected leader of the IPP.
	29 September–12 October	General election: Conservative victory.
	30 September	Foundation of Cumann na nGaedheal by Arthur Griffith.
	9 November	George Wyndham appointed Chief Secretary.
1901	31 March	Census taken: population recorded as 4,458,775.
	5 June	T.W. Russell founds the Ulster Farmers' and Labourers' Union and Compulsory Purchase Association.
1902	31 May	Treaty of Vereeniging marks end of South African war.
	18 August	T.H. Sloan (Independent Unionist) captures South Belfast seat.
	20 December	Land Conference brings together landlords and tenants.
1903	11 June	Foundation of the Independent Orange Order.
	14 August	Land Act: comprehensive scheme of land purchase launched.
	22 October	Death of W.E.H. Lecky, historian.
1904	2 January	Arthur Griffith begins 'The Resurrection of Hungary' articles in the *United Irishman*.
	26 August	Irish Reform Association (centrist) launched: promotes private discussion of the possibility of devolution for Ireland.
	2 December	Ulster Unionist conference calls for the creation of an Ulster Unionist Council.
	27 December	Opening of the Abbey Theatre.

1905	3 March	Ulster Unionist Council launched (Belfast).
	6 March	Resignation of George Wyndham.
	8 March	Formation of the Dungannon Clubs (Belfast).
	13 July	Independent Orange Order publishes the 'Magheramorne Manifesto'.
	28 November	Griffith proposes the Sinn Féin policy to the National Council.
1906	13–27 January	General election: Liberal victory.
	14 October	Laurence Ginnell advocates cattle driving (Downs, County Westmeath).
	21 October	Death of Colonel Edward Saunderson, Unionist leader.
1907	28–30 January	Riots at the premiere of the *Playboy of the Western World*.
	29 January	Augustine Birrell appointed as Chief Secretary.
	21 April	Sinn Féin League formed from Cumann na nGaedheal and Dungannon Clubs.
	6 May	James Larkin launches a dock strike in Belfast.
	21 May	Irish Party conference declares against Irish Council Bill.
	2 August	Pius X issues the Ne Temere decree on mixed marriages.
	5 September	Sinn Féin formed from the union of the National Council with the Sinn Féin League.
	December	Return of Tom Clarke, veteran Fenian, to Dublin.
1908	21 February	North Leitrim by-election: first parliamentary outing for Sinn Féin.
	1 August	Irish Universities Act passed: formation of the National University of Ireland and Queen's University, Belfast.
	8 September	Opening of St Enda's School by Patrick Pearse.
	11 November	Irish Women's Franchise League established.
	29 December	Proposal for Irish Transport Workers' Union.
1909	4 January	Larkin founds the ITGWU.
	9–10 February	'Baton' Convention of the United Irish League.
	30 November	House of Lords rejects the 'People's Budget': precipitates constitutional crisis.
	3 December	Passage of the Birrell Land Act.
1910	15–28 January	General election: Liberals retain power under Asquith.
	21 February	Edward Carson elected as leader of the Irish Unionist Parliamentary Party.
	June–November	Constitutional conference, London, fails.
	December	General election: Liberals retain power.
1911	23 January	Ulster Women's Unionist Council founded.
	1 April	SS *Titanic* launched by Harland and Wolff.
	2 April	Census taken: population recorded as 4,381,951.

	18 August	Parliament Act (abolishes absolute veto of the Lords).
	21 August	Formation of the Irish Women's Suffrage Federation.
	23 September	Ulster Unionist demonstration at Craigavon, Belfast.
	13 November	Andrew Bonar Law elected Conservative leader.
1912	9 April	Bonar Law pledges unconditional support for Ulster Unionist resistance to Home Rule (Balmoral, Belfast).
	11 April	Introduction of the third Home Rule Bill.
	14–15 April	*Titanic* disaster.
	11 June	Agar-Robartes exclusion amendment to the Home Rule Bill.
	28 June	Irish Labour Party founded.
	28 September	Ulster Solemn League and Covenant (of opposition to Home Rule) signed by Unionists.
1913	1 January	Carson's exclusion amendment to the Home Rule Bill.
	31 January	Formation of the Ulster Volunteer Force.
	26 August	Start of the ITGWU strike in Dublin.
	24 September	Provisional Government of Ulster launched by the UUC, Belfast.
	19 November	Formation of the Irish Citizen Army.
	25 November	Foundation of the Irish Volunteers under Eoin MacNeill.
1914	20 March	Curragh Incident.
	2 April	Foundation of Cumann na mBan.
	24–5 April	Larne gun-running.
	23 June	Government of Ireland (Amendment) Bill proposes exclusion through county option in Ulster.
	21–4 July	Buckingham Palace Conference fails to reach an agreement on Ulster exclusion from Home Rule.
	26 July	Howth gun-running: four killed at Bachelor's Walk, Dublin, in a confrontation between the army and protestors.
	3 August	Outbreak of war between Germany and France: Redmond pledges the support of the Irish Volunteers for the defence of Ireland.
	4 August	Outbreak of war between Britain and Germany.
	15 September	Home Rule suspensory measure passed.
	18 September	Home Rule enacted but suspended.
	20 September	Redmond at Woodenbridge, County Wicklow: he commits the Irish Volunteers to serving outside Ireland.
	24 September	Split opens up within the Volunteers between supporters and opponents of Redmond's position.
1915	25 May	Coalition government formed under Asquith.
	May	Foundation of the Military Committee of the IRB Supreme Council.

	29 July	Gaelic League votes to take a more directly political line: Hyde resigns from the presidency.
	December	Military Council of the IRB expanded.
1916	19–22 January	Military Council of the IRB agrees on a rising no later than Easter.
	3 April	Plans published for Irish Volunteer 'manoeuvres' on 23 April (Easter Sunday).
	20–1 April	German arms shipment intercepted by the Royal Navy: the *Aud* captured and scuttled.
	21 April	Roger Casement arrives from Germany and is arrested.
	22 April	Eoin MacNeill countermands the order for manoeuvres.
	23 April	MacNeill's countermanding order published. Military Council of the IRB agrees to proceed with its plans for rebellion.
	24 April	Initial military operations of the rebels: key buildings (including the GPO) seized and reinforced.
	29 April	The unconditional surrender of the insurgents.
	3–12 May	The leaders of the Rising executed.
	May–July	Lloyd George attempts to negotiate a deal between the Irish Party and the Ulster Unionists on the basis of exclusion.
	1 July	Opening of the Somme offensive.
	3 August	Execution of Casement.
	7 December	Lloyd George replaces Asquith as PM.
	22–3 December	The first of those interned after the Rising return to Ireland.
	29 December	James Joyce's *Portrait of the Artist* published (New York).
1917	5 February	Roscommon by-election: Count Plunkett returned for Sinn Féin. The first of a series of decisive by-election victories for the party.
	9 May	Longford South by-election: Joseph McGuinness (Sinn Féin) victorious.
	16 May	Proposal for an Irish Convention launched.
	10 July	Clare East by-election: Eamon de Valera (Sinn Féin) victorious.
	25 July	First meeting of the Convention: it survives until 5 April 1918.
	25–6 October	Sinn Féin ard-fheis: Eamon de Valera elected President of the party; the constitution of the party is modified.
	27 October	De Valera elected President of the Irish Volunteers.
1918	6 February	Representation of the People and Redistribution of Seats Acts.
	6 March	Death of John Redmond.

	18 April	Military Service Act raises the possibility of conscription in Ireland: Mansion House Conference of nationalist protestors.
	21 April	Anti-Conscription pledge signed by nationalists.
	17–18 May	Arrest of Sinn Féin leadership.
	11 November	Armistice.
	14–28 December	General election: Sinn Féin wins 73 seats to the six captured by the nationalists. The Unionists win 26 seats.
1919	21 January	Soloheadbeg ambush, County Tipperary: two RIC men shot. First meeting of Dáil Éireann in opening of Anglo-Irish war.
	3 June	Local Government (Ireland) Act.
	18 June	Dáil Éireann founds 'arbitration courts'.
	28 June	Treaty of Versailles signed.
	4 July	Sinn Féin and IRA proscribed.
	12 September	Dáil Éireann proscribed.
	11 November	First number of the *Irish Bulletin*.
1920	15 January	Local elections: sweeping Sinn Féin victories.
	25 February	Government of Ireland Bill introduced into the Commons.
	20 March	UUC, Belfast, accepts the Government of Ireland Bill.
	20 March	Tomas MacCurtain killed, Cork.
	14 October	Seán Treacy killed in gun-battle, Dublin.
	25 October	Death of Terence MacSwiney on hunger strike.
	1 November	Enrolment begins of Ulster Special Constabulary; execution of Kevin Barry.
	21 November	'Bloody Sunday'.
	28 November	Kilmichael ambush, County Cork: IRA kill 18 auxiliaries.
	11 December	Burning of parts of Cork city centre by the auxiliaries.
	23 December	Government of Ireland measure enacted: devolved administration launched in Northern Ireland.
1921	4 February	James Craig succeeds Carson as Ulster Unionist leader.
	5 May	Craig and de Valera meet in Dublin.
	24 May	General election, Northern Ireland: Ulster Unionists win 40 out of 52 seats.
	25 May	Burning of the Customs House, Dublin.
	22 June	Opening of the Northern Ireland parliament, Belfast: George V makes a conciliatory address.
	9 July	Truce proclaimed between the crown forces and the IRA.
	16 August	Second Dáil formed.

	11 October	Negotiations launched between representatives of the British government and that of the Dáil.
	6 December	Anglo-Irish Treaty signed.
	14 December	Debate on the Treaty within Dáil Éireann begins.
1922	7 January	Dáil accepts the Treaty.
	9 January	Arthur Griffith elected as President, following the resignation of de Valera.
	14 January	Formation of the Provisional Government of Ireland.
	16 January	Hand-over of power: the end of the Castle administration.
	2 February	Joyce's *Ulysses* published.
	26–7 March	Anti-Treaty IRA repudiate the authority of the Dáil.
	30 March	Craig–Collins pact signed in an effort to ease sectarian confrontation in Northern Ireland.
	14 April	Republican forces opposed to the Treaty seize the Four Courts.
	20 May	Collins–de Valera electoral pact.
	16 June	General election in the Irish Free State: electorate endorses the Treaty.
	22 June	Assassination of Sir Henry Wilson, London.
	28 June	Irish Free State forces move to dislodge Irregulars from the Four Courts: effective beginning of the civil war.
	5 July	Cathal Brugha shot at the Hammam Hotel, Dublin.
	12 July	Michael Collins appointed commander-in-chief, Free State army.
	12 August	Death of Arthur Griffith.
	22 August	Michael Collins shot dead in the Béal na mBláth ambush.
	9 September	Third Dáil: W.T. Cosgrave elected as president.
	11 September	Abolition of proportional representation for local elections in Northern Ireland.
	25 October	Passage of the Irish Free State constitution through the Dáil.
	15 November	General election, United Kingdom.
	17 November	Beginning of the execution of republican prisoners by the Free State authorities.
	24 November	Execution of Erskine Childers.
	6 December	Irish Free State formally established.
	7 December	Assassination of Seán Hales: government executes four imprisoned republicans in retaliation.
1923	7 March	Ballyseedy, County Kerry: eight republicans killed.
	10 April	Liam Lynch, commander of the anti-Treaty IRA, shot.
	24 May	Republican military campaign ended.
	9 August	Hogan Land Act (Irish Free State).
	27 August	General election, Free State: Cumann na nGaedheal victory.

	10 September	Ireland enters the League of Nations.
	14 November	W.B. Yeats awarded the Nobel Prize for Literature.
	6 December	General election, United Kingdom.
1924	6–19 March	Army Mutiny.
	21 April	Ministers and Secretaries Act passed.
	29 October	General election, United Kingdom.
	6 November	First meeting of the Boundary Commission.
1925	3 April	General election in Northern Ireland.
	7 November	Boundary Commission proposals leaked to the press.
	3 December	Tripartite Agreement.
1926	18 April	Census taken, Irish Free State and Northern Ireland: population recorded as 2,971,992 (IFS) and 1,256,561 (NI).
	16 May	Foundation of Fianna Fáil.
	11 November	George Bernard Shaw receives the Nobel Prize for Literature.
1927	28 May	Agricultural Credit Corporation launched.
	9 June	General election, Irish Free State.
	10 July	Assassination of Kevin O'Higgins.
	20 July	Introduction of Public Safety legislation.
	4 August	Death of John Dillon.
	11 August	Establishment of the Electricity Supply Board.
	12 August	Fianna Fáil deputies take their seats in Dáil.
	15 September	General election, Irish Free State.
	9 November	Electoral (Amendment No. 2) Act.
1928	25 February	Death of William O'Brien.
	May	Joseph Devlin forms the National League of the North.
1929	16 April	Proportional representation abolished for parliamentary contests in Northern Ireland.
	22 May	General election, Northern Ireland.
	30 June	General election, United Kingdom.
	21 October	Opening of the Shannon hydro-electric scheme.
	29 October	Wall Street Crash.
1930	17 September	Irish Free State elected to the League of Nations Council.
1931	26 September	Foundation of Saor Éire.
	17 October	Constitution (Amendment No. 17) Act passed: a severe public safety measure.
	27 October	General election, United Kingdom.
	11 December	Statute of Westminster.
1932	16 February	General election: Fianna Fáil victory.
	9 March	First Fianna Fáil government formed.
	22–6 June	Eucharistic Congress.
	30 June	Land annuities withheld from the British: beginning of the economic war.
	4–13 October	Unemployed riot in Belfast.
	16 November	Opening of the Stormont parliament building.

	anuary	General election, Irish Free State.
	3 May	Oath of allegiance removed from the Free State constitution.
	20 July	National Guard (Blueshirts) formed from the Army Comrades' Association: proscribed, 22 August.
	2 September	United Ireland (Fine Gael) formed from Cumann na nGaedheal, National Guard and the Centre Party.
	2 November	Legislation curtails power of the governor general.
	16 November	Legislation restricting right of appeal to the privy council.
	30 November	General election, Northern Ireland.
1934	18 January	Death of Joseph Devlin.
	7–8 April	Republican Congress formed.
	21 December	Coal–Cattle Pact signals relaxation of the economic war.
1935	6–9 May	Rioting in Belfast during celebrations of George V's Jubilee.
	12–21 July	Rioting in Belfast after Orange demonstrations.
	22 October	Death of Edward Carson.
	14 November	General election, United Kingdom.
1936	26 April	Census taken, IFS: population recorded as 2,968,420.
	27 May	Aer Lingus inaugurated.
	29 May	Irish Free State Senate abolished.
	18 June	IRA proscribed.
	10 December	Abdication of King Edward VIII.
	11 December	Amending Act removes references to the crown from the Free State constitution.
	12 December	External Relations Act.
1937	28 February	Census taken, Northern Ireland: population recorded as 1,279,745.
	14 June	De Valera's new constitution approved by the Dáil.
	1 July	General election and constitutional referendum, Irish Free State.
1938	9 February	General election, Northern Ireland.
	25 April	Anglo-Irish Agreement: settlement of the economic war; return of the Treaty ports.
	17 June	General election, Éire: Fianna Fáil victory.
	25 June	Douglas Hyde inaugurated as first President of Ireland.
1939	16 January	IRA launches bombing campaign in England.
	28 January	Death of W.B. Yeats.
	14 June	Legislation suppressing the IRA passed by the Dáil.
	25 August	IRA bomb, Coventry: five killed.
	3 September	Beginning of the Second World War.
1940	24 November	Death of James Craig.
	25 November	John M. Andrews succeeds as Prime Minister of Northern Ireland.

	27 December	John Charles McQuaid consecrated as Archbishop of Dublin.
1941	13 January	Death of James Joyce, Zurich.
	April–May	German air-raids on Belfast: raid of 15–16 April kills 745.
	7 December	Japan attacks US naval base at Pearl Harbor, Hawaii.
1943	28 April	John Andrews resigns as Prime Minister of Northern Ireland, and as Ulster Unionist leader.
	1 May	Basil Brooke appointed Prime Minister of Northern Ireland.
	22 June	General election, Éire: Fianna Fáil victory.
1944	14 January	Split within the Irish Labour Party: formation of National Labour.
	30 May	General election, Éire: Fianna Fáil victory.
	6 June	D-Day: Allied invasion of France.
1945	2 May	De Valera offers condolences on the death of Hitler.
	8 May	Victory in Europe Day.
	13, 16 May	Churchill and de Valera's broadcasts on the end of the war in Europe.
	14 June	General election, Northern Ireland.
	16 June	Seán T. O'Kelly elected President.
	5 July	General election, United Kingdom.
	14 August	Surrender of Japan.
1946	19 February	National Insurance (Northern Ireland) Act passed.
	12 May	Census taken, Éire: population recorded as 2,955,107.
	6 July	Foundation of Clann na Poblachta.
1947	27 March	Education Act (Northern Ireland) passed.
1948	4 February	General election: first Inter-Party government takes office under John A. Costello.
	7 September	Costello announces the Irish intention to declare a republic.
	21 December	Republic of Ireland Act passed by the Dáil.
1949	10 February	General election, Northern Ireland.
	18 April	Ireland becomes a republic and leaves the Commonwealth.
	2 June	Ireland Act passed by the British parliament.
	12 July	Death of Douglas Hyde.
1950	23 February	General election, United Kingdom.
	2 November	Death of George Bernard Shaw.
	20 December	Foundation of the Industrial Development Authority.
1951	4 April	Catholic hierarchy condemns Noel Browne's 'mother and child' scheme.
	8 April	Census taken, Republic of Ireland and Northern Ireland: population recorded as 2,960,593 (ROI) and 1,370,921 (NI).
	30 May	General election, Republic of Ireland: Fianna Fáil victory.
	25 October	General election, United Kingdom.

1952	3 July	Establishment of Bord Fáilte.
1953	31 January	*Princess Victoria* ferry disaster: 128 drowned.
	22 October	General election, Northern Ireland.
	29 October	Health Act (Republic of Ireland).
1954	6 April	Flags and Emblems Act passed in Northern Ireland.
	18 May	General election, Republic of Ireland: second Inter-Party government formed.
1955	26 May	General election, United Kingdom.
	14 December	Republic of Ireland admitted to the United Nations.
1956	8 April	Census taken, Republic of Ireland: population recorded as 2,898,264.
	30 May	T.K. Whitaker appointed as Secretary to the Department of Finance.
	12 December	IRA launches its Border Campaign.
1957	5 March	General election: Fianna Fáil returned to power.
1958	20 March	General election, Northern Ireland.
	29 May	First draft of Whitaker's Economic Development presented to the government.
	2 July	Industrial Development Act.
	11 November	Programme for Economic Expansion presented to the Dáil.
1959	17 June	De Valera elected President.
	23 June	Seán Lemass succeeds as Taoiseach.
	8 October	General election, United Kingdom.
1960	20 September	F.H. Boland elected President of the General Assembly, UN.
	8 November	Niemba ambush, Congo: ten Irish UN soldiers killed.
1961	9 April	Census taken, Republic of Ireland: population recorded as 2,818,341.
	23 April	Census taken, Northern Ireland: population recorded as 1,425,042.
	4 October	General election, Republic of Ireland: Fianna Fáil victory.
	31 December	Radio Telefís Éireann begins transmissions.
1962	26 February	IRA calls off its Border Campaign.
	31 May	General election, Northern Ireland.
	11 October	Opening of the Second Vatican Council, Rome.
1963	25 March	Terence O'Neill appointed Prime Minister of Northern Ireland.
	26–9 June	President John F. Kennedy visits Ireland.
	22 August	Publication of the Second Programme for Economic Expansion.
1964	January	Campaign for Social Justice founded in Dungannon, County Tyrone.
	2 June	Eddie McAteer elected leader of the nationalists, Stormont.
	18 September	Death of Seán O'Casey.
	15 October	General election, United Kingdom.

1965	14 January	Lemass and O'Neill meet at Stormont.
	9 February	Lemass and O'Neill meet in Dublin.
	7 April	General election, Republic of Ireland: Fianna Fáil returned.
	16 November	Death of William T. Cosgrave.
	25 November	General election, Northern Ireland.
	14 December	Anglo-Irish Free Trade Agreement signed by Lemass and Harold Wilson.
1966	31 March	General election, United Kingdom.
	10–17 April	Commemorations of the fiftieth anniversary of the Easter Rising.
	17 April	Census taken, Republic of Ireland: population recorded as 2,884,002.
	19 May	Séamus Heaney's *Death of a Naturalist* published.
	6 June	Reverend Ian Paisley's supporters conflict with nationalists, Cromac Square, Belfast.
	26 June	Malvern Street Murders by the UVF.
	20 July	Ian Paisley gaoled for unlawful assembly.
	10 September	Donogh O'Malley announces free secondary education.
	9 October	Census taken, Northern Ireland: population recorded as 1,484,775.
	10 November	Lemass resigns: replaced by Jack Lynch.
1967	1 February	Formation of the Northern Ireland Civil Rights Association.
	30 November	Death of Patrick Kavanagh.
1968	24 August	NICRA lead march from Coalisland to Dungannon, County Tyrone.
	5 October	Civil rights march, Derry: RUC conflict with marchers.
	9 October	Evolution of the People's Democracy, Belfast; Derry Citizens' Action Committee formed.
	22 November	O'Neill announces five-point programme of reform.
	30 November	Civil rights march in Armagh.
	9 December	O'Neill delivers 'Ulster at the Crossroads' speech on television.
	11 December	William Craig, Minister of Home Affairs, Northern Ireland, sacked.
1969	1–4 January	PD march from Belfast to Derry: Burntollet clash.
	11 January	PD demonstration, Newry, County Down.
	24 February	General election, Northern Ireland: Unionists divided over O'Neill's leadership.
	28 April	Resignation of O'Neill: James Chichester-Clark succeeds as Prime Minister of Northern Ireland.
	18 June	General election, Republic of Ireland: Fianna Fáil victory.
	14 July	First death of the 'Troubles': Dungiven, County Londonderry.

	August	Rioting in Derry and Belfast: introduction of British troops onto the streets.
	12 September	Cameron Commission report (into disturbances of 1968) published.
	10 October	Hunt Committee report into Northern Ireland policing published.
	23 October	Samuel Beckett awarded the Nobel Prize for Literature.
	18 December	Creation of the Ulster Defence Regiment (following recommendation of the Hunt report on policing).
1970	11 January	Split within the republican movement: formation of Provisional Sinn Féin.
	March–April	Phased disbandment of the B Specials in Northern Ireland.
	21 April	Foundation of the Alliance Party in Northern Ireland.
	May–June	Arms controversy: Haughey and Blaney sacked from the government and arrested.
	29 May	Macrory report on local government in Northern Ireland published.
	18 June	General election, United Kingdom.
	21 August	Social Democratic and Labour Party formed.
1971	6 February	First British soldier killed by PIRA.
	20 March	Resignation of Chichester-Clark as Prime Minister, Northern Ireland.
	23 March	Brian Faulkner succeeds Chichester-Clark as Prime Minister of Northern Ireland.
	18 April	Census taken, Republic of Ireland: population recorded as 2,978,248.
	20 April	Census taken, Northern Ireland: population recorded as 1,536,065.
	11 May	Death of Seán Lemass.
	16 July	SDLP withdraw from the Northern Ireland parliament.
	9–10 August	Internment introduced in Northern Ireland.
	14 September	Formation of the Democratic Unionist Party.
	4 December	Loyalist bomb attack on McGurk's pub, Belfast: 15 killed.
1972	22 January	Republic signs the treaty of accession to the EEC.
	30 January	Bloody Sunday, Derry: 13 demonstrators shot by soldiers.
	24 March	Stormont prorogued: introduction of direct rule.
	19 April	Widgery Tribunal (on Bloody Sunday) reports.
	10 May	Referendum, Republic of Ireland, on EEC membership.
	7 July	Willie Whitelaw (Secretary of State, NI) meets PIRA leaders.

	21 July	Bloody Friday, Belfast: 11 killed by PIRA bombs.
	7 December	Special position of the Roman Catholic Church removed from the Irish constitution after a popular referendum.
	20 December	Diplock Commission (on judicial procedure) reports.
1973	1 January	Republic's membership of the EEC formalized.
	26 February	Report of the Commission on the Status of Women published.
	28 February	General election, Republic: Fine Gael–Labour coalition formed.
	20 March	Northern Ireland Constitutional Proposals published.
	30 May	Local elections, Northern Ireland: first contest conducted under proportional representation since 1920.
	28 June	Northern Ireland Assembly elections.
	18 July	Northern Ireland Constitution Act formally abolishes local parliament.
	31 July	First meeting of Northern Ireland Assembly.
	18 August	Death of Viscount Brookeborough (Basil Brooke).
	6–9 December	Conference on the future government of Northern Ireland (Sunningdale, Berkshire).
1974	1 January	Power-sharing Executive takes office in Northern Ireland.
	4 February	PIRA bomb, Catterick: 11 killed.
	28 February	General election, United Kingdom.
	14 May	Start of the Ulster Workers' Council strike.
	17 May	Loyalist bombs in Dublin and Monaghan: 33 killed.
	28 May	Resignation of Faulkner and the fall of the Executive.
	29 May	Direct rule resumed: UWC strike called off.
	8 October	Seán MacBride shares Nobel Prize for Peace.
	10 October	General election, United Kingdom.
	21 November	Birmingham car bombings: 21 killed.
1975	1 May	Elections to Northern Ireland Constitutional Convention.
	29 August	Death of Eamon de Valera.
1976	4–5 January	15 killed (ten Protestants and five Catholics) in sectarian onslaughts in County Armagh.
	5 January	Death of John A. Costello.
	21 July	Assassination of Christopher Ewart-Biggs, British ambassador to Ireland.
	23 October	Resignation of President Ó Dálaigh (Patrick Hillery succeeds).
	30 November	Máiread Corrigan and Betty Williams share Nobel Prize for Peace.
1977	3 March	Death of Brian Faulkner.
	16 June	General election, Republic: Fianna Fáil victory.

1978	17 February	La Mon Hotel bomb: 16 killed.
1979	3 May	General election, United Kingdom: Margaret Thatcher and the Conservatives returned to power.
	27 August	Assassination of Earl Mountbatten and three others at Mullaghmore, County Sligo. IRA ambush, Warrenpoint, County Down: 18 soldiers killed.
	29 September	First papal visit to Ireland.
	28 November	John Hume succeeds Gerry Fitt as leader of the SDLP.
	7 December	Charles Haughey elected leader of Fianna Fáil and subsequently as Taoiseach.
	December	Census, Republic of Ireland: population recorded as 3,364,881.
1980	21 May	Margaret Thatcher and Charles Haughey meet in London.
1981	14 February	Fire at the Stardust Ballroom, Artane, Dublin: 48 die.
	1 March	Hunger strike at the Maze Prison begins, led by Bobby Sands.
	9 April	Sands elected as MP for Fermanagh and South Tyrone.
	5 May	Death of Sands on hunger strike.
	May–August	Deaths of ten hunger-striking prisoners.
	11 June	General election, Republic: Fine Gael–Labour coalition formed.
	14 November	Assassination of Reverend Robert Bradford, MP for South Belfast.
	December	Census, Northern Ireland: population recorded as 1,481,959.
1982	18 February	General election, Republic: Fianna Fáil victory.
	20 July	IRA attack on Household Cavalry, London: eight killed.
	20 October	Northern Ireland Assembly elections.
	24 November	General election, Republic: Fine Gael–Labour coalition in power.
	6 December	INLA bomb, Droppin' Well bar, Ballykelly, County Londonderry: 17 killed.
1983	30 May	First meeting of the New Ireland Forum, Dublin Castle.
	9 June	General election, UK: Conservative victory. Gerry Adams returned for West Belfast.
	7 September	'Pro-life' amendment to the constitution carried in a popular referendum.
	21 September	Death of F.S.L. Lyons, historian.
	7 November	First meeting of the Anglo-Irish Intergovernmental Council.
1984	2 May	New Ireland Forum report published.
	12 October	PIRA bomb, Grand Hotel, Brighton, during the Conservative Party conference: five killed.

1985	28 February	PIRA attack on Newry police station: nine killed.
	15 November	Hillsborough Agreement signed.
	11 December	First meeting of the Anglo-Irish Intergovernmental Conference.
	21 December	Foundation of the Progressive Democrats.
1986	23 January	By-elections held in Northern Ireland (caused by Unionist protest resignations).
	26 June	Divorce referendum in the Republic: prospect of divorce rejected.
	24 December	Single European Act signed by President Hillery: referendum ordered for 26 May 1987.
	December	Census, Republic of Ireland: population recorded as 3,537,195.
1987	14 February	General election, Republic: Fianna Fáil victory.
	11 March	Garret FitzGerald retires from the leadership of Fine Gael.
	27 March	Fianna Fáil government's strictly deflationary budget.
	8 May	Loughgall, County Armagh: eight PIRA members shot dead by security forces.
	26 May	Single European Act approved in referendum.
	8 November	Enniskillen, County Fermanagh: 11 die in PIRA bomb during Remembrance Day commemorations.
	22 December	Assassination of UDA leader, John McMichael.
1988	11 January	John Hume and Gerry Adams meet in Belfast for talks.
	6 March	Three PIRA members shot dead in Gibraltar.
	March–July	Intermittent SDLP–Sinn Féin talks.
	20 August	PIRA bomb at Ballygawley, County Tyrone: eight soldiers killed.
1989	15 June	General election, Republic: inconclusive result.
	12 July	Fianna Fáil–Progressive Democrat coalition formed.
	22 September	PIRA bomb at Royal Marine barracks, Deal, Kent: ten killed.
1990	17 May	Stevens report completed.
	18 May	David Trimble elected MP, Upper Bann constituency.
	13 June	Terence O'Neill (Lord O'Neill of the Maine) dies.
	30 July	Ian Gow (Conservative MP and prominent Unionist) killed.
	24 October	PIRA detonates human bombs: seven die.
	31 October	Brian Lenihan dismissed as Tánaiste by Charles Haughey.
	9 November	Mary Robinson elected President of Ireland.
	13 November	Alan Dukes resigns from the leadership of Fine Gael: John Bruton succeeds.
	27 November	John Major succeeds to the Conservative leadership after the deposition of Mrs Thatcher.

1991	7 February	IRA mortar bomb attack on 10 Downing Street.
	14 March	Birmingham Six freed.
	21 March	Census taken, Northern Ireland: population recorded as 1,577,836.
	26 June	Maguire Seven cleared.
	3 July	End of the cross-party talks sponsored by Peter Brooke (Secretary of State, Northern Ireland).
	9 July	Plan published to merge Ulster Defence Regiment and Royal Irish Rangers.
1992	17 January	Teebane, County Tyrone: eight Protestants killed.
	5 February	Seán Graham's bookmakers, Ormeau Road, Belfast: five Catholics killed.
	6 February	Albert Reynolds elected as leader of Fianna Fáil.
	22 February	Split within the Workers' Party: Democratic Left formed.
	9 April	General election, United Kingdom.
	10 August	UDA proscribed.
	10 November	Final collapse of the Brooke–Mayhew inter-party talks.
	25 November	General election, Republic of Ireland; abortion referendum.
1993	12 January	Fianna Fáil–Labour coalition government formed in Dublin.
	24 April	Hume–Adams statement on the future of Northern Ireland.
	25 September	Hume–Adams agreement.
	23 October	PIRA bomb a fish shop, Shankill Road, Belfast: ten killed.
	30 October	UFF attack on the Rising Sun bar, Greysteel, County Londonderry: seven killed.
	20 November	Hume–Adams joint statement.
	15 December	John Major and Albert Reynolds issue their Joint Declaration on Northern Ireland.
1994	9 March	Select Committee on Northern Ireland Affairs established in the House of Commons.
	2 June	RAF helicopter crashes, Mull of Kintyre: 25 British anti-terrorist experts killed.
	18 June	UVF attack on The Heights bar, Loughinisland, County Down: six killed.
	31 August	PIRA announces 'a complete cessation of hostilities'.
	13 October	The Combined Loyalist Military Command announces that it will 'universally end all operational hostilities'.
	16 November	Labour ministers resign from the Irish coalition government.
	17 November	Resignation of Albert Reynolds as Taoiseach.

	19 November	Bertie Ahern elected leader of Fianna Fáil.
	15 December	John Bruton is elected Taoiseach at the head of a coalition government containing Fine Gael, Labour and Democratic Left.
1995	22 February	Frameworks for the Future document published by the British and Irish governments.
	18 March	James Molyneaux re-elected as Ulster Unionist leader (but a protest candidate wins 88 votes to Molyneaux's 521).
	15 June	By-election, North Down: Robert McCartney elected, defeating Ulster Unionist candidate.
	9 July	The RUC prevent Orangemen from marching along the nationalist Garvaghy Road, Portadown, after a church service at Drumcree: a stand-off and loyalist violence ensues.
	11 July	The Drumcree stand-off ends: 500 Orangemen, without bands, march down the Garvaghy Road.
	28 August	James Molyneaux resigns from the Ulster Unionist leadership.
	8 September	David Trimble elected as leader of the Ulster Unionists.
	5 October	Séamus Heaney awarded the Nobel Prize for Literature.
	24 November	Divorce referendum, Republic of Ireland: narrow majority accepts the right to divorce.
	28 November	Launch of the twin-track British–Irish strategy to reactivate inter-party talks and to establish an 'international body' to examine the decommissioning question.
	30 November–1 December	President Clinton in Northern Ireland.
1996	9 February	Canary Wharf bomb, and the end of the IRA ceasefire.
	28 February	British and Irish governments attempt to restart the talks process: all-party talks planned for 10 June.
	30 May	Elections held for the Northern Ireland Forum.
	10 June	Talks begin at Stormont.
	14 June	First meeting of the Northern Ireland Forum.
	7 July	Stand-off develops between Orangemen and police at Drumcree, County Armagh: loyalist violence escalates.
	11 July	RUC backs down over the Drumcree march in the face of loyalist pressure: the banned march proceeds.
	13 July	SDLP withdraws from the Forum.
1997	30 January	Independent Review of Parades and Marches report: recommends the creation of an independent Parades Commission.

	5 March	Adjournment of the (stalled) multi-party talks.
	1 May	General election, United Kingdom: Labour victory.
	16 May	Tony Blair delivers a key-note, pro-Union address in Belfast.
	2 June	Alban Maginness (SDLP) is elected the first nationalist Lord Mayor of Belfast.
	3 June	Multi-party talks resume at Stormont.
	6 June	General election, Republic of Ireland: Fianna Fáil–Progressive Democrat coalition returned to power under Bertie Ahern.
	6 July	Orangemen permitted to walk the Garvaghy Road: widespread nationalist protest and violence ensues.
	19 July	The IRA announces a resumption of their ceasefire, offering 'a complete cessation of military operations'.
	9 September	Sinn Féin joins the multi-party talks process.
	15 September	All-party talks formally begin.
	24 September	The international panel on decommissioning (headed by General de Chastelain) begins its work.
	31 October	Mary McAleese elected President of Ireland.
	10 December	A Sinn Féin delegation meets Tony Blair in Downing Street.
	27 December	Billy Wright, LVF leader, killed by INLA prisoners in the Maze.
1998	20 February	Temporary expulsion of Sinn Féin from talks process because of recent republican killings.
	7 April	Tony Blair flies to Belfast in order to support the endangered talks process at Stormont.
	10 April	The signing of the Good Friday Agreement.
	11 April	The executive of the Ulster Unionist Party endorses the deal.
	18 April	The Ulster Unionist Council endorses the Agreement.
	6 May	Tony Blair and John Major jointly visit Belfast to support the Agreement.
	10 May	Sinn Féin ard-fheis endorses the Agreement.
	22 May	Referenda in Northern Ireland and the Republic of Ireland: the Good Friday Agreement is endorsed by 71 per cent of the Northern Irish electorate. The Agreement and proposed changes to articles two and three of the Irish constitution are approved by 94 per cent of the southern electorate.
	3 June	Independent commission on policing in Northern Ireland named.
	25 June	Elections to the Northern Ireland Assembly.
	29 June	Parades Commission announces the re-routing of the annual Orange march from Drumcree Church, Portadown.

	12 July	Three Catholic brothers – Jason Quinn (aged 9), Mark (10) and Richard (11) – are killed by a fire-bomb thrown into their home in Ballymoney, County Antrim.
	8 August	Last remaining loyalist belligerents, the LVF, announce ceasefire.
	15 August	The Omagh car bomb: 29 people killed by dissident republicans in the Real IRA.
	22 August	INLA ceasefire announced.
	8 September	Real IRA ceasefire.
	16 October	John Hume and David Trimble awarded the Nobel Peace Prize.
1999	9 September	Publication of the Patten Report on Policing.
	11 October	Peter Mandelson replaces Mo Mowlam as Secretary of State for Northern Ireland.
	2 December	First meeting of the Northern Ireland Executive.
2000	11 February	Suspension of the Executive.
	6 May	IRA statement on decommissioning (putting arms 'completely and verifiably beyond use').
	27 May	Return of devolution.
2001	24 January	Resignation of Mandelson from NIO: appointment of John Reid as Secretary of State.
	29 April	Census taken, Northern Ireland: population recorded as 1,685,267.
	June	First referendum on the Treaty of Nice, Republic of Ireland (54% oppose).
	7 June	General Election, United Kingdom: UUP 6 seats (26.8% of poll), DUP 5 seats (22.5%), SF 4 seats (21.7%), SDLP 3 seats (21%). SF overtakes SDLP for the first time.
	1 July	David Trimble resigns as First Minister.
	6 August	Arrest of three Irish republicans in Colombia.
	11 September	Twin Towers attack, New York.
	26 October	IRA begins decommissioning.
	6 November	David Trimble reinstated as First Minister.
2002	6 March	Referendum on abortion, Republic of Ireland (50.42% of the electorate reject government-supported 'pro-life' amendment).
	23 April	Census, Republic of Ireland: population recorded as 3,917,203.
	17 March	Raid on the headquarters of Special Branch, PSNI, Castlereagh, Belfast.
	17 May	General election, Republic of Ireland: Fianna Fáil/ Progressive Democrat coalition returned under Bertie Ahern.
	4 October	PSNI 'spy-ring' raid on the offices of Sinn Féin at Stormont.

	15 October	Executive suspended.
	16 October	Second referendum on the Treaty of Nice, Republic of Ireland (63% in favour).
	17 October	Tony Blair speaks at Harbour Commissioners' Offices, Belfast.
	24 October	John Reid replaced as Secretary of State for NI by Paul Murphy.
2003	26 November	Assembly elections: DUP 30 seats (25.7% of poll), UUP 27 seats (22.7%), SF 24 seats (23.5%), SDLP 18 seats (17%).
2004	11 June	Local government and European elections, Republic of Ireland.
	20 December	Armed raid on the Northern Bank headquarters, Belfast: £26 million stolen.
2005	30 January	Killing of Robert McCartney, Belfast.
	5 May	General Election, United Kingdom: DUP (33.7%); SF 5 seats (24.3%); SDLP 3 seats (17.5%); UUP 1 seat (17.7%). Paul Murphy replaced as Secretary of State for NI by Peter Hain.
	28 July	IRA statement ordering 'an end to the armed campaign'.
	26 September	IMC Report: disposal of 'the totality of the arsenal of the IRA'.
2006	4 April	Killing of Denis Donaldson.
	23 April	Census, Republic of Ireland: population recorded as 4,239,848.
	13 June	Death of Charles Haughey.
	11–13 October	Negotiation of the St Andrews Agreement.
	22 November	Northern Ireland (St Andrews Agreement) Act passed.
	24 November	Northern Ireland Assembly meets and is adjourned.
2007	28 January	Sinn Féin Ard Fheis on the issue of policing and justice.
	7 March	Elections, Northern Ireland Assembly: DUP (36 seats), SF (28 seats), UUP (18 seats), SDLP (16 seats).
	26 March	First face-to-face meeting between DUP and SF leaderships.
	8 May	Northern Ireland Assembly elects Ian Paisley and Martin McGuinness as First and Deputy First Minister.
	12 May	Sinn Féin Ard Chomhairle nominates members to the Policing Board, Northern Ireland.
	15 May	Bertie Ahern addresses the British Parliament.
	24 May	General election, Republic of Ireland: Fianna Fáil/Green coalition returned under Bertie Ahern.
	27 June	Gordon Brown succeeds Tony Blair as Prime Minister of the United Kingdom.

		Peter Hain succeeded by Shaun Woodward as Secretary of State for NI.
	13 September	Bertie Ahern commences his testimony to the Mahon Tribunal.
2008	30 April	Bertie Ahern addresses the United States Congress.
	5 June	Peter Robinson succeeds Ian Paisley as First Minister of Northern Ireland.
	6 May	Bertie Ahern resigns as Taoiseach of Ireland: Brian Cowen succeeds.
	13 June	Referendum on the Treaty of Lisbon: 53.4 per cent of poll reject Treaty.
2009	20 January	Nationalization of Anglo Irish Bank by the Irish government.
	11 February	State recapitalization of Bank of Ireland and Allied Irish Bank.
	7 March	Two soldiers killed by the Real IRA at Massereene Barracks, Antrim.
	9 March	PSNI officer, Constable Stephen Carroll, killed by Continuity IRA sniper.
	20 May	Publication of the Ryan Report on Child Abuse.
	7 June	European Elections: SF tops poll, with the DUP vote down by 13.8 per cent.
	2 October	Second referendum on Treaty of Lisbon: 67.1% of poll approve Treaty.
	26 November	Publication of the Report into Child Sex Abuse in the Dublin Diocese.
	28 December	Iris Robinson announces her retirement from politics.
2010	7 January	BBC *Spotlight* programme on Iris and Peter Robinson.
	11 January	Peter Robinson steps down as First Minister for six weeks.
	5 February	Deal brokered between DUP and Sinn Fein on devolution of administration of policing and justice.

Sources: Paul Bew and Gordon Gillespie (eds), *Northern Ireland: A Chronology of the Troubles, 1968–1993* (Dublin, 1993); Paul Bew and Gordon Gillespie (eds), *The Northern Ireland Peace Process, 1993–1996: A Chronology* (London, 1996); J.E. Doherty and D.J. Hickey, *A Chronology of Irish History since 1500* (Dublin, 1989); T.W. Moody, F.X. Martin and F.J. Byrne (eds), *A New History of Ireland VIII: A Chronology of Irish History to 1976* (Oxford, 1982). I am grateful to Gordon Gillespie for permitting me to use material from his ongoing chronicle of Northern Ireland politics.

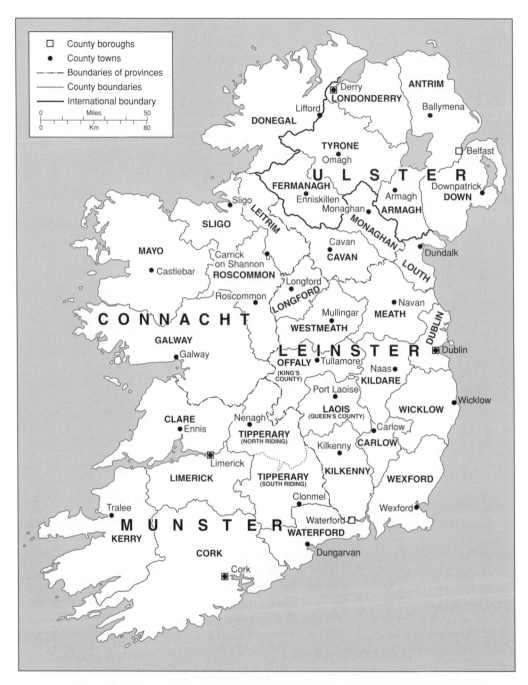

Map 1 Ireland: provinces, counties and county towns.
Source: T.W. Moody, F.X. Martin and F.J. Byrne (eds), *A New History of Ireland IX.*
Maps, Genealogies, Lists: A Companion to Irish History, Part II (Oxford, 1983).

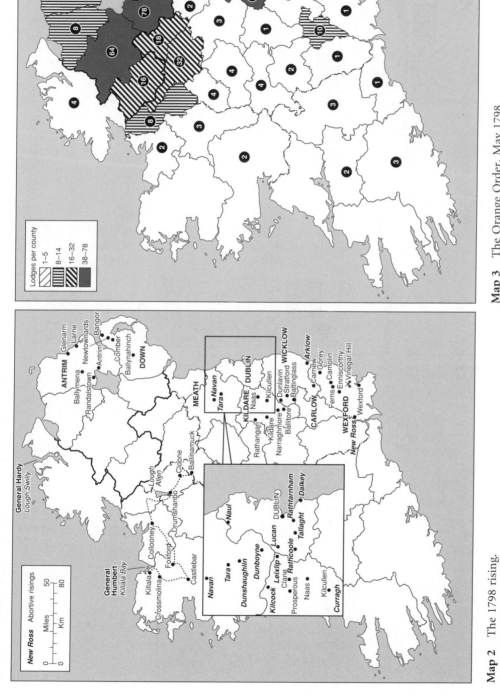

Map 2 The 1798 rising.
Source: Ruth Dudley Edwards, *An Atlas of Irish History,* 2nd edition (London, 1981).

Map 3 The Orange Order, May 1798.
Source: Ruth Dudley Edwards, *An Atlas of Irish History,* 2nd edition (London, 1981).

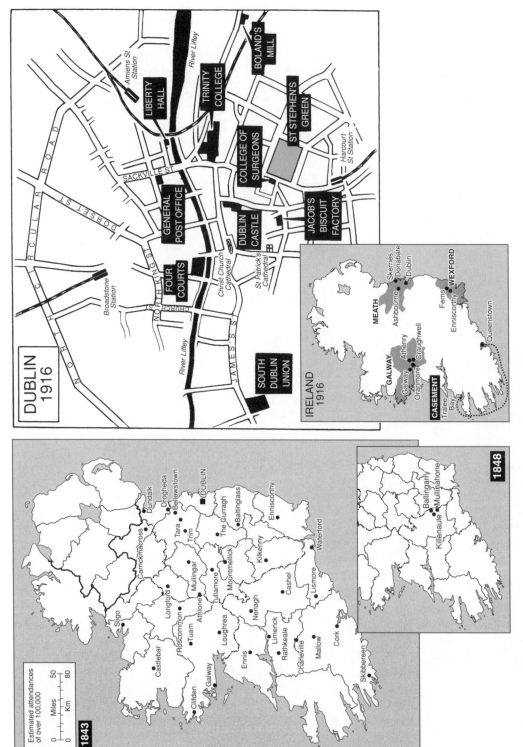

Map 4 O'Connell and Young Ireland: the repeal meetings, 1843; 1848 rising.
Source: Ruth Dudley Edwards, *An Atlas of Irish History*, 2nd edition (London, 1981).

Map 5 The 1916 rising.
Source: Ruth Dudley Edwards, *An Atlas of Irish History*, 2nd edition (London, 1981).

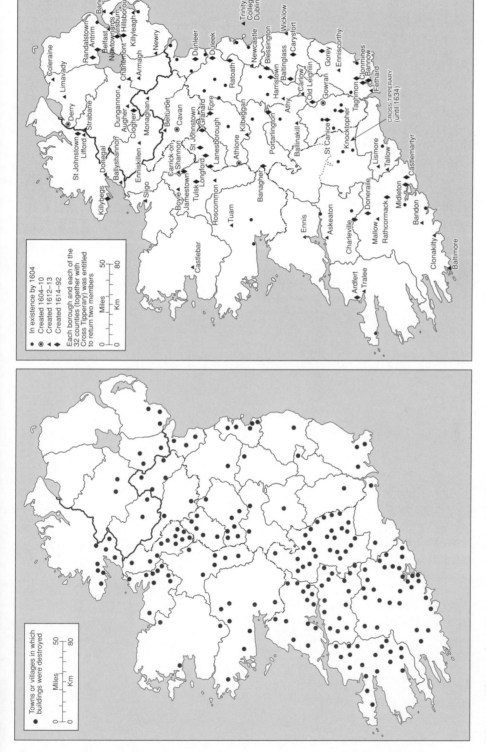

Map 6 The Anglo-Irish war: reprisals by British forces, September 1919–July 1921.
Source: Ruth Dudley Edwards, *An Atlas of Irish History*, 2nd edition (London, 1981).

Map 7 Parliamentary constituencies, 1604–1800.
Source: T.W. Moody, F.X. Martin and F.J. Byrne (eds), *A New History of Ireland IX. Maps, Genealogies, Lists: A Companion to Irish History, Part II* (Oxford, 1983).

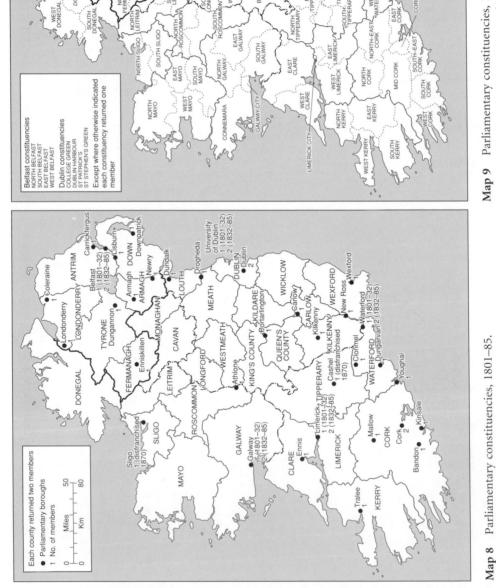

Map 8 Parliamentary constituencies, 1801–85.
Source: T.W. Moody, F.X. Martin and F.J. Byrne (eds), *A New History of Ireland IX. Maps, Genealogies, Lists: A Companion to Irish History, Part II* (Oxford, 1983).

Map 9 Parliamentary constituencies, 1885.
Source: T.W. Moody, F.X. Martin and F.J. Byrne (eds), *A New History of Ireland IX. Maps, Genealogies, Lists: A Companion to Irish History, Part II* (Oxford, 1983).

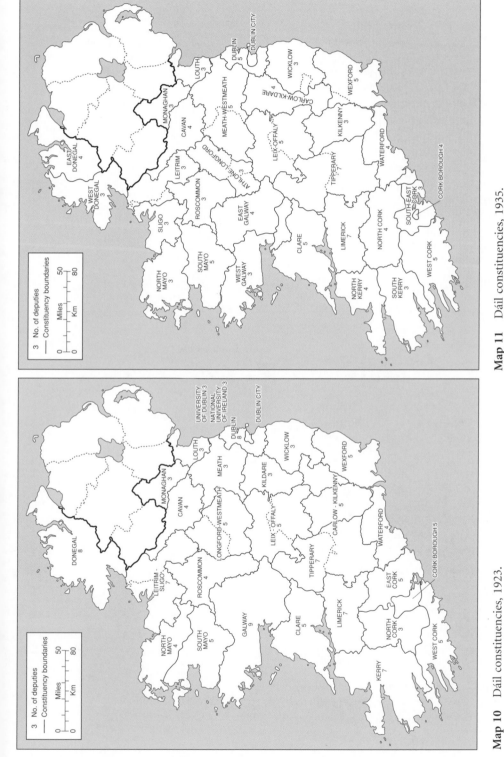

Map 10 Dáil constituencies, 1923.

Source: T.W. Moody, F.X. Martin and F.J. Byrne (eds), *A New History of Ireland IX. Maps, Genealogies, Lists: A Companion to Irish History, Part II* (Oxford, 1983).

Map 11 Dáil constituencies, 1935.

Source: T.W. Moody, F.X. Martin and F.J. Byrne (eds), *A New History of Ireland IX. Maps, Genealogies, Lists: A Companion to Irish History, Part II* (Oxford, 1983).

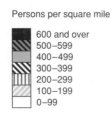

Persons per square mile

- 600 and over
- 500–599
- 400–499
- 300–399
- 200–299
- 100–199
- 0–99

Map 12   Population density, 1841–91, by baronies.
Source: T.W. Moody, F.X. Martin and F.J. Byrne (eds), *A New History of Ireland IX.
Maps, Genealogies, Lists: A Companion to Irish History, Part II* (Oxford, 1983).

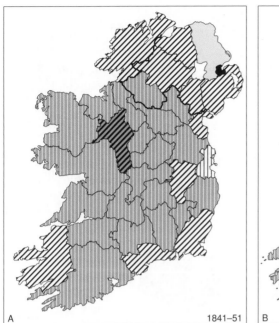

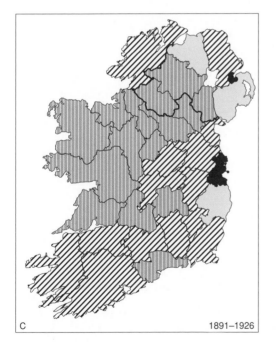

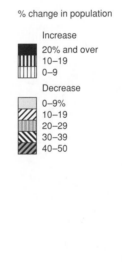

% change in population

Increase
20% and over
10–19
0–9

Decrease
0–9%
10–19
20–29
30–39
40–50

A   1841–51

B   1851–91

C   1891–1926

Map 13   Population change, 1841–1926, by counties.
Source: T.W. Moody, F.X. Martin and F.J. Byrne (eds), *A New History of Ireland IX.*
Maps, Genealogies, Lists: A Companion to Irish History, Part II (Oxford, 1983).

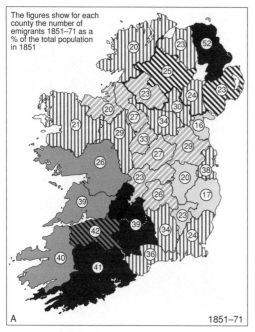

The figures show for each county the number of emigrants 1851–71 as a % of the total population in 1851

A   1851–71

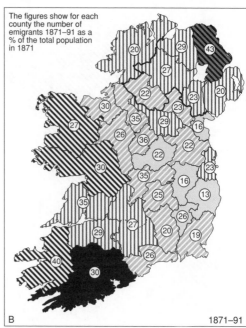

The figures show for each county the number of emigrants 1871–91 as a % of the total population in 1871

B   1871–91

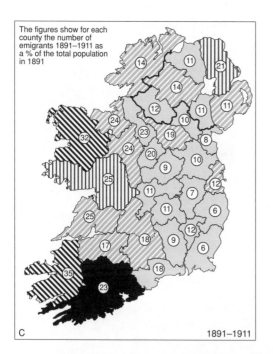

The figures show for each county the number of emigrants 1891–1911 as a % of the total population in 1891

C   1891–1911

Number of emigrants in 1,000s

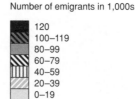

■	120
	100–119
	80–99
	60–79
	40–59
	20–39
	0–19

Map 14   Emigration, 1851–1911, by counties.
Source: T.W. Moody, F.X. Martin and F.J. Byrne (eds), *A New History of Ireland IX. Maps, Genealogies, Lists: A Companion to Irish History, Part II* (Oxford, 1983).

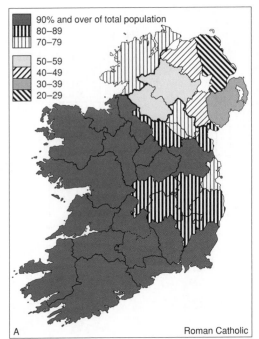

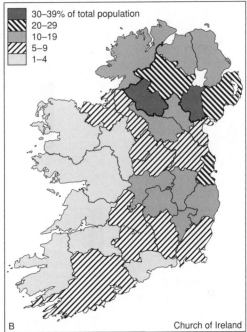

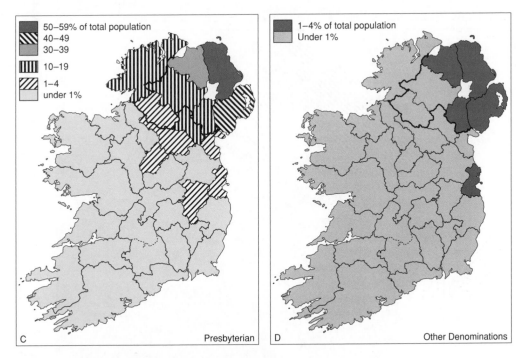

Map 15 Religious denominations, 1871, by counties.
Source: T.W. Moody, F.X. Martin and F.J. Byrne (eds), *A New History of Ireland IX. Maps, Genealogies, Lists: A Companion to Irish History, Part II* (Oxford, 1983).

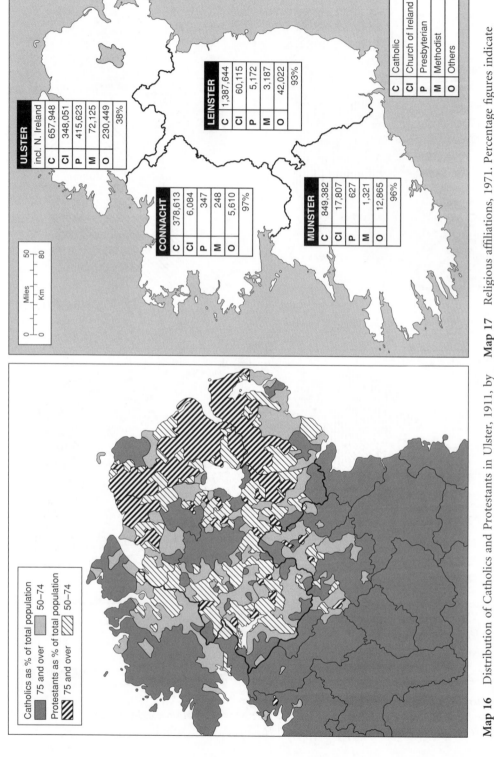

ULSTER	incl. N. Ireland	
C	657,948	
CI	348,051	
P	415,623	
M	72,125	
O	230,449	
	38%	

LEINSTER		
C	1,387,644	
CI	60,115	
P	5,172	
M	3,187	
O	42,022	
	93%	

CONNACHT		
C	378,613	
CI	6,084	
P	347	
M	248	
O	5,610	
	97%	

MUNSTER		
C	849,382	
CI	17,807	
P	627	
M	1,321	
O	12,865	
	96%	

C	Catholic
CI	Church of Ireland
P	Presbyterian
M	Methodist
O	Others

Miles 0 — 50
Km 0 — 80

Map 16 Distribution of Catholics and Protestants in Ulster, 1911, by district electoral divisions.

Source: T.W. Moody, F.X. Martin and F.J. Byrne (eds), *A New History of Ireland IX. Maps, Genealogies, Lists: A Companion to Irish History, Part II* (Oxford, 1983).

Catholics as % of total population
75 and over
50–74

Protestants as % of total population
75 and over
50–74

Map 17 Religious affiliations, 1971. Percentage figures indicate number of Roman Catholics in each province.

Source: Ruth Dudley Edwards, *An Atlas of Irish History*, 2nd edition (London, 1981).

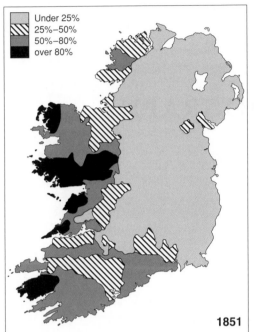

1851

1891

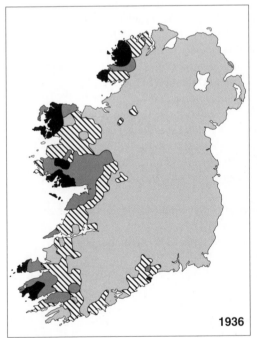
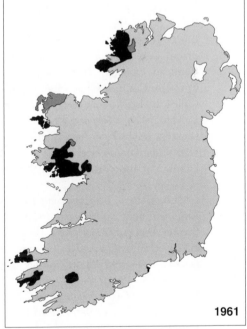

1936

1961

Map 18   Irish speakers, 1851–1961.
Source: Ruth Dudley Edwards, *An Atlas of Irish History*, 2nd edition (London, 1981).

SELECT BIBLIOGRAPHY

1 General Works

Bardon, Jonathan, *A History of Ulster* (Belfast, 1992).

Bartlett, Thomas, *Concise History of Ireland* (Cambridge, 2010).

Beckett, J.C., *The Making of Modern Ireland, 1603–1923* (London, 1966).

Bew, Paul, *Ireland: The Politics of Enmity, 1789–2006* (Oxford, 2006).

Boyce, D. George, *Nineteenth Century Ireland: The Search for Stability* (Dublin, 1990).

Boyce, D. George, *Nationalism in Ireland*, 2nd edition (London, 1991).

Boyce, D. George, *Ireland 1828–1923: From Ascendancy to Democracy* (Oxford, 1992).

Brown, Terence, *Ireland: A Social and Cultural History, 1922–79* (London, 1981).

Buckland, Patrick, *A History of Northern Ireland* (Dublin, 1981).

Comerford, R.V., *Ireland: Inventing the Nation* (London, 2003).

Cullen, L.M., *The Emergence of Modern Ireland, 1600–1900* (London, 1981).

Daly, Mary E., *A Social and Economic History of Ireland since 1800* (Dublin, 1981).

Dickson, David, *New Foundations: Ireland, 1660–1800* (Dublin, 1987).

Elliott, Marianne, *The Catholics of Ulster: A History* (London, 2000).

Elliott, Marianne, *When God Took Sides: Religion and Identity in Modern Ireland* (Oxford, 2009).

English, Richard, *Irish Freedom: The History of Nationalism in Ireland* (London, 2007).

Fanning, Ronan, *Independent Ireland* (Dublin, 1983).

Ferriter, Diarmaid, *The Transformation of Ireland, 1900–2000* (London, 2004).

Fitzpatrick, David, *The Two Irelands, 1912–1939* (Oxford, 1998).

Flackes, W.D. and Elliott, Sydney, *Northern Ireland: A Political Directory (1968–1993)* (Belfast, 1994).

Foster, R.F., *Modern Ireland, 1600–1972* (London, 1988).

Garvin, Tom, *The Evolution of Irish Nationalist Politics* (Dublin, 1981).

Harkness, David, *Northern Ireland since 1920* (Dublin, 1983).

Hennessey, Thomas, *A History of Northern Ireland, 1920–1996* (Dublin, 1997).

Hoppen, K. Theodore, *Ireland since 1800: Conflict and Conformity*, 2nd edition (London, 1999).

Keogh, Dermot, *Twentieth Century Ireland: Nation and State* (Dublin, 1994).

Kiberd, Declan, *Inventing Ireland: The Literature of the Modern Nation* (London, 1995).

Lee, J.J., *The Modernisation of Irish Society, 1848–1918* (Dublin, 1973).

Lee, J.J., *Ireland 1912–1985: Politics and Society* (Cambridge, 1989).

Loughlin, James, *The Ulster Question since 1945* (London, 1998).

Lyons, F.S.L., *Ireland since the Famine*, 2nd edition (London, 1973).

McBride, Ian, *Eighteenth-Century Ireland: The Isle of Slaves* (Dublin, 2009).

McCartney, Donal, *The Dawning of Democracy: Ireland, 1800–1870* (Dublin, 1987).

MacDonagh, Oliver, *Ireland: The Union and its Aftermath* (London, 1977).

MacDonagh, Oliver, *States of Mind: A Study of Anglo-Irish Conflict, 1780–1980* (London, 1983).

Mulholland, Marc, *The Longest War: Northern Ireland's Troubled History* (Oxford, 2002).

Murphy, John A., *Ireland in the Twentieth Century* (Dublin, 1975).

O'Farrell, Patrick, *Ireland's English Question: Anglo-Irish Relations, 1534–1970* (London, 1971).

O'Farrell, Patrick, *England and Ireland since 1800* (Oxford, 1975).

Ó Gráda, Cormac, *A New Economic History of Ireland, 1780–1939* (Oxford, 1994).

Ó Gráda, Cormac, *A Rocky Road: The Irish Economy since the 1920s* (Manchester, 1997).

Ó Tuathaigh, Gearóid, *Ireland before the Famine, 1798–1848* (Dublin, 1972).

Patterson, Henry, *Ireland since 1939* (Dublin, 2006).

Strauss, Eric, *Irish Nationalism and British Democracy* (London, 1951).

Travers, Pauric, *Settlements and Divisions: Ireland, 1870–1922* (Dublin, 1988).

Vaughan, W.E. (ed.), *A New History of Ireland V: Ireland Under the Union I: 1801–1870* (Oxford, 1989).

Vaughan, W.E. (ed.), *A New History of Ireland VI: Ireland Under the Union II: 1870–1921* (Oxford, 1996).

Walker, Brian M., *Parliamentary Election Results in Ireland, 1801–1922* (Dublin, 1978).

Walker, Brian M., *Parliamentary Election Results in Ireland, 1918–1992* (Dublin, 1992).

Wichert, Sabine, *Northern Ireland since 1945*, 2nd edition (London, 1999).

2   Contemporary Works

Adams, Gerry, *Before the Dawn: An Autobiography* (London, 1996).

Adams, Gerry, *Hope and History: Making Peace in Ireland* (Dingle, 2003).

Adams, Gerry, *A New Ireland: A Vision for the Future* (Dingle, 2005).

A.E. (Russell, George William), *Thoughts for a Convention: Memorandum on the State of Ireland* (Dublin, 1917).

Ahern, Bertie, *Autobiography* (London, 2009).

Arnold, Bruce, *What Kind of Country: Modern Irish Politics, 1968–83* (London, 1984).

Barry, Tom, *Guerrilla Days in Ireland* (Dublin, 1949).

Beckett, Ian (ed.), *The Army and the Curragh Incident, 1914* (London, 1986).

Bloomfield, Kenneth, *A Tragedy of Errors: The Government and Misgovernment of Northern Ireland* (Liverpool, 2007).

Bryce, James, *Studies in Contemporary Biography* (London, 1903).

Connolly, James, *Socialism and Nationalism: A Selection from the Writings of James Connolly* (Dublin, 1948).

Connolly, James, *Labour in Ireland. I: Labour in Irish History. II: The Reconquest of Ireland* (Dublin, n.d.).

Crawford, Fred H., *Guns for Ulster* (Belfast, 1947).

Dunraven, Lord, *The Crisis in Ireland: An Account of the Present Condition of Ireland and Suggestions towards Reform* (Dublin, 1905).

Dunraven, Lord, *The Outlook in Ireland: The Case for Devolution and Conciliation* (Dublin, 1907).

Faulkner, Brian, *Memoirs of a Statesman* (London, 1978).

FitzGerald, Garret, *All in a Life: An Autobiography* (Dublin, 1991).

Gavan Duffy, Sir Charles, *The League of North and South: An Episode in Irish History, 1850–1854* (London, 1886).

Gavan Duffy, Sir Charles, *Thomas Davis: The Memoirs of an Irish Patriot, 1840–1846* (London, 1890).

Hume, John, *A New Ireland: Politics, Peace and Reconciliation* (Boulder, Colo., 1996).

Hurd, Douglas, *Memoirs* (London, 2003).

Hussey, Gemma, *At the Cutting Edge: Cabinet Diaries, 1982–87* (Dublin, 1990).

Hussey, Gemma, *Ireland Today: Anatomy of a Changing State* (Dublin, 1993).

Gwynn, Stephen, *John Redmond's Last Years* (London, 1919).

'I.O.' (C.J.C. Street), *Ireland in 1920* (London, 1921).

Jones, Thomas, *Whitehall Diary III: Ireland, 1918–25* (Oxford, 1971).

Lenihan, Brian, *For the Record* (Dublin, 1991).

Macardle, Dorothy, *Tragedies of Kerry, 1922–23* (Dublin, 1924).

Macardle, Dorothy, *The Irish Republic*, 4th edition (Dublin, 1951).

Macdonald, John, *Diary of the Parnell Commission* (London, 1890).

Macknight, Thomas, *Ulster as it is: or Twenty Eight Years' Experience as an Irish Editor*, 2 vols (London, 1896).

Macready, Sir Nevil, *Annals of an Active Life*, 2 vols (London, n.d.).

Marjoribanks, Edward and Colvin, Ian, *The Life of Lord Carson*, 3 vols (London, 1932–6).

McDonald, Henry, *Colours: Ireland – From Bombs to Boom* (Edinburgh and London, 2004).

Mitchell, George, *Making Peace* (London, 1999).

Moody, T.W. and Hawkins, R.A.J., with Moody, Margaret, *Florence Arnold-Forster's Irish Journal* (Oxford, 1988).

Mowlam, Mo, *Momentum: The Struggle for Peace, Politics and the People* (London, 2002).

Neill, Ivan, *Church and State* (Dunmurry, 1995).

O'Brien, Conor Cruise, *My Life and Themes* (Dublin, 1998).

O'Brien, R. Barry, *The Life of Charles Stewart Parnell*, 2 vols (London, 1898).

O'Brien, R. Barry, *Dublin Castle and the Irish People*, 2nd edition (London, 1912).

O'Brien, William, *An Olive Branch in Ireland, and its History* (London, 1910).

O'Brien, William, *The Downfall of Parliamentarianism: A Retrospect for the Accounting Day* (Dublin, 1918).

O'Brien, William, *The Irish Revolution and How it Came About* (Dublin, 1923).

O'Brien, William and Ryan, Desmond (eds), *Devoy's Post-Bag, 1871–1928*, 2 vols (Dublin, 1948–53).

O'Callaghan, Seán, *The Informer* (London, 1998).

O'Connor, T.P., *Memoirs of an Old Parliamentarian* (New York, 1929).

O'Donnell, F.H., *A History of the Irish Parliamentary Party*, 2 vols (London, 1910).

O'Malley, Ernie, *On Another Man's Wound* (London, 1936).

O'Neill, Terence, *Ulster at the Crossroads* (London, 1969).

O'Neill, Terence, *The Autobiography of Terence O'Neill, Prime Minister of Northern Ireland, 1963–1969* (London, 1972).

O'Toole, Fintan, *The Lie of the Land: Irish Identities* (London, 1997).

Paul-Dubois, L., *Contemporary Ireland* (Dublin, 1908).

Pearse, Padraic H., *Collected Works*, 5th edition (Dublin, 1922).

Phillips, W. Alison, *The Revolution in Ireland, 1906–1923*, 2nd edition (London, 1926).

Powell, Jonathan, *Great Hatred, Little Room: Making Peace in Northern Ireland* (London, 2008).

Reynolds, Albert, *My Autobiography* (Dublin, 2009).

Ross, Charles, *Correspondence of Charles, First Marquess of Cornwallis*, 3 vols (London, 1859).

Skinner, Liam, *Politicians by Accident* (Dublin, 1946).

Stanhope, Earl, *Life of the Right Honourable William Pitt*, 4 vols (London, 1862).

Street, C.J.C., *Ireland in 1921* (London, 1922).

Winter, Ormonde, *Winter's Tale: An Autobiography* (London, 1955).

3   Articles and Monographs

Adams, W.F., *Ireland and Irish Emigration to the New World from 1815 to the Famine* (New Haven, 1932).

Akenson, Donald Harman, *The Irish Education Experiment: The National System of Education in the Nineteenth Century* (London, 1970).

Akenson, Donald Harman, *The Church of Ireland: Ecclesiastical Reform and Revolution, 1800–1885* (New Haven, 1971).

Akenson, Donald Harman, *Conor: A Biography of Conor Cruise O'Brien* (Montreal and Kingston, 1994).

Allen, Kieran, *Fianna Fáil and Irish Labour: 1926 to the Present* (London, 1997).

Allen, Kieran, *The Celtic Tiger: The Myth of Social Partnership in Ireland* (Manchester, 2000).

Arthur, Paul, *The People's Democracy, 1968–73* (Belfast, 1974).

Aughey, Arthur, *Under Siege: Ulster Unionism and the Anglo-Irish Agreement* (Belfast, 1989).

Augusteijn, Joost, *From Public Defiance to Guerrilla Warfare: The Experience of Ordinary Volunteers in the Irish War of Independence, 1916–1921* (Dublin, 1996).

Barr, Colin, '"Imperium in Imperio": Irish Episcopal Imperialism in the Nineteenth Century', *English Historical Review*, 123, 502 (June, 2008).

Barrington, Ruth, *Health, Medicine and Politics in Ireland, 1900–70* (Dublin, 1987).

Bartlett, Thomas, 'An End to Moral Economy: The Militia Riots of 1793', *Past & Present*, 99 (May 1983).

Bartlett, Thomas, *The Fall and Rise of the Irish Nation: The Catholic Question, 1690–1830* (Dublin, 1992).

Bartlett, Thomas, *Theobald Wolfe Tone* (Dublin, 1997).

Bartlett, Thomas, *Acts of Union: An Inaugural Lecture delivered at University College Dublin on 24 February 2000* (Dublin, 2000).

Bartlett, Thomas, 'Ireland, Empire and Union, 1690–1801', in Kevin Kenny (ed.), *Ireland and the British Empire* (Oxford, 2004).

Bartlett, Thomas and Hayton, David W. (eds), *Penal Era and Golden Age: Essays in Irish History, 1690–1800* (Belfast, 1979).

Bartlett, Thomas and Jeffery, Keith, *A Military History of Ireland* (Cambridge, 1996).

Barton, Brian, *Brookeborough: The Making of a Prime Minister* (Belfast, 1988).

Barton, Brian, 'Relations between Westminster and Stormont during the Attlee Premiership', *Irish Political Studies*, 7 (1992).

Bayly, C.A., 'Ireland, India and the Empire, 1780–1914', *Transactions of the Royal Historical Society*, Sixth Series, Vol. 10 (Cambridge, 2000).

Beames, Michael, *Peasants and Power: The Whiteboy Movements and their Control in Pre-Famine Ireland* (Brighton, 1983).

Beckett, J.C., *The Anglo-Irish Tradition* (London, 1976).

Bence-Jones, Mark, *Twilight of the Ascendancy* (London, 1987).

Bernstein, George L., 'Liberals, the Irish Famine and the Role of the State', *Irish Historical Studies*, xxix, 116 (November 1995).

Bew, John, *The Glory of Being Britons: Civic Unionism in Nineteenth-Century Belfast* (Dublin, 2008).

Bew, Paul, *Land and the National Question, 1858–82* (Dublin, 1979).

Bew, Paul, *C.S. Parnell* (Dublin, 1980).

Bew, Paul, *Conflict and Conciliation in Ireland, 1890–1910: Parnellites and Agrarian Radicals* (Oxford, 1987).

Bew, Paul, *Ideology and the Irish Question: Ulster Unionism and Irish Nationalism, 1912–1916* (Oxford, 1994).

Bew, Paul, *John Redmond* (Dublin, 1996).

Bew, Paul, 'Moderate Nationalism and the Irish Revolution, 1916–23', *Historical Journal*, 42, 3 (September, 1999).

Bew, Paul, Gibbon, Peter and Patterson, Henry, *Northern Ireland, 1921–94: Political Forces and Social Classes* (London, 1995).

Bew, Paul and Gillespie, Gordon (eds), *Northern Ireland: A Chronology of the Troubles, 1968–1993* (Dublin, 1993).

Bew, Paul and Gillespie, Gordon (eds), *The Northern Ireland Peace Process, 1993–1996: A Chronology* (London, 1996).

Bew, Paul, Hazelkorn, Ellen and Patterson, Henry, *The Dynamics of Irish Politics* (London, 1989).

Bew, Paul and Patterson, Henry, *Seán Lemass and the Making of Modern Ireland, 1945–66* (Dublin, 1982).

Bew, Paul, Patterson, Henry and Teague, Paul, *Between War and Peace: The Political Future of Northern Ireland* (London, 1997).

Biagini, Eugenio, *British Democracy and Irish Nationalism, 1876–1906* (Cambridge, 2007).

Biggs-Davison, John and Chowdharay-Best, George, *The Cross of Saint Patrick: The Catholic Unionist Tradition in Ireland* (Bourne End, 1984).

Bielenberg, Andrew (ed.), *The Irish Diaspora* (London, 2000).

Bishop, Patrick and Mallie, Eamonn, *The Provisional IRA* (London, 1987).

Blackstock, Allan, ' "A Dangerous Species of Ally": Orangeism and the Irish Yeomanry', *Irish Historical Studies*, xxx, 119 (May 1997).

Blackstock, Allan, *An Ascendancy Army: The Irish Yeomanry, 1796–1834* (Dublin, 1998).

Blackstock, Allan, *Loyalism in Ireland, 1789–1829* (London, 2007).

Bobotis, A, 'Rival Maternities: Maud Gonne, Queen Victoria and the Reign of the Political Mother', *Victorian Studies* (Autumn, 2006).

Bogdanor, Vernon, *Devolution* (Oxford, 1979).

Bogdanor, Vernon, *Devolution in the United Kingdom* (Oxford, 2001 edition).

Bolton, G.C., *The Passing of the Irish Act of Union* (Oxford, 1966).

Boulton, David, *The UVF, 1966–73: An Anatomy of Loyalist Rebellion* (Dublin, 1973).

Bourke, Joanna, *Husbandry to Housewifery: Women, Economic Change and Housework in Ireland, 1890–1914* (Oxford, 1993).

Bowen, Desmond, *Souperism: Myth or Reality?* (Cork, 1970).

Bowen, Desmond, *The Protestant Crusade in Ireland, 1800–70: A Study of Protestant–Catholic Relations between the Act of Union and Disestablishment* (Dublin, 1978).

Bowen, Desmond, *Paul Cullen and the Shaping of Modern Irish Catholicism* (Dublin, 1983).

Bowen, Desmond and Bowen, Jean, *Heroic Option: The Irish in the British Army* (London, 2005).

Bowman, John, *De Valera and the Ulster Question, 1917–73* (Oxford, 1982).

Bowman, Timothy, 'The Ulster Volunteer Force and the Formation of the 36th (Ulster) Division', *Irish Historical Studies*, 33, 128 (November, 2001).

Bowman, Timothy, *Carson's Army: The Ulster Volunteer Force, 1910–22* (Manchester, 2008).

Bowyer Bell, James, *The Secret Army: A History of the IRA, 1916–70* (London, 1970).

Boyce, D.G., *Englishmen and Irish Troubles: British Public Opinion and the Making of Irish Policy, 1918–1922* (London, 1972).

Boyce, D. George (ed.), *The Revolution in Ireland, 1879–1923* (London, 1988).

Boyce, D. George, Eccleshall, Robert and Geoghegan, Vincent (eds), *Political Thought in Ireland since the Seventeenth Century* (London, 1993).

Boyce, D. George and O'Day, Alan (eds), *Parnell in Perspective* (London, 1991).

Boyce, D. George and O'Day, Alan (eds), *The Making of Modern Irish History: Revisionism and the Revisionist Controversy* (London, 1996).

Boyce, D.G. and O'Day, Alan (eds), *Defenders of the Union: A Survey of British and Irish Unionism since 1800* (London, 2001).

Boyce, D.G. and O'Day, Alan (eds), *The Ulster Crisis, 1885–1921* (London, 2006).

Boyle, John W., 'The Belfast Protestant Association and the Independent Orange Order, 1901–10', *Irish Historical Studies*, xiii, 50 (September 1962).

Boyle, John W., *The Irish Labor Movement in the Nineteenth Century* (Washington, DC, 1988).

Bradshaw, Brendan, 'Nationalism and Historical Scholarship in Modern Ireland', *Irish Historical Studies*, xxvi, 104 (November 1989).

Brewer, John with Gareth Higgins, *Anti-Catholicism in Northern Ireland, 1600–1998: The Mote and the Beam* (Basingstoke, 1998).

Brooke, Peter, *Ulster Presbyterianism: The Historical Perspective, 1610–1970* (Dublin, 1987).

Brotherstone, Terry, Clarke, Anna and Whelan, Kevin (eds), *These Fissured Isles: Ireland, Scotland and British History, 1798–1848* (Edinburgh, 2005).

Brown, Michael, Geoghegan, Patrick and Kelly, James (eds), *The Irish Act of Union, 1800* (Dublin, 2003).

Brown, Stewart J., *The National Churches of England, Ireland and Scotland, 1801–46* (Oxford, 2001).

Bruce, Steve, *'God Save Ulster!': The Religion and Politics of Paisleyism* (Oxford 1986).

Bruce, Steve, *The Red Hand: Protestant Paramilitaries in Northern Ireland* (Oxford, 1992).

Bruce, Steve, *The Edge of the Union: The Ulster Loyalist Political Vision* (Oxford, 1994).

Buckland, Patrick, *Irish Unionism I: The Anglo-Irish and the New Ireland, 1885–1922* (Dublin, 1972).

Buckland, Patrick, *Irish Unionism II: Ulster Unionism and the Origins of Northern Ireland, 1886–1922* (Dublin, 1973).

Buckland, Patrick, *The Factory of Grievances: Devolved Government in Northern Ireland, 1921–39* (Dublin, 1979).

Buckland, Patrick, *James Craig* (Dublin, 1980).

Budge, Ian and O'Leary, Cornelius, *Belfast: Approach to Crisis: A Study of Belfast Politics, 1613–1970* (London, 1973).

Bull, Philip, 'The United Irish League and the Reunion of the Irish Parliamentary Party, 1898–1900', *Irish Historical Studies*, xxvi, 101 (May 1988).

Bull, Philip, 'The Significance of the Nationalist Response to the Irish Land Act of 1903', *Irish Historical Studies*, xxviii, 111 (May 1993).

Bull, Philip, *Land, Politics and Nationalism: A Study of the Irish Land Question* (Dublin, 1996).

Bull, Philip, 'The Formation of the United Irish League, 1898–1900: The Dynamics of Irish Agrarian Agitation', *Irish Historical Studies*, 33, 131 (May, 2003).

Callanan, Frank, *The Parnell Split, 1890–91* (Cork, 1992).

Callanan, Frank, 'Parnell: the Great Pretender?', *History Ireland* (Autumn, 1993).

Callanan, Frank, *T.M. Healy* (Cork, 1996).

Cameron, Ewen, 'Communication or Separation? Reactions to Irish Land Agitation and Legislation in the Highlands of Scotland, c.1870–1910', *English Historical Review*, cxx, 487 (June 2005).

Campbell, Colm, *Emergency Law in Ireland, 1918–25* (Oxford, 1994).

Campbell, Fergus, 'Irish Popular Politics and the Making of the Wyndham Land Act, 1901–3', *Historical Journal*, 45, 4 (December 2002).

Campbell, Fergus, *Land and Revolution: Nationalist Politics in the West of Ireland, 1891–1921* (Oxford, 2005).

Campbell, Fergus, 'Who Ruled Ireland? The Irish Administration, 1879–1914', *Historical Journal*, 50, 3, (September, 2007).

Campbell, Fergus, *The Irish Establishment, 1879–1914* (Oxford, 2009).

Canning, Paul, *British Policy towards Ireland, 1921–41* (Oxford, 1985).

Carroll, Joseph T., *Ireland in the War Years* (Newton Abbot, 1975).

Clark, Samuel, *Social Origins of the Irish Land War* (Princeton, 1979).

Clark, Samuel and Donnelly Jr, James S. (eds), *Irish Peasants: Violence and Political Unrest, 1780–1914* (Manchester, 1983).

Clarke, Peter, *Lancashire and the New Liberalism* (Cambridge, 1971).

Clayton, Pamela, *Enemies and Passing Friends: Settler Ideologies in Twentieth Century Ulster* (London, 1996).

Clear, Catriona, *Nuns in Nineteenth Century Ireland* (Dublin, 1987).

Cochrane, Feargal, *Unionist Politics and the Politics of Unionism since the Anglo-Irish Agreement* (Cork, 1997).

Coldrey, B.M., *Faith and Fatherland: The Christian Brothers and the Development of Irish Nationalism, 1838–1921* (Dublin, 1988).

Collins, Peter (ed.), *Nationalism and Unionism: Conflict in Ireland, 1885–1921* (Belfast, 1994).

Collins, Stephen, *The Cosgrave Legacy* (Dublin, 1996).

Comerford, R.V., *Charles J. Kickham: A Study in Irish Nationalism and Literature* (Dublin, 1979).

Comerford, R.V., *The Fenians in Context: Irish Politics and Society, 1848–1882* (Dublin, 1985).

Connell, K.H., *The Population of Ireland, 1750–1845* (Oxford, 1950).

Connolly, Claire, 'Writing the Union', in Daire Keogh and Kevin Whelan (eds), *Acts of Union: The Causes, Contexts and Consequences of the Act of Union* (Dublin, 2001).

Connolly, Claire, 'Completing the Union: The Irish Novel and the Moment of Union', in Michael Brown, Patrick Geoghegan and James Kelly (eds), *The Irish Act of Union, 1800: Bicentennial Essays* (Dublin, 2003).

Connolly, S.J., *Priests and People in Pre-Famine Ireland, 1780–1845* (Dublin, 1982).

Connolly, S.J., *Religion and Society in Nineteenth Century Ireland* (Dundalk, 1985).

Connolly, S.J. (ed.), *Kingdoms United? Great Britain and Ireland since 1800: Integration and Diversity* (Dublin, 1999).

Coogan, Tim Pat, *The IRA* (London, 1980).

Coogan, Tim Pat, *Michael Collins: A Biography* (London, 1990).

Coogan, Tim Pat, *De Valera: Long Fellow, Long Shadow* (London, 1993).

Cook, Scott, 'The Irish Raj: Social Origins and Careers of Irishmen in the Indian Civil Service, 1855–1919', *Journal of Social History*, 20 (Spring, 1987).

Cook, Scott, *Imperial Affinities: Nineteenth-Century Analogies and Exchanges between India and Ireland* (New Delhi, 1993).

Cooke, A.B. and Vincent, John, *The Governing Passion: Cabinet Government and Party Politics in Britain, 1885–6* (Brighton, 1974).

Corish, Patrick J., *The Irish Catholic Experience: A Historical Survey* (Dublin, 1985).

Costello, Francis J., *Enduring the Most: The Life and Death of Terence MacSwiney* (Dingle, 1995).

Cote, Jane McL., *Fanny and Anna Parnell: Ireland's Patriot Sisters* (London, 1991).

Coulter, Colin and Coleman, Steve, *The End of Irish History? Critical Reflections on the Celtic Tiger* (Manchester, 2003).

Cox, Michael, Guelke, Adrian and Stephen, Fiona (eds), *A Farewell to Arms? From 'Long War' to Long Peace in Northern Ireland* (Manchester, 2000).

Cronin, Mike, 'The Socio-Economic Background and Membership of the Blueshirt Movement', *Irish Historical Studies*, xxix, 114 (November 1994).

Cronin, Mike, *The Blueshirts and Irish Politics* (Dublin, 1997).

Crossman, Virginia, *Politics, Law and Order in Nineteenth Century Ireland* (Dublin, 1996).

Cullen, Louis, 'Alliances and Misalliances in the Politics of the Union', *Transactions of the Royal Historical Society*, Sixth Series, Vol. 10 (2000).

Cullen, Mary and Luddy, Maria (eds), *Women, Power and Consciousness in Nineteenth Century Ireland: Eight Biographical Studies* (Dublin, 1995).

Curran, Joseph M., *The Birth of the Irish Free State, 1921–23* (Alabama, 1980).

Curtin, Nancy, 'The Transformation of the Society of United Irishmen into a Mass-based Revolutionary Organisation, 1794–6', *Irish Historical Studies*, xxiv, 96 (November 1985).

Curtin, Nancy J., *The United Irishmen: Popular Politics in Ulster and Dublin, 1791–1798* (Oxford, 1994).

Curtis, L.P., *Coercion and Conciliation in Ireland, 1880–1892: A Study in Conservative Unionism* (Princeton, 1963).

Curtis, L.P., 'Incumbered Wealth: Landed Indebtedness in Post-Famine Ireland', *American Historical Review*, lxxxv (April 1980).

d'Alton, Ian, 'Southern Irish Unionism: A Study of Cork Unionists, 1884–1914', *Transactions of the Royal Historical Society*, 5th series, 23 (London, 1973).

d'Alton, Ian, *Protestant Society and Politics in Cork, 1812–1844* (Cork, 1980).

Daly, Mary E., *Dublin, the Deposed Capital: A Social and Economic History, 1860–1914* (Cork, 1985).

Daly, Mary E., *The Famine in Ireland* (Dublin, 1986).

Daly, Mary E., *Industrial Development and Irish National Identity, 1922–1939* (Dublin, 1992).

Davis, Richard, *Arthur Griffith and Non-Violent Sinn Féin* (Dublin, 1974).

Davis, Richard, *The Young Ireland Movement* (Dublin, 1987).

De Bréadún, Deaglán, *The Far Side of Revenge: Making Peace in Northern Ireland* (Cork, 2001).

Delaney, Enda, *Demography, State and Society: Irish Migration to Britain, 1921–71* (Liverpool, 2000).

Delaney, Enda, *The Irish in Post-War Britain* (Oxford, 2008).

Denman, Terence, 'The Catholic Irish Soldier in the First World War: The "Racial Environment"', *Irish Historical Studies*, xxvii, 108 (November 1991).

Denman, Terence, '"The Red Livery of Shame": The Campaign against Army Recruitment in Ireland, 1899–1914', *Irish Historical Studies*, xxix, 114 (November 1994).

Devine, T.M. (ed.), 'The End of Disadvantage? The Descendants of Irish Catholic Immigrants in Modern Scotland since 1945', in Martin Mitchell (ed.), *New Perspectives on the Irish in Scotland* (Edinburgh, 2008).

Devine, T.M. and Dickson, David (eds), *Ireland and Scotland, 1600–1850: Parallels and Contrasts in Economic and Social Development* (Edinburgh, 1983).

Dickson, David, Keogh, Daire and Whelan, Kevin, *The United Irishmen: Republicanism, Radicalism and Rebellion* (Dublin, 1993).

Doherty, Gabriel, 'National Identity and the Study of Irish History', *English Historical Review*, 111, 441 (1996).

Dolan, Anne, 'Killing and Bloody Sunday, November 1920', *Historical Journal*, 49, 3 (September 2006).

Dolan, Anne, *Commemorating the Irish Civil War: History and Memory, 1923–2000* (Cambridge, 2006).

Donnelly, James S., *The Land and the People of Nineteenth Century Cork: The Rural Economy and the Land Question* (London, 1975).

Douglas, R.M., 'The Pro-Axis Underground in Ireland, 1939–42', *Historical Journal*, 49, 4 (December 2006).

Doyle, Eugene J., *Justin McCarthy* (Dublin, 1996).

Dudley Edwards, Ruth, *Patrick Pearse: The Triumph of Failure* (London, 1977).

Dudley Edwards, Ruth, *James Connolly* (Dublin, 1981).

Dudley Edwards, R. and Williams, T. Desmond (eds), *The Great Famine: Studies in Irish History, 1845–52* (Dublin, 1956).

Duggan, John P., *Neutral Ireland and the Third Reich* (Dublin, 1989).

Duggan, John P., *A History of the Irish Army* (Dublin, 1991).

Dunleavy, Janet Egleson and Dunleavy, Gareth W., *Douglas Hyde: A Maker of Modern Ireland* (Berkeley, 1991).

Dunphy, Richard, *The Making of Fianna Fáil Power in Ireland, 1923–1948* (Oxford, 1995).

Dwyer, T. Ryle, *Irish Neutrality and the USA, 1939–47* (Dublin, 1977).

Dwyer, T. Ryle, *Eamon de Valera* (Dublin, 1980).

Elliott, Marianne, *Partners in Revolution: The United Irishmen and France* (New Haven and London, 1982).

Elliott, Marianne, *Wolfe Tone: Prophet of Irish Independence* (New Haven and London, 1989).

Elliott, Marianne, *Robert Emmet: The Making of a Legend* (London, 2003).

English, Richard, *Radicals and the Republic: Socialist Republicanism in the Irish Free State, 1925–1937* (Oxford, 1994).

English, Richard, '"The Inborn Hate of Things English": Ernie O'Malley and the Irish Revolution', *Past and Present*, 151 (May 1996).

English, Richard, *Ernie O'Malley: IRA Intellectual* (Oxford, 1998).

English, Richard, *Armed Struggle: The History of the IRA* (London, 2003).

English, Richard and Walker, Graham (eds), *Unionism in Modern Ireland: New Perspectives on Politics and Culture* (Dublin, 1996).

Ervine, St John, *Craigavon: Ulsterman* (London, 1949).

Fanning, Bryan, *Racism and Social Change in the Republic of Ireland* (Manchester, 2002).

Fanning, Bryan (ed.), *Immigration and Social Change in the Republic of Ireland* (Manchester, 2007).

Fanning, Ronan, *The Irish Department of Finance, 1922–1958* (Dublin, 1978).

Farrell, Brian, *The Founding of Dáil Éireann: Parliament and Nation-Building* (Dublin, 1971).

Farrell, Brian, *Seán Lemass* (Dublin, 1983).

Farrell, Michael, *Northern Ireland: The Orange State* (London, 1976).

Farrell, Michael, *Arming the Protestants: The Formation of the Ulster Special Constabulary and the Royal Ulster Constabulary, 1920–27* (London, 1983).

Farrington, Christopher, *Ulster Unionism and the Peace Process in Northern Ireland* (Basingstoke, 2006).

Feingold, William L., *The Revolt of the Tenantry: The Transformation of Local Government in Ireland, 1872–1886* (Boston, 1981).

Fergusson, James, *The Curragh Incident* (London, 1964).

Ferriter, Diarmaid, *Judging Dev: A Reassessment of the Life and Legacy of Eamon de Valera* (Dublin, 2009).

Ferriter, Diarmaid, *Occasions of Sin: Sex and Society in Modern Ireland* (London, 2009).

Fisk, Robert, *In Time of War: Ireland, Ulster and the Price of Neutrality, 1939–45* (London, 1983).

Fitzpatrick, David, *Politics and Irish Life, 1913–21: Provincial Experience of War and Revolution* (Dublin, 1977).

Fitzpatrick, David, 'The Geography of Irish Nationalism, 1910–21', *Past and Present*, 78 (1978).

Fitzpatrick, David, *Irish Emigration, 1801–1921* (Dundalk, 1984).

Fitzpatrick, David (ed.), *Ireland and the First World War* (1986).

Fitzpatrick, David, *Harry Boland's Irish Revolution, 1887–1922* (Cork, 2003).

Foley, Tadhg and O'Connor, Maureen (eds), *Ireland and India: Colonies, Culture and Empire* (Dublin, 2006).

Follis, Bryan, *A State under Siege: The Establishment of Northern Ireland, 1920–1925* (Oxford, 1995).

Foster, R.F., *Charles Stewart Parnell: The Man and his Family* (Hassocks, 1976).

Foster, R.F., *Lord Randolph Churchill: A Political Life* (Oxford, 1981).

Foster, R.F., *Paddy and Mr Punch: Connections in Irish and English History* (London, 1993).

Foster, R.F., *The Story of Ireland: An Inaugural Lecture delivered before the University of Oxford on 1 December 1994* (Oxford, 1995).

Foster, R.F., *W.B. Yeats: A Life. I: The Apprentice Mage* (Oxford, 1997).

Foster, R.F., *The Irish Story: Telling Tales and Making it Up in Ireland* (London, 2001).

Foster, R.F., *W.B. Yeats: A Life, 2: The Arch-Poet, 1915–39* (Oxford, 2003).

Foster, R.F., *Luck and the Irish: A Brief History of Change, 1970–2000* (Oxford, 2007).

Foster, R.F. and Jackson, Alvin, 'Parnell and Carson', in *European History Quarterly*, 39, 3 (July 2009).

Gailey, Andrew, *Ireland and the Death of Kindness: The Experience of Constructive Unionism, 1890–1905* (Cork, 1987).

Gallagher, Michael, *The Irish Labour Party in Transition, 1957–82* (Manchester, 1982).

Gallagher, Michael, *Political Parties in the Republic of Ireland* (Dublin, 1985).

Garvin, Tom, *Nationalist Revolutionaries in Ireland, 1858–1928* (Oxford, 1987).

Garvin, Tom, *1922: The Birth of Irish Democracy* (Dublin, 1996).

Garvin, Tom, *Preventing the Future: Why Was Ireland so Poor for so Long?* (Dublin, 2004).

Geary, Laurence M., *The Plan of Campaign, 1886–1891* (Cork, 1986).

Geoghegan, Patrick, *The Irish Act of Union: A Study in High Politics, 1798–1801* (Dublin, 1999).

Geoghegan, Patrick, 'The Irish House of Commons, 1799–1800', in Michael Brown, Patrick Geoghegan and James Kelly (eds), *The Irish Act of Union: Bicentennial Essays* (Dublin, 2001).

Geoghegan, Patrick, *Robert Emmet: A Life* (Dublin, 2002).

Geoghegan, Patrick, *King Dan: The Rise of Daniel O'Connell, 1775–1829* (Dublin, 2008).

Gibbon, Peter, *The Origins of Ulster Unionism: The Formation of Popular Protestant Politics and Ideology in Nineteenth Century Ireland* (Manchester, 1975).

Girvin, Brian, *Between Two Worlds: Politics and Economy in Independent Ireland* (Dublin, 1989).

Girvin, Brian, *From Union to Union: Nationalism, Democracy and Religion in Ireland – Act of Union to EU* (Dublin, 2002).

Gleeson, James, *Bloody Sunday*, paperback edition (London, 1963).

Godson, Dean, *Himself Alone: David Trimble and the Ordeal of Unionism* (London, 2004).

Gordon, David, *The O'Neill Years: Unionist Politics, 1963–1969* (Belfast, 1989).

Gough, Hugh and Dickson, David (eds), *Ireland and the French Revolution* (Dublin, 1990).

Gray, Peter, *The Irish Famine: New Horizons* (London, 1995).

Gray, Peter, *Famine, Land and Politics: British Government and Irish Society, 1843–50* (Dublin, 1999).

Gray, Peter, 'National Humiliation and the Great Hunger: Fast and Famine in 1847', *Irish Historical Studies*, 32, 126 (November 2000).

Gray, Peter, 'Famine and Land in Ireland and India, 1845–80: James Caird and the Political Economy of Hunger', *Historical Journal*, 46, 1 (March 2006).

Gray, Peter, *The Making of the Irish Poor Law, 1815–43* (Manchester, 2009).

Gray, Tony, *The Orange Order* (London, 1972).

Gwynn, Denis, *The Life of John Redmond* (London, 1932).

Harkness, David W., *The Restless Dominion: The Irish Free State and the British Commonwealth of Nations, 1921–1931* (London, 1969).

Harris, Mary, *The Catholic Church and the Foundation of the Northern Irish State, 1912–30* (Cork, 1993).

Hart, Peter, 'Michael Collins and the Assassination of Sir Henry Wilson', *Irish Historical Studies*, xxviii, 110 (November 1992).

Hart, Peter, 'The Geography of Revolution in Ireland, 1917–23', *Past and Present*, 155 (1997).

Hart, Peter, *The IRA and its Enemies: Violence and Community in County Cork, 1916–1923* (Oxford, 1998).

Hart, Peter, 'The Social Structure of the Irish Republican Army, 1916–23', *Historical Journal*, 42, 1 (March 1999).

Hart, Peter, ' "Operations Abroad": The IRA in Britain, 1919–23', *English Historical Review*, 115, 460 (2000).

Hart, Peter, *Mick: The Real Michael Collins* (London, 2005).

Hempton, David and Hill, Myrtle, *Evangelical Protestantism in Ulster Society, 1740–1890* (London, 1992).

Hennessey, Thomas, *The Northern Ireland Peace Process: Ending the Troubles?* (Dublin, 2000).

Hennessey, Thomas, *Northern Ireland: The Origins of the Troubles* (Dublin, 2005).

Hennessey, Thomas, *The Evolution of the Troubles, 1970–72* (Dublin, 2007).

Hepburn, A.C., *A Past Apart: Studies in the History of Catholic Belfast, 1850–1950* (Belfast, 1996).

Hepburn, A.C., *Catholic Belfast and Nationalist Ireland in the Era of Joe Devlin, 1871–1934* (Oxford, 2008).

Hill, J.R., 'Ireland without Union: Molyneux and his Legacy', in John Robertson (ed.), *A Union for Empire: Political Thought and the Union of 1707* (Cambridge, 1995).

Hill, Jacqueline, *From Patriots to Unionists: Dublin Civic Politics and Irish Protestant Patriotism, 1660–1840* (Oxford, 1997).

Holmes, Janice and Urquhart, Diane (eds), *Coming into the Light: The Work, Politics and Religion of Women in Ulster, 1840–1940* (Belfast, 1994).

Holmes, R. Finlay, *Henry Cooke* (Belfast, 1981).

Holmes, R. Finlay, *Our Irish Presbyterian Heritage* (Belfast, 1985).

Hopkinson, Michael, *Green against Green: The Irish Civil War* (Dublin, 1988).

Hopkinson, Michael, 'The Craig–Collins Pact of 1922: Two Attempted Reforms of the Northern Ireland Government', *Irish Historical Studies*, xxvii, 106 (November 1990).

Hopkinson, Michael, *The Irish War of Independence* (Dublin, 2002).

Hoppen, K. Theodore, *Elections, Politics and Society in Ireland, 1832–1885* (Oxford, 1984).

Hoppen, K. Theodore, 'Grammars of Electoral Violence in Nineteenth Century England and Ireland', *English Historical Review*, cix (June 1994).

Hoppen, K. Theodore, 'An Incorporating Union: British Politicians and Ireland, 1800–30', *English Historical Review*, cxxiii, 501 (April 2008).

Horgan, John, *Seán Lemass: The Enigmatic Patriot* (Dublin, 1997).

Howe, Stephen, *Ireland and Empire: Colonial Legacies in Irish History and Culture* (Oxford, 2000).

Hume, David, *The Ulster Unionist Party, 1972–1992: A Political Movement in an Era of Conflict and Change* (Belfast, 1996).

Hutchinson, John, *The Dynamics of Cultural Nationalism: The Gaelic Revival and the Creation of the Irish Nation State* (London, 1987).

Hyde, H. Montgomery, *Carson: The Life of Sir Edward Carson, Lord Carson of Duncairn* (London, 1953).

Hyde, H. Montgomery, *The Londonderrys: A Family Portrait* (London, 1979).

Hyland, J.L., *James Connolly* (Dublin, 1997).

Jackson, Alvin, 'Irish Unionism and the Russellite Threat, 1894–1906', *Irish Historical Studies*, xxv, 100 (November 1987).

Jackson, Alvin, *The Ulster Party: Irish Unionists in the House of Commons, 1884–1911* (Oxford, 1989).

Jackson, Alvin, 'Unionist Politics and Protestant Society in Edwardian Ireland', *Historical Journal*, xxxiii, 4 (1990).

Jackson, Alvin, 'Unionist Myths, 1912–1985', *Past and Present*, 136 (August 1992).

Jackson, Alvin, *Sir Edward Carson* (Dublin, 1993).

Jackson, Alvin, *Colonel Edward Saunderson: Land and Loyalty in Victorian Ireland* (Oxford, 1995).

Jackson, Alvin, 'Irish Unionists and Empire, 1880–1920: Classes and Masses', in Keith Jeffery (ed.), *An Irish Empire? Aspects of Ireland and the British Empire* (Manchester, 1996).

Jackson, Alvin, 'British Ireland: What if Home Rule Had Been Enacted in 1912?', in Niall Ferguson (ed.), *Virtual History: Alternatives and Counterfactuals* (London, 1997).

Jackson, Alvin, 'The Irish Act of Union, 1801–2001', *History Today* (January 2001).

Jackson, Alvin, *Home Rule: An Irish History, 1800–2000*, paperback edition (London, 2004).

Jackson, Alvin, 'Ireland, the Union and the Empire, 1800–1960', in Kevin Kenny (ed.), *Ireland and the British Empire*, paperback edition (Oxford, 2006).

Jackson, Daniel, *Popular Opposition to Irish Home Rule in Edwardian Britain* (Liverpool, 2009).

Jalland, Patricia, *The Liberals and Ireland: The Ulster Question in British Politics to 1914* (Brighton, 1980).

Jeffery, Keith (ed.), *An Irish Empire? Aspects of Ireland and the British Empire* (Manchester, 1996).

Jeffery, Keith, *Ireland and the Great War* (Cambridge, 2000).

Jeffery, Keith, *Field Marshal Sir Henry Wilson: A Political Soldier* (Oxford, 2006).

Johnson, David, *The Inter-war Economy in Ireland* (Dundalk, 1985).

Johnson, Nuala, *Ireland, the Great War, and the Geography of Remembrance* (Cambridge, 2007).

Johnston, Edith Mary, *Great Britain and Ireland, 1760–1800* (Edinburgh, 1963).

Jordan, Donald, *Land and Popular Politics in Ireland: County Mayo from the Plantation to the Land War* (Cambridge, 1994).

Jordan, Donald, 'The Irish National League and the "Unwritten Law": Rural Protest and Nation-Building in Ireland, 1882–1890', *Past and Present*, 158 (February 1998).

Jupp, Peter, *The Governing of Britain, 1688–1848: The Executive, Parliament and the People* (London, 2006).

Kaufmann, Eric, *The Orange Order: A Contemporary Northern Irish History* (Oxford, 2007).

Kaufmann, Eric, 'The Orange Order in Scotland since 1860: A Social Analysis', in Martin Mitchell (ed.), *New Perspectives on the Irish in Scotland* (Edinburgh, 2008).

Kavanaugh, Ann C., *John Fitzgibbon, Earl of Clare: Protestant Reaction and English Authority in Late Eighteenth Century Ireland* (Dublin, 1997).

Kearney, Hugh, *The British Isles: A History of Four Nations* (Cambridge, 1989).

Kee, Robert, *The Laurel and the Ivy: The Story of Charles Stewart Parnell and Irish Nationalism* (London, 1993).

Keenan, D.J., *The Catholic Church in Nineteenth Century Ireland* (Dublin, 1983).

Kelly, James, 'The Origins of the Act of Union: An Examination of Unionist Opinion in Britain and Ireland, 1650–1800', *Irish Historical Studies*, xxv (May 1987).

Kelly, James, *Prelude to Union: Anglo-Irish Politics in the 1780s* (Cork, 1992).

Kelly, James, 'The Act of Union: Its Origins and Background', in Daire Keogh and Kevin Whelan (eds), *Acts of Union: The Causes, Contexts and Consequences of the Act of Union* (Dublin, 2001).

Kelly, James, 'The Failure of Opposition', in Michael Brown, Patrick Geoghegan and James Kelly (eds), *The Irish Act of Union: Bicentennial Essays* (Dublin, 2001).

Kelly, James, 'The Historiography of the Act of Union', in Michael Brown, Patrick Geoghegan and James Kelly (eds), *The Irish Act of Union: Bicentennial Essays* (Dublin, 2001).

Kelly, Matthew, 'Dublin Fenianism in the 1880s: "The Irish Culture of the Future?"', *Historical Journal*, 43, 2 (June 2000).

Kelly, Matthew, ' "Parnell's Old Brigade": The Redmondite-Fenian Nexus in the 1890s', *Irish Historical Studies*, 33, 130 (November 2002).

Kelly, Matthew, 'The Politics of Protestant Street Preaching in 1890s Ireland', *Historical Journal*, 48, 1 (March 2005).

Kelly, Matthew, *The Fenian Ideal and Irish Nationalism, 1882–1916* (London, 2008).

Kendle, John, *Ireland and the Federal Solution: The Debate over the United Kingdom Constitution, 1870–1921* (Kingston and Montreal, 1989).

Kendle, John, *Federal Britain: A History* (London, 1997).

Kennedy, Denis, *The Widening Gulf: Northern Attitudes to the Independent Irish State, 1919–49* (Belfast, 1988).

Kennedy, Kieran, Giblin, Thomas and McHugh, Deirdre, *The Economic Development of Ireland in the Twentieth Century* (London, 1988).

Kennedy, Liam, *The Modern Industrialisation of Ireland, 1940–1988* (Dublin, 1989).

Kennedy, Liam and Ollerenshaw, Philip, *An Economic History of Ulster, 1820–1940* (Manchester, 1985).

Kennedy, Michael, *Ireland and the League of Nations, 1919–46: International Relations, Diplomacy and Politics* (Dublin, 1996).

Kenny, Kevin (ed.), *Ireland and the British Empire*, paperback edition (Oxford, 2006).

Keogh, Daire and Whelan, Kevin (eds), *Acts of Union: The Causes, Contexts, and Consequences of the Act of Union* (Dublin, 2001).

Keogh, Dermot, *The Vatican, the Bishops and Irish Politics, 1919–1939* (Cambridge, 1986).

Keogh, Dermot, *Ireland and Europe, 1919–89* (Cork and Dublin, 1989).

Keogh, Dermot, *Jack Lynch: A Biography* (Dublin, 2008).

Kerr, Donal, *Peel, Priests and Politics: Sir Robert Peel's Administration and the Roman Catholic Church in Ireland, 1841–6* (Oxford, 1982).

Kerr, Donal, *'A Nation of Beggars?': Priests, People and Politics in Famine Ireland, 1846–1852* (Oxford, 1994).

Kiely, David M., *John Millington Synge: A Biography* (Dublin, 1994).

Kinealy, Christine, *This Great Calamity: The Irish Famine, 1845–52* (Dublin, 1994).

Kinealy, Christine, *The Culture of Commemoration: The Great Irish Famine – A Dangerous Memory?* (n.p., 1996).

Kinealy, Christine, *A Death-Dealing Famine: The Great Hunger in Ireland* (London, 1997).

Kinealy, Christine, *Repeal and Revolution: 1848 in Ireland* (Manchester, 2009).

Kinealy, Christine and Parkhill, Trevor (eds), *The Famine in Ulster: The Regional Impact* (Belfast, 1997).

Kissane, Bill, *The Politics of the Irish Civil War* (Oxford, 2005).

Knowlton, Steven R., *Popular Politics and the Irish Catholic Church: The Rise and Fall of the Independent Irish Party, 1850–59* (New York and London, 1991).

Kotsonouris, Mary, *Retreat from Revolution: The Dáil Courts, 1920–24* (Dublin, 1994).

Laffan, Michael, 'The Unification of Sinn Féin in 1917', *Irish Historical Studies*, xvii, 67 (March, 1971).

Laffan, Michael, *The Partition of Ireland, 1911–1925* (Dundalk, 1983).

Laffan, Michael, *The Resurrection of Ireland: The Sinn Féin Party, 1916–25* (Cambridge, 1999).

Lane, Fintan, 'P.F. Johnson, Nationalism, and Irish Rural Labourers, 1869–82', *Irish Historical Studies*, 33, 130 (November 2002).

Larkin, Emmet, *James Larkin: Irish Labour Leader, 1876–1947* (London, 1965).

Larkin, Emmet, *The Roman Catholic Church and the Creation of the Modern Irish State, 1878–86* (Dublin, 1975).

Lawlor, Sheila, *Britain and Ireland, 1914–23* (Dublin, 1983).

Lawrence, R.J., *The Government of Northern Ireland: Public Finance and Public Services, 1921–64* (Oxford, 1965).

Lee, J.J. (ed.), *Ireland, 1945–70* (Dublin, 1979).

Leersen, Joep, *Remembrance and Imagination: Patterns in the Literary and Historical Representation of Ireland in the Nineteenth Century* (Cork, 1996).

Legg, Marie-Louise, *Newspapers and Nationalism: The Irish Provincial Press, 1850–92* (Dublin, 1999).

Loughlin, James, *Gladstone, Home Rule and the Ulster Question, 1882–93* (Dublin, 1986).

Loughlin, James, *Ulster Unionism and British National Identity since 1885* (London, 1995).

Loughlin, James, *The British Monarchy and Ireland: 1800 to the Present* (Cambridge, 2007).

Luddy, Maria, *Women and Philanthropy in Nineteenth Century Ireland* (Cambridge, 1995).

Luddy, Maria, *Women in Ireland, 1900–18: A Documentary History* (Cork, 1995).

Luddy, Maria, *Hanna Sheehy Skeffington* (Dublin, 1995).

Luddy, Maria and Murphy, Cliona (eds), *Women Surviving* (Swords, 1989).

Lynn, Brendan, *Holding the Ground: The Nationalist Party in Northern Ireland, 1945–72* (Aldershot, 1997).

Lyons, F.S.L., *The Irish Parliamentary Party, 1890–1910* (London, 1951).

Lyons, F.S.L., *The Fall of Parnell, 1890–91* (London, 1960).

Lyons, F.S.L., *John Dillon: A Biography* (London, 1968).

Lyons, F.S.L., *Charles Stewart Parnell* (London, 1977).

Lyons, F.S.L., *Culture and Anarchy in Ireland, 1890–1939* (Oxford, 1979).

MacBride, Lawrence, *The Greening of Dublin Castle: The Transformation of Bureaucratic and Judicial Personnel in Dublin Castle in Ireland, 1892–1922* (Washington, 1991).

McBride, Ian, 'When Ulster Joined Ireland: Anti-Popery, Presbyterian Radicalism and Irish Republicanism in the 1790s', *Past and Present*, 157 (November 1997).

McBride, I.R., *Scripture Politics: Ulster Presbyterians and Irish Radicalism in the Late Eighteenth Century* (Oxford, 1998).

McCabe, Ian, *A Diplomatic History of Ireland, 1948–49: The Republic, the Commonwealth and NATO* (Dublin, 1991).

McCartney, Donal, 'The Writing of History in Ireland, 1800–1830', *Irish Historical Studies*, x, 40 (September 1957).

McCartney, Donal (ed.), *The World of Daniel O'Connell* (Dublin, 1980).

McCartney, Donal (ed.), *Parnell: The Politics of Power* (Dublin, 1991).

McCartney, Donal (ed.), *W.E.H. Lecky: Historian and Politician, 1838–1903* (Dublin, 1994).

McConnel, James, 'The Franchise Factor in the Defeat of the Irish Parliamentary Party, 1885–1918', *Historical Journal*, 47, 2 (June, 2004).

MacDonagh, Oliver, *O'Connell: The Life of Daniel O'Connell, 1775–1847* (London, 1991).

McDonald, Henry, *Trimble* (London, 2000).

McDowell, R.B., *The Irish Convention, 1917–18* (London, 1970).

McDowell, R.B., *The Church of Ireland, 1869–1969* (London, 1975).

McDowell, R.B., *Ireland in the Age of Imperialism and Revolution, 1760–1801* (Oxford, 1979).

McDowell, R.B., *Crisis and Decline: The Fate of Southern Unionism* (Dublin, 1997).

McGarry, Fearghal (ed.), *Republicanism in Modern Ireland* (Dublin, 2003).

McGarry, Fearghal, *Eoin O'Duffy: A Self-Made Hero* (Oxford, 2005).

McGarry, Fearghal, *The Rising: Ireland, Easter 1916* (Oxford, 2010).

McGee, Owen, *The IRB: The Irish Replication Brotherhood from the Land League to Sinn Féin* (Dublin, 2005).

McIntosh, Gillian V., 'Unionist Culture and Literature, 1920–60', PhD thesis (Queen's University, Belfast, 1998).

McIntosh, Gillian V., *The Force of Culture: Unionist Identities in Twentieth-Century Ireland* (Cork, 1999).

Macintyre, Angus, *The Liberator: Daniel O'Connell and the Irish Party, 1830–1847* (London, 1965).

McKee, Eamon, 'Church–State Relations and the Development of Irish Health Policy: The Mother and Child Scheme, 1944–53', *Irish Historical Studies*, xxv, 98 (November 1986).

McKittrick, David, Kelters, Seamus, Feeney, Brian and Thornton, Chris (eds), *Lost Lives: The Stories of the Men, Women and Children who Died as a Result of the Northern Ireland Troubles* (Edinburgh and London, 1999).

McMahon, Deirdre, *Republicans and Imperialists: Anglo-Irish Relations in the 1930s* (New Haven and London, 1984).

MacManus, M.J. (ed.), *Thomas Davis and Young Ireland, 1845–1945* (Dublin, 1945).

Macmillan, Gretchen, *State, Society and Authority in Ireland: The Foundations of the Modern State* (Dublin, 1993).

McMinn, J.R.B., 'Liberalism in North Antrim, 1900–1914', *Irish Historical Studies*, xxiii, 89 (May 1982).

Maguire, Martin, 'The Organisation and Activism of Dublin's Protestant Working Class, 1883–1935', *Irish Historical Studies*, xxix, 113 (May 1994).

Maguire, Martin, *The Civil Service and the Revolution in Ireland, 1912–1938: 'Shaking the Blood-Stained Hand of Mr Collins'* (Manchester, 2008).

Maguire, W.A., *Belfast* (Keele, 1993).

Maher, Jim, *The Flying Column: West Kilkenny, 1916–21* (Dublin, 1987).

Malcolm, Elizabeth, *'Ireland Sober, Ireland Free': Drink and Temperance in Nineteenth Century Ireland* (Dublin, 1986).

Malcomson, A.P.W., *John Foster: The Politics of the Anglo-Irish Ascendancy* (Oxford, 1978).

Mandle, W.F., *The Gaelic Athletic Association and Irish Nationalist Politics, 1884–1924* (Dublin, 1987).

Manning, Maurice, *The Blueshirts* (Dublin, 1970).

Manning, Maurice, *James Dillon: A Biography* (Dublin, 1999).

Mansergh, Nicholas, *The Unresolved Question: The Anglo-Irish Settlement and its Undoing, 1912–72* (New Haven and London, 1991).

Mansergh, Nicholas, *Grattan's Failure: Parliamentary Opposition and the People in Ireland, 1779–1800* (Dublin, 2005).

Martin, F.X. (ed.), *Leaders and Men of the Easter Rising: Dublin, 1916* (London, 1967).

Matthews, Kevin, 'Stanley Baldwin's Irish Question', *Historical Journal*, 43, 4 (December, 2000).

Matthews, Kevin, *Fatal Influence: The Impact of Ireland upon British Politics, 1920–25* (Dublin, 2004).

Maume, Patrick, *'Life that is Exile': Daniel Corkery and the Search for Irish Ireland* (Belfast, 1993).

Maume, Patrick, *D.P. Moran* (Dublin, 1995).

Maume, Patrick, 'Parnell and the IRB Oath', *Irish Historical Studies*, xxix, 115 (May 1995).

Maume, Patrick, *The Long Gestation: Irish Nationalist Life, 1891–1918* (Dublin, 1999).

Maye, Brian, *Arthur Griffith* (Dublin, 1997).

Miller, David W., *Church, State and Nation in Ireland, 1898–1921* (Dublin, 1973).

Miller, David W., *Queen's Rebels: Ulster Loyalism in Historical Perspective* (Dublin, 1978).

Miller, David W. (ed.), *Peep o'Day Boys and Defenders: Selected Documents on the County Armagh Disturbances, 1784–96* (Belfast, 1990).

Miller, Kerby A., *Emigrants and Exiles: Ireland and the Irish Exodus to North America* (New York, 1985).

Mitchell, Arthur, *Labour and Irish Politics, 1890–1930: The Irish Labour Movement in an Age of Revolution* (Dublin, 1974).

Mitchell, Arthur, *Revolutionary Government in Ireland: Dáil Éireann, 1919–22* (Dublin, 1995).

Mokyr, Joel, *Why Ireland Starved: A Quantitative and Analytical History of the Irish Economy, 1800–1850*, 2nd edition (London, 1985).

Moloney, Ed, *A Secret History of the IRA* (London, 2002).

Moody, T.W. (ed.), *The Fenian Movement* (Cork, 1968).

Moody, T.W., *The Ulster Question, 1603–1973* (Dublin, 1974).

Moody, T.W., *Davitt and Irish Revolution, 1846–82* (Oxford, 1981).

Moran, Gerald, 'James Daly and the Rise and Fall of the Land League in the West of Ireland, 1879–82', *Irish Historical Studies*, xxix, 114 (November 1994).

Morgan, Austen, *Labour and Partition: The Belfast Working Class, 1905–23* (London, 1991).

Morgan, Hiram, 'An Unwelcome Heritage: Ireland's Role in British Empire Building', *History of European Ideas*, 19 (July, 1994).

Morrow, John, 'Thomas Carlyle, "Young Ireland", and the "Condition of Ireland Question"', *Historical Journal*, 51, 3 (September, 2008).

Mulholland, Marc, 'The Evolution of Ulster Unionism, 1960–69: Causes and Consequences', PhD thesis (Queen's University, Belfast, 1997).

Mulholland, Marc, *Northern Ireland at the Cross Roads: Ulster Unionism in the O'Neill Years, 1963–69* (London, 2000).

Mulholland, Marc, '"The Best and Most Forward Looking" in Ulster Unionism: The Unionist Society (est. 1942)', *Irish Historical Studies*, 33, 129 (May, 2002).

Murphy, Cliona, *The Women's Suffrage Movement and Irish Society in the Early Twentieth Century* (Hemel Hempstead, 1989).

Murphy, James H., *Abject Loyalty: Nationalism and Monarchy in Ireland During the Reign of Queen Victoria* (Washington, 2001).

Murray, Gerard, *John Hume and the SDLP: Impact and Survival in Northern Ireland* (Dublin, 1998).

Newby, Andrew, *Ireland, Radicalism and the Scottish Highlands, 1870–1912* (Edinburgh, 2006).

Ní Dhonnchadha, Máirín and Dorgan, Theo (eds), *Revising the Rising* (Derry, 1991).

Norman, E.R., *The Catholic Church and Ireland in the Age of Rebellion, 1859–73* (London, 1965).

Norstedt, Johann, *Thomas MacDonagh: A Critical Biography* (Charlottesville, 1980).

Nowlan, Kevin B., *The Politics of Repeal: A Study in the Relations between Britain and Ireland, 1841–50* (London, 1965).

Nowlan, Kevin B., *The Making of 1916: Studies in the History of the Rising* (Dublin, 1969).

Nowlan, Kevin B. and O'Connell, Maurice R. (eds), *Daniel O'Connell: Portrait of a Radical* (Belfast, 1984).

Nowlan, Kevin B. and Williams, T. Desmond (eds), *Ireland in the War Years and After* (Dublin, 1969).

O'Brien, Conor Cruise, *Parnell and his Party, 1880–90* (Oxford, 1957).

O'Brien, Conor Cruise, *Writers and Politics* (London, 1965).

O'Brien, Conor Cruise, *States of Ireland* (London, 1972).

O'Brien, Gerard, *Anglo-Irish Politics in the Age of Grattan and Pitt* (Dublin, 1987).

O'Brien, Justin, *The Arms Trial* (Dublin, 2000).

Ó Cadhla, Stiofán, *Civilising Ireland: Ordnance Survey, 1824–42: Ethnography, Cartography, Translation* (Dublin, 2006).

O'Callaghan, Margaret, 'Language, Nationality and Cultural Identity in the Irish Free State, 1922–27', *Irish Historical Studies*, xxiv (1984).

O'Callaghan, Margaret, *British High Politics and a Nationalist Ireland: Criminality, Land and the Law under Forster and Balfour* (Cork, 1994).

O'Callaghan, Margaret, 'New Ways of Looking at the State Apparatus and State Archive in Nineteenth-Century Ireland: "Curiosities from that Phonetic Museum" – Royal Irish Constabulary Reports and Their Political Uses', *Proceedings of the Royal Irish Academy*, 104c (2004).

O'Carroll, J.P. and Murphy, John A., *De Valera and his Times* (Cork, 1983).

Ó Cathain, Mairtin, *Irish Republicanism in Scotland, 1858–1916: Fenians in Exile* (Dublin, 2007).

Ó Ciasain, Niall, *Print and Popular Culture in Ireland, 1750–1850* (London, 1997).

O'Connell, Maurice R. (ed.), *Daniel O'Connell: Political Pioneer* (Dublin, 1991).

O'Connor, Emmet, *A Labour History of Ireland, 1824–1960* (Dublin, 1992).

O'Connor, Thomas H., *The Boston Irish: A Political History* (Boston, 1995).

O'Day, Alan, *The English Face of Irish Nationalism: Parnellite Involvement in British Politics, 1880–86* (Dublin, 1977).

O'Day, Alan, *Parnell and the First Home Rule Episode, 1884–87* (Dublin, 1986).

O'Day, Alan (ed.), *Reactions to Irish Nationalism* (London, 1987).

O'Day, Alan (ed.), *Political Violence in Northern Ireland: Conflict and Conflict Resolution* (London, 1997).

O'Day, Alan, *Irish Home Rule, 1867–1921* (Manchester, 1998).

O'Day, Alan, *Charles Stewart Parnell* (Dublin, 1998).

O'Day, Alan, 'Ireland and Scotland: The Quest for Devolved Political Institutions, 1867–1914', in R.J. Morris and Liam Kennedy (eds), *Ireland and Scotland: Order and Disorder, 1600–2000* (Edinburgh, 2005).

O'Ferrall, Fergus, *Catholic Emancipation: Daniel O'Connell and the Birth of Irish Democracy, 1820–30* (Dublin, 1985).

Ó Gráda, Cormac, *Ireland Before and After the Famine: Explorations in Economic History, 1800–1925* (Manchester, 1988).

Ó Gráda, Cormac, *The Great Irish Famine* (Dublin, 1989).

O'Halloran, Clare, *Partition and the Limits of Irish Nationalism: An Ideology under Stress* (Dublin, 1987).

O'Halpin, Eunan, *The Decline of the Union: British Government in Ireland, 1892–1920* (Dublin, 1987).

O'Halpin, Eunan, 'Parliamentary Party Discipline and Tactics: The Fianna Fáil Archives, 1926–32', *Irish Historical Studies*, xxx, 120 (November 1997).

O'Halpin, Eunan, *Defending Ireland: The Irish State and its Enemies since 1922* (Oxford, 1999).

O'Halpin, Eunan, *Spying on Ireland: British Intelligence and Irish Neutrality during the Second World War* (Oxford, 2008).

O'Leary, Cornelius, *Irish Elections, 1918–77: Parties, Voters and Proportional Representation* (Dublin, 1979).

O'Malley, Kate, *Ireland, India and Empire: Indo-Irish Radical Connections, 1919–64* (Manchester, 2008).

O'Malley, Padraig, *The Uncivil Wars: Ireland Today* (Belfast, 1980).

O'Malley, Padraig, *Biting at the Grave: The Irish Hunger Strikes and the Politics of Despair* (Belfast, 1990).

O'Neill, Kevin, *Family and Farm in Pre-Famine Ireland: The Parish of Killashandra* (Wisconsin, 1984).

O'Shea, James, *Priest, Politics and Society in Post-Famine Ireland: A Study of County Tipperary, 1850–1891* (Dublin, 1983).

Oldstone-Moore, Christopher, 'The Fall of Parnell: Hugh Price Hughes and the Nonconformist Conscience', *Éire-Ireland* (Fall, 1996).

Owens, Gary, '"A Moral Insurrection": Faction Fighters, Public Demonstrations, and the O'Connellite Campaign, 1828', *Irish Historical Studies*, xxx, 120 (November 1997).

Pakenham, Thomas, *The Year of Liberty: The Story of the Great Irish Rebellion of 1798* (London, 1969).

Palmer, Stanley, *Police and Protest in England and Ireland, 1780–1850* (Cambridge, 1988).

Paseta, Senia, 'Nationalist Responses to Two Royal Visits to Ireland, 1900 and 1903', *Irish Historical Studies*, 31, 124 (November, 1999).

Paseta, Senia, *Before the Revolution: Nationalism, Social Change and Ireland's Catholic Elite, 1879–1922* (Cork, 1999).

Paseta, Senia, *Thomas Kettle* (Dublin, 2009).

Patterson, Henry, *Class Conflict and Sectarianism: The Protestant Working Class and the Belfast Labour Movement, 1868–1920* (Belfast, 1980).

Patterson, Henry, *The Politics of Illusion: Republicanism and Socialism in Modern Ireland* (London, 1989).

Patterson, Henry, 'Party versus Order: Ulster Unionism and the Flags and Emblems Act', *Contemporary British History*, 13, 4 (1999).

Patterson, Henry, 'Brian Maginess and the Limits of Liberal Unionism', *Irish Review*, 25 (1999–2000).

Patterson, Henry, 'In the Land of King Canute: the Influence of Border Unionism on Ulster Unionist Politics, 1945–63', *Contemporary British History*, 20, 4 (2006).

Patterson, Henry and Kaufmann, Eric, *Unionism and Orangeism in Northern Ireland since 1945* (Manchester, 2007).

Peatling, Gary, *British Opinion and Irish Self-Government, 1865–1925: From Unionism to Liberal Commonwealth* (Dublin, 2001).

Philpin, C.H.E. (ed.), *Nationalism and Popular Protest in Ireland* (Cambridge, 1987).

Phoenix, Eamon, *Northern Nationalism: Nationalist Politics, Partition and the Catholic Minority in Northern Ireland, 1890–1940* (Belfast, 1994).

Prager, Jeffrey, *Building Democracy in Ireland: Political Order and Cultural Integration in a Newly Independent Nation* (Cambridge, 1986).

Prince, Simon, 'The Global Revolt of 1968 and Northern Ireland', *Historical Journal*, 49, 3 (September, 2006).

Purdie, Bob, *Politics in the Streets: The Origins of the Civil Rights Movement in Northern Ireland* (Belfast, 1990).

Rafferty, Oliver, *The Church, the State and the Fenian Threat, 1861–75* (London, 1999).

Rafferty, Oliver, *The Catholic Church and the Protestant State: Nineteenth-Century Irish Realities* (Dublin, 2008).

Regan, John M., 'The Politics of Reaction: The Dynamics of Treatyite Government and Policy, 1922–33', *Irish Historical Studies*, xxx, 120 (November 1997).

Regan, John, *The Irish Counter-Revolution, 1921–36: Treatyite Politics and Settlement in Independent Ireland* (Dublin, 1999).

Regan, John, 'Southern Irish Nationalism as a Historical Problem', *Historical Journal*, 50, 1 (March, 2007).

Richardson, David, 'The Career of John M. Andrews, 1871–1956', PhD thesis (Queen's University, Belfast, 1998).

Ridden, Jennifer, 'Britishness as an Imperial and Diasporic Identity: Irish Elite Perspectives, c.1820s–1870s', in Peter Gray (ed.), *Victoria's Ireland? Irishness and Britishness, 1837–1901* (Dublin, 2004).

Ruane, Joseph and Todd, Jennifer, *The Dynamics of Conflict in Northern Ireland: Power, Conflict and Emancipation* (Cambridge, 1996).

Rumpf, Erhard and Hepburn, A.C., *Nationalism and Socialism in Twentieth Century Ireland* (Liverpool, 1977).

Ryan, A.P., *Mutiny at the Curragh* (London, 1956).

Salmon, Trevor, *Unneutral Ireland: An Ambivalent and Unique Security Policy* (Oxford, 1989).

Savage, D.C., 'The Origins of the Ulster Unionist Party, 1885–6', *Irish Historical Studies*, xii, 47 (March, 1961).

Savage, Robert J., *Irish Television: The Political and Social Origins* (Cork, 1996).

Scally, Robert James, *The End of Hidden Ireland: Rebellion, Famine and Emigration* (New York, 1995).

Scoular, Clive, *James Chichester-Clark: Prime Minister of Northern Ireland* (Killyleagh, 2000).

Seaver, George, *John Allen Fitzgerald Gregg: Archbishop* (London and Dublin, 1963).

Senior, Hereward, *Orangeism in Ireland and Britain, 1795–1836* (London, 1966).

Sexton, Brendan, *Ireland and the Crown, 1922–36: The Governor Generalship of the Irish Free State* (Dublin, 1989).

Shannon, Catherine B., *Arthur J. Balfour and Ireland, 1874–1922* (Washington, 1988).

Share, Bernard, *The Emergency: Neutral Ireland, 1939–45* (Dublin, 1978).

Sheehy, Jeanne, *The Rediscovery of Ireland's Past: The Celtic Revival, 1830–1930* (London, 1980).

Shields, Andrew, *The Irish Conservative Party, 1852–68: Land, Politics and Religion* (Dublin, 2006).

Small, Stephen, *Political Thought in Ireland, 1776–1798: Republicanism, Patriotism and Radicalism* (Oxford, 2002).

Smith, James, *Ireland's Magdalen Laundries and the Nation's Architecture of Containment* (Manchester, 2008).

Smith, Jeremy, *The Tories and Ireland, 1910–14: Conservative Party Politics and the Home Rule Crisis* (Dublin, 2002).

Smith, Jeremy, '"Ever Reliable Friends"? The Conservative Party and Ulster Unionism in the Twentieth Century', *English Historical Review*, 121, 490 (February, 2006).

Smyth, Clifford, *Ian Paisley: Voice of Protestant Ulster* (Edinburgh, 1986).

Smyth, Jim, *The Men of No Property: Irish Radicals and Popular Politics in the Late Eighteenth Century* (Dublin, 1992).

Smyth, Jim (ed.), *Revolution, Counter-revolution and Union: Ireland in the 1790s* (Cambridge, 2001).

Solow, Barbara, *The Land Question and the Irish Economy, 1870–1903* (Cambridge, Mass., 1971).

Steele, E.D., *Irish Land and British Politics: Tenant Right and Nationality, 1865–70* (Cambridge, 1974).

Stewart, A.T.Q., *The Ulster Crisis: Resistance to Home Rule, 1912–14* (London, 1967).

Stewart, A.T.Q., *The Narrow Ground: Aspects of Ulster, 1609–1969* (London, 1977).

Stewart, A.T.Q., *Edward Carson* (Dublin, 1981).

Takagami, Shin-ichi, 'The Fenian Rising in Dublin, March 1867', *Irish Historical Studies*, xxix, 115 (May 1995).

Taylor, Peter, *Provos: The IRA and Sinn Féin* (London, 1997).

Thompson, D.I., *The Imagination of an Insurrection: Dublin, Easter 1916* (New York, 1967).

Thompson, Frank, *The End of Liberal Ulster: Land Agitation and Land Reform, 1868–86* (Belfast, 2001).

Thornley, David, *Isaac Butt and Home Rule* (London, 1964).

Tierney, Michael (ed.), *Daniel O'Connell: Nine Centenary Essays* (Dublin, 1949).

Townend, Paul, 'Between Two Worlds: Irish Nationalists and Imperial Crisis, 1878–80', *Past & Present* (February, 2007).

Townshend, Charles, *The British Campaign in Ireland, 1919–1921: The Development of Political and Military Policies* (Oxford, 1975).

Townshend, Charles, *Easter 1916: The Irish Rebellion* (London, 2005).

Townshend, Charles, *Political Violence in Ireland: Government and Resistance since 1848* (Oxford, 1983).

Travers, Pauric, *Eamon de Valera* (Dublin, 1994).

Turner, Michael, *After the Famine: Irish Agriculture, 1850–1914* (Cambridge, 1996).

Urquhart, Diane, *Women in Ulster Politics, 1890–1940: A History Not Yet Told* (Dublin, 2000).

Urquhart, Diane, *The Ladies of Londonderry: Women and Political Patronage* (London, 2007).

Valiulis, Maryann Gialanella, *Almost a Rebellion: The Army Mutiny of 1924* (Cork, 1985).

Valiulis, Maryann Gialanella, *Portrait of a Revolutionary: General Richard Mulcahy and the Founding of the Irish Free State* (Dublin, 1992).

Vaughan, W.E., *Landlords and Tenants in Ireland, 1848–1904* (Dundalk, 1984).

Vaughan, W.E., *Landlords and Tenants in Mid-Victorian Ireland* (Oxford, 1994).

Walker, Brian M., *Ulster Politics: The Formative Years, 1868–86* (Belfast, 1989).

Walker, Brian M., *Dancing to History's Tune: History, Myth and Politics in Ireland* (Belfast, 1996).

Walker, Graham, *The Politics of Frustration: Harry Midgley and the Failure of Labour in Northern Ireland* (Manchester, 1985).

Walker, Graham, *A History of the Ulster Unionist Party: Protest, Pragmatism and Pessimism* (Manchester, 2004).

Wallace, Martin, *Drums and Guns: Revolution in Ulster* (London, 1970).

Wallace, Martin, *British Government in Northern Ireland: From Devolution to Direct Rule* (Newton Abbot, 1982).

Ward, Margaret, *Unmanageable Revolutionaries: Women and Irish Nationalism*, 2nd edition (London, 1989).

Ward, Margaret, *Hanna Sheehy Skeffington: A Life* (Cork, 1997).

Ward, Paul, *Unionism in the United Kingdom, 1918–74* (London, 2005).

Ward, Rachel, *Women, Unionism and Loyalism in Northern Ireland: From Teamakers to Political Actors* (Dublin, 2006).

Warren, Alan, 'Disraeli, the Conservative Party and the Government of Ireland, 1868–81', *Parliamentary History*, 18 (1999).

Warren, Alan, 'Disraeli, the Conservatives and the National Church, 1837–81', *Parliamentary History*, 19 (2000).

West, Trevor, *Horace Plunkett: Cooperation and Politics: An Irish Biography* (Gerrards Cross, 1986).

Wheatley, Michael, *Nationalism and the Irish Party: Provincial Ireland, 1910–16* (Oxford, 2005).

Whelan, Irene, *The Bible War in Ireland: The 'Second Reformation' and the Polarisation of Protestant–Catholic Relations, 1800–40* (Chicago, 2005).

Whelan, Kevin, *The Tree of Liberty: Radicalism, Catholicism and the Construction of Irish Identity, 1760–1830* (Cork, 1996).

Whelan, Yvonne, *Reinventing Modern Dublin: Streetscape, Iconography and the Politics of Identity* (Dublin, 2003).

White, Jack, *Minority Report: The Protestant Community in the Irish Republic* (Dublin, 1975).

White, Terence de Vere, *Kevin O'Higgins* (London, 1948).

Whyte, J.H., *The Independent Irish Party, 1850–59* (Oxford, 1958).

Whyte, J.H., 'Interpretations of the Northern Ireland Problem: A Reappraisal', *Economic and Social Review*, ix, 4 (July 1978).

Whyte, J.H., *Church and State in Modern Ireland, 1923–1979*, 2nd edition (Dublin, 1980).

Whyte, J.H., *Interpreting Northern Ireland* (Oxford, 1990).

Wilkinson, David, 'The Fitzwilliam Episode, 1795: A Reinterpretation of the Role of the Duke of Portland', *Irish Historical Studies*, xxix, 115 (May, 1995).

Wilkinson, David, 'How Did they Pass the Union? Secret Service Expenditure', *History*, 82, 266 (April, 1997), pp. 223–51.

Williams, T. Desmond (ed.), *The Irish Struggle, 1916–26* (London, 1966).

Wills, Claire, *That Neutral Island: A History of Ireland during the Second World War* (London, 2007).

Wilson, Tom, *Ulster: Conflict and Consent* (Oxford, 1989).

Wood, Ian, *Crimes of Loyalty: A History of the UDA* (Edinburgh, 2006).

Woodham-Smith, Cecil, *The Great Hunger: Ireland, 1845–49* (London, 1962).

Wright, Frank, *Northern Ireland: A Comparative Analysis* (Dublin, 1988).

Wright, Frank, *Two Lands on One Soil: Ulster Politics Before Home Rule* (Dublin, 1996).

INDEX

Note: page numbers in italics denote illustrations or maps

Abbey Theatre 175
Abbot, Charles 28
abdication crisis 292
Aberdeen, Earl of 90
abortion debate 404
Academical Institutions (Ireland) Act 52
Adams, Gerry
  assassination attempt 396
  and Collins 425
  elected 392
  and Hume 387–8, 392, 402–3, 407
  and Lynch 425
  and Paisley 421
  St Andrews Agreement 421
  on Trimble 418
Adams, W.F. 82
Aer Lingus 288
Afghan War 114
Agar-Robartes, T.G. 163
Agence Générale pour la Défense de la
  Liberté Religieuse 57
Agricultural Credit Act 280
agricultural exports 316
agricultural growth 323
Agriculture and Technical Instruction,
  Dept of 147
Ahern, Bertie *413*
  and Paisley 419–20
  resignation 412–13, 415
  separated from wife 424

sovereignty 390
  as Taoiseach 388–9
  and Trimble 379, 409, 414
Aiken, Frank
  ceasefire 268–9
  foreign policy 318–19
  and Lemass 313
  and Lynch 325
  and McGilligan 304–5
  neutrality 299
  reunification 298
  WWII 349
air raids, Belfast 348, 349–50
aircraft industry 347
Aldous, Richard 414
Alexandra, Queen 174
Aliens Act 292
All for Ireland League 157
Allen, Kieran 308–9, 313
Alliance Party 370, 416
All-Ireland Committee 147, 148
Allister, Jim 422
Alter, Peter 57
American Civil War 93, 97–8
American note affair 300
American War of Independence 93
Amnesty Association 95, 104–5, 108–9
Andrews, John 349, 350–1
Anglesey, Marquis of 34
Anglicanism 4, 65–6, 169

Anglo-American war 93
Anglo-Irish Agreement (1938) 294, 295–6
Anglo-Irish Agreement (1985)
  aftermath 395, 405
  challenged 385
  FitzGerald 383, 386–7, 401
  Hume 407–8
  Long War 416
  Paisley 419
  Ulster Unionist Party 406–7
Anglo-Irish Free Trade Agreement 319
Anglo-Irish literary revival 168, 169, 174,
  175
Anglo-Irish trade 295, 345
Anglo-Irish Treaty (1921) 416
  and Craig 337
  Cumann na nGaedheal 277, 279–80
  end of 292, 294
  governor generalship 290–1
  IRA 248, 249–50
  and RIC 334
Anglo-Irish war (Irish War of
  Independence) 56, 225, 248, 252–4,
  334, 391, 419, *481*
anti-burgher schism 65
anti-clericalism 102, 186
anti-Parnellites 142–3, 149–50
Anti-Partition League (1919) 230, 231
Anti-Partition League (1945) 353–4
anti-semitism 294
Antrim, Battle of 19
Apprentice Boys' demonstration 369
Archdale, E.M. 220
Ardilaun, Lord (Guinness, A.E.) 173–4,
  226
Arianism 65
Armagh, Archbishop of 51, 52
Armagh, County 8, 9, 14, 366, 368, 397
arms affair 325, 326
arms raids 354, 395
Army Comrades' Association (Blueshirts)
  296
Army Convention 261–2
Army Council 275
Army Mutiny 278
Arnold, Bruce 376
Ashbourne, Lord (Gibson, E.) 126, 177, 225

Ashbourne Purchase Act 133, 150
Ashe, Thomas 203
Ashtown ambush 246
Asquith, Herbert 47, 160–1, 162, 164, 194,
  197, 221
Association, Treaty of 258–60, 272
Athanasianism 65
Atlantic, Battle of 297–8
Attlee, Clement 351–2, 354
Aud 200
Augusteijn, Joost 247
Auxiliaries 252, 253

Bachelor's Walk massacre 167, 196
Balbriggan, sacking of 252
Baldwin, Stanley 339
Balfour, Arthur James 132, 133, 134, 147,
  148
Balfour, Gerald 145, 147, 155, 221, 223, 228
Ball, F.E. 226
ballads 9–10, 27
Ballaghadereen shootings 384
Ballinamuck, Battle of 20
Ballingarry, Battle of 55
Ballot Act 109, 215
Ballybay confrontation 48
Ballymena, captured 19
Ballynahinch, Battle of 17, 19, 21
Ballynure insurgents 17
Ballyseedy killings 268
Baltinglass, Battle of 308
Barbour, John Milne 349, 350
barley crop 289
Barren Land Act 11
Barrett, Dick 268, 269
Barrie, H.T. 238
Barry, Kevin 247
Barry, Tom 247, 248–9, 254, 265
Bartlett, Thomas 1, 9, 12, 29
Barton, Robert 255, 266
Bates, John 60, 61, 64
Bates, Richard Dawson 332–3, 339, 349,
  350
'Baton Convention' 144, 157, 166–7
Batten, Henry 252
Beach, Michael Hicks 111, 132
Béal na mBláth ambush 263

Beckett, J.C. 1, 4–5, 17, 21
Belfast 4, 20, 332, 348, 349–50, 398
    see also Stormont Assembly
Belfast Conservative Society 61, 64
Belfast Regional Survey and Plan (Matthew)
    358
Belfast Telegraph 410
Belleek fort 335
Benson report 358
Bentham, Jeremy 45, 54
Beresford, John 7
Beresford family 32–3
Bertaud, Jean-Paul 20
Beveridge, William 300, 301, 305
Bew, Paul 86, 104, 114, 118, 127, 131, 138,
    146, 196, 198, 305, 312, 328, 352, 361,
    387, 401, 409
Biggar, J.G. 110, 112, 115, 118, 187
Binchy, Daniel 279
Birkenhead, Lord (Smith, F.E.) 291
Birmingham Six 393
Birrell, Augustine 153, 156, 158–9, 162–4,
    199
bishops 29, 30, 51, 88
Black and Tans 252, 253
Black Friday 355
Blackstock, Allan 15
Blair, Tony 68, 388, 389, 409, 414, 417–20
Blaney, Neil 314, 325
Bleakley, David 371
Bloody Friday 392
Bloody Sunday (1920) 245, 253, 315
Bloody Sunday (1972) 371–2, 391, 398
Bloomfield, Kenneth 357
Blueshirts 296, 297
Blythe, Ernest 276–7, 283, 337–8
Boers 107, 149, 189, 235, 254–5
Bogdanor, Vernon 128–9
Boland, Gerry 314
Boland, Kevin 314, 325, 385
Boland's Mill 203
Bolshevism 284
Bompard's expedition 101
Bono *402*
Border Campaign: *see* Operation Harvest
Boundary Commission 256, 270, 276,
    277–8, 336–8, 340–1

Bowman, John 298
Boyce, D. George 54, 76, 211, 243
boycotts 119, 122, 276, 341
Boyne, Battle of the 17
'The Boys of Sandy Row' 58
Bradford, Robert 393
Bradlaugh, Charles 99, 124
Bradshaw, Brendan 3
Braghall, Thomas 11
Breen, Dan 265
Brett, Sergeant 101
brewing industry 8, 160
Brighton bombing 393–4
Britain
    Crimean War 79, 92
    and France 92–3
    and Great Famine 77, 84–5, 87
    House of Commons 118
    House of Lords 26, 161
    intelligence network 253, 417
    Irish Land Acts 159–60
    and Parnell 38
    post-WWI 250
    protectionism 347
    and Redmond 38
    social reforms 168–9
    war debt 278
Britain, Battle of 299
British Army 195–6, 199, 369–70, 371,
    398
British Relief Association 73, 75
British-Irish Council 389, 409
British–Irish Inter-governmental
    Conference 389
Brodrick, St John: *see* Midleton, Lord
Brooke, Basil (Lord Brookeborough)
    and Attlee 354
    dissenters 366–7
    ennobled 355
    reports 358
    reunification 298
    unemployment 356
    Unionism 353
    UVF 223
    World War II 351
    see also Brooke–Mayhew talks
Brooke, Peter 387, 389

Brookeborough: *see* Brooke, Basil
Brooke–Mayhew talks 387, 402, 408
'Brothers Grim' 421, 423
Brown, Gordon 421
Browne, Michael 309
Browne, Noel 302, 307–8, 309
Bruce, Steve 397
Brugha, Cathal 181, 244, 259, 265, 270
Brunswick clubs 35, 59–60
Bruton, John 388
Bryce, James 138
Buckingham Palace Conference 196, 206, 236, 237
Buckland, Patrick 346
Bull, Philip 152
Buller, Redvers 132
Burdett, Francis 31–2
burial-ground question 30
Burke, Edmund 12
Burke, Richard (Edmund's son) 12
Burke, Richard (of IRB) 103
Burke, T.H. 122, 134
Burntollet bridge ambush 366, 369
Bush, George W. 413, 417
business class 221, 344
Butler, Máire 184
Butler Act (1944) 352
Butt, Isaac
    death of 114
    Dublin corporations 47
    Dublin University Magazine 172–3
    electoral success 216
    farmer movement 105–6
    and Gladstone 104–5
    Home Government Association 109
    Home Rule League 113
    Home Rule movement 96, 106, 110–12
    Irish language 176, 179
    Irish Metropolitan Conservative Society 60
    Unionism 47
Buttites 110, 111–12, 116
Byrne, Edward 293

Cabra demonstration 95, 104
Cahera, Great Famine *74*
Cahirciveen killings 268

Callaghan, Gerard and Daniel 59
Callan Society 86–7
Callanan, Frank 138, 143
Cameron Commission 371
Campaign for Democracy in Ulster 364
Campaign for Social Justice 364
Campbell, Gordon 274
Campbell, J.H.M. 226, 227, 274
Campbell, Sheena 396
Campbell-Bannerman, Henry 153
Canary Wharf bomb 388, 393
Canning, George 28, 33
Capital Investment Advisory Committee 311
Carlow 18
Carlyle, Thomas 54
Carnarvon, Lord 126, 129
Carrickshock ambush 41
Carroll, William 113–14
Carson, Edward *228*
    as attorney general 194
    Catholic university 156
    and Craig 237
    Criminal Law Amendment Act 132–3
    as influence 425
    loyalist militancy 236
    and O'Connell, compared 31, 47
    and Stephens, compared 98
    Ulster Unionism 163–4, 226–7, 240–1
    UUC 229
    Wilde 134
Castle Document 201
Castlebar, Battle of 20
Castlereagh, Lord 7, 21, 25, 27, 28
Castlereagh holding centre 397
Castlereagh raid 416–17
Castlerock killings 396
Catalpa episode 107
Cathleen ni Houlihan (Gregory and Yeats) 175
Catholic Association 31, 34, 35, 58–9, 62
    see also New Catholic Association
Catholic Board 29
Catholic Church
    child abuse 390, 415
    Cumann na nGaedheal 283
    and Gaelicism 172
    and Marx 4

Catholic Church (*cont'd*)
  Maynooth 51–2
  parliamentarianism 207
  priests 37, 76, 84, 88, 116
  propertied 2
  republicanism 308–9
  veto question 7, 28–32, 35
  see also emancipation
Catholic Committee (1760) 11–12, 13, 14
Catholic Committee (1804) 29
Catholic Convention 12, 36
Catholic Defence Association 88, 89
Catholic Emancipation Act 12, 36, 59
Catholic population
  burials 30
  discriminated against 360
  disenfranchised 7, 8, 27–8
  education 352–3
  40-shilling freeholders 11, 12, 31–3, 35, 36, 37
  growth 2, 9
  identity 390
  middle class 361, 364
  in North 340–1, 342–3, 352–3, 363
  response to claims 11–12
  universities 52, 53, 155, 156
  Whig appointments 45–6
  workers, expelled 340
  see also emancipation
Catholic Question 27–36
Catholic relief bill 28, 30, 31–2
Catholic rent 32, 33, 48
Catholic University 96
cattle-driving campaign 157, 166–7
Cavan election 210
Cavendish, Frederick 122
ceasefire 1, 3, 268–9, 388, 389, 392, 402, 408, 409
Celtic Literary Society 183
Celtic Tiger 410–12, 413
Celticism 3, 104, 164
censorship 311, 327–8
censuses 176, 274, 310, 412
Central Board scheme 130
Central Conservative Society 61–2, 63, 215, 225
Central Protestant Defence Association 219

Centre Party: *see* National Centre Party
Chamberlain, Annie 295
Chamberlain, Joseph 125–6, 128, 129–30
Chamberlain, Neville 294–6, 298, 345
Charitable Donations and Bequests (Ireland) Act 51, 52
Charles, Prince 393
Chester raid 99, 100
Chichester-Clark, James 369–70
child abuse 390
Child Abuse Inquiry 415
Childers, Erskine 246, 264, 268, 270, 303, 320
Christian Brothers 247, 390
Christian Democracy 57, 304
'Chuckle Brothers' 421
Church of Ireland
  anti-O'Connell 64, 65
  clergy's living conditions 41
  disestablishment 42, 91, 103, 105, 169, 215, 217–19
  evangelicalism 216
  and House of Commons 7
  O'Connell 41–2
  Parnell 124–5
  and Presbyterians 214
  restructured 218–19
  souperism 76, 86, 191
  tithe 40–1
  Unionism 216–17
Church Temporalities Act 41, 42
church-building 84
Churchill, Randolph 126, 221
Churchill, Winston 162, 163, 253–4, 270–1, 296, 299, 335
Civil Authorities (Special Powers) Act 334
Civil List Act 11
civil rights 361, 362–3, 381
civil unrest 345–6, 369–70
An Claidheamh Soluis 178
Clan na Gael 106, 113–14, 130–1
Clann Éireann 278
Clann na Poblachta 302, 306, 312, 353
Clann na Talmhan 303
Clare, Lord (Fitzgibbon, J.) 17, 21, 23, 28
Clare by-election 34
Clark, Ernest 333, 340

Clarke, Kathleen 281
Clarke, Thomas J. 166, 181
class 4, 352
  see also middle classes; working classes
Clerkenwell gaol rescue 103
Clery's speech 311
clientelism 37–8, 414
Clinton, Bill 409
Clontarf meeting banned 47–8, 50, 51
Close, Maxwell 181
coal 347
Coal–Cattle Pact 290
Cochrane, Feargal 357, 396, 401, 405, 409
Colley, George 323, 373–4, 378
Collins, Michael
  and Adams 425
  and Craig 334, 337
  and de Valera 260–1
  as director of intelligence 245, *264*
  on Downing Street talks 255
  Dublin Castle 259
  and Fenians 107
  Free State army 263
  GAA 181
  IRA in North 276
  Jordan's film 3, 248, 425
  killed 263, 267, 269, 276, 337
  Squad 275, 315
Colwyn Committee 345
Comerford, Vincent 90, 95–6, 99, 105,
  217–18
Commission on the Status of Women 381
Common Agricultural Policy 318, 380
Common Sense, An Agreed Process 395
Commonwealth, British 23, 328, 382
community schools 326
compulsory purchase 159–60
Comyn, David 176
Conditions of Employment Act 282, 287
Connaught Rangers 196, 197, 247
Connolly, James
  Easter Rising 200, 201, 203
  Famine 69
  feminism 187
  Irish National League of Great Britain 190
  Labour in Irish History 4
  Marxism 171

The Reconquest of Ireland 4
  socialism 189, 192
Connolly, Seán 83–4
conscription 198, 209
consensual politics 357
Conservative Party, Irish 46, 59, 147, 215
  see also Toryism
Constabulary (Ireland) Act 334–5
Constabulary (Northern Ireland) Act 334–5
Constitution (1922) 274, 275, 291, 297
Constitution (1937) 292, 293, 294
Constitution (Amendment No. 17) Act 284
Constitution (Amendment No. 27) Act 292
Constitutional Amendment (Removal of
  Oath) Act 290
construction industry 412
constructive unionism 146, 155, 156, 164,
  221
consumer boom 374
Continuity IRA 422
Control of Manufactures legislation 288
Convention, Irish 207, 209, 230, 236
Convention Act 11, 12
'Convention of Misunderstandings' 154,
  155, 156–7
Coogan, Tim Pat 285, 320, 325
Cooke, Edward 24–5
Cooke, Henry 42, 49, 63–6, 214, 218
Cooper, Bryan Ricco 225, 264–5, 274
Cork 59, 100, 226, 252
Corn Laws repealed 71
Cornwallis, Lord 21, 24, 25
Corporation Act 34
corporations 10, 42–3, 47
Corrupt Practices Act 215
Corry, J.P. 221
Corydon, John Joseph 99
Cosgrave, Liam 311–12, 327, 375, 378,
  384, 406
Cosgrave, William T.
  and Baldwin 339
  and Craig 321, 338
  customs duties 288
  Fine Gael 297
  religion 283
  senators 274
  state-building 275

Costello, John Aloysius
   and de Valera 309
   Irish republic 306, 352
   national/religious identity 308
   as Taoiseach 303, 305–7, 310, 318
cottiers 55, 69, 80–1, 83, 85–6
Council for the Status of Women 381
Council of Europe 306, 312
Council of Ireland 332, 339, 385, 400, 404
Cousins, Margaret 187
Cowan, Peadar 309
Cowen, Brian 415
Craig, James (Lord Craigavon)
   Anglo-Irish trade 295, 345
   Anglo-Irish Treaty 337
   and Bates 332–3
   Boundary Commission 340
   cabinet 213
   and Carson 237
   and Collins 334, 337
   and Cosgrave 321
   and de Valera 336
   death of 350
   dissenters 366–7
   elected 335
   gamesmanship 326
   institutions 335–6
   IRA 333–4
   and Lloyd George 336–7
Craig, William 358, 363
Craigavon, Lord: *see* Craig, James
Craigavon demonstration 233
Craig–Collins pact 334, 337
Cranbrook, Earl of 102
Crawford, Fred 107, 216, 234
Crawford, Lindsay 225, 367
Crawford, William Sharman 50, 86, 88
Crichton, Lord 220
Crimean War 79, 92
Criminal Law Amendment Act 132–3
Croke, Thomas William 124, 181
Croke Park 252, 301
Crolly, William 52
Crosbie, Talbot 149
Crosland, Tony 383
Crown Jewels affair 291
Cullen, Louis 18

Cullen, Paul 52, 83, 89, 95, 96, 102, 103
cultural identity 382, 383
cultural nationalism 169, 171–2, 192
Cumann na mBan 188, 232, 248
Cumann na nGaedheal (1900) 184, 242
Cumann na nGaedheal (1923) 273–5
   Anglo-Irish Treaty 277, 279–80
   Brian Ricco Cooper 265
   Catholic Church 283
   leadership 343
   nation/state 282–3
   Protestants in North 277
   Redmondite ideas 280
   values 308
Cumann na Poblachta 265
Cumann na Saoirse 266
Cumberland, Duke of 62, 219
Cumming, T. 246
Curragh Incident 196, 235–6
currency crisis 375
Curtin, Nancy 7, 9, 14
Curtis, Lionel 292
Cusack, Michael 176, 180, 181
Cushendall killings 334
Customs Duties (Provisional Imposition)
   Act 287–8
Customs House, Dublin 248, 267
customs union 26
Cuthbert, N. 356, 358

Dáil Éireann 211, 243, 249–50, 258, 265,
   483
Dalton, Charlie 275
Dalton, Emmet 267
Daly, Mary 76, 81, 83, 280, 288
Daly, Miriam 396
Daly, Paddy 268
dance halls 328
Davis, Thomas
   cultural nationalism 169
   and Duffy 3, 171–2
   Irish language 54, 83, 176
   Nation 52, 54
   and O'Connell 48, 52–3, 54
   Young Ireland 53
Davitt, Michael
   GAA 180

Lalorite 115
land nationalization 118, 122, 125, 189
and MacCormack 245–6
National League 123
on O'Brien 151
socialism 189
De Chastelain, John 418
De Gaulle, Charles 327, 380
De Grey, Lord 50
de Valera, Eamon *285, 412*
annuities 289
anti-conscription 210
Boland's Mill 203
and Chamberlain 294–5
and Churchill 299
and Collins 260–1
consensual approach 320
and Costello 309
and Craig 336
Cumann na Poblachta 265
Downing Street talks 255, 256
External Relations Act 305
Fianna Fáil 285–7
as influence 245, 412, 425
and IRA 297
leadership 285–6
League of Nations 282
and Lemass 300
oath of allegiance 258
and Parnell 211–12
partition 313
as President of Irish Republic 255
as President of Sinn Féin 242
replaced 258, 304, 322
revisionism 278–9
and son 290
sovereignty 293
WWII 349
de Valera, Vivion 290
Deasy, Timothy 101
debt 27, 76, 374–5, 376, 377
Declaratory Act 7
decommissioning of weapons 416, 418, 422
Defenders 13–14, 17, 19, 20
Delors, Jacques 382
Democratic Left 377

Democratic Unionist Party (DUP)
Anglo-Irish Agreement 395, 399
elections 418–19
European Union 404
formation of 370
St Andrews Agreement 421
and Sinn Féin 419
Unionism 403–4
Dempsey, Larry 17
Derry, Bishop of 41
Derry Housing Action Committee 365
Derry (Londonderry)
Apprentice Boys' demonstration 369
Bloody Sunday 371–2, 391, 398
demonstration 365
Destitute Poor (Ireland) Act 73
Devlin, Bernadette (McAliskey) 364, 366, 396
Devlin, Joseph 153, 154, 164, 194, 197, 208, 341
Devlin's Hotel incident 275–6
devolution 152–6, 168
Devon Commission 86
Devonshire, Duke of 223
'devotional revolution' 83, 84
Devoy, John 92, 98, 106, 113–14, 115
Diamond, Battle of the 14, 45, 62
Diana, Princess 393
Dickens, Charles 68, 71
Dickson, David 10, 13
Diderot, Denis 9
Dillon, James 296, 303
Dillon, John
anti-Parnellites 143
boycotting 122
on Easter Rising 205
and Healy 145
Home Rule 114, 129, 164
IPP 209, 210
Irish Reform Association 155
Land League 119
Land War 132
leadership 209
Liberalism 146–7, 156
and O'Brien 146–7
on Parnell 139
and Redmond 151

Dillon, John (*cont'd*)
 Tories 147–8
 and Ulster Unionists 152, 153
Dillon, John Blake 89–90, 105
disease 73, 75, 76, 78, 307
disestablishment, Church of Ireland 42,
 91, 103, 105, 169, 215, 217–19
dispensary doctors 283
Disraeli, Benjamin 114
distilling industry 8, 160
divorce 283, 294, 322, 381, 390, 424
Dockrell, Maurice 225
Dockrell family 274
Dolan, C.J. 185
dominion status 256, 279
Donaldson, Denis 417
Donegan, Patrick 384
dot.com bubble 411–12
Dowden, Edward 139, 225
Down, County 19
Down and Connor, Bishop of 51
Downing Street Declaration 387–8, 403,
 404, 408
Downs policy 157
Downshire, Marquess of 221
Dowra affair 376
Droppin' Well pub 393
Drumm, Máire 396
Drummond, Thomas 45, 46, 76
Dublin
 bombings 384, 396
 Customs House 248, 267
 Easter Rising map 480
 Fenian uprising 100
 Four Courts 6, 203, 260–1, 263, 271
 poverty 188
 Toryism 225
 Unionism 24–5, 224–5
 see also General Post Office
Dublin Castle 6
 Collins 259
 informants 19
 press campaigns 10
 repression 14–15
 1798 uprising 20–1
 and Sinn Féin 254
 Union Act 25
Dublin corporation 10, 38, 43, 47

Dublin Evening Mail 103
Dublin Liberties 22
Dublin Metropolitan Police 245, 252–3, 273
Dublin Protestant Operative movement 63
Dublin Unemployed Association 310–11
Dublin United Irishmen 13
Dublin University Magazine 172
Dublin University Review 173
Duffy, Charles Gavan
 and Davis 171–2
 death of 56
 Independents 89, 90
 My Life in Two Hemispheres 56
 Nation 53
 and O'Connell 30
 Parnellites and Tories 116
 tenants 87
 Thomas Davis 3, 56
 Young Ireland 49, 53
 Young Ireland 56
Duffy, George Gavan 255
Duggan, Eamon 255
Dukes, Alan 377
Dunbar-Harrison, Letitia 283
Dundalk 192
Dungannon 363, 365, 366
Dungannon Clubs 184
Dunmanway killings 252
Dunne, Catherine 398
Dunphy, Richard 279, 287, 294
Dunraven, Lord 151, 153, 155
DUP: *see* Democratic Unionist Party

East Down 227
Easter Rising (1916) *202, 480*
 aftermath 204–7, 237
 casualties 204
 fiftieth anniversary 319–20
 martyrs 206, 207
 Pearse 167, 200–1, 203–7
 Redmond 164
 Sinn Féin 242
 suppressed 204–6
 see also General Post Office
Ecclesiastical Titles Act 88, 116
Economic Council 358
economic crisis 377, 415
economic growth 8, 327, 373, 383, 412–14

economic modernization 333, 358, 360
Economic Survey of Northern Ireland (Isles
    and Cuthbert) 356, 358
Economic War 288, 289
education
    community schools 326
    employment 410
    English language 83
    free 362
    higher 155–6, 362
    Irish language 177
    national schools 83, 177
    reform 326
    state-schools 352–3, 362
    see also universities
Education Act (1944) 352
Education Act (1947) 352–3
Edward VII 184
Edward VIII 292
Edwards, Robin Dudley 193
Eighty Club 134
Éire Nua policy 392
Eksund 391
Electoral Amendment Act 281
Electricity Supply Board 280
Eliot, Lord 51
Elliott, Marianne 13
emancipation 7, 28, 29, 34, 35–6, 58–9
Emancipation Act 36, 59
emergency import tariffs 288
Emergency Powers Act 384
emigration 68, 81–2, 327, 328, *486*
Emmet, Robert 21–2, 203
Emmet rising 93
Employer–Labour Conference 317
Employers' Federation 191
employment 43–4, 301, 410
    see also unemployment
Employment Equality Act 381
Employment Equality Agency 381
Encumbered Estates Act 76
enfranchisement
    40-shilling freeholders 11, 12, 31–3, 35,
        36, 37
    £10 households 37, 43
    women 186–7, 231, 232
English, Ada 258
English language 83

Enlightenment 4, 9
Ennis boycott 119
Enniscorthy 18
Enniskillen, Earl of 219
Enniskillen bomb 393
Erin's Hope 101
Erne, Lord 219
Erne, Lough 300
Erskine, Lord 368
Ervine, David 395–6, 403
Ervine, St John 175
espionage 417
Etreux, Battle of 197
Eucharistic Congress 346
European Court of Human Rights 397
European Economic Community 318, 327,
    328–9, 373, 379–83, 411
European exchange rate mechanism 411
European Monetary System 383, 411
European Union 380–3, 404, 424
evangelicalism 66–7, 216, 367–8
evictions 80, 86, 120–1, 122–3, 138
Ewart, William 221
Ewart-Biggs, Christopher 384
Executive Authority (External Relations)
    Act 292, 305, 306
Expiring Laws Continuance Act 112
Export Profits Tax Relief 316
External Affairs, Dept of 293
external association 291, 293, 297
External Relations Act: *see* Executive
    Authority (External Relations) Act

Falkiner, C.L. 226
Famine, Great 4
    accountability 77–80, 84–5, 87
    Cahera *74*
    cottiers 81, 85–6
    death toll 68–70, 79, 80–2
    disease 73, 76, 78
    emigration 81–2
    food distribution 70, 71
    food exports 78, 79
    food prices 72, 73–4, 75
    impact of 52, 80–5
    landlords 75–6
    and poor law 44
    public works 71–2, 73, 78

Famine, Great (*cont'd*)
  Quakers 73, 76–7
  relief 72–3, 77
  Relief Commission 70
  and repeal 55
  revisionism 68, 78
  Whigs 71–2
Fanning, Ronan 249, 275, 277, 289, 327
Fanny 107
farmer movement 87, 103, 105
farming community
  after Famine 81
  British politicians 169
  EU 380
  Fianna Fáil 289
  IRA 247
  Parnell 169
  political vulnerability 225
  prosperity 96–7, 169
  tenant organizations 86–7
  tithes 41
Farnham, Lord 223
Farrell, Brian 326
Farrell, Michael 4
Farren, Thomas 191, 198
Farrington, Christopher 419
Faulkner, Brian
  and Cosgrave 406
  Economic Council 358
  and Heath 405–6
  leadership 370–2
  and O'Neill 356
  Sunningdale 385, 409
  and Trimble, compared 406
  as young Unionist 353
federalism 55, 110, 114, 236, 392
Feetham, Richard 278, 338–9
feminism 186–7, 232, 266, 294
Fenian Brotherhood 95–6
Fenian Proclamation 97
Fenian rising (1867) 98–100
Fenianism
  cultural fusion 172–3
  Home Rule movement 108
  international influences 92, 93–4
  IPP 166
  Irish Confederation 91

  leaders 96–7
  middle classes 93–4
  Parnell 117, 131, 166
  popular culture 107
  popularization 104
  and Redmondites 241
  risings 56, 92, 204
  sports and recreation 94–5
  survival of 107
  tenant right 103–4
  Yeats 173
  Young Irelanders 91
  see also Irish Republican Brotherhood
Ferguson, Samuel 171, 172, 183
Fetherstonhaugh, Godfrey 226
Fianna Fáil
  anti-Treaty 266
  constitution 294
  and Cumann na nGaedheal 273–4
  and de Valera 278–9, 285–7
  in decline 304, 312
  early days 280
  economic growth 412–14
  elections 282, 312–13, 326–7
  executions of IRA men 304
  farming community 289
  feminism 294
  Free State institutions 281
  green left 284–5
  hegemony 375
  industrial strategy 288–9
  Inter-Party government 310
  and Labour Party 287
  Lemass 303
  neoliberalism 377
  and opposition 302
  and republicans 281–2
  rural employment 289–90
  tariff protection 313
  women's issues 281–2
Field, William 180
film censorship 328
Finance Department 286, 293, 313, 315
Fine Gael party 287, 288, 296–7, 327, 377
Fine Gael–Labour government 375–6
Fisher, J.R. 278, 338, 339
Fisher, Warren 295

Fitt, Gerry 392, 400
Fitzgerald, Edward 17, 148–9
FitzGerald, Garret
    AIA 383, 386–7, 401
    economic measures 374–6, 377
    in EU 382, 383
    and Haughey 377–9
    New Ireland Forum 385–6, 401
    and Ulster Unionism 379
    on Unionism 403
Fitzgerald, William Vesey 34
Fitzgibbon, Gerald 225
Fitzgibbon, John (Lord Clare) 7
Fitzpatrick, David 203
Fitzwilliam, Earl 12, 13
Flags and Emblems Act 353
Flatley, Michael 3
Follis, Bryan 332
food prices 72, 73–4, 75
food shortage 70, 71, 78, 79
    see also Great Famine
Foreign Affairs Dept 419
foreign-aid men 19
Forster, W.E. 120, 121
40-shilling freeholders 11, 12, 31–3, 35,
    36, 37
Forum (1996) 385, 388, 401
Foster, John 7
Foster, R.F. (Roy) 4, 27, 31, 73, 91, 173,
    249, 303, 410
Four Courts, Dublin 6, 203, 260–1, 263,
    271
Fox, Billy 383–4
Fox, Charles James 303
Foyle, Lough 299–300
Framework Documents 404, 408
France 9, 15, 17, 19, 20, 57, 92–3
    see also French revolution
franchise reform 11, 363
    see also enfranchisement
Franco, Francisco 297, 306
Franco-Austrian war 92
Free Presbyterians 367
Free Staters 266–7, 273
    see also Irish Free State
free trade 8, 71
Freeman's Journal 105, 112, 151

French, Lord 393
French revolution (1789) 2, 6–7, 9–11,
    14, 66
French revolution (1848) 55
Frongoch camp 205, 207
Fukuyama, Francis 423

Gaelic Athlete 181
Gaelic Athletic Association (GAA) 176,
    180–3, 181, 192, 200, 247
Gaelic Journal 176
Gaelic League 175, 176–7, 178–9, 192
Gaelic Literary Society 242
Gaelic revival 39, 172, 193
Gaelic Union 176
Gael-Linn 329
Gallipoli 197
Galway City 225
Galway Mutiny 136, 154
Garda Síochána 273
Garvin, Tom
    army recruitment 263
    Britain/Sinn Féin 257
    Cavan 244
    on Dáil Éireann 250
    GAA/IRB 181
    IRA 247
    Irish Party 211
    Land League 124
    on O'Connell 60
    repeal movement 58
    republicans/Free Staters 266–7
GDP per capita 410, 411
Geary, Laurence 132
General Post Office 167, 192, 201, *202*, 203
    see also Easter Rising (1916)
George III 6, 10, 28, 39
George IV 62
George V 257, 258, 260, 336, 338, 346
George VI 294
gerrymandering 342, 363, 366
Gibbon, Peter 214, 352, 361
Gibraltar shootings 399
Gibson, Edward (Lord Ashbourne) 126,
    177, 225
Ginnell, Laurence 157
Girvin, Brian 57

Gladstone, Herbert 121
Gladstone, W.E.
  and Butt 104–5
  disestablishment 217–18
  and Healy 142
  Home Rule 144–5, 333
  Independent Irish Party 90–1
  Irish Universities Act 109
  justice for Ireland 105
  kidnap plot 107
  Landlord and Tenant (Ireland) Act 106
  and Parnell 117, 120, 127, 134–5
  religious concepts 420–1
  resignation 51
  Vatican Decrees 109
Glenavy, Lord: *see* Campbell, J.H.M.
Glencullen police station 101
GNP 323, 373–4, 410, 411
Goderich, Viscount (Robinson, F.J.) 33
gombeenmen 80
Gonne, Maud 174, 187, 188
Good Friday Agreement 390–1, 392, 403,
    404, 409, 414, 416, 423
Gordon, David 356
Gough Barracks 354
Goulburn, Henry 33
Goulding, Cathal 363
Government of Ireland Act 251
  Craig 336, 337, 339
  May 1921 elections 253
  Midleton 230
  NI Constitution 332
  Northern Ireland administration 343–4
  revised 278
  symbolism 259–60
  Ulster Unionist Party 236, 405
  UUC 239–40
Graham, Edgar 393
Graham, James 51
Grand Hotel, Brighton 393
Grand Orange Lodge 63
Grattan, Henry 3, 12, 26, 27, 28–9, 39, 272
Gray, Edmund Dwyer 112
Gray, John 105
Greco-Turkish war 173
Green Party 412–14
Greenwood, Hamar 248, 250

Greer, S.M. 87
Gregg, John Allen Fitzgerald 293
Gregg, Tresham 63, 215
Gregory, Augusta 171, 173, 175
Gregory clause 75, 79–80
Grey, Lord 40, 43
Greysteel killings 396
Griffith, Arthur *182*
  anti-clericalism 186
  Cavan election 210
  and Davis 56
  Downing Street talks 255
  as influence 287, 425
  in IRB 186
  journalism 183, 185
  and Larkin 191
  Redmondites 185–6
  replacing de Valera 258–9
  separatism 258
  Sinn Féin 171, 242
  social issues 188–9
  suffragism 187
  on Synge 174
  United Irishman 178, 183–4
GUBU 376
guerrilla tactics 235, 244–5, 254
Guinness, Arthur Edward (Lord Ardilaun)
    173–4, 226
Gunpowder Act 11
gun-running 107, 167, 233, 234–5, 236
Gwynn, Denis 48
Gwynn, Stephen
  constitutionalism 168
  Easter Rising 204
  feminism 187
  GAA 180
  Gaelic League 179
  on Lloyd George 206
  on McDowell 208
  and Redmond 194, 198, 212
  War Office 196
  and Yeats 174

Habeas Corpus Act 98
Hain, Peter 419
Hales, Seán 268
Hall, Robert 356, 358

Hall-Thompson, Colonel 352–3
Halpin, General 100, 101
Hamilton, Claud 219, 221
Hamilton, George 223
handbills 9–10
Hanna, George B. 353
Harcourt, William 128
Hardiman, James 176
Harney, Mary 410
Harrington, T.C. 129, 132, 180
Hart, Peter 243, 244, 247
Haughey, Charles J. 320, 325–6, 374–6,
    377–9, 414
Hawarden Kite 127, 128
Hayden, Mary 3
Headfort killings 245
Health Act 307, 308, 309, 311
Healy, Cahir 341–2
Healy, Maurice 179
Healy, T.M. (Tim)
    and Dillon 145
    elected 125
    and Gladstone 127, 142
    Irish language 179
    and Murphy 191
    and O'Connell 116
    on Orangeism 220
    and Parnell 137–8, 139
    People's Rights Association 141
    in power 291
    as pseudo-radical 118
Heaney, Séamus 23, 382
Hearth Tax Act 11
Heath, Edward 371, 405
Hermon, Sylvia 418
Heytesbury, Lord 51, 52
Hibernians, Ancient Order of 154, 166–7,
    187, 191, 198–9, 210
Hicks Beach, Michael 111, 132
Hill, Arthur 221
Hillery, Patrick 384
Hillsborough 386–7
    see also Anglo-Irish Agreement
Hillsborough gathering 63–4
Hill-Trevor, Lord 220
historiography 3, 5
Hobart's Relief Act 11, 12, 14

Hobson, Bulmer 167, 184, 200, 204
Hoche, Lazare 15
Hogan Land Act 280
Holmes, Finlay 65
Holy Cross Primary School 416
Home Government Association 105, 109,
    110, 214–15
Home Rule 108–16
    Asquith, 160–1
    Butt 96, 106, 110–12
    defeated 220–1
    doggerel 193
    emancipation 36
    Fenianism 108
    Gladstone, W.E. 333
    Independent Irish Party 108
    Liberalism 168–9, 216
    Parnellites 129
    six-county exclusion 237–8, 239
    stalled 192
    Unionism against 220–1
Home Rule Bills 3, 194
    (1886) 129–30
    (1893) 144–5, 173, 227
    (1914) 161, 165, 175, 221, 229, 233, 236,
        241, 250
Home Rule Confederation 110, 113, 114
Home Rule League 110, 112, 113, 114
Home Rule Party 110, 215, 243
Home Rule within Home Rule 163–4
Homeless Citizens' League 363–4
homosexuality debate 404
Hopkinson, Michael 261, 265
Hoppen, K.T. 58, 61, 88, 108–9, 215, 225,
    259, 295, 302
Horgan, John 287, 305, 320, 328
House of Commons, Irish 7, 10, 11, 25
House of Commons, UK 118
House of Lords, UK 26, 161
Household Cavalry barracks 393
housing 83, 412
    see also public housing
Houston, Edward Caulfield 134
Howth 167
Hughes, Hugh Price 137
human rights 389
Humbert, J.J.A. 20

Hume, John *402*
  and Adams 387–8, 392, 402–3, 407
  AIA 401, 407–8
  external arbiters 424
  and O'Connell 425
  SDLP 399–400
  and Sinn Féin 389, 408
hunger strikes 302, 385–6, 392, 401
Hunt, Lord, report 397
Hunt, Michael 245
Hussey, Gemma 374, 376, 381
Hutchinson, John 169, 177
Hyde, Douglas 172, 176–7, 179

ICTU (Irish Congress of Trade Unions)
    311
IDA: *see* Industrial Development Authority
immigration 412
imperialism 257, 275
Indemnity Act 15
Independent Irish Party 61, 88–9, 90, 116
Independent Orange Order 367
Indian 'Mutiny' 92, 247
Industrial Credit Company 280, 288
Industrial Development Authority (IDA)
    305, 313, 411
Industrial Development (Encouragement
    of External Investment) Act 316
industrial development programme 361
Industrial Efficiency Act 305
Industrial Relations Act 301
information technology 411
informers 19, 100, 245
Inghinidhe na hEireann 188
INLA: *see* Irish National Liberation Army
Insurrection Act 15
Intermediate Education (Ireland) Act 176
International Commission on
    Decommissioning 418
internment 205, 354, 371
Inter-Party government 302–4, 305–6,
    308, 310, 311
investment 381, 384, 410, 411
IRA (Irish Republican Army) 3
  Anglo-Irish Treaty 248, 249–50
  anti-partition 335
  arrest of members 248

British Army service 247
Canary Wharf bomb 388
ceasefires 392
Craig 333–4
cultural influences 247
and de Valera 297
decommissioning of weapons 418
educational level of members 247
farming community 225
and Fenianism 107
Fianna Fáil executions 304
guerrilla tactics 244–6
as Irish Free State army 265
membership 252–3
Operation Harvest 312, 354–5, 356, 362
and Sinn Féin 243
US support 248
  see also Continuity IRA; Provisional
    IRA; Real IRA
IRAO (Irish Republican Army
    Organization) 275
Iraq War 414
Ireland Act (1949) 352
Irish Brigade 88
Irish Bulletin 246, 248
Irish Catholic Association 29–30
Irish Church Act 105, 109, 150, 218–19
Irish Church Temporalities Commission
    218
Irish Citizen Army 191, 203
Irish Civil War 231, 263, 267, 273–7, 280,
    286, 290, 314, 322
Irish Confederation 55, 91, 92
Irish Congress of Trade Unions (ICTU)
    311
Irish Constabulary 55, 100, 101
Irish Council Act 153, 154–5, 156
Irish Enlightenment tradition 273
Irish Franchise Act 61, 125, 215
Irish Free State 272–85
  army 263–4
  Boundary Commission 338
  British Commonwealth 382
  constitution 260, 274
  early days 271
  name of 258
  and Northern Ireland 337

Sinn Féin vote 210
taxes 344
Irish Free State Act 332
Irish Free State Constitution Act 230
  see also Constitution (1922)
Irish Freedom 192
Irish Guards 196
Irish Historical Studies 3
Irish Independent 191
Irish Irelanders 175, 176, 185–6
Irish Landowners' Convention 149
Irish language 54, 83, 176–9, 390, *489*
Irish Literary Revival 169
Irish Literary Society of London 173
Irish Literary Theatre 173–4
Irish Loyal and Patriotic Union 134, 220,
  221, 224
  see also Irish Unionist Alliance
Irish Medical Association 309
Irish Metropolitan Conservative Society 60
Irish Nation League 207
Irish National Brotherhood 181
Irish National Land League 87, 97, 115,
  117, 124, 129–220, 132, 146
Irish National League 123–4, 131, 141,
  219, 220
Irish National League of Great Britain 145,
  190
Irish National Liberation Army (INLA)
  393, 401
Irish National Teachers' Organization 301
Irish National Theatre 173–4, 175
Irish National Volunteers 197
Irish Nationality and Citizenship Act 292
Irish Parliamentary Party
  and British Army 195–6
Irish Parliamentary Party (IPP) 87
  and British Army 195–6, 199
  Dillon 209, 210
  (1891–1914) 141–68
  electoral failures 207, 211
  and Fenians 166
  and Gaelic League 178–9
  Home Rule movement 108
  and Irish National League 123
  Labour Party 190
  land reform 152

  leaders 154
  Liberalism 144–5, 160, 162, 164,
    193–4
  Lloyd George 206
  localization 211
  O'Brien 145
  O'Connell influence 91
  parliamentarianism 180
  Parnell 116–17, *136*
  Redmond 154
  Sinn Féin 144
  Ulster Unionism 144
  Unionism 90, 227
  women 187–8
Irish People 94, 97, 98, 103
Irish Press 314, 322
Irish Protestant 225
Irish Protestant Conservative Society 60
Irish Reform Association 152, 153, 155
Irish Republican Army: *see* IRA
Irish Republican Brotherhood (IRB) 92,
  96
  and Butt 109
  and GAA 181
  and labour movement 192
  and liberalism 105
  Military Council 200
  New Departure 181
  oath of allegiance 257
  parliamentarianism 113
  Parnell 137–8, 165
  see also Fenianism
Irish Sugar Company 288
Irish Tenant League 86–8, 89, 105–6,
  116–17
Irish Times 308, 314
Irish Trades Union Congress 210, 308
Irish Transport and General Workers'
  Union 190–1, 317
Irish Unionist Alliance 226, 230, 239
  see also Irish Loyal and Patriotic Union
Irish Unionist Parliamentary Party 216,
  220, 221, 235
  see also Ulster Party
Irish Universities Act (1873) 109
Irish Universities Act (1908) 53, 156
Irish Volunteers (1778) 10

Irish Volunteers (1913) *166,* 167, 181, 188,
    234, 241
Irish War of Independence: *see* Anglo-Irish
    War
Irish Women's Franchise League 187
Irish Worker 191
iron curtain 424
Irregulars, republican 261, 262, 265, 267,
    270, 335
Isles, K.S. 356, 358

Jacob's biscuit factory 203
Jameson, Andrew 225
Jameson family 274
Japan/Pearl Harbor 299
job creation 311, 355, 373
John XXIII 358, 368
Johnston, Roy 362
Johnston, William 215, 219, 225, 232
Jordan, Neil 3, 248, 425
Joyce, James 174
Jubilee Coercion Act 132
Jubilee riots 346
Judaism 293–4

Kane, R.R. 177
Katholischer Verein Deutschlands 57
Kearney, Richard 5
Kearns, Linda 281
Kelly, Liam 354
Kelly, Samuel 347
Kelly, T.J. 99, 101
Kenmare, Lord 11
Kennedy, Geraldine 376
Kennedy, John F. 319
Keogh, Dermot 378
Keogh, John 11, 34, 36
Keogh, William 90, 117, 194
Kernan, James 51
Kerr, Donal 52, 53
Kerry killings 268
Kettle, A.J. 120
Kettle, T.M. 167, 175, 185, 187, 197
Keynesianism 300, 305, 313
Kickham, Charles 94, 96, 97, 104, 106–7
Kildare 18
Killakee 100

Killala, Battle of 20
Killarney mine killings 268
Kilmainham Gaol 120
Kilmainham party 120
Kilmainham treaty 121, 122, 125–6,
    131
Kilmallock police station 100
Kilmichael ambush 245, 247, 248, 252,
    253, 254
Kilwarden, Viscount 22
Kinealy, Christine 72, 78, 79
King, Martin Luther, Jr. 365
King-Harman, Edward 109
Kingstown and District Unionist Club
    229–30, 232
Kitchener, Earl 196
Knights of Columbanus 308
Knocknagoshel killings 268
Kohn, Leo 257
Korean war 355
Kotsonouris, Mary 250

La Mon Hotel bombing 393
Labouchere, Henry 121
Labour Leader 190
labour market 287
    see also employment
labour movement 186–7, 188, 192, 311
Labour Party of Britain 190, 287, 388
Labour Party of Ireland 170, 189, 190, 210,
    282, 287, 301, 356, 375, 377
Lacordaire, Henri 57
Ladies' Land League 120–1, 122–3, 130
Lake, Gerard 15, 17, 18–19
Lalor, James Fintan 55, 56, 85, 115, 172
Lamennais, Félicité de 57
Land Acts
    (1870) 109, 150, 223
    (1881) 120, 131, 133, 151, 223
    (1887) 133
    (1896) 147
    (1903) 150, 151, 157, 158, 368
    (1909) 158, 159, 199
    see also Land Purchase Acts
Land Commission 119
Land Conference 106, 152
Land Law (Ireland) Act 119

Land League: *see* Irish National Land League
land nationalization 122, 125, 189
land purchase 223–4, 289, 294
Land Purchase Acts 199
  (1885) 128, 133, 150, 199
  (1888) 133
  (1903) 150, 151, 157, 158, 368
  (1923) 280
Land War 97, 121, 132, 138
Landlord and Tenant (Ireland) Act 106
landlordism
  debt 76
  in decline 158, 221, 223–4, 227, 230
  evangelicalism 67
  evictions 80
  Famine 75–6
  and Fenians 96
  Irish Landowners' Convention 149
  paternalistic 357–8
  Presbyterian businessmen 214
  Protestantism 169
  tithes 76
  Toryism 67
  Unionism 169
landmines 268, 398
Langan, Peter 92
Langrishe's Act 12
Larkin, Jim 189, 190, 191
Larkinism 170
Larne 233, 234–5, 236
Lavelle, Patrick 95, 102
Law, Andrew Bonar 253
Law, Hugh 187
Lawless, John 48
Lawrence, R.J. 332
Leader 169, 178, 179, 186
League of Nations 297, 312, 328, 382
Lecky, W.E.H. 4, 225
Lee, J.J. 86, 203, 204, 305, 307, 312, 318–19, 374, 378
Leech Commission 341, 342, 363
legislative independence 3, 6, 8, 23, 27, 272
Leinster 17–18, 19
Leinster Regiment 196
Lemass, Noel 269

Lemass, Seán *321*
  and Aiken 313
  anti-partitionism 385
  Conditions of Employment Act 287
  and de Valera 300
  EC membership 329
  economic growth 373, 383
  Fianna Fáil 281–2, 303
  and Haughey 379
  internment 354
  in IRA 246
  Irish Times 314
  Irish Transport and General Workers' Union 317
  job creation 311
  Keynesianism 305
  National Industrial and Economic Council 317–18
  nationalism 320
  pragmatism 314–16
  retirement 321–3
  reunification 298
  as Tánaiste 301
  and Unionists 330
  visiting Stormont 359
  wage restrictions 301
Lenihan, Brian 328
Leo XIII 133
Liberal Party of Britain 90, 104, 237
  Dillon 144, 146–7, 156
  Home Rule 144, 168–9
  and IPP 144–5, 160, 162, 164, 193–4
  see also Gladstone; Lloyd George
Liberal Party of Ireland 35, 88, 104, 117, 122, 132, 133, 143, 216–18, 230
Liberal unionism 147, 216
Liberal Unionists 216
Liberty Hall 200
'Library of Ireland' 54, 56, 171
Libyan arms 391, 395
Lichfield House compact 37, 38
Ligoniel pub killings 370, 398
Limerick Junction 100
Lindsay, Mrs, of Cork 246
linen manufacturing 8, 14, 346, 347–8, 355–6, 361
Lisbon Treaty 415

List, Friedrich 184
literacy levels 9, 83, 410
literary censorship 327–8
Little, P.J. 179
Liverpool, Lord 33
living standards 288, 380–1
Lloyd George, David
  and Churchill 163
  and Craig 336–7
  and Curtis 292
  Easter Rising aftermath 237–8
  Home Rule 162
  IPP 206
  Military Service Act 209
  negotiations 206, 207, 230–1, 238, 239
  People's Budget 159, 160, 199
  six-county exclusion 206
  and Unionists 256
Loans Guarantee Acts 347
local government 147, 250, 341, 342, 363,
  366, 369, 372, 419
Local Government (Ireland) Act 147
Locke distillery sale 301
Lock-Out 191, 192
Lockwood Committee 359
Lomasney, William 130–1
Londonderry, Lord 234, 331
Londonderry, Theresa 231, 232
Londonderry Corporation 363, 369
Long, Walter 229, 239
Long March 366, 369
Long War 391, 393, 396, 397–8, 399, 416,
  417
Longford South by-election 207
Longley, Michael 1
Loughborough, Lord 28
Loughgall killings 399
Loughinisland killings 396
Loyal Irish Union 220
Loyal National Repeal Association 39, 46,
  47, 51, 52–3, 55
loyalism 1, 2, 11, 236, 365–6, 368, 389
Loyalist Volunteer Force 389
Luby, T.C. 98
Lucas, Charles 10
Lucas, C.H.T. 246, 252, 253
Lucas, Frederick 87, 89

Lynch, Jack 314, 322–6, 375, 378
Lynch, Liam 185, 265, 267, 268, 270, 425
Lynch, Michael 297
Lynn Committee 341
Lyons, F.S.L. 5, 112, 120, 125, 132, 137,
  139, 260
Lyttle, Tommy 397

McAleese, Mary 3
Macardle, Dorothy 281
McBride, Ian 17, 65
McBride, Lawrence 251
MacBride, Seán
  Clann na Poblachta 302, 308, 312, 353
  External Relations Act 306
  IRA 247
  as Minister for External Affairs 303
  mother and child debacle 307–9
  on republic 307
McCabe, Edward 124
McCarthy, Justin 129, 137, 145, 180
McCartney, Robert 417
McCartney sisters 417
McCaughey, Seán 302
McCluskey, Patricia and Conn 363–4
MacCormack, Captain 245
McCracken, Henry Joy 6, 13, 19
McCracken, Mary Anne 50
McCullough, Denis 184
MacDermot, Frank 296
MacDiarmada, Seán 201
MacDonagh, Oliver 30, 81, 82
MacDonagh, Thomas 192, 203
MacDonald, Malcolm 298
Macdonald, Norman 45
MacDonnell, Antony 149, 152–3
McDowell, Alexander 208
McDowell, R.B. 24–5, 238
McElligott, J.J. 293
MacEntee, Seán 300–1, 302, 305, 310, 313,
  314
MacEoin, Seán 308
McGilligan, Patrick 303, 304–5, 310
McGrath, Joe 276
McGuiness, Martin 392, 417, 419, *420,*
  421, 422
MacHale, John 51, 52, 102

Macintyre, Angus 43
McKelvey, Joe 268, 269
MacKenna, Stephen 171, 172
McMahon, Deirdre 291
McMahon murders 334
MacManus, Terence Bellew 95–6
McMichael, Gary 395
McMichael, John 395, 396
McMinn, J.R.B. 213
McNally, Leonard 19
MacNeill, Eoin
  Boundary Commission 278, 338, 339
  brother 291
  Irish language 177
  Irish Volunteers 167, 191, 196, 200
  resignation 339
McNeill, James 291
McQuaid, John Charles 294, 301, 309, 311
Macready, Neville 243, 251–2, 253, 261
MacRory, Joseph 293
MacSwiney, Mary 258
Maffey, John 298, 306
Magee College 359
Mageean, Nicholas 19
Magennis, Brian 351, 353
Magennis, James Joseph 299
Maher, E. 299
Mahon Tribunal 414
Major, John 387–8, 389
Malcomson, A.P.W. 7
Mallin, Michael 203
Mallon, Séamus 403
Malthus, Thomas 8
Manchester Martyrs 97, 102, 107, 108, 111
Mandelson, Peter 416
Mandle, W.F. 180
Mansergh, Nicholas 337
Mansion House Conference 210
manufacturing industries 26, 316, 346–7
marching 353, 365
market forces 74
Markievicz, Constance 187, 188, 203, 258, 281
marriage 8, 81, 82
Marshall Aid 306–7
martial law 15
Martyn, Edward 173

martyrs 101–2, 247, 354
  see also Manchester Martyrs
Marxism 4, 171
Massey, General 100
Matthew, Robert 358
Maume, Patrick 131, 178–9
Maxwell, Somerset 220
Maye, Brian 183, 186
Mayhew, Patrick 387, 402, 408
Maynooth Act 51
Maynooth College 52, 156, 177, 218
Maynooth seminary 52, 218
Mayo 17–18, 115, 117, 146
Meath 18
media 327
medical services, socialized 307–8
Meehan, F.E. 185
Mellowes, Liam 268, 269
Mendicity Institution 203
Mercier, Vivian 169
Messines, Battle of 207
Methodist Church 66, 346
Metropolitan Conservative Society 225
Michael Collins (Neil Jordan) 3, 248, 425
middle classes 93–4, 169, 361, 364
Midleton, Lord (Brodrick, St John) 208, 223, 226, 230, 231, 238, 240–1
militancy 167, 232–3, 241–2, 366–7
militant loyalism 1, 2, 107, 395
militant republicanism 1, 2, 21–2, 99–100, 165, 385, 424
Military Service Act 209
  see also conscription
Militia Act 11
Millardet, Alexis 81
Miller, David 8
Ministers and Secretaries Act 273
Ministry of Development 358
Mitchel, John
  British/Famine 84–5
  as influence 116, 169, 171
  Jail Journal 56
  Nation 53, 54
  on O'Connell 48, 56
  on potato blight 78
  United Irishman 55
  Young Irelanders 49–50

Mitchell, Arthur 250
Mitchell, George 408–9, 416
Mitchelstown Massacre 133
Mokyr, Joel 77
Molyneaux, James 351, 404, 407
Molyneux, William 23
Monaghan bombings 384, 396
monster meetings 47, 54, 104
Montalembert, Charles de 57
Monteagle, Lord 82
Montesquieu, C. de S. 9
Montgomery, Henry 66
Moody, T.W. 96
Moore, F. Frankfort 291
Moore, George 183
Moore, George Henry 90, 91, 104, 108
Moore, William 225
Moran, D.P. 183, 362
   Catholic Gaelicism 172, 177, 186
   and Larkin 191
   Leader 169, 178, 179
   Sinn Féin electoral victory 207
   suffragism 187
Moriarty, David 102
Morley, John 129, 134–5
Morning Post 338, 339
Morpeth, Lord 45, 46
Morris, Michael 225
Morris, Tom 'Trigger' 247
Morrison, Danny 392
mother and child affair 307–9, 354
Mountbatten, Louis 384, 393
Moynihan, Maurice 286
Mulcahy, Richard 203, 244, 248, 254, 260,
   263, *264*, 276, 303, 308
Mulgrave, Earl of 45–6
Mulholland, H.L. 221
Municipal Corporations Act 43, 46, 60–1
Munro, Henry 17, 19, 21
Murphy, Cliona 187
Murphy, John 18
Murphy, John A. 413
Murphy, William Martin 191
Murray, Daniel 51, 52
mutinies
   India 92, 247
   Ireland 275–6, 278
mysticism 170–1

Naas, Lord 91
Nagle, Pierce 98
Nannetti, J.P. 189
Napoleon III 92
Napoleonic wars 27, 29
Nappagh Fleet 14
Nation (1842) 49, 52, 53–4
Nation (1927) 281
National Army 261, 275
National Association for Full and Prompt
   Justice or Repeal 38
National Association of Ireland 103
National Centre Party 296–7, 303
National Coalition Panel 260
National Convention of the Volunteers 10
National Corporate Party 297
National Council 184
National Farmers' Association 323
National Federation 141, 145
National Guard 296–7
   see also Blueshirts
National Industrial and Economic Council
   317–18
National Institutes for Higher Education
   326
National Insurance Act 199
National Labour Party 301
National League: *see* Irish National League
National League of Great Britain 145
National League of the North 341–2
National Literary Society 173
national schools 83, 177
National Union of Journalists 326
National University of Ireland 156, 177,
   179, 326
National Volunteers 167, 191, 197, 209
nationalism 2–3
   advanced 92, 93, 173, 174
   Celtic 164
   constitutional 143–4, 386
   cultural 169, 171–2, 192
   feminism 186–7
   gentry 54
   Irish Liberalism 216
   labour movement 188
   Lemass 320
   militant 3
   modern 172

new 168, 182–3, 188
O'Connell 36, 39, 40
popular 251, 357, 399
secular 21
shifting 328
violent 133–4
NATO 306
Neave, Airey 393
Neill, Ivan 353
Nelson, Brian 395, 397
neutrality 297, 298–300, 306, 307, 328
New Catholic Association 31, 32, 59
New Catholic rent 33
New Departures 106, 115, 165, 181, 403
New Industries (Development) Acts 347
New Ireland Forum 385, 401
New Ross 18
New Ulster Political Research Group 395
New University of Ulster 358, 359, 360
Newe, G.B. 371
Newtownbarry killings 41
Nice Treaty 414
Nicholls, George 44
Nicholson, W.P. 368
Niemba ambush 319
Nixon, J.W. 396–7
No Rent manifesto 120
Nolan, Father 176
North, Lord 24, 303
North Eastern Boundary Bureau 339
North Fermanagh 227
North of Ireland Women's Suffrage
    Committee 231
Northern Bank raid 417
Northern Ireland Assembly 389
Northern Ireland Civil Rights Association
    363, 364–6
Northern Ireland Executive 416
Northern Ireland government 240, 270,
    331–2, 336
    see also Stormont Assembly
Northern Ireland Labour Party 355, 356,
    366, 375, 376
Northern Ireland Troubles 241–54, 384,
    397–8, 421, 423
Northern Whig 213, 338
Northern Whig Club 10
Norton, Willie 308, 311

Novick, Peter 5
Nugent, George 19
Nugent, Oliver 223

Ó Buachalla, Dónal 291
Ó Dálaigh, Cearbhall 384
Ó Faoláin, Seán 56–7, 311
Ó Gráda, Cormac 26, 27, 77, 79
Ó Moráin, Micheál 326
O'Brien, Conor Cruise 308, 376, 379
O'Brien, Cruise 185
O'Brien, Peter 133
O'Brien, R. Barry 45, 118, 120, 124
O'Brien, William
    anti-Parnellites 149–50
    Davitt on 151
    and Dillon 146–7
    GAA 180
    IPP 145
    Irish Convention 207
    Land War 132
    and Parnell 132, 137
    on Redmond 143, 168, 212
    resignation 156–7
    UIL 148, 179
O'Brien, William (labour leader) 195, 301
O'Brien, William Smith 55
O'Callaghan, Katherine 258
O'Callaghan, Margaret 122, 131
O'Callaghan, Seán 365
O'Casey, Seán 191, 224–5
O'Connell, Charles 45
O'Connell, Daniel 29
    acquitted *49*
    background and career 30–2
    biography 56–7
    Catholic Association 58–9
    Christian Democracy 57
    Church of Ireland 41–2
    constitutionalism 48
    corporations 43
    and Davis 48, 52–3, 54
    death of 84
    and Duffy 30
    electoral success 34–5, 59
    federalism 55
    as influence 57, 116, 425
    Kilkenny speeches 47

O'Connell, Daniel (*cont'd*)
  Mallow speeches 47, 48
  and Mitchel 56
  monster meetings 54
  nationalisms 36, 39, 40
  Orange Order 40
  and Parnell, compared 56–8
  and Peel 50–1, 52
  platform style 158
  poor law reform 44
  repeal 37–40, 47, 50, 58
  Tara meeting 47
  and Wellington 34
  Whigs 37, 44–5, 79–80
  and Young Irelanders 50, 53, *480*
O'Connell, J.J. 263
O'Connell, John 29, 46
O'Connell, Maurice 411
O'Connor, Emmet 189, 190
O'Connor, Fergus 38, 50
O'Connor, John 99
O'Connor, Rory 185, 260, 268, 269
O'Connor, T.P. 125
O'Donnell, F. Hugh 109, 110, 112, 121, 123
O'Donoghue, Martin 373–4
O'Duffy, Eoin 267, 296–7
O'Ferrall, Fergus 32, 34
O'Flaherty, Eamon 11, 12
O'Flanagan, Michael 256
O'Gorman Mahon, The 116
O'Grady, Standish 171, 172, 193
O'Growney, Eugene 177
O'Hegarty, P.S. 266
O'Higgins, Kevin 269, 270, 274, 276, 279,
  280, 281, 384
O'Higgins, T.F. 311
O'Kelly, J.J. 124
O'Kelly, Seán T. 287, 295
O'Leary, Cornelius 61
O'Leary, John 96, 97, 121, 173, 184
O'Mahony, John 92, 97–8, 104
O'Malley, Desmond 326, 384
O'Malley, Donough 326, 410
O'Malley, Ernie 193, 247–9, 254, 255, 263,
  265
O'Malley, Frank 247
O'Neill, Phelim 370

O'Neill, Terence *321*, 351, 355
  Catholic school visit 358–9
  economic modernization 333, 358, 360
  electoral failure 356–7
  and Fitzwilliam 331
  and Lemass 320–1, 329
  liberalism 361
  modernization 363
  paternalism 357–8
  resignation 369
O'Neill, T.P. 71, 72
O'Rahilly, T.F. 178
O'Shea, Katherine 120, 131, 135–6
O'Shea, W.H. 118, 121, 126, 129, 131, 136,
  138, 143
O'Shiel, Kevin 339
O'Sullivan, Joseph 247
O'Toole, Fintan 390
oath of allegiance 257, 258, 260
obstructionist campaign 112–13
Offences against the State (Amendment)
  Act 326, 384
oil crisis 327, 373, 374
old age pension reductions 280
Omagh bomb 393, *394*
Omagh District Council 363
Omagh scandal 145
Operation Harvest 312, 354–5, 356, 362
Orange Order *479*
  anti-unionism 39, 40
  Ballybay confrontation 48
  Central Conservative Society 63
  condemnation of 45
  demonstrations 30
  dissolved 59, 62, 63
  influence 127
  Irish Protestant Constitution 24
  membership 62
  O'Connell 40, 58–9
  outlawed 31
  parades 353
  Presbyterianism 63
  sectarianism 47
  1798 rising 15
  territorial dynasties 219
  and Toryism 62–3
  Unionism 216, 219–20

Unlawful Oaths Act 31
working class 4
Orde, Hugh *422*
Ordnance Survey 176
Ormeau road bookmaker's shooting 396
Orsini bomb 92

Pacelli, Eugenio 293
paedophilia 390
paganism 171
Paget, H.W.: *see* Anglesey, Marquis of
Paine, Thomas 9
Paisley, Ian 367–8, *420*
  and Adams 421
  and Ahern 419–20
  AIA 419
  and Blair 420
  boycotting talks 404
  on EU 404
  imprisoned 368
  popularity 385
  Protestant Unionists 370
  supporters 403
Palmerston, Dublin 100, 101
Palmerston, Lord 90
Parachute Regiment 371
paramilitarism 40, 233–4, 235, 270, 370,
  415–16
Parker, Stewart 6
Parliament Act 161, 194, 233
parliamentary constituencies *481, 482*
parliamentary reform 10, 11, 26–7, 28,
  37–8, 40, 59, 62, 90, 125
Parliamentary Reform Act 123, 125
Parnell, Anna 120, 121
Parnell, Charles Stewart 124–5
  achievements 138, 139–40
  alliance 141
  and British government 38
  and Buttites 110, 111–12
  by-elections 139
  and Carroll 114
  Church of Ireland 124–5
  and de Valera 211–12
  death of 139, 168, 170, 173, 176, 180
  and Devoy 106, 115
  evictions 122–3

farmers 169
Fenianism 96, 115, 117, 131, 166
GAA 180, 181–2
and Gladstone 117, 120, 127, 134–5
and Healy 137–8, 139
Home Rule 129–30
Home Rule Confederation 114
in House of Commons 118
Independent Irish Party 116–17
as influence 211–12
Irish Republican Brotherhood 137–8,
  165
Kilmainham Gaol 120
Land League 132
Manchester Martyrs 111
mistress 131
New Departures 115, 165
non-violence 118–19
and O'Connell, compared 56–8
Plan of Campaign 132, 133, 135, 138,
  146, 149, 179
Protestants 169
and Redmond 142–3
re-elected *136*
rural problems 117–18
Split 131–40, 141–2, 143, 158, 189–90
Toryism 134
working classes 189
Parnell, Fanny 116
Parnell, John 25
Parnell manifesto 127
partition 221, 236–9, 424
  Agar-Robartes 163
  Chamberlain 294, 296
  Collins 270
  Costello 308
  de Valera 298, 306–7, 313, 320, 325
  Faulkner 385
  Fianna Fáil 302, 303, 304, 329
  Irish Party 207
  Lemass 380, 384
  and nationalism 390
  Redmondites 256
  Ulster Unionists 405
  see also six-county exclusion
Party Processions Act 219
pastoral farming 41, 81, 82

patriarchy 232, 424

patronage 7, 25, 42–3, 50, 76, 308, 351

Patten report 416

Patterson, Henry 305, 312, 328, 352, 361, 387, 401

Patton, K.F. 299

Peace Preservation (Ireland) Act 112

peace process 414, 419, 423

Pearce, Edward Lovett 6

Pearl Harbor 299

Pearse, Margaret 281

Pearse, Patrick 170, *201*
  Easter Rising 167, 200–1, 203–7
  eulogy for O'Donovan, Rossa 95
  Gaelic League 178
  Lock-Out 191–2
  and MacNeill 200
  mysticism 171
  pamphlets 171–2
  passion play 175
  and Redmond 194
  'Renunciation' 272
  St Enda's 193
  United Irishmen 257

Peel, Robert 46, 70–1
  Catholic Board 29–30
  Catholic clergy 51–2
  colleges created 87–8
  emancipation 33–4, 35
  free trade 71
  Irish Conservatism 59
  and O'Connell 50–1, 52
  relief from Famine 70
  Toryism 52
  university reform 52, 53

Peep o'Day Boys 14

People's Budget 159, 160, 199

People's Democracy 366, 367–8

People's Rights Association 141

Petrie, George 171

Pettigo triangle 335

Phoenix literary societies 92

Phoenix Park murders 122, 130–1

Pigott forgeries 130, 131, 134

Pilot 52

PIRA: *see* Provisional IRA

Pitt, William 10, 21, 24, 28

Pius IX 52, 88

Pius XII 306, 309

Place Act 11

Plain Truth 364

Plan of Campaign 132, 133, 135, 138, 146, 149, 179

plastic bullets 397

The Playboy of the Western World riot 174

Plunket, William 28, 30

Plunkett, G.N. 207

Plunkett, Horace
  and Balfour 147, 221
  bourgeoisie 225
  IPP 158
  loyalist militancy 236
  ousted 226, 270
  political economy 287
  Recess Committee 143, 148

Plunkett, Joseph 171, 201, 207

police 245, 393, 397–8
  see also Police Service of Northern Ireland; Royal Ulster Constabulary

Police (Northern Ireland) Act 416

Police Service of Northern Ireland (PSNI) 415, 416, 421

Policing Board of Northern Ireland 421

Pollock, H.M. 345, 347

Ponsonby Estate 133

Poor Law Amendment (Ireland) Act 74–5, 76, 78

Poor Law Extension Act 70

poor law system 43–4, 75, 76, 78

Poor Relief (Ireland) Act 44

popular culture 3–4, 107, 108

population *484, 485*

Portland, Duke of 25

potato consumption 8, 83

potato crop failure 50, 53, 69, 81, 86

poverty 43–4, 158–9, 188, 411, 424

Powell, Enoch 403

Powell, Jonathan 414, 419, 420

Power, John O'Connor 112

Poynings' Law 7

Prager, Jeffrey 272–3, 284

Pratley, Michael 334

Precursor Society 38

Presbyterianism 7
  and Anglicanism 65–6
  Belfast 20
  and Church of Ireland 214
  embourgeoisement 213, 214
  landlordism 214
  non-subscribing 65
  Orangeism 63
  radical 17
  reform of Church of Ireland 42
  secessionist schism 65
  and Toryism 65
  and Ulster Unionism 64, 65
Primrose Committee 161–2
Proclamation, Fenian (1867) 97, 105
Proclamation (1916) 203, 319–20
Programmes for Economic Expansion 315,
  316–18, 323
Progressive Democratic Party 376–7,
  412–14
Progressive Unionist Party 399
proportional representation 274, 326, 342
Protection of Person and Property
  (Ireland) Act 119
protectionism
  Britain 347
  Fianna Fáil 282, 287–8, 290, 313, 315,
    317, 329, 347
  scaled down 329
  tariffs 10, 184, 282, 313, 347
protest marches 365
Protestant ascendancy 1, 12, 28, 32–3, 40,
  42, 62, 65, 172
Protestant rent 60
Protestant Unionist Party 370
Protestantism
  clergy 76
  Conservatives 109
  Cumann na nGaedheal 277
  dispensary doctors 283
  distrust within 21
  evangelicalism 66–7, 367–8, 404
  gangs 14
  land holders 169
  liberals 35–6
  militancy 127, 366–7
  Parnell 169

  Russell 88
  Ulster 162
  Wexford 18
  see also Protestant ascendancy
Prout, J.T. 267
Provisional Government (1867) 99
Provisional Government (1916) 203
Provisional Government (1922) 261, 262,
  263, 267–9, 337–8
Provisional Government (Ulster) 232, 235
Provisional IRA (PIRA) 371, 385–6, 391,
  398, 401, 416–18
Provisional Sinn Féin 140, 391–2
PSNI: *see* Police Service of Northern
  Ireland (PSNI)
public housing 359–60, 363–4
Public Order legislation 353
Public Record Office 270
public spending 375, 376
public works 44, 71–2, 73, 78
Purdie, Bob 362

Quakers 73, 76–7
Queen's College Belfast 156
Queen's Colleges (Cork, Galway) 155, 156

Radio Telefís Éireann 327
Rahilly, Michael Joseph 167
railways 95, 100, 358, 359, 360
ranch war 157, 158, 199
Randalstown, Battle of 17, 19, 21
Real IRA 422
Recess Committee 143, 147, 148
Red Hand Commandos 395
red scare 284–5
Redmond, John *142*
  achievements 208–9
  and Asquith 161, 162
  and British government 38
  as constitutionalist 399–400
  death of 209
  and Dillon 151
  Easter Rising 164
  and Hyde 179
  IPP 154
  Irish Volunteers 241
  land sale 158

Redmond, John (*cont'd*)
  leadership 166–7, 212
  and Lloyd George 230
  and McDowell 208
  Midleton, Lord 208
  O'Brien on 168
  Parnellites 142–3
  voluntary Irish army 209–10
  Woodenbridge speech 195
Redmond, W.C. 245
Redmond, William 167, 187, 197
Redmond, William Archer 210
Redmondites 89, 167, 181, 185–6, 241
referenda 322, 326, 327, 409, 414, 415
Reform Act (1832) 60, 62
Reform Act (1867) 123
Reformed Presbyterian Church
    (Covenanters) 65, 367
Regency Crisis 10
Reilly, Thomas Devin 78
Relief Act, Hobart 12, 14
relief petitions 12
religious denominations *487, 488*
religious practice, post-Famine 83–4
religious tolerance 138
rent strike 120–1
Renunciation Act 7, 8
Repeal Association: *see* Loyal National
    Repeal Association
repeal movement
  O'Connell 37–40, 47, 50, 58
  post-Famine 86
  and Ulster Unionism 47
Report of the Joint Working Party on the
    Economy of Northern Ireland (Hall)
    356
Representation of the People Act (1884) 125
Representation of the People Act (1918) 210
republicanism 1
  Catholicism 308–9
  and feminism 266
  Fianna Fáil 281–2
  flourishing 362
  vs Free Staters 266–7, 273
  and imperialism 257
  militant 1, 2, 21–2, 99–100, 165, 385, 424
  removal of British 392

Sinn Féin 242–3
  Wexford 18
  women activists 247–8, 266
Restoration of Order in Ireland Act 267,
    334
reunification 298, 311, 388, 391–2
revisionism 4, 68, 78, 193, 278–9
revival (1859) 66
Reynolds, Albert 328, 387, 388, 402
Reynolds, Hanna 121
Reynolds, Thomas 19
ribbon movement 104
Richardson, George 233
Ridgeway, Joseph West 132
rioting 88, 346, 369–70
risings
  1798 15, 17–19, 20–1, 93, 173, *479*
  1803 22
  1848 56, 92
  1867 98–100, 101–2
  see also Easter Rising (1916)
Riverdance (Flatley) 3
Robinson, F.J. (Goderich) 33
Robinson, Mary 377, 382, 424
Robinson, Peter 421–2, *422*
Rooney, William 183
Roscommon by-election 207
Rosebery, Lord 145
Rossa, Jeremiah O'Donovan 92, 95, 98
Rosslea affair 220
Rossmore, Lord 220
Rousseau, Jean-Jacques 9
Royal Dublin Fusiliers 196
Royal Highland Fusiliers 398
Royal Irish Constabulary 129, 133, 252–3,
    334
Royal Irish Regiment 197
Royal Munster Fusiliers 196, 197
Royal Ulster Constabulary (RUC)
  disarmed 370
  formation of 334–5
  Long War 397–8
  loyalist paramilitaries 396–7
  officers targeted 398
  renamed 416
  and Ulster Special Constabulary 270
  Unemployed Workers' Committee 345

Russell, Charles 134
Russell, George 170, 191, 192
Russell, John 71, 88, 116
Russell, Thomas 22
Russell, T.W. 150, 151, 153, 216, 227–8, 332
Ryan, Desmond 97
Ryan, James 307, 309, 311, 314, 315
Ryan, Richie 374
Ryan, Sean 415
Ryan Report 415

Sadleir, John 90, 117, 194
St Andrews Agreement 414, 419, 420, 421
St Enda's School 193
St Stephen's Green 203, 226
Saintfield, Battle of 19
Salazar, António de Oliveira 306
Salisbury, Lord 126, 135
Sampson, Colin 397
Samuel, Herbert 161–2
Sands, Bobby 392
Saorstát Éireann: *see* Irish Free State
Sarsfield, Patrick 226
SAS (Special Air Service) 398–9
Saunderson, Edward 67, 118, 125, 140, 147, 216, *217*, 220, 221, 351, 368
Saunderson, Somerset 238
Saurin, W.H. 24, 38, 62
Savage, Robert 329
Scanlan, Thomas 196
Scappaticci, Freddie 417
Scullabogue, Battle of 18, 20
SDLP: *see* Social Democratic and Labour Party
Seánad Éireann (Senate) 274, 283, 290
secessionist schism 65
secret societies 170–1
sectarianism 9, 109
    Armagh 14
    Defenderism 20
    1803 rising 22
    loyalism 354–5
    marching 365
    O'Connell 57–8
    Orange Order 47
    rioting 88

UFF 396
Ulster 19
UVF 396
secularization 390
separatism 1
    cultural nationalism 192
    feminism 187
    Griffith 258
    parliamentary nationalism 165
    and patriots 272
    post-Easter Rising 207
    Sinn Féin 184, 185
Sèvres, Treaty of 250
Sexton, Thomas 120
Shankill Road bomb 393
Shannon hydro-electrics 280
Shaw, William 114
Shawe-Taylor, John 149, 150, 151, 158
Sheehy Skeffington, Francis 185, 187, 204
Sheehy Skeffington, Hanna 187, 232, 266, 281, 294
Shiel, Richard Lalor 31
shipbuilding 340, 346, 348, 356, 361
Shops Act 287
Silver Jubilee, George V 346
Simms, Robert 19
Simon, John 295
Simpson, David 418
Simpson, Wallis 292
Sinclair, Betty 365
Sinclair, Maynard 351
Single Market 411
sink estates 411
Sinn Féin (1905) 54, 56, 144, 154, 171, 175, 184–5, 206–7, 210, 241–2, 243, 251, 254, 336
Sinn Féin (1970) 399, 408, 416–17, 419, 421
Sinn Féin 184
Sinn Féin League 184
six-county exclusion
    accepted 341
    Carson 163, 230
    Home Rule 237–8, 239, 332
    Lloyd George 206
    Ulster Unionist Council 237–8
Skibbereen funeral *72*

Skibbereen speech 48
Skinner, Liam 286, 318
Slattery, Michael 45
sleaze 301, 413–14
Sloan, T.H. 153, 367, 368
slum-clearance 286–7
Smiddy, Timothy 279
Smith, F.E. (Birkenhead) 291
Smith, Paddy 323
Smith, P.J. 318
Smuts, Jan 255
Smyth, G.B. 340
Social Democratic and Labour Party
    (SDLP) 362, 371, 387, 399–400, 401
social mobility 94, 169
social welfare 301, 352
socialism 189, 192
Socialist Party of Ireland 190
Society for the Preservation of the Irish
    Language 176, 179
Soloheadbeg ambush 243, 245
Somme, Battle of 207, 220, 349
soup kitchens 73–4
souperism 76, 86, 191
South Africa Act 113
South African war 149, 159, 173, 195–6,
    254–5, 332
South Antrim 227
South Down parades 353
South Dublin Union 203
South Irish Horse 197
sovereign authority 255–6, 257, 260, 293
Spanish Civil War 297, 306
Special Air Service (SAS) 398–9
Special Commission 131, 133, 134, 138
Special Criminal Court 326, 384
Special Powers Act 334, 335
Spencer, Earl 122, 133, 134, 291
Spender, Wilfrid 233, 295
Spring, Dick 377, 402
Stalker, John 397
Stanhope, Earl 28
state schools, non-denominational 352–3
Stepaside police station 101
Stephens, James 92, 93, 97–8, 101
Stevens Inquiry 396–7
Stewart, Robert: *see* Castlereagh, Lord

stock market crisis 375
Stockport riots 88
Stokes, William 79
Stormont Assembly 354, 372, 405, 417
    see also Northern Ireland government
Strickland, Peter 246, 252
strikes 191–2, 210, 301, 302, 348–9, 385
Stuart, Villiers 32
suffragism 186–7
sugar-beet industry 289
Sullivan, T.D. 85, 107
Sunday Independent 307
Sunningdale Agreement 385, 400, 404, 409
Suppression Act 31, 34
Sutherland, Peter 382
Swanzy, O.R. 340
Sweetman, Gerard 310, 311, 315
Swift, Jonathan 183
Swinford Revolt 143, 151, 156–7
Synge, J.M. 169, 174, 175

Taca 318
Tallaght doctrine 377
Tallaght Hill 100, 101
Tammany Hall 123
Tamworth manifesto 64
tariff protection 10, 184, 282, 313, 347
Taylor, John 393
teachers 341
Teague, Paul 387, 401
television 329
£10 household franchise 37, 43
Tenant League: *see* Irish Tenant League
tenant organizations 86–7
Tenant Protection Society 86–7
tenant right 88, 91, 103–4
tenurial system 85, 223
Test Act 34
Thatcher, Margaret 397, 407
Thornley, David 112
Thurles, Synod of 88
Tierney, Michael 56, 57
tillage farming 41, 81, 82, 289
The Times 47, 133–4, 218
Tipperary 100
Tithe Composition Act 41
Tithe Rent Charge Act 41, 42, 43

tithes 40–1, 42, 76
Tobin, Liam 275
Tod, Isabella 231
Tone, Theobald Wolfe 12, 101, 172
  Argument on behalf of the Catholics of Ireland 13
  captured 20
  Griffiths on 183–4
  public readings 9
Topping, Walter 353
Toryism 45, 60–1, 91
  Dillon 147–8
  as influence 67
  landlords 67
  Orange Party 58–9, 62–3
  Parnell 134
  Peel 52
  and Presbyterianism 65
  Ulster Unionism 160
  see also Irish Conservative Party
Townshend, Charles 200, 235, 244–5, 251, 267
trade agreement 319
Trade Union Acts 300–1
trade unions 170, 189–90, 411
Traditional Unionist Voice 422
Treacy, E.W. 49
Treaty ports 294
Trent episode 93
Trevelyan, Charles 71, 73, 77, 78
Trevelyan, G.O. 128
Trimble, David *402*
  Adams on 418
  and Ahern 379, 409, 414
  and Blair 417–18
  and Carson 425
  and Craig, compared 336
  as devolutionist 408–9
  electoral defeat 418
  and Faulkner, compared 371, 406
  and Mitchell 416
  and Molyneux 404–5
  and Paisley 403, 404
  Sinn Féin 416
  Ulster Unionists 389
Trinity College 155, 156
Troubles, Northern Ireland: *see* Northern Ireland Troubles

Truce (1921) 230, 248–9, 254–5, 259
tuberculosis 346
Tudor, Henry 252
Twaddell, W.J. 334, 393
typhus 73, 76, 78

UDA: *see* Ulster Defence Association
UDP: *see* Ulster Democratic Party
UDR: *see* Ulster Defence Regiment
UFF: *see* Ulster Freedom Fighters
UIL: *see* United Irish League
Ulster 2, 17–18, 19, 162
Ulster Constitution Defence Committee 368
Ulster Constitutional Club 215
Ulster Constitutional Union 215, 219
Ulster Covenant 210, 238
Ulster custom 86, 106
Ulster Day protest 407
Ulster Defence Association (UDA) 370, 395, 399
Ulster Defence Regiment (UDR) 395, 396–7, 398
Ulster Democratic Party (UDP) 395, 399
Ulster Freedom Fighters (UFF) 393, 395, 396
Ulster Loyalist Democratic Party 395
Ulster Loyalist Union 221
Ulster Party 216, 220, 221, 225
Ulster Protestant Defence Association 219
Ulster Protestant Volunteers 368
Ulster Provisional Government 232, 235
Ulster Special Constabulary 223, 270, 333–4, 335, 370
Ulster Unionist Convention 221
Ulster Unionist Convention Building *222*
Ulster Unionist Council 223, 228–9, 233, 235, 237–8, 239–40
Ulster Unionist Party
  AIA 395, 399, 406–7
  Asquith 47
  Carson 226–7, 240–1
  Cooke's influence 65
  devolutionist 372
  and Dublin Unionism 224
  electoral success/failure 418
  and Home Rule 162, 221, 223, 241, 340, 405

Ulster Unionist Party (*cont'd*)
  and Irish Unionism 226–7, 238
  Liberal government 237
  militancy 144, 167, 232–3
  1920 settlement 254–5
  Paisley 368
  paramilitarism 233–4
  semi-constitutional agitation 35
  Tories 160
  see also Trimble, David
Ulster Volunteer Force (UVF) (1912) 94,
  107–8, 197, 223, 232–5
Ulster Volunteer Force (UVF) (1966) 384,
  395, 396, 422
Ulster Women's Unionist Council 232
Ulster Workers' Council 385, 400–1
Ulster Workers' strike 385, 404, 405
Unemployed Workers' Committee 345
unemployment
  Brooke 356
  civil unrest 345–6
  funds for 352
  job creation 310–11
  levels of 376, 381, 410, 412
  poverty 411
  Republic of Ireland 373
  WWII 351
Union, Act of (1800) 2, 3, 23–7, 213, 319,
  331, 343
Unionism 212–14
  Belfast 4, 332
  Butt 47
  Carson 163–4
  Church of Ireland 216–17
  Cork 226
  development of 215–16
  Dillon 152, 153
  disestablishment 219
  disintegration of 221
  DUP 403–4
  electoral successes 225–6
  and evangelicalism 67, 216
  against Home Rule 220–1
  Independent Irish Party 90
  industrial development programme 361
  Irish Toryism 59
  landowners 169

  Lemass 330
  North/South 226, 231
  Orange Order 216, 219–20
  and patriotism 109–10
  police 397
  Presbyterian 64
  social changes 224
  strengths 213–14
  women's participation 231–2
  working class 4
  see also constructive unionism; Ulster
    Unionist Party
Unionist Party of Northern Ireland
  (UPNI) 405–6
Unionist Women's Franchise Association
  232
unitarianism 171
United Ireland 120
United Ireland Party: *see* Fine Gael party
United Irish League (UIL) 146, 148, 157,
  179, 185
United Irish Society 12–13, 15, 21–2, 50
United Irishman (1848) 55, 78
United Irishman (1899) 178, 183
United Irishmen 13–14, 15, *16*, 17, 19,
  213, 257
United Nations 312, 318–19, 328, 382,
  414
United States of America
  Fenianism 106
  investment 410, 411
  and Ireland 424
  Irish-born population 82, 93
  weapons 391
  see also American Civil War; American
    War of Independence
United Ulster Unionist Council 404
universities 52, 53, 155–6, 362
  see also specific universities, by name
University College Cork 177
University College Dublin (Trinity) 155,
  156, 247
Unlawful Oaths Act 31
UPNI (Unionist Party of Northern
  Ireland) 405–6
utilitarianism 76, 77
UVF: *see* Ulster Volunteer Force

Vanoni Plan 311
Vaughan, W.E. 214, 224, 231
Verner, Thomas 45
Versailles, Treaty of 250
veto question 7, 28–32, 35
Victoria, Queen 39
Vinegar Hill, Battle of 18
Voltaire 9
Voluntary Health Insurance Board 311
volunteering 93, 94

wages
  Lemass 301
  post-Famine 83
  public works 72
  rises 323, 374
  work schemes 70
Wages Standstill Order 300–1
Walsh, John 226, 230
Walsh, William 124, 207
Walshe, Joseph 293
Ward, Alan 258, 259, 292, 332
Ward, Margaret 188
Warnock, Edmond 351
Warren, John Borlase 20
Waterford contest 32–3, 34
Waterloo, Battle of 27, 29
weavers 8–9
Weber, Max 169
welfare reforms 351–2, 356
Wellington, Duke (Wellesley) 33–4
Westminster Statute 279, 282
Wexford, County 17–19, 64
Wexford Bridge, Battle of 18
Wexford town 18
Whately, Richard 43
Whelan, Kevin 18
Whigs
  Catholic appointments in Ireland 45–6
  fall of 46
  French revolution 10–11
  Great Famine 71–2, 71–5
  market forces 74
  O'Connell 37, 44–5, 79–80
  reform 10
Whitaker, T.K. 285, 310, 313–14, 320–1, 359
Whitaker–Lemass revolution 315–17, 320–1

White, J.R. 191
Whyte, J.H. 21, 86–7, 88
Wilde, Oscar 28, 134
William IV 39
Williams, T. Desmond 57, 309
Wilson, Harold 370
Wilson, Henry 246, 247, 250, 261, 393
Wilson, Tom 358
Wilson Report 358, 359
Wiseman, Nicholas 88
Wolfe, Arthur 22
Wolfe Tone societies 362
women
  Covenant 232
  Dáil Éireann 258
  Fianna Fáil 281–2
  in labour market 287
  priesthood 390
  republicanism 247–8, 266
  rights 187, 381–2
  suffrage 186–7, 231–2
  Unionism 231–2
  in UVF 232
Women Graduates Association 294
Women's Coalition 416
Women's Prisoners' Defence League 266
Women's Social and Progressive League 294
Wood, Charles 71
Woodenbridge speech 195, 196, 199
Workers' Party 377
workhouses 44, 75
working classes 4, 189
World War I 165, 192, 196–8, 209, 230–1, 348
World War II 299–300, 348, 349, 351–2
  see also neutrality
Wyndham, George 145, 148–9, 155, 174, 228, 233, 368–9
Wyndham Act 151, 152, 156, 157, 159
Wyse, Thomas 37

Yeats, W.B.
  Cathleen ni Houlihan 175
  clericalism 283
  Countess Cathleen 174
  as critic 183
  on de Valera 304

Yeats, W.B. (*cont'd*)
  Fenianism 173
  Fine Gael 297
  intellectual revival 168
  mysticism 170
  nationalism 173, 175
  Parnell's death 176
  politics 171, 192

Yelverton's Act 7
yeomanry 15, 21, 22, 41
York, Duke of 33
Young Ireland Branch 179, 185
Young Irelanders 48–50, 53–4, 55–6, 91,
  480

Zeuss, Johann Kasper 176